# Intellectual Property Branding in the Developing World



*Intellectual Property Branding in the Developing World* identifies success stories in the areas of intellectual property (IP) and branding for non-technological innovation in the developing world. The author examines the relationship between IP, branding, and innovation to demonstrate that innovation, in general, and non-technological innovation, in particular, must go hand in hand with branding. Branding of non-technological innovations should be a good strategic tool to be used by countries in the developing world mainly in the areas where they have competitive advantages.

This book will assist scholars and academics dealing with innovation, branding, and IP issues, providing context and guidance to policymakers from the developing world. It is also relevant to researchers and students in the fields of intellectual property law, commercial law, international law, management, and innovation.

**Tshimanga Kongolo** has been with the World Intellectual Property Organization (WIPO) Academy for almost 18 years. Prior to joining WIPO, he taught IP at Osaka University, Osaka, Japan. He also spent seven months as a Research Fellow (while being with Osaka University) at Max Planck Institute for Foreign and International Patent, Copyright and Competition Law, Munich, Germany, in 2000. His key areas of expertise involve international IP law; branding and innovation; African IP systems; and global IP challenges, including traditional knowledge and IP and public health. He has widely published books and articles on those areas in peer-reviewed top international IP journals (see Google Scholar).

# Routledge Research in Intellectual Property

**Intellectual Property Branding in the Developing World**
A New Approach to Non-Technological Innovations
*Tshimanga Kongolo*

**Intellectual Property Policy, Law and Administration in Africa**
Exploring Continental and Sub-Regional Co-Operation
*Caroline Bongiwe Ncube*

**Intellectual Property Rights and Competition in Standard Setting**
Objectives and Tensions
*Valerio Torti*

**Re-Thinking Intellectual Property**
The Political Economy of Copyright Protection in the Digital Era
*YiJun Tian*

**The Development of Intellectual Property Regimes in the Middle East**
*David Price*

**Intellectual Property, Community Rights and Human Rights**
The Biological and Genetic Resources of Developing Countries
*Marcelin Tonye Mahop*

**Intellectual Property in Global Governance**
The Crisis of Equity in the Knowledge Economy
*Chidi Oguamanam*

**Intellectual Property Overlaps**
Theory, Strategies, and Solutions
*Robert Tomkowicz*

For more information about this series, please visit: https://www.routledge.com

# Intellectual Property Branding in the Developing World

## A New Approach to Non-Technological Innovations

**Tshimanga Kongolo**

Routledge
Taylor & Francis Group
LONDON AND NEW YORK

First published 2019
by Routledge
2 Park Square, Milton Park, Abingdon, Oxon OX14 4RN

and by Routledge
605 Third Avenue, New York, NY 10017

First issued in paperback 2021

*Routledge is an imprint of the Taylor & Francis Group, an informa business*



Publisher's Note
The publisher has gone to great lengths to ensure the quality of this reprint but points out that some imperfections in the original copies may be apparent.

*British Library Cataloguing-in-Publication Data*
A catalogue record for this book is available from the British Library

*Library of Congress Cataloging-in-Publication Data*
Names: Kongolo, Tshimanga, author.
Title: Intellectual property branding in the developing world: a new approach to non-technological innovations / by Tshimanga Kongolo.
Description: Abingdon, Oxon; New York, NY: Routledge, 2019. |
Series: Routledge research in intellectual property |
Includes bibliographical references and index.
Identifiers: LCCN 2019003448 | ISBN 9781138298965 (hbk)
Subjects: LCSH: Brand name products—Law and legislation—Developing countries. | Intellectual property—Economic aspects—Developing countries.
Classification: LCC K1569 .K665 2019 | DDC 346/.124048—dc23
LC record available at https://lccn.loc.gov/2019003448

ISBN 13: 978-1-03-224117-3 (pbk)
ISBN 13: 978-1-138-29896-5 (hbk)

DOI: 10.4324/9781315098272

Typeset in Galliard
by codeMantra

To my son Kazadi and my daughter Awoi

# Contents

# Preface

If a strong belief is considered a religion, the intellectual property (IP) system is my religion. I do believe in its power to transform a society and contribute to the well-being of people. I started writing on IP when IP was still unknown by non-experts and when it could easily be categorized as science fiction, whereby imaginative concepts were the baselines, and the future was more inspiring/exciting than the present. I made a choice to be part of this unidentified journey. IP was unpopular in the developing world. Needless to recall, one of the reasons for the unpopularity of the IP system stemmed from its misuse by colonial powers during the colonial period to protect their interests and serve as an instrument of commerce to the detriment of the colonized countries. Up until recently, the standards of most international IP norms were decided/defined by developed countries and were based on their own IP environment and needs.

Nowadays, the landscape of IP has changed, and the developing world has contributed to this change. Recently, IP has more and more been deemed a strategic tool, enhancing innovation both at a country's and at a company's levels. This shift is likewise perceived in the area of innovation, which has changed face and geography from West to East. In the current world, knowledge and skills are key factors, enabling economic and technological growth. In the arena of non-technological innovation, with the growing importance of cosmetics; textiles; and agriculture, including foods, where raw material and knowledge belong to the developing world, the latter has a comparative advantage. Branding of their products should be encouraged and implemented. The main question to be asked and answered in this book is how the developing world is coping in the areas of non-technological innovation and branding.

IP-Innovation-Branding constitute the major pillars for any successful innovation system. Innovation does take place in low-income economies, lower middle-income economies, upper middle-income economies, and high-income economies. In several countries from the developing world, it is difficult to capture and assess the status of innovation due to the coexistence of formal and informal economies. Meanwhile, it is true that innovation is rendered visible, thanks to branding.

Through success stories in the realm of both non-technological innovation and branding, it is demonstrated that the developing world is progressing well in these areas. The link between non-technological innovation and branding is illustrated through case studies. In my view, innovation goes hand in hand with branding, and in the very near future, no innovation will be able to reach the market if it is not branded. **Branding innovations** should be a good strategic tool to be used by countries in the developing world, mainly in the areas where they have competitive advantages.

Writing a book involves a number of challenges from different angles. I spent a long time researching in this exciting field of innovation and branding in order to capture its benefit for the developing world. Collecting success stories from the developing world was part of my research that I could not have achieved without the assistance of Ms. Nardie Daniel, to whom I am grateful. Finally, I am appreciative of my children, who were part of the scenario when I was writing this book without being aware that I was doing a serious work. I still remember the day my daughter (11 years old) made fun of me while I was writing the introduction of this book as I was able to produce only a page of writing after spending 8 hours (of concentration?). She thought she could do better.

This book has a wide scope and may assist scholars, entrepreneurs, academics, IP advisors, and marketing and brand promoters in understanding the connection between branding and innovation. This work is also expected to provide both context and guidance to policy makers, mainly from the developing world, helping them to benefit from the innovation system at large.

Tshimanga Kongolo

# Acknowledgements

The author is grateful to his son Kazadi and daughter Awoi for their patience and unspoken support.

He is thankful to the following companies, which provided permission to include images of their products in this book: TopFruit, Pink Lady, South Africa; Himalayan Bio Trade Private Limited (HBTL), Nepal; Inaya Zanzibar, Tanzania; Malée Cosmetics Pty Ltd., South Africa; Guanomad, Madagascar; Grenada Chocolate Company, Grenada; Ly Ly Foods, Cambodia; Pure Fiji Export Limited, Fiji; Akoma Cooperative Multi-Purpose Society (AKOMA), Ghana; soleRebels, Ethiopia; and Beauty Bee Company Limited, Kenya.

## Disclaimer

# Abbreviations and acronyms

| | |
|---|---|
| IP | Intellectual Property |
| IPRs | Intellectual Property Rights |
| R&D | Research and Development |
| TK | Traditional Knowledge |
| TCEs | Traditional Cultural Expressions |
| OVOP | One Village, One Product |
| OTOP | One Town, One Product |
| OTOI | One Town, One Innovation |
| GIs | Geographical Indications |
| AI | Artificial Intelligence |
| DI | Digital Intelligence |
| CSR | Corporate Social Responsibility |
| GNI | Gross National Income |
| LDCs | Least-Developed-Countries |
| PCT | Patent Cooperation Treaty |
| BRICS | Brazil, Russia, India, China, South Africa |
| DST | Data Stream Technology |
| SIJBCO | Sunny Isle Jamaican Black Castor Oil |
| APROMAIZ | Productores De Maiz Blanco Gigante Del Cusco |
| PDCI | Pecuaria Development Cooperative Inc. |
| UMFI | Upland Marketing Foundation, Inc. |
| NGO | Non-Governmental Organization |
| AO | Appellation of Origin |
| HBTL | Himalayan Bio Trade Private Limited |
| FSC | Forest Stewardship Council |
| EU | European Union |
| USPTO | United States Patent and Trademark Office |
| OHIM | Office for Harmonization in the Internal Market |
| EUIPO | European Union Intellectual Property Office |
| JNTBGRI | Jawaharlal Nehru Tropical Botanical Garden and Research Institute |
| TBGRIC | Tropical Botanical Garden and Research Institute |
| AICRPE | All India Coordinated Research Project on Ethnobiology |

| | |
|---|---|
| HYX | Heng Yuan Xiang Group |
| SCC | Saigon Cosmetics Corporation |
| SME | Small and Medium-Sized Enterprise |
| CIPC | Companies and Intellectual Property Commission |
| CORBANA | Corporación Bananera Nacional Corbana, S.A. |
| BMBC | Banana Molecular Biology Center |
| F&B | Food and Beverage |
| EIPO | Ethiopian Intellectual Property Office |
| GDP | Gross Domestic Product |
| CTS | Ceylon Tea Services Limited |
| UAE | United Arab Emirates |
| ALCOTEXA | Alexandria Cotton Exporters Association |
| ASEAN | Association of Southeast Asian Nations |
| MSMEs | Micro, Small and Medium Enterprises |
| HUL | Hindustan Unilever Limited |
| P&G | Procter and Gamble |
| FMCG | Fast-Moving Consumer's Goods |

# General introduction

In the current world, knowledge and skills are key factors enabling economic and technological growth. Innovation occupies a considerable place and plays an important role in enhancing progress. The scope of innovation is broad and difficult to delimit and may relate to the implementation of a new product, process, marketing method, and organizational method.

As indicated in the title, this book covers three main concepts: namely, intellectual property (IP), innovation, and branding. In the view of the author, the three concepts are interlinked (IP-Innovation-Branding) and constitute the major pillars for any successful innovation system. IP goes along with creativity, which is also an important element for both innovation and branding. IP may serve as an innovation indicator, as well as, an innovation incentive.

The main question is how the developing world is managing the link between ***IP-Innovation-Branding***. In this connection, case studies and success stories taking place in the developing world will be scrutinized to illustrate this relationship.

Within the IP landscape, trademarks, designs, and geographical indications play a significant role in identifying and distinguishing products (goods and services). Traditional knowledge, which is considered a newcomer in the IP field, has contributed tremendously to the global value chain, and should not be underestimated or overlooked.

Recently at the global level, innovation has changed face and geography, moving from West to East, and from North to South. Innovation does take place in low-income economies, lower-middle-income economies, upper-middle-income economies, and high-income economies. Innovation is no longer a reserved domain for high-tech countries and does not relate necessarily to Research and Development (R&D). As it will be seen through the book, several countries from the developing world are using many existing innovation techniques to catch up the gap and to become more competitive at the international market.

The Oslo Manual has attempted to define an innovation as the implementation of a new or significantly improved product (good or service), or process, a new marketing method, or a new organizational method in business practices, workplace organization, or external relations.[1] A variety of factors may positively or negatively impact an innovation. Innovation activities take place in all parts of an economy, such as manufacturing, service industries, public administrations, the health sector and, even private households.[2]

The concept of innovation pertains to both technological and non-technological innovations. Technological innovations are usually associated with product and process innovation, whereas non-technological innovations are generally associated with marketing and organizational innovations. It should be underlined that technological and non-technological innovations are highly interconnected.

In the developing world, many questions are on the table as to the impacts of innovations on the overall economy of a country. Most of the time, a particular emphasis is put on technological innovations to the detriment of non-technological innovations. In several countries from the developing world, it is difficult to capture and assess the status of innovation due to the coexistence of formal and informal economies. As it will be demonstrated, in the developing world, a large number of innovations are taking place in the non-technological sector, including in diverse industries such as foods, agriculture, service, textile/fashion, cosmetics, tourism, and creative industries. In the developing world, there are more and more non-technological innovations or innovations without research compared to technological innovations.

The impacts of non-technological innovations on development will be highlighted. Nowadays, it seems insufficient to see innovation only through the lens of new product development and process innovation or traditional R&D. Recent literature on innovation highlights the interactive feature of innovation processes where non-technological activities play a crucial role, stressing that non-technological factors are a requirement for getting the most of firms' capacity for technological innovation.

Agriculture is the most active sector in the developing world. Some countries have taken advantage of their strength to encourage innovation in this sector by setting up incentives and building up adequate infrastructure to escort innovation activities. Horticulture, a sub-sector of agriculture, has shown remarkable growth in certain countries as demonstrated through case studies.

As it will be shown through this study, innovation has economic value, thanks to commercialization. In this context, branding plays a very important role in the commercialization of innovative products. It can serve as a mirror of success to an innovation. An innovation is rendered visible thanks to branding. Branding is another area where the developing world is making a lot of progress to promote their innovations in general and products in particular.

In the present world with the existence of high competition level among competitors worldwide, branding is another concept which adds value to innovation. Branding a product (goods and service) to reach the market is gaining more and more significance in commerce. Branding goes along with marketing. New marketing methods that may qualify as innovations came to light to support branding which is supposed to be an old concept. In the field of IP, it is well recognized that trademarks, designs and geographical indications are tools or instruments that may support the branding of both technological and non-technological innovations. In this context, more and more companies from the developing world are utilizing these tools to compete among themselves and the big players at the global level.

The concepts of brand and branding are multifaceted in nature and may be perceived differently by different actors. A brand should not be confused with a trademark, which is one form of protection of a brand. A brand can as well be protected through design, geographical indication or unfair competition. For an entrepreneur, a brand goes beyond protection. It reflects the image of the product (good or service), reputation, and a trustful relationship between a customer and a producer.

A brand cannot be created suddenly. It is a result of a tremendous effort requiring investments and good strategies. As a result, a brand is personal to an individual. A brand is registered in the mind of each consumer. When a brand is damaged, the effect is huge in the minds of consumers. Consequently, the minds of consumers would be likewise damaged and the trust destroyed. One bad experience over a brand may destroy its reputation. Normally, consumers are loyal to their brands. There is an emotional attachment to the brand. To remain relevant and maintain consumers' preference in the changing and competitive world, brands owners must continue to be innovative. For a brand to survive, innovation is the key to keep pace with the changes. Every touch point that a consumer has with the product can be a brand creating or destroying moment.

Looking at the IP data, the trend of growth in trademark and industrial design applications and registrations in the developing world is evident. In a large number of countries in the developing world consumers are more and more keen on seeing enterprises promoting their products through trademarks and designs. Under the same reasoning, several enterprises file for registration of their marks to be able to identify their products and serve as a certificate of quality. A trademark may be considered as a highway used to bring products to the market. It is a valuable source of information on the products. Trademarks may relate to both product and marketing innovations. In the developing world, the number of registrations could be higher but because of the coexistence of both formal and informal economies, there are numerous marks that are unregistered. It is true that those unregistered marks or designs serve the same function, which is to enable consumers to identify their goods or services in the informal economy.

In the developing world, the contribution to the global value chain of traditional knowledge (TK), which is a newcomer in the purview of IP, is well recognized. TK is present in most of the fields as are innovation and branding. As it will be seen in this study, TK constitutes a baseline for knowledge and skill utilized in many domains.

This study aims to lend support to the hypothesis that "innovation" is no longer exclusively synonymous with technological research and development or scientific expertise. Non-technological marketing innovation, for instance, that is facilitated by brands and branding is equally important. Further, this study purports to demonstrate that despite a lack of technological and scientific infrastructure the developing world is progressing and innovating in non-technological ways, across multiple non-technological sectors, in manners that allow them to harness and leverage their intellectual property assets.

This study attempts to identify success stories in both areas: namely, branding and non-technological innovations in the developing world. The research seeks to highlight real-life examples of people and business organizations, from the developing world that operate in these areas and who have achieved success to learn from. Through success stories, it will be demonstrated that innovation, in general, and non-technological innovation, in particular, must go hand in hand with branding. **Branding innovations** should be a good strategic tool to be used by countries in the developing world mainly in the areas where they have competitive advantages.

This book is divided into six chapters as follows:

The first chapter entitled "Conceptual Framework" will attempt to define key concepts forming the core pillars of this study. First, intellectual property landscape, whereby the role of trademarks in identifying products and geographical indications will be stressed together with the importance of designs in the modern world before highlighting the added value of traditional knowledge in the global value chain. Second, fundamentals of innovation will be underlined by displaying its different types, which are product innovation, process innovation, marketing innovation, and organizational innovation, and also by showing the interconnection between technological and non-technological innovations. Third, the essentials of branding will be examined to capture the scope of branding in the global economy before stressing different factors used to build up a strong brand which impacts on how a brand should be managed in the current world where the interface between trademarks, designs, and geographical indications commence to occupy an important place.

Chapter 2, entitled "Intellectual Property Trends in the Developing World from 2011 to 2016 Based on Income Status," will put forward the trends of IP in the developing world from 2011 to 2016 through the evaluation of trademark, design, and patent figures of selected countries grouped by their income status as classified by the World Bank: namely, low-income economies, lower-middle-income economies, upper-middle-income economies, and high-income economies.

Chapter 3 titled, "Non-Technological Innovations and Intellectual Property in the Developing World," will emphasize through success stories and case studies the role of a trademark as an innovation indicator before looking at innovation in the service sector, innovation in agro-industry, and innovation in the area of traditional knowledge.

Chapter 4, entitled "Branding of Local Products in Diverse Industries in the Developing World," will underscore success stories from the developing world relating to branding in the following areas: global branding strategies, local branding strategies, branding in coffee/tea industry, branding in food industry, branding in cosmetic industry, and branding in various sectors.

Chapter 5, titled "Branding Innovations in the Developing World," will underline why branding is so important for innovations mainly in the developing world through One Village, One Product (OVOP) or One Town, One Product (OTOP) model before showing the multidimensional facets of branding and innovations in the current world and new era by examining Patanjali Ayurved

Limited from India which is a very good example to follow. In addition, branding traditional knowledge in the innovation era will be advocated prior to looking forward to the future of branding and innovations in the new era with a focus on the developing world.

Chapter 6, entitled "General Conclusion," will summarize different findings and propose the way forward.

## Notes

1 Oslo Manual, Guidelines for Collecting and Interpreting Innovation Data, Third Edition, OECD-EUROSTAT, 2005.
2 Oslo Manual, Guidelines for Collecting and Interpreting Innovation Data, Third Edition, OECD-EUROSTAT, 2005.

# 1 Conceptual framework

## Intellectual property landscape

Within the IP landscape, trademarks, designs, and geographical indications play a significant role in identifying and distinguishing products (goods and services). Traditional knowledge, which is considered a newcomer in the IP field, has contributed tremendously to the global value chain, which should not be underestimated or overlooked.

### *Role of trademarks in identifying products (goods and services)*

The conventional trademark system encompasses some well-established general principles that most national laws provide in conformity with international trademark norms.[1] There is no doubt that trademarks are the most visible IP subject matter. A trademark may be any sign, any combination of signs, colors, symbols, letters, words, and drawing, capable of distinguishing the goods or services of one undertaking from those of the other.

To be eligible for protection, the principle is that the sign should be inherently distinctive enough to enable consumers to make the choice, with the aim of not misleading them or creating a likelihood of confusion. Actually, some countries have agreed to provide protection to signs that have acquired distinctiveness through use, creating a second meaning to these signs to be identified as such by consumers.

A trademark enables consumers to differentiate the products of one enterprise from those of the other. It provides exclusive right to its owner to prevent competitors from using the protected mark in the course of commerce. It is a very useful tool used in business to identify the origin of products as well as their quality, empowering consumers to make a trustworthy decision either to purchase the products or not to do so. Thus, a trademark is a source of valuable information on the products and conveys a message about the quality of the products to the consumers. The uniqueness of the products is perceived through the distinctive character of the trademark. Through a trusting and faithful relationship, consumers will no longer question the qualities embodied in the products. A trademark allows a consumer to save a search cost. It provides information to potential consumers and allows them to mentally compare products in order to decide within seconds without using complex search tools.

A trademark, being the most tangible intangible property, is easily identifiable by consumers. In the past, consumers were deemed to be laymen who had no knowledge of the products they intended to purchase. As a matter of fact, they were less demanding. Nowadays, things have changed, and consumers are very knowledgeable, and they know exactly what they intend to purchase. This has led producers to level up the quality of their products to meet consumers' demands and needs, and at the same time to compete against other competitors. In the past, consumers' needs were limited territorially, so the satisfaction effort and assessments from entrepreneurs were limited to a defined location.

***Currently, with the globalization of the world, producers have to satisfy the needs and expectations of a large number of consumers spread all over the world.*** Consequently, the behavior of customers is well scrutinized before any investment in the product is made in order to respond effectively to their expectations. Consumers from the developing world are as demanding as consumers from the developed world. The main difference may reside in the fact that those of the developing world have two coexisting and complementary markets: formal markets and informal markets. A consumer may opt for the first or second market depending on his/her purchasing power.

Trademark data may reflect the trend in trademark applications and registrations in the developing world. This goes together with business activities. Trademarks are in principle registered or protected where business activities are to be carried out or for strategic competition purposes. So, data on trademark registration is nowadays a very good indicator of both innovation and business activities.[2]

It should be underlined that two new factors have changed the current trademark landscape: namely, the Internet and the increased uses of human senses for business purposes to create new distinct signs which were not considered as such before, known as non-traditional marks or non-conventional marks.

Internet, being the new commercial platform, has enhanced e-commerce and generated new issues relating to the use of trademarks on the internet, including online infringement acts, on the one hand, and those pertaining to the potential liability of Internet intermediaries, on the other hand. Presence on the internet for any enterprise or firm is not an option but essential. It is a must, leading to the visibility of its products in a wide sphere. This assertion is valid in both developed and developing worlds. Lawful uses and unlawful uses of trademarks both coexist on the internet. It may be difficult in some instances to separate the two. The geographical delimitation of the use of a trademark on the Internet is a big challenge, given its global nature. In addition, it should be underlined that, in business, the use of a trademark to maintain registration is required prior to renewing the protection period. Nowadays, more businesses take place on the Internet. Given the global nature of the internet, it is not always easy to prove the territorial uses of trademarks on the internet to maintain registration. Legislations different from one country to another and components considered to determine the use are not necessarily similar.

The second current issue brought out by the internet pertains to the potential liability of intermediaries, including the liability of search engines for the sale of trademarks as keywords (e.g. Google), the liability of Internet auction sites for trademark infringement (e.g. eBay), and trademark infringement in social media and virtual worlds (e.g. Facebook). The main question is "who is liable?" Is it the intermediary (e.g. Internet providers) or the owners of the sites or users? Under the current perspectives, two schools of thought exist: (1) to consider online intermediaries as secondary trademark liable (safe harbor) and (2) to strengthen the liability of online intermediaries by taking into consideration their state of mind and the necessity of anti-counterfeit measures. Meaning that the online intermediaries must prove that they took reasonable steps to prevent the unlawful behavior.

The third issue generated by the internet in the context of trademarks pertains to the combination of the first and second issues: namely, the question of the use of keywords that are supposed to belong to a competitor as metatags in advertising and whether this amounts to an infringement. In other words, does the use of keywords for search purposes qualify as the use of a trademark? In most jurisdictions, an act is deemed as an infringing act only if it qualifies or is considered the "use of a trademark." The question may be extended to other stakeholders in the Internet auction sites and in social media.

Nowadays, enterprises knowing the positive effects of trademarks in the minds of consumers have set up distinct signs which did not exist before, using more and more of the five human senses. The aim is to attract consumers and enable them to differentiate between products based on their color, smell, touch/feel, taste, and sound. The new category of marks is called non-traditional or non-conventional marks. Within the non-traditional marks, signs are grouped into visible signs and non-visible signs. Visible signs include three-dimensional marks, color marks, position marks, gesture marks, motion or multimedia signs, holograms, slogans, and titles of films and books. Non-visible signs comprise olfactory marks (smell marks), sound marks, taste marks, and texture or feel marks.

It is well recognized that to be protected, a trademark must be distinct. The challenge is how the new category of marks would meet this requirement. It is likewise agreed that non-traditional marks should not be descriptive. Meaning that, in principle, smell marks should not be used for perfume nor taste marks for drinks or foods, etc. Under the same perspectives, the unsettled question is whether a single color may be distinct enough to qualify as a trademark. In some legislation, some types of non-visible signs are provided protection, provided that the distinctiveness is acquired through use. A distinctiveness test is still challenging for most non-traditional marks.

How do you prove that consumers purchase your products because of the secondary meaning or distinctiveness that they have acquired on the market? How do you prove that consumers have purchased your tires because they smell like rose? Is the smell the first distinctive sign that consumers assess to buy your products? The same questions may be asked for sound, single color, texture, and taste marks. Other issues relate to the representation of those non-visible signs as a large number of legislations require that a mark be graphically represented for the registration purposes. To overcome the representation issue, a number of countries have opted for a description of the mark. The latter does not adequately solve this issue as in most of the cases defining a smell or sound by a description generate further issues on the interpretation and delimitation of the scope.

There is still a long way to go as many countries are still reluctant to provide full trademark protection for non-traditional marks, mainly for the non-visible signs. Meanwhile, it is true that if all the five senses of a human being become the hostage of business and trade, concerns over the availability of marks as well as other issues pertaining to public interest and public domain may come to light. The developing world is likewise divided. Some countries from the developing world have amended their trademark laws to provide protection to some non-traditional marks, such as single colors, smells, sounds, and 3D objects.

### *Importance of designs in the modern world*

In the current world, designs have gained more and more notoriety in trade by offering additional useful information on the products that may not be provided by trademarks. In the area of industrial designs, for instance, as prescribed under international norms,[3] the aesthetic aspect and the shape of the products are the key features that attract the eyes of consumers and make them purchase the products. People buy with their eyes. An industrial design makes the product appealing vis-à-vis consumers and increases its marketability and its commercial value. When selecting between a diversity of products of the same nature, the visual appeal of a product plays a great role in its choice by consumers.

Currently, a design is an important tool for business the same way as trademarks. Designs influence very much the judgment of consumers. Designs may relate to the automobile industry, the fashion industry, architecture, the aircraft industry, sports equipment, furniture, heavy equipment, cosmetics, electronics, telephones, etc. The aim is to make the product appealing and marketable. As for trademarks, consumers will associate the product quality with its design or look. The relationship between consumers and producers is built on trust. ***The appealing aspect of the design will be the decisive factor inducing a consumer to buy a product.***

Design is an area of IP whereby consumers may easily be grouped into two categories: namely, skilled or informed consumers and unskilled consumers. The knowledge of a consumer may be limited to the category of product he/she is interested in. Outside the area of his/her interest or expertise, the same consumer may have no ability to make a well-informed decision. A skilled/informed consumer in the fashion industry may be an outsider in the automobile industries, and vice versa. The same may be observed, even in some sectors that may be deemed related, such as cosmetics and fashion. A skilled or skillful consumer in the fashion industry may not be knowledgeable in the perfume or cosmetics industry.

The role of designs in the modern world is significant. In the developing world, in many countries, traditional designs are products of culture, and each design may have a specific meaning. Traditional designs are more and more used in the fashion industry. ***The visual appearance of the product is a determinant.*** Even in ancient times, the shape of the product was valuable vis-à-vis consumers. In the modern age, designs go along with investments. Enterprises being aware of the design importance have invested in the presentation and packaging of the products they sell to their clients.

In the area of design, another new component that will change the design industry is the so-called artificial intelligence (AI). The author prefers the term digital intelligence (DI), reflecting well the environment or platform where the creation takes place. The two terms will be used concurrently where appropriate. AI/DI encompasses both the technical part protectable under patents and the shape or look (if visible) protectable under design. The current design system may not always be suitable to protect AI/DI, mainly in relation to the functionality character (of the shape) that may be considered under design laws of many countries as non-protectable.

### *Added value of geographical indications in promoting local products*

Geographical indications perform the same role of identifying products and their qualities as prescribed under international norms.[4] The difference between a geographical indication, a trademark, and a design is that in respect of a geographical indication, the quality of the product is due to its geographical location or its place of production/origin. ***A geographical indication is a tool for promoting local products by displaying their original quality, making them unique compared with similar products produced elsewhere.*** This is to say that a geographical indication adds tremendous value to the product.

Depending on the legal regime of protection chosen by a country, a geographical indication may be protected under a sui generis regime or through a trademark system.[5] Conditions of protection and eligibility are different. Some countries have opted to protect geographical indications under one of the following regimes of trademark: collective marks, authentication marks, or certification marks. With respect to the developing world, the choice in the regime of protection should be taken seriously, keeping in mind national interests.

In most cases, a geographical indication involves long-standing techniques and knowledge used to produce the product. Know-how developed from generation to generation may constitute the core skills and knowledge enabling the uniqueness of the production method that generates the unique quality. In the agro-sector, the weather and climate may influence the product's quality. Certain qualities may be generated by the presence of a climate condition deemed adequate. Unlike in Europe, in the developing world and in a large number of countries, the geographical indication system is a new concept and a new business tool to promote local products.

It should also be stated that geographical indications might be present in both the agro-sector and the non-agro-sector. Although most of the renowned geographical indications are in the agro-sector, there are new geographical indications in the non-agro-sector, such as in the textile industry, forming part of their cultural heritage. These new geographical indications are more and more seen in the developing world.

The challenges in the developing world with regard to geographical indications are enormous. Compliance with established standards of production to maintain the quality of the geographical indication product is among the main issues. Likewise, the cost involved in production, coupled with quality control put in place, is not always favorable to countries which have only a few geographical indications to protect. In addition, the geographical limitation/boundaries of the areas of production are not always easy to define.

Notwithstanding existing challenges with regard to certain countries in the developing world, it should be recognized that if used efficiently, the GI system may enable the promotion of local products.

### *Interfaces among trademarks, designs, copyright, and patents*

In the current world of business and commerce, the interface among trademarks, designs, patents, and copyright is a new reality that any entrepreneur must be aware of. The simultaneous use of the four intellectual property rights (IPRs) by an entrepreneur has become a strategic tool whereby the merit of each regime of protection and business advantages are considered. The entrepreneur may decide to protect one, two, or three aspects of IP in a product, provided that the set of conditions is met for each.

In the conventional world of IP, the division or separation is made among the IP branches or categories. In the business sector, the division does not always make sense. This division is left to lawyers or attorneys. All these IPRs may constitute a package in a transaction or in a license agreement. The combination of protections in one product is becoming common nowadays. The functionality part of the product may be protected under patent; the visual aspect, under design or copyright; and the distinctiveness aspect, under the trademark. A good example of a combination of protection is a three-dimensional object, such as a mobile telephone.

The advantage of the combination of protections is that it enables the entrepreneur to recoup his/her investment and choose the best option(s). That is to say that an entrepreneur will have diverse means to take advantage of his/her rights. Meanwhile, the demerit of the combination of protections is that the owner of the rights will have unlimited time of protection by excluding third parties or potential competitors. Moreover, the combination of protections may prevent or delay the IPRs from falling into the public domain, which is considered the normal place to be after the expiration of the protection period(s).

It should be stressed that as far as the interface among trademarks, designs, patents, and copyright is concerned, in terms of protection, despite the fact that the cumulus of protection is the trend, under the IP laws of some countries in both developed and developing worlds, a non-cumulus protection regime is still the rule. Meaning that the same product may be prevented from enjoying several protection regimes.

The question to be asked in the future is whether excess combination of protections may lead to a brand fatigue vis-à-vis consumers.

### *Significance of traditional knowledge in the global value chain*

Traditional knowledge (TK) is a newcomer in the field of IP. It is constituted by knowledge and skills passed from generation to generation and having economic value.[6] Currently, its contribution to the global value chain is recognized. TK is present not only in the field of biotechnology, including medical sciences, but also in many fields in the non-technological sector, such as cosmetics, fashion/textiles, the agro-industry, and food.[7]

The main question at the beginning of the debate was whether TK was an IP.[8] After longstanding discussions for many years not only at the international level but also at the regional and national levels, it is now well recognized that TK is an IP. Some argue that TK does not qualify as an IP because it is old and collective, it has no time limit, and the owner is not identifiable. It should be pointed out that some conventional IPRs may be collective, and some may be protected indefinitely, such as trademarks. It has been demonstrated that TK is dynamic and that a community or a group of people and individuals in some circumstances may own TK. In addition, denying TK protection just because it is different compared to other conventional IPRs does not make sense. TK is a product of human intellect deserving protection. The main issue is to find out the best way of protecting TK. Some have argued that protecting TK through a sui generis regime whereby specific features or characteristics of TK are first considered should be given preeminence. The sui generis system does not exclude TK matters protectable under the conventional IP regime to be protected if conditions are met.

TK in a broad sense encompasses traditional cultural expressions, known as TCEs.[9] TCEs have tremendously contributed to the modern design industries, including textiles and fashion.

With globalization, free movement of ideas, knowledge, and skills are enabled. Consequently, unrelated persons may easily misappropriate TK without any payment to the right holders or, in most cases, with no permission. With the increased value of genetic resources that are widely located in the South, unrelated persons may take advantage of free access to misappropriate not only the skills but also these genetic resources for their own benefit. Some may use existing IPRs to exclude the original right holders from using their TK for commercial purposes. ***As will be seen through case studies, TK is fully in commerce and trade, and has extended to various sectors or industries, including pharmaceuticals, cosmetics, textiles, coffee, tea, and agriculture.***

Within the debate, despite the fact that some countries are still reluctant, the disclosure of country of origin is proposed as part of the solution for better protection of TK. The disclosure may somehow enable TK owners to control their TK and select who should have access. This could also be a strong mechanism to fight against misappropriation of TK. There is a global recognition of the contribution of TK to the global value chain. Under the same perspectives, the regime of prior informed consent and access, and sharing of benefits have been advocated under certain international laws, such as the Nagoya Protocol and the Convention on Biological Diversity (CBD).

It should be underscored that under the World Intellectual Property Organization (WIPO) Intergovernmental Committee on Intellectual Property and Genetic Resources, Traditional Knowledge and Folklore (IGC), negotiations with the objective of reaching agreement on the text(s) of an international legal instrument(s), which will ensure the effective protection of TK, TCEs, and genetic resources (GRs), are proceeding.

## Fundamentals of innovation

Innovation is like an ice cream with multiple flavors, and IP is one of the flavors that may influence the taste. ***The choice of the right flavor is the key.*** IP may serve as an innovation incentive and an innovation indicator as well. A good IP infrastructure, in a broad sense, may induce creativity and secure return on investments. At the same time, the volume of new IP products on a market may signal the innovation shape of that market.[10]

Although the concept of innovation is not novel, its definition is still unsettled because of its wide coverage, which is hard to delimit. The Oslo Manual has attempted to define an innovation as the implementation of a new or significantly improved product (good or service) or process; a new marketing method; or a new organizational method in business practices, workplace organization, or external relations.[11]

The Oslo Manual distinguishes four categories of innovations as follows: product innovation, process innovation, marketing innovation, and organizational innovation.

Product innovation is the introduction of goods or services that are new or significantly improved with respect to their characteristics or intended uses.

Process innovation is the implementation of a new or significantly improved process or delivery method.

A marketing innovation is the implementation of a new marketing method involving significant changes in the delivery of the product. Marketing innovation encompasses three dimensions[12]:

1 Product strategy
2 Price strategy
3 Promotion strategy

These strategies lead to tactical marketing actions, such as changes in design or packaging, changes in sales or distribution methods, changes in advertising or permanent exhibitions. The objectives are to increase the attractiveness of the firms' goods or services and/or to enter new markets. Firms focusing attention on marketing initiatives are likely to have a better ability to increase customer satisfaction compared to competitors.

An organizational innovation is the implementation of a new organizational method in a firm's business practices, workplace organization, or external relations.[13]

Organizational innovations can be understood both as enablers for other types of innovations and as a distinct form of innovation (direct source of competitive advantage). The measurement of an organizational innovation and its effects is methodologically challenging due to its complexity. Organizational innovation comprises three types of practice[14]:

1 Management practice (teamwork, knowledge management, flexible work arrangements)
2 Production approaches (change to the work organization, total quality management, business re-engineering).
3 External relations (outsourcing, networking, customer relations).

There is a link between marketing and organizational innovation strategies on technological innovation performance.[15]

***A shared feature of any innovation is that it must have been implemented.*** A new or improved product is implemented when it is introduced on the market. New processes, marketing methods, or organizational methods are implemented when they are brought into actual use in the firm's operations.[16] At the end of the day, innovation is about product upgrading, process upgrading, marketing approaches upgrading, and structural or managerial upgrading. An innovation may relate also to a new application of the existing technology to a new or different environment responding and corresponding to the needs of the stakeholders.

The Global Innovation Index has added that today, innovation capacity is seen more and more as the ability to exploit new technological combinations; it embraces the notion of incremental innovation and innovation without research.[17]

The set of issues one must deal with across the spectrum of science, technology, and innovation is quite immense.[18]

It is not the purpose of this study to discuss the different approaches to the definition of an innovation. The common denominator is that for any innovation, there should be a degree of novelty.

The combination of two or three types of innovations is not rare or exceptional, each having its own attributes and implementation scheme. Innovation is in principle difficult to measure. A key challenge is to find metrics that capture innovation as it actually happens in the world today.[19] It is always challenging to single out the main factor that has contributed to an innovation. A variety of factors may positively or negatively have impact on an innovation. Innovation activities take place in all parts of economy: manufacturing, the service industries, public administrations, the health sector, and even private households.[20]

Regional differences in levels of innovation activity can be substantial, and identifying the main characteristics and factors that promote innovation activity and the development of specific sectors at the regional level can help in understanding innovation processes and be valuable for the elaboration of policy.[21] This is where the environment or the infrastructure plays an important role in setting up incentives for innovation activities to result in innovations.

Several obstacles hamper innovation activities in the developing world, including cost, knowledge, market, and institution/infrastructure. A number of exogenous systemic factors shape the innovation landscape in the developing world, such as: macroeconomic uncertainty, instability, physical infrastructure (lack of basic services, such as electricity, or "old" communications technologies), institutional fragility, lack of social awareness about innovation, risk-averse nature of enterprises, lack of entrepreneurs, existence of barriers to business start-up, and lack of public policy instruments for business support and management training.[22] As in most of the countries in the developing world, technological knowledge is introduced to these countries through foreign direct investment, importation, and technology licensing, and the core challenges are the adaptation, imitation, and absorptive capacity of local entities to translate this knowledge to implementable ones for the benefit of the firms or the country.

An innovation is not an end by itself. It is a process that leads to the end, which could be progress, growth, or development. This is valid, likewise, when a government designs the innovation policy of a country. In other words, the innovation policy should be seen as a means for achieving the development goal and not the goal itself.

Hence, innovation is a driving force to achieve sustainable development.

IP may not only drive change in the field of innovation but also is itself impacted by the changing innovation system. In the new innovation landscape, IP is a vehicle for knowledge transfer and protection, facilitating the vertical disintegration of knowledge-based industries.[23]

Trade is one of the framework conditions that can strengthen innovation in the business sector. It can serve as an avenue for knowledge diffusion. It affects the incentives of firms toward innovative activities. Trade in tangible goods can facilitate the exchange of intangible ideas. Access to foreign technology and knowledge can accelerate domestic innovation and growth. Trade in technology, such as through the licensing of intellectual property, is another channel of technology diffusion. Trade can affect innovation through competition. Regulations can affect trade and innovation in multiple ways. They can negatively affect the rate of innovation by imposing additional burdens on innovation. Capacity and incentives for new technology adoption for firms may be affected by the broader regulatory infrastructure.[24]

Under this framework, policy makers are expected to intervene when the system of knowledge generation and diffusion does not achieve its objectives of contributing to innovation and technological progress in an efficient manner because of the lack of well-developed networks between the different actors of the system or because of institutional or infrastructural weaknesses. For example, systemic failures may include the inefficient flow of information, the lack of collaboration among firms, the lack of university-industry collaboration, and the inadequacy between basic research done in universities and firms' needs.[25]

Innovation does take place in the informal economy in the form of new products, product improvements, process improvements, and the utilization of new tools. This type of innovation has been characterized as "quick responses to market demand and supply," solving problems to overcome shortcomings of the formal economy and/or to adapt foreign products to local conditions.[26] Connections between the formal and informal economies lead to knowledge being shared, exchanged, combined, and applied to create new products, services, and processes. Lacking are studies assessing the role of innovation emanating within and from the informal sector.

It is critical to consider how innovation works in the informal sector, given that it represents the main source of income for a large proportion of the population in low- and middle-income countries. Clearly, innovation in this context is not normally based on R&D but rather on incremental and non-technological innovation. However, the informal sector does not appear in official statistics, and knowledge of how to assess and promote innovation in informal contexts is still lacking.[27] In the developing world, the informal economy is often a greater source of innovation than the formal sector.[28]

In the developing world, innovation impacts the lives of people. It is present in any field. It is not reserved only for the technological sector. Among non-technological innovation, trademarks, designs, geographical indications, and traditional knowledge play a predominant role.

In accordance with the Oslo Manual, marketing innovation and organizational innovation are considered non-technological innovations.

Under this study, the focus will be on non-technological innovations or innovations without research in the developing world: namely, marketing innovation. To be more pragmatic, success stories and case studies from this sector taking place in the developing world will be highlighted.

## Essentials of branding

The concepts of brand and branding are multifaceted in nature and may be perceived differently by different actors. A brand should not be confused with a trademark, which is one form of protection of a brand. A brand can also be protected through design, geographical indication, or unfair competition. For an entrepreneur, a brand goes beyond protection. It reflects the image of the product (good or service), reputation, and a trustful relationship between a customer and a producer.

As stated, branding is another concept that should always escort both IP and innovation. It is a process enabling the promotion of products with an aim of creating a strong link/relationship with the clients/customers so that they may purchase the product without having to visualize it. In other words, branding is a mechanism that is used to create a strong product image, allowing consumers to recognize the product, including the embodied quality, with no effort. A brand is what consumers purchase. The name of the product itself suffices for the clients to identify it and to rely on its quality. A consumer is linked emotionally and intuitively with a brand. ***The relationship between the producer and the customers is like that between members from the same club or cooperative.***

What the consumer is looking for behind the brand is the guarantee of a specific quality, generally considered to be superior. Brands exist in all sectors, but with different modalities. The industrial sector defines, among other things, the ways in which the brand can be differentiated and the modes of accessibility of the product.[29]

A brand cannot be created suddenly. It is a result of tremendous effort requiring investments and good strategies. As a result, a brand is personal to an individual. A brand is registered in the mind of each consumer. When a brand is damaged, the effect is huge in the minds of consumers. ***Consequently, the minds of consumers would be likewise damaged and the trust destroyed.*** One bad experience with a brand may destroy its reputation. Normally, consumers are loyal to their brands. There is an emotional attachment to the brand.

Globalization is among the most important challenges facing companies today, whether operations are global or conducted in a single country.[30]

***To remain relevant and maintain consumers' preferences, in the changing and competitive world, brand owners must continue to be innovative.*** For a brand to survive, innovation is the key to keep pace with the changes. Every touch point that a consumer has with the product can be a brand creating or brand destroying moment.

It should be pointed out that a distinction is made between a corporate brand and a product brand. The promotion of a corporate brand or a product brand is a matter of strategy specific to each commercial entity or a firm. Neither are exclusive. They do coexist. It is said that corporate brands aim at supporting all aspects of the firm and differentiate the firm from its competitors. Corporate branding enables firms to use the vision and culture of the whole organization explicitly as part of its uniqueness. Corporate brands can increase the firm's visibility, recognition, and reputation to a greater extent than can product brands. It is also said that corporate brand failure produces more damage to the corporate image than that of a product brand. The focus of a product brand is on customers, while that of a corporate brand is on stakeholders. When products vary and change over time and across markets, customers usually use corporate brand names and corporate identities to recognize and comprehend products or services.

It should be stressed that each brand holds a distinct position in its product category. Therefore, the positioning of a brand is always a strategic decision for a company or a brand because the position can be central to customers' perception and choice decisions. The position of a brand is how the brand is perceived in the minds of consumers relative to competitive offerings. Three sets of features are considered to be the baseline for a good position for a brand: (1) perception of uniqueness (vis-à-vis competitors), (2) prevalence (e.g. how many customers are aware of it), and (3) strength. Branding requires a strategic method to make the brand a unique one vis-à-vis consumers. A strong brand does not mean a dominant brand. An enterprise may well position its brand as the second brand on the market to be able to replace the first brand in case of deficiency or to target the second level of consumers of that product.

The common objective of brands is to introduce differentiation within a given sector, through the promotion of the specific values on which their identity is built.[31]

A brand is normally represented by a logo or a sign, making products recognizable by the customers and enabling them to distinguish those products from products emanating from other competitors.

Logos are to modern communication and consumption activities what numbers are to mathematics and words to language. The logo plays a role in social relations for two complementary reasons: on the one hand, for the informational content it communicates to the consumer before the purchase; on the other hand, for the perception it will create of the same consumer after the purchase.[32]

When one talks about a brand, the intrinsic value of the brand, namely financial value and social value, should not be underestimated. In addition, effective brand communication should always be stressed. Given the fact that consumers are more interconnected now than before, failure to deliver the brand promise is punished by the market faster than before.

Brands must remain relevant to customers. That is the reason why the owners of brands continue to invest in their brands by being innovative. Brand owners may create social value via innovation as well as social changes. Some brands are creating social value by the manner in which they design their products and the way they communicate with consumers. Innovation is the main driver of brands. Branded businesses innovate more than non-branded businesses.

Given the trust consumers have in their brands, owners of brands may take several risks in investing in a new range of products. In the same line of reasoning, some brands have involved themselves in existing social issues and challenges in attempting to respond to them by being innovative. The social benefit of brands is more and more stressed. Corporate social responsibility (CSR) has become an increasingly de rigueur part of the corporate landscape.[33]

It is often stated that the growing usage of information and communication technologies has expanded the scope of services and enhanced their tradability.[34]

Innovation has economic value, thanks to commercialization. In this context, branding plays an important role in the commercialization of innovative products. It can serve as a mirror of success to an innovation.[35] Brands reduce search costs and are a crucial and decisive element in the value chain of an innovation. Branding may be considered a highway, bringing products to the market. It is a valuable source of information about the products.[36] It is part of marketing innovation, introducing new technology to promote products and to make them available to the consumers.

Accordingly, branding may have two effects on product innovation: when firms invest in branding activities to sell an innovation-based product, branding complements innovation. But when firms rely on these activities to sell an image-based product, branding may substitute for innovation.[37]

In particular, many low- and middle-income countries see companies intensively filing for trademarks, even if they make comparatively less use of other IP forms.[38] How effective branding channels will be in terms of promoting innovation depends on the quality of information communicated to consumers.[39]

In sum, in the present world, with the existence of high competition levels among competitors worldwide, branding adds value to innovation. Branding a product (goods and service) to reach the market is gaining more and more significance in commerce. New marketing methods that may qualify as innovations have come to light to support branding, which is supposed to be an old concept. In the field of IP, it is well recognized that trademarks, designs, and geographical indications are tools or instruments that may support the branding of both technological and non-technological innovations. In this context, more and more companies from the developing world are utilizing these tools to compete among themselves and the big players at the global level.

***At the end of the day, consumers of branded products become/behave like fanatics of a sport team who are ready to support their teams in any desirable (win) or undesirable situation (loss). However, unlike in sports, where fanatics may continue to support their teams, even after several losses, in business, the judgment of deceived consumers is very tough and may lead to full rejection of products produced by the company and cause destruction of the longstanding relationship that has been built with them.*** And the loss may be difficult to overcome or repair in the future. So, having loyal customers is a blessing that one cannot underestimate. It is a big asset for a company. Individual consumers control the brand and have a say in its success.

Every touch point with consumers may affect the brand negatively or positively. *Good examples of a brand are remembered, but bad examples are unforgettable.* So, the line of demarcation is very slim. A reputed brand may be damaged by a single behavior of a service provider of the brand. For a brand to survive, an innovation is an imperative, not an option, in order to remain the product of choice.

Unlike in the past, social media is another new reality that should be taken into consideration in the branding exercises of products. Social media enables individual consumers to inform large numbers of other consumers in a very short time frame by co-creating and spreading brand-related content through their digital networks. This environment of social media networks sets new, digital forms of word of mouth apart from their analog predecessors by enabling, for instance, real-time access to large numbers of friends and followers.

As a result, social media firestorms can constitute an important threat to firms' brand assets, in line with many corporate leaders' sense that "reputation risk" is a grave threat. This approach anticipates that the power of social media firestorms will not be "strong" or "weak" in general but rather will vary, according to certain contingencies.[40]

In Chapter 4, success stories and case studies on branding may facilitate the understanding of the close relationship between the owner of a brand and its customers. Unlike in the previous years, nowadays, communication through public mediums is common. So, brands are more and more conscious of keeping a clean image of their brands. This is also illustrated through the personality endorsement of a brand. The private/social life of the personality may have positive or negative impacts on the brand. This is the reason why, in order to prevent damage to the reputation of a brand from the disgusting behavior of an endorsing personality, corporations are ready to revoke their contract with the personality, publicly cutting the link between them so that customers cease to perceive the personality as the brand endorser, which may be detrimental to the image of the brand.

## Notes

1 Article 15 of the TRIPs Agreement defines a trademark and ascertains the realm of protection. Paragraph 1 of Article 15 defines a trademark as follows:

> 1 Any sign, or any combination of signs, capable of distinguishing the goods or services of one undertaking from those of other undertakings, shall be capable of constituting a trademark. Such signs, in particular words including personal names, letters, numerals, figurative elements and combinations of colors as well as any combination of such signs, shall be eligible for registration as trademarks. Where signs are not inherently capable of distinguishing the relevant goods or services, Members may make registrability depend on distinctiveness acquired through use. Members may require, as a condition of registration, that signs be visually perceptible.

2 Tshimanga Kongolo, An Analysis of IP Data in Africa from 2011 to 2015 and Assessment of Innovation Trends, *Oxford Journal of IP Law and Practice*, Vol. 12, Issue 12, December 2017.

3 Article 25 of the TRIPs Agreement:

> 1 Members shall provide for the protection of independently created industrial designs that are new or original. Members may provide that designs are not new or original if they do not significantly differ from known designs or combinations of known design features. Members may provide that such protection shall not extend to designs dictated essentially by technical or functional considerations.
> 2 Each Member shall ensure that requirements for securing protection for textile designs, in particular in regard to any cost, examination or publication, do not unreasonably impair the opportunity to seek and obtain such protection. Members shall be free to meet this obligation through industrial design law or through copyright law.

4 Article 22(1) of the TRIPs Agreement:

> 1 Geographical indications are, for the purposes of this Agreement, indications which identify a good as originating in the territory of a Member, or a region or locality in that territory, where a given quality, reputation or other characteristic of the good is essentially attributable to its geographical origin.

5 Tshimanga Kongolo, Any New Developments with regard to the GI Issues debated under WTO? *European Intellectual Property Review (EIPR)*, Vol. 33, Issue 2, 2011.

6 See The Protection of Traditional Knowledge: Draft Articles - REV. 2, WIPO/GRTKF/IC/37/FACILITATORS TEXT TK REV.2 (August 31, 2018), www.wipo.int

**Traditional knowledge** for the purposes of this instrument is knowledge that is created, maintained, and developed by indigenous [peoples], local communities, [other beneficiaries], and that is linked with, or is an integral part of the national or social identity and/or cultural heritage of indigenous [peoples], local communities; that is transmitted between or from generation to generation, whether consecutively or not; which subsists in codified, oral, or other forms; and which may be dynamic and evolving, and may take the form of know-how, skills, innovations, practices, teachings or learnings.

See also Tshimanga Kongolo, African Contribution to Shaping the Worldwide Intellectual Property System, Ashgate Publishing/Taylor & Francis Publishing, 2013.

7 See Tshimanga Kongolo, *African Contributions in Shaping the Worldwide Intellectual Property System*, Ashgate Publishing/ Routledge/Taylor and Francis, March 2013.

8 See Tshimanga Kongolo, *Unsettled International Intellectual Property Issues*, Kluwer Law International, February 2008.

9 The Protection of Traditional Cultural Expressions: Draft Articles Facilitators' Rev.2 (August 31, 2018), www.wipo.int

**Traditional cultural expression** means any form of [creative or spiritual] [artistic and literary] expression, tangible or intangible, or a combination thereof, such as actions, materials, music and sound, or verbal forms, as well as their adaptations, which may subsist in written/codified, oral or other form], that is created, generated, expressed or maintained [in a collective context] by indigenous [peoples] and local communities; that is the unique product of and/or [directly] linked with the cultural and/or social identity and cultural heritage of indigenous [peoples] and local communities; that may be dynamic and evolving; and that is transmitted from generation to generation, whether consecutively or not.]

See also Tshimanga Kongolo, *African Contribution to Shaping the Worldwide Intellectual Property System*, Ashgate Publishing/Taylor & Francis Publishing, 2013.

10 Tshimanga Kongolo, Innovation Shapes and Intellectual Property in Africa, *European Intellectual Property Review (EIPR)*, Vol. 35, Issue 10, 2015, p. 653.

11 *Oslo Manual, Guidelines for Collecting and Interpreting Innovation Data*, Third Edition, OECD-EUROSTAT, 2005.

12 Caroline Mothe and Thuc Uyen Nguyen Thi, The Link between Non-Technological and Technological Innovations, *European Journal of Innovation Management*, Vol. 13, Issue 3, 2010, pp. 313–332.

13 *Oslo Manual, Guidelines for Collecting and Interpreting Innovation Data*, Third Edition, OECD-EUROSTAT, 2005.

14 Caroline Mothe and Thuc Uyen Nguyen Thi, The Link between Non-Technological and Technological Innovations, *European Journal of Innovation Management*, Vol. 13, Issue 3, 2010, pp. 313–332.

15 See Tshimanga Kongolo, L'innovation et la propriete intellectuelle en Afrique, in Melanges Edou Edou, Regards sur la propriete intellectuelle en Afrique, LGDJ, 2017.

16 *Oslo Manual, Guidelines for Collecting and Interpreting Innovation Data*, Third Edition, OECD-EUROSTAT, 2005.

17 Global Innovation Index, 2014.

18 Nicholas S. Vonortas, International Perspectives on Innovation: Introduction, *Journal of Technology Transfer*, Vol. 43, 2018, pp. 259–262. See also Krause, Ulrike, Innovation: The New Big Push or the Post-Development Alternative? *Development*, Vol. 56, 2013, pp. 223–226.

19 Global Innovation Index, 2014.

20 *Oslo Manual, Guidelines for Collecting and Interpreting Innovation Data*, Third Edition, OECD-EUROSTAT, 2005.

21 *Oslo Manual, Guidelines for Collecting and Interpreting Innovation Data*, Third Edition, OECD-EUROSTAT, 2005.

22 *Oslo Manual, Guidelines for Collecting and Interpreting Innovation Data*, Third Edition, OECD-EUROSTAT, 2005.

23 2011 World Intellectual Property Report, The Changing Face of Innovation, WIPO, 2011.

24 Nobuo Kiriyama, Trade and Innovation, OECD Trade Policy Working Paper, N.135, 2012. See also Yi Hsu, Cross National Comparison of Innovation Efficiency and

Policy Application, *African Journal of Business Management*, Vol. 5, Issue 4, 2011, pp. 1378–1387.

25 José Guimon and Natalia Agapitova, Why Should Governments of Developing Countries Invest in R&D and Innovation? *African Journal of Business Management*, Vol. 7, Issue 12, 28 March, 2013, pp. 899–905. See also Les Levidow and Theo Papaioannou, Which Inclusive Innovation? Competing Normative Assumptions Around Social Justice, *Innovation Development*, Vol. 8, Issue 2, 2017, pp. 1–18.

26 Erika Kraemer-Mbula and Sacha Wunsch-Vincent, *The Informal Economy in Developing Nations: Hidden Engine of Innovation?* Cambridge University Press, 2016.

27 José Guimon and Natalia Agapitova, Why Should Governments of Developing Countries Invest in R&D and Innovation? *African Journal of Business Management*, Vol. 7, Issue 12, pp. 899–905, 28 March, 2013.

28 Erika Kraemer-Mbula and Sacha Wunsch-Vincent, *The Informal Economy in Developing Nations: Hidden Engine of Innovation?* Cambridge University Press, 2016.

29 Michel Chevalier and Gerald Mazzalovo, *Pro Logo: Brands as a Factor of Progress*, Palgrave Macmillan, 2004.

30 Hans Ruediger Kaufmann, Sandra Maria Correia Loureiro and Agapi Manarioti, Exploring Behavioural Branding, Brand Love and Brand Co-creation, *Journal of Product & Brand Management*, Vol. 25, Issue 6, 2016, pp. 516–526.

31 Michel Chevalier and Gerald Mazzalovo, *Pro Logo: Brands as a Factor of Progress*, Palgrave Macmillan, 2004.

32 Michel Chevalier and Gerald Mazzalovo, *Pro Logo: Brands as a Factor of Progress*, Palgrave Macmillan, 2004.

33 Stefanie Robinson and Stacy Wood, A "good" New Brand — What Happens When New Brands Try to Stand Out Through Corporate Social Responsibility, *Journal of Business Research*, Vol. 92, 2018, 231–241.

34 Timon Bohn, Steven Brakman and Erik Dietzenbacher, The Role of Services on Globalization, *The World Economy*, 41, 2018, pp. 2732–2749.

35 2013 World Intellectual Property Report, Brands – Reputation and Image in the Global Marketplace, WIPO, 2013.

36 Tshimanga Kongolo, Intellectual Property and Misappropriation of the Public Domain, *European Intellectual Property Review (EIPR)*, Vol. 33, Issue 12, 2011.

37 2013 World Intellectual Property Report, Brands *–Reputation and Image in the Global Marketplace*, WIPO, 2013.

38 2013 World Intellectual Property Report, Brands *–Reputation and Image in the Global Marketplace*, WIPO, 2013.

39 2013 World Intellectual Property Report, Brands *–Reputation and Image in the Global Marketplace*, WIPO, 2013.

40 Nele Hansen, Ann-Kristin Kupfer and Thorsten Hennig-Thurau, Brand Crises in the Digital Age: The Short- and Long-Term Effects of Social Media Firestorms on Consumers and Brands, *International Journal of Research in Marketing*, Vol. 35, Issue 4, 2018, pp. 557–574. See also Thorsten Hennig-Thurau, Edward C. Malthouse, Christian Friege, Sonja Gensler, Lara Lobschat, Arvind Rangaswamy and Bernd Skiera, The Impact of Newmedia on Customer Relationships. *Journal of Service Research*, Vol. 13, Issue 3, 2010, pp. 311–330. Philipp A. Rauschnabel, Nadine Kammerlander and Björn S. Ivens, Collaborative Brand Attacks in Social Media: Exploring the Antecedents, Characteristics, and Consequences of a New Form of Brand Crises. *Journal of Marketing Theory and Practice*, Vol. 24, Issue 4, 2016, pp. 381–410. Yuchi Zhang, Wendy W. Moe and David A. Schweidel, Modeling the Role of Message Content and Influencers in Social Media Rebroadcasting. *International Journal of Research in Marketing*, Vol. 34, Issue 1, 2017, pp. 100–119.

# 2 Intellectual property trends in the developing world from 2011 to 2016 based on income status

## Selected low-income economies in the developing world

Under this section, trademark class count in applications and registrations, industrial design count in applications and registrations, and patent applications and patent grants of selected low-income economies in the developing world from 2011 to 2016 will be examined. Gross national income per capita (GNI) for each country will be considered. Low-income economies are countries falling within the GNI per capita of $995 or less.

*Table 2.1* Trademark class count in applications (Direct and via Madrid system)

| | *2011* | *2012* | *2013* | *2014* | *2015* | *2016* |
|---|---|---|---|---|---|---|
| Gambia | 407 | 441 | 406 | 562 | 544 | 1,165 |
| Liberia | 1,813 | 2,011 | 1,799 | 1,864 | 1,730 | 2,039 |
| Madagascar | 4,693 | 4,795 | 4,450 | 5,132 | 4,954 | 6,050 |
| Malawi | 1,199 | 1,164 | 983 | 1,059 | 1,264 | 1,167 |
| Mozambique | 4,468 | 5,040 | 4,665 | 5,272 | 5,324 | 5,337 |
| Nepal | 3,583 | 3,961 | 4,551 | 4,738 | 4,276 | 5,078 |
| Rwanda | – | 517 | 274 | 2,180 | 2,363 | 2,377 |
| Sierra Leone | 1,710 | 2,299 | 2,043 | 2,333 | 1,707 | 1,874 |
| Uganda | 3,050 | 2,306 | 2,079 | 2,666 | 2,815 | 3,044 |
| Zimbabwe | – | 1,877 | 1,574 | 1,992 | 2,683 | 3,232 |

Source: www.wipo.int/ipstats/en/wipi/index.html (last accessed December 15, 2018).

As it can be observed through the table, among the low-income economies, which are likewise least-developed countries (LDCs), in terms of trademark class count in applications, three countries, namely, Madagascar, Mozambique, and Nepal, have taken the lead to reach each a total of more than 5,000 trademarks in 2016. Progression has been remarkable in Madagascar with trademark class count in applications of 4,693 in 2011 to 6,050 in 2016. The same trend of increase is observed for Nepal.

*Table 2.2* Trademark class count in registrations (Direct and via the Madrid system)

| | *2011* | *2012* | *2013* | *2014* | *2015* | *2016* |
|---|---|---|---|---|---|---|
| Gambia | 462 | 441 | 406 | 562 | 502 | 956 |
| Liberia | 1,659 | 1,673 | 1,797 | 1,566 | 1,875 | 1,896 |
| Madagascar | 3,714 | 5,479 | 4,541 | 3,781 | 4,567 | 6,304 |
| Malawi | 962 | 1,817 | 949 | 876 | 915 | 1,247 |
| Mozambique | 2,071 | 4,601 | 4,453 | 4,670 | 5,490 | 5,198 |
| Nepal | 1,381 | 1,916 | 2,610 | 1,862 | 2,253 | 2,786 |
| Rwanda | – | 517 | 198 | 2,015 | 3,081 | 2,288 |
| Sierra Leone | 1,907 | 2,358 | 2,485 | 2,419 | 2,125 | 1,965 |
| Uganda | 372 | 1,106 | 1,106 | 1,486 | 2,255 | 2,094 |
| Zimbabwe | – | 1,610 | 2,866 | 1,558 | 2,284 | 3,311 |

Source: www.wipo.int/ipstats/en/wipi/index.html (last accessed December 15, 2018).

In terms of trademark class count in registrations, Madagascar and Mozambique have performed well, with more than 5,000 registrations in 2016. In 2016, Zimbabwe registered more trademarks, with 3,311, than Nepal, which registered only 2,786 trademarks.

*Table 2.3* Design count in applications (Direct and via the Hague system)

| | *2011* | *2012* | *2013* | *2014* | *2015* | *2016* |
|---|---|---|---|---|---|---|
| Madagascar | 309 | 303 | 169 | 207 | 206 | 170 |
| Mozambique | – | 132 | 221 | 146 | 118 | 32 |
| Nepal | 21 | 16 | 56 | – | 35 | 34 |
| Rwanda | 5 | 78 | 73 | 77 | 69 | 69 |

Source: www.wipo.int/ipstats/en/wipi/index.html (last accessed December 15, 2018).

The performance of low-income countries in the area of design count in applications is disappointing. All the selected countries have poorly performed.

Madagascar is the only country that kept the total number above 100 design count in applications between 2011 and 2016. Mozambique had a mixed picture. What is surprising is that among the selected countries, there is none showing progression. The tendency is toward regression of numbers of design count in applications.

*Table 2.4* Design count in registrations (Direct and via the Hague system)

| | *2011* | *2012* | *2013* | *2014* | *2015* | *2016* |
|---|---|---|---|---|---|---|
| Madagascar | 271 | 295 | 274 | 172 | 244 | 185 |
| Mozambique | | 36 | 131 | 230 | 131 | 26 |
| Nepal | | 20 | | 9 | 1 | 21 |
| Rwanda | 5 | 54 | 73 | 72 | 69 | 99 |

Source: www.wipo.int/ipstats/en/wipi/index.html (last accessed December 15, 2018).

Madagascar maintained the lead in the extent of design count in registrations between 2011 and 2016 with regard to low-income countries and LDCs. As said, the trend is toward reduction of the total number of design count in registrations, which is the opposite of other income economies. And Madagascar is not an exception.

*Table 2.5* Patent applications (Direct and via the PCT)

| | *2011* | *2012* | *2013* | *2014* | *2015* | *2016* |
|---|---|---|---|---|---|---|
| Ethiopia | 15 | 13 | 9 | 4 | – | – |
| Madagascar | 61 | 44 | 51 | 34 | 19 | 36 |
| Malawi | | 69 | 4 | 5 | 6 | 4 |
| Mozambique | 23 | 40 | 41 | 60 | 102 | 40 |
| Nepal | 23 | 17 | 30 | – | 82 | 37 |
| Tanzania | 2 | – | 3 | 4 | 2 | 16 |
| Rwanda | – | 70 | – | 12 | 6 | 128 |
| Uganda | – | – | 14 | 8 | 9 | 16 |
| Zimbabwe | – | – | 23 | 27 | 28 | 13 |

Source: www.wipo.int/ipstats/en/wipi/index.html (last accessed December 15, 2018).

Patent has always been the most challenging area for low-income economies in general and LDCs in particular. As illustrated, patent applications are filed at a low level in terms of number, and few countries have reached annually a total number of 50 applications. This is to say that in these countries, a patent system is not playing its role of inducing creativity and responding to social needs as part of the solution for those countries. In 2016, for instance, only Rwanda received more than 100 patent applications. As Rwanda is a Contracting State to the PCT, this may be due to the filing through the PCT system.

*Table 2.6* Patent grants (Direct and via PCT)

| | *2011* | *2012* | *2013* | *2014* | *2015* | *2016* |
|---|---|---|---|---|---|---|
| Madagascar | 41 | 44 | 40 | 24 | 23 | 19 |
| Malawi | 1 | 4 | 3 | – | 1 | 7 |
| Mozambique | – | – | 43 | 60 | 54 | 35 |
| Nepal | 2 | 2 | 1 | – | 74 | – |
| Tanzania | 2 | – | 3 | 4 | 1 | – |
| Uganda | 1 | 1 | 3 | 1 | – | – |

Source: www.wipo.int/ipstats/en/wipi/index.html (last accessed December 15, 2018).

As pointed out, the same observation is relevant as regards patent grants, which are very low compared with other income economies. Another characteristic of low-income economies is that data are not always available. The author was unavailable to get data from Rwanda in the area of patent grants.

## Selected lower-middle-income economies in the developing world

Under this section, trademark class count in applications and registrations, design count in applications and registrations, and patent applications and patent grants of selected lower middle-income economies in the developing world from 2011 to 2016 will be evaluated. GNI for each country will be considered. Lower-middle-income economies are countries falling within the GNI per capita between $996 and $3,895.

*Table 2.7* Trademark class count in applications (Direct and via the Madrid system)

| | *2011* | *2012* | *2013* | *2014* | *2015* | *2016* |
|---|---|---|---|---|---|---|
| Bangladesh | 11,645 | 11,429 | 11,581 | 11,541 | 12,809 | 12,375 |
| Cambodia | 4,567 | 5,168 | 5,854 | 4,888 | 1,513 | 4,099 |
| Egypt | 23,211 | 23,323 | 23,242 | 24,870 | 26,068 | 35,122 |
| Ghana | 2,003 | 4,993 | 5,308 | 6,111 | 5,120 | 5,519 |
| India | 198,547 | 190,853 | 208,837 | 237,727 | 289,713 | 313,623 |
| Indonesia | – | – | 67,210 | 46,452 | 49,534 | 63,721 |
| Lesotho | 1,498 | 1,811 | 1,464 | 1,727 | 1,672 | 1,715 |
| Moldova | 12,687 | 12,671 | 12,774 | 11,394 | 10,180 | 11,067 |
| Mongolia | 3,713 | 3,982 | 8,915 | 9,082 | 11,638 | 12,040 |
| Morocco | 9,781 | 27,215 | 25,942 | 26,638 | 26,006 | 29,046 |
| Pakistan | 18,478 | 19,665 | 20,822 | 25,267 | 28,056 | 36,126 |
| Philippines | – | 32,933 | 36,993 | 41,505 | 42,889 | 47,953 |
| Sao Tome and Principe | 1,264 | 1,486 | 1,334 | 1,374 | 1,440 | 1,439 |
| Tunisia | 3,906* | 4,110* | 9,951 | 12,747 | 13,223 | 11,667 |
| Vietnam | 53,834 | 55,614 | 57,718 | 61,061 | 67,746 | 82,041 |
| Kenya | 3,361 | 3,706 | 3,676 | 4,052 | 10,872 | 4,791 |
| Zambia | 3,198 | 4,019 | 4,005 | 3,934 | 2,209 | 2,417 |
| OAPI | 3,265* | 3,780* | 7,743 | 8,702 | 9,835 | 12,487 |

Source: www.wipo.int/ipstats/en/wipi/index.html (last accessed December 15, 2018).
*Reflects the number of trademark applications (not the class count).

Among the lower middle-income economies, with a population of 1 billion and 311 million, India breaks the record with 313,623 trademark class count in applications. Since 2012 this number is on steady increase. Vietnam is another lower middle-income country showing progress since 2011 to today without any drop and with a total of 82,041 trademark class count in applications.

Indonesia, ranked second after India in 2013, suffered from a drop both in 2014 and 2015. A recovery was seen in 2016. Philippines, Pakistan, and Egypt showed a steady progress almost with no drop since 2011 by reaching each a total of more than 30,000 trademark class count in applications in 2016. The performance of Morocco should be stressed with a steady rise of number of trademark class count in applications since 2013 to reach its highest record in 2016 with 29,046.

*Table 2.8* Trademark class count in registrations (Direct and via the Madrid system)

| | 2011 | 2012 | 2013 | 2014 | 2015 | 2016 |
|---|---|---|---|---|---|---|
| Bangladesh | 1,409 | 2,520 | 3,021 | 4,172 | 4,522 | 3,378 |
| Cambodia | 3,671 | 3,706 | 5,821 | 4,215 | 1,150 | 3,812 |
| Egypt | 15,465 | 13,897 | 16,241 | 14,872 | 15,912 | 16,938 |
| Ghana | 1,882 | 3,597 | 3,513 | 3,299 | 4,114 | 4,429 |
| India | 142,943 | 55,191 | 61,924 | 69,667 | 84,764 | 201,988 |
| Indonesia | – | – | 18,750 | 35,274 | 46,588 | 19,622 |
| Lesotho | 1,362 | 1,487 | 1,509 | 1,262 | 1,943 | 1,636 |
| Morocco | 9,534 | 24,393 | 23,467 | 23,564 | 24,058 | 23,758 |
| Moldova | 12,095 | 12,125 | 12,244 | 11,882 | 11,121 | 8,972 |
| Mongolia | 4,272 | 4,578 | 4,624 | 9,870 | 11,579 | 9,247 |
| Pakistan | 6,111 | 6,442 | 9,305 | 9,183 | 9,436 | 12,578 |
| Philippines | – | 23,802 | 26,955 | 29,337 | 36,014 | 44,643 |
| Sao Tome and Principe | 1,577 | 1,519 | 1,612 | 1,447 | 1,727 | 1,238 |
| Tunisia | – | – | 9,640 | 13,088 | 15,464 | 12,598 |
| Vietnam | 41,636 | 39,064 | 41,075 | 42,596 | 42,101 | 41,348 |
| Kenya | 3,131 | 3,131 | 3,574 | 3,585 | 9,414 | 4,601 |
| Zambia | 2,915 | 2,624 | 2,963 | 2,716 | 2,357 | 2,327 |
| OAPI | 3,200* | 3,750* | 6,326 | 9,294 | 1,461 | 5,177 |

Source: www.wipo.int/ipstats/en/wipi/index.html (last accessed December 15, 2018).

India maintained its lead over the number of trademark class count in registrations, with 201,988, in 2016, the highest number between 2011 and 2016 in this income group. However, it should be stressed that a huge drop in the number of registrations is noticed in 2012 before a slight recovery in 2015. Vietnam and the Philippines both followed with a total number of more than 40,000 trademark class count in registrations each in 2016. As long as low middle-income economies in Africa are concerned, Morocco is in the leading position, followed by Egypt. Both countries suffered some drops. It should, however, be stressed that Morocco's class count in registrations increased dramatically from 9,534 in 2011 to 24,393 before keeping the same path with a few drops.

*Table 2.9* Design count in applications (Direct and via the Hague system)

| | 2011 | 2012 | 2013 | 2014 | 2015 | 2016 |
|---|---|---|---|---|---|---|
| Bangladesh | 1,297 | 1,198 | 1,232 | 1,379 | 1,376 | 1,456 |
| Cambodia | 47 | 47 | 30 | 82 | 69 | – |
| Egypt | 3,230 | 3,053 | 2,681 | 2,890 | 2,663 | 951 |
| Ghana | 139 | 146 | 94 | 110 | 101 | 569 |
| India | 8,216 | 8,545 | 8,497 | 9,309 | 10,290 | 10,673 |
| Indonesia | 4,196 | 4,612 | 4,259 | 3,731 | 3,972 | 3,893 |
| Morocco | 5,394 | 4,596 | 5,061 | 5,526 | 5,950 | 6,143 |
| Moldova | 1,854 | 2,193 | 2,565 | 1,150 | 2,206 | 902 |
| Mongolia | 765 | 744 | 1,016 | 930 | 791 | 823 |
| Namibia | 168 | 154 | 169 | 114 | 96 | 118 |
| Philippines | 1,112 | 1,225 | 1,376 | 1,348 | 1,103 | 1,569 |
| Tunisia | 200 | 639 | 1,455 | 1,420 | 1,578 | 1,509 |

(*Continued*)

| | *2011* | *2012* | *2013* | *2014* | *2015* | *2016* |
|---|---|---|---|---|---|---|
| Sao Tome and Principe | 83 | 74 | 49 | 70 | 50 | 88 |
| Vietnam | 2,104 | 2,107 | 2,429 | 2,609 | 2,885 | 3,394 |
| Kenya | 114 | 103 | 86 | 95 | 85 | 104 |
| Zambia | 16 | 12 | 43 | 40 | – | – |
| OAPI | 799 | 904 | 899 | 836 | 799 | 824 |

Source: www.wipo.int/ipstats/en/wipi/index.html (last accessed December 15, 2018).

The picture is a bit mixed in relation to the total number of design count in applications as regards the lower middle-income economies. India and Morocco are the only countries where numbers are stable between 2011 and 2016. India is the only country that has reached a total of more than 10,000 design count in applications mainly in the last two years (2015 and 2016). Morocco, coming second, is the only country after India which has obtained more than 5,000 design count in applications in the last four years. Indonesia and Philippines have each achieved a total of more than 3,000 design count in applications. Moldova and Egypt have shown a "ping pong" performance between 2011 and 2016, with ups and downs. It is difficult to provide a coherent explanation of why there are drops for some countries in 2016 and increases for some others. The good performance of Tunisia with a total number of 200 design applications in 2011 to reach a total of 1,509 in 2016 deserves recognition.

*Table 2.10* Design count in Registrations (Direct and via the Hague system)

| | *2011* | *2012* | *2013* | *2014* | *2015* | *2016* |
|---|---|---|---|---|---|---|
| Bangladesh | 646 | 1,056 | 984 | 802 | 771 | 804 |
| Cambodia | 40 | 47 | 30 | 29 | 99 | – |
| Egypt | 2,022 | 1,953 | 1,378 | 1,201 | 1,627 | 901 |
| Ghana | 139 | 146 | 94 | 110 | 101 | 116 |
| India | 6,237 | 6,778 | 6,975 | 7,057 | 7,461 | 7,331 |
| Indonesia | – | – | 3,014 | 3,878 | 3,505 | 2,831 |
| Morocco | 1,826 | 1,854 | 5,017 | 5,223 | 5,134 | 6,075 |
| Moldova | 1,204 | 1,592 | 1,719 | 1,857 | 1,481 | 1,427 |
| Mongolia | 829 | 744 | 884 | 754 | 791 | 641 |
| Philippines | 665 | 1,061 | 1,346 | 1,141 | 1,051 | 1,721 |
| Tunisia | 200 | 639 | 1,454 | 1,418 | 1,571 | 1,507 |
| Sao Tome and Principe | 83 | 74 | 49 | 70 | 50 | 88 |
| Vietnam | 1,331 | 1,405 | 1,557 | 1,963 | 1,681 | 1,659 |
| Kenya | 40 | 50 | 38 | 34 | 57 | 163 |
| Zambia | 12 | 20 | 33 | 22 | – | – |
| OAPI | 765 | 831 | 881 | 928 | 746 | 816 |

Source: www.wipo.int/ipstats/en/wipi/index.html (last accessed December 15, 2018).

In terms of design count in registrations, India maintained the lead over Morocco but with a narrow gap. The two are the only countries with a total each of more than 5,000 design count in registrations in the last four years in respect to the lower middle-income economies. The very bad picture emanates from Egypt, which showed a steady decrease of design count registrations to reach a total of 901 in 2016 while in 2011 it was among the highest with 2,022 design count in registrations.

*Table 2.11* Patent applications (Direct and via the PCT system)

| | *2011* | *2012* | *2013* | *2014* | *2015* | *2016* |
|---|---|---|---|---|---|---|
| OAPI | 516 | 550 | 552 | 578 | 529 | 506 |
| Bangladesh | 306 | 354 | 303 | 293 | 340 | 344 |
| Cambodia | 43 | 53 | 75 | 67 | 65 | – |
| Egypt | 2,209 | 2,211 | 2,051 | 2,136 | – | 2,149 |
| India | 42,291 | 43,955 | 43,031 | 42,854 | 45,658 | 45,057 |
| Indonesia | 5,830 | – | 7,450 | 8,023 | 9,153 | 8,538 |
| Morocco | 1,049 | 1,040 | 1,144 | 1,090 | 1,020 | 1,303 |
| Moldova | 108 | 115 | 96 | 139 | 124 | 155 |
| Mongolia | – | – | 265 | 265 | 237 | 219 |
| Pakistan | 953 | 894 | 934 | 922 | 886 | 840 |
| Philippines | 3,196 | 2,994 | 3,285 | 3,589 | 3,734 | 3,419 |
| Tunisia | 680 | 626 | 549 | 542 | 589 | 583 |
| Vietnam | 3,560 | 3,805 | 3,995 | 4,447 | 5,033 | 5,228 |
| Kenya | 257 | 259 | 241 | 207 | 193 | 203 |
| Zambia | 24 | 38 | 39 | 39 | – | – |

Source: www.wipo.int/ipstats/en/wipi/index.html (last accessed December 15, 2018).

In the area of patent applications, in the grouping of lower-middle-income economies, India is the only country that obtained more than 40,000 applications in the last six years (2011–2016). Besides India, Indonesia is also the only country in this income grouping to reach a total of more than 5,000 patent applications in the last six years. Efforts carried out by Vietnam with more than 5,000 patent applications in the last two years and Philippines with more than 3,000 applications the last four years should be stressed. Egypt and Morocco are showing a stable trend though the total numbers are not great. Each received more than 1,000 patent applications yearly.

*Table 2.12* Patent grants (Direct and via the PCT system)

| | *2011* | *2012* | *2013* | *2014* | *2015* | *2016* |
|---|---|---|---|---|---|---|
| OAPI | 405 | 380 | 430 | 550 | 526 | 360 |
| Bangladesh | 85 | 153 | 134 | 121 | 101 | 106 |
| Egypt | 483 | 634 | 465 | 415 | 472 | 450 |
| India | 5,168 | 4,328 | 3,377 | 6,153 | 6,022 | 8,248 |
| Morocco | 979 | 979 | 937 | – | – | 352 |
| Moldova | 63 | 51 | 61 | 54 | 61 | 70 |
| Mongolia | – | – | 212 | 216 | 234 | 157 |
| Pakistan | 469 | 312 | 282 | 185 | 131 | 214 |
| Philippines | 1,135 | 1,111 | 2,207 | 2,159 | 2,200 | 4,006 |
| Tunisia | 674 | 613 | 535 | 552 | 589 | 583 |
| Vietnam | 1,006 | 1,068 | 1,182 | 1,397 | 1,388 | 1,423 |
| Kenya | 59 | 76 | 71 | 53 | 24 | 26 |
| Zambia | 15 | 32 | 21 | 23 | – | – |

Source: www.wipo.int/ipstats/en/wipi/index.html (last accessed December 15, 2018).

In respect to the patent grants in lower middle-income economies, obviously India retained its lead with more than 8,000 patents issued in 2016 and more than 6,000 the last three years. India is followed by the Philippines with 4,006 patent grants in 2016. Vietnam may be said to be the third with just over 1,000 patents grants in the last six years. The performance of other countries from the same income grouping is disappointing with less than 600 patents issued yearly since 2013.

## Selected upper-middle-income economies in the developing world

Under this section, trademark class count in applications and registrations, design count in applications and registrations, and patent applications and patent grants of selected upper middle-income economies in the developing world from 2011 to 2016 will be analyzed. GNI for each country will be considered. Upper-middle-income economies are countries falling within the GNI per capita between $3,896 and $12,055.

It should be pointed out that given its wide scope, this income grouping encompasses likewise economies which are closer to the lower middle-income and those that are closer to the high-income economies. As an illustration, Algeria with the GNI per capita of 4,850$ and Jamaica with 4,930$ are closer to lower middle-income economies. Likewise, Malaysia with a GNI per capita of 10,570$ is closer to the high-income economies.

*Table 2.13* Trademark class count in applications (Direct and via the Madrid system)

| | *2011* | *2012* | *2013* | *2014* | *2015* | *2016* |
|---|---|---|---|---|---|---|
| Algeria | 11,061 | 10,636 | 3,662 | 3,676 | 26,448 | 7,059 |
| Botswana | 2,657 | 3,182 | 2,887 | 2,980 | 3,274 | 3,271 |
| Brazil | 152,699 | 151,711 | 163,422 | 157,016 | 158,709 | 166,368 |
| China | 1,414,576 | 1,647,511 | 1,878,384 | 2,220,703 | 2,828,083 | 3,697,916 |
| Colombia | 29,084 | 32,777 | 36,080 | 37,822 | 41,901 | 42,737 |
| Cuba | 4,249 | 4,406 | 4,825 | 5,324 | 10,505 | 9,858 |
| Jordan | 6,812 | 6,751 | 6,510 | 6,958 | 7,485 | 7,346 |
| Iran | 6,476 | 6,054 | 6,281 | 6,275 | 6,842 | – |
| Jamaica | 5,185 | 4,323 | 4,245 | 4,553 | 6,503 | 5,349 |
| Malaysia | 28,833 | 31,876 | 32,225 | 34,571 | 35,923 | 39,107 |
| Mauritius | 1,884 | 1,836 | 1,758 | 1,855 | 2,049 | 2,328 |
| Mexico | 100,281 | 105,830 | 111,359 | 119,912 | 131,429 | 141,726 |
| Namibia | 2,067 | 4,300 | 3,704 | 3,943 | 5,406 | 4,849 |
| Peru | 28,766 | 29,553 | 29,845 | 30,427 | 32,300 | 30,708 |
| Romania | 29,074 | 26,548 | 28,831 | 26,188 | 24,497 | 24,984 |
| Russian Federation | 207,152 | 224,156 | 235,641 | 239,707 | 219,052 | 251,549 |
| South Africa | 33,484 | 34,604 | 36,070 | 35,418 | 36,973 | 37,976 |
| Thailand | 38,950 | 44,963 | 46,097 | 45,661 | 52,344 | 56,131 |
| Turkey | 182,236 | 225,751 | 221,549 | 231,624 | 227,179 | 227,159 |

Source: www.wipo.int/ipstats/en/wipi/index.html (last accessed December 15, 2018).

China, a country of 1 billion, 371 million inhabitants, is ranked first over trademark class count in applications for all economies for the last six years (2011–2016) with a record of 3,697,916 in 2016. China has not suffered any drop of trademark applications between 2011 and 2016. China has contributed to the overall ranking of its income grouping (upper-middle-income economies) and its region, to be number one. It should be underlined that a great number of trademark applications in China are also filed through the Madrid System. China was able to double the number of trademark class count in applications in five years.

Four countries within the same income grouping, namely, Turkey, the Russian Federation, Brazil, and Mexico, have performed a high score with more than 100,000 trademark class count in applications. Mexico showed a steady growth with no drop between 2011 and 2016. The same may be said for the Russian Federation, notwithstanding a reduction in 2015.

Malaysian and Colombia did not suffer any reduction of trademark class count in applications between 2011 and 2016 in addition to the steady increase. Some of the countries like Thailand, South Africa, Peru, and Romania performed well but with a few drops.

*Table 2.14* Trademark class count in registrations (Direct and via the Madrid system)

| | *2011* | *2012* | *2013* | *2014* | *2015* | *2016* |
|---|---|---|---|---|---|---|
| Algeria | 10,048 | 11,519 | 4,211 | 5,110 | 11,226 | 7,349 |
| Botswana | 3,189 | 2,451 | 2,791 | 3,109 | 3,213 | 2,581 |
| Brazil | 60,485 | 55,230 | 36,911 | 85,738 | 96,050 | 99,938 |
| China | 1,040,970 | 1,030,592 | 1,020,274 | 1,382,122 | 2,239,413 | 2,270,810 |
| Colombia | 22,138 | 26,896 | 24,914 | 33,334 | 36,472 | 30,061 |
| Cuba | 4,325 | 4,379 | 4,617 | 4,208 | 6,745 | 6,243 |
| Iran | 8,001 | 8,015 | 7,180 | 7,262 | 9,578 | – |
| Jordan | 5,435 | 4,624 | 4,777 | 5,737 | 5,794 | 7,248 |
| Jamaica | 4,429 | 5,379 | 3,839 | 2,975 | 4,341 | 4,195 |
| Malaysia | 23,819 | 26,076 | 26,979 | 27,428 | 28,800 | 32,806 |
| Mauritius | 1,946 | 1,570 | 1,797 | 1,550 | 1,925 | 2,061 |
| Mexico | 68,234 | 82,170 | 88,708 | 96,829 | 109,342 | 120,357 |
| Namibia | 2,455 | 2,747 | 2,830 | 2,503 | 2,951 | 2,509 |
| Peru | 21,595 | 21,902 | 22,978 | 25,864 | 25,404 | 26,189 |
| Romania | 23,340 | 23,340 | 20,552 | 21,855 | 18,993 | 19,644 |
| Russian Federation | 105,150 | 118,091 | 117,655 | 122,956 | 129,361 | 149,187 |
| South Africa | 31,286 | 29,230 | 27,225 | 31,778 | 27,206 | 11,281 |
| Thailand | 18,707 | 19,825 | 19,563 | 20,617 | 21,177 | 35,809 |
| Turkey | 91,137 | 138,055 | 174,254 | 194,215 | 196,244 | 218,137 |

Source: www.wipo.int/ipstats/en/wipi/index.html (last accessed December 15, 2018).

In terms of trademark class count in registrations, like in the applications, China is a leading country. Unlike in the applications, from 2011 to 2013, a slight reduction in the number of trademark class count in registrations was observed in China before a takeoff in 2014. Despite the drop, China was able to double the number of the trademark class count in registrations again after five years from 2011.

Turkey made a rebound to reach 218,137 of trademark class count in registrations in 2016 despite its slow start in 2011 with 91,137. Mexico is another country within this income grouping which almost doubled the number of trademark class count in registrations between 2011 and 2016. The Russian Federation showed a steady growth with no drop in terms of trademark class count in registrations from 2011 to 2016.

Brazil has suffered several drops between 2011 and 2013, showing a mixed performance in the area of trademark class count in registrations, notwithstanding the good performance of the last three years (2014–2016). South Africa is another country that suffered several drops to reach 11,281 trademark class count in registrations in 2016 although the number was 31,286 in 2011. The same assertion is valid for both Algeria and Romania.

*Table 2.15* Design count in applications (Direct and via the Hague system)

| | *2011* | *2012* | *2013* | *2014* | *2015* | *2016* |
|---|---|---|---|---|---|---|
| Algeria | 803 | 1,067 | 260* | 920 | – | – |
| Botswana | 38 | 46 | 148 | 93 | 56 | 105 |
| Brazil | 6,835 | 6,563 | 6,847 | 6,590 | 6,039 | 6,057 |
| China | 521,468 | 657,582 | 659,563 | 564,555 | 569,059 | 650,344 |
| Colombia | 384 | 490 | 766 | 577 | 718 | 533 |
| Cuba | 13 | 9 | 9 | 11 | – | 8 |
| Iran | 4,292 | 3,759 | 4,825 | 8,864 | 11,856 | 15,979 |
| Jordan | 77 | 81 | 70 | 52 | 110 | 101 |
| Jamaica | 64 | 112 | 175 | 75 | 66 | 183 |
| Malaysia | 1,871 | 2,082 | 2,053 | 1,882 | 1,762 | 1,427 |
| Mauritius | 82 | 71 | 15 | – | – | – |
| Mexico | 4,149 | 4,137 | 4,011 | 4,080 | 3,999 | 4,296 |
| Peru | 334 | 407 | 499 | 319 | 358 | 303 |
| Romania | 1,164 | 1,298 | 1,735 | 1,235 | 1,016 | 1,337 |
| Russian Federation | 6,077 | 7,870 | 6,935 | 7,313 | 6,002 | 6,565 |
| South Africa | 2,044 | 2,361 | 2,237 | 1,973 | 1,960 | 2,194 |
| Thailand | 3,749 | 3,481 | 3,802 | 4,077 | 4,461 | 4,857 |
| Turkey | 41,219 | 46,330 | 51,097 | 48,799 | 45,852 | 46,305 |

Source: www.wipo.int/ipstats/en/wipi/index.html (last accessed December 15, 2018).

All the selected countries under this income grouping experienced drops between 2011 and 2016 in terms of design count in applications. Reasons may vary from one country to another. China, leading also in the area of design count between 2011 and 2016 with 650,344 in 2016, is not an exception. China experienced first a growth in the number in two consecutive years in 2012 and 2013 before a drop in 2014. The recovery came back in 2015 but with lesser design count in applications than in 2012.

Turkey showed a consecutive growth of design count in applications from 2011 to 2013 before suffering a drop in 2014 and 2015. Turkey is second in the overall performance within the same income grouping economies after China with 46,305 design count in applications in 2016.

Brazil suffered slight drops in terms of number of design count in applications in 2012, 2014, and 2015. The Russian Federation, showing a mixed picture, experienced a drop after any growth between 2011 and 2016 in relation to the design count in applications.

Iran had only one drop in 2012, before showing a constant growth from 2013 to 2016. The overall performance of Iran is positive. In 2011, the total number of the design count in applications was 4,292, with a sustainable progression since 2013, it reached a total of 15,979 in 2016.

*Table 2.16* Design count in registrations (Direct and via the Hague system)

| | *2011* | *2012* | *2013* | *2014* | *2015* | *2016* |
|---|---|---|---|---|---|---|
| Algeria | 148 | 493 | 101* | 121 | – | – |
| Botswana | 30 | 39 | 139 | 84 | 56 | 105 |
| Brazil | 4,646 | 4,332 | 2,656 | 4,334 | 3,285 | 6,972 |
| China | 380,290 | 466,858 | 412,467 | 361,576 | 482,659 | 446,135 |
| Colombia | 772 | – | 526 | 526 | 501 | 490 |
| Cuba | 18 | 6 | 9 | 8 | – | 10 |
| Iran | 1,947 | 1,519 | 1,912 | 3,268 | 4,150 | 5,126 |
| Jordan | 85 | 87 | 42 | 56 | 87 | 92 |
| Jamaica | 51 | 90 | 173 | 189 | 71 | 120 |
| Malaysia | 1,641 | 1,924 | 2,001 | 1,891 | 1,301 | 1,900 |
| Mauritius | 59 | 35 | 66 | – | – | – |
| Mexico | 2,443 | 2,644 | 2,851 | 2,371 | 2,852 | 2,547 |
| Peru | 229 | 327 | 372 | 427 | 381 | 168 |
| Romania | 1,537 | 1,975 | 1,469 | 1,853 | 1,565 | 1,660 |
| Russian Federation | 5,747 | 5,585 | 5,716 | 5,874 | 8,585 | 5,476 |
| South Africa | 1,276 | 1,255 | 1,701 | 892 | 1,016 | 1,130 |
| Thailand | 1,253 | 2,107 | 2,858 | 2,477 | 3,711 | 3,755 |
| Tunisia | 200 | 639 | 1,454 | 1,418 | 1,571 | 1,507 |
| Turkey | 37,607 | 42,246 | 47,721 | 47,568 | 48,088 | 48,687 |

Source: www.wipo.int/ipstats/en/wipi/index.html (last accessed December 15, 2018).
*Reflects the number of trademark applications (not the class count).

In terms of design count in registrations, China maintained the lead for the years in consideration. Turkey scored second and retained a sustainable growth despite one slight drop in 2014. Brazil and the Russian Federation continued to show mixed pictures over design count in registrations with growth and drops between 2011 and 2016.

*Table 2.17* Patent applications (Direct and via PCT)

| | *2011* | *2012* | *2013* | *2014* | *2015* | *2016* |
|---|---|---|---|---|---|---|
| Algeria | 897 | 900 | 840 | 818 | 805 | 672 |
| Botswana | 9 | 14 | 9 | 9 | | 7 |
| Brazil | 28,649 | 30,435 | 30,884 | 30,342 | 30,219 | 28,010 |
| China | 526,412 | 652,777 | 825,136 | 928,177 | 1,101,864 | 1,338,503 |
| Colombia | 1,953 | 2,061 | 2,032 | 2,158 | 2,242 | 2,203 |
| Cuba | 248 | 178 | 170 | 150 | – | 195 |
| Iran | 11,636 | 12,018 | 11,054 | 13,802 | 14,279 | 15,632 |
| Jordan | 400 | 394 | 392 | 379 | 335 | 278 |

(*Continued*)

| | *2011* | *2012* | *2013* | *2014* | *2015* | *2016* |
|---|---|---|---|---|---|---|
| Jamaica | 113 | 107 | 119 | 155 | 70 | 78 |
| Lebanon | 282 | – | 355 | 341 | 304 | – |
| Malaysia | 6,452 | 6,940 | 7,205 | 7,620 | 7,727 | 7,236 |
| Mauritius | 20 | 18 | 20 | 21 | 21 | 38 |
| Mexico | 14,055 | 15,314 | 15,444 | 16,135 | 18,071 | 17,413 |
| Peru | 1,168 | 1,190 | 1,266 | 1,287 | 1,249 | 1,163 |
| Romania | 1,463 | 1,077 | 1,046 | 1,038 | 1,053 | 1,063 |
| Russian Federation | 41,414 | 44,211 | 44,914 | 40,308 | 45,517 | 41,587 |
| South Africa | 7,245 | 7,444 | 7,295 | 7,552 | 7,497 | 9,711 |
| Thailand | 3,924 | 6,746 | 7,404 | 7,930 | 8,167 | 7,820 |
| Turkey | 4,113 | 4,666 | 4,661 | 5,097 | 5,841 | 6,848 |

Source: www.wipo.int/ipstats/en/wipi/index.html (last accessed December 15, 2018).

China displayed continuous growth in the area of patent applications between 2011 and 2016. The progression in number since 2011 has been very significant to reach a total of 1,338,503 in 2016, representing an increase of over 100% compared to 2011. During the years 2011–2016, China did not suffer any drop of patent applications. Needful to mention also that the performance of China is remarkable in the PCT filing.

The overall performance of Brazil, Iran, Mexico, and the Russian Federation between 2011 and 2016 over patent applications is considerably positive despite some drops.

Within the BRICS upper middle-income economies, South Africa scored less in this income grouping in trademarks, designs, and patents.

The steady performance of Malaysia should be stressed with an annual increase of patent applications from 2011 despite an insignificant drop in 2016.

*Table 2.18* Patent grants (Direct and via PCT)

| | *2011* | *2012* | *2013* | *2014* | *2015* | *2016* |
|---|---|---|---|---|---|---|
| Algeria | 1,546 | 352 | 183 | 281 | 351 | 383 |
| Botswana | 6 | 1 | 3 | – | – | 1 |
| Brazil | 3,439 | 2,830 | 2,972 | 2,749 | 3,411 | 4,194 |
| China | 172,113 | 217,105 | 207,688 | 233,228 | 359,316 | 404,208 |
| Colombia | 617 | 1,667 | 2,264 | 1,212 | 1,003 | 917 |
| Cuba | 154 | 84 | 125 | 94 | – | 93 |
| Jamaica | 48 | 20 | 42 | 28 | 74 | 5 |
| Lebanon | 305 | 317 | 325 | 316 | 279 | – |
| Malaysia | 2,353 | 2,460 | 2,660 | 2,705 | 2,877 | 3,324 |
| Mauritius | 2 | 6 | 5 | 9 | 4 | 2 |
| Mexico | 11,485 | 12,358 | 10,368 | 9,819 | 9,338 | 8,652 |
| Peru | 385 | 431 | 287 | 332 | 362 | 403 |
| Romania | 430 | 384 | 451 | 356 | 305 | 355 |
| Russian Federation | 29,999 | 32,880 | 31,638 | 33,950 | 34,706 | 33,536 |
| South Africa | 5,296 | 6,205 | 4,756 | 5,065 | 4,499 | 4,255 |
| Thailand | 900 | 1,008 | 1,211 | 1,276 | 1,364 | – |
| Turkey | 893 | 1,004 | 1,211 | 1,276 | 1,723 | 1,764 |

Source: www.wipo.int/ipstats/en/wipi/index.html (last accessed December 15, 2018).

As a matter of consequence, China maintained the lead with regard to patent grants between 2011 and 2016. China achieved a total of 404,208 patent grants in 2016, representing more than 200% increase from 2011. The Russian Federation is ranked second after China in the overall performance of countries of the same income grouping in the area of patent grants.

The performance of Brazil and Turkey is below the expectation between the years 2011 and 2016. Mexico continues to experience a decrease in the number of patent grants since 2013 to reach a level of 8,652 in 2016. The overall performance of South Africa in terms of patent grants from 2011 to 2016 is better than Brazil despite several drops.

Despite their low number of patent grants, Malaysia, Thailand, and Turkey are the only countries besides China that have not suffered any drop since 2011 with a steady annual growth in terms of patent grants.

## Selected high-income economies in the developing world

In this section, trademark class count in applications and registrations, design count in applications and registrations, and patent applications and patent grants of selected high-income economies in the developing world from 2011 to 2016 will be scrutinized. GNI will be considered. High-income economies are countries falling within the GNI per capita of $12,056 or more.

The general observation is that there are few countries in this income grouping from the developing world performing well in the IP area.

*Table 2.19* Trademark class count in applications (Direct and via the Madrid system)

| | *2011* | *2012* | *2013* | *2014* | *2015* | *2016* |
|---|---|---|---|---|---|---|
| Argentina | 77,494 | 60,170 | 55,295 | 58,486 | 66,272 | 71,058 |
| Barbados | 1,371 | 1,398 | 1,182 | 1,153 | 1,337 | 1,094 |
| Chile | 43,936 | 41,853 | 42,961 | 42,640 | 42,964 | 45,368 |
| Korea | 171,744 | 182,357 | 200,089 | 207,383 | 236,086 | 231,978 |
| Oman | 4,281 | 4,410 | 4,560 | 4,642 | 5,033 | 5,551 |
| Qatar | 7,043 | 6,773 | 7,979 | 7,608 | – | – |
| Singapore | 34,997 | 37,224 | 38,433 | 41,775 | 41,999 | 45,332 |
| Uruguay | 10,670 | 9,949 | 10,792 | 9,881 | 9,463 | – |

Source: www.wipo.int/ipstats/en/wipi/index.html (last accessed December 15, 2013).

Korea has shown a remarkable performance in the area of trademark class count in applications between 2011 and 2016. The total amount continues to grow despite a slight drop in 2016. It should be stressed that Korea is also among the leading countries in the Madrid system.

Argentina's performance looks well with more than 70,000 trademark class count in applications received in 2016 and with a minimum of 50,000 yearly since 2011.

Chile and Singapore both have performed well in terms of trademark class count in applications between 2011 and 2016. Chile suffered two slight drops in

2012 and 2014. Singapore has not suffered any drop between 2011 and 2016, and the total number of trademark class count in applications is on the increase.

The good performance of Oman should be acknowledged for two reasons. The number of trademark class count in applications continues to grow, and Oman has not experienced any drop between 2011 and 2016.

Uruguay had a mixed picture with three slight declines in number in 2012, 2014, and 2015. Qatar, the highest GNI per capita in the developing world, suffered a number of drops between 2011 and 2016.

*Table 2.20* Trademark class count in registrations (Direct and via the Madrid system)

| | *2011* | *2012* | *2013* | *2014* | *2015* | *2016* |
|---|---|---|---|---|---|---|
| Argentina | 67,279 | 68,861 | 75,151 | 89,219 | 50,719 | 59,065 |
| Barbados | 216 | 398 | 324 | 765 | 181 | 402 |
| Chile | 27,431 | 20,970 | 26,613 | 35,814 | 35,970 | 34,107 |
| Korea | 115,858 | 110,223 | 135,229 | 134,825 | 159,901 | 161,106 |
| Oman | 5,570 | 5,842 | 5,953 | 5,733 | 6,764 | 5,916 |
| Qatar | 7,043 | 6,773 | 7,979 | 6,533 | – | – |
| Singapore | 27,230 | 29,208 | 30,084 | 36,728 | 46,193 | 49,609 |
| Uruguay | 8,215 | 18,257 | 11,576 | 10,108 | 6,390 | – |

Source: www.wipo.int/ipstats/en/wipi/index.html (last accessed December 15, 2018).

Korea maintained its lead with regard to trademark class count in registrations between 2011 and 2016 in its income grouping. Notwithstanding two drops in 2012 and 2014, its performance continues to be on the right track.

Notwithstanding its second ranking after Korea, Argentina has a mixed performance between 2011 and 2016 in the area of trademark class count in registrations.

Singapore experienced a steady growth in terms of trademark class count in registrations between 2011 and 2016 without any drop.

Other countries of the same income grouping showed a mixed picture on their performances. This is the case of Uruguay, Qatar, and Oman.

*Table 2.21* Design count in applications (Direct and via the Hague system)

| | *2011* | *2012* | *2013* | *2014* | *2015* | *2016* |
|---|---|---|---|---|---|---|
| Argentina | 1,444 | 1,574 | 1,465 | 1,384 | 1,581 | 1,653 |
| Barbados | 7 | 4 | 5 | – | 4 | 4 |
| Chile | 529 | 538 | 762 | 465 | 402 | 401 |
| Korea | 58,571 | 65,469 | 70,054 | 68,441 | 72,458 | 69,120 |
| Singapore | 3,985 | 4,092 | 4,320 | 4,268 | 4,262 | 4,337 |
| Uruguay | 110 | 117 | 93 | 77 | 57 | – |

Source: www.wipo.int/ipstats/en/wipi/index.html (last accessed December 15, 2018).

In the area of design count in applications between 2011 and 2016 in respect to high-income economies from the developing world, Korea continues to lead despite casual drops in 2014 and 2016. Singapore also is on the right track. Uruguay showed a mixed picture.

*Table 2.22* Design count in registrations (Direct and via the Madrid system)

| | *2011* | *2012* | *2013* | *2014* | *2015* | *2016* |
|---|---|---|---|---|---|---|
| Argentina | 1,377 | 1,457 | 1,545 | 1,271 | 1,482 | 1,476 |
| Barbados | 3 | 3 | – | – | 3 | 1 |
| Chile | 219 | 279 | 455 | 723 | 427 | 412 |
| Korea | 43,634 | 47,670 | 49,039 | 57,029 | 56,256 | 55,736 |
| Singapore | 3,972 | 3,929 | 4,314 | 4,314 | 4,359 | 4,376 |
| Uruguay | 27 | 111 | 42 | 92 | 47 | – |

Source: www.wipo.int/ipstats/en/wipi/index.html (last accessed December 15, 2018).

As long as design count in registrations is concerned, Korea maintained its lead over other countries of the same income grouping, despite consecutive drops from 2015. The good performance of Singapore between 2011 and 2016 without a single drop in terms of design count in registrations should be stressed.

*Table 2.23* Patent applications (Direct and via the PCT)

| | *2011* | *2012* | *2013* | *2014* | *2015* | *2016* |
|---|---|---|---|---|---|---|
| Argentina | 4,821 | 4,813 | 4,772 | 4,682 | 4,125 | 3,809 |
| Barbados | 71 | 36 | 42 | 39 | 45 | 41 |
| Chile | 2,792 | 3,019 | 3,072 | 3,105 | 3,274 | 2,907 |
| Korea | 178,924 | 188,915 | 204,589 | 210,292 | 213,694 | 208,830 |
| Singapore | 9,794 | 9,685 | 9,722 | 10,312 | 10,814 | 10,980 |
| Uruguay | 687 | 700 | – | 676 | 558 | – |

Source: www.wipo.int/ipstats/en/wipi/index.html (last accessed December 15, 2018).

Korea took a lead over patent applications between 2011 and 2016 in relation to the high-income economies from the developing world. A slight drop in number is observed in 2016 although the country enjoyed a steady growth of the number of patent applications from 2011 to 2015.

Singapore demonstrated a good performance between 2011 and 2016 in terms of patents applications notwithstanding a slight drop in 2012.

Argentina saw the number of patent applications dropping since 2012 notwithstanding its third place in ranking for this income grouping.

*Table 2.24* Patent grants (Direct and via the PCT)

| | *2011* | *2012* | *2013* | *2014* | *2015* | *2016* |
|---|---|---|---|---|---|---|
| Argentina | 1,291 | 932 | 1,297 | 1,360 | 1,559 | 1,879 |
| Barbados | 6 | 16 | 9 | 3 | 10 | 26 |
| Chile | 1,013 | 770 | 898 | 1,168 | 1,058 | 2,077 |
| Korea | 94,720 | 113,467 | 127,330 | 129,786 | 101,873 | 108,875 |
| Singapore | 5,949 | 5,633 | 5,575 | 5,538 | 7,054 | 7,341 |
| Saudi Arabia | 252 | | 233 | 561 | 763 | 595 |
| Uruguay | 13 | 22 | | 31 | 19 | – |

Source: www.wipo.int/ipstats/en/wipi/index.html (last accessed 30 June 2018).

Korea maintained the lead as regards patent grants between 2011 and 2016 for high-income countries. It should be stressed that Korea sustained the growth in number from 2011 to 2014 before experiencing a drop in 2015.

Singapore, despite three consecutive years of reduction of patent grants between 2012 and 2014, showed an increase in number in the last three years.

## Assessment of IP trends in the developing world between 2011 and 2016

As stated, this chapter aimed at assessing IP trends in the developing world from 2011 to 2016 based on income grouping as classified by the World Bank. Through the review of trademark class count in applications and registrations, design count in applications and registrations, and patent applications and patent grants with regard to low-income economies, lower middle-income economies, upper middle-income economies, and high-income economies in the developing world, it has been observed that the global trends depend mostly on each IP category, economic situation of the country, and GNI per capita, where applicable.

Regarding the low-income economies grouping as regards trademark class count in applications and registrations between 2011 and 2016, the findings revealed that in accordance with the level of development and economic situation, Madagascar, Mozambique, and Nepal performed well in this income grouping.

With regard to the low-income economies grouping in relation to design count in applications and registrations between 2011 and 2016, the findings showed that in this area, the performance of countries from this income grouping is disappointing. All the selected countries poorly performed, and the trend is toward regression of numbers. Madagascar had the lead and Mozambique had a mixed picture.

Concerning the low-income economies grouping in connection with patent applications and patent grants between 2011 and 2016, the findings displayed that patent applications are filed at a low level and only few countries from this income grouping have reached annually 50 applications. This may sound unbelievable but the reality is that few patent applications are filed in low-income countries given the level of development of their industries, research, and development (R&D), as well as large potential market enabling business. Looking in depth, a few patent applications received emanate from non-resident applicants who are most of the time foreigners.

In regard to the lower middle-income economies grouping in respect to trademark class count in applications and registrations between 2011 and 2016, the findings demonstrated that India performed well in the income grouping from the years 2011 to 2016. Vietnam showed progress with no drop since 2011. Indonesia ranked second after India suffered drops in 2014 and 2015 before a recovery in 2016. The Philippines, Pakistan, and Egypt showed a steady progress.

As for the lower middle-income economies grouping in regard to design count in applications and registrations between 2011 and 2016, the findings displayed a mixed picture in relation to the total number of design count both in applications and registrations. India and Morocco are the only countries where numbers are stable between 2011 and 2016 as regards both design count in applications and registrations.

In respect to the lower middle-income economies grouping as for patent applications and patent grants between 2011 and 2016, the findings revealed that India has been the only country in this income grouping to receive more than 40,000 patent applications from 2011 to 2016. India maintained the lead in respect to patent grants but with a narrow margin or gap on the Philippines.

As regards upper middle-income economies grouping in relation to the trademark class count in applications and registrations between 2011 and 2016, the findings confirmed the great performance of China, ranking number one, not only with regard to the same income grouping but also toward all income economies. China was able to double the trademark class count numbers in five years in both applications and registrations. In the same income grouping, Turkey, the Russian Federation, Brazil, and Mexico performed well with more than 100,000 trademark class count in applications and registrations annually.

Regarding the upper middle-income economies grouping with regard to design count in applications and registrations between 2011 and 2016, the findings demonstrated that all selected countries under this income grouping suffered drops on design count in applications between 2011 and 2016, with no exception. China is the leading country in both design count in applications and registrations.

In relation to the upper middle-income economies grouping as regards patent applications and patent grants between 2011 and 2016, the findings showed the continuous growth of China in both patent applications and patents grants in the consecutive years (2011–2016). Despite some drops, Brazil, Iran, Mexico, and the Russian Federation performed well between 2011 and 2016 as long as patent applications are concerned. As to patent grants, Brazil and Turkey performed below the expectation.

Concerning high-income economies grouping in regard to trademark class count in applications and registrations between 2011 and 2016, the findings confirmed the remarkable performance of Korea. Singapore experienced a steady growth with no drop on trademark class count in registrations between 2011 and 2016.

As long as the high-income economies grouping is concerned with regard to design count in applications and registrations between 2011 and 2016, the findings displayed the continuous good performance of Korea by maintaining the lead in respect to the same income economies, despite a few drops.

With regard to the high-income economies grouping concerning patent applications and patent grants between 2011 and 2016, the findings confirmed the lead of Korea with a high score between 2011 and 2016. It should also be pointed out the good performance of Singapore.

Actually, the world population consists of 7 billion, 346.7 inhabitants. The low-income economies are made of 638.3 (in million) inhabitants, with an average GNI per capita of 619$. The lower middle-income economies are composed of 2 billion, 927.5 inhabitants, with an average of 2,032 GNI per capita. Under this income grouping, India itself has a population of over 1.1 billion. The upper middle-income economies have a total of 2 billion, 593.9 inhabitants, with an average of 8,260 $ of GNI per capita. This income grouping encompasses China that has a population of over 1.3 billion. The high-income economies have a total population of 1 billion, 187.1 inhabitants, with an average GNI per capita of 41,932 $.

The question is what is the ratio of each income group to the world total of trademark class count in applications and registration, design count in applications and registrations, and patent applications and patent grants in 2016, for instance? The world total in terms of trademark class count was 9,768,200 in applications in 2016 and 6,549,100 in registrations. The low-income economies received a total of 66,300 trademark class count in applications and a total of 49,200 in registrations in 2016.

The lower middle-income economies obtained a total of 916,700 trademark class count in applications and a total of 593,800 in registrations in 2016. The upper middle-income economies received in 2016 a total of 5,201,000 trademark class count in applications and a total of 344,200 in registrations. High-income economies showed a total of 3,584,200 trademark class count in applications and 2,561,900 in registrations.[1]

The world total for design count in applications in 2016 was 1,240,600. The low-income economies had a total of 1,700 designs in applications.[2] In the area of design count in applications in 2016, lower middle-income economies received a total of 47,400.[3] The upper middle-income economies received 751,000 design counts in applications in 2016. The high-income got a total of 440,500 design count in applications in 2016.

The overall worldwide total of patent applications in 2016 was 3,127,900 and a total of 1,351,600 for patent grants. The low-income economies received only 10,000 patent applications in 2016 and granted only 7,500 patents. In 2016, the lower middle-income economies received a total of 76,000 patent applications and 22,100 patents were granted. The total patent application filed in 2016 in respect to the upper middle-income economies was 1,489,100 and for patent grants a total of 474,400. The high-income countries received 1,552,800 patent applications in 2016 and granted 847,600 patents.

As revealed by the findings, the IP trends in the developing world depend on the income status of countries and on the categories of IPRs.

## Notes

1 WIPO (2017), World Intellectual Property Indicators 2017.
2 There was no data for design count in registration for 2016.
3 There was no data for design count in registration for 2016.

# 3 Non-technological innovations and intellectual property in the developing world

## Trademark as an innovation indicator

As illustrated in the second chapter, trademark and design data present various practical advantages to be used as an innovation indicator, mainly in the area of non-technological innovation.

Contrary to patents, trademarks are obviously linked to the commercialization of products, as they are fundamentally used to sell goods or services on the market. Consequently, trademarks may shed more light onto innovation, being less focused on the technological dimension and more on the commercial side. Moreover, trademarks may help to appreciate non-technological innovations that are not based on technological research reflected by patents.

There is a significant correlation between trademarks, branding, and innovation in various sectors, suggesting that trademarks could be used as an indicator for certain kinds of innovations and complete the information brought by other innovation indicators.

It should also be stressed that a trademark is also linked to product innovation. The relationship between trademark registration and product innovation is easy to capture. In many cases, enterprises set up new trademarks to escort new innovative products and to assist in the commercialization of these new products on the market. This association would enable consumers to easily identify the innovative products and their benefits.

With regard to marketing innovations, the link with trademark registrations is more complex. The connection is more perceptible in the branding strategy of a firm.

There are many case studies and success stories in the developing world in relation to trademark used as innovation indicators that are worth to review.

### *The Havaianas brand of rubber flip-flop sandals, Brazil*[1]

The Havaianas brand of rubber flip-flop sandals started life 50 years ago as a basic shoe for poor plantation workers in Brazil. Brazilian manufacturing company Alpargatas currently owns it. The brand became a staple in the country before gaining fresh impetus in the mid-1990s, when parent company Alpargatas decided to reposition the declining brand as an aspirational fashion product. It hired leading designers to come up with attractive colors and designs and soon Brazilian and then international celebrities were wearing the new, colorful and stylish, higher-priced sandals. Sales grew rapidly.

However, the market was saturated in Brazil, where Havaianas sold 850 pairs of flip-flops for every 1,000 people in 2007. Although Havaianas was enjoying strong overseas sales growth in 65 countries, no strategy for international expansion was thought and available. In 2008, Marcio Luiz Simoes Utsch, Alpargatas, chief executive, decided to try to turn Havaianas into Brazil's first truly global brand.

Making Havaianas a global brand required further expansion in Europe, the United States, and Asia. To compete in this global market, there was a need to revise the Havaianas marketing strategy. To fit into this global market, Havaianas had to adapt itself to the taste of this new range of consumers. Consequently, it had to expand its range of colors and designs to appeal to consumers who were more sophisticated and who did not have either the same flip-flop culture or climate as Brazilians. It was necessary to invest in sales, marketing, and production.

The key elements of Havaianas's strategy were a constant focus on product innovation; a consistent global marketing and communications strategy; and fast, flexible responses to consumer tastes. The company introduced new sandals with closed tops for cooler climates, sandals with straps around the ankle, and even sandals with real diamonds for fashion shows. It also kept the Havaianas brand fresh by introducing socks; bags; and softer, washable shoes.

The revised marketing message suggested innovation and aspiration. It also built on Brazil's positive image overseas by portraying Havaianas as a colorful, joyful, simple product. This general message still allowed the company to tailor its approach to different countries. For instance, in the United States, Havaianas was careful not to promote its sandals to college students so much that it threatened the brand's "cool" edge in this demographic; in France, sales took off when the French importer positioned the brand in the luxury market alongside design names such as Lacoste and Jean Paul Gautier.

To help maintain a consistent message, the company preferred to run its own operations rather than work through local importers and distributors. The main exception was Europe, where it has 5 offices but 18 distributors.

The company reacted fast to market intelligence. Sales slumped when the flip-flops were made outside Brazil. As such, Havaianas opened a new plant in the southeast of the country. When it realized customers liked shops with a full range of its flip-flops, it opened stores in Rome, Paris, London, and New York.

The brand has managed to meet the needs of all classes of people in Brazil while selling its products as luxury products abroad. The brand is sold in more than 80 countries. Havaianas officially became a global brand in 2000.

The Havaianas trademark(s) is consistently ranked among the most valuable Brazilian trademarks and is registered in many countries in the world. Havaianas flip-flops are popular in the world, with 200 million pairs being sold every year.

The hallmark of Havaianas's success is innovation. Creative styles with various colors were manufactured in addition to closed-toed sandals for customers who live in cooler climates.

### *Bio Mada, Madagascar*[2]

Hanta Tiana Rajaonarisoa founded Bio Mada, a natural essential oils social enterprise, in 2011, in response to a gap that existed in the market for affordable, hypo-allergenic mosquito repellent. Rajaonarisoa noticed that Madagascar was rich in the type of natural flora-pine and lemongrass from which high quality insect repellents could be produced at minimal cost.

With the assistance of her core team, Rajaonarisoa made-up two products: namely, an all-natural mosquito repellent that could be applied directly on to the skin or sprayed into the air and an anti-perspiring deodorant, "Fresh Oil," that reduces perspiration and helps prevent body odor.

Today, Bio Mada supplies its products to 40 retail pharmacies across Madagascar and sells 2,000 bottles of their product per month. The company's most popular product is the mosquito repellent. Future plans for expansion of the company's product line include hairspray and fly repellent that will comprise all natural essential oils.

Hanta Tiana Rajaonarisoa and her company Bio Mada are making use of plant resources that are naturally available in Madagascar to create new types of products that are completely free of synthetic chemicals. The newly created products from the Bio Mada company fill a gap that existed within the market for all-natural mosquito repellent; provide an environmentally safe and hypo-allergenic solution to the public health problem of mosquito-borne diseases/mosquitoes transmitting diseases to humans; reduce perspiration to help prevent body odor; generate employment in Madagascar's poor, rural communities; and help protect Madagascar's biodiversity (by harvesting sustainable levels of raw materials in a manner that allows nature to self-replenish in a manner that is sustainable).

In 2015, Bio Mada won the Indian Ocean's Best Developmental Stage Company of the Year.. Products currently are sold in pharmacies, schools, and hotels throughout Madagascar. The Bio Mada brand was not built in one day. Heavy advertising and product sampling at local trade and health fairs, in pharmacies, and in the hospitality industry contributed to its expansion.

### *Dry Bath, South Africa*[3]

Ludwick Marishane, a South African college student, created an innovative product called "Dry Bath," enabling a person to take a shower without using water. The gel called "Dry Bath" kills germs, moisturizes the skin, and exudes a pleasant and light smell. The gel is packaged in small, easy-to-open sachets that were also a South African innovation. One small packet replaces one bath, and users never need any water.

Ludwick Marishane created a product that is the first of its kind in respect of it being completely safe for use on the entire body, inclusive of hair. Dry Bath is an innovative, bacteria-killing, and odor-eliminating gel that uses the motion of one's hands to remove dead skin cells and foul body scents without damaging the skin's natural protective barrier.

Marishane's creation has been featured in international media as a substance with the potential for use in the following service areas:

1. The military
2. Non-governmental organizations who deploy personnel into high conflict zones
3. Aid agency personnel and residents of natural disaster recovery areas
4. Long haul air travel
5. Guest services within the hospitality industry

In 2011, Ludwick Marishane was awarded the Global Student Entrepreneur of the Year Award.

In recognizing the importance of protecting his intellectual property asset, Ludwick Marishane, via Headboy Industries, has ensured that the Dry Bath product has been formally registered as a trademark. Further, both the Dry Bath process and the Dry Bath product are patented.

The brand strategy implemented by Headboy Industries incorporates heavy use of real-time, interactive social media. It also encourages public use of product samples to elevate brand awareness and the unique attributes of the product.

### *Booomers International, Ghana*[4]

Booomers International is an enterprise, incorporated in 2014, which designs, produces, and markets bicycles with frames comprised entirely of bamboo. The company is a subsidiary of the Yonso Project and manufactures a range of different types of bamboo bicycles and accessories for the local Ghanaian, regional African, and international markets. Booomers International aims to help improve the accessibility of transportation in rural communities and the effect of transportation on the environment with a view to mitigating the adverse effects of climate change.

The company also aims to help alleviate poverty by providing jobs to persons in rural communities. The ultimate goal of Booomers International is "to provide the poor in rural Ghana the means to gain economic freedom."

Booomers International is using its trademark and trade name to commercially exploit its range of bamboo bicycle products across local, regional, and international fora. It has also embarked upon a brand strategy that champions and promotes the place of origin of the product as a signifier of the product's quality and authenticity: "Made in Ghana."

## Innovation in the service sector

Service industries have a different focus. They concentrate more on marketing and organizational innovations than on product and process innovations. It is said that in the service sector, a large number of firms are driven by organizational innovations which impact on new ways of delivering services.

Organizational innovation can be conductive to service innovation and may serve as a precondition to the integration and development of new service functions. From the opposite angle, it may also be said that service innovation brings the need for more effective organizational arrangements to occur, given the increase of firms' interactions with providers, suppliers, clients, and other external institutional agents in the search for information and knowledge.[5] As mentioned, organizational innovation frequently favors a shift or re-design of service's provision, enabling firms to attain productivity gains in design, logistics, marketing, R&D, and management functions, among others.[6]

It should be stressed that services are no longer a secondary instrument of the value chain. Instead, they have become essential and may add value from their involvement, for instance, in product design, business management, procurement in global markets, and support to customers' participation in value creation.

Service-based innovation enables firms to be closer to their customers, to raise barriers to market entry, to make businesses less vulnerable to economic cycles, and to promote efficiency through the use of business services.

The introduction of new service functions or service innovations contributes toward changing traditional value chains through, for instance, the provision of new service delivery channels.

Increasingly, industry leaders are complementing their product offerings with service innovations to develop solutions that generate greater customer value, improve brand preference, and create greater cross-selling opportunities. In some service areas, customers are more and more associated with the promotion of the positive image of the service (e.g. Internet companies).

Providing additional services to accompany the sale of products is increasingly central to the strategies of manufacturing companies. In a number of instances, consumers may benefit from additional services if they purchase more than two products of the company.

The increasing tradability of services and the ease with which they can be transmitted over long distances facilitate the internationalization of services providers that generate, transfer, and spread knowledge. Thus, they play a crucial role in the creation and commercialization of new products and processes.[7]

It should be stressed that common branding strategies may apply for a single service (single brand), a bunch of similar services (family brand), all services of the company (umbrella brand), or the company itself (company brand).[8]

First, most innovations in services appear to be non-technical and the result of small, incremental changes in processes and procedures that do not require much formal research and development (R&D). Second, services make greater use of trademarks, designs, and copyright to protect their innovations.[9]

The service sector is huge and comprises various industries, such as hotel, information technology (IT), airline, restaurant, tourism, car rental, Internet provider, and garages (car repair). With new technology, new services have been created to respond to novel needs.

While some firms such as Sony, Samsung, LG, and Apple have a long history of design-focused innovation, others are new to this game. In industries that are primarily design driven (for instance, furniture and homeware), design innovations could be a source of both value creation and value capture. Creation is often about creating product offerings with profound differences in features, reliability, and other performance attributes. Thus, marketing/sales investments in the promotion of design-oriented advantages should be more impactful in the pursuit of value capture.[10]

Conversely, the shorter development cycles generally associated with design innovation, often consisting of nothing more than a sketch of a unique shape or pattern, are better suited to the rapidly changing competitive dynamics of relatively smaller markets. In a situation of evolving customer tastes and the rapid entry of new competitors, design may constitute a more powerful strategic approach than traditional, engineering-driven innovation efforts.[11]

Under this section, some success stories in the developing world in the service sector will be highlighted.

### *DataStream Technology Sdn Bhd (DST), Brunei Darussalam*[12]

DataStream Technology Sdn Bhd (DST) was formed in 1995 as a response to the government of Brunei Darussalam's call for the privatization of communication services. Since its inception, the company, called the DST Group, has grown substantially and has diversified into nine core businesses.

Initially, the three letters "DST," derived from Data Stream Technology, formed the main focal point and were central to the development of the group's trademarks.

Aware of the importance of IP, the group evolved with further branding exercises when DSTCom introduced two trademarks: namely, "Prima" for post-paid mobile phone services and "Easi" for prepaid services. These new initiatives gave customers the choice to select the services which most met their needs and led to an increase in the group's business activities.

With the expansion of business, there was again the need to create more trademarks. The DST Group created three additional trademarks and brand names – "FasCom," "Simpur," and "Zippi" – which were more easily recognized by consumers than the names of the companies themselves: DST Technical Services Sdn Bhd (a service provider of nationwide two-way trunk radios), DST

Multimedia Sdn Bhd (an Internet service provider), and DST Payphone Sdn Bhd (an operator of prepaid phone cards and fixed phone booths).

It should be stressed that there are now over 1,000 licensed vendors for the brand name "Easi," 250 licensed vendors for the brand name "Simpur," and 350 licensed vendors for the brand name "Zippi."

The DST Group has become one of the country's most successful private enterprises as a network operator, a service and entertainment provider for communications. It occupies a dominant place in the market.

The important success factor of the DST Group is its innovative way of creating "easy-to-remember" trademarks and brand names to differentiate its multiple communication services among the group, while the group commits itself to providing quality services for all its customers.

## *theSOFTtribe Limited (SOFT), Ghana*[13]

Herman Chinery-Hesse, former software developer in London in 1990, with no start-up capital beyond limited personal savings, no infrastructure, and no equipment other than his old computer, took a risk and a big challenge in returning to his country, Ghana, to set up a software company first called S.O.F.T. and renamed theSOFTtribe Limited in 2004 to have a more distinctive brand name and prevent potential confusion with other businesses, products, and imitators, registered – deliberately or not – under similar variants. In the meantime, there was no Ghanaian software industry.

On the basis of a single software package which he had developed when freelancing in the United Kingdom, Chinery-Hesse landed his first contract with a Ghanaian travel firm while still en route to Accra. The payment enabled him and his founding partner, Kojo Gyakye, to buy a second computer. When they managed to receive their first contract to write a network application, the company still did not even have a network of its own on which to run the program. The young entrepreneurs had an early breakthrough when the Switzerland-based Nestlé corporation, contracted theSOFTtribe to develop production management software for its operations in Ghana. At that time, theSOFTtribe did not have a proper office to be called as such. They had a couple of desks in the bedroom in Chinery-Hesse parent's home.

As an African start-up company, theSOFTtribe had to persuade each potential new client that it was a better choice than the international, big-name competitors. The company's strategy was to offer systems specifically designed to be more reliable in the African context, and to back these up with a professional support service better than that provided by competitors.

theSOFTtribe's products are not necessarily very sophisticated, but the company realizes that simplicity can be an advantage in Ghana. Key to the company's success is their innovative and core concept of "tropical tolerance," which takes into account the unique characteristics of the African business and social environment. theSOFTtribe's systems are designed to meet the more challenging conditions of the developing world.

Later theSOFTtribe developed a strategic partnership with Microsoft Corporation and also with BusyInternet, Ghana's largest privately owned and operated information and communication technology (ICT) center. One of the most important aspects of the deal with Microsoft is that although Chinery-Hesse's company uses the product platform from Microsoft, IP rights (IPRs) of all subsequent developments done on the product are retained by the Ghanaian company. The deal thus encourages innovation and ensures a framework for preserving theSOFTtribe's intellectual capital.

One of theSOFTtribe's recently developed and increasingly used product is its microfinance management software which is based on the Microsoft Dynamics platform. Based on well-established microcredit approaches to reduce poverty and foster social development, the software enables small-scale lending to promote grassroots enterprises. The company licenses the software to microfinance organizations in the region. In accordance with the deal with Microsoft, the IPRs of the software and the revenue from the licensing are retained by theSOFTtribe.

Today, theSOFTtribe is the market leader in Ghana. Its systems include payroll management, cybercafé billing, airline reservation and ticketing, micro-finance fund management, plantation management, and bespoke software, such as the one developed for the Ghanaian timber industry.

It serves over 250 clients, prominent among which are major multinationals such as Pepsi, Unilever, and oil giant Total S.A. It exports to 11 other countries in the region. All this has been accomplished without having had access to business loan financing.

### *Beauty Gems Group Co., Ltd., Thailand*[14]

In 1964, the husband and wife team of Mr. Pornsit Sriorathaikul and Dr. Sunee Sriorathaikul started Beauty Gems Group Co., Ltd. (Beauty Gems), then a small family-run gem and jewelry export business in Bangkok, Thailand. Committed to producing beautiful, high quality, competitively priced jewelry and gems for the global market, their business grew quickly by taking advantage of the parallel emergence of the Thai gem and jewelry industry.

In 1973, Beauty Gems opened its first manufacturing factory with 3 million Thai baht (฿) in capital and 300 employees, and by 1983, the company's staff doubled, and its capital went up to ฿13.5 million. To meet the increasing demand for custom cut diamonds, Beauty Gems diversified and in 1990 set up two subsidiary companies to provide top quality diamonds to its subsidiary companies and customers.

Focusing on export markets from the start, Beauty Gems is now one of the largest jewelry and gem exporters in Asia, with over 3,500 employees and an annual turnover of over ฿5 billion. The company is a one-stop subcontractor that combines state-of-the-art technology with traditional Thai craftsmanship to meet all of its clients' needs in jewelry outsourcing, design, and manufacture.

Since Beauty Gems is a wholesaler, many of its export products are not sold under company brand names but of the names of its customers.

Continuous research and development (R&D) has always been an integral part of Beauty Gems' success. Perhaps the most important factor is the company's emphasis on the originality of the designs of its products. Each market is different, and the company research styles that are popular in each target market to design products that will appeal to the tastes of its consumers. This approach has facilitated the company's success in many markets, the most successful of which has been Japan. Beauty Gems took the time to research what kind of designs would appeal to discerning Japanese consumers, and as a result became one of the first Thai jewelry companies to penetrate the Japanese market. It is now one of the top gem and jewelry exporters to Japan.

Beauty Gems' R&D department also fosters innovation among its workforce by encouraging employees to take part in design and production contests and educating them on the importance of intellectual property (IP) and IP rights (IPRs). The company also places an importance on the use of design and patent information when researching new products, technologies, and processes.

Beauty Gems also played an important role in creating a reliable body in Thailand that awards certification to gold and silver products.

The role of IPRs is very important to Beauty Gems and this is underscored in the company's unique IP management strategy, which is facilitated by dedicated IP personnel and divided into two categories: company-owned IP and client owned IP.

For company-owned IP, starting in 1999, the company has filed for protection for its trademarks and industrial designs with the Department of Intellectual Property of Thailand (DIP Thailand). The company also maintains copyright protection for all material related to the development and marketing of its products. This strategy allows the company to emphasize product quality and improvement over price competition, which enhances the company's corporate image, builds customer loyalty, and attracts more investment.

For client owned IP, Beauty Gems considers safeguarding it an essential part of its business strategy. The company does its best to protect its clients' designs and trade secrets, which has been a key factor in establishing the strong reputation that it enjoys.

The combination of being a one-stop contractor with a commitment to protecting IP has made Beauty Gems one of the largest manufacturers in Asia in the gem and jewelry business. This philosophy has built up the reputation of the company, with many of the world's best known jewelry brands trusting Beauty Gems for their subcontracting needs. The company has gone from a small family-run business to a key player in the international market, with products sold in major markets, such as France, Germany, Hong Kong, Japan, Saudi Arabia, Switzerland, and the United States, among others. Every year, Beauty Gems exports ฿4 billion worth of products.

A focus on R&D and commitment to protecting IP of both the company and its clients has been the key factors to Beauty Gems' success.

## Innovation in agro-industry

As mentioned, an innovation may occur in any sector, including the agro-industry. In this area, as agriculture is at the heart of economies of many countries from the developing world, numerous innovations take place in this area as it will be demonstrated through success stories.

### *Javara, Indonesia*[15]

Inspired by Indonesia's food biodiversity, indigenous wisdom, and spiritualism, JAVARA was founded by Helianti Hilman in 2008. JAVARA works across agricultural value chains from production to distribution in order to preserve such biodiversity and bring community-based, organic products to broader markets.

Working with over 50,000 farmers and 2,000 food artisans, selling over 600 premium artisan food products, JAVARA is currently known as the leading social enterprise in Indonesia that works with a vast range of bio-diverse community-based organic food products using ethical principles.

Prior to JAVARA, Helianti founded a number of social enterprises in Indonesia. Her signature brand, JAVARA, is one of Indonesia's leading purveyors of artisanal products. Originally trained as a lawyer who advised the Indonesian government on intellectual property development, Helianti was also a rural economic development consultant for international development organizations. Inspired by the wealth of Indonesia's biodiversity and the dedication of the indigenous farmers, Helianti brings her passion for community-based business and expertise in agribusiness to grow her social enterprise to the next level.

At JAVARA, working hand-in-hand with local indigenous farmers, food artisans, and biodiversity warriors to revive and sustain the existence of the heritage is the goal. At the same time, producing added-value products based on such food ingredients, building local capacity to create quality community-based artisan food products are the principles. At JAVARA, among other things, branding of the product origin using local packaging materials is encouraged.

The company intervenes along the supply chains to strengthen supplier's production capacity, improve workplace safety, and sell products nationally and internationally, securing premium prices for the farmers and processors.

JAVARA's value chain includes farmers with small landholdings, organized into farmer collectives. JAVARA creates local farm-entrepreneurs and helps them develop high market potential products and supports them to adopt sustainable and economically beneficial farming practices such as crop rotation or inter-cropping.

JAVARA works with over 25 partners across 18 countries in Europe, America, and Asia. The company engages in co-branding partnerships and has 60 domestic partners, which include large retailers, premium supermarkets, and hotel chains that carry JAVARA labeled products.

### *Pecuaria Development Cooperative Inc., PDCI, Philippines*[16]

Pecuaria Development Cooperative Inc. (PDCI) is a cooperative for agrarian reform established in 1991, in Lanipga, Bula, a municipality in the province of Camarines Sur, in the Republic of the Philippines (Philippines). Consisting of 426 producers (in 2012), the cooperative was created following land reforms in the country in the early 1990s. During this period, hundreds of hectares of arable land in Lanipga were made available for the organization's use by the Philippine government.

Having initially struggled to implement an efficient, profitable, and sustainable rice production process and strategy, PDCI subsequently managed a positive improvement in production in Lanipga while enhancing the environment and supporting the farming community.

The cooperative, moreover, has invested in new research and development (R&D) facilities and created new marketing policies and commercialization strategies for its rice farmers. To this end, PDCI entered strategic partnerships with local, national, and international organizations. As a result, the cooperative's rice farmers modernized and streamlined production process created quality brands and entered the niche market of organic rice produce.

PDCI's members, furthermore, diversified their product-range to include sugar, organic fertilizer, and poultry goods. By 2012, the organization had emerged from the margins of the Philippine economy to become a major player in the organic rice-producing industry in the country.

A key factor in the improved prospects of PDCI's producers was the incorporation of a robust branding and commercialization strategy.

In order to break into new markets with quality goods and brands, PDCI relied on the services of a marketing organization called Upland Marketing Foundation, Inc. (UMFI) – a brand creation NGO based in Manila, the capital of the Philippines.

As of 2012, PDCI and UMFI had a variety of value-added, branded products including organic white, brown, black, and pink rice.

Rather than positioning the cooperative's rice and sugar goods in the "organic" foods sector, however, UMFI chose to position them as "healthy" food products. This decision was made following consumer surveys in Manila that showed a higher percentage of buyers were willing to pay premium prices for products labeled "healthy" than for those labeled "organic." As a result, the marketing organization created a "Healthy Rice" brand for PDCI's rice. A second rice brand – "High Fiber Rice" – was also created.

With secure IP assets, UMFI (and its farming partner) has been able to develop and promote organic rice and sugar brands with confidence across the Philippines and into the international market.

## *Asociacion De Productores De Maiz Blanco Gigante Del Cusco, Peru*[17]

For generations, giant white maize has been cultivated around Cusco City (Cusco), in the Urubamba Valley of the Andes Mountains, the Republic of Peru (Peru). Since the 1950s, the city's farmers have leveraged their illustrious maize-growing history in order to preserve their farming traditions, develop a marketable reputation for their grain, and preserve the local environment.

In 2005, a milestone was reached when 17 of Cusco's mainly small- and medium-sized farming communities joined hands and established the *Asociacion De Productores De Maiz Blanco Gigante Del Cusco* (APROMAIZ) – the association of giant white maize producers of Cusco. Since its foundation, APROMAIZ has united the voice and strengthened the bargaining power of its members.

Subsequently, the cooperative has collaborated with local and national government in Peru and with international agencies. As a result, the farming skill of the association's members has been improved while the quality of the region's maize has been enhanced. In addition, Cusco's famous crop growing culture and environment has been conserved while the economic status of producers in the region has been developed.[18]

Indeed, maize cultivation know-how and culture in Cusco had been passed down the generations of farmers as traditional knowledge. Traditionally, the region's farmers prepared the land (which was turned by ox-pulled plough or by a *chakitaqlla*, a hand plough) between June and July of each year.

In order to grow maize in the traditional way, healthy seeds were mixed with *guano* (a manure made of droppings from bats or sea-birds), *muña* (an herb – *minthostachys setosa* – that is native to South America), and ash from a stove. This ancient yet effective process secured the seeds against microbes that may otherwise have destroyed them. Thereafter, the crop's kernels were sown into ground.

In order to win new customers and to compete in the national and international market, APROMAIZ has produced quality maize supported by attractive brands and enhanced by the region's Appellation of origin (AO) certification. In support of these branding initiatives, the cooperative has developed a comprehensive commercialization strategy.

APROMAIZ, furthermore, has ensured that all its products are organically produced and have not undergone genetic modification. Having established a sanitary, natural, and well-organized regime of maize production, the farmers' association developed a robust commercialization strategy.

To this end, the cooperative developed two separate but overlapping streams for generating income: (a) maize produced for human and non-human consumption that is sold to the national and international market, and (b) maize for re-planting and for industrial use.

APROMAIZ's maize has been packaged and commercialized in a variety of snacks and flavors that have been sold within various retail outlets. Moreover, the cooperative's grain product has been sold via a number of national and international brokers including Peru Inka S.R.L. (Peru Inka), an agro-industrial company based in La Florida Los Kantus, Cusco.

The farmers' association, however, has flexibly adjusted its packaging to suit the specific requirements of each of the countries where it exports its products. As of 2012, APROMAIZ's giant white maize was sold to customers throughout Peru and around the world including in France, Japan, Spain, and the United States.

## *TopFruit, South Africa*[19]

TopFruit was founded in 1983 by three nurserymen: Dr. Jim Button, Richard Hill, and Roy Jeffery. Their collective aim was to efficiently import, test, and commercialize new varieties in the fruit industry.

Through plant breeding, a strong program of intellectual property management, robust brand development, and innovative marketing initiatives, TopFruit, as the Master Licensee for Pink Lady® apples in the African Territory (South Africa, Africa and the Indian Ocean Islands), has succeeded in growing the Pink Lady® business in their territory. Apple and Pear Australia Limited (APAL) is the owner of this one widely recognized in the world: Pink Lady Apples. Sustainability is a key touchstone at TopFruit. The company strives always to effect environmentally sound business practice. TopFruit is focused on sourcing fruit varieties and brands that are easier to grow, require less chemicals, and therefore reduce its impact on the environment (Figure 3.1).

*Figure 3.1* Apple variety.

TopFruit has continuously strived to unlock the commercial potential of all products within the company's portfolio. One of TopFruit's most successful brands to date is Pink Lady apples (Figure 3.2).

TopFruit has successfully launched Pink Lady apples into the South African market via a customized promotional campaign that was tailored specifically for the market. For TopFruit, branding and building brand awareness of Pink Lady® apples went far beyond simply selling the product. A large part of the company's marketing strategy for Pink Lady apples entailed focusing on the appearance, taste, and health benefits of the fruit – for example, its nutritional benefits – to promote the product as well as the Pink Lady® story (Figure 3.3).

*Figure 3.2* TopFruit registered logo.

*Figure 3.3* Pink Lady registered logo.

### *Sunny Isle Jamaican Black Castor Oil, Jamaica*[20]

Castor oil has been used for over 4,000 years for a variety of purposes – from hair and skin care to healing aches and pains and as massage oil. The castor bean travelled to Jamaica during the slave trade from its native home of Eastern Africa, and for many years, Jamaicans have been using castor oil as their home-made remedy for medicinal purposes as well as skin care, hair care, and every-day aches and pains. Today, many persons use castor oil to moisturize, thicken, strengthen, and grow their hair.

Sunny Isle Jamaican Black Castor Oil (SIJBCO), manufactured by JBC Distributors Incorporated, is processed the "old-fashioned" Jamaican way. Its organic castor beans are roasted and ground by a manual grinder. Then they are boiled to extract the 100% pure, dark brown organic castor oil.

Sunny Isle is dedicated to bringing authentic, high quality, Jamaican Black Castor Oil and other organic hair and skin care products to women and men of all hair types, skin types, and ethnicities. The rapid success of the Sunny Isle Jamaican Black Castor Oil brand stems from the fact that, at its core, Sunny Isle Jamaican Black Castor Oil (SIJBCO) is a quality product. SIJBCO has been able to leverage the universal appeal of healthy hair and skin to market a product, once thought to be used solely by one ethnic group, across all ethnicities and nationalities.

Sunny Isle is the only brand of Jamaican Black Castor Oil that is formally approved for export by the Jamaican Government.

## Innovation in the area of Traditional Knowledge

Traditional knowledge (TK) in a broad sense, encompassing traditional cultural expressions, is the newcomer in the field of IP. It comprises knowledge passed from generation to generation having economic value. TK is dynamic and evolves with its time and environment. It is not static. TK is present in many fields such as agriculture, cosmetics, biotechnology, creative industries, foods, and fashion or textile. As it will be demonstrated through case studies in the developing world, knowledge used through generations form the foundation of many so-called innovations nowadays. TK remains innovative.

With the development of biotechnology, cosmetic, and creative industries, TK is more and more utilized in commerce than before. Its great contribution to the global value chain is no longer questionable as illustrated via success stories.

### *Himalayan Bio Trade Private Limited (HBTL), Nepal*[21]

Based in Kathmandu, the capital of the Federal Democratic Republic of Nepal (Nepal), Himalayan Bio Trade Private Limited (HBTL) was founded in 2000 in order to process and market forest-derived products made by members of the Nepalese rural community.

Desiring to enter the international market, HBTL has worked hard on diversifying and distinguishing its brands, establishing international standards in its production processes, and developing a sound marketing strategy. Working with stakeholders, the community-based organization took the strategic decision to enter the niche market of organically produced goods.

In support of this decision, HBTL has invested in industry certification for organic production including those provided by WFEN (an internationally renowned certifier of naturally produced goods) and the Forest Stewardship Council (FSC) – an independent NGO that has promoted sustainable forest management policies and accreditation services around the world.

The farmers' organization, for instance, has implemented FSC's Cradle-to-Cradle certification which ensures progressive production processes (including the use of organic farming methods void of chemical fertilizers) that are favorable to human health while protecting the environment. With sound organic credentials and other international certifications at the core of its production processes, HBTL has been able to market its products in the EU – a region which has had a thriving market for organic products.

Moreover, in order to reach clients and customers around the world, HBTL has established a strong marketing strategy that includes participation in well-known industry trade fairs and events such as BioFach – a global trade fair for organic goods producers based in Nuremburg in Germany. Timed to coincide with the 2011 BioFach fair, the producers' organization and its partners – including other Nepali cooperatives – joined forces and produced a collective brand called "Nepali Delegation."

Intended to create awareness among clients of Nepalese products, the brand has appeared on HBTL's product brochures and thus helped to stimulate general interest in Nepalese goods. In addition to marketing its products via collaborations with international fairs organizers, the producers' organization has relied on commercialization partnerships with major cosmetics manufacturers such as Aveda – a skincare and hair products producer with a well-established reputation for sourcing materials from marginalized communities.

Since 2007, Aveda has sourced attractive blue, black, red, yellow, and green hand-made Lokta paper from HBTL in order to package its range of "Holiday Gift Set" cosmetic brands – called Hand Relief and Foot Relief (both being moisturizers). Not only have these brands raised the corporate profile of Aveda; they have also enhanced the profile and reputation of HBTL and its producers while opening new commercialization avenues for their products (Figure 3.4).

Aveda, moreover, has been keen to promote its procurement relationship with the Nepali organization including via direct marketing campaigns for consumers on the company's corporate website. Furthermore, the Nepali crafts organization has itself developed a stylish and customer friendly website (where customers can peruse HBTL's products), further enhancing its reputation on the Internet and internationally.

*Figure 3.4* Hand-made paper cards.

Having established a strong brand image on the Internet, raised Nepali Delegation brand awareness internationally, and entrenched high quality production processes, the organization has diversified its product portfolio to meet a growing market for non-timber forest products. HBTL offers a vast range of certified, natural, and organic products, including Nepali hand-made Lokta paper, hemp, and nettle clothing and accessories (such as folders, journals, notebooks, lampshades, and business cards) (Figure 3.5).

Other products in the organization's portfolio include wildcrafted essential oils (such as Abies oil, Anthopogon oil, Artemisia oil, Calamus oil, Jatamansi oil, Juniper oil, Valerian oil, Wintergreen oil, and Zanthoxylum oil); cultivated items of essential oils (such as Chamomile oil, Citronella oil, Eucalyptus oil, French basil oil, Lemongrass oil, Mentha oil, and Palmarosa oil); raw herbs; and vegetable oils.

As of 2012, the community-based organization commercialized its products both locally (through networks of distributors in Nepal such as Deudhunga Cooperative Ltd, Malika Handmade Paper Pvt. Ltd and Everest Gateway Herbs Pvt. Ltd) and internationally to several countries and regions including the Commonwealth of Australia, the EU, India, Japan, the Republic of Korea, and the United States.

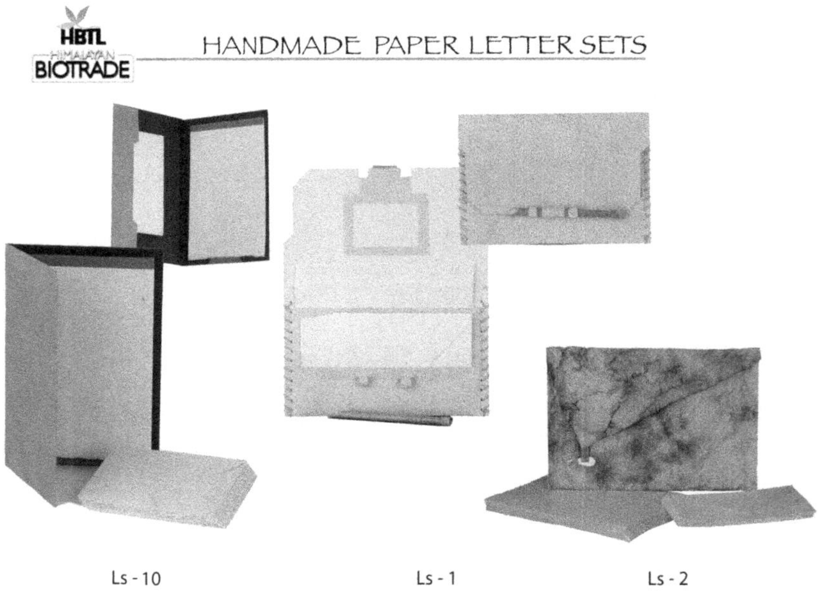


*Figure 3.5* Hand-made paper letter set.

HBTL and its partners have been aware of the importance of the intellectual property (IP) system as a means of securing IP assets, distinguishing goods in a competitive global market, and reaping a return on investment. To this end, Aveda registered two trademarks (in 2008) for Foot Relief and Hand Relief via the United States Patent and Trademark Office (USPTO). Both brands' external packaging was made of attractive paper sourced from HBTL.

In 2010, moreover, the cosmetics maker secured its IP in the European Union (EU) via a trademark registration for Aveda Hand Relief at the Office for Harmonization in the Internal Market (OHIM), now called the European Union Intellectual Property Office (EUIPO). In part, because these trademarked brands have had success in the market, and due to Aveda's product promotion campaigns (which have highlighted the relationship with HBTL), both the community organization and the cosmetics maker have benefited financially from the goodwill and product awareness achieved by Aveda's IP protected assets (Figure 3.6).

As Aveda's trademarked products have flourished, the cosmetics company has not only been able to continue sourcing products from rural communities including HBTL; Aveda has also supported the Nepali organization's development by making investments in order to raise its paper production standards. Due to the alliance with Aveda, the producers' organization was awarded the Chain of Custody accreditation (which ensures traceability of forest products to their place of origin in aid of sustainability) by the FSC (Figure 3.7).

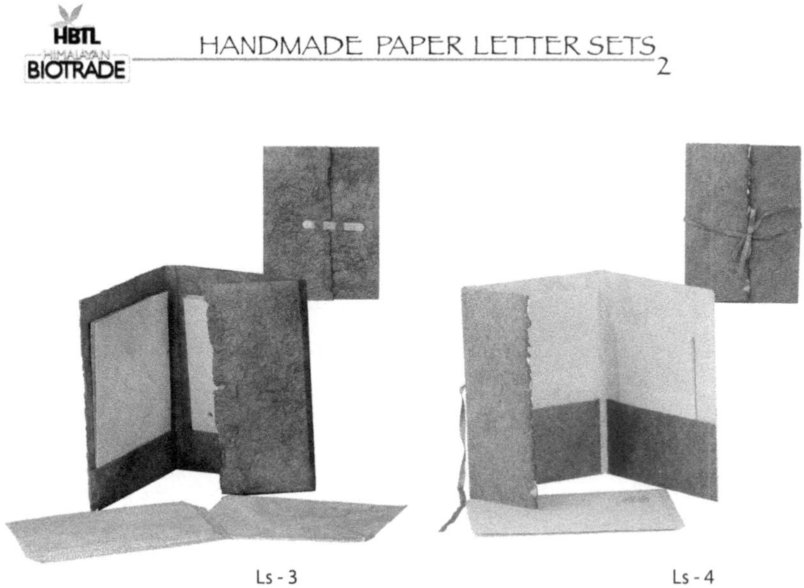


*Figure 3.6* Hand-made paper letter sets 2.

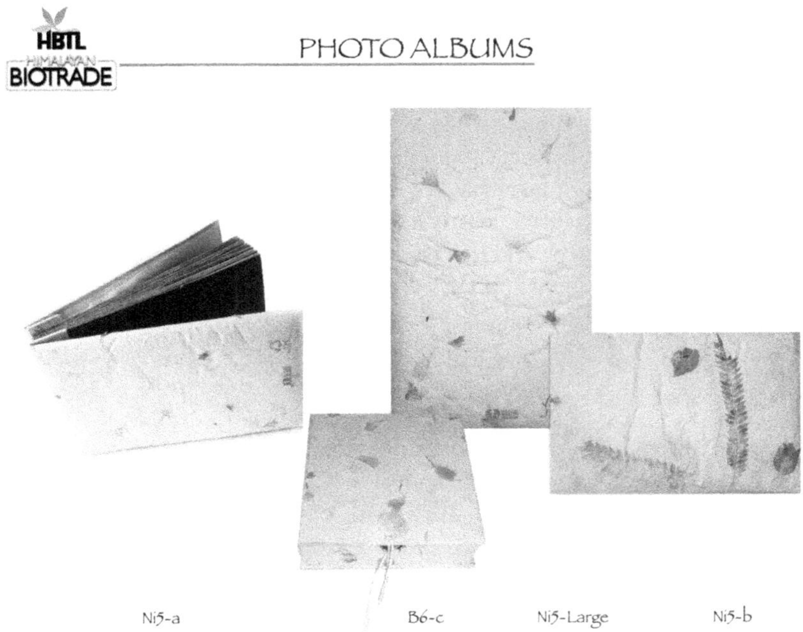


*Figure 3.7* Photo albums.

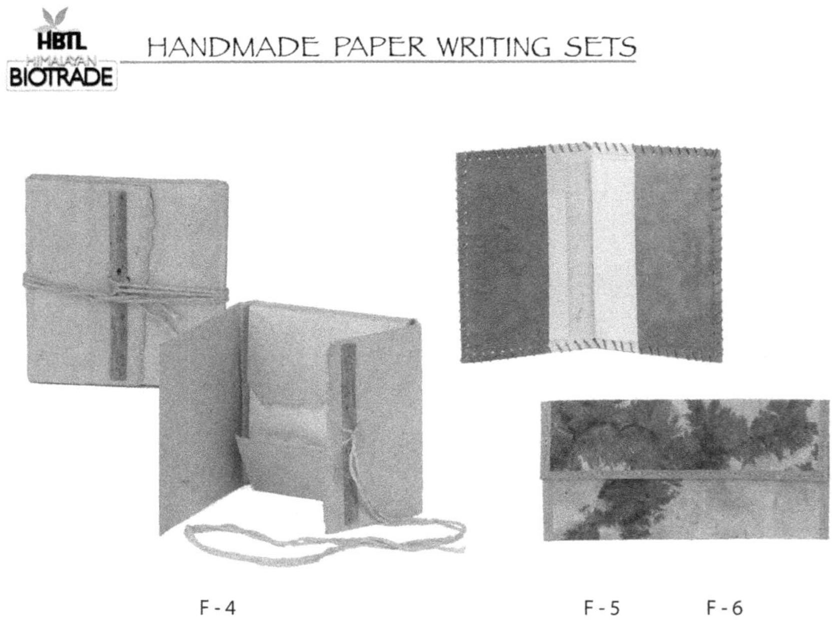


*Figure 3.8* Hand-made paper writing sets.

HBTL has managed to tap into the cultural and natural resources of Nepal, inspire its people, and enter the international market with well made, high quality and desirable products. Having formed key national and international partnerships, the community-owned organization entered commercialization agreements with companies such as Aveda whose successful products and brands, some of which are sourced from HBTL and supported by IP assets, have resulted in mutually beneficial returns on investment. As the capacity and income of its members continue to grow and diversify, HBTL has ensured that the environment on which they depend is preserved for future generations of humans and other flora and fauna (Figure 3.8).

### *Inaya Zanzibar, Tanzania*[22]

Cheherazade Cheikh co-founded Inaya Zanzibar in 2013. As a former employee of the Zanzibari hotel and tourism industry, Cheikh noticed that there was a need for guest amenities, such as soaps, bath oils, lip balms, and spa products made in Zanzibar, from natural products found in Zanzibar and throughout the African continent. Inaya Zanzibar draws inspiration from Africa's rich nature and diverse cultures when creating its natural bath and body care products. Its team makes luxurious and unique natural bath and body care products in small batches in the company's workshop in Zanzibar. All of Inaya Zanzibar's

*Figure 3.9* Product sets.

products are handmade, eco-friendly, and biodegradable; free of parabens, SLS, phthalates, and artificial colors.

Today, Inaya Zanzibar produces three ranges of products: (1) Guest Amenities, (2) Spa Range, (3) Retail Range for shops and boutiques. The company continues to develop luxury soaps and other bath and body care products using oils, butters, herbs, and flowers sourced all over the continent. Inaya Zanzibar currently offers guest amenity products to the hospitality sector and has its products sold at multiple locations across Tanzania (Figure 3.9).

Cheherazade Cheikh has recognized the importance of intellectual property protection through formal registration. She has officially trademarked the name Inaya Zanzibar as a means of safeguarding her brand as she embarks upon a business/brand growth strategy. To increase brand awareness regarding the Inaya Zanzibar products, Cheherazade Cheikh adopted a direct marketing approach, promoting her brand by going door to door to hotels throughout the island of Zanzibar with product samples in hand. As the hotels began to stock the Inaya Zanzibar products in their guest rooms, additional consumer interest was generated by the guests themselves, who actually used the Inaya Zanzibar bath and body care products and, thereafter, actively sought retail products from the company directly (Figure 3.10).

Today, demand for Inaya Zanzibar products has increased so greatly that an online store is currently being developed to service regional and international customers (Figure 3.11).

Inaya Zanzibar uses traditional, hand-made/semi-industrialized techniques to create its soap products.

*Figure 3.10* Body sets.

*Figure 3.11* Bath sets.

## *Tropical Botanical Garden and Research Institute (TBGRI), India*[23]

In December 1987, Dr. Palpu Pushpangadan, then director of the Jawaharlal Nehru Tropical Botanical Garden and Research Institute (JNTBGRI) in Kerala, was leading a team from the All India Coordinated Research Project on Ethnobiology (AICRPE) on an ethnobotanical expedition to the Western Ghats.

Knowing that the Kani knew the area better than anyone, Dr. Pushpangadan employed some of them as guides. While traversing through the rough terrain, the team was surprised that after several hours their Kani guides did not feel tired, while they themselves were constantly feeling fatigued. Curious as to why, they observed their guides and saw them continuously munching black fruits of some plants. Seeing their exhaustion, the Kani guides offered some of the fruit to the AICRPE team. Upon eating the fruit, the team immediately felt full of energy and vitality.

The Kani has a rich tradition of using wild plants found in the region for health reasons, and their tribal physicians – known as Plathi – are the exclusive holders of the traditional medicinal knowledge of the tribe. According to Kani tribal customs, only the Plathi have the right to transfer and disseminate their traditional medicinal knowledge. Because of this, the Kani guides were reluctant to share with the AICRPE team the source of the revitalizing fruit. However, after great pressure, the Kani led the team to a plant known locally as "arogyapacha" (known scientifically as trichopus zeylanicus ssp. Travancoricus).

With first-hand experience of the medicinal benefits of arogyapacha, Dr. Pushpangadan knew that the effect of the plant's berries was unusual, and that it had significant sales potential if it proved to be safe.

Their research over eight years discovered that not only did the plant (particularly the fruit and leaves) have anti-stress and immune-stimulating properties, but it also boosts stamina, relieves fatigue, helps control tumors, and activates the body's natural defenses and cellular immune system.

After seven years, JNTBGRI's research isolated 12 active chemical compounds in the plant that yielded the effects they experienced. The traditional way in which the Kani used arogyapacha was to eat its fruit. JNTBGRI discovered that crushing the plant's leaves was the most effective way to get to the 12 compounds.

JNTBGRI's research scientifically demonstrated the important medicinal benefits of the arogyapacha plant and proved that when used alone or combined with other ingredients, it can be more effective and safer than ginseng.

JNTBGRI has applied the success of Jeevani to other R&D projects and it believes that the project is a model for bringing beneficial traditional medicinal plants to the world market.

Combined with the fact that without the Kani people JNTBGRI would have never even known about arogyapacha, their traditional knowledge cannot be ignored.

They knew the importance of the Plathis in Kani culture and their role of passing down traditional knowledge and medicine through generations, and they had no desire to take advantage of them.

The benefit sharing agreement between JNTBGRI and the Kani people has been acclaimed as a model for similar agreements around the world.

## Notes

1 WIPO, IP Advantages, www.wipo.int (accessed on October 30, 2018). See www.havaianas-store.com/en
2 www.biomada.com/. See WIPO IP Advantages, www.wipo.int
3 www.dst-group.com. See WIPO IP Advantages, www.wipo.int
4 WIPO IP Advantages, www.wipo.int. See www. softtribe.com
5 Jorge Gallego, Luis Rubalcaba and Christiane Hipp, Services and Organizational Innovation: The Right Mix for Value Chain, *Management Decision*, Vol. 51, Issue 6, 2013, pp. 1117–1134.
6 Jorge Gallego, Luis Rubalcaba and Christiane Hipp, Services and Organizational Innovation: The Right Mix for Value Chain, *Management Decision*, Vol. 51, Issue 6, 2013, pp. 1117–1134.
7 Jorge Gallego, Luis Rubalcaba and Christiane Hipp, Services and Organizational Innovation: The Right Mix for Value Chain, *Management Decision*, Vol. 51, Issue 6, 2013, pp. 1117–1134.
8 Matthias Gotsch and Christiane Hipp, Using Trademarks to Measure Innovation in Knowledge-Intensive Business Services, *Technology Innovation Management Review*, Vol. 4, May 2014, pp. 18–30.
9 See Matthias Gotsch and Christiane Hipp, Using Trademarks to Measure Innovation in Knowledge-Intensive Business Services, *Technology Innovation Management Review*, May 2014.
10 Sujan M. Dan, Brian I. Spaid and Charles H. Nobles, Exploring the Sources of Design Innovations: Insights from the Computer, Communications and Audio Equipment Industries, *Research Policy*, Vol. 47, 2018, 1495–1504.
11 Sujan M. Dan, Brian I. Spaid and Charles H. Nobles, Exploring the Sources of Design Innovations: Insights from the Computer, Communications and Audio Equipment Industries, *Research Policy*, Vol. 47, 2018, 1495–1504.
12 WIPO IP Advantages, www.wipo.int.
13 www.softtribe.com. See WIPO IP Advantages, www.wipo.int
14 www.beautygems.com/. See WIPO IP Advantages, www.wipo.int
15 WIPO IP Advantages, www.wipo.int. See www.javara.co.id/?DA
16 WIPO IP Advantages, www.wipo.int. See www.pecuariacoop.com/
17 WIPO IP Advantages, www.wipo.int. See www.asocam.org
18 See Mario Pansera and Richard Owen, Framing Inclusive Innovation Within the Discourse of Development: Insights from Case Studies in India, *Research Policy*, Vol. 47, 2018, pp. 23–34. See also Riccardo Crescenzi and Luisa Gagliardi, The Innovative Performance of Firms in Heterogeneous Environments: The Interplay Between External Knowledge and Internal Absorptive Capacities, *Research Policy*, Vol. 47, 2018, pp. 782–795.
19 WIPO IP Advantages, www.wipo.int. See www.topfruit.co.za/
TopFruit is a Master Licensee for Pink Lady® apples, African Territory (Africa, South Africa & Indian Ocean Islands).
20 https://jamaicanblackcastoroil.com/. See WIPO IP Advantages, www.wipo.int
21 WIPO IP Advantages, www.wipo.int. See www.himalayanbiotrade.com/
22 www.inayazanzibar.com. See WIPO IP Advantages, www.wipo.int
23 WIPO IP Advantages, www.wipo.int. See www.jntbgri.res.in/

# 4 Branding of local products in diverse industries in the developing world

## Global branding strategies

The internalization of a brand may force the change in strategy of the brand as well as its appearance to become easily identifiable.[1] Several enterprises in the world, to be competitive, have changed their branding strategies to think globally. With the globalization of the world economy, any enterprise may compete at the global level, provided that it has something to offer. The best scenario would be to have a competitive advantage vis-à-vis other players, including the big ones. Shifting from a local brand to a global one is not an easy affair. It requires the knowledge of the huge market and the aggressive promotion of the products to be offered to that market.

It should be underscored that being present at the global market does not mean that the brand is successful.

Under this section, selected success stories pertaining to global branding strategies from the developing world will be highlighted.

### *HYX Group, China*[2]

Founded in 1927, the Heng Yuan Xiang Group (HYX) was a small wool store in Shanghai for 60 years before Mr. Liu Ruiqi who had a vision took over as General Manager and Chairman of HYX in 1987. Although HYX was small and had minimal tangible assets, Mr. Liu quickly identified that the company's name carried a considerable amount of fame and recognition, and without wasting time developed a brand strategy.

For Mr. Liu, the most important thing for a company to do to achieve success is to form its own brand culture. So his first plan of action was to register the company's well-known name as a trademark. To make the trademark more appealing, he added a cartoon image of a little girl beside the three Chinese characters that represented the company name. This made the trademark eye-catching, easy to identify, and easy to remember.

Under the branding strategy, all products produced in collaboration with national and international partners would be united under the HYX brand name. Because the company's name was already so well known in China, the factories could save on advertising and marketing costs and at the same time reduce internal operational costs, allowing for more investment in further market development. This initial collaboration was a resounding success, and the company moved from producing only 75 tons of wool annually in 1991 to over 10,000 tons annually in 1997.

A turning point for the company came in 1992, when it launched a unique five-second television commercial, paying heavily to have it played during one of the most popular television series of the time. The commercial was repeated several times during each episode of the television series. The HYX brand name became a household word synonymous with wool textiles in China.

Beyond the creation of new products, an important part of the company's R&D portfolio is its research and investment into brand promotion and developing innovative advertising campaigns. As Mr. Liu said, "If you do not invest, your brand will gradually disappear." After achieving "household name" status domestically, HYX sought to develop its name into a worldwide brand. To achieve this, in 1995 the company launched a campaign to become an official sponsor of the Olympic Games. Its goal was realized when it became an official sponsor of the 2008 Beijing Olympic Games.

Another branding strategy is the sponsorship of sports, which brings even more exposure to its brand. Since 1997 the company has sponsored domestic women and youth soccer teams and has sponsored the Chinese national soccer team in the World Cup on numerous occasions. It was also the official designer for national team uniforms in the 2008 Olympics and the 2010 Asian Games.

In 1991, it registered its newly designed name and logo as a trademark with the Trademark Office in China. In line with its international branding strategy, in 2008 the company registered its trademark under the Madrid system.

Similar to the collaborations with the textile factories, the company licenses its intangible assets, including its trademarks and know-how, to its franchisees.

The company's branding strategies have allowed it to expand into international markets. Its first subsidiary abroad opened in Uruguay in 1996 and by 2010 it enjoyed annual revenues of over US$ 3 billion.

With strong brand names and high value-added products and services, the company has made significant headway on its commitment to bring a quality Chinese brand to the international market.

### *Saigon Cosmetics Corporation (SCC), Vietnam*[3]

Saigon Cosmetics Corporation (SCC) is a Vietnamese company based in Ho Chi Minh City, specializing in fragrance, cosmetics, and toiletries production and distribution.

SCC currently owns more than 200 trademarks and industrial designs, many of them at the international level. SCC is also actively engaged in licensing activities both as a licensor of its own intellectual property rights (IPRs) and as a licensee of IPRs from foreign companies.

SCC registered some of its trademarks abroad using the Madrid system for the international registration of marks. In particular, Miss Saigon, one of SCC's leading brands, was filed for registration in several countries using the Madrid system. All SCC brands, including Anderman, Cindy, DeAndre, Essy, Fantasy, and Jackson, have specific consumer targets.

SCC has entered into licensing, franchising, and manufacturing agreements with reputable local and foreign corporations. SCC franchised with Walt Disney Company to produce and distribute the Walt Disney perfume in Vietnam, featuring famous Disney characters such as Snow White, The Little Mermaid, and Mickey Mouse, popular with young consumers. The company also collaborated with French cosmetics company "Laura Beaumont" in launching a new natural fragrance brand called "Aroma Link." Moreover, SCC supplies toiletries to METRO Cash & Carry and Big-C supermarkets under the manufacturing agreement.

In 2007, SCC launched the first ever celebrity fragrance in Vietnam (called mytime) in collaboration with My Tam, a famous Vietnamese pop singer. SCC is the exclusive manufacturer and distributor for all mytime products, including a new body wash launched in 2009, in Vietnam and foreign markets.

Furthermore, SCC has a long-term strategic co-operative agreement with the US-based Liz Claiborne Cosmetics, assuring mutual support in sourcing materials, manufacturing technology, and quality assurance.

Saigon Cosmetics Corporation is the leading cosmetics, perfume, and detergent manufacturer in Vietnam, employing more than 300 staff. SCC's products are exported to over 20 countries, including Angola, Cambodia, China, Japan, Myanmar, Russia, South Africa, the Philippines, and the United States. Export revenue accounts for about 40% of total revenue.

SCC has won many honorable awards and prizes for its achievements including "Best Vietnamese Brand in the cosmetics industry." In 2007, SCC won the WIPO Innovative Enterprise Trophy for its active use of the IP system in its research and development (R&D), production and commercial activities. SCC's products won the consumer-opinion based "Vietnamese High Quality Goods Awards" (organized by Saigon Marketing Magazine) for the 13th time in a row.

Early awareness of the importance of the effective use of the IP system played a key role in SCC's success:

> Without investing in the protection of our IP assets, it would have been significantly easier for free riders to take advantage our ingenuity, creativity and reputation making it more difficult if not impossible, for the company to establish itself as a leader in cosmetics manufacturing in Viet Nam,

say SCC's managers.

## *Malée Cosmetics Pty Ltd., South Africa*[4]

Malée Cosmetics Pty Ltd (also trading as Malée Natural Science) is a manufacturer and retailer of premium bath and body care products established in 2009 in Johannesburg, South Africa.

Founded by Zeze Oriaikhi, a Nigerian-born entrepreneur, the small- and medium-sized enterprise (SME) has quickly developed a reputation for quality natural products including soaps, moisturizers, fragrances, shampoos, and conditioners.

As of 2012, the SME was in a strong position within a niche eco-luxury market of the hospitality industry in South Africa. In addition, the cosmetics maker was looking to grow out of Africa and into the European and North American market.

Eager to find a solution to her skincare concerns, Ms. Oriaikhi – who did not have a network of business partners to rely on at this stage – initially conducted research and development (R&D) through inquiries and investigations into consumer trends and supplier networks.

During this early R&D process, the entrepreneur visited a number of cosmetics retailers in the country and studied their products' ingredients in order to gauge the cosmetics' effectiveness in the South African environment.

Because these products did not alleviate her skin problems, nor did many of them have wholly natural ingredients, Ms. Oriaikhi recognized a niche in the market and thereafter seized the opportunity to create her own 100% natural skincare brand.

With the creation of an R&D team with complementary skills sets, Malée Natural Science's founder was finally in a position to move the company forward and to produce its first cosmetics.

In order to develop a wholly African product, moreover, Ms. Oriaikhi felt that it was necessary to source all of its ingredients (such as avocado oil and shea butter) from within the continent. The cosmetic's packaging, in addition, would be manufactured with materials that were procured and made within South Africa (Figure 4.1).

Parallel to Malée Natural Science's emphasis on natural ingredients and attractive packaging, the SME has created a wide and growing range of products under the "Natural Science" brand name, including products for the skin (such as creams, body scrubs, and perfumes), products for bathing (including moisturizers, cleansers, soaps, shampoos, and conditioners), and products that include lip balms and cuticle balms. In 2012 the company had over 40 products under the Natural Science brand.

In order to commercialize its many products globally, the company has engaged in international industry fairs and events. The SME has promoted its products via a specialized stand at Top Drawer London, an event in the United Kingdom's capital that showcases the latest international retail products and designs, and the Food Wine Design Fair (2010, 2011 and 2012), one of the premiere lifestyle goods trade shows held at Hyde Park Corner Shopping Center in Johannesburg (Figure 4.2).

*Figure 4.1* Hand cream.

*Figure 4.2* Conditioning body cream.

In addition to enhancing the company's reputation among business partners, Ms. Oriaikhi has ensured that the SME's Internet presence and interaction with a global clientele is maintained via an easy-to-use E-commerce shop. Malée Natural Science's online shop features all of the company's products accompanied with colorful photographs and well-illustrated explanations of ingredients and directions for best use (Figure 4.3).

The cosmetics maker, moreover, has promoted its products and engaged its customers through extensive use of social networking sites (including Facebook and Twitter) and via up-to-date commentary and news feeds via the entrepreneur's personal blog (Figure 4.4).

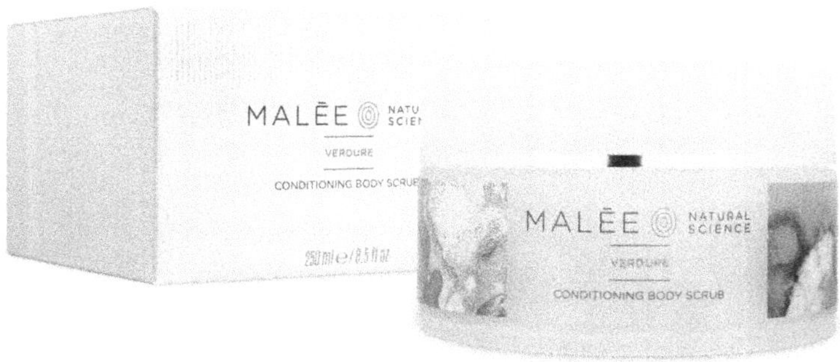


*Figure 4.3* Conditioning body scrub.

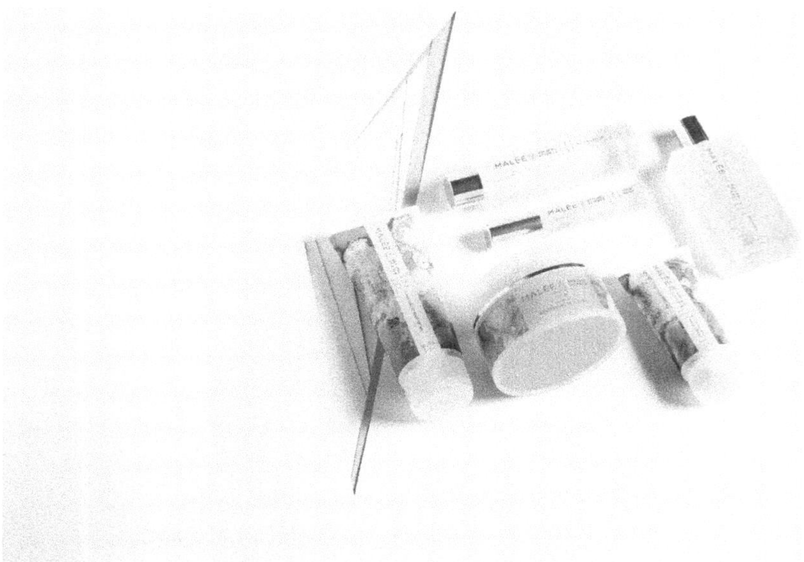

*Figure 4.4* Bath sets.

To this end, the company registered a trademark for Malee Cosmetics (2009) via the Companies and Intellectual Property Commission (CIPC)– South Africa's IP office.

Relying on the IP system to protect her company's good name, Ms. Oriaikhi's company established a strong Internet presence and set its sights on the international market.

### *Guanomad, Madagascar*[5]

Erick Rajaonary, an accountant-turned-entrepreneur, decided to switch careers and start mining bat droppings in order to create organic fertilizer. Intent on developing and commercializing this idea, Mr. Rajaonary, a native of Madagascar, created a company called Guanomad S. A. (Guanomad).

Established in 2006, Guanomad has expanded its fertilizer production capacity and created a wide portfolio of brands – including *GuanofertiN Engrais 100% Bio*. In the process, the company has become the number one brand in Madagascar of fertilizer based on bat droppings – usually known as *guano*. As of 2014, Guanomad was not only commercializing its products globally; the company had also become a multiple award winner.

In order to compete globally, Guanomad has developed a robust branding and commercialization strategy – which includes implementing quality in its production standards, creating a variety of distinct brands, and raising brand awareness.

One of the earliest challenges facing the small- and medium-sized enterprise (SME) was to re-brand the negative image that was sometimes associated with guano – such droppings were thought to be unsafe as fertilizer, especially compared to chemical fertilizers. Bats, moreover, can produce a strong smell that has given them an unfavorable image.

To re-imagine guano, the SME linked the word to a new sense of national identity and pride – hence Guanomad, a conflation of guano and "mad" (an abbreviation of Madagascar) (Figure 4.5).

*Figure 4.5* Guanomad registered logo.

Guanomad also ensures sensitivity when mining a cave (especially those within ancestral lands of indigenous communities) and engages benefits-sharing agreements with local councils – for each kilogram (kg) of extracted guano, an agreed upon portion is given freely to local producers.

In line with revamping guano – a word at the core of the company's corporate identity – the SME has created three separate brands of fertilizer (apart form Guanomad), such as GuanofertiN (highly optimized nitrogen composition), GuanofertiK (K for Potassium) a powerful organoleptic enhancer, fully organic, for an awesome result on fruits and Guanosol (enriched with organic matters to optimize the soil)

The company, moreover, has ensured its brands are produced in compliance with national and international standards. Guanomad, for instance, achieved certifications for its production processes (operations, processing, hygiene, and health and safety) awarded by the Ministry of Breeding of the Malagasy Government – the department responsible for ensuring quality for Malagasy agriculture.

Guanomad has also fulfilled industry standards including that of *Organisme de contrôle et de certification* (Ecocert), one of the largest organic certifications organizations in the world.

With quality ensured and a positive brand image created, the company has positioned itself within the niche market of guano-based organic fertilizer.

The company, furthermore, prioritizes industry trade fairs, its own distribution centers and community events (via meetings with smallholder farmers or through its own model farms – a variety of crops are grown on them using the SME's fertilizer) as vehicles for promoting its products, business ethos, and brands.

Distinct, safe, and actively branded and marketed, approximately 50% of Guanomad's products have been exported to the European Union (EU), North America and, more recently, Africa – the remainder has been commercialized domestically.

### *Corporación Bananera Nacional Corbana S. A, Costa Rica*[6]

The Corporación Bananera Nacional Corbana, S.A. (CORBANA) – the national banana corporation – was established in 1971 in Zapote, San Jose, Costa Rica. Partly owned and managed by the banana producers themselves, CORBANA is a public entity.

By developing banana marketing and commercialization strategies, the company has been able to exploit new branding methods and open new markets for the country's farmers.

To achieve its many aims, CORBANA has worked with several partners including banana growers; government departments (such as the Ministry of Agriculture – MOA); and academia (including the University of Costa Rica – UCR). Between 2007 and 2009, moreover, CORBANA established two new research facilities including the Banana Molecular Biology Center (BMBC) in La Rita de Guapliles, the province of Limon, Costa Rica.

As of 2012, hundreds of banana plantations dotted the country's landscape and millions of cases of banana fruits were exported from Costa Rica annually.

CORBANA has relied on the country's illustrious banana farming tradition in order to develop a distinct reputation for the fruit in the international market.

In order to achieve a GI for Costa Rican bananas, CORBANA collaborated over a three-year period (beginning in 2008) with several stakeholders, such as the government of Costa Rica (specifically the Ministry of Foreign Trade), members of academia (including UCR), and international partners (such as the European Union – EU).

In 2010 "Banano de Costa Rica" became the first GI to be registered in the country via the Registro Nacional – the country's IP office. The following year, "Banano de Costa Rica"– Bananas of Costa Rica – was registered via the Lisbon System for the International Registration of Appellations of Origin.

CORBANA has utilized the "Banano de Costa Rica" GI label in order to consolidate its market position and to break into new commercialization opportunities around the world. Banano de Costa Rica is exported to the EU, a market with strong GI tradition.

CORBANA has engaged in high profile product placement and advertising campaigns in some of its most lucrative markets in Europe such as Norway. The company was the official sponsor (and the only fruit vendor) of the 2008 marathon in Oslo, Norway. As of 2012, CORBANA produced and commercialized bananas within Costa Rica and exported the fruit not only to Europe but also to the United States and, increasingly, to the Arabian Gulf region.

CORBANA was established in order to empower farmers, open market access for their products, and improve their communities and environment. By developing a comprehensive R&D and commercialization strategy, and by relying on IP assets and value-added banana products, the farmer-owned company increased competitiveness, consolidated its market position, and entered new commercialization opportunities internationally.

## Local branding strategies

Unlike in the first section whereby success stories dealt with aimed at showing how originally small enterprises or SMEs could target the global market by adopting strategies involving/utilizing IP mechanisms to reach their goals, in this section a number of local success stories will be underscored. In this context, international success, if any, should be considered as a consequence and not the goal.

### *Es Teler 77, Indonesia*[7]

Es Teler 77 is a family-owned Indonesian fast food restaurant. The idea of starting a business came in 1982 when Mrs. Murniati Widjaja won the first prize in the Ice Making Competition in Indonesia. The award-wining drink, named "Es Teler," was comprised of jackfruit (a tropical mulberry fruit), young coconut, and avocado enriched with condensed milk and crushed ice with a special syrup made by Mrs. Murniati Widjaja. Her husband then came up with the idea to sell the drink with a catch-phrase of "Juara Indonesia" (Indonesian Champion). With the growth of the business, the kiosk was turned into a family-owned company.

To meet the increasing demand, Mr. Sukyatno, Mrs. Murniati Widjaja's son-in-law, built a large new restaurant with support from his family members. He also created a new slogan: "Drunk the world over Es Teler 77" and their family business continued to grow.

Mr. Sukyatno realized the importance of trademark protection early on. Through trademark registration, he protected the company's Es Teler 77 name as well as its service mark, Juara Indonesia, in many categories including restaurants, cafeterias, hotels, catering, beverages, food services, meatballs, mixed fruit ices, ice creams, crackers, and syrups. Realizing the power and benefits of using trademarks, he created and registered another service mark; Mie Tek Tek for restaurants specializing in serving many kinds of noodles cooked in the traditional manner.

Es Teler 77 has been franchising its business since 1987. A franchisee receives the company's business strategy and support from its team of experts.

Despite strong competition from foreign and domestic fast food rivals, the company's customer base has grown day by day and the ES Teler 77 brand name has become widely known in Indonesia. As of 2010, the company had more than 200 outlets throughout Indonesia and five restaurants in Australia and Singapore. In addition, Mie Tek Tek has about 20 locations in Indonesia. The company commits itself to providing the best Indonesian food and beverages to its customers.

### *Radix Guitars, Indonesia*[8]

Like in many other countries, in Indonesia it is not easy to compete with well-known brands. In an interview with WIPO Magazine, Mr. Toein Bernadhie, founder of Radix Guitars, maintained that at the beginning, many people thought he was crazy to build and design guitars for the Indonesian market because consumers were used to purchasing imported brands.

Mr. Toein Bernadhie built Radix Guitars as he felt that there was a local need and market for an Indonesian brand. To reach this goal the entrepreneur decided to develop partnerships with famous musicians.

This synergy has allowed Mr. Bernadhie to offer something unique: Indonesian-made guitars, produced mostly by hand, designed together with famous Indonesian musicians who also promote the Radix brand. Using this technology, Mr. Bernadhie decided to apply his woodworking experience to designing, manufacturing, and selling electric guitars.

Mr. Bernadhie needed to differentiate his guitars from the flood of popular imported guitars in the Indonesian market. He found it by creating guitars designed with popular domestic professional guitarists, allowing his company to provide Indonesian consumers with the chance to not only own the same guitar their favorite musicians use but also one they designed.

"Design is very important for the guitar business," he said. "I believe people first choose a guitar based on the design, so we work very carefully and closely with musicians to design guitars that capture their technical requirements and vision." According to Mr. Bernadhie, this strategy allowed him to develop guitars that meet the quality requirements of professional musicians, provide a high level of reliability, and give professionals and amateurs alike pride in using an Indonesian-made guitar.

"Competition is tough in the Indonesian guitar market," he says.

> It is hard to introduce an Indonesian-made guitar in a market dominated by imported brands. I realized that if I wanted to compete I needed not only unique designs but also a strong brand that sounds good, is easy to remember, and can convey the image of my company.

Doing so, he explained, would help him obtain what he believed to be integral to his success: partnerships with professional Indonesian musicians. "We collaborate and cooperate with famous Indonesian guitarists to design and create signature artist guitars. We believe this approach helps us attain a strong foothold in the Indonesian market," said Mr. Bernadhie.

Trademark registration goes hand-in-hand with Radix's use of branding. As Mr. Bernadhie said, "in this kind of business a trademark registration is especially important because unless you have a trademark you cannot claim or defend your brand." Mr. Bernadhie believes his company has reached its current level of success because of his trademark registration.

Radix has developed a successful niche company through a business model based on branding, trademarks, and partnerships with guitarists to develop a popular, well-known line of Indonesian guitars. "I'm very proud of Radix because today it has become one of the top guitars for many of the most popular Indonesian musicians," says Mr. Bernadhie. As Mr. Bernadhie explained, "our sponsors and customers are very confident in our brand and feel Radix is not just the company's brand, but also their brand."

## *RG Brands, Kazakhstan*[9]

RG Brands, which was formed in 1994 by the Resmi Group Limited, LLP (Resmi), a Kazakhstani wholesale trader of retail goods and provider of transportation and logistics services within the country. RG Brands was first established as a distributor of imported products in the food and beverage (F&B) industry. Through a series of successful partnerships and contracts with international companies, and with a strong set of original brands protected by the intellectual property (IP) system, RG Brands has become one of Kazakhstan's largest companies and the owner of some of the country's most recognizable F&B brands.

Developing, producing, marketing, and distributing popular brands in the F&B industry was not RG Brands' first goal. Taking advantage of a burgeoning market, the company was initially founded in 1994 to import foreign F&B products. Indeed, with demand for such goods increasing in Kazakhstan, the company was keen to become competitive in this market. To that end, during RG Brands' first few years of operation it focused on importing, distributing, and marketing various types of natural and artificial fruit juice products in flavors such as apple, orange, or grapefruit.

Following this successful initial, in 1998 RG Brands entered into research and development (R&D) on the viability of creating new brands specifically for the Kazakhstan market. Through industry research the company learned that, at the time, over 60% of the F&B market was made of importers. Furthermore, over 20% of the total cost of products came from transportation costs, which kept the price of these products to the end-consumers very high.

Further R&D into market patterns revealed that while demand for fruit juices was growing, it was not substantial compared to other beverages. The company's research found that this was partly due to a lack of seasonal products in the F&B industry.

RG Brands decided to shift its primary focus. While it would still import F&B products, the company's R&D provided a window into another possibility; the creation of new, high quality brands in Kazakhstan that are delivered to consumers at more affordable prices.

This new vision brought about the development of RG Brands' first natural juice products, creating original recipes that catered to the tastes and demands of the Kazakhstani consumers. In 1999, the company introduced 12 varieties of natural fruit juices in two types of sizes – 1 liter and 250 milliliters. Following their successful reception, RG Brands continued its tradition of R&D to successfully develop new products.

For RG Brands to transform from a distributor to a producer, it not only had to create high quality products but also needed recognizable brands. Before RG Brands shifted the company's focus, there were not many local brands that were popular. Indeed, the popularity of multinational brands, such as those from PepsiCo, led RG Brands to partner with PepsiCo and PLI. Recognizing a lack of well-known Kazakhstani brands, RG Brands went about to change that. Following the company's shift to brand creator, it realized that branding – which along with the physical products and packaging represents a vital part of the company's IP – would be essential to their success.

Developing the company's first brand (Da-Da) in 1999 marked the beginning of the implementation of RG Brands' strategy. The combined factors of strong R&D, acquisitions of production facilities, and leveraging its assets for financing led to the company's successful shift to the producers and owners of some of Kazakhstan's leading brands. In 2004, distribution of imported brands only represented one-fourth of RG Brands' operations. By 2013 the company's original brands were among the most popular in Kazakhstan and represented the bulk of RG Brands' operations.

With the introduction of the Grizzly brand in 2007, the company develops, produces, and distributes brands in four major categories: juices, water, beverages (such as tea and carbonated drinks that are not juice or water), and food.

In the juices category, the company's brand portfolio includes Da-Da, Da-Da Day, Da-Da Kids, Gracio, and Sunny Nectar.

In the water category, the company developed its popular a'su brand in 2010. RG Brands markets a'su as a brand of purified natural mineral water from mountain glaciers that targets active people.

In the beverages category (which RG Brands separates into a different category and includes carbonated beverages but does not include water or juice), the company has two original brands: Aport Schorle and Yeti.

In the food category, the company has three major brands: Piala Tea, Moë milk, and Grizzly potato chips (or potato crisps).

Building a strong presence, RG Brands rely on the IP system to protect the company's brands. RG Brands has a number of trademark registrations, both in Kazakhstan through the Committee of Intellectual Property Rights authority and abroad through the Madrid system of international registration of marks.

The diversity of RG brands enables Resmi Group Limited, LLP to position itself in a number of industries.

### *Chocolate Mamas, Tanzania*[10]

Chocolate Mamas is a gourmet Tanzanian chocolate company that is the country's first and only producer of fine chocolate. The company sources its premium cocoa beans directly from local farmers' cooperatives to ensure home-grown, organic chocolate of the highest quality. Chocolate Mamas prides itself on producing environmentally friendly, fair trade chocolate that's also gluten free with no mixed vegetable oils, fat additives, emulsifiers, chemicals, or preservatives. Chocolate Mamas' chocolate is 100% Tanzanian, with even its sugar and cocoa-butter produced in-house or sourced locally, with the entire chocolate making process taking place in Tanzania: from hand selection of the best beans to the innovative roasting and production process. Packaging for Chocolate Mamas' products is made of recycled maize husks produced by a local NGO for disabled persons.

Chocolate Mamas uses very basic, hand-made/non-industrialized techniques to create their chocolate product. To promote their products and raise awareness regarding their brand, Chocolate Mamas employs an online, web-based marketing strategy. The company also promotes its product in a unique way by catering sample size servings of their chocolate delicacies for tasting at various events in which they open up bespoke, portable, chocolate bars.

## Branding in coffee/tea industries

In the growing coffee/tea market, it is getting tougher for coffee business owners to find their niches. In coffee/tea industries, building a strong brand identity is the dream of many enterprises that are involved in this business. Coffee and tea are becoming a more and more specific business. To attract consumers, a personalized and strong brand is required. This is true for both large enterprises and SMEs.

Coffee is gradually becoming a cultural product. As a result, most major brands have launched varietal products, offering, for example, "Coffee of the World" collections available in super markets.[11]

This section will highlight some successful brands from the developing world that have imposed themselves in the global market by using well-thought-out branding strategies.

## *Ethiopian Coffee Industry, Ethiopia*[12]

Coffee production occupies a major place in the economy of Ethiopia. It generates about 60% of Ethiopia's total export earnings. According to the Ethiopian Coffee Annual Report 2018,[13] coffee is the first export item in Ethiopia and Ethiopia is Africa's leading coffee producer and the fifth largest in the world, with about half of its production going for export. Harrar, Sidamo, and Yirgacheffe are the three most famous coffee brands of Ethiopia.

In 2004, the government launched the Ethiopian Coffee Trademarking and Licensing Initiative to provide a practical solution to overcome the divide between what coffee farmers received for a sack of their beans and what retailers charge for that coffee when they sold it in retail outlets in different countries.[14] The main goal of the initiative was to recognize the exceptional qualities of Ethiopian coffees as brands on the one hand, and to place them in a better position strategically in the expanding specialty coffee market on the other hand. The aim was likewise, at the end of the day to protect Ethiopia's ownership of the names so as to prevent their misappropriation.

The Ethiopian government had to make a decision on how best to use IPRs to obtain exclusive ownership of Ethiopian coffee names, achieve wider international recognition, and maximize returns.[15] The government of Ethiopia decided to protect the coffee names through trademark registration instead of geographical indications regime, which could be easily thought in the present case. Thanks to the dispute between the American coffee chain Starbucks Coffee Corporation and the Ethiopian Intellectual Property Office (EIPO), which was settled out of Court, the Ethiopian coffee gained more popularity worldwide. Consequently, the most famous Ethiopian coffee secured their registration as trademarks in many countries by signing trademark licensing agreements.

In addition, the Initiative has helped Ethiopia to differentiate Ethiopian coffees from coffees of other countries, which strengthened the confidence and bargaining position of the coffee growers and exporters of the country. There is an increasing demand for Ethiopian fine coffee in the world market. The innovation of the Initiative is that it enabled the growers and producers to become part of price setters instead of being price takers.[16]

Coffee is vital to the cultural and socio-economic life of Ethiopians and contributes 25%–30% of the country's foreign exchange, half of GDP, 90% of exports, 85% of total employments in the country and part of the culture.[17]

It should be kept in mind that decrease of coffee production may be influenced by other factors of the economy at a given time.

Lessons learned in this case study suggest similar benefits could be garnered for other developing countries' agricultural products under certain conditions.[18]

### *Trung Nguyen Coffee, Vietnam*[19]

Dang Le Nguyen Vu, a student-turned-entrepreneur, established Trung Nguyen –formerly called Trung Nguyen Coffee Factory Central Highlands. Mr. Vu established the company while he was still studying medicine in Buon Ma Thuot, the capital of Đắk Lắk province, Vietnam.

Mr. Vu stressed that Vietnam had the potential of achieving high economic growth and becoming a powerful economy if the coffee sector could be improved and upgraded.

Without much business experience but with a strong love of coffee and a desire to explore its economic potential, Mr. Vu (and a small group of fellow students) established a small coffee shop in Buon Ma Thuot named "Trung Nguyen" – which roughly translates to "central highlands." The single-roomed coffee shop initially relied on a revenue-sharing agreement with coffee producers.

First delivering coffee drinks to clients in the area via bicycle, the entrepreneur and his colleagues soon advanced to motorcycle based deliveries in order to meet increasing demand. To expand the company's capacity and gain the knowledge required to be successful in the coffee production business, Mr. Vu recognized the need to engage in research and development (R&D) activities. The entrepreneur also saw the need to strategically develop the company's human resources department. Mr. Vu noted: "You need to use your passion to drive your plans and move your organization forward, through [comprehensive] planning and excellent execution."

An early development in the company's R&D strategy was to ensure that it became a vertically integrated business, where a single owner manages the supply chain. To this end, Mr. Vu learned from rivals and relied on business models from around the world to ensure that the company had the capability to manufacture, package, and distribute coffee products independently.

Trung Nguyen understood that Vietnam up until then had simply exported raw coffee beans while European countries were making money through excellent branding of a product they could not grow. This is why [the company] decided to produce Vietnam's first branded coffee. Being vertically integrated permitted Trung Nguyen to add value to its products. Rather than simply selling unroasted coffee in an unpredictably priced global market (as had been the case for traditional coffee producers in Vietnam), the company created ready-for-sale, premium brands for the domestic and international market. As a result, the then small- and medium-sized enterprise (SME) gained greater control of its production processes, products, and prices – even though it procured raw coffee beans from networks of independent farmers.

As of 2013, the company's products were sold in over 50,000 retail outlets in over 50 countries and territories, such as the People's Republic of China (PRC) and the European Union (EU). In the same year, Trung Nguyen managed over 60 of its own cafés and had become Vietnam's biggest coffee processing company and brand – with over 3,000 employees and an associated network of over 400 coffee farm workers. Mr. Vu, meanwhile, had become popularly known in Vietnam as "The Coffee King."

Trung Nguyen has distinguished its products in the market by creating a number of coffees. Vietnam's terroir produces a coffee with bold and intense flavor as well as 71 brands and products. At the same time, the company has enhanced quality in its production processes, promoted and commercialized its products via its own network of cafés and distribution networks, and collaborated with industry partners.

With hundreds of millions of dollars invested in its production, branding, and commercialization strategy, Trung Nguyen has also ensured protection for its corporate identity, including the identity of its many brands.

## *Darjeerling Tea, India*[20]

Tea planting in the Indian district of Darjeeling began in 1841 by Archibald Campbell, a civil surgeon of the Indian Medical Service. Campbell was transferred as superintendent of Darjeeling in 1839 from Kathmandu, Nepal. In 1841, he brought seeds of the Chinese tea plant (*Camellia sinensis*) from Kumaun and began to experiment with tea planting in Darjeeling. The British government also established tea nurseries during that period (1847). Commercial development began during the 1850s.

By 1866, Darjeeling had 39 gardens producing a total of 21,000 kilograms of tea per year. Tea cultivation in Darjeeling has continued to prove to be a profitable venture, and today, nearly 17,400 hectares in 87 tea gardens produce over 10 million kilograms of tea every year. The tea industry in India in general and in Darjeeling in particular is operated by the private sector. The Darjeeling Planters Association, formed in 1892, is the sole producers' forum for Darjeeling tea. The Association works in close cooperation with the Tea Board of India, a government-controlled organization that administers all stages of tea cultivation, processing, and sale, including that of the Darjeeling segment.

Darjeeling tea comprises just over 1% of the total tea production in India (10.85 million kilograms of Darjeeling tea as compared to 981 million kilograms of total production). Yet the quality, reputation, and characteristics of Darjeeling tea have made the region a hallmark, underscoring that the incomparable quality of this tea is essentially attributable to its geographical origin.

Traders as well as individual buyers, while purchasing Darjeeling tea, expect the tea to be cultivated, grown, and produced in the defined region of the district of Darjeeling. Consequently, Darjeeling tea that is worthy of its name cannot be grown or manufactured anywhere else in the world.

The Tea Board of India underscores its role in authenticating the regional origin of Darjeeling tea. To safeguard the special characteristics associated with this tea and its high reputation, both the Tea Board and the Darjeeling Planters Association have been involved at various levels in protecting this common heritage.

Both the logo and the word "Darjeeling" are registered domestically under the Geographical Indications of Goods (Registration and Protection) Act of 1999 of India. Internationally, the logo has been registered in various jurisdictions including Canada, Egypt, some European countries, Japan, Lebanon, the United Kingdom, and the United States of America as a trademark/certification mark/collective mark.

To ensure domestic and international protection of Darjeeling as a certification trademark and a geographical indication, as well as the supply of genuine Darjeeling tea, the Tea Board initiated in 2000 a compulsory system of certifying the authenticity of Darjeeling tea under the provisions of the Tea Act of 1953. The system requires all dealers in Darjeeling tea to compulsorily enter into a license agreement with the Tea Board and pay an annual license fee.

## *Dilmah Tea, Sri Lanka*[21]

In 1974, Mr. Fernando bought his first few estates to try his hand at producing pure Sri Lankan tea, and set up Ceylon Tea Services Limited (CTS) in 1981. As the company grew and more subsidiaries were launched in various countries, CTS, and all other companies Mr. Fernando owned, would later become wholly owned subsidiaries of MJF Holdings, Limited (MJF Holdings).

In the early years, the young entrepreneur found it difficult to compete with the more established multinational tea corporations and make his dream a reality. It was difficult for him to find buyers for his tea and he struggled to keep his fledgling estates afloat. For much of the early part of his career, Mr. Fernando sold his tea to multinational tea companies like Lipton and Tetley which they marketed under their own brand names. In the 1970s, these and other major international tea companies started purchasing less Sri Lankan tea, as they were blending it with cheaper teas from other countries.

Mr. Fernando decided to bring prosperity back to the tea industry in his homeland by creating, producing, selling, and promoting a new pure Sri Lankan tea brand called Dilmah (an amalgam of the names of his two sons, Dilhan and Malik). Mr. Fernando positioned his new company as a seller of pure Sri Lankan tea and remained steadfast in his commitment not to mix it with other teas.

The new family-run company first tried to sell Dilmah tea directly to major international companies and foreign supermarkets, but most had never heard of the new brand and it was hard to persuade them to take a chance on the new company.

Things changed dramatically in the mid-1980s when Mr. Fernando finally entered the Australian market through a partnership with Coles, one of the largest retailers in Australia. Coles decided to initially test the new tea at a single retail outlet, and its popularity proved to be so high that within six months the retailer increased this to five locations. Within two years Mr. Fernando's tea could be found on the shelves of Coles stores throughout Australia. This success gave his tea respect among consumers and gave him the ability to launch his tea under his own brand name.

The strong consumer reaction to the resurgence of pure Sri Lankan tea and positive early sales gave Mr. Fernando some leverage with Coles and other tea buyers, and in 1988 he officially launched Dilmah as an independent brand. With sales booming in Australia, Dilmah was soon on sale in nearby New Zealand and other countries in Oceania and Asia. Sale of Dilmah tea spread quickly, and throughout the 1990s it became one of the most popular teas in Europe and North America.

By 2011, these strategies had made Dilmah the only international Sri Lankan tea company and one of the few vertically integrated tea companies in the world, growing tea on its own estates (some of Sri Lanka's best) and using state-of-the-art facilities to print, package, ship, and market the tea.

Protected with trademark registrations, the entrepreneur has been able to use his brand to grow his company, give back to the community and environment, and make a positive impact on the lives of over a million people involved in the tea industry in Sri Lanka.

### *Blue Mountain Coffee, Jamaica*[22]

Coffee was first introduced on the island in 1728 and gained prominence during the nineteenth century when many of the natives turned to growing coffee on their own lands. The plants flourish nicely in this region and give the beans a good shape, unique flavor, intense aroma, delicate acid balance, and sweetness. A unique, special flavor comes out when these beans are roasted.

Jamaica Blue Mountain coffee is grown and processed by skilled local farmers in an artistic manner. Experienced reapers select the finest bright red cherries and pulp within the Blue Mountains. The specific area in which coffee defined as "Blue Mountain" can be grown and how and where it is "processed or manufactured" is defined in regulations made under the Coffee Industry Regulation Act, 1948 of Jamaica. Only coffee grown at elevations between 3,000 and 5,500 feet in the parishes of Saint Andrew, Saint Thomas, Portland, and Saint Mary can be called Jamaica Blue Mountain.

As early as 1944, the authorities realized the potential of the coffee grown on the Blue Mountains and recognized the need for quality control and branding.

The CIB processes and commercializes three types of coffees produced on the island: Jamaica Blue Mountain, Jamaica High Mountain Supreme, and Jamaica Prime. Among them, the Blue Mountain coffee is the most cherished and enjoys a worldwide reputation. Blue Mountain Coffee is registered with the United States Patent and Trademark Office (USPTO) as a certification mark, protected as a community trademark in the European Union and as a certification trademark with the Intellectual Property Office (IPO) of the United Kingdom.

Jamaica Blue Mountain coffee is an example of how developing countries can benefit from the increased value of their branded products protected through intellectual property rights.

### *Coffee Planet, United Arab Emirates*[23]

Coffee Planet LLC brews coffee in the United Arab Emirates and internationally. Founded in Dubai in 2005, Coffee Planet aimed to help people experience the finest global Arabica coffee. Its first task was to improve the quality of coffee sold on-the-go in highway convenience stores. The company also roasts Arabica coffee beans and supplies beans, machines and equipment, as well as other coffee-related solutions for office, hotel, and restaurant markets.

In 2007, Coffee Planet expanded its operations to offer a complete coffee solution to leading five-star hotels, catering companies, airlines, and offices in the United Arab Emirates (UAE). In 2008, the company opened a new roaster in Dubai, which enabled them to control the roasting of its specialty blends and single origin coffees. They also expanded into retail across the UAE, selling coffee in supermarkets and specialist food stores. In 2009, it launched its first franchised café concept within the UAE. Two years later, the company's global expansion of franchised cafes took place in international markets.

Today, Coffee Planet provides turnkey solutions for the commercial coffee industry, which include planning, designing, and building as well as project management services. The company is involved in the development of a chain of coffee shops for various brands and provides its products on a franchise basis. Coffee Planet is now a multi-million dollar success story, through its own brand and via roasting private label coffee for leading companies across the globe.

## Branding in food industry and agro-sector

Branding undertakings are likewise taking place in the food industry and agro sector where many actors are playing a great role in the developing world. Some success stories in these areas from the developing world will be examined. It should be acknowledged from the outset that in the agro-sector different techniques of production have been developed for many centuries. The added value is that current branding strategies enable farmers to get from their products and to have a say on the distribution of their products.

### *Grenada Chocolate Company, Grenada*[24]

The Grenada Chocolate Company was founded in 1999 by Mott Green, Doug Browne, and Edmond Brown with the idea of creating an Organic Farmers' and Chocolate-Makers' Cooperative. The company produces high quality, organic, dark chocolate on the Caribbean island of Grenada from their world famous cocoa beans (Figure 4.6).

*Figure 4.6* Organic chocolate.

*Figure 4.7* Round chocolate.

The factory produces high quality, organic, dark chocolate in Grenada using the world famous Trinitario cocoa beans that grow right on their own doorstep. The chocolate factory is nestled in lush cocoa groves in Grenada's pristine rainforest. The internationally award-winning organic dark chocolate has the complex flavor of Grenada's fine-flavored organic cocoa beans, processed carefully in small batches (Figure 4.7).

*Figure 4.8* Organic dark chocolate.

Producing the chocolate right where the cocoa grows allows the cooperative to do its own fermenting which gives a real advantage in creating the finest, most complex phenolic profile from the beans. The other important factor is that fresh beans are used to make the chocolate rather than ones that have been shipped half way around the world might be months or even years old (Figure 4.8).

The Grenada Chocolate factory is one of very few small-scale chocolate-makers producing fine chocolate where the cocoa physically grows. Small batch chocolate making is rare. For this reason, the Grenada Chocolate Company had to innovate and create many of their own processing methods, designing specialist small-scale machines and refurbishing antique equipment to meet the requirements of its unique situation. Sustainability is at the core of the Grenada Chocolate Factory's values. Many of the machines had to be reconfigured and to be powered by solar-electric energy.

Cocoa from the Grenada Chocolate Company is grown naturally without the use of any chemical pesticides, herbicides, or fertilizers and has been certified as organic.

### *The Egyptian Cotton Industry*[25]

The Egyptian cotton industry has a long tradition. It has evolved through many years since the ancient period. Barbadense cotton is of the highest quality and the renowned cotton of Egypt. The cotton industry became more organized through private initiatives when cotton stakeholders established the

Alexandria Cotton Exporters Association (ALCOTEXA) in 1932. ALCOTEXA operates as a non-profit organization with a goal of fostering cotton trade and works as a forum for exporters, importers, spinners, and other relevant entities dealing with cotton from Egypt. It maintains close cooperation with the Egyptian government and is mandated to register all cotton export deals from Egypt.

In 2001, the Egyptian Ministry of Economy and Foreign Trade along with ALCOTEXA developed a logo consisting of figurative elements (the drawing of a cotton flower) and the words "Egyptian Cotton" to promote and increase the export of cotton products from Egypt.[26]

The use and protection of the logo combined with promotional activities were part of the branding strategy employed to increase consumer recognition of the high quality and specific attributes of Egyptian cotton that differentiate it from cotton produced elsewhere and justify its premium price.[27]

Faced with the challenges from cotton producers from other countries, such as the United States of America, China, India, and other countries, the Egyptian government recognized the need for developing new cotton varieties with improved quality and yields to retain Egyptian cotton's competitive advantage in the global market.[28]

The Egyptian government maintains a licensing scheme for commercialization and promotion of Egyptian cotton. The scheme allows any use of the name/logo of Egyptian cotton only through a licensing agreement.[29]

The protection of the Egyptian cotton name and logo and complementary licensing scheme established by the government have paved the way toward a positive future for Egyptian cotton.[30]

## *Jollibee, Philippines*[31]

Today, the biggest fast food chain in the Philippines is Jollibee Foods Corporation. Tony Tan Caktiong, the president and CEO of the corporation, went from modest beginnings to the top of the world. Born in a poor family who migrated from south-eastern China to the Philippines in search of a better life, Tony Caktiong became involved in the restaurant business from an early age when his father opened a restaurant.

At the age of 22, inspired by a visit to an ice cream plant, he set out to gain his own foothold in the restaurant business. Relying on family savings, he seized a franchising opportunity with Magnolia Dairy Ice Cream and opened two ice cream parlors. In response to customer requests, he added hot meals and sandwiches to the menu. A menu which soon proved a lot more popular than ice cream. In 1978, Mr. Caktiong decided to capitalize on this development. He discontinued the Magnolia franchise and converted his parlors into fast food outlets.

Jollibee invested millions of pesos to register the "bee" trademark in the Philippines and other key countries. Helped by savvy marketing and advertising strategies, the mark struck a chord with the public. Since its establishment at the end of the 1970s, Jollibee Foods Corporation has grown spectacularly; today, Jollibee is the leading fast food chain in the Philippines with over 50% market share and hundreds of restaurants all over the country.

Today, Jollibee Foods Corporation uses eight proprietary brands (including "Jollibee" for their core fast food business, "Greenwich" for their pizza and pasta chain, and "Chowking" for their oriental food outlets); owns many trademarks (including "Bee Happy," "Yumburger," "Chickenjoy," and "Amazing Aloha"); and has registered all of its logos, some of them in several countries.

Protecting their brands through national and international trademark registration has been instrumental in Jollibee's remarkable success.

### *Chuao Cocoa Bean, Venezuela*[32]

Among all the varieties of cocoa, criollo is often referred to as the most noble and is used as the basis for some of the finest chocolates in the world. In the plantation of Chuao, one of the first villages founded in Venezuela in the middle of the 16th century, unique soil conditions and a microclimate including high equatorial humidity and heavy rains (that wash rich and fertile silt down the mountainsides into the 140-hectare plantation) create perfect cocoa growing conditions.

Although said to give the most subtle, sweet, and complex beans, criollo trees are very difficult to farm and are particularly susceptible to disease. Expert caring and specific geographic conditions are essential for coaxing the high quality beans from these trees which are the least productive of all cocoa varieties.

To the local indigenous people, Chuao cocoa is not just an agricultural product; it represents much more. It is their life, their identity, their pride. For them, the cocoa nuts that they have planted, bred, and selected for centuries are inseparable from their lives, their culture, their land, and their language.

To protect this considerable national asset, an application for an appellation of origin (AO) with respect to Chuao was filed in Venezuela on August 10, 2000 by Campesina. The Declaration of Recognition was granted and published in the Official Journal of Industrial Property of Venezuela in November 2000. The registration protects the name Chuao and restricts its use to beans and cocoa products from that specifically defined geographical area, recognizing the influence of climatic and human factors on the quality of those products.

The protection of the Chuao AO has proved to be a very effective tool for marketing and branding of the Chuao cocoa; the name itself denotes the unique character of the product and serves as a guarantee of quality and enhances consumer recognition. The recognized quality and protection of Chuao cocoa allowed the Campesina cooperative to work out an agreement in 2000 with a chocolate company – Amedei s.r.l. of Italy – for supplying cocoa.

Following the agreement with Campesina, Amedei sought further protection for the name "Chuao" by registering it as a trademark through the Madrid system. Recognition of the market potential of the special characteristics of Chuao cocoa and their protection through intellectual property rights (IPRs) have enabled the farmers to increase their income substantially.

Chuoa criollo cocoa is an example of how IP rights can be used by agricultural communities to generate wealth. The AO led to the creation of a trusted brand which helped chocolate producers and consumers differentiate Chuoa from other cocoa varieties.

## *Pancholo's, Paraguay*[33]

In 1992, two high school friends decided to open their own fast food business. Helped by a municipal ordinance prohibiting fast food stalls in the street, but not on vacant lots, they sold food out of a wagon in a vacant lot in the busy Mariscal Lopez Avenue area of Paraguay. Emprendimientos Fast S.A. was born.

The quality of their fast food quickly won the business a robust customer base. With the ever-growing popularity of their business, the fast food wagon became too small to cater to increasing consumer demand. This gave rise to the establishment of the first Pancholo's bricks and mortar restaurant.

In 1997, while defining their expansion strategy, Emprendimientos Fast S.A realized that trademark registration was necessary to protect the level of distinctiveness that their product had acquired in the minds of customers, and to prevent unauthorized third parties from using their brand in bad faith. Pancholo's was officially trademarked. The company expanded the scope of their IP protection by securing trademark registration for subsequent product extensions as the organization continued to grow: Pizzolos, Pastolos, Lomitolos, Autocholos.

The opening of the first Pancholo's subsidiary in 1997 marked the start of rapid growth. Today, ten Pancholo's restaurants, with almost 150 employees can be found all around Asuncion. The company, Emprendimientos Fast S.A, owns more than five trademarks. Pancholo's sells hot dogs, hamburgers, steak sandwiches, fries, pizzas, pasta, and ice cream.

## *Ly Ly Foods, Cambodia*[34]

Mrs. Keo Mom started a small food manufacturing business out of her home thanks to a rice-cracker processing machine purchased from a foreign company approximately US 50,000, in 2002 and producing jasmine rice crackers in small quantities sold at markets in Phnom Penh, the capital and largest city of the Kingdom of Cambodia and its outskirts.

After consultations with relevant agencies of the Cambodian government, Mrs. Mom decided to register the business as a handicraft manufacturing plant under the name Ly Ly Food Industry Co. Ltd. (Ly Ly Food). Ly Ly Food's core vision is not only to create attractive, healthy, quality snacks; indeed, the company was also in part established with the goal of providing employment for underprivileged Cambodians.

*Figure 4.9* Rice cracker.

Rather than importing raw materials (such as jasmine rice and corn) necessary to make the SME's snacks, Ly Ly Food sources them from a local network of farmers in Cambodia, thus shortening supply chains and saving costs. At the same time, the company is able to enhance the capacity of farmers (many of whom are illiterate and on low incomes), allowing them to establish sustainable revenue streams (Figure 4.9).

Today, Ly Ly Food has become one of the most well-known local producers of Jasmine rice snacks in the country while supporting local producers and employing hundreds of previously unemployed people. At the same time, Mrs. Mom and the company she founded have become role models for how to establish a successful SME, especially in the Association of Southeast Asian Nations (ASEAN) region (Figure 4.10).

Ly Ly Food's products are easy to distinguish in the market and thereby enhancing the SME's profile with customers. Furthermore, the company has registered trademarks and industrial designs with the IP office in Cambodia; boosted consumer confidence by implementing international quality standards for its production processes; and promoted awareness of its corporate identity, products, and brands through participation in exhibitions and industry events (Figure 4.11).

*Figure 4.10* Fish cracker.

*Figure 4.11* BBQ & sea food.

*Figure 4.12* Roasted duck.

In addition to raising the SME's corporate profile and protecting the company name, from 2003, Mrs. Mom has protected images relating to the company's brands as trademarks, including a stylized image of a cow and a rabbit. Ly Ly Food subsequently registered a number of trademarks that have been actively promoted (Figure 4.12).

In 2014, Ly Ly Food expanded to international markets such as the United States of America and the Republic of the Union of Myanmar. Such international success has prompted further growth.

## Branding in cosmetics industry

Unlike the food industry that is deemed to be an everlasting business, the recent cosmetic industry is a result of modernization. A huge increase of cosmetic products has been noticed in the last ten years in the global market. Consequently, the competition among cosmetic companies on the one hand and among cosmetic products on the other hand is tough. The choice of a cosmetic product is subjective in the human mind. Hence, branding is a very important tool in this area to make consumers choose one product to the detriment of another. To become a brand of choice, what is required is not only tremendous promotional undertakings of the product, but more importantly the trust of the consumers to believe that your product is better than those of the competitors.

Recently, aggressive branding strategies in the cosmetic industry in the developing world are on the rise. It should be mentioned at the outset that the use of plants, leaves, or fruits for making cosmetics is not new in the developing world. In the ancient time, indigenous people knew the importance of cosmetics by mixing ingredients to obtain a cosmetic product that not only smells nice but also performs further functions, such as relaxing the skin, washing hair, polishing nails, and relaxing the body, on the other hand. Although the techniques of making these products used in the past sound rudimentary, the final purpose is the same, to produce a product which is smell-friendly vis-à-vis consumers and efficient in terms of functions.

Innovative techniques have improved the quality of cosmetics offered to the consumers. However, the contribution of traditional knowledge to the global value chain should not be underestimated. Ancient practices of indigenous people constitute the foundation of the current cosmetic industry.

Under this section, different success stories from the developing world in the domain of cosmetics will be highlighted.

### *JO'M Cosmetics, South Africa*[35]

JO'M Cosmetics was established by Johannah Moriti in 2005 to provide a natural cosmetic range for skin and hair. Today, the JO'M range includes hair care, skin care, makeup, and cosmetics products that are specially formulated for all ethnicities. JO'M products are produced using 100% plant extracts, natural oils, and essential oils.

The brand has a local and regional online presence. JO'M has also established a presence in Europe. Its international headquarters are situated in Spain, affording access to 28 European Union countries.

The JO'M brand was introduced to the consumer market by its seminal product: hair softener that elongates that coils in Afrocentric hair making it softer and more manageable, without the use of chemical relaxers. A wide range of hair and skincare products, for all ethnicities, have since been created by JO'M that are sold in local, regional, and international markets. Johannah Moriti has recognized the importance of protecting her brand to build her brand and retain the product quality with which her brand is currently associated.

### *Shea Terra Organics, Uganda*[36]

*Shea Terra Organics* was the vision of Tammie Umbel with a quest to carve and redefine a market for natural products from African countries that would help alleviate poverty; yet still assist with the preservation of natural habitats for native wildlife.

Shea butter is indigenous to the tropical regions of Africa. It is extracted from the nut of the Shea-Karite tree, a plant which only begins to bear its first fruit after 15 years.

Shea butter straight from the African source was really cheap. Many people needed it for its therapeutic benefits, but could not afford it due to the artificially high price that wholesalers and retailers set in the market. Women across the shea butter belt literally had tons of the products that they could not sell due to the low demand of this "costly" butter. What Tammie Umbel did was to make high quality, shea butter products available to everyone at unheard of prices. The result was a shea butter revolution.

Realizing the immense impact that a single ingredient like shea butter could have on the world, Tammie Umbel began seeking out other rare ingredients indigenous to Africa that could enhance or compliment the benefits of shea butter.

With an aggressive commercialization strategy, Tammie Umbel harnessed the power of intellectual property and branding to transform what was formerly known as *The African Shea Butter* Company, into *Shea Terra Organics.* With a quality product renowned for its geographic origin and therapeutic properties, direct access to networks of local suppliers, and increasing global demand for East African shea butter, Tammie Umbel was able to leverage the *Shea Terra Organics* brand into a burgeoning industry powerhouse.

### *Pure Fiji Export Limited, Fiji*[37]

Formed through a combination of volcanic and tectonic activity and heavily forested for thousands of years, inhabitants of the Fijian islands have relied on the resources of the forest and ocean for survival and prosperity.

Oils extracted from the leaves, branches, and nuts of Fiji's flora are one such resource that has played an important role in the country's communities. Long valued for their medicinal and beauty purposes, Fijian oils help to protect, nourish, moisturize, and heal skin and hair. In 2000, Pure Fiji Export Ltd. (Pure Fiji) was launched as a small and medium-sized enterprise (SME) to bring these products and traditions to international markets (Figure 4.13).

*Figure 4.13* Bath sets.

*Figure 4.14* Bath sets 2.

Started by Ms. Gaetane Austin and her daughter Andree, Pure Fiji has become one of the country's most successful SMEs. With an innovative branding strategy and brand names and products protected by the intellectual property (IP) system, the company continues to bring the traditions, smells, and essences of the lush islands of Fiji to consumers throughout the world.

While the country enjoys an abundance of traditional knowledge in handcrafts, agriculture, fishing, and medicine, much of it has not been harnessed. Pure Fiji is one company, however, that has been able to tap into this traditional knowledge, imbue it with modern techniques, and utilize natural ingredients to develop Fijian products that can be appreciated throughout the world (Figure 4.14).

In addition to the main Pure Fiji brand under which a wide variety of products are sold such as beauty, skin and hair care, and oil, the company has developed other brands to differentiate some of its products. The *Reniu* brand was created to serve as a platform for many of the SME's coconut-derived products, including coconut oil, lotion, and soaps. In an effort to appeal to a wider market, Pure Fiji developed the *Mana'Ia* brand name of products specifically for men. Eschewing the typical Pure Fiji logo and colors, *Mana'Ia* uses darker blues and greens and is accompanied with a *Pure Fiji Man* slogan (Figure 4.15).

By 2014, Pure Fiji was producing and exporting products in ten different categories. In addition to its line of beauty products, the SME also commercializes ambience products (such as candles, mists, and aroma sticks) based on natural Fijian ingredients; skin repair products using the *dilo* tree and marketed as Dilo Rescue; coconut oil marketed under the Reniu brand name; and the Mana'ia line of treatment products for men, which includes lotions, gels, and oils again made from natural Fijian ingredients.

*Figure 4.15* Body sets.

## *Akoma Cooperative Multi-Purpose Society (AKOMA), Ghana*[38]

Akoma Cooperative Multi-Purpose Society (AKOMA) is a farmers' non-governmental organization (NGO) founded in 2006 in the village of Pusu-Namogo, in the Upper East region of Ghana. Shea trees are indigenous to Africa and can be found across the West, Central, and Eastern regions of the continent – including Ghana. For generations, many people across these regions relied on the tree and its health properties to provide products for food, medicines, and cosmetics.

With an all-woman membership, AKOMA has created sustained employment for hundreds of previously unemployed residents in the village based mainly on the production and sale of shea butter – a by-product of vitellaria paradoxa, the African shea tree (Figure 4.16).

The nuts of the shea tree in this part of the world are gathered and crushed in order to produce oil for cooking. Moreover, the yellow cream – shea butter – that can be derived from the crushing process is applied to the belly by some pregnant Ghanaian women (to ease the pains associated with childbirth) or used on some newborn infants as a moisturizer.

In order to unite shea tree farmers in Pusu-Namogo, develop new commercialization opportunities for their products, and enhance their shea tree farming tradition, AKOMA was created.

AKOMA, which means heart, was established by Angus Klufio, an entrepreneur of Ghanaian heritage. Mr. Klufio – who also founded Akoma International UK Limited (AIL), a cosmetics manufacturer and supplier based in Derby, United Kingdom – established the farmers' NGO initially in order to create a steady supply of shea butter for his cosmetics company (Figure 4.17).

*Figure 4.16* Raw shea butter.

*Figure 4.17* Raw shea butter 2.

In order to support AKOMA's entry into the international market for shea butter, Mr. Klufio has relied on the capacity of AIL and TAG and developed a strong branding and commercialization strategy. To this end, the entrepreneur focused on developing a diverse range of quality products with a strong ethical identity for the NGO and its affiliated companies (Figure 4.18).

With certification marks AKOMA and AIL have been able to distinguish their raw materials and product ingredients from those of others. At the same time, AIL has positioned the cosmetic products sourced from the NGO in the niche market of certified and ethically procured goods and assured customers on product safety. Not only has AKOMA's shea butter been strategically positioned in

*Figure 4.18* Raw shea butter 3.

*Figure 4.19* Shea million.

this manner; it has also been marketed by AIL as a healthy product. Furthermore, AIL has enhanced its commercial activities by diversifying its products portfolio to include four lines of skincare goods (as of 2012) based on coconut oil, bath salts, and cocoa pods and powders (Figure 4.19).

AKOMA and its manufacturing branch have also commercialized shea butter via agreements to supply a number of cosmetics companies in the United Kingdom, such as Bulldog Natural Grooming (Bulldog) – a cosmetics maker that caters for men's products from its base in the West of London.

Through a strategic process of quality improvements, niche market product placing, product development, and via collaboration with an international cosmetics maker, the NGO's quality raw materials have entered the international market.

## Branding in various sectors

Under this section, a number of success stories from the developing world on branding in the following sectors will be stressed: Travel and tourism, fashion, footwear, beverage, and health.

### *Nature Air Holding Company SA (Nature Air), Costa Rica*[39]

Nature Air Holding Company SA (Nature Air) is an award winning airline established in 1990 in San Jose, Costa Rica. Since its foundation, the small and medium size enterprise (SME) has been at the forefront of airlines that have combined a successful business model with a proactive socio-economic and environmentally friendly strategy. Having gained a firm foothold in the tourism industry of Costa Rica, Nature Air successfully developed its range of services and expanded into the surrounding region. In addition, the airline has set new standards for responsible tourism and aviation whilst supporting the local community and sustaining the country's richly varied environment.

Nature Air – formerly known as Travel Air Alaska (TAA, up until 2000) – has been Managed since 2000 by Alex Khajavi who had a worldwide experience.

The entrepreneur was hired in 2000 as a consultant by Nature Air (TAA at the time) in order to rescue the company's unstable business model. Although the airline only had a single plane, the businessman successfully created a new research and development (R&D) strategy at the company. However, Mr. Khajavi was faced with a new challenge shortly thereafter, in September 2001, when the global economy (including the airline and tourism industries) took a downturn. As a consequence, some of Nature Air's investors pulled out of the company and Mr. Khajavi became its majority shareholder and director.

After taking charge of Nature Air, the businessman managed a number of R&D projects that improved the company's capacity and diversified its services.

With a growing capacity and staff of pilots who were trained as tourism guides, the company was able to extend its services and expand its client base and destinations to countries such as the Republic of Panama (Panama) and the Republic of Nicaragua (Nicaragua). As of 2012, Nature Air serviced 74 short haul flights daily to 15 destinations in Central America.

Nature Air has invested in a broad-range branding and commercialization plan in order to attract international customers and establish a firm position within a niche market of eco-tourism in Central America. For example, shortly after Mr. Khajavi's directorship began in 2001, the company rebranded its corporate identity and adopted a new trade name – Nature Air – so as to open up new avenues for commercialization and development. Based on the new corporate image, the company has entered the eco-tourism market as a fun yet environmentally and socially conscious SME. The airline, moreover, has established a firm reputation for quality service.

The airline has registered over 20 trademarks at home and abroad.

## *Gobi Cashmere, Mongolia*[40]

Formed in 1981, Gobi was originally a state-run enterprise that was partially privatized in 1999 and fully privatized in 2007 through a joint venture between a Mongolian company and two Japanese companies.

Today, the Gobi Corporation is the fifth largest producer of cashmere wool in the world, offering its international customers the finest cashmere available from its own indigenous nomadic herders in Mongolia.

Developing the GOBI brand was one of the Gobi Corporation's most important strategies for market diversification and business growth. A key strategy was a detailed plan to revitalize the Gobi brand while emphasizing the pride it has in being produced in Mongolia. The company's management used diverse ways in achieving this.

First, in 2008 Gobi launched its Factory Store (also known as an outlet store) next to its complex in Ulaanbaatar, the capital city. The store displayed the luxurious attributes of Gobi products and gives customers an opportunity to see and feel for themselves some of the finest Mongolian cashmere in the world.

Second, Gobi has intensified its effort to make higher quality products that can command a higher premium, thus intensifying the company's image as a luxury brand and lessening its reliance on the sale of raw or semi-processed cashmere.

Third, the company has developed new product types that target a younger and higher-income demographic, and its products are also made with specific markets and climates in mind.

Gobi successfully built on its heritage and name to create a new brand identity for itself. Mongolian cashmere has traditionally enjoyed a competitive edge in international markets since it holds a positive image as a product with a long traditional heritage from a vast, pastoral, and unspoiled land.

In order to ensure that customers are aware of what they are purchasing, in 2002, and with the assistance of the United States Agency for International Development, Gobi worked with three other Mongolian cashmere companies (Goyo, Altai Cashmere, and Mongol Nekhmel) to establish the Mongolian Fiber Mark Society (the Society). A non- profit organization (NPO), the Society is dedicated to developing the Mongolian cashmere industry's competitiveness, promoting Mongolian cashmere in international markets, and implementing associated marketing activities.

The development of a new brand image for Gobi and the creation of certification marks to protect these assets is vital to Gobi, the Society, and the entire Mongolian cashmere industry.

As a matter of fact, it should be recalled that Gobi realized the importance of protecting its name early on. In 1988 it filed for trademark protection for the Gobi name and its logo through the Madrid System for the International Registration of

Marks. The Pure Mongolian Cashmere and "Made With Mongolian Cashmere" marks were registered with the Office for Harmonization of the Internal Market (currently call EUIPO), in November 2004 and June 2005, respectively.

## *soleRebels, Ethiopia*[41]

soleRebels is a family owned brand and manufacturer of hand-crafted footwear based in Zenabwork village, Addis Ababa, Ethiopia that was co-founded by Bethlehem Tilahun Alemu in 2005.

Based on Ethiopia's long history of handmade goods built with recycled and environmentally friendly raw materials, soleRebels products – which include sandals, slippers, shoes, and boots for men, women, and children – are not only comfortable and stylish; they are also durable and affordable. The company and its brand have expanded international market access for hundreds of Ethiopian artisans across Africa, the European Union (EU), North America, and Asia. In order to win new customers and retain loyal clientele, soleRebels has focused on creating attractive brands and ecologically viable, value-added, and quality goods (Figure 4.20).

*Figure 4.20* Shoes.

Some of the company's brands include coZEES (boots for women in 15 models and various colors); Slip-Ons (comfortable and easy-to-wear shoes in 232 types and several colors); sandals and flip-flops (in 294 models and myriad colors); Lace-Ups (or laced shoes, in 212 models and a variety of color combinations); and, b*knd (a brand made of non-animal products that is aimed at a niche market of vegetarians and vegans) (Figure 4.21).

Moreover, the company has made the strategic decision to develop an image for its products that is ancient yet young, independent, and rebellious (Figure 4.22).

*Figure 4.21* Shoes 2.

*Figure 4.22* Shoes 3.

*Figure 4.23* Shoes 4.

As of 2012, soleRebels' products were commercialized in several countries around the world including Canada, France, Japan, the Kingdom of Denmark, the United Kingdom, and the United States (Figure 4.23).

## *Beauty Bee Company Limited/Baby Banda brand, Kenya*[42]

Beauty Bee Company Limited a Kenyan company that specializes in products for mothers-to-be and children. The company was founded in 2006 and entered the consumer market with its flagship product: the breastfeeding pillow. In 2008, Beauty Bee Company Limited rebranded its operation to begin trading under a new brand name: Baby Banda. In 2008, the company successfully launched Kenya's largest fair dedicated to young parents, mothers-to-be, and babies: The Baby Banda Pregnancy and Baby Fair, which has been hosted successfully each year for the past seven years. The Baby Banda company also hosts workshops for mothers-to-be: The Baby Banda Motherhood 101 Workshops that bring medical experts together to educate young parents about various issues that pertain to parenting.

*Figure 4.24* Baby Banda-pillows.

Today, the Baby Banda brand produces a wide range of products in four categories (Figure 4.24):

1 Pregnancy and after
2 Breastfeeding
3 Baby and Toddler
4 Diaper Bags

Since the establishment of the company in 2006, Carol Ngige has recognized the importance of branding to growing her business and the importance of establishing positive brand identity through the creation of quality products. The strategic decision to rebrand her company in 2008 better positioned Carol Ngige to expand her business' range of complementary product and service offerings while still holding true to its target market – young parents, mothers-to-be – and still operating under the main umbrella brand "Baby Banda." By ensuring that the original Baby Banda label is placed on each Baby Banda product and inserting authentic Baby Banda product brochures inside each product as it is packaged (Figure 4.25).

Carol Ngige has "innovated" in terms of marketing strategy. Since opening their first retail store in Nairobi in 2006, Carol Ngige has continued to implement a business strategy that was structured around leveraging the brand to increase industry presence locally and regionally. By conceptualizing the Baby Banda Pregnancy and Baby Fair Ngige created a bricks-and-mortar environment

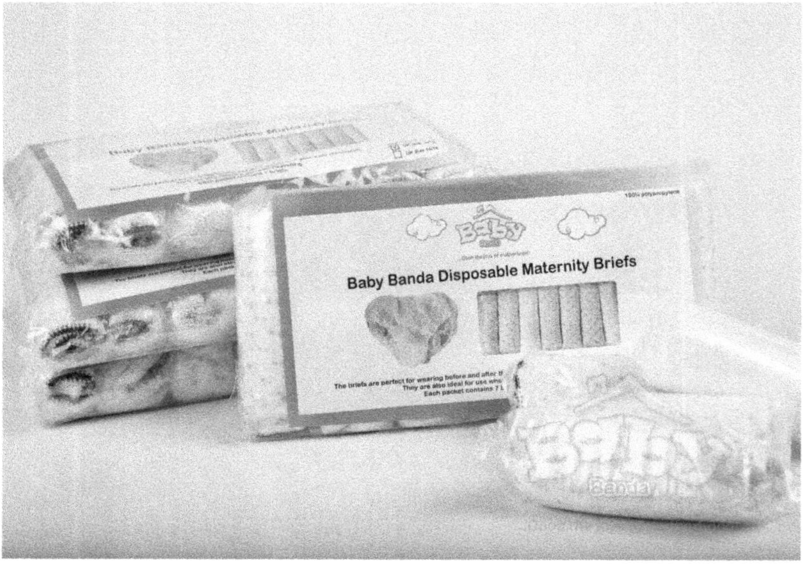


*Figure 4.25* Disposal maternity briefs.

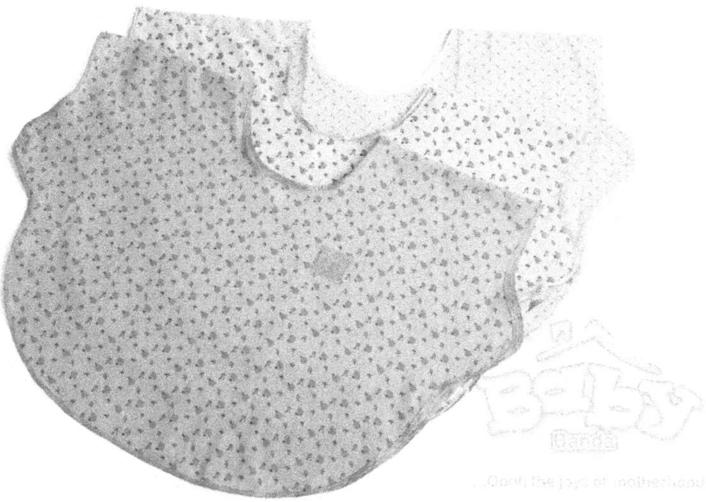


*Figure 4.26* Napkin.

in which to promote her products and increase awareness of her brand. Similarly, by employing the strategic use of social media and web-based platforms to market her goods directly to customers, Carol Ngige has minimized capital expenditure on marketing middlemen (Figure 4.26).

### *Panama Springs S.A, Panama*[43]

In 2003, Panama Springs S.A, one of Panama's leading bottling companies, launched a new product: Panama Blue; a bottled, natural spring water sourced from the same aquifers that have sustained life in the Cerro Azul region of Panama for eons.

Developing an award- winning bottle design that is protected by the IP system, Panama Blue has become one of Panama's most popular national products and exports. It is also one of the few brands indigenous to Panama that uses the country's name.

Panama Blue is bottled at the water source. The factory is located at the top of the mountain very near to where the natural aquifers are located. Panama Springs' operations provide employment opportunities for more than 50 families in the region. One of the major reasons why the water from the Cerro Azul region retains its level of quality is because it comes from aquifers that have not been exposed to outside air.

By collecting the water close to the source, the water does not come into contact with the outside air until a fresh bottle of Panama Blue is opened. This ensures the water's quality and long shelf life. When Panama Springs designed the Panama Blue bottle and label, the company was not only eyeing the domestic market, but also international markets.

In 2008, Panama Blue files a trademark application with the United States Patent and Trademark Office (USPTO). The complete trademark – Panama Blue 100% Rainforest Pure – was formally registered with the USPTO in 2010. That same year, Panama Blue received official registration of its trademark – Panama Blue Rainforest Pure Spring Water – in the European Union via the Office for Harmonization in the Internal Market, actually called European Union Intellectual Property Office (EUIPO).

Backed by the IP system, Panama Springs has developed a robust and successful branding strategy for Panama Blue. The company has developed a branding image that evokes the beauty of Panama, the clearness and freshness of natural spring water and the vital role that fresh water plays in an active lifestyle and rehydration of the human body.

In only a few years, Panama Springs has been able to tap into an abundant natural resource, develop an innovative product design and name, and become one of the leading bottled water companies in Panama. The unique design of the Panama Blue bottle and label has been recognized internationally.

## Notes

1 Brand identity is the capacity of a brand to be recognized as unique, overtime, without confusion, thanks to the elements that individualize it. See also Michel Chevalier and Gerald Mazzalovo, *Pro Logo: Brands as a Factor of Progress*, Palgrave Macmillan, 2004.

2 WIPO IP Advantages, www.wipo.int (last visited, December 15, 2018). See www.hoyxn.com

3 WIPO IP Advantages, www.wipo.int (last visited, December 15, 2018). See www.vietnambiz.org

4 WIPO IP Advantages, www.wipo.int (last visited, December 15, 2018). See www.maleeonline.com/
5 WIPO IP Advantages, www.wipo.int (last visited, December 15, 2018). See www.guanomad.com
6 WIPO IP Advantages, www.wipo.int (last visited, December 15, 2018). See www.corbana.co.cr
7 WIPO IP Advantages, www.wipo.int (last visited, December 15, 2018).
8 WIPO IP Advantages, www.wipo.int (last visited, October 30, 2018). See www.radixguitars.com/
9 www.brands.kz/en. See WIPO IP Advantages, www.wipo.int (last visited, December 15, 2018).
10 https://www.zoomtanzania.com. See WIPO IP Advantages, www.wipo.int (last visited, December 15, 2018).
11 Michel Chevalier and Gerald Mazzalovo, *Pro Logo: Brands as a Factor of Progress*, Palgrave Macmillan, 2004, p. 23.
12 WIPO Advantages, The Coffee War: Ethiopia and the Starbucks Story (see www.wipo.int).
13 United States Department of Agriculture (USDA), Foreign Agricultural Service, Ethiopia Coffee Annual, May 29, 2018.
14 WIPO Advantages, The Coffee War: Ethiopia and the Starbucks Story (see www.wipo.int).
15 WIPO Advantages, The Coffee War: Ethiopia and the Starbucks Story (see www.wipo.int).
16 WIPO IP Advantages, The Coffee War: Ethiopia and the Starbucks Story (see www.wipo.int).
17 Alemayehu Asfaw Amamo, Coffee Production and Marketing in Ethiopia, *European Journal of Business and Management*, Vol. 6, Issue 37, 2014.
18 Heran Sereke-Brhan, Coffee, Culture, and Intellectual Property: Lessons for Africa from the Ethiopian Fine Coffee Initiative, *The Pardee Papers*, No. 15, Boston University, July 2010.
19 www.trung-nguyen-online.com. See WIPO IP Advantages: www.wipo.int
20 www.darjeeling.gov.in/darj-tea.html. See WIPO IP Advantages: www.wipo.int
21 WIPO IP Advantages, www.wipo.int. See www.dilmahtea.com
22 WIPO IP Advantages, www.wipo.int. See www.bluemountaincoffeejamaica
23 https://coffeeplanet.com/. See WIPO IP Advantages, www.wipo.int (last visited, December 15, 2018).
24 WIPO IP Advantages, www.wipo.int. See www.grenadachocolate.com
25 WIPO IP Advantages, www.wipo.int
26 WIPO-Case studies, Cotton from the Land of the Pharaos, WIPO (www.wipo.int).
27 WIPO-Case studies, Cotton from the Land of the Pharaos, WIPO (www.wipo.int).
28 WIPO-Case studies, Cotton from the Land of the Pharaos, WIPO (www.wipo.int).
29 WIPO-Case studies, Cotton from the Land of the Pharaos, WIPO (www.wipo.int).
30 WIPO-Case studies, Cotton from the Land of the Pharaos, WIPO (www.wipo.int).
31 WIPO IP Advantages, www.wipo.int. See www.jollibee.com.ph
32 WIPO IP Advantages, www.wipo.int. See www.amanochocolate.com
33 WIPO IP Advantages, www.wipo.int
34 World Intellectual Property Organization (2014), IP *Successes in the ASEAN Region – Case Studies: The Kingdom of Cambodia – Crunching Success*, www.wipo.int. See also, www.lylyfood.com
35 WIPO IP Advantages, www.wipo.int. See www.jomcosmetics.co.za/
36 WIPO IP Advantages, www.wipo.int. See www.sheaterraorganics.com
37 WIPO IP Advantages, www.wipo.int. See www.purefiji.com
38 WIPO IP Advantages, www.wipo.int. See www.akomacooperative.com

39 WIPO IP Advantages, www.wipo.int. See www.natureair.com
40 WIPO IP Advantages, www.wipo.int. See www.gobicashmere.com
41 www.solerebels.com. See, WIPO IP Advantages, www.wipo.int (last visited, December 15, 2018).
42 WIPO IP Advantages, www.wipo.int. See www.babybandafair.com
43 WIPO IP Advantages, www.wipo.int. See www.paginasamarillas.com.pa

# 5 Branding innovations in the developing world

## One Village, One Product/One Town, One Product Model

The concept of one village, one product is not new. It originated in Japan in 1979 and has been spread mainly in Asia and with a few implementations in a number of countries in the developing world. The background and main objectives, fundamental principles, implementation in Asian and other countries, and challenges, will be highlighted before stressing its potential as a tool for enhancing innovation and branding in the developing world.

### *Background and main objectives*

The concept "One Village, One Product (OVOP)" originated in Oita Prefecture[1] in Japan in 1979 by the initiative of then the Governor of Oita Prefecture, Mr. Morihito Hiramatsu, before it has been spread in other countries. Other Asian countries, such as Thailand, Vietnam, China, Malaysia, Mongolia, and the Philippines, have adopted the concept. These countries benefitted from the assistance of the government of Japan to embark on this movement, project, or program. In Africa, this program has been introduced as a technical assistance means in Malawi and Senegal by the government of Japan through its agencies.[2]

In many countries where this model has been introduced, the concept has been renamed, "One Town, One Product (OTOP)." This does not change the basis of the concept and its objectives.[3] The two terms are used interchangeably in the book to mean the same.

The main idea behind OVOP or OTOP is to empower local villages or towns to concentrate on one product that they promote and market. When it was initiated in Oita, the uniqueness of the OVOP was that the movement was mainly left under the hands of local people, and the local government only gave technical support, encouragement, and marketing promotion, not much of financial subsidies, because too much dependence on government might weaken the dynamism of the movement.

The OVOP movement encourages locals to have/develop a particular product or products that best represent the village or town to gain sales revenue in the market, thereby generating income in the villages and improving the local economy. OVOP (Oita) movement provides an important model of success in regional development policy. The movement encouraged and empowered local citizens to unearth opportunities for economic growth and develop local industry with a global outlook.[4]

In other words, the main purpose of OTOP project is to support community to create products and markets by promoting self-reliance within community, entrepreneurs who participated in OTOP have to put their energy, creativity and desire in order to utilize their surrounding resources and contribute wealth to society.[5]

### *Fundamental principles*

The initial Oita OVOP was based on three powerful principles as follows[6]:

1 Local yet global: creating globally accepted products that reflect pride in the local culture
2 Self-reliance and creativity: realization of OVOP through independent actions utilizing potential of the region
3 Human resource development: fostering of people with a challenging and creative spirit

The basic philosophy of the OVOP movement, wherever it is promoted, is to mobilize local human and material resources for value-added activities to create marketable goods/services. All OVOP or OTOP cases share this spirit. It is, however, true that the level of development of the country may impact on its implementation strategy and final objective.

For the Oita OVOP, the purpose was to revitalize local communities which were being left out from the development process of the nation. The Thai OTOP is much more inclined to the economic purpose of national restructuring. The Malawi OVOP is somewhere between social and economic objectives.[7]

The initiators of the movement/project/program could also be different. In Oita, they were prefectural and municipal governments while the central government played the key role in Thailand and Malawi.[8]

The common denominator is that local chief executives of each city and municipality take the lead in identifying, developing and promoting a specific product or service, which has a competitive advantage. OTOP, Philippines, for instance, supports micro, small and medium enterprises (MSMEs) to manufacture, offer, and market distinctive products or services through the use of indigenous raw materials and local skills and talents.[9]

One community creates one marketable product with identical brand by using own resources, and brushes up the product, upgrades the value, establishes the own brand, and merchandises in the global markets.[10]

### *Implementation of OVOP/OTOP in Asian countries and elsewhere*

OVOP/OTOP model offers locals the opportunity to promote indigenous raw materials, inbred skills and talents to come up with distinctive products worthy of both domestic and foreign markets.

As stated, the level of involvement of the stakeholders, including the main actors may influence the implementation process of OVOP/OTOP. To illustrate this, Thai OTOP is under strong government initiatives, which is different from the Japanese OVOP model which empowered locals to take the lead for the benefit of the local communities.[11] In the case of Thailand, central government established OTOP central committee and OTOP coordination office. Four Ministries, namely, Ministry of Industry, Ministry of Agriculture and Cooperative, Ministry of Home Affairs, and Ministry of Trade, were directly participating through five small committees including market promotion.[12]

The OVOP movement is expected to correct the deficiency by encouraging the mobilization of local human, material, and cultural resources to create value-added goods and services for domestic and external markets.[13]

In order to promote local entrepreneurship, the government may organize product championship contests and publicly grant special "awards" to innovative local products.[14] With regard to Thailand, for instance, the OTOP championship is an innovative product contest initiated by the OTOP National Administrative Committee and the Ministry of Interior. Community groups, SMEs and individual entrepreneurs must register as manufacturers of OTOP products to participate in this contest. Each producer can submit only one product. The general criteria for the contest are (i) the product is exportable and has a brand quality, (ii) production can be sustainable and with consistent quality, (iii) the product can provide customer satisfaction, and (iv) the product has an impressive background story.[15]

In the Philippines, the OTOP was widely implemented. In Ilocos Norte, Philippines, the project has been successfully implemented.

Table 5.1 shows the different OTOP products of the different towns including its descriptions (Philippines).[16]

*Table 5.1* OTOP products of the different towns

| *Municipality* | *One-Town-One-Product Project* | *Description* |
|---|---|---|
| Bacarra | Sugar cane Vinegar Industry | **VINEGAR/BASI**<br>Vinegar is made from an upgraded variety of sugarcane juice. Its rich and lush taste can be attributed to the generations old process of fermenting vinegar done the traditional "Ilokano way," 100% pure and organic. This product is also known for its therapeutic and healing properties. |

| *Municipality* | *One-Town-One-Product Project* | *Description* |
|---|---|---|
| | | Basi (sugarcane wine) is made from the Juice of the crushed red-rinded sugarcane variety compounded with elements like barks and fruits of an indigenous *samak* (Macaranga) tree. The resultant brew is a mellow pale red drink as an outcome of the mixture of aromatic fruit of the *samak* tree. |
| San Nicolas | Terra Cotta Industry (Pottery/ Ceramics) | **CERAMICS**<br>Pottery and brick making are among the major industries of Ilocos Norte. This industry has been in existence for centuries now. These products are known for their durability, functionality and symmetry. They were for a long period of time, indigenous as they became an integral part of the way of life of the native inhabitants of the province. |
| Sarrat | Binakol (Loom woven) Products | **LOOMWOVEN PRODUCTS**<br>Hand loom weaving is a process where threads that make up the warp and weft are interwoven in an upright loom by one or two weavers. These products are widely accepted not only in the Philippines but also in other countries. Handloom products include blankets, pillow cases, towels, placemats, table napkins, table runners are clothing materials. |
| Paoay | Chichacorn (fried corn snack) | **CHICHARON (CORNICK) – FRIED CORN SNACKS**<br>Chicharon / cornick is a crunchy corn kernel made from glutinous white corn. Its taste enhanced by garlic and other flavoring such cheese barbecue, sweet and spicy and *adobo*, makes it a deliciously tempting snack. Mega Bawang is the brand being used by the Paoay Chicharon Producers Association, however, the producers have their respective brand names for their products. |
| Batac | Batac Empananda | **EMPANADA**<br>When it comes to *empanda*, Batac empanada is the best. It has the distinct taste that makes it different. It is made of a savory filling of green papaya, mongo, chopped Ilocano sausage (*longganisa*) and/or egg. The dough that serves as a wrapper to enclose the filling is thin and crisp made from rice flour. It is deep fried rather than baked. |
| Currimao | Native delicacies | **NATIVE DELICACIES**<br>Native delicacies such as *bibingka*, *suman*, *tupig* and *puto* are always commercially available in the province specifically in the Municipality of Currimao. These products, except *puto* are made from glutinous rice and are enhanced by coconut oil and brown/white sugar or molasses. |
| Pagudpod | Shell Craft | **SHELL CRAFT**<br>Beautiful shells and pebbles lay along the magnificent ivory beach shore of Pagudpud. These are gathered by the residents and are manufactured into fashion accessories and functional items. The unique designs and craftsmanship of these products are sought after or taken as *pasalubong* by tourist. |

Source: Eric S. Parilla, Economic Promotion through One-Town One Product, International Jour*nal of Academic Research in Business and Social Sciences*, Vol. 3, Issue 7, July 2013.

### *Challenges*

Any human innovation is not without setback. OVOP/OTOP is not an exception. While the new initiative had been implemented efficiently in Oita, Japan, its introduction in the developing world faces many challenges to produce similar results as those of Oita. Some misinterpretations of the model may be among the causes of unsuccessful implementation.

From the viewpoint of ideology and also sustainability, there should be self-help movement, but in some countries which are lacking in the basic structure for community-based movement, the involvement of central government may be necessary.[17]

Though the OVOP movement recorded successful results in Japan, the expected achievements seemed to be less than expected in other countries where the model had been advocated due to different development approaches, country background, stakeholders' involvement and understanding of the concept.[18]

Challenges are more profound when the OVOP/OTOP model is implemented in Africa. The illustrative examples are Malawi and Senegal. Malawi faced a number of issues from the outset of the implementation of the model.[19] OVOP movement can also contribute to rural development in terms of poverty reduction.

Insufficient development of infrastructure such as transport and communication in Africa are disadvantageous conditions for competing in the international market.

This limitation, which is shared by many other African countries, is inadequate transport infrastructure that obstructs OVOP producers successful participation in national and global value chains. In addition, African producers need to improve the quality of their products and establish their brands. One big concern in the Malawian OVOP movement is its sustainability.

With relation to domestic market, because of the low buying power by the people, market scale is limited and demand is not sufficient for developing many products.

Moreover, domestic market is not mature so that there is not big demand of unique products.[20]

The Major challenge of any OVOP/OTOP relying on the central government's contribution or leadership is that the full budget allocation may be problematic which entails that local entities subject of the project may seek external assistance from other countries.[21] The spirit behind the OVOP/OTOP model being the empowerment of locals may be undermined. In Africa, for instance, local people and local administrative officials have not acquired enough empowerment or experience in regional development.

Some suggest that if the OVOP/OTOP model is introduced on such scale and standard in African countries, it should be treated as a core project of government, like for Thailand, with heavy contribution in budget, human resources, and time, even to the level that other government projects may have to be reduced.[22] The author has some reservations on this approach.

It may be stressed that, in order to make OVOP take off in Africa, it will need prompt actions in several fronts.

### *One Town, One Product model as an innovation incentive and branding tool in the developing world*

Through the evolution of the concept One Village, One Product, despite a number of challenges on its implementation in some least-developed countries, the merit to serve as innovation incentive and branding tool in the developing world is enormous.

It has been seen that even in the situation whereby this model is implemented throughout an assistance package, branding and innovation incentive may be encouraged. In the Philippines, for instance, the best feature of the OTOP assistance package is the product packaging or the product enhancement and design program under the marketing assistance package wherein the Department of Trade and Industry provides full support in the packaging and labeling of its product.[23]

It is also maintained that the effectiveness of the OTOP assistance package in terms of skills development and training, the marketing assistance package, and the financial assistance program offered by the implementing agencies is moderately effective.[24]

In the best scenario, the entrepreneur should not rely on the assistance package offered by implementing agencies but to seek for more opportunities through undergoing training or proper study in marketing strategies and entrepreneurship principles that will strengthen its sales competitiveness in the local and international market.[25]

Historical evidence indicates that countries in the developing world that rely on foreign aid do not develop their economies as efficiently as those states that pursue their own economic development.[26]

The OVOP/OTOP may take several forms in the implementation process, such as cooperative, private-public partnership, SMEs, etc.[27]

Promotion of production of local specialties is expected to make great contributions to the promotion of diversification of rural economy, increase of income, promotion of rural industry and of SMEs including micro-scale enterprises. OTOP-Philippines, for instance, encourages the country's MSMEs to produce and market distinct products using indigenous raw materials and manpower.[28]

As stated, ownership of a project by stakeholders implicates ensuring the widest possible participation of those who are supposed to be the beneficiaries of the project. The essence of ownership is that the recipients drive the process.

Although Japan is a highly developed economy and advanced in technological infrastructure compared to other developing nations, the OVOP experience in rural economies within that setting provides a lesson for developing economies.[29]

First, fundamental principles and lessons of the One-Village One-Product movement are confirmed through the examination of experiences of the movement in Japan and other Asian Countries, and the applicability of the movement to Africa is considered.[30]

Second, OVOP movement is not a top-down project that is carried out by donors or central government from outside, but a movement whose subject is local people and central government is a facilitator to support or build that environment.[31]

It is evident that the success of OVOP in Oita is also due to the concerted efforts of the prefectural government in opening and expanding distribution channels and market accessibility; ranging from local street markets, numerous "Oita Fairs" in big Japanese cities to the establishment of retail stores for OVOP products locally and overseas.[32]

It should be stressed that much of the success of Thai OTOP is due to the highly developed road networks and the availability of pick-up trucks for villagers. Japanese OVOP also benefited from the development of highway networks and motorization. For OVOP model to succeed in Sub-Sahara Africa, nationwide delivery services and transportation networks need to be expanded and improved quickly.[33]

Notwithstanding a number of challenges over the implementation of One Village, One Product/One Town, One Product model, merits are enormous mainly for the developing world. ***As mentioned, branding goes alongside with innovation nowadays and OVOP/OTOP model can well induce innovation and branding of local products.***

OVOP/OTOP model can be adapted in the developing world to take into consideration local realities, impediments, and challenges. To start with, according to the author, the model may be renamed: One Town, One Innovation **(OTOI).** The merit of the new title is that it will level up the effort to put into place to come up with an innovation that may relate to goods or services (products), process, new organization methods, and new marketing approaches. As perceived, the innovation may be technological or non-technological.

The main principles of **OTOI** will be almost the same as OTOP/OVOP, but with different emphasis, namely:

1 Local yet global
2 Self-reliance and **innovation**
3 Human resource development

Each town or village subject to implementing this model will be empowered to initiate an innovative project in one area where it has competitive advantage. The project will be entirely local and financed locally by each town from funds generated by itself. From these perspectives, to make this model work, emulation among towns could be encouraged to come up with an innovative product or branding methods. The innovation should meet global standards. Unlike the OTOP/OVOP model, under the OTOI model, innovative products will be made principally to supply the national market. The external market may be utilized to sell these products only if it is needed to support the local economy (e.g. export to the neighboring countries) or in case of overproduction.

As learned from existing OVOP/OTOP, the involvement of the central government should be very limited. It should have a supportive role in one dimension of the activity, such as guidance on marketing strategies. At the end of the sequence, each town would come up with an innovation that responds and corresponds to their needs and adapted to their level of development.

To encourage local entrepreneurs to invest in producing the said products or generating an innovation, tax incentives may be an option or the way to go. The creation of new markets for local producers is needed. From the same perspectives, products/innovation contest may be set up to award good performances.

The implementation of the model may be fixed to three years from the initiation stage to close of the project. After the three years, each town may initiate another project based on a different innovation target. The implementation of the model in a continuous manner will empower communities and town to fly by themselves counting less on the central government or external aids. Registration of generated IPRs should be guaranteed.

## Patanjali Ayurved Limited (India)

Patanjali Ayurved Limited is an Indian consumer goods company that is performing very well and which has become a very strong competitor to existing multinational companies established in India carrying on business in the same range of sectors and producing similar products.

The background of the enterprise will be highlighted before looking at its products. Patanjali Ayurved Limited's branding strategies will be examined to find out lessons to learn from the developing world's perspectives before putting forward current challenges faced by Patanjali Ayurved Limited to keep the pace and the way forward to overcome those challenges.

### *Background*

Baba Ramdev established the Patanjali Ayurved Limited in 2006 along with Acharya Balkrishna Acharya with the objective of establishing science of Ayurveda in accordance and coordination with the latest technology and ancient wisdom.[34] The company grew multifold in a very short time. Baba Ramdev strategically launched the brand Patanjali.[35] Patanjali Ayurved Ltd has achieved a tremendous presence across India and around the globe in a very small time since its inception in 2006.[36] Patanjali company completely marketing its products on the basis of healthy, natural, farm fresh without any pesticides and chemical has gained the lot of attention from the consumers which has helped it to compete against the conglomerates P&G, ITC, Hindustan Unilever, Nestle, etc.[37] The company is set up with an aim to provide superior quality of products at fair price and to get their customers rid of the chronic diseases by providing products which are organic and natural.[38]

In India, Ayurveda or Ayurvedic products are the traditional holistic medical system. After centuries of experiments, studies, and meditations, natural scientists and early psychics developed this system. Basically, the word Ayurveda has been formed by "ayus," meaning life, and "veda," meaning knowledge. It can be said that Ayurveda is about knowing more about life.[39]

The company has a production capacity of Rs. 350 billion (US$4.9 billion) and is in the process of expanding to a capacity of Rs. 60,000 (equivalent to Rs.610 billion or US$8.5 billion in 2017) through its new production units at several places, including Noida, Nagpur, and Indore.

## *Products*

Patanjali Ayurved Ltd produces a wide range of products in various categories: namely, natural food products, natural health care products, natural personal care products, ayurvedic medicines, and herbal home care products (e.g. detergent).

The company manufactures more than 900 products including 45 types of cosmetic products and 30 types of food products. According to Patanjali, all the products manufactured by Patanjali Ayurved Ltd are made from Ayurveda and natural components.[40] It has also manufactured around 300 types of medicines for curing many diseases like from common cold to acute paralysis.[41]

Among the products, the following five have made Patanjali Ayurved Ltd very popular and successful:[42]

1 Cow's ghee

Ghee is commonly used in India and Middle East countries and is one of the classes of clarified butter. Traditionally ghee is made from cow's milk which is considered sacred in the Hindu religion. It is a major ingredient in the Hindu kitchen and is mainly used on chapatis in Northern India. While ghee has a lot more uses rather than just in the kitchen.[43]

Ghee is 100% butterfat and primarily contains butter, milk proteins, and water. It is a great alternative to butter. As it is low in fat, ghee can also reduce cholesterol in intestines.

Patanjali earned a revenue of Rs. 1,467 crore from cow's ghee, a fragmented market with several unorganized players. In the organized branded ghee market, Patanjali is a direct rival to Amul. Branded ghee accounts for about 44% of volumes in the overall market. Patanjali is the only brand that seems to have a good presence across zones. It has the highest volume share, followed by Amul, Krishna, Milma, Nandini and others.[44]

2 Dant Kanti toothpaste

Patanjali Dant Kanti Toothpaste is herbal toothpaste containing herbs and some ayurvedic ingredients. It improves the health of the teeth and gums and helps to protect the teeth and gums from infections.

Dant kanti toothpaste earned a revenue of Rs. 940 crore from the segment. The company said its share in market stood at 14% at the end of March. Rivals include market leader Colgate Palmolive India Ltd and Dabur India Ltd. Colgate Palmolive saw its share fall to 55.6% in 2016 compared to 57.4% in the previous year. Dabur India, maker of Dabur Red and Meswak brands, said that its share in the herbal and ayurvedic toothpaste market rose 1% in the year ended March amid consumers' growing preference for such products.[45]

3 Ayurvedic medicines

As stated, Pantajali Ayurved Ltd produces a wide range of medicinal products for curing a large number of diseases based on traditional knowledge.

Patanjali earned Rs. 870 crore revenue from ayurvedic medicines, nearly four times compared to its direct rival Dabur India.[46]

4 Keshkanti shampoo

Patanjali keshkanti shampoo is an herbal hair shampoo or cleanser. It nourishes the hair and enhances hair glow.

Keshkanti shampoo contributed a revenue of Rs. 825 crore for Patanjali. Hindustan Unilever is the market leader with a 45% share in shampoos. India's largest consumer goods maker earned Rs. 16,304 crore from the personal care segment, which includes shampoo and soap brands like Dove, Sunsilk, Tresemme and Lux, and skincare products like Fair & Lovely and Ponds cream.[47]

5 Soaps

Patanjali produces a great number of herbal soap. Patanjali's herbal soap segment mopped up a revenue of Rs. 574 crore. HUL, the maker of Lifebuoy, is the market leader in soaps, followed by rivals like Nirma, and Godrej Consumer Products.[48]

Overall, Patanjali's products satisfy the need of consumers and are not high end products.[49] And the Patanjali products initially priced anywhere between 10% and 30% cheaper than competitors.[50]

It should be mentioned that Patanjali Ayurved Ltd has manufacturing units in Nepal under the trademark Nepal Gramudhyog and imports majority of herbs in India from Himalayas of Nepal.

Baba Ramdev maintained that Patanjali will be the largest fast-moving consumer goods (FMCG) brand in the world by 2015. The top FMCG companies in India are Pantanjali's competitors such as Hindustan Unilever Limited (HUL), Colgate-Palmolive, ITC Limited, Nestle, and Procter & Gamble.

### *Branding strategies*

Patanjali enjoys an edge over its competitors due to its branded house marketing strategy. Unlike foreign players Patanjali promotes its entire product under one single brand house which has helped them to infuse a sense of trust and loyalty in the customers. Patanjali is able to create a brand perception of health and wellness among the Indian masses, primarily because of Baba Ramdev's association with the brand who is considered to be a veteran of yoga.[51]

Strong innovation and new products pipeline, pricing discounts to the peers (15%–30%), ayurvedic and natural propositions with low A&P spends (leveraging Baba Ramdev's brand pull) lend Patanjali's products an edge over the competition.[52]

This is to say that the rising awareness about the importance of a healthy lifestyle and increasing awareness regarding alternative therapies like yoga and Ayurveda became instrumental in generating acceptance for Patanjali products.[53]

Patanjali is not only attracting price sensitive customers but also brand loyal customers. Patanjali Ayurveda differentiated its products mainly by its go herbal scheme which set the chemical products aside.[54]

Within a very short period of time, Patanjali products captured a number of consumers. From 2008 to 2012 there is a huge increment in the number of products which is from 26 to 120. Patanjali has increased its market share within a very brief time but shortage of these products is the major problem faced by consumers these days.[55]

It is said that the most important reasons for the popularity of Patanjali products and that increased market share are as follows:[56]

1 Effective communication strategy
2 Better quality at affordable prices
3 Easy availability and wide range of products
4 Brand image based on the credibility of Baba Ramdev
5 Consumer awareness of Patanjali products

Whether it is the assurance of purity conveyed by its natural and herbal product line or the influence of Ramdev, Patanjali Ayurved Ltd has become a key player in the market and is giving its competitors a run for their money.[57]

### *Challenges*

As highlighted earlier, competitors did not see the success of Patanjali the same way. The main competitors redesigned their branding strategies to better compete further in the areas where Patanjali had competitive advantages. Under the same line of reasoning, companies like Hindustan Unilever Limited (HUL), Nestle, and others plan a strong come back in the market by developing distribution channels and changing marketing strategies.[58] Colgate-Palmolive for example competes with Patanjali by using Ayurvedic herb for its toothpaste Colgate to attempt to regain market in this area.

As the company doubled sales targets every year and set its sights on total domination over the Indian consumer, it developed an uncontrolled hunger for new distributors and new channels of trade, often at the expense of older allies. Initially, popularity of Patanjali products grew due to its own Chikitsalayas which later helped bring general trade on board at much lower margins than they would get from competing products of big FMCG companies.[59]

The problems with the distribution network come as Patanjali is in the middle of a debt-fuelled expansion. Increased overhead costs because of the expansion, higher distribution and selling expenses, advertising and promotion expenses and higher dealer discounts and commissions will keep its performance subdued in the medium term.[60]

According to a recent Credit Suisse report, consumer offtake has declined in many product categories. While the company continues to hold sway over toothpastes with Dant Kanti, and in ghee, incremental gains in these categories are said to have declined. Several categories are seeing declining offtake levels, most prominent among them being honey and hair care.[61]

A number of reasons for a slowdown of Patanjali have been pointed out both by scholars and mass media. These are as follows:[62]

1 Brand fatigue setting due to the lack of renovation

Patanjali saw a massive surge in household penetration in calendar year 2017 from 27% to 45%, driven mainly by non-core users who bought into the ayurvedic and naturals positioning of the brand rather than core loyalists. Many of these consumers lapsing out as the novelty value and buzz around the brand has gone down and other companies are offering similar products.

2 Inability to crack general trade distribution

Patanjali started out by selling its products from its own network of chikitsalayas and then spread to the general trade distribution. That is where it found itself pitched against giant incumbents such as Hindustan Unilever, Colgate, and Nestle. According to an ET report, Patanjali products were available in 2016 in two lakh traditional retail outlets popularly called as kirana shops. That was 1/30th the presence of FMCG market leader Hindustan Unilever in the kirana universe (over 60 lakh outlets). For Colgate and Nestle, the numbers were 47 lakh and 35 lakh, respectively. According to a recent ET Prime report, Patanjali's own chikitsalaya network faces stress as the company is focusing on new distribution and trade channels. The report said Patanjali had developed an uncontrolled hunger for new distributors and new channels of trade, often at the expense of older allies. General trade distribution remains a challenge for the company.

3 Dilution of the ayurvedic credentials due to excessive extension

Patanjali started out as an ayurvedic pharmacy and expanded into herbal and organic food products. Slowly, as its popularity grew, it started expanding away from its standard ayurvedic portfolio into products such as biscuits, noodles, and toothbrushes. Patanjali is now planning to foray into apparel and frozen vegetables. This might have diluted its image of an Ayurvedic company.

4 Strong competitive response from large companies with their own Ayurvedic offerings

FMCG companies like Colgate and HUL are investing heavily in natural products to lure back consumers who may have drifted to the rival camp, says the report. Competitors like DaburNSE 0.43% and Colgate have been defending their turf. While Dabur responded with strategic pricing, HUL launched nationally an ayurvedic range of products. Colgate, too, was forced to come up with an ayurvedic offering.

5 Sharp drop in advertising spends by the company

According to a May report (2018) by exchange4media.com, out of the 16 weeks this year, the company did not appear in BARC's list of Top 10 Advertisers for six weeks. Even in the other nine weeks, the brand featured at the bottom end of the category (between 5 and 10). In fact, in week 16 (April 14–20), Patanjali was at the bottom spot with 16,539 insertions.

6 Low media coverage of Patanjali

This is probably again the result of brand fatigue. Patanjali brand leader Baba Ramdev has been an aggressive promoter. Low media coverage could be a result of over-exposure and consequential peaking of interest in the brand.

### *Way forward*

After facing strong competitive response from large FMCG companies with their own Ayurvedic offerings, Patanjali Ayurved is trying to find a new route to growth: agri and food-processing business. It has already entered the dairy sector with products such as cow milk, curd, buttermilk, and cheese. It has also started selling frozen greens such as peas, sweet corn, and mixed vegetables.[63] Ramdev pointed out that Patanjali was now focusing more on agriculture and accordingly he encourages organic farming.

Patanjali is taking a new course after facing several challenges in its current business.

General trade distribution remains a challenge for the company due to a stronghold of big FMCG companies.

Dairy, agri business and food processing could be Patanjali's new route to revenue growth even as it struggles to consolidate existing business. According to market research firm Euromonitor, after edible oils, dairy is the second-largest segment in India's packaged-foods business, valued at Rs. 1.2 trillion as of 2017.

## Branding Traditional Knowledge in innovation era

The title of this section may not please people who still believe that traditional knowledge (TK) is the opposite of innovation, thinking that it is an old concept and static. Needless to highlight that as stated it earlier, TK is dynamic and has contributed enormously to the global value chain as illustrated through success stories and case studies. TK is an IP which does not fall within the conventional IP system in which main principles are decided from the outset.

Until now, fighting against misappropriation of TK has been debated under the scope of many international organizations and civil societies but a consensus is still far from being reached. Various ways have been proposed through the mechanisms of prior informed consent and benefit sharing of benefit but do not always satisfy the stakeholders. In addition, the disclosure of country of origin/source of genetic resources or associated TK has been put forward but there are still some resistances for its endorsement. Putting aside debates, *denying recognition of TK nowadays is like drinking milk but refuting to believe that it comes from a cow.*

TK is more and more contributing to the making of products as displayed throughout case studies in a large number of industries such as cosmetics, agriculture, and textile. Many cosmetic products, for instance, are made off of traditional technology passed from generation to generation. The developing world is rich of plants, herbs, fruits used in modern cosmetic industry. Modernization of techniques should not become an usurpation.

***Branding TK may be one of the ways to fight against its misappropriation.*** Unlike in the past whereby the contribution of TK was unnoticed, nowadays, it is easy to trace the source of TK. As TK skills are tremendously used in business, it is time to brand TK, unless it is considered secret. It will be difficult for an entity that is not related to it to claim the ownership. The branding of TK through different means should be encouraged. As seen, the OTOP/OVOP/OTOI model and Patanjali case are two branding mechanisms which are based to a large extent on TK.

As seen through success stories, TK may be branded throughout creation of cooperatives, SMEs, private-public partnership. Empowering local communities to take care of their own destiny is recommended as the case has been in respect to the OVOP-Oita model. In addition, at the level of States, tax incentives may be provided to SMEs embarking on business to support local production or offering local products.

Using TK's technology should also be encouraged to set up new brands. Patanjali is a good example to follow. Products generated locally may compete with other products from the same sector provided that the quality is good and that the packaging is also well thought.

## Notes

1 Oita Prefecture is located on the north-eastern coast of Kyushu Island, Japan.

2 See Japan Association for International Collaboration of Agriculture and Forestry (JAICAF), One-Village One Product movement in Africa, March 2007.

3 Moses B. Appoy, Analysis of the Marketing Management Strategies of the OTOP in Ifugao towards a Sustainable OTOP Implementation, *Asian Journal of Business and Management*, Vol. 3, Issue 4, August 2015, pp. 230–252.

4 Kunio Igusa, Globalization in Asia and Local Revitalization Efforts: A View from One Village One Product (OVOP) Movement in Oita, Ritsumeikan Asia Pacific University.

5 Annabelle, Bughao, The Impact of One Town One Product Program on Business Environment on Selected Areas in Cavite, Philippines, International Conference on Language, Education, Humanities and Innovation, January, 21, 22, 2017.

6 Kunio Igusa, Globalization in Asia and Local Revitalization Efforts: A View from One Village One Product (OVOP Movement in Oita, Ritsumeikan Asia Pacific University.

7 Kiyoto Kurokawa (JICA), Fletcher Tembo (ODI) and Dirk Willem te Velde (ODI), Challenges for the OVOP movement in Sub-Saharan Africa: -Insights from Malawi, Japan and Thailand, April 2010.

8 Kiyoto Kurokawa (JICA), Fletcher Tembo (ODI) and Dirk Willem te Velde (ODI), Challenges for the OVOP movement in Sub-Saharan Africa: -Insights from Malawi, Japan and Thailand, April 2010.

9 Rana, Erec Cutaran, Sustainable Local Development through One Town One Product (OTOP): The Case of Mindanao, Philippines, International Conference on OVOP, 2008.

10 Fred R. Schumann, A Study of One Village One Product (OVOP) and Workforce Development: Lessons for Engaging Rural Communities around the World, Tokyo, March 28, 2016.

11 See OECD-UNESCO, International Workshop on Innovation for Development: Converting Knowledge to Value, January 28–30, 2009, OCDE, Conference Center, Paris.

12 Japan Association for International Collaboration of Agriculture and Forestry (JAICAF), One-Village One Product movement in Africa, March 2007.

13 Kiyoto Kurokawa (JICA), Fletcher Tembo (ODI) and Dirk Willem te Velde (ODI), Challenges for the OVOP movement in Sub-Saharan Africa: -Insights from Malawi, Japan and Thailand, April 2010.

14 Kiyoto Kurokawa (JICA), Fletcher Tembo (ODI) and Dirk Willem te Velde (ODI), Challenges for the OVOP movement in Sub-Saharan Africa: -Insights from Malawi, Japan and Thailand, April 2010.

15 Kiyoto Kurokawa (JICA), Fletcher Tembo (ODI) and Dirk Willem te Velde (ODI), Challenges for the OVOP movement in Sub-Saharan Africa: -Insights from Malawi, Japan and Thailand, April 2010.

16 Eric S. Parilla, Economic Promotion through One-Town One Product, *International Journal of Academic Research in Business and Social Sciences*, Vol. 3, Issue 7, July 2013.

17 Nguyen Thi Anh, One Village One Product (OVOP) in Japan to One Tambon One Product (OTOP) in Thailand: Lessons for Grass Root Development in Developing Countries, *Journal of Social and Development Sciences*, Vol. 4, Issue 12, 2016, pp. 529–537.

18 NDIONE Joseph Sega & SUZUKI Kanichiro, The OVOP as a Tool to Develop Small and Medium-Sized Enterprises: Insights from OVOP Entrepreneurial Experience in Senegal, *International Journal of Education and Research*, Vol. 6, Issue 3, March 2018.

19 See Eric S. Parilla, Economic Promotion through One-Town One Product, *International Journal of Academic Research in Business and Social Sciences*, Vol. 3, Issue 7, July 2013.

20 Kiyoto Kurokawa (JICA), Fletcher Tembo (ODI) and Dirk Willem te Velde (ODI), Challenges for the OVOP movement in Sub-Saharan Africa: -Insights from Malawi, Japan and Thailand, April 2010.

21 Kanako Mukai and Ryo Fujikura, "One Village One Product: Evaluations and Lessons Learnt from OVOP Aid Projects," *Development in Practice*, Vol. 25, Issue 3, 2015, pp. 389–400.

22 See Eric S. Parilla, Economic Promotion through One-Town One Product, *International Journal of Academic Research in Business and Social Sciences*, Vol. 3, Issue 7, July 2013.
23 See Eric S. Parilla, Economic Promotion through One-Town One Product, *International Journal of Academic Research in Business and Social Sciences* Vol. 3, Issue 7, July 2013.
24 See Eric S. Parilla, Economic Promotion through One-Town One Product, *International Journal of Academic Research in Business and Social Sciences*, Vol. 3, Issue 7, July 2013.
25 Moses B. Appoy, Analysis of the Marketing Management Strategies of the OTOP in Ifugao towards a Sustainable OTOP Implementation, *Asian Journal of Business and Management*, Vol. 3, Issue 4, 2015.
26 See Nguyen Thi Anh, "One Village One Product (OVOP) in Japan to One Tambon One Product (OTOP) in Thailand: Lessons for Grass Root Development in Developing Countries, *Journal of Social and Development Sciences*, Vol. 4, Issue 12, 2016, pp. 529–537.
27 Binod Ghimire, "One Village, One Product," Development Advocate Nepal. Kathmandu: United Nations Development Programme (UNDP), October 2013–March 2014, pp. 23–25.
28 See Eric S. Parilla, Economic Promotion through One-Town One Product, *International Journal of Academic Research in Business and Social Sciences*, Vol. 3, Issue 7, July 2013.
29 Fred R. Schumann, A Study of One Village One Product (OVOP) and Workforce Development: Lessons for Engaging Rural Communities around the World, Tokyo, March 28, 2016.
30 Japan Association for International Collaboration of Agriculture and Forestry (JAICAF), One-Village One Product movement in Africa, March 2007
31 See Timur Dadabaev, *Japan in Central Asia: Strategies, Initiatives, and Neighboring Powers*. London: Palgrave Macmillan, 2016. See also Ning Li and Fred Schumann, "The One Village One Product (OVOP) Model and Economic Development on Guam," *Journal of Economics and Economic Education Research*, Vol. 14, Issue 3, 2013.
32 NDIONE Joseph Sega & SUZUKI Kanichiro, The OVOP as a Tool to Develop Small and Medium-Sized Enterprises: Insights from OVOP Entrepreneurial Experience in Senegal, *International Journal of Education and Research*, Vol. 6, Issue 3, March 2018.
33 Kiyoto Kurokawa (JICA), Fletcher Tembo (ODI) and Dirk Willem te Velde (ODI), Challenges for the OVOP movement in Sub-Saharan Africa: -Insights from Malawi, Japan and Thailand, April 2010.
34 Wikipedia, accessed on November 29, 2018.
35 Simnalika Kushwaha, Strategies that Unpaid Brand Ambassador Baba Ramdev Employed to Create Brand Patanjali, *Indian Journal of Applied Research*, Vol. 8, Issue 4, April 2018.
36 www.patanjaliayurved.org
37 Reema Agnes Frank, Consumer Purchase Behavior Towards Patanjali Brand in Mangalore, *Journal of Management*, Vol. 2, Issue 1, June 2018.
38 Preeti Shukla and Payal Shrivastav, Patanjali- The Swadesi Titan: A Case Study Analysis on Pal, *International Journal of Current Research*, Vol. 8, Issue 11, pp. 41487–41490.
39 Ajeet Kumar and Anshu Ahuja, Consumer Behavior Towards Patanjali Products: A Study on Consumers with Reference to Rohtak District of Haryana, *Kaav International Journal of Economics, Commerce & Business Management*, Vol. 4, Issue 2, April–June, 2017.
40 Wikipedia, accessed on November 29, 2018.

41 Ajeet Kumar and Anshu Ahuja, Consumer Behavior Towards Patanjali Products: A Study on Consumers with Reference to Rohtak District of Haryana, *Kaav International Journal of Economics, Commerce & Business Management*, Vol. 4, Issue 2, April–June, 2017.
42 *The Economic Times*, These five products made Ramdev's Patanjali a mega business, January 19, 2018.
43 www.cashkaro.com
44 www.cashkaro.com
45 www.cashkaro.com
46 www.cashkaro.com
47 www.cashkaro.com
48 www.cashkaro.com
49 Simnalika Kushwaha, Strategies that Unpaid Brand Ambassador Baba Ramdev Employed to Create Brand Patanjali, *Indian Journal of Applied Research*, Vol. 8, Issue 4, April 2018.
50 See Sandhya Rani and Chhaya Shukla, Trend of Patanjali Products: An Ayurvedic Magic Wand for Healthy Living, Paripex, *Indian Journal of Research*, Vol. 1, Issue 9, 2012, pp. 93–94. See also Irshad Ali and Manmohan Yadav, A Study of Consumer Perception of Herbal Products in Bhopal, *International Journal of Management Studies*, Vol. 2, Issue 1, 2015, pp. 69–80.
51 Simnalika Kushwaha, Strategies that Unpaid Brand Ambassador Baba Ramdev Employed to Create Brand Patanjali, *Indian Journal of Applied Research*, Vol. 8, Issue 4, April 2018.
52 Ajeet Kumar and Anshu Ahuja, Consumer Behavior Towards Patanjali Products: A Study on Consumers with Reference to Rohtak District of Haryana, *Kaav International Journal of Economics, Commerce & Business Management*, Vol. 4, Issue 2, April–June, 2017.
53 Ruchi Jaggi and Munmun Ghosh, Consumer Perception of Patanjali Products: An Analytical Study, The IUP Journal of Brand Management, Vol. XIV, Issue 1, 2017. See Ramakrishna Bandaru, Factors Influencing the Customers towards Patanjali Natural Food Products: A study in Hyderabad City, *International Journal of Scientific & Engineering Research*, Vol. 8, Issue 7, July–2017.
54 Simnalika Kushwaha, Strategies that Unpaid Brand Ambassador Baba Ramdev Employed to Create Brand Patanjali, *Indian Journal of Applied Research*, Vol. 8, Issue 4, April 2018. See D. T. Shinde and S. J. Gharat, Product Positioning of Patanjali Ayurved ltd, *Pune Research Discovery*, Vol. 1, Issue 3, 2017, pp. 1–6.
55 Rupali Khanna, Customer Perception Towards Brand: A Study on Patanjali, *Global Journal of Management and Business Research: e-marketing*, Vol. 15, Issue 9, 2015, pp. 41–45. See also Ajeet Kumar and Anshu Ahuja, Consumer Behavior Towards Patanjali Products: A Study on Consumers with Reference to Rohtak District of Haryana, *Kaav International Journal of Economics, Commerce & Business Management*, Vol. 4, Issue 2, April–June, 2017.
56 Ruchi Jaggi and Munmun Ghosh, Consumer Perception of Patanjali Products: An Analytical Study, *The IUP Journal of Brand Management*, Vol. XIV, Issue 1, 2017. See Anudeep Arora, Conquering Miles to Reach A Milestone: How Baba Ramdev turned Patanjali into 5000 Crores Business, *Journal of Modern Management & Entrepreneurship (JMME)*, Vol. 7, Issue 4, October 2017, pp. 41–47.
57 Ruchi Jaggi and Munmun Ghosh, Consumer Perception of Patanjali Products: An Analytical Study, *The IUP Journal of Brand Management*, Vol. XIV, Issue 1, 2017.
58 See R. K Gopal and Brijesh Singh, Demystifying the Brand Patanjali - A Case on Growth Strategies of Patanjali Ayurved ltd, *PES Business Review*, Vol. 11, Issue 1, 2016.
59 *The Economic Times*, Pain in Patanjali chain: Sales drop first time in five years, November 22, 2018.

60 *The Economic Times*, Pain in Patanjali chain: Sales drop first time in five years, November 22, 2018.
61 *The Economic Times*, Yoga pause? Ramdev's Patanjali is caught in 6 body locks, October 9, 2018.
62 *The Economic Times*, Yoga pause? Ramdev's Patanjali is caught in 6 body locks, October 9, 2018.
63 *The Economic Times*, Agri Yoga: Will Ramdev's new asana put Patanjali back on growth path? October 9, 2018.

# 6 General conclusions

It has been demonstrated through this book that intellectual property, innovation, and branding are interlinked and they constitute the main pillars of any innovation system. The common denominator is that the three concepts involve creativity.

Within the framework of IP landscape, the role of trademarks in identifying products, the importance of designs in the modern world, the added value of geographical indications (GIs) in promoting local products, the interfaces among trademarks, designs, copyright, and patents, and significance of traditional knowledge in the global value chain have been demonstrated.

In the area of innovation, it has been stressed that both technological and non-technological innovations are related. With regard to non-technological innovations, the developing world is doing well and in some of the areas, they have competitive advantages compared with the rest of the world.

Branding is a very important tool, enabling innovations to be present at the market. An innovation will be deemed successful if products or processes reach the market. This requires strategic promotion of products to get them to the market and help them become favorites in the eyes of consumers.

Through the review of trademark class count in applications and registrations, design count in applications and registrations, and patent applications and patent grants with regard to low-income economies, lower middle-income economies, upper-middle-income economies, and high-income economies in the developing world, it has been observed that the global trends depend mostly on each IP category, economic situation of the country and GNI per capita, where applicable.

Regarding the low-income economies grouping as regards trademark class count in applications and registrations between 2011 and 2016, the findings revealed that in accordance with the level of development and economic situation, Madagascar, Mozambique, and Nepal performed well in this income grouping.

With regard to the low-income economies grouping in relation to design count in applications and registrations between 2011 and 2016 the findings showed that in this area, the performance of countries from this income grouping is disappointing. All the selected countries poorly performed and the trend is toward regression of numbers. Madagascar had the lead and Mozambique had a mixed picture.

Concerning the low-income economies grouping in connection with patent applications and patent grants between 2011 and 2016, the findings displayed that patent applications are filed at a low level and only few countries from this income grouping have reaching annually 50 applications. This may sound unbelievable but the reality is that few patent applications are filed in low-income countries given the level of development of their industries, research, and development (R&D), as well as large potential market enabling business. Looking in depth, a few patent applications received emanate from non-resident applicants who are most of the time foreigners.

In regard to the lower middle-income economies grouping in respect to trademark class count in applications and registrations between 2011 and 2016, the findings demonstrated that India performed well in the income grouping from the years 2011 to 2016. Viet Nam showed progress with no drop since 2011. Indonesia ranked second after India suffered drops in 2014 and 2015 before a recovery in 2016. Philippines, Pakistan, and Egypt showed a steady progress.

As for the lower middle-income economies grouping in regard to design count in applications and registrations between 2011 and 2016, the findings displayed a mixed picture in relation to the total number of design count both in applications and registrations. India and Morocco are the only countries where numbers are stable between 2011 and 2016, as regards both design count in applications and registrations.

In respect to the lower middle-income economies grouping as for patent applications and patent grants between 2011 and 2016, the findings revealed that India has been the only country in this income grouping to receive more than 40,000 patent applications from 2011 to 2016. India maintained the lead in respect to patent grants but with a narrow margin or gap on the Philippines.

As regards upper-middle-income economies grouping in relation to the trademark class count in applications and registrations between 2011 and 2016, the findings confirmed the great performance of China ranked number one, not only with regard to the same income grouping but also towards all income economies. China was able to double the trademark class count numbers in five years in both applications and registrations. In the same income grouping, Turkey, the Russian Federation, Brazil, and Mexico performed well with more than 100,000 trademark class count in applications and registrations annually.

Regarding the upper-middle-income economies grouping with regard to design count in applications and registrations between 2011 and 2016, the findings demonstrated that all selected countries under this income grouping suffered drops on design count in applications between 2011 and 2016, with no exception. China is the leading country in both design count in applications and registrations.

In relation to the upper-middle-income economies grouping as regards patent applications and patent grants between 2011 and 2016 the findings showed the continuous growth of China in both patent applications and patents grants in the consecutive years (2011–2016). Despite some drops, Brazil, Iran, Mexico, and the Russian Federation performed well between 2011 and 2016 as long as patent applications are concerned. As to patent grants, Brazil and Turkey performed below the expectation.

Concerning high-income economies grouping in regard to trademark class count in applications and registrations between 2011 and 2016, the findings confirmed the remarkable performance of Korea. Singapore experienced a steady growth with no drop on trademark class count in registrations between 2011 and 2016.

As long as the high-income economies grouping is concerned with regard to design count in applications and registrations between 2011 and 2016 the findings displayed the continuous good performance of Korea by maintaining the lead in respect to the same income economies, despite a few drops.

With regard to the high-income economies grouping concerning patent applications and patent grants between 2011 and 2016 the findings confirmed the lead of Korea with high score between 2011 and 2016. It should also be pointed out the good performance of Singapore.

Non-technological innovations have been illustrated through case studies and success stories in diverse domains taking place in the developing world, such as innovation in the service sector, innovation in agro-industry, and innovation in the area of traditional knowledge. Each success story has been dealt under its appropriate sector or industry as follows: Trademark as an Innovation Indicator: The Havaianas brand of rubber flip-flop sandals, Brazil; Bio Mada, Madagascar; Dry Bath, South Africa; Booomers International, Ghana; Innovation in the Service Sector: DataStream Technology Sdn Bhd (DST), Brunei Darussalam; theSOFTtribe Limited (SOFT), Ghana; Beauty Gems Group Co., Ltd., Thailand; Innovation in Agro-Industry: Javara, Indonesia; Pecuaria Development Cooperative Inc., PDCI, Philippines; Asociacion De Productores De Maiz Blanco Gigante Del Cusco, Peru; TopFruit, Pink Lady, South Africa; Sunny Isle Jamaican Black Castor Oil, Jamaica

Innovation in the Area of Traditional Knowledge (TK): Himalayan Bio Trade Private Limited (HBTL), Nepal; Inaya Zanzibar, Tanzania; Tropical Botanical Garden and Research Institute (TBGRI), India.

Success stories from the developing world relating to IP branding in the following areas have been highlighted: Global branding strategies, local branding strategies, branding in coffee/tea industry, branding in food industry, branding in cosmetic industry, and branding in various sectors.

As it has been seen, some of the most known brands from the developing world have a long history in their developments to reach their current level of recognition. Among these examples or success stories, to illustrate a few of them there are Café de Colombia of Colombia, Egyptian Cotton of Egypt, Ethiopian Coffee of Ethiopia, Pure Fiji of Fiji, Darjeeling Tea of India, Jamaica Blue Mountain Coffee of Jamaica, Panama Blue Spring Water of Panama, Jollibee Foods of the Philippines, Malée Cosmetics of South Africa and Chocolate Mamas of Tanzania.

Brands boost innovation. First, in order to exist, a brand must cultivate its own identity, must differentiate itself. Innovation is a powerful means of achieving that. A degree of novelty is required for a brand to become innovative. The capacity for an enterprise to read the needs of the market and innovate new ways to respond to them is a big challenge that any serious and innovative enterprise is obliged to go throughout.

In the global market, the "uniqueness" in terms of products or marketing methods may be a plus and may provide a competitive advantage vis-à-vis competitors, including the big ones. Some enterprises and their products started by being local before imposing themselves to the world market. Branding of local products may be preferable than imitating external products or strategies. In the areas of cosmetics and traditional knowledge, including traditional designs, the developing world has the knowledge to offer to the world. Branding innovation should become a new business approach that may enable further innovations.

In the current world, specifically in the near future, no innovation will last if it is not branded. This is true both in the areas of technological and non-technological innovations. In the same line of reasoning, branding activities will gain more and more importance to become the main route for an innovation to reach the market. It is in the view of the author that branding may also contribute to fighting against misappropriation of traditional knowledge, unless the traditional knowledge is deemed secret. As illustrated through success stories, in the area of agro-sector, cosmetics and textile, traditional knowledge has tremendously contributed to the global value chain that no honest person would deny.

To illustrate the importance of branding for innovations the "One Village, One Product (OVOP)" known also as "One Town, One Product" Model was scrutinized first before suggesting some slight amendments of the major principles to include the innovation dimension in the process, to be renamed "One Town, One Innovation (OTOI)." OVOP/OTOP/OTOI model is presented as an option that the developing world may explore to brand on the one hand their products given its early success in a number of countries in Asia, including Thailand, Malaysia, China and Philippines, and also on the other hand to set it as a tool inducing innovations, both technological and non-technological.

From the same perspectives, the recent success story of Patanjali Ayurved Limited, an Indian consumer goods company, expanding its business through strong branding strategy of local products, promoting the uses of traditional knowledge in general and local know-how in particular, may well illustrate the multifaceted aspects of both branding and innovation.

To sum up, through lessons learned from case studies and success stories with regard to both innovation and branding, it is recommended that the innovation be adapted to the taste of consumers to respond to their current needs in order to fill the gap in the market. Good marketing strategies adapted to the social environment where products would be launched should be considered. Moreover, empowering locals to take care of their destiny by creating a supporting environment for business would be a plus for the whole economy and trade. From the developing world perspectives, the availability of natural material, such as plants, herbs may serve as a comparative advantage to produce products which are entirely organic. For enterprises aiming to be present at the global market, building strategic partnerships may be the way to go.

Finally, brands must always be innovative to prevent brand fatigue on the eyes of consumers who may be attempted to look for another innovative brand.

# Index

www.ingramcontent.com/pod-product-compliance
Ingram Content Group UK Ltd.
Pitfield, Milton Keynes, MK11 3LW, UK
UKHW011019180926
475701UK00004B/829

*9781032241173*

vices Act of 1991, local authorities in Norway were permitted to institute work requirements as a condition of eligibility for social assistance. As Dahl and Dropping (chapter 9) explain, this reform reflected a renewed emphasis on work and activity as opposed to the provision of passive aid. However, they note that there has been considerable variance in implementation, with recent figures showing workfare programs operated by only 25 percent of local social assistance administrations. Similarly, as public expenditure on social assistance nearly doubled during the first half of the 1990s in Sweden, reforms were initiated to qualify the social right to cash assistance; thus, the Uppsala model (named after Sweden's fifth largest municipality) required applicants for public aid to search actively for employment and to confer with social welfare officers and employment counselors in developing individual career plans. As in Norway, however, Hort (chapter 8) reports that the Swedish approach to workfare in public assistance was confined to a relatively small percent of the municipalities.

Just as public assistance reforms are incorporating behavioral incentives and work requirements in efforts to activate welfare recipients, the trend in unemployment policy has been to forge closer ties between the cash benefits of unemployment compensation and measures to promote employment. Even the semantics have changed. In Australia "unemployment benefits" have become a "Job Search Allowance" for the short-termed unemployed (Eardley, 1997). The changes in unemployment policies are more evident in Europe than the U.S. because European unemployment compensation schemes tend to offer benefits that are comparatively higher, last longer, and are often available to teenagers with no work record. Thus, according to the previous work record, the period of coverage by unemployment insurance ranges from around five months to two years in Germany, between three months and five years in France, and six months to five years in the Netherlands (Van Langendonk, 1997). These relatively generous arrangements create less of an incentive for recipients to seek work than in the U.S., where benefits are usually limited to six months (with an extension of 13 weeks in states where the unemployment rate is high) and provide a relatively low replacement rate; in 1993, for example, the average weekly benefit amount in the U.S. was 37 percent of the average weekly covered wage (U.S. House of Representatives, 1994).

In the United Kingdom, as Judge (chapter 1) indicates, the Work Trials program introduced in 1993 is one of various reforms underway to promote a more active approach to unemployment policy. Devised to help jump-start work opportunities for people unemployed for six months, the program involves three-week trial periods during which participants continue to receive unemployment benefits while being placed in jobs, providing labor for which employers do not have to pay any wages. After the trial period both parties decide whether the worker will continue to stay on as a regular employee. In 1998, the New Labor government expressed its intention to advance work-oriented initiatives through a series of "New Deals"—programs designed for different groups of unemployed people. Initial measures have been concentrated on the unemployed, aged 18 to 24, who have been continuously out of work and collecting benefits for six months and those aged 25+ who have been claiming benefits for two years. These New Deal programs involve mandatory participation in several months of work-readiness and job-search activities conducted through the Employment Service and partner agencies. Participants who do not find unsubsidized jobs during the initial phase are offered various options including six months of subsidized employment and full-time enrollment in education and training courses.

Although not as extensive as the British reforms, Merrien (chapter 7) notes that Switzerland also made a major shift in unemployment policy introducing requirements for mandatory participation of the unemployed in active labor-market programs. In 1995 Swiss legislation reduced entitlement to passive unemployment benefits from 400 to 150 days, after which recipients are required to work in temporary job programs created by the Cantons. Along similar lines, Italy's law 223 of 1991 introduced expressed limits on eligibility for unemployment benefits and their duration. For example, to qualify for benefits, unemployed workers are required to attend training programs or to perform socially useful jobs. However, as Fargion (chapter 2) reveals, in the process of implementation the new measures binding the unemployed to a more active orientation have been substantially loosened, if not completely unfastened. Despite the attenuation that marked law 223's course from policy to practice, Fargion sees the law as representing an important change in the framework of Italian social policy, the implications of which have not yet been fully realized.

As evidenced by these various efforts at welfare reform, over the last decade there has been a conspicuous alteration in the policy framework for social protection of unemployed people in modern welfare states. This book analyzes the recent flourish of diverse policy initiatives to activate the unemployed in nine countries—Britain, France, Italy, the Netherlands, New Zealand, Norway, Sweden, Switzerland, and the United States. The studies of these countries each provide a systematic account of the background, design, implementation, and results of employment-oriented measures, allowing us to compare their organized responses to common problems. In illuminating these national experiences, the chapters that follow seek to broaden our perspective on the policy options, the issues raised and lessons learned in the course of activating the unemployed.

## References

Eardley, Tony. (1997) "New Relations of Welfare in the Contracting State: The Marketisation of Services for the Unemployed in Australia," Social Policy Research Center Discussion Paper 79. SPRC, University of New South Wales.

International Social Security Association. (1989) "Developments and Trends in Social Security 1978-1989," *International Social Security Review* (3/89).

Kalisch, David. (1991) "The Active Society," *Social Security Journal* (August).

Marklund, S. (1992) "The decomposition of social policy in Sweden." *Scandinavian Journal of Social Welfare* 1:1 (July).

Danziger, Sheldon, Robert Moffitt and LaDonna Pavetti. (1999) *Is Welfare Reform Working? The Impact of Economic Growth and Policy Changes: A Congressional Briefing*.
Washington D.C.: Consortium of Social Science Associations.

Organization for Economic Cooperation and Development. (1988) "The Future of Social Protection: The General Debate," in *The Future of Social Protection*. Paris: OECD.

OECD. (1989) "Editorial: The Path to Full Employment: Structural Adjustment for an Active Society," *Employment Outlook* (July).

Torfing , Jacob. (1997) "From the Keynesian Welfare State to a Schumpeterian Workfare Regime—the Offensive Neo-Statist Case of Denmark." Paper presented at the 9th International Conference on Socio-Economics, Montreal, Canada, July 5-7.

U.S. House of Representatives. (1994) *Overview of Entitlement Programs: 1994 Green Book.* Washington D.C.: Government Printing Office.

Van Langendonck, Jef. (1997) "The Social Protection of the Unemployed," *International Social Security Review* 50:4, pp. 29-43.

# 1

# Evaluating Welfare to Work in the United Kingdom

*Ken Judge*

## Introduction

Although Britain experienced several years of sustained economic growth during the mid- to late-1990s it continues to face a number of serious employment problems, some of a deep and long-standing nature. First, the second half of the twentieth century has witnessed a marked gender difference in employment trends. Whereas female participation in the labor market has steadily increased there has been a marked reduction in employment levels among men. A comparison with the employment rate for men in 1951 suggests that there may be as many as 1.5 million men, aged between 25 and 49, who are not working as the millenium approaches and who could be in employment. Secondly, there remains a hard core of long-term unemployment especially among young people and members of many ethnic minority groups. Unemployment rates often exceed 20 percent among these groups and they can easily reach 50 percent and more in the most disadvantaged parts of the country. Thirdly, there has been a dramatic increase in the numbers of people entirely dependent on state benefits and who have lost all contact with the labor market. For example, one million single parents, nearly all of whom are women, are not in work. Similarly, approaching 2 million people, mainly men, are dependent on long-term sickness or incapacity benefits. The size of both of these groups has doubled since the late 1980s.

In response to these and related problems there has been a growing interest in the UK in what are generally described as welfare to work or active employment policies. There is nothing particularly new about the adoption of such policies to address the economic and social costs of long-term unemployment. Prior to 1997 the Thatcher and Major governments invested considerable amounts of political capital in promoting welfare to work policies. But there has been a dramatic change in the ordering of political priorities since Tony Blair's landslide election victory in 1997. Welfare reform in general and welfare to work in particular are at the very center of New Labour's domestic policy agenda.

Alan Deacon (1998) suggests that welfare to work strategies have three main goals. First, to increase job opportunities for those reliant on social security benefits by providing employment subsidies, creating new jobs or offering training and work experience schemes. Secondly, to change the characteristics and motivation of long-term welfare recipients through the provision of a range of advice and counseling services and training and development opportunities. Finally, to reform the structure of the tax and benefit system so that welfare claimants have clearer incentives to take advantage of work opportunities. To varying extents all three of these distinct aspects of a welfare to work strategy can be found among changes implemented or planned by the Blair government since 1997. However, before turning to a review of the main features of New Labour's welfare to work strategy it is important to consider what relevant research evidence was available in the UK at the time of the 1997 general election.

## Evaluating Welfare-to-Work in the Mid-1990s

The best available study of British experience with welfare to work schemes prior to Labour's election victory in 1997 was commissioned by the Joseph Rowntree Foundation. Karen Gardiner's *Bridges from Benefit to Work: A Review* (1997) identifies 42 schemes for evaluation. The basis of the selection of such schemes is described below.

> In theory welfare-to-work is any policy intervention that encourages or facilitates a transition from benefits to paid employment. In practice this could cover a vast range of issues, from provision of nursery places to subsidised public transport. The approach in this paper is to include all designated welfare-to-work schemes currently being operated by the UK Government under the auspices of the Department of Social Security, the Department for Education and Employment and the Employment Service. Hence policies are only included that have getting people into work as a prime objective. (Gardiner, 1997, p. 2)

The 42 welfare-to-work schemes identified by Gardiner are listed by eight different categories in table 1.1. A large number of the schemes reflect different levels of investment in *education and training*, with a particular emphasis on youth training schemes and apprenticeships together with various initiatives to relax regulations about benefit entitlement whilst studying. Such schemes directly address employment problems associated with lack of educational qualifications, skills and experience. The second group of 12 initiatives are focused on *job search assistance*. These are intended to improve job search skills and knowledge about vacancies as well as providing practical assistance in the form of access to computers and telephones. The third category includes three schemes aimed at providing financial *incentives to employers* by providing tax exemptions, wage subsidies or the continuation of out-of-work benefits for an initial period of employment. Such schemes can directly lower labor costs and so stimulate demand for workers or they can help to overcome uncertainty among employers about the advisability of giving particular workers an opportunity to prove themselves in a real work situation. The next category of *public job creation* is much more rare in modern Britain, although there are still some examples of attempts to establish new jobs for this purpose especially in the public and voluntary sectors. *Out-of-work benefits* are perhaps somewhat surprisingly included in Gardiner's classification for three reasons. First, she argues that benefit claimants have to meet strict criteria about looking for work to qualify for benefits. Secondly, many of the other schemes shown in table 1.1 such as education, training and job assistance are "hung" on the framework of benefit receipt. Finally, the actual structure of the benefits themselves are an important part of the set of incentives and disincentives that influence transitions into and out of employment. The next category of *in-work benefits* is much more clear-cut.

The main aim of these schemes is to provide direct incentives to low-paid workers, especially those with high child care or housing costs. *Assistance with job-related costs* is a potentially very important category because they do have an important influence on the perception of "reservation wages" among those seeking work. However, Gardiner identifies only one example; the child care disregard. The final category relates to *transitional financial assistance* and a number of specific and self-explanatory examples are shown in table 1.1.

**Table 1.1**
**Typology of Welfare-to-Work Schemes**

| Education/ Training | Job Search Assistance | Incentives/ Requirements for Employer | Public Job Creation | Out-of-work Benefits | In-work Benefits | Assistance with Job-Related Costs | Transitional Financial Assistance |
|---|---|---|---|---|---|---|---|
| Training for Work | Restart Interviews | Employers' National Insurance Contributions Holiday | Project Work (p) | Jobseeker's Allowance (JSA)/ Income Support | Family Credit/ Disability Working Allowance | Child Care Disregard | Run-on of Housing Benefit/Council Tax Benefit |
| Youth Training | Restart Courses | Workstart (p) | | JSA/Unemploy-ment Benefit | Full-time Credit in Family Credit | | Faster Family Credit |
| Youth Credits | Jobplan Workshops | Work Trials | | Income Support | Earnings Top-up (p) | | Back to Work Bonus |
| Modern Apprenticeships | Job Search Seminars | | | Housing Benefit | Jobmatch | | Child Maintenance Bonus |
| Career Development Loans | Job Review Interviews and Workshops | | | Council Tax Benefit | Housing Benefit | | Jobfinder's Grant |
| Career Development Loans Plus | Travel to Interview Scheme | | | | Council Tax Benefit | | |
| Workskill (p) | Jobclubs | | | | | | |
| Pre-vocational Program (p) | Workwise | | | | | | |
| Other forms of studying while on benefits | Job Interview Guarantee | | | | | | |
| | 1-2-1 | | | | | | |
| | Parent Plus (p) | | | | | | |
| | Contract for Work (p) | | | | | | |

Note: (p) = pilot scheme
*Source:* Gardiner (1997)

The main aim of the Gardiner review is to synthesize evidence about the success of the 42 welfare to work schemes that were in place in Britain in 1997. This proved to be very difficult. Decent evaluation data was and remains in very short supply. Nevertheless, wherever possible Gardiner tried to obtain information about additionality, take-up and net costs for each scheme. Further information about her evaluation criteria is shown in box 1.1.

It is relatively easy to collect data about the number of participants and the total investment made in each of the welfare-to-work schemes. Unfortunately, it is much harder to obtain information about additionality and even more difficult to estimate the savings associated with successfully getting "additional workers" into employment. Of the 42 schemes reviewed by Gardiner, only 9 lend themselves to a very crude attempt at estimating the annual unit gross cost per additional person in work. These results are summarized in table 1.2.

**Box 1.1**
**Evaluation Criteria for Welfare-to-Work Schemes**

**Additionality** — the success of the scheme in helping people to find work; this is the percentage of participants who find a job who would not have done so without the welfare-to-work program.

**Take-up** — the scope of the scheme to assist people into employment; this is the proportion of the population who choose to take part in the program.

**Net costs** — the cost of getting someone into work under each scheme. The measurement of *gross costs* per "additional worker" requires information on unit costs and additionality for each scheme. To calculate the *net costs* of welfare-to-work, the *savings* need to be taken into account. These include improved tax take and reductions in benfit expenditure for the government and, in addition, there are a wide range of potential gains for the economy and society. The amount of savings for government depends on the wages that the "additional workers" are paid and how long they remain in employment. Wider gains are determined by a much broader range of factors.

Source: Gardiner, 1997, pp. vii-viii.

**Table 1.2**
**Welfare-to-Work Schemes: Value for Money and Additionality**

| Scheme | Annual Unit cost (£) | Additionality | Annual unit cost per | | Additional person in work | |
|---|---|---|---|---|---|---|
| | | | £1,000 to £3,000 | £3,000 to £6,000 | £6,000 to £10,000 | £40,000 plus |
| **Education/training** | | | | | | |
| Training for Work | 1,444[1] | 3% | | | | ∘ |
| **Job search assistance** | | | | | | |
| Jobplan Workshops | 104 | 2% | | ∘ | | |
| Jobclubs | 172 | 4% | | ∘ | | |
| Workwise | 195 | 2% | | | ∘ | |
| 1-2-1 | 64 | 2% | | ∘ | | |
| Travel to Interview | 42 | 3% | ∘ | | | |
| **Incentives/requirementsfor employers** | | | | | | |
| Workstart (pilot) | 1,250 | 17% | | | ∘ | |
| **In-work benefits** | | | | | | |
| Jobmatch | 1,667 | 28% | | ∘ | | |
| **Transitional financial assistance** | | | | | | |
| Jobfinder's Grant | 200 | 8% | ∘ | | | |

Notes:

I. Figures for Training are based on evaluation of predecessor scheme, Employment Training.

II. Additionality estimates are not completely consistent. Estimates for Workstart and Jobmatch represent proportions of participants who took work under the scheme who otherwise would not have done so. Estimates for Travel to Interview and Jobfinder's Grant represent proportions of participants who found work due to this assistance who otherwise would not have done so. Estimates for Training for Work (one year), Jobplan Workshops (four months), Jobclubs (five months) Workwise (four months) and 1-2-1 (six months) are the proportions of participants who entered employment as a result of the skills/assistance provided by the scheme, as measured in evaluations at some time (given in brackets) after completion of the scheme.

1. The unit cost figures for Training for Work are adjusted to exclude the element of costs that covers benefit entitlement. This provides for a fair comparison with other schemes where the costs do not include benefits received.

Source: Gardiner (1997)

In many respects the estimates shown in table 1.2 should be regarded as "heroic guesstimates." There are a number of important caveats in respect to each of them. For example, the very high costs associated with training and education reflect the fact that the benefits in terms of additional workers may take some years to show. A key issue for evaluation concerns the length of time over which additionality should be measured. Nevertheless, the data in table 1.2 do serve to provide a broad indication of the *initial* costs and benefits associated with British welfare-to-work schemes in the mid-1990s. Perhaps the most important finding is that overall welfare–to-work schemes do appear to have a significant impact in assisting people to move from benefits to paid employment. However, they do not help very much in providing good policy guidance about the relative cost-effectiveness of different schemes. It is clear that a continued emphasis on welfare-to-work must place a greater premium on the design and collection of better data for evaluation. One attempt to do this that was published after the completion of Gardiner's review, and which is regarded as a particularly successful example of a British welfare-to-work scheme, can be used to illustrate both what is required in terms of research design and also the continuing difficulties that can arise.

## Work Trials

The Work Trials program is the responsibility of the Employment Service, which "is responsible for operating a wide range of labor market services in Britain, some of which are available to all job seekers, while others are restricted to unemployed people or to others meeting eligibility criteria" (White et al., 1997, p. 1). A brief description of what a Work Trial provides and what its potential benefits might be is shown in box 1.2.

There are a number of ways in which Work Trials ought to be able to contribute to making the labor market more effective. The fact that unemployed participants are selected by Jobcenter staff reduces the search costs faced by employers. This should increase the number of vacancies that are notified. Secondly, it is widely believed that one problem faced by the long-term unemployed in the labor market is the notion that they have low work capability, a view which is held by many employers. The Work Trials gives the long-term unemployed claimant an opportunity to demonstrate that this belief is not a valid one at relatively little cost to the employer. There is also the problem that people who have experienced long-term unemployment can lose work-related confidence, which might make them reluctant to apply for jobs. Work Trials help to overcome this particular difficulty because participants are placed in Work Trials vacancies directly by Jobcenter staff, thus avoiding the need to rely on or go through conventional application and interview procedures. In general, White et al. (1997) suggest that "these factors should lead to a reduction in unemployment and an increase in employment as a result of the program" (p. 15).

The evaluation of the Work Trials program was based on a matched comparison group design. Data were collected on two samples: an intervention group and a set of controls matched in a number of important respects. The intervention group consisted of all individuals admitted to the program in May-June 1994 at 250 selected Jobcenters. The comparison group was selected from Employment Service data about individuals in each region based on gender, age group and duration of current unemployment episode. Both samples were interviewed at the end of 1994, i.e., approximately six months after the intervention group was admitted to the program. One problem that arose immediately was that the response rate among the comparison group (47 percent) was substantially lower than among the intervention group (64 percent). Moreover, there were statistically significant differences in the characteristics of the two samples. For example, Work Trials participants had lower reservation wages, more recent contact with the Employment Service and a higher probability that their spouses were in paid employment. All of these factors might have been expected to increase the employment chances of people in the intervention group.

One of the key findings to emerge from the evaluation of the Work Trials program is that after six months 59 percent of the intervention group reported that they had a job compared with only 25 percent of the control group. This result strongly suggests that the Work Trials program is successful. However, from a theoretical point of view a slightly different comparison is required. What is required is to calculate the employment rate for participants with the particular set of characteristics most representative of the sample as a whole, and then compare this with the employment rate for individuals with the identical characteristics who did not take part in the program. On this basis, the Work Trials program is estimated to increase the chances of employment by 34-40 percentage points, "a result which (to the best of our knowledge) has no parallel in previous studies of national market programmes" (White et al., 1997, p. 123).

However, there are at least two important qualifications about the results that need to be borne in mind. First, the findings relate to a six-month period of follow-up. Are these a good indication of what might be expected in terms of medium-to-long-term outcomes? Secondly, the findings from this study may prove to be highly context specific. "An obvious question, for example, is whether Work Trials could be extended to a larger number of participants, with a similarly positive effect on employment chances" (White et al., 1997, p. 124). Nevertheless, whatever the answers to these and related questions, the most important point to make is that welfare-to-work was perceived to be successful.

**Box 1.2**
**Work Trials**

Work Trials are designed to increase the employment chances of people who have experienced a continuous period of six months' unemployment. Introduced in 1993-94, the program had 20,000 places available in 1994-95. The Work Trials consists of a period of up to three weeks in which an unemployed person is placed in a job notified to Jobcenter staff by an employer registered under this program. During this time, the job seeker continues to receive benefits and is also compensated for travel and meal expenses where appropriate. The employer receives the services of a worker without having to pay a wage. At the completion of the three-week "trial" period, either participant can decide that the job should end. In the case of the unemployed person, this would mean that his unemployment claim would be treated as uninterrupted. If both sides agree to the continuation of the job, the claimant signs off the register and is taken on as an employee.

The main criteria taken into account by Jobcenter staff in recommending unemployed people for participation in the program are set out below:

- A checkable work history
- Qualifications or experience relevant to the types of job available through Work Trials and a desire to work in such jobs
- Possessing a telephone at home and being able to come into the Jobcenter at short notice
- Being highly motivated and job-ready, that is, not in need of the types of skills taught in Jobclubs
- Registered unemployed for at least the previous six months.

Source: White et al., 1997, pp. 13-15.

At the time that the Blair government was being elected, a range of evidence was becoming available in Britain that lent support to the notion that active employment policies could make a positive contribution to improving the employment chances of people experiencing long-term unemployment. This helps to explain the renewed emphasis on welfare to work adopted by New Labour.

## New Labour

In March 1998 the Blair government published a consultative paper on welfare reform (Cm 3805, 1998) that set out a number of key principles that ought to guide the future development and adaptation of the British welfare state. The first of these principles emphasized the central importance of work. "The new welfare state should help and encourage people of working age to work where they are capable of doing so" (Cm 3805, 1998, p. 2). Starting from this principle the government set itself the task of rebuilding the welfare state around work. It aims to do this in five main ways (Cm 3805, 1998, p. 23):

- Helping people move from welfare to work through the New Deals and Employment Zones;
- Developing flexible personalized services to help people into work;
- Lowering the barriers to work for those who can and want to work;
- Making work pay, by reforming the tax and benefit system, including a Working Families Tax Credit, reforming National Insurance and income tax, and introducing the national minimum wage; and
- Ensuring that responsibilities and rights are fairly matched.

The government aims to monitor progress and invest in substantial evaluation of new initiatives and it has clearly identified the success measures by which it will be judged in due course (see box 1.3).

It is clear that the Blair government has embarked on a very ambitious agenda of social reform and many of its new policy initiatives are expected to have beneficial consequences in terms of increasing employment opportunities. However, two strands of policy development are probably the most significant. The first is a series of "New Deals" for particular groups where long-term unemployment is regarded as especially serious. The second element reflects a more general commitment to "making work pay."

**Box 1.3**
**Success Measures for Work-Related Policies**

1. A reduction in the proportion of working-age people living in workless households.
2. A reduction in the proportion of working-age people out of work for more than two years.
3. An increase in the number of working-age people in work.
4. An increase in the proportion of single parents, people with a long-term illness, and disabled people of working age in touch with the labor market.

Source: Cm 3805, 1998, p. 31.

**Box 1.4**
**New Deal for Young People**

**Eligibility**
Those aged 18 to 24 who have been unemployed and claiming Jobseekers Allowance (JSA) continuously for six months become eligible for New Deal when they reach the six-month threshold. At that point their participation is mandatory. Those who have already been unemployed for six months are required to enter New Deal when they reach their next six-monthly Restart interview date, but are entitled to request immediate entry before then. A number of groups who are at particularly high risk of social exclusion are entitled to entry to New Deal before the six-month point.

**Outline of Process**
Those joining New Deal first enter a Gateway period lasting up to four months, during which the Employment Service and their partners will work with them to improve their employability, and to find unsubsidized jobs for as many as possible. Those who do not find a job will then move on to one of four options:

1. A period of subsidized employment lasting six months, and including opportunities for self-employment.
2. A course of full-time education or training.
3. A job with an Environment Task Force.
4. A job in the voluntary sector.

As far as possible, young people will be offered a choice of options. They do not however have the option of remaining on JSA. If the client reaches the end of their option, and still has not obtained a job, they will normally reclaim JSA, and will enter a Follow-through period. During this, they will remain on JSA, but receive intensive help to find a job.

Source: DfEE, 1999, Notes for Editors.

## *The New Deals*

The biggest single investment of public expenditure and political capital made by the Blair government during its first phase in office has been made in a large-scale welfare to work program focused on five main groups:

- Young unemployed people
- Long-term unemployed people
- Single parents
- People with a disability or long-term illness
- Partners of the unemployed

To date most of the investment and attention has been concentrated on the first two of these so-called New Deals. Boxes 1.4 and 1.5 summarize the key features of each scheme.

**Box 1.5**
**New Deal for Long-Term Unemployed People**

**Eligibility**
Those aged 25+ who have been claiming JSA continuously for 2 years become eligible for New Deal when they reach the 2-year threshold. At that point, their participation is mandatory. Those who have already been unemployed for 2 years are required to enter New Deal when they reach their next annual Restart interview date, but are entitled to request immediate entry before then. There are a number of additional groups who are entitled to entry to New Deal before reaching the 2-year point.

**Outline of Process**
Those joining New Deal first enter an Advisory Interview Process lasting between 3-6 months with an average of 7 interviews during which Employment Service (ES) and their partners will work with them to improve their employability, and to find unsubsidized jobs for as many as possible. Those who do not find a job may transfer to other provision or move on to one of the two New Deal specific measures:

- a period of subsidized employment, lasting 6 months
- a course of full-time education/training lasting up to a year whilst remaining on JSA

If the client reaches the end of their Advisory Interview Process without taking up an opportunity, they may return to their normal jobseeker activity and will re-enter at their next full-year Restart Interview. A further series of interviews are available as part of the Follow-Through for those returning from subsidized/unsubsidized employment or existing training provision within 13 weeks of leaving JSA/completing the provision, and those completing Education and Training Opportunities.

Source: DfEE, 1999, Notes for Editors.

*Making Work Pay*

The means by which the government intends to "make work pay" include: the introduction of a national minimum wage, reducing the starting rate of income tax and the threshold for national insurance contributions, and the replacement of Family Credit by Working Families' Tax Credit. A brief description of each of these key elements of policy is set out below.

## The National Minimum Wage

One of the most significant of the reforms introduced since the Blair government was elected in May 1997 is the introduction of a national minimum wage. This policy was implemented in April 1999 when the minimum hourly wage for most adult workers was set at £3.60. The minimum wage has great potential to improve the net incomes of low-paid workers and, all other things being equal, it might be expected to have a beneficial incentive effect on encouraging unemployed people to take jobs. However, we do not live in a *ceteris paribus* world. The potential impact of the minimum wage on the demand for labor has been a fiercely contested area of debate and it is simply too early to make an impartial assessment of its consequences.

## Tax Reform

Since its election in May 1997 the Blair government has introduced a large number of tax changes. Some of the most important of these in relation to welfare to work policies were described by the Chancellor of the Exchequer, Gordon Brown, in his budget speech in March 1999:

> Today's Budget encourages a dynamic Britain of enterprise and fairness because for too long governments have taken too much in taxes from people who work hard but are not wealthy, this Budget now reforms tax and benefits and delivers tax cuts that reward work and make work pay for everyone in Britain. Most fundamentally the tax reforms of this Budget provide a better deal for the hard working majority—a ladder of opportunity for those who want to work their way up, a chance to keep more of what they earn and, for all, a fundamental guarantee that work will pay. Our reforms in national insurance will give employers an overall tax cut of 1.5 billion pounds and employees an overall tax cut of 2.5 billion pounds—an average of 130 pounds per year per employee. We said in our manifesto that we would introduce a 10p starting rate of income tax for individuals when it was prudent to do so it will take effect in April 1999, a 10p starting rate on the first 1,500 pounds of income, the lowest starting rate of tax since 1962 (Brown, 1999).

## Working Families' Tax Credit (WFTC)

The working families' tax credit, planned to come into operation in autumn 1999, is a reform of the system of in-work support for working families with children. It will replace the previous system, family credit (FC), which has operated since 1988. Although FC operates through the benefit system and WFTC is planned to operate as a tax credit through the wage packet, the principle behind the operation of both schemes is the same. Families with at least one child and an adult working 16 hours or more per week whose net income falls below a certain "eligible amount" are entitled to a certain amount of benefit which helps top up their earnings. The principal changes that the introduction of WFTC is expected to make to this system of in-work support are the following:

- The credit for each child aged under 11 in the family is to be increased by £2.50 per week.
- The taper threshold is to be raised. The threshold is the amount of net income families can earn before their entitlement to FC or WFTC starts to be reduced. Currently, the FC threshold is £79; for WFTC, it will be raised to £90.
- The taper rate is to be lowered from 70 percent to 55 percent. This means that, for families whose income is above the threshold level, with each extra pound of net income received, the amount of credit paid will fall by 55p rather than by 70p.
- FC is normally paid to the female partner in a couple with children. With WFTC the credit will normally be paid to the principal earner in the household (although couples will be able to nominate the other member of the household to receive the credit if they so desire).
- A childcare credit of up to £150 is expected to be included in the final version of WFTC. Credit will be available to families with two or more children spending £150 or more on childcare per week.

## Assessing the Third Way

It is very early in the life of the Blair government to offer a comprehensive review of its welfare to work policies. Some new initiatives have not yet been implemented and even those that are in place have only been operational for a few months. Nevertheless, there are three useful pieces of evidence available with which to make a tentative assessment of the direction of travel of New Labour. The first of these is a set of largely descriptive statistics about participation in the New Deals for young people and the long-term unemployed people. The second is an assessment of the ways in which the government appears to be addressing the main barriers to work for disadvantaged groups. The third is a policy simulation exercise that attempts to evaluate a number of aspects of the government's emphasis on making work pay.

*New Deal Statistics*

All of the New Deals for unemployed people are relatively new. However, some statistics about two of the New Deals have recently been made available.

*Young People Aged 18 to 24*

Table 1.3 summarizes the numbers entering and leaving New Deal over the eleven months of January to November 1998. The total number participating built up from just over 6,000 at the end of January to over 14,000 at the end of March; since the national roll-out at the beginning of April the total has risen to 125,500 at the end of November. Seventy-three percent of all those joining have been male. Around 13 percent of total entrants to date have been people with a disability. There have been over 27,000 starts from ethnic minority groups, of which one in five are Pakistani, one in three Black African / Caribbean, and one in eight Indian.

Table 1.4 shows where those participating at the end of November were in the New Deal process. As one would expect, with the Gateway period designed to last for up to 4 months from the date of the first New Deal interview, the majority, around two-thirds, were still on the Gateway. Of the 42,300 who were on an option, over half were on the Full-Time Education and Training option, a quarter were on the subsidized Employment option, and the rest were split evenly between the Voluntary Sector and Environment Task Force options. There are now a small number of people in the Follow-Through phase of New Deal, although it is anticipated that some of these will later re-join an option.

Again, there are differences between males and females, between those with disabilities and other participants, and between those from ethnic minority groups and the overall figures. Whilst there is a small difference between males and females in the proportion who have

**Table 1.3**
**18-24 New Deal Summary Figures**
**Great Britain (Thousands)**

| Month | Number on New Deal at month end (4) | | | Number of starts (2) in month | | | Number of leavers (3) in month | | |
|---|---|---|---|---|---|---|---|---|---|
| | Male | Female | Total (4) | Male | Female | Total | Male | Female | Total |
| Jan-98 | 4.5 | 1.6 | 6.3 | 4.7 | 1.8 | 6.6 | 0.2 | 0.1 | 0.4 |
| Feb-98 | 7.5 | 2.6 | 10.3 | 3.6 | 1.2 | 4.8 | 0.5 | 0.2 | 0.8 |
| Mar-98 | 10.3 | 3.6 | 14.2 | 3.5 | 1.3 | 4.9 | 0.7 | 0.3 | 1.1 |
| Apr-98 | 26.2 | 9.2 | 35.8 | 17.2 | 6.1 | 23.5 | 1.3 | 0.5 | 1.9 |
| May-98 | 47.4 | 16.3 | 64.3 | 25.7 | 8.9 | 34.9 | 4.6 | 1.8 | 6.4 |
| Jun-98 | 59.7 | 20.5 | 81.6 | 17.5 | 6.2 | 24.5 | 5.1 | 2.0 | 7.3 |
| Jul-98 | 73.1 | 25.4 | 100.5 | 20.6 | 7.8 | 29.1 | 7.1 | 2.9 | 10.2 |
| Aug-98 | 80.2 | 27.8 | 110.1 | 14.0 | 5.2 | 19.5 | 6.9 | 2.8 | 9.9 |
| Sep-98 | 84.6 | 29.3 | 116.1 | 13.8 | 5.2 | 19.3 | 9.3 | 3.8 | 13.3 |
| Oct-98 | 87.4 | 30.0 | 119.6 | 15.0 | 5.5 | 20.9 | 12.3 | 4.7 | 17.4 |
| Nov-98 | 88.1 | 30.2 | 120.5 | 10.6 | 4.0 | 14.8 | 9.9 | 3.8 | 14.0 |
| **Total** | | | | **146.2** | **53.2** | **203.1** | **58.1** | **23.0** | **82.6** |

Notes:

(1) Figures refer to the last Friday of each month.

(2) Those identified by ES as having joined New Deal, including those who have received an initial invitation but not yet attended their first interview.

(3) Those who have left during Gateway either to go into an unsubsidized job or for some other reason; plus those who have left an option without returning to ES.

(4) Totals include those for whom gender is not recorded. For this reason, and also because of rounding, components will not necessarily sum to totals.

Source: DfEE (1999)

moved onto options, people with disabilities are more likely to be on an option (40 percent against 35 percent overall). People from ethnic minorities are less likely to have moved onto options (29 percent compared to 37 percent for white participants).

Overall, 24 percent of those on options are on the Employer option. Within this, a slightly greater proportion of men than women—but a significantly smaller proportion of people from ethnic minority groups—are on the Employer option. Within ethnic groups, Black Africans are least likely to be on the Employer option (8 percent)—and Indians, Pakistani's and Bangladeshi's most likely (18 percent). People with disabilities are just as likely to be on the Employer option as all participants.

Fifty-two percent of those on options are on the Full-Time Education and Training option. Within this, there are a greater proportion of women (55 percent) than men (50 percent), and a significantly greater proportion of people from ethnic groups (68 percent). People

Table 1.4
Numbers Participating in 18-24 New Deal at End of November 1998
Great Britain (Thousands)

| | | | Options | | | | | |
|---|---|---|---|---|---|---|---|---|
| | Total | Gateway (1) | Total | Employer | Education & Training | Voluntary sector | Environment Task Force | Follow - Through (2) |
| All (3) | 120.5 | 75.8 | 42.27 | 10.00 | 21.77 | 5.54 | 4.96 | 2.39 |
| Male | 88.1 | 55.7 | 30.43 | 7.36 | 15.21 | 3.8 | 4.58 | 1.90 |
| Female | 30.2 | 18.6 | 11.15 | 2.51 | 6.15 | 2.17 | 0.32 | 0.47 |
| People with disabilities | 16.9 | 9.7 | 6.80 | 1.55 | 3.46 | 1.05 | 0.74 | 0.37 |
| People from ethnic minority groups (4) | 16.5 | 11.6 | 4.81 | 0.71 | 3.28 | 0.62 | 0.19 | 0.18 |

Notes:
(1) Including those awaiting their first Gateway interview.
(2) Individuals join the Follow-Through stage only after completing their New Deal option. With all options designed to last six months or more, there will be very few in this stage of the New Deal process.
(3) Totals include those for whom gender is not recorded. For this reason, and also because of rounding, components will not necessarily sum to totals.
(4) Excluding those who, when asked their ethnic origin, were recorded as "Prefer not to say."

Source: DfEE (1999)

with disabilities are just as likely to be on the Full-Time Education and Training option as all participants.

Table 1.5 shows the immediate destinations of the 127,300 young people who have left the New Deal Gateway. These are made up of 77,200 who left the New Deal altogether and 50,100 who left to take up an option. Of those who left the New Deal altogether, 37,300 are known to have gone into an unsubsidized job. A further 17,100 went into other known destinations—mainly transfers to other benefits, but also, for example, starts on training courses. Of those whose destination is not known, a proportion will have gone into jobs, but have not been recorded as such in the systems which generate the data. In total, nearly 50,000 have gone into jobs from the Gateway, three-quarters of those being unsubsidized jobs.

**Table 1.5**
**Numbers Leaving Gateway by Immediate Destination (1)**
**Great Britain (Thousands)**

| | | | Options | | | | | Other | | |
|---|---|---|---|---|---|---|---|---|---|---|
| Quarter/ Month of leaving | Total | Unsubsidised employment (2) | Total | Employer | Education & Training | Voluntary sector | Environment Task Force | Transfer to other benefits | Other (3) | Not known (4) |
| Jan-Mar 98 | 3.3 | 1.08 | 1.10 | 0.62 | 0.36 | 0.07 | 0.05 | 0.29 | 0.19 | 0.64 |
| Apr-Jun 98 | 21.5 | 8.02 | 6.26 | 3.12 | 2.11 | 0.57 | 0.46 | 1.71 | 0.93 | 4.61 |
| Jul- Sep 98 | 56.5 | 15.15 | 24.61 | 5.51 | 14.22 | 2.51 | 2.37 | 4.00 | 3.68 | 9.12 |
| Oct 98 | 26.3 | 7.45 | 10.62 | 1.96 | 5.03 | 1.85 | 1.79 | 2.02 | 1.69 | 4.52 |
| Nov 98 | 19.6 | 5.62 | 7.53 | 1.28 | 3.40 | 1.50 | 1.36 | 1.62 | 0.95 | 3.87 |
| **Total** | **127.3** | **31.37** | **50.12** | **12.49** | **25.11** | **6.49** | **6.02** | **9.63** | **7.45** | **22.76** |

Notes:

(1) Includes those leaving before receipt of a first interview.

(2) Those who are recorded by ES as having been placed into unsubsidized employment, plus those who are recorded as having terminated their JS claim in order to go into a job. This will undercount the total number going into a job: some who go into a job will not, for whatever reason, record this as the reason for the termination of their JSA claim. These will be counted as "not known." Past research indicates that the destinations of those who do not give a reason for termination follow a similar pattern to those who do give a reason. As further data are added, the numbers going into jobs in recent months may be revised upwards.

(3) Includes for example transfer to a training program, gone abroad.

(4) Where there is no leaving code recorded on JUVOS, or where the leaving code is recorded as "not known," or simply "ceased claiming" or "failed to attend." As more data are added, the numbers in this category may be revised downwards for recent months.

Source: DfEE (1999)

## Long-Term Unemployed People Aged 25+

Table 1.6 summarizes the numbers entering and leaving New Deal over the five months of July to November 1998. The total number participating built up from 13,100 at the end of July to 60,100 at the end of November. Eighty-four percent of all those joining have been male. Nineteen percent of total entrants to date have been people with a disability. There have been nearly 6,000 starts from ethnic minority groups. In common with the New Deal for young people, females are slightly more likely than males to have left New Deal by the end of November: 17 percent of all females who started in July to November have left, against 15 percent of males.

Table 1.7 shows where those participating at the end of November were in the New Deal process. As one would expect, with the Advisory Interview Process designed to last for 3-6 months from the date of the first New Deal Interview, the majority, around 93 percent, are still on it. The remainder were on a New Deal specific measure: 1,300 on the Employer Subsidy and 990 on Education and Training Opportunities; 1,960 are on Work Based Training for Adults.

**Table 1.6**
**25+ New Deal Summary Figures**
**Great Britain (Thousands)**

| | Number on New Deal at month end (1) | | | Number of starts (2) in month | | | Number of leavers (3) in month | | |
|---|---|---|---|---|---|---|---|---|---|
| Month | Male | Female | Total (4) | Male | Female | Total | Male | Female | Total |
| Jul-98 | 11.0 | 2.0 | 13.1 | 11.4 | 2.1 | 13.6 | .4 | .1 | .5 |
| Aug-98 | 20.6 | 3.9 | 24.6 | 10.7 | 2.0 | 12.8 | 1.0 | .2 | 1.2 |
| Sep-98 | 29.3 | 5.4 | 35.0 | 10.5 | 2.0 | 12.5 | 1.8 | .4 | 2.2 |
| Oct-98 | 41.5 | 7.5 | 49.3 | 14.7 | 2.7 | 17.4 | 2.5 | .6 | 3.1 |
| Nov-98 | 50.5 | 9.2 | 60.1 | 12.0 | 2.3 | 14.5 | 3.0 | .6 | 3.7 |
| **Total** | | | | **59.2** | **11.1** | **70.9** | **8.7** | **1.9** | **10.7** |

Notes:

(1) Figures refer to the last Friday of each month.

(2) Those identified by ES as having joined New Deal, including those who have received an initial invitation but not yet attended their first interview.

(3) Those who have completed the Advisory interview Process and not taken up an opportunity, plus those who have left JSA for reasons other than starting on the Employer subsidy or other provision. Subsequent data may be revised upwards as leavers from WBTZ/TfW and current ES provision are monitored.

(4) Totals include those for whom gender is not recorded. For this reason, and also because of rounding, components will not necessarily sum to totals.

Source: DfEE (1999)

People with disabilities and those from ethnic minority groups are just as likely to have moved onto a New Deal specific measure, or be on Work Based Training for Adults.

Table 1.8 shows the immediate destinations of the 15,000 people who have left the Advisory Interview Process. Twenty-eight percent have left for employment (2,800 unsubsidized and 1,400 subsidized), 7 percent for Education and Training Opportunities, 13 percent for Work Based Training for Adults, 10 percent to normal jobseeker activity, and 42 percent for other reasons. Men are slightly more likely to have left for subsidized employment than women; but no more likely to have left for unsubsidized employment. Conversely, women are more likely to have left to transfer to another benefit.

**Table 1.7**
**Numbers Participating in 25+ New Deal at End of November 1998**
**Great Britain (Thousands)**

| Total | Advisory Interview Process (1) | | Employer Subsidy | Education & Training Opportunities | Work Based Training for Adults (2) | Follow-Through (3) |
|---|---|---|---|---|---|---|
| All (4) | 60.1 | 55.8 | 1.32 | .99 | 1.96 | .02 |
| Male | 50.5 | 46.9 | 1.15 | .81 | 1.60 | .02 |
| Female | 9.2 | 8.5 | .16 | .17 | .35 | .00 |
| People with disabilities | 11.2 | 10.3 | .28 | .23 | .41 | .01 |
| People from ethnic minority groups (5) | 4.8 | 4.4 | .05 | .10 | .20 | .00 |

Notes:

(1) Including those awaiting their first Advisory interview. Whilst on the Advisory process, clients may participate in provisions such as Program Centers, Jobclub, Jobplan or Worktrials.

(2) In Scotland, Training for Work is the equivalent program.

(3) Individuals join the Follow-Through stage on returning from the Employer Subsidy, unsubsidized employment, or WBTA/TfW within 3 months of completing training/leaving JSA; plus those completing Education and Training Opportunities.

(4) Totals include those for whom gender is not recorded. For this reason, and also because of rounding, components will not necessarily sum to totals.

(5) Excluding those who, when asked their ethnic origin, were recorded as "Prefer not to say."

Source: DfEE (1999)

**Table 1.8**
**25+ Numbers Leaving the Advisory Interview Process by Destination (1)**
**Great Britain (Thousands)**

| Month of of leaving **Total** | **Total** | **Left New Deal:** Left JSA Unsubsidized Employment (2) | Transfer to other benefits | Other (3) | Not Known (4) | **Still on New Deal:** On JSA (5) | Left JSA Employer Subsidy | Work Based Training for Adults/TfW | On JSA Education & Training Opportunities |
|---|---|---|---|---|---|---|---|---|---|
| Jul-98 | .6 | .21 | .15 | .06 | .12 | .00 | .01 | .03 | .00 |
| Aug-98 | 1.6 | .45 | .37 | .17 | .25 | .00 | .09 | .20 | .04 |
| Sep-98 | 3.4 | .69 | .59 | .29 | .42 | .18 | .35 | .42 | .44 |
| Oct-98 | 4.5 | .68 | .53 | .14 | 1.29 | .41 | .52 | .65 | .31 |
| Nov-98 | 4.9 | .74 | .67 | .22 | 1.08 | .88 | .42 | .70 | .25 |
| Total | 15.0 | 2.76 | 2.31 | .88 | 3.15 | 1.47 | 1.40 | 2.00 | 1.04 |

Notes:

(1) Including those leaving before receipt of a first interview.

(2) Those who are recorded by ES as having been placed into unsubsidized employment, plus those who are recorded as having terminated their JSA claim in order to go into a job. This will undercount the total number going into a job: some who go into a job will not, for whatever reason, record this as the reason for termination of their JSA claim. These will be counted as "not known." Past research indicates that the destinations of those who do not give a reason for termination follow a similar pattern to those who do give a reason. As further data are added, the numbers going into jobs in recent months may be revised upwards.

(3) Includes for example gone abroad.

(4) Where there is no leaving code recorded on JUVOS, or where the leaving code is recorded as "not known," or simply "ceased claiming" or "failed to attend." As more data are added, the numbers going into jobs in recent months may be revised downwards.

(5) At the end of the Advisory Process, client may return to normal jobseeker activity including regular fortnightly reviews.

Source: DfEE (1999)

People with disabilities and ethnic minority groups are both less likely to have left the Advisory process to return to their normal pattern of jobseeker activity. People from ethnic minority groups are more likely to have left for unsubsidized jobs (21 percent against 18 percent overall); but less likely to have left for the Employer Subsidy (4 percent against 9 percent overall). They are also more likely to have left for education/training opportunities (24 percent against 20 percent overall).

An initial assessment of the New Deal for young unemployed people conducted by the independent Institute for Employment Studies (Atkinson,1999) is generally optimistic about the progress made during 1998. A summary of the first evaluation report is shown in box 1.6.

*Removing the Barriers to Work*

The Joseph Rowntree Foundation has taken a special interest in undertaking studies that investigate the changing nature of the labor market and its interaction with the tax-benefit system. As a result, Fran Bennett and Robert Walker (1999) were commissioned to reflect on the implications of these and related studies for the Blair government's new approach to welfare to work. The aims of the review are to:

- Identify both the potential and the limits of the proposed welfare to work strategy in general
- Assess the merits of the principal elements in the strategy and the scope for improvement
- Address specific limitations and unresolved issues (p. ix)

In an earlier review also commissioned by the Joseph Rowntree Foundation, Karen Gardiner (1997) identified 38 barriers that prevent people from working. Bennett and Walker (1998) use Gardiner's list to attempt a prelimary assessment of the government's welfare to work strategy. Table 1.9 summarizes their evaluation. Each of the 38 barriers to work is marked in one of the following ways:

- with an asterisk (*) to indicate that it is a primary focus of welfare reform
- with a tick (·) to show that it is being addressed to some extent
- with a cross (x) to suggest that it is being ignored and may even be exacerbated by current policy developments

**Box 1.6**
**The New Deal for Young Unemployed People: A Summary of Progress**

Delivery through local partnerships is a key feature of New Deal and in a relatively short time, complex arrangements for delivery have been put in place. New and previously untried delivery models have been put in place, strategic and delivery "partnerships" have been established, and new service providers have been contacted.

When the program was initiated, there was a stock of about 112,000 young people who had been claiming Jobseeker's Allowance (JSA) for six months or more. The early months of the program aimed to take them in, as well as "new" individuals, as their spell of unemployment reached the six-month mark. By the end of November 1998, some 203,000 individuals had joined the New Deal, and of them, just over 80,000 had already left it. So, at the end of that month, 120,500 people were taking part in it. The initial scale of entry had therefore been sufficient to take in the existing stock, and was settling down to accommodate new entrants, about 20,000 a month.

At this point, over one-third of the entrants (38 percent) were still in the Gateway, a period of assessment and advice designed to help them find the most beneficial route through the program. Some required relatively little or fairly straightforward help, and some 19 percent had found an unsubsidized job. Rather more, 23 percent had moved through into one of the four options, and the rest had left the program. Of those joining an option:

- 25 percent had taken a subsidized job with an employer. Generally, taking jobs, whether subsidized or not, tended to be more common among those with the shorter spells of unemployment.
- 50 percent had taken a course of full-time education or training; the least well-qualified leavers from the Gateway were well represented among those joining this option. Further, the overwhelming proportion of them were aiming to secure a qualification at NVQ/SVQ Level 2.
- 13 percent had taken a job in the voluntary sector, and 12 percent with an Environment Task Force. Much less was known about how these options were operating.

While early indications are encouraging, it would be wrong to suppose that the client group is universally and uncritically "pro" the New Deal. Qualitative research suggests, however, that most have a generally hopeful attitude towards it, and what it is trying to do. This is reflected in the low use of benefit sanctions to enforce participation.

At this time, employers too were joining the program, but tending to reserve judgment about their longer term participation. Those not joining were mainly doing so for lack of information and opportunity, rather than from a positive decision to stay out.

Early indications of the effects of the New Deal on individual and employer participants are generally positive. Broader effects on the labor market as a whole will take longer to come through, but by November 1998 there was already evidence of a positive effect of outflows from unemployment, without corresponding evidence of negative side-effects on other groups of jobseekers.

Source: Atkinson (1999), pp. 1&2.

Table 1.9 suggests that in many respects the reforms are targeted on the key barriers to work. There are 9 asterisks and 22 ticks with only 7 crosses. At first sight this is an impressive achievement for any government let alone one that had been in the political wilderness for 18 years prior to its 1997 election victory and with only 18 months or so to take action prior to Bennett and Walker's (1998) assessment. It would be somewhat churlish and perhaps unrealistic to expect too much in a relatively short space of time. On the other hand, it is important to reflect on the possible downsides of the approach adopted by the Blair government.

Some of the issues that deserve more attention include the following:

- Has the government struck the right balance between trying to improve the human capital of workers on the margins of the labor market relative to stimulating the demand for such labor?
- Is there too much emphasis on the need to promote a culture of attachment to the labor market?
- Can more be done to ease the transition between the loss of benefits and an increased reliance on earnings from employment?

These are not easy questions to answer. Moreover, as Bennett and Walker (1998) conclude:

> Which of the outstanding barriers are the most important to address is perhaps more a matter of political judgement than empirical fact and, in any case, will change over time: supply side measures will not address deficits in labour demand, be they the result of recession or structural change. (p. 27)

### *Making Work Pay*

A new study from the IFS has used data from the Quarterly Labour Force Survey (QLFS), which follows approximately 12,000 people each quarter for five quarters on a rolling-panel basis, to identify individual characteristics that influence decisions about whether or not to enter work. In particular, it examines how individual attributes and characteristics, labor market conditions and the tax and benefit system influence "entry or re-entry into work by men and women who are unemployed or inactive in the labor market" (Gregg et al., 1999, vii).

Gregg et al. (1999) develop statistical models to estimate the impact of changes in in-work and out-of-work incomes on the prob-

## Table 1.9
## Government Action to Tackle Potential Barriers to Securing Employment

| *Economically inactive* | |
|---|---|
| *Individual characteristics* | *Benefits system and employment services* |
| ⊙ (a) Lack of educational qualifications | ⊙ (a) Benefit levels are too high |
| * (b) Lack of work experience | ⊙ (b) Benefit levels are too low |
| ⊙ (c) Lack of basic skills | * (c) Difficulties and delays in payment of benefits |
| ⊙ (d) Lack of practical skills/access to facilities | ⊙ (d) Disincentives for couples |
| ⊙ (e) Long-term sickness/disability | ⊙ (e) Disincentives to work whilst on benefits |
| * (f) Caring responsibilities | x (f) Treatment of housing costs |
| ⊙ (g) High living costs (dependents and housing) | x (g) Loss of passport benefits |
| | ⊙ (h) Lack of suitable training |
| | ⊙ (j) Lack of assistance with job search |
| | * (k) Lack of flexibility and responsiveness of the system to people's needs |
| *Desire for job* | |
| *Individual attachment to the labor market* | *Lack of information* |
| * (a) Cultural/social values that restrict job search | ⊙ (a) Job opportunities |
| * (b) Lack of flexibility about work one would consider | ⊙ (b) Benefits |
| | ⊙ (c) Take-home pay |
| * (c) Lack of motivation | ⊙ (d) Training and other employment services |
| * (d) Unrealistic reservation wages | x (e) Rules concerning working while on benefits |
| * (e) Insufficient job search | |
| *Job search* | |
| *Job market and employers* | *Uncertainty* |
| x (a) Lack of jobs at the national or local level | ⊙ (a) Net income in work |
| x (b) Lack of suitable kinds of work | x (b) Managing financially during transition |
| ⊙ (c) Lack of jobs with adequate wages | ⊙ (c) New job |
| ⊙ (d) Prejudice of employers | ⊙ (d) Need to reclaim benefits |
| ⊙ (e) Employment conditions | |
| *Securing employment* | |
| *Work-related arrangements and costs* | |
| (a) Childcare | |
| (b) Travel, clothing and tools | |

Key: * focus of reforms . addressed by reforms x not addressed by reforms ability of moving into work. Out-of work income is calculated using a model of the UK tax and benefit system (TAXBEN). In-work income is derived from the distribution of earnings actually observed among people who move into work in the QLFS. The results obtained from investigating the relationship between the net financial rewards from entering work and the information on which people actually move into work are employed to undertake sophisticated simulations of policy options. By using TAXBEN it is possible to simulate the impact of key features of the Blair government's welfare reform agenda on the probability of movements into work and their associated costs. Three principal options are considered:

- The replacement of Family Credit by the Working Families' Tax Credit, planned for October 1999.
- Two changes to employee National Insurance contributions that lower the costs to low-paid workers and achieve harmonization with the income tax system.
- The introduction of a 10p starting rate of income tax. (A slight complication here is that the IFS team assumed that the 10p tax rate would apply to the first £2,000 of taxable income whereas in the event this rate applies only to the first £1,500. Nevertheless, it is a useful illustration.)

The results of these three policy options are summarized in table 1.10. Each of the options has a beneficial effect on average levels of estimated income gained from being in work with larger benefits in each case for men rather than women. The results imply that the reforms would increase the expected financial return to work by around 7.7 percent for men and around 6.5 percent for women. These gains are sufficient to create incentives for people to rejoin the labor market. However, in a separate analysis, Gregg et al. (1999) estimate that the national minimum wage would yield similar benefits for men and even greater benefits for women. The average gain in income per week being £2.54 and £3.82, respectively. Unfortunately, because it is impossible to predict what, if any, impact the national minimum wage will have on the availability of jobs it is inappropriate to produce estimates of what effect this policy will have on the total stock of unemployment. Nevertheless, it is estimated that the minimum wage "is likely to have a greater impact on 'entry jobs' than on the labor market as a whole" (Gregg et al., 1999, p. ix).

**Table 1.10**
**Summary of IFS Policy Simulations**

| | New Policies | | |
|---|---|---|---|
| **Consequences** | **WFTC** | **NI Changes** | **10p Tax Rate** |
| Average £ gain from work | | | |
| - men | 2.67 | 2.65 | 1.65 |
| - women | 0.88 | 1.95 | 1.20 |
| Reduction in stock of unemployment | 91,720 | 115,280 | 75,970 |
| Estimated net cost (±) per job | 8,300 | 17,700 | 39,400 |

Source: Gregg et al. (1999), table 4.

Each of the reforms shown in table 1.10 is estimated to reduce the stock of unemployment with the proposed changes to national insurance contributions having the largest effect. However, using a relatively crude measure of cost-effectiveness the WFTC appears to provide the best value. The estimated annual net cost to the taxpayer of each new job entrant ranges from £8,300 for WFTC to £39,400 for a 10p tax rate. However, it is important to remember that policies often have more than one goal and so they cannot be judged solely by reference to this particular criterion. Nevertheless, the combined effect of these three sets of policies is estimated to reduce unemployment by almost 300,000 or approximately 4 percent of the stock of unemployed people. Gregg et al. (1999) conclude that:

> Although this decrease is unlikely to be large enough to completely transform the labor market, the finding is good news for those (including the present government) who see "welfare to work" programs as a means of reducing unemployment and economic activity rates amongst the working-age population. Our findings seem to fit in with the general pattern suggested by other research both in the UK and elsewhere. (p. 141)

## Summary and Conclusion

There is clear evidence that the tax and benefit system has failed the people in Britain who have most needed help in recent years as a result of changes in the demand for labor associated with the growing globalization of the economy. As a direct result, welfare to work policies are critical to the economic and social strategy being pursued by the Blair government in the UK. There are two main strands to policy development. The first is based on the so-called New Deals for specific groups of people who have been marginalized in the labor market. Key to these initiatives is active investment in counseling and practical support. The early evidence suggests that progress is being made but it remains very early in the life of such initiatives to make definitive evaluative judgements. The same is also largely true of the cluster of policies aimed at "making work pay." There are grounds for believing that changes to the tax and benefit system and the introduction of a national minimum wage will have a positive effect on encouraging people to rejoin the labor force but there are many unknowns. For example, it remains very unclear how the raft of initiatives introduced by "New Labour" will fare if the economy experiences a serious downturn. However, for the moment the signs are promising. Welfare to work is perceived to be working. The challenge for the future is to invest in more sophisticated evaluation efforts so as to produce convincing evidence about what aspects of policy work best for which people in what circumstances. There is a clear commitment to support independent research but it will take some time for findings to emerge in forms that might influence future policy development.

## References


Atkinson, J. (1999). *The New Deal for Young Unemployed People: A Summary of Progress.* Sheffield: Employment Service.

Bennett, F., & Walker, R. (1998). *Working with Work: an initial assessment of welfare to work.* York: Joseph Rowntree Foundation.

Brown, G. (1999). *Budget Speech,* www.hm-treasury.gov.uk/budget99/speech. html.

Cm 3805. (1998). *New Ambitions for Our Country: a new contract for welfare,.* London: The Stationery Office.

Deacon, A. (1998). "Public welfare and private behaviour: the case of 'welfare to work' programmes." Paper delivered to the 2nd International Research Conference of the International Social Security Association, Jerusalem.

Department for Education and Employment (DfEE). (1999). *New Deal for Young People and Long-Term Unemployed People Aged 25+: Statistics.* www.dfee.gov.uk/news/ 38.wtm

Gardiner, K. (1997). *Bridges from Benefit to Work: a review.* York: Joseph Rowntree Foundation.

Gregg, P, Johnson, P., & Reed, H. (1999). *Entering Work and the British Tax and Benefit System.* London: Institute for Fiscal Studies.

White, M., Lissenburgh, S., & Bryson, A. (1997). *The Impact of Public Job Placing Programmes,* London: Policy Studies Institute.

# 2

# Creeping Workfare Policies: The Case of Italy

*Valeria Fargion*

The Italian record on unemployment is one of the worst in Europe. Yet, the policies pursued to tackle this dramatic problem have been for a long time extremely limited and out of tune with respect to leading trends in western countries. In sharp contrast with the Anglo-Saxon countries, the workfare logic has only very recently crept into the political debate and its impact on policy measures is still very mild and quite contradictory.

Fighting unemployment is now considered a top priority by the Italian government and an unparalleled amount of resources is being funneled in this direction. The results are still unclear and so far the efforts largely have been aimed at setting up the relevant legislative framework. To be sure, a full-fledged strategy to reinsert the unemployed into the labor market is just beginning to develop. Nevertheless, until the mid-nineties the scenario looked quite different: active labor policies were almost nonexistent and passive policies represented a maze of measures characterized by all sorts of disparities and inequity.

To understand the peculiarities—or perhaps the anomalies—of the Italian case, we certainly need to examine the policy legacy of the country's welfare model. However, before going into the institutional background of current policy making it will be useful to provide some basic information on the main features of unemployment in Italy and its development over the last decade.

### Unemployment in Italy: A Quantitative Overview

If we take a long-term perspective, the performance of the Italian labor market can hardly be considered satisfactory. Table 2.1 provides the relevant data to substantiate the point by illustrating the postwar trends for the main labor market indicators. Let's start by considering activity rates. As one can easily notice, in the mid-1990s the Italian labor force only represented around 40 percent of the total population as compared with an average of 46.9 percent for OECD countries and 45.2 percent for the European Union. This level is nearly the same as forty years ago and it places Italy at the bottom of European rankings along with Greece and Spain.

The primary explanation for this particular feature of the Italian economy is the very low participation of women in the labor market. As table 2.2, illustrates, in 1996 the activity rate for Italian women aged 15 to 64 was the lowest in Europe. Official statistics might not be fully accurate, given the diffusion of irregular female work in the informal economy. However, while throughout the 1980s female

**Table 2.1**
**Unemployment, Employment, and Labor Participation Rates in Italy, Selected Years (1956-1995)**

| | Unemployment rate | Employment rate | Activity rate |
|---|---|---|---|
| 1956 | 9,4 | 36,7 | 40,6 |
| 1960 | 5,6 | 41,5 | 44,1 |
| 1965 | 5,4 | 38,4 | 40,5 |
| 1970 | 5,4 | 36,6 | 38,7 |
| 1975 | 5,9 | 35,9 | 38,1 |
| 1980 | 7,6 | 36,8 | 39,8 |
| 1981 | 8,4 | 36,8 | 40,2 |
| 1982 | 9,1 | 36,6 | 40,3 |
| 1983 | 9,9 | 36,6 | 40,6 |
| 1984 | 10,4 | 36,6 | 40,9 |
| 1985 | 10,6 | 36,7 | 41,1 |
| 1986 | 11,1 | 36,9 | 41,5 |
| 1987 | 12,0 | 36,8 | 41,8 |
| 1988 | 12,0 | 37,2 | 42,3 |
| 1989 | 12,0 | 37,0 | 42,0 |
| 1990 | 11,0 | 37,4 | 42,0 |
| 1991 | 10,9 | 37,8 | 42,5 |
| 1992 | 11,5 | 37,5 | 42,4 |
| 1993 | 10,2 | 36,3 | 40,4 |
| 1994 | 11,3 | 35,6 | 40,1 |
| 1995 | 12,0 | 35,3 | 40,1 |

Source: Gualmini 1997

participation in the labor market steadily went up, 1992 marks a turning point and the country's position starts to deteriorate. In the mid-eighties Spain, Greece and Ireland shared with Italy a similar—if not worse—situation, but during the nineties these countries have gradually come closer to the European average, while Italy is still 14 percentage points below. In short, Italy remains very distant from the Nordic countries, including the Netherlands,[1] as well as from the main continental countries of France and Germany, but it also ends up as a laggard even within Southern Europe.

**Table 2.2**
**Female Labor Force Activity Rates in the European Union, 1986-1996**

| | 1986 | 1987 | 1988 | 1989 | 1990 | 1991 | 1992 | 1993 | 1994 | 1995 | 1996 |
|---|---|---|---|---|---|---|---|---|---|---|---|
| EUR 15 | | | | | | 55.8 | 55.7 | 55.9 | 56.4 | 56.7 | 57.2 |
| Belgium | 45.8 | 45.5 | 45.3 | 45.6 | 46.1 | 48.2 | 49.3 | 50.3 | 51.2 | 51.7 | 52.0 |
| Denmark | 76.1 | 76.5 | 76.6 | 76.4 | 77.6 | 78.0 | 78.2 | 77.4 | 73.8 | 73.3 | 73.6 |
| Germany | 52.5 | 52.7 | 53.8 | 54.4 | 57.6 | 61.2 | 61.1 | 60.7 | 61.4 | 61.3 | 61.3 |
| Greece | 41.0 | 41.1 | 42.6 | 43.0 | 42.6 | 40.2 | 41.7 | 42.3 | 43.2 | 44.3 | 45.8 |
| Spain | 33.7 | 37.1 | 39.2 | 39.7 | 40.6 | 40.7 | 41.8 | 42.6 | 44.2 | 44.9 | 45.7 |
| France | 57.8 | 57.6 | 57.7 | 57.9 | 58.0 | 58.2 | 58.9 | 59.6 | 60.1 | 60.6 | 61.3 |
| Ireland | 39.6 | 41.0 | 40.4 | 40.8 | 41.9 | 42.7 | 43.4 | 45.4 | 46.7 | 47.1 | 48.6 |
| Italy | 41.1 | 41.7 | 42.8 | 43.4 | 43.2 | 44.2 | 42.0 | 42.0 | 42.2 | 42.5 | 43.3 |
| Luxembourg | 42.4 | 43.4 | 41.8 | 42.4 | 42.4 | 44.6 | 47.5 | 46.1 | 47.0 | 44.1 | 45.7 |
| Netherlands | | 49.3 | 49.7 | 50.4 | 52.4 | 53.6 | 55.3 | 56.0 | 57.4 | 58.3 | 59.6 |
| Austria | 51.4 | 52.7 | 53.5 | 54.1 | 55.2 | 56.1 | 57.8 | 58.5 | 62.3 | 62.3 | 61.8 |
| Portugal | 53.7 | 55.0 | 56.0 | 56.7 | 57.1 | 59.9 | 58.6 | 58.7 | 58.8 | 59.1 | 59.5 |
| Finland | 72.8 | 72.5 | 72.5 | 73.0 | 72.5 | 71.7 | 70.4 | 69.7 | 69.6 | 69.4 | 69.3 |
| Sweden | 80.0 | 80.9 | 81.6 | 81.9 | 82.3 | 81.4 | 79.6 | 77.3 | 75.7 | 78.2 | 75.2 |

*Note:* Activity rates for females aged 15-64.
Source: Eurostat Yearbook 1997

Turning to the central issue of unemployment, what first needs to be stressed is that Italy has been living with double digit unemployment rates since the early to mid-eighties (table 2.1). To fully grasp the main aspects of the problem, once more it might be useful to analyze the Italian case in a comparative perspective. From this standpoint, one can appreciate the somewhat distinct path followed by Italy compared to the rest of Europe. While EU countries in general experienced a decrease in the level of unemployment during the late eighties which was followed by a consistent upward trend starting with 1990, Italy seems to be trapped since the early eighties in an upward spiral with the only exception being the 1990-1993 period. But perhaps it is even more interesting to focus on the breakdown of unemployment rates by sex. As shown in table 2.3, what is most notable is the very high level of female unemployment. Indeed, the level of male unemployment is quite close to the European average ranging from around 7 percent in 1991 to around 10 percent in 1996. Female unemployment is instead consistently higher than the European average. As a result, while in the 1990s the difference between male and female unemployment is about 2½- 3 percentage points at the EU level, the corresponding figure for Italy lingers around 7 percent.

An examination of the relevant data in greater detail reveals that the gap between male and female unemployment actually narrows over the period 1986-1996. However, this is essentially because male unemployment increases while female unemployment remains roughly at the same level, which corresponds to 16.6 percent in 1996 compared to a European average of 12.5 percent. A similar situation can be found in Greece and Finland—there is only one country displaying a worse record, namely Spain.

The problem in Italy is further complicated by the age composition of unemployment. As in many other European countries youth unemployment in Italy is the most critical issue. However, to place the Italian situation into perspective one needs to recall that: (a) employment for both men and women is heavily concentrated in the 25 to 49 age group; and (b) the 1990s witnessed a sharp and sudden drop in the activity rates of men aged 50 to 64. What I intend to stress with the latter point is that one needs to consider the effects of early-retirement policies, in order to fully appreciate the dynamics at work in the Italian case. Such policies forced out of the labor force a substantial number of workers close to retirement age, thereby

Table 2.3
**Male and Female Unemployment Rates in the European Union, 1986-1996**

| | | 1986 | 1987 | 1988 | 1989 | 1990 | 1991 | 1992 | 1993 | 1994 | 1995 |
|---|---|---|---|---|---|---|---|---|---|---|---|
| EUR 15 | Men | | | | | | 7.0 | 7.9 | 9.6 | 10.3 | 9.6 |
| | Women | | | | | | 10.3 | 10.9 | 12.0 | 12.8 | 12.5 |
| Belgium | Men | 7.2 | 7.3 | 7.0 | 5.3 | 4.6 | 4.6 | 4.8 | 6.2 | 7.7 | 7.4 |
| | Women | 18.0 | 17.7 | 15.2 | 13.0 | 11.5 | 10.7 | 9.5 | 10.9 | 12.5 | 12.3 |
| Denmark | Men | 4.6 | 5.3 | 5.9 | 7.6 | 8.0 | 8.4 | 8.5 | 10.6 | 7.3 | 5.7 |
| | Women | 7.9 | 7.2 | 7.4 | 9.0 | 9.0 | 10.1 | 10.0 | 11.2 | 9.0 | 8.6 |
| Germany | Men | 5.6 | 6.1 | 5.3 | 4.6 | 4.1 | 4.5 | 4.9 | 6.5 | 7.6 | 7.1 |
| | Women | 8.3 | 8.0 | 8.0 | 7.5 | 6.2 | 6.6 | 8.3 | 9.4 | 10.4 | 9.7 |
| Greece | Men | 5.2 | 5.3 | 5.0 | 4.7 | 4.4 | 4.9 | 5.0 | 5.8 | 6.2 | 6.4 |
| | Women | 11.9 | 11.7 | 12.8 | 12.6 | 12.0 | 13.1 | 13.2 | 13.9 | 14.0 | 14.1 |
| Spain | Men | 19.8 | 17.2 | 15.8 | 13.3 | 12.1 | 12.1 | 13.7 | 18.7 | 20.2 | 18.2 |
| | Women | 25.4 | 28.3 | 28.4 | 25.6 | 24.4 | 23.4 | 25.3 | 28.8 | 31.6 | 30.5 |
| France | Men | 8.7 | 8.7 | 8.2 | 7.4 | 7.2 | 7.2 | 8.2 | 9.7 | 11.2 | 10.1 |
| | Women | 12.3 | 13.5 | 12.9 | 12.7 | 12.2 | 11.7 | 12.9 | 13.5 | 14.6 | 14.2 |
| Ireland | Men | 17.9 | 18.1 | 17.5 | 16.4 | 14.0 | 15.8 | 15.3 | 15.9 | 14.8 | 12.3 |
| | Women | 19.7 | 19.2 | 18.6 | 16.7 | 15.2 | 16.8 | 15.4 | 16.0 | 14.8 | 12.1 |
| Italy | Men | 7.1 | 7.6 | 7.5 | 7.5 | 6.5 | 6.9 | 6.9 | 7.8 | 9.0 | 9.3 |
| | Women | 17.2 | 16.8 | 17.6 | 17.5 | 15.8 | 15.9 | 14.1 | 14.9 | 15.7 | 16.3 |
| Luxembourg | Men | 1.9 | 1.8 | 1.5 | 1.2 | 1.2 | 1.1 | 1.6 | 1.9 | 3.0 | 2.1 |
| | Women | 4.0 | 3.8 | 2.9 | 2.4 | 2.4 | 2.1 | 2.8 | 3.1 | 4.3 | 4.4 |
| Netherlands | Men | | 7.5 | 7.4 | 6.8 | 5.7 | 5.6 | 4.1 | 5.4 | 6.6 | 6.2 |
| | Women | | 14.0 | 12.7 | 11.9 | 10.9 | 10.0 | 7.8 | 7.7 | 8.1 | 8.7 |
| Austria | Men | 3.2 | 3.6 | 3.3 | 2.9 | 3.0 | 3.4 | 3.5 | 4.1 | | 4.0 |
| | Women | 3.1 | 4.1 | 4.0 | 3.6 | 3.6 | 3.7 | 3.8 | 4.5 | | 4.9 |
| Portugal | Men | 7.0 | 6.0 | 4.5 | 3.6 | 3.4 | 2.7 | 3.5 | 4.7 | 6.1 | 6.8 |
| | Women | 11.9 | 9.9 | 8.6 | 7.6 | 6.7 | 5.8 | 4.9 | 6.5 | 8.0 | 8.1 |
| Finland | Men | 6.2 | 5.8 | 5.1 | 3.6 | 4.1 | 9.4 | 15.5 | 20.0 | 20.0 | 18.0 |
| | Women | 4.6 | 4.4 | 4.0 | 3.4 | 2.8 | 5.8 | 10.6 | 15.7 | 16.7 | 16.3 |
| Sweden | Men | 2.6 | 2.1 | 1.7 | 1.4 | 1.7 | 3.4 | 6.2 | 9.7 | 9.1 | 8.9 |
| | Women | 2.7 | 2.2 | 1.7 | 1.5 | 1.6 | 2.6 | 4.2 | 6.6 | 6.7 | 7.4 |
| United | Men | 12.0 | 11.5 | 9.3 | 7.6 | 7.3 | 9.5 | 11.7 | 12.5 | 11.5 | 10.2 |
| Kingdom | Women | 11.0 | 10.5 | 8.7 | 7.2 | 6.7 | 7.4 | 7.5 | 7.8 | 7.4 | 7.4 |

Source: Eurostat Yearbook 1997

shifting most of the unemployed belonging to this age group into the non-active population. In detail, while the activity rate of men aged 50 to 64 dropped from 65 to 55 percent in just five years (from 1991 to 1996), the unemployment rate for the same age group remained at around 50 percent of the European average.

**Table 2.4**
**Youth Unemployment in the European Union, 1986-1996**

| | | 1986 | 1987 | 1988 | 1989 | 1990 | 1991 | 1992 | 1993 | 1994 | 1995 | 1996 |
|---|---|---|---|---|---|---|---|---|---|---|---|---|
| EUR 15 | Women | | | | | | 17.6 | 18.2 | 20.8 | 21.8 | 22.5 | 22.9 |
| | Men | | | | | | 14.9 | 16.3 | 20.1 | 21.3 | 20 | 20.9 |
| Belgium | Women | 27 | 28.7 | 23.4 | 20.2 | 19.2 | 17.1 | 15.2 | 19.6 | 23.4 | 23.7 | 24.4 |
| | Men | 15.5 | 14.7 | 13 | 11.4 | 10.1 | 11 | 11.3 | 17.4 | 20.5 | 19.7 | 17.3 |
| Denmark | Women | 9.5 | 10 | 9 | 12.4 | 11.6 | 12.3 | 12.6 | 14.7 | 10.2 | 12.3 | 12.4 |
| | Men | 7 | 8 | 8.1 | 10.7 | 11.4 | 10.7 | 12.1 | 14.5 | 10.2 | 7.8 | 9 |
| Germany | Women | 9 | 7.6 | 7.3 | 5.9 | 4.7 | 5.8 | 6.5 | 7.7 | 8.4 | 8.2 | 8.6 |
| | Men | 6.8 | 7.4 | 6.3 | 5.2 | 4.4 | 5.2 | 5.4 | 7.6 | 9.4 | 8.7 | 10.5 |
| Greece | Women | 34.2 | 33.8 | 36 | 34 | 32.6 | 33.5 | 34.2 | 36 | 36.9 | 37.7 | 41.3 |
| | Men | 16 | 17.5 | 17 | 17 | 15.1 | 16.9 | 17.2 | 18.8 | 19.8 | 19.4 | 21.5 |
| Spain | Women | 49.6 | 49.6 | 48.3 | 42.6 | 39.3 | 37.1 | 39.8 | 46.6 | 49.7 | 48.1 | 48.3 |
| | Men | 44.2 | 38.4 | 35.2 | 27.5 | 25.7 | 25.2 | 28 | 39.1 | 41.4 | 36.4 | 36.6 |
| France | Women | 26.4 | 27.1 | 25.3 | 23 | 23 | 22.6 | 25 | 27.7 | 30.5 | 30.7 | 30.3 |
| | Men | 21.5 | 20 | 19.1 | 16.2 | 16.8 | 17 | 18.6 | 23.6 | 27.2 | 23.7 | 25.1 |
| Ireland | Women | 22.6 | 22.8 | 22.8 | 19.6 | 18.2 | 21.1 | 20.8 | 22.8 | 20.5 | 17.3 | 17 |
| | Men | 29.1 | 28.6 | 27.1 | 23.7 | 20.9 | 24.7 | 24.3 | 26.9 | 25.1 | 20.3 | 19.1 |
| Italy | Women | 40.3 | 39.7 | 39.5 | 38.5 | 35.4 | 33.5 | 32.2 | 34.4 | 35.4 | 37.6 | 39.2 |
| | Men | 27.3 | 28.7 | 27.9 | 25.9 | 23.4 | 23.8 | 23.3 | 26.3 | 28.7 | 29 | 30 |
| Luxembourg | Women | 6.7 | 6.6 | 4.8 | | | | | | 7.3 | 7.8 | 8.3 |
| | Men | 5.5 | 4.2 | 4.6 | | | | 4.2 | 4.4 | 8.5 | 6.7 | 10.1 |
| Netherlands | Women | | 18 | 14.5 | 13.9 | 11.9 | 12 | 8.5 | 9.5 | 9 | 12.7 | 11.6 |
| | Men | | 15.7 | 14 | 12.4 | 10.2 | 10.2 | 7.7 | 11.3 | 13.6 | 11.5 | 11.3 |
| Austria | Women | 4.4 | 5.4 | 5 | 4.7 | 3.8 | 3.4 | 4 | 4.6 | | 6.2 | 6.5 |
| | Men | 3.5 | 4.6 | 4.2 | 3.6 | 3.8 | 4 | 4.2 | 4.7 | | 5.7 | 7.1 |
| Portugal | Women | 25.5 | 22 | 19.3 | 15.8 | 13.3 | 11.7 | 10.8 | 14.7 | 16.9 | 17.1 | 20 |
| | Men | 16.3 | 14 | 10.2 | 8.2 | 7.9 | 6.2 | 8.7 | 9.9 | 12.5 | 15.1 | 14.6 |
| Finland | Women | | | | | | | | | | 41.1 | 41.2 |
| | Men | | | | | | | | | | 41.9 | 41.3 |
| Sweden | Women | 5.3 | 4.6 | 3.6 | 3 | 3.7 | 5.7 | 9.1 | 15.2 | 14.3 | 17.8 | 20.6 |
| | Men | 5.7 | 4.4 | 3.3 | 3.2 | 3.7 | 7.5 | 13.7 | 21.6 | 19 | 22.4 | 20.2 |
| United Kingdom | Women | 17 | 15 | 11.9 | 9.3 | 9.3 | 11.4 | 11.7 | 13.4 | 12.8 | 12.5 | 11.3 |
| | Men | 19.8 | 17.2 | 14.3 | 11.2 | 11.4 | 15.9 | 19 | 20.9 | 19.3 | 17.9 | 17.9 |

*Notes:* Unemployment rates for men and women aged 15-24
Luxembourg data 1986-1995 unreliable due to small sample size

*Source: Eurostat Yearbook 1997*

Taking a closer look at the figures for youth unemployment (table 2.4), the magnitude of the problem is immediately evident. Once more Italy falls into the bottom rankings along with its southern neighbors Greece and Spain, and with Finland. In fact, in 1996 the unemployment rate of men aged 15 to 24 reached a high of 30 percent as against a European average of 20.9 percent. The corresponding rates for women appear even more unbalanced with a percentage of 39.2 in the Italian case compared to a European average of 22.9 percent.

So far we have highlighted the particular relevance of youth and female unemployment in the Italian case. However, our understanding of the country's situation might be very misleading if we don't put into focus the impact of the North-South cleavage. According to a recent report commissioned by the EU, "the problem of employment in Italy can be identified with the regional problem. Three figures sum it up: in 1996 the South of Italy accounted for 36 percent of the population and just 28 percent of employment, but a full 57 percent of unemployment" (European Commission 1996, 4).

Table 2.5 provides the relevant information to grasp how deep the divide is between the Center-North and the South of Italy. If we just take a look at the figures in columns four and ten—which refer to employed and total population in the different regions—one is immediately struck by the fact that in most northern regions about one person out of two is employed, while in Sicily or Calabria the equivalent ratio is one in four. To put it more vividly, in the most depressed areas of the Mezzogiorno there are as many as four people sharing the income generated by a working person compared to two in Emilia or Lombardy. In sum, as we move from North to South the employment rate steadily declines.

To be sure, when considering the size of employment in the two parts of the country we need to take into account the persistent difference in the corresponding activity rates. Participation in the labor market has always been substantially lower in Southern Italy: in 1996 the distance between the region at the top and the region at the bottom of the ranking was as much as 15 percentage points. Yet, we might add that since the recession of 1992 the gap is actually widening because of activity rates dropping more markedly in the South. The "discouragement effect" has apparently been more diffused in those parts of the country where the prospects for a recovery of the economy were particularly bleak.

**Table 2.5**
**Population by Employment Status, Sector of Employment, and Region; Italy 1996 (in thousands)**

| Region | Employed | | | | Unemployed | | Total Active | | Inactive | Total Active and Inactive |
|---|---|---|---|---|---|---|---|---|---|---|
| | Agri-culture | Ind-ustry | Other | Total | N | % labor force | N | % pop-ulation | N | |
| Piedmont | 87 | 676 | 930 | 1,693 | 159 | 8.3 | 1,852 | 43.7 | 2,386 | 4,238 |
| Val d'Aosta | 4 | 12 | 36 | 52 | 3 | 5.6 | 55 | 46.6 | 63 | 118 |
| Lombardy | 102 | 1,536 | 2,036 | 3,674 | 235 | 6.1 | 3,909 | 44.1 | 4,964 | 8,873 |
| Trentino | 39 | 109 | 250 | 398 | 17 | 3.9 | 415 | 45.8 | 491 | 906 |
| Veneto | 100 | 766 | 983 | 1,849 | 103 | 5.6 | 1,952 | 44.4 | 2,446 | 4,398 |
| Friuli | 23 | 162 | 282 | 467 | 34 | 7.1 | 501 | 42.7 | 671 | 1,172 |
| Liguria | 23 | 127 | 426 | 576 | 74 | 11.7 | 650 | 39.9 | 981 | 1,631 |
| E. Romagna | 121 | 592 | 981 | 1,694 | 109 | 5.6 | 1,803 | 46.2 | 2,097 | 3,900 |
| Tuscany | 57 | 463 | 833 | 1,353 | 125 | 8.4 | 1,478 | 42.4 | 2,010 | 3,488 |
| Umbria | 20 | 92 | 188 | 300 | 29 | 10.2 | 329 | 40 | 494 | 823 |
| Marches | 39 | 221 | 304 | 564 | 45 | 6.5 | 609 | 42.4 | 826 | 1,435 |
| Lazio | 80 | 362 | 1,375 | 1,817 | 259 | 12.8 | 2,076 | 40.2 | 3,085 | 5,161 |
| Abruzzo | 36 | 145 | 265 | 446 | 46 | 9.6 | 492 | 39 | 770 | 1,262 |
| Molise | 17 | 29 | 60 | 106 | 22 | 16.5 | 128 | 39 | 200 | 328 |
| Campania | 158 | 349 | 987 | 1,494 | 520 | 25.5 | 2,014 | 35 | 3,737 | 5,751 |
| Puglia | 145 | 285 | 697 | 1,127 | 268 | 17.7 | 1,395 | 34.5 | 2,653 | 4,048 |
| Basilicata | 26 | 52 | 93 | 171 | 41 | 18.1 | 212 | 35.2 | 391 | 603 |
| Calabria | 77 | 94 | 350 | 521 | 167 | 25.2 | 688 | 33.8 | 1,345 | 2,033 |
| Sicily | 157 | 259 | 877 | 1,293 | 416 | 23.5 | 1,709 | 33.8 | 3,343 | 5,052 |
| Sardinia | 61 | 114 | 317 | 492 | 131 | 21 | 623 | 37.8 | 1,023 | 1,646 |
| Italy | 1,370 | 6,448 | 12,267 | 20,085 | 2,805 | 12.1 | 22,89 | 40.3 | 33,978 | 56,868 |
| Center-North | 694 | 5,12 | 8,623 | 14,437 | 1,192 | 7.7 | 15,629 | 43.2 | 20,515 | 36,144 |
| South | 677 | 1,329 | 3,644 | 5,650 | 1,612 | 21.7 | 7,262 | 35 | 13,461 | 20,723 |

Source: Annuario Statistico Italiano 1998

Finally, unemployment is almost three times as high in the South compared to the Center-North. What is actually masked by national averages is the polarization between the two parts of the country. While in many northern areas, particularly in the North-East, small and medium size firms are experiencing a labor shortage, especially for skilled workers, the opposite holds true for most of Southern Italy. The progressive deterioration of the labor market in the South reflects the structural inability to create jobs in a context where demographic pressures are much greater than in the North. Whereas in the North the expansion of labor demand has been sufficient to draw in a substantial flow of immigration, in the South there has been a labor glut, affecting chiefly women and young people.

But one can hardly appreciate the dynamics currently at work in the southern economy without referring to the strategy pursued by the central government from the 1950s onwards to spur economic development in this area. Such a strategy was centered on the public establishment of huge industrial plants in the petrochemical, steel and metalwork sectors. However, the total failure of this approach became clearly evident during the 1980s and triggered the dismantling of many of the "desert cathedrals"—as the media labeled these industrial plants. The hemorrhage of job places stemming from this policy reversal accounts for the bulk of the estimated 600,000 jobs which were lost over the period 1991-1996.

As many economists have pointed out, the Mezzogiorno has moved into de-industrialization without having really industrialized, thereby rapidly turning from an agricultural to a service society with all the negative consequences that go along with such an abrupt shift. The data presented in table 2.5 on the regional size of employment by sector illustrate the point. Despite a substantial decrease during the 1980s, in 1996 industrial employment still represents 35 percent of total employment in the Center-North while in the South it is only 24 percent. At the same time, in this area the service sector accounts for as much as 64 percent, i.e., four percentage points above the northern level.

## Italian Unemployment Policies and the Southern Model of Welfare

As illustrated in the previous section, the problem of unemployment in Italy, especially in the southern part of the country is quite dramatic and surely calls for urgent measures to alleviate the situation. However, before discussing the kinds of policies currently being enacted in Italy and the extent to which they reflect mainstream workfare strategies, we need to shed some light on the policy legacy which characterizes this particular sector of the welfare state.

Most notably, unemployment policies have always played a marginal role within the Italian system of social protection. For instance, if we consider the development of social expenditure over the thirty-year period from the early 1950s to 1980, we can find clear evidence to support the point. Over this period expenditure for pensions increased from around 45 percent of total expenditure for income maintenance programs to as much as 80 percent, but outlays for the unemployment insurance constantly remained at a level of around 2 percent (Ferrera 1984).

Nor did the situation change during the 1980s when the jobless total started to soar. Throughout the decade expenditure for passive labor policies never exceeded 1 percent of GDP, placing Italy at the bottom of European rankings. Such an outcome might appear less surprising if we consider the labor market regime in which the Italian system of shock absorbers is embedded. In contrast to Britain's voluntarist approach, Italy developed a high level of labor market regulation. It goes beyond the scope of this paper to discuss at length either the legalism of continental industrial relations or its Mediterranean version. However, by focusing on the basic assumptions underpinning the Italian labor market regime we are in a better position to understand the path followed by unemployment policies.

In a nutshell, labor legislation since the 1960s has strengthened workers' rights and entitlements at employers' expense. However, this has had a pernicious, albeit unintended, consequence, namely it has reinforced the division between workers who are regular labor market participants and growing numbers of outsiders. The strategy pursued by the trade unions and formally sanctioned in the Workers Code of 1970 was aimed at reinforcing workers representation in the workplace and strictly limiting employers' freedom to hire and fire. Perhaps the most important restriction is the heavy penalty levied on the employer if a dismissal is judged "unfair": in such case economic compensation and mandatory re-hiring are imposed on the employer. Together with the favorable rulings traditionally handed down by the Courts to workers appealing dismissals, this has made outright dismissal extremely rare. Legislation has recently moved to reduce the stringency of such regulations and exemptions have been granted to small firms. From a different perspective the Code of 1990 also meant erecting high barriers around those who already had regular permanent jobs. Indeed, excessive and ill-advised regulation hampering both external and internal flexibility is what is usually lamented by the advocates of the Euro-sclerosis thesis. Without necessarily having to agree with the solutions suggested by this stream of thought, it is certain that over-regulation has favored the consolidation of a dual labor market, with highly negative implications from economic, social, political and fiscal points of view. Not surprisingly such a dual market reiterates the North-South cleavage: according to current estimates, non-regular work represents some 34 percent of total employment in the South as against 18 percent in the North. But how does this relate to the specific measures which have developed over time to protect the unemployed?

Let's start by considering the ordinary unemployment benefit. Throughout the postwar period only minor adjustments were introduced with respect to this program. In detail, the qualifying conditions have remained two years of employment with the relevant contributions, plus registration with the job placement agency. The benefit was and still is payable for a maximum of 180 days and consisted until 1988 of a ridiculously low daily flat rate. From 1988 to 1994 something started to change and the level of the benefit increased first to 28 percent and then to 30 percent of the previous wage.

These conditions and in particular the totally inadequate level of the benefit are largely responsible for spurring the clientelistic misuse of invalidity pensions, which has been for a long time a major distortion of the Italian social protection system. Patronage and the clientelistic exchange of invalidity pensions for political support could thrive on the basis of: (a) very low contributory requirements (only five years); and (b) the discretionary assessment of workers claims which was handled by local commissions comprising political, administrative and unions representatives. The rationale underlying the practical operation of the program was explicitly sanctioned in the early seventies. Parliament passed a provision stating that the local Commissions should take into account the level of social and economic deprivation in the area (!), when assessing invalidity claims. As the literature on the Italian welfare state largely documents, invalidity pensions have widely been used as a functional substitute for unemployment benefits, especially in the agricultural sector and more so in the southern part of the country. A few figures are in order to illustrate the extent of the phenomenon: (a) the pension fund for independent farmers was paying out by 1975 as many as 1,537,000 invalidity pensions as opposed to 601,000 old-age pensions; (b) from 1959 to 1972 old-age pensions grew from 3 to 4 million, while invalidity pensions soared from 1 to 4 million. The trend continued to the point that in 1978 invalidity pensions outnumbered old-age benefits reaching a peak level of 5,300,000.

It was only in the mid-eighties that legislative restrictions were finally introduced in order to curb the disproportionate growth of invalidity benefits. But apart from the particulars of these perverse effects, the point is that providing an adequate safety net against the risk of unemployment has certainly not been a top priority on the agenda of Italian policy makers. In sharp contrast, temporary unemployment has attracted a good deal of attention. Over time a number of different measures have been put in place to protect workers who were at risk of losing their jobs, rather than workers who had already lost them.

The first program providing short-term compensation in case of temporary layoffs or working time reductions was introduced back in 1941 for northern industries. After the war the coverage was gradually extended to the whole industrial sector, including white-collar workers. The benefits could be drawn in case of temporary difficulties experienced by the firm during broader economic or sector downturns. INPS (the major Italian social insurance agency), was entrusted with the management of the program and a specific fund therein was set up for the purpose. During the seventies and the eighties the relevance of this fund increased to the point that public opinion held the *Cassa Integrazione Guadagni* (Wage Compensation Fund) almost synonymous for unemployment policies altogether. Indeed, short-term compensation absorbed a disproportionate amount of total expenditure for unemployment in Italy, creating a situation unmatched in the other Western countries.

This outcome was brought about by the introduction in 1968 and the subsequent misuse of a special short-term unemployment benefit intended to be used in the event of industrial restructuring and re-organization. The trade unions successfully pressed for the extension of the original short-term compensation program in order to avoid massive layoffs during the economic downturn and industrial readjustments triggered by the first oil shock. The measure was extremely generous, offering a replacement rate of 80 percent of previous earnings and protecting redundant workers from job-loss. However, to understand how the program was actually implemented we should consider that: (a) eligibility was subject to negotiation between trade unions and employers and (b) up until 1988 the program was entirely financed by the state.

Under these circumstances, this particular option soon became very attractive for both unions and employers. On the one hand the program allowed for a freezing of firings—in line with the rigidity of labor market regulation strongly pursued by the trade unions, especially in the seventies—and on the other hand the financial and the social costs of industrial restructuring could be largely externalized by the firms. Highly unionized large firms were clearly in a better position to take advantage of the discretionary procedures involved in the operation of special short-term unemployment compensation. The result was such that this type of benefit entirely lost its temporary nature. Irrespective of whether or not the restructuring process would eventually create new working opportunities within the firm, coverage renewals, especially in large industrial plants, were granted for up to as many as ten years!

From the early seventies to the mid-eighties the number of hours compensated by the special fund constantly increased and in 1985 reached a peak level equivalent to around 400,000 workers reporting zero hours of work. "According to Tronti's estimates, a one percentage point increase in the number of hours covered by the CIG resulted, in the period 1972-1988, in a 0.75 percent slowdown in industrial hiring. This worsened the segmentation of the Italian labor market, discouraging labor mobility for protected workers and increasing the difficulties in finding 'secure jobs' for workers with little or no labor experience—the lower risk of income loss increased the power of insider workers in the unionized sectors by reducing competition from unemployed outsiders" (Dell'Aringa and Samek Lodovici 1996, 188).

While short-term compensation offers perhaps the clearest evidence of the allocative distortion typical of Italian shock absorbers, early retirement measures further reinforce such distortion. Along with France, Italy is the country that has most extensively used this measure. During the 1980s early retirement schemes involved on average 32,000 workers a year. Once more, this option was largely confined to the core sectors of the labor force.

Despite the high level of protection guaranteed by these two policy measures, the Italian system of protection offers no public assistance program for those workers whose ordinary unemployment benefits have expired or for those who do not even qualify for such "second-class" measures, including first-job seekers. Indeed, the lack of any social protection coverage for a young unemployed person in search of first employment is identified by Ferrera (1996) as an indicator of a distinct southern model of welfare. As highlighted by the author, the absence of a basic safety net and the unevenness of coverage among workers places Mediterranean countries in a very different position compared to the rest of Europe.

In greater detail, the coverage offered by the various programs operating in southern Europe remained low throughout the 1980s and continues to be the lowest in the European Union. According to Eurostat data, in 1993 only around a third of unemployed men 25 years of age and over received a benefit in Greece, Italy and Portugal[2] in contrast to virtually all men in Belgium, Denmark, Germany, Ireland and the UK. Not surprisingly in the same three countries the proportion drops even more for men under age 25, falling below 20 percent (European Commission 1998). Because there is still no universal public assistance scheme[3] in Italy, the only alternative for the vast majority of the unemployed is to resort to the discretionary benefits granted by municipalities. However, whereas regional governments in central and northern Italy have passed legislation promoting the establishment of minimum income programs by local authorities, quite the opposite holds true for the South (Fargion 1996, 1997). As shown in section one, this is exactly the area where the bulk of unemployment is concentrated and where two-thirds of Italian people living below the poverty line are located. The unquestionable result is a severe mismatch between social needs on the one hand and institutional capabilities and policy responses on the other.

The evidence provided so far most clearly illustrates the dualism of the Italian income maintenance system, which Spain, Portugal, and Greece also share. Ferrera (1996, 20) neatly and concisely summarizes this polarization as follows:

> On the one hand we find in these countries a group of hyper-protected beneficiaries who are (or have been) included in the citadels of garantismo: typically public employees, white collar workers and private wage-earners of medium and large enterprises

working on a full contract, with job security (the occupazione garantita). These categories receive generous replacement benefits for short-term risks (sickness, maternity, temporary or partial unemployment, etc.) and very high earnings related pensions when they retire. On the other hand we find large numbers of under-protected workers and citizens, who only (occasionally) draw meager benefits and may thus find themselves in conditions of severe hardship: typically irregular workers in weak sectors without job security (small enterprises, traditional services and agriculture, etc.) workers of the informal economy, young and long-term unemployed people.

Although this scenario on the whole still represents the current situation, the underpinnings of the Italian labor market regime started to erode during the 1980s. The blatant inequities inherent in the system could hardly be concealed as the number of unemployed started to soar during the economic recession of the early 1980s. Indeed, even the trade unions which had strongly supported demand management policies and strict employment protection legislation reluctantly began considering supply-side adjustments as possible strategies for dealing with labor market difficulties.

The first crack in the system can perhaps be identified with the tripartite agreement of 1983. As a result of this agreement, a 1984 law introduced work and training contracts to promote employment for youth in the age group 15 to 29 (for a maximum of two years) and legislation was also passed providing for work-sharing and part-time contracts.[4] From the point of view of the trade unions, these all represented concessions to the employers in order to ease the problem of unemployment. But in fact the trade unions wanted to maintain control over the application of the new rules, moving just one step ahead: from total rigidity to "flexibility controlled by the unions."

Some active measures were also introduced from the mid-eighties onwards, challenging what had been so far the almost exclusive reliance on passive policies. Yet such measures were primarily reactions to contingent pressures and can hardly be considered a full-fledged strategy. In fact, the titles of the relevant laws explicitly refer to "urgent," "special" or "extraordinary" provisions. For instance, the title of law 1137 of 1986 is "Special plan for youth employment"; in the same vein, law 44 of the same year refers to "Special measures to promote entrepreneurship."

Practically all of the active measures passed in the eighties are targeted at youth unemployment. In addition, they all call for a decentralization of this policy field at the regional and local level. After many years of unsuccessful claims, the Regions succeeded in being legitimated as relevant actors in this policy arena.[5] However, the new political bodies and administrative structures were simply juxtaposed over the old system of public job placement dependent on the national Labor Ministry. The result was inevitably an intricate maze of highly inefficient and largely ineffective institutional arrangements.

In short, the legislation of the 1980s did in fact introduce some innovative elements but their impact was overwhelmed by pre-existing policy arrangements in a context dominated by the kind of inclusive coalitions typical of distributive politics. Bargaining over the concession of early retirement to one group of workers or the reiteration of special short-term benefits to another largely concealed the steps taken to develop the first active labor policies at the local level. In a broader perspective one can note that Government and Parliament were involved in passing some restrictive measures aimed at cost-containment—such as the introduction of co-payments in the health sector or tighter selection of beneficiaries in the case of family allowances and disability pensions. However, the predominant approach reflects the entrenched difficulty Italian policy makers have in using equitable criteria in the distribution of costs and benefits and their long-term inability to address structural problems as epitomized by the ever delayed reform of the pension system. In contrast to most other European countries Italy did not contain its growing fiscal imbalance and lingered on playing distributive games and spending freely throughout the 1980s. As a result the country witnessed an unrestrained growth of the public debt—from 54 to 104 percent of GDP—and budget deficits reaching as much as 11 percent of GDP by the end of the decade.

## The Early 1990s: Transition Under Emergency Conditions

The 1990s mark a definite turning point in the development of postwar Italy, to the extent that in the domestic debate this period has been labeled as the transition from the First to the Second Republic. Not surprisingly the collapse of the old party system reflects a deep change in the style and the content of policy making. Such change is most clearly visible in macro-economic and financial policies, but also in social policy reforms where there have been open attempts to redress the major distortions of the Italian welfare model. The pension reform of 1995 is certainly the best case in point, but a similar trend can be detected in most areas of social protection. As might be expected, difficulties and hesitations have slowed down this process of painful adjustment. This also holds true for unemployment policies. While the intention to reach international standards and procedures shapes policy formulation, it is somehow undermined by the demands of coping with the dramatic legacy of the previous decades.

More precisely, the principles and the philosophical justification underpinning mainstream workfare strategies throughout Europe clearly filtered into the measures passed during the 1990s in Italy. Yet, one might better identify the new policy course as embryonic workfare under emergency constraints. Indeed, while the main provisions adopted from 1991 onwards clearly set unemployment policies on a new track, their implementation cannot avoid coming to terms with the dismal record of job creation in the Italian economy and with the quite problematic outcomes of previous programs. To put it differently, the disruptive effects of such pieces of legislation as law 223 of 1991 are dampened by a series of ad hoc measures prompted by the (socially and politically) intolerable concentration of unemployment in particular geographical areas.

Most certainly, law 223 represents a critical disjuncture with previous developments in the field, in particular the misuse of short-term earnings compensation programs. The explicit aim of the law is in fact to put an end to the improper freezing of employment status for redundant workers that have no real possibility of being reintegrated into the firm. Considering the evidence presented in the previous section, there can be little doubt as to whether this is actually a departure from the existing policy path. If we extend the analysis to the rationale underlying particular provisions, the above consideration is strengthened even further. Law 223 is couched in the language of supply-side adjustments and touches on the basic elements that make up the workfare logic. By discouraging the passive collection of benefits and promoting unemployed workers' "employability"—as suggested by the EU jargon—emphasis has clearly shifted to reintegrating the unemployed into the workforce as swiftly as possible.

The law covers three main subjects. As already mentioned, the first refers to the *Cassa Integrazione...guadagni*. In order to bring this policy instrument back to its original purpose, namely providing coverage in case of temporary lay-off of workers, strict limitations are set on both duration and eligibility for benefits. However, to make this policy instrument more equitable and in tune with the changes occurring within the Italian economy, the use of it is extended to firms in the trade sector employing more than 200 workers and to industrial handicraft. Instead of simply relying on negotiations with the workers' trade unions, firms which request the special short-term compensation scheme are required to present a detailed restructuring plan and to scale up their financial contribution to the relevant fund. Under these circumstances, it was not so surprising that during the debate over the law a reversal of roles apparently took place between the major trade unions and the leading employers' association. Indeed, the former—finding it increasingly difficult to sustain the privileges and the anomalies connected to the old system—strongly pushed for its reform. The latter instead moved to a very cautious and to some extent ambiguous position, realizing that the new system would be far more burdensome for employers and would also place a clear responsibility on their shoulders. After all the previous arrangement "allowed industrial restructuring to take place at a lower cost and with less social tension compared to other European countries where collective dismissals were more traumatic" (Reyneri 1996).

Secondly, the law introduces "mobility" rolls as a standard procedure to deal with redundancies. Registration of dismissed workers on mobility rolls—while definitely severing every link with previous employers—provides a very generous twelve months allowance for workers dismissed from firms which employ more than fifteen people.[6] However, as in most other European workfare programs, the benefit is progressively scaled down providing an indirect incentive for workers to speed up their job search. Furthermore, workers are formally required to attend training programs or to engage in "socially useful jobs," lest they be disqualified from receiving the benefit. In a broader perspective this clearly sanctions some form of conditionality and obligation in return for the benefit, as highlighted by workfare ideology in both the Anglo-Saxon and milder European versions. On the other hand, the new emphasis on supply-side adjustments prompts Regional Labor Agencies to assume a primary role in active labor policies by entrusting them with the responsibility for training, job orientation and job creation initiatives.

The third crucial topic addressed by law 223 refers to redundant workers close to retirement who have a long history of contributions. The provisions dealing with this matter explicitly break with the widespread use of early retirement typical of the 1980s. The law actually provides for a phasing out of early retirement schemes, setting a well-defined ceiling for the on-going year. Whereas this very costly instrument is ruled out from future prospects, the law envisages a "long mobility" allowance as an alternative. This particular allowance is intended to cover the beneficiaries close to retirement age until they are eligible for pension benefits. Qualifying conditions are extremely restrictive, however, and severely limit the possibility of resorting to the scheme.

In summary, there is ample evidence to consider this law as a watershed in the development of Italian unemployment policies. But as we have anticipated, it would be misleading to limit our analysis to what is formally sanctioned in the law. Each of the aforementioned measures were immediately followed by an intricate and detailed set of provisions which undermined the most disruptive effects of the original rulings. The result is such that when jurists approach the subject they usually refer to a "regulatory galaxy" (Giubboni 1999). Without attempting to disentangle the legal setting in this area, it is useful to highlight at least some points. Let's start with the special short-term compensation scheme (GIGS). Between 1992 and 1996 the different cabinets in power issued a whole chain of relevant legislative decrees—which were eventually turned into three main laws.[7] These provisions extended coverage to new sectors, but, more importantly, they repeatedly extended the original duration of special compensation, once again loosening the temporary nature of this type of benefit. Moreover, according to Reyneri (1996, 370) "the particularistic management of the scheme remains intact: hardly any applications to CIGS are rejected during preliminary administrative proceedings on the grounds of inadequate restructuring planning with the usual political-administrative bargaining continuing instead to take place." The latter comment is perhaps too pessimistic but it certainly points to the difficulty of reversing entrenched practices and policies.

We see a similar outcome with the second major innovation introduced by law 223, namely the establishment of mobility rolls and of a connected mobility allowance. What we find is a series of dispensations from the originally set time limits for mobility allowances. This continued until 1995 when a legislative decree issued by the government[8] overrode the chaotic reiteration of individual time extensions. The interesting part is that this was accomplished by establishing a brand-new benefit—the "*sussidio*"—for all workers whose benefit had expired—be it short-term compensation or mobility allowance—provided they agreed to be engaged in "socially useful jobs." Given the relevance of this policy instrument in the emerging scenario of unemployment policies, the issue will be discussed at length in the next section. At present we shall only comment that one could hardly understand such a policy choice without considering: (a) the persistent inability of the Italian labor market to reintegrate expelled workers and (b) mounting social pressure in areas such as Apulia or Campania where a very heavy concentration of long-term industrial unemployment resulted from the crumbling of state-assisted industrialization.

To complete the picture, we should finally focus on legislative developments dealing with redundant workers close to retirement age. Here we are confronted with a progressive relaxation of the stringent conditions set by the 1991 law regarding eligibility for the "long mobility" allowance. At the same time, access to early retirement does not come to a halt with as many as 11,300 and 12,391 new entries respectively in 1994 and 1995.[9] Under these circumstances, one can understand why early retirement was made the object of a Parliamentary inquiry launched by the Labor and Social Security Committee of the Chamber of Representatives in October 1996. Indeed, the final report openly criticizes early retirement as the most blatant example of the asymmetric coverage offered by Italian shock absorbers. According to the Commission, whereas insider workers belonging to the industrial and the building sector of the economy have largely taken advantage of this costly program, occupational groups in less protected sectors such as the tertiary sector could only rely on ordinary unemployment benefits.

How can we pull all these different threads together? Should we conclude that the attempt to reform passive labor policies pursued by the 1991 law was a substantial failure? If so, was this law just a symbolic exercise? I argue that the answer cannot be so straightforward. The law has actually set this policy field on new ground, but the transition has apparently turned out to be more controversial than originally expected. Perhaps the seeds sown in 1991 could hardly be expected to mature overnight and are just now starting to produce their fruit.

Results, especially from the first half of the decade, appear rather mixed. Yet, we can find some further evidence pointing to the emergence of a new trend by turning from legislation to spending levels and, more precisely, to the distribution of expenditure by type of benefit. Table 2.6 provides all the relevant information for the period 1989-1995. We can start by focusing on early retirement, which notably represented the single largest item of expenditure at the end of the eighties. Although the program was not abruptly phased out (as envisaged by the 1991 law), the table documents a downward trend in the level of spending from 1991 onwards.

If we look at short-term benefits what we notice is a substantial increase in expenditure, particularly in connection with the 1992-93 recession. This increase was followed, however, by a reversal of the trend at the end of the period. Actually between 1993 and 1995 resources allocated for this purpose were cut by half. It is clear that the latter down-turn as well as the internal redistribution of resources from special to standard benefits were obviously congruent with the reiterated objective of scaling down the *Cassa Integrazione Guadagni* and its special scheme in particular. Furthermore, the decrease in expenditure for short-term benefits was compensated by a sharp rise in spending for mobility allowances and steadily growing outlays for ordinary unemployment benefits. In other words, we are confronted with a consistent, albeit not massive, shift of resources from

**Table 2.6**
**Unemployment Benefits by Type, 1989-1995 (in billions of lira)**

| Benefits | 1989 | 1990 | 1991 | 1992 | 1993 | 1994 | 1995 |
|---|---|---|---|---|---|---|---|
| Short-term Standard Benefits – Industry | 144 | 275 | 764 | 976 | 1.427 | 789 | 326 |
| Short-term Standard Benefits – Construction | 214 | 229 | 393 | 432 | 486 | 499 | 359 |
| Short-term Special Benefits | 1.731 | 1.229 | 1.395 | 1.683 | 1.734 | 1.683 | 1.154 |
| Total short-term benefits | 2.089 | 1.733 | 2.552 | 3.091 | 3.647 | 2.971 | 1.839 |
| Ordinary Unemployment Benefits | 2.506 | 3.225 | 3.109 | 3.251 | 3.851 | 4.345 | 4.032 |
| "Mobility" benefits | 0 | 0 | 123 | 685 | 1.502 | 2.362 | 1.880 |
| Early-retirement | 3.159 | 3.248 | 3.549 | 3.497 | 3.369 | 2.902 | 2.914 |
| Total benefits | 7.754 | 8.206 | 9.333 | 10.524 | 12.369 | 12.58 | 10.665 |

*Source:* Onofri Commission, Document no. 2

over-protected to under-protected workers. On the basis of our previous discussion of the Italian system of shock absorbers, this certainly appears as a prerequisite for any further reform. While this effort might seem small or insufficient in light of, for example, the amount of resources funneled to the pension system, the direction of reform is quite clear.

## "Socially Useful Jobs": Workfare or Welfare?

When discussing the workfare component of 1990s Italian unemployment policies, one can hardly avoid talk about "socially useful jobs." Although from a quantitative point of view "socially useful jobs" are definitely less relevant than most other employment related programs, they represent perhaps the most controversial issue in this policy domain. In order to appreciate why they have become and still are such a hot topic of debate, it is informative to review their development.

"Socially useful jobs" were introduced back in 1981 with reference to redundant workers from public infrastructure projects in Southern Italy. The aim of the relevant law was to allow workers receiving short-term compensation to top-up their earnings by engaging in community jobs organized by public agencies. A subsequent law in 1984 extended the possibility of organizing such jobs to the rest of the country, but in fact both provisions remained largely ineffective with only scattered local initiatives actually getting off the ground. As mentioned in the previous section, the issue was brought up again by law 223 of 1991. However, in just a few years the approach to the program was almost completely reversed suggesting the necessity for a more detailed temporal analysis.

### *Phase I: Legislation without Implementation*

According to the 1991 law, involvement in socially useful jobs was an obligation for beneficiaries of short-term compensation or the mobility allowance. Yet, the whole issue was substantially ignored until 1993 when the topic of socially useful jobs entered the tripartite agreement reached by the Ciampi government. As we might recall, this agreement along with the one signed in 1992 by the Amato government, marks the beginning of a new phase in industrial relations allowing for wage moderation and the reform of collective bargaining. A phase—we might add—that witnesses the resurgence of neo-corporatist arrangements, whereby the governments of the transition period attempt to bypass their political weakness by getting the social partners directly involved in decision-making on crucial labor market issues. Within this context, socially useful jobs were viewed as a means for expanding working opportunities and thereby legitimated as a relevant component of the overall strategy to fight inflation and unemployment.

As a byproduct of the Ciampi protocol, a comprehensive regulation of this policy instrument was provided for the first time through a series of more or less identical government decrees, eventually converted into law 451 of 1994. Retrospectively, it appears quite useful to isolate the period 1993-1994, which covers the initial definition of the program. We should first of all point out that the relevant legislative provisions envisage a bifurcation in socially useful jobs corresponding to the identification of two distinct categories of beneficiaries. Workers enjoying short-term compensation or the mobility allowance compose the first category, while unemployed workers without any social insurance coverage, particularly long-term unemployed and first-job seekers, make up the second. One can easily note how this reflects the distinction between the original nucleus of policy intervention of the early eighties and the new perspective stemming from the tripartite agreement of 1993. At the risk of being tedious, we need to focus more closely on the specific arrangements for each of the two groups in order to fully grasp what has been at stake in this particular policy area.

Starting with the first group of workers, participation in the program is openly depicted as an obligation which is sanctioned by suspension of the benefit in case of noncompliance. It also offers workers the possibility of topping up their earnings through the monetary integration provided by the agency engaging them. Most clearly, the underlying objective is to avoid irregular work by unemployed workers receiving social insurance benefits, thus enhancing transparency of the labor market and counteracting the expansion of the informal sector of the economy. The second group of beneficiaries are limited to no more than twelve months of engagement with a maximum working time of 80 hours per month at a fixed hourly compensation.

Despite the fact that the two beneficiary groups work under quite different financial arrangements, with the latter receiving far less generous benefits, in both cases emphasis is placed on the obligations as well the rights of claimants. In short, the relevant legislative provisions appear to be influenced by the workfare ideology and clearly reflect the idea that it is legitimate to ask people to fulfil some obligations in return for benefits. As for the content of working programs the law excludes routine activities and instead earmarks funds for the development of special projects in innovative sectors such as environmental protection or urban renewal. Within this context, "socially useful jobs" are essentially public jobs that can be created by any branch of the public administration at the central, regional or local level and also by the non-profit sector. The procedures are quite burdensome with a lot of bureaucratic red tape and a centralist leaning, as exemplified by the establishment of a national board of experts located within the Ministry of Labor that is responsible for screening proposals.

However, turning from legislation to facts one gets the impression that during this first phase politicians and the social partners were not seriously invested in getting the new program off the ground and were essentially paying lip-service to the workfare approach being developed in the rest of Europe. A 1994 study by CNEL (National Council for the Economy and Labor) documents very little activity by the various branches of public administration which were supposed to set up the relevant projects and a similar—albeit perhaps more surprising—lack of interest by worker trade unions. The behavior of Regional Employment Commissions in charge of approving local projects is even more indicative as it openly undermined the goals officially stated in the law. Unemployed workers were asked to participate in "socially useful jobs" exclusively on the basis of voluntary requests!

*Phase II: From Workfare Language to Welfare Practice*

Starting with 1995 a second and quite distinct phase can be detected. During the new phase we are confronted with an explosion of "socially useful jobs" and at the same time by a systematic distortion of the features and goals set down in the 1994 law. At first glance, the new trend appears surprising, given that Parliament had only just converted into law (December 1994) the chain of government decrees provisionally regulating the subject. But what actually triggered this contradictory outcome is the emergency situation which emerged at this very point in time. As many as 300,000 of the benefits granted under the recently introduced mobility allowance program in fact expired in December 1994, with almost no beneficiaries reintegrated into the workforce. Despite all the incentives envisaged by the 1991 law to encourage firms to hire unemployed workers on "mobility" rolls, in fact these soon turned out to be only entry rolls offering no real possibility of being re-employed. As a result, a vast number of workers were about to be canceled from the lists and left without any kind of income support, thus creating a socially explosive problem especially in some southern regions. The situation was particularly dramatic in Campania and Puglia, which had heavy concentrations of unemployed workers.

Under these circumstances what happened seems quite understandable: expanding "socially useful jobs"—or perhaps for the first time really initiating them—was the only way to avoid social unrest in hot areas such as Naples or Turin where unemployed workers were highly mobilized and vociferous. Some solution had to be found and it had to be found quickly! Along these lines a number of provisions laid down in the 1994 law were suspended and criteria for setting up the relevant projects were relaxed.[10] The goal of providing some alternative before losing control of the whole situation resulted first of all in simplifying procedures and decentralizing the approval, financing and monitoring of relevant projects. Certainly, removing some red tape could be interpreted as a healthy measure but the strategy was actually intended to speed up the process[11] regardless of the content and profile that "socially useful jobs" might acquire along the way. The trade-off was obviously between quantity and quality. Indeed, most of the projects initiated in the period refer to routine administrative activities in the public sector, which were openly excluded in the original rulings.

The driving force behind the move appears most clearly if we look at the kind of workers engaged in the newly set up programs. As many as 53,000 positions are created from scratch in just a few months and over 66 percent of them are occupied by unemployed workers whose benefits expired in December 1994 (Perrone 1996, 9). In essence, "socially useful jobs" swiftly became a new type of social shock absorber that allowed for the continuation of social protection to the advantage of only a limited group of unemployed workers. In the wording of legislative decree no. 31 of 1995, workers are obliged to participate in "socially useful jobs" in order to receive an extra 12 months of coverage at 64 percent of temporary unemployment compensation. As the new policy came into effect—

triggering a progressive expansion in the number of "socially useful jobs"—the paramount importance of insured workers as opposed to first-job seekers became more evident. Indeed, in 1996 a government decree stipulated that at least 15 percent of earmarked national funds allocated to the regional level be reserved to workers not enjoying any social insurance benefit. In short, the particular component of "socially useful jobs" stemming from the tripartite agreement of 1993 and largely aimed at reaching the outsiders of the labor market almost vanished during this phase. Once more, a privileged category takes shape and a new divide develops between insiders and outsiders.

The picture we have outlined is largely confirmed by relevant developments in the subsequent two years. Actually, detailed information on the subject is scanty for 1995 and mostly produced by workers trade unions and regional employment agencies. However, starting in 1996 the Ministry of Labor began to produce a special report to Parliament every six months. The report has actually circulated very little but it contains a great deal of statistical data. Yet, if we consider that the program increasingly acquired a welfare scope and that relevant projects essentially consisted of dead-end jobs, one could hardly expect to find the kind of monitoring and performance-driven ideology typical of British workfare policies. Under these circumstances, the available information is perhaps sufficient to grasp the basics of the story.

First, we should note that the original allocation of 495 billion lira in 1995 went up to 1,150 billion lira in 1996, stabilizing at roughly the same level in 1997. These figures represent the total amount of resources funneled through the National Employment Fund to the regions and to inter-regional projects.[12] Since the latter are consistently less relevant, the largest share of funding has regularly gone to the regions which in turn provided for the distribution of funding among the local projects selected by the Regional Employment Commission. As indicated in table 2.7, by 1997 "socially useful jobs" organized within regions reached a total figure of 75,119 people. However, to have an accurate picture we should also consider the 13,425 further jobs that stemmed from inter-regional projects.[13] Focusing on the break-down by age group, it is most interesting to note that only 10 percent of workers are under 30 years old. The bulk is represented by prime age male blue collar workers. Indeed, as many as 67 percent of workers fall in the age group between 30 and 49. Gender composition is really weighted towards male workers (62 percent versus 38 percent) and finally blue-collar workers represent 83 percent of the total as against 18 percent of white-collar workers.

There is ample evidence to support how biased the program actually turned out to be. But the table also points to substantial subnational variations. As we might expect, the largest concentration of jobs can be found in Campania (the Region where Naples is located), Puglia and Lazio. The three Regions account by themselves for about 60 percent of all "socially useful jobs." Yet, territorial differences do not simply reflect how severe the unemployment problem has been in the various geographical areas. If we take a look at what type of workers are engaged in "socially useful jobs," two quite distinct patterns emerge reflecting the north-south divide.

**Table 2.7**
**"Socially Useful Jobs": Currently Employed Workers in Regional Projects by Age, Sex, Professional Status, and Region, 1997**

| Region | age < 29 years | age 30-39 years | age 40-49 years | age > 50 years | Blue-collar workers | White-collar workers | Men | Women | Total engaged workers |
|---|---|---|---|---|---|---|---|---|---|
| Val d'Aosta | 8 | 27 | 52 | 44 | 102 | 29 | 44 | 87 | 131 |
| Piedmont | 978 | 929 | 777 | 792 | 2,347 | 1,129 | 959 | 2,517 | 3,476 |
| Lombardy | 112 | 126 | 199 | 194 | 449 | 182 | 318 | 313 | 631 |
| Liguria | 422 | 460 | 312 | 173 | 726 | 641 | 732 | 635 | 1,367 |
| Trentino-AA | 1 | | 4 | 1 | 6 | | 6 | | 6 |
| Veneto | 141 | 125 | 187 | 290 | 453 | 290 | 400 | 343 | 743 |
| Friuli | 42 | 69 | 70 | 168 | 251 | 98 | 174 | 175 | 349 |
| E.Romagna | 115 | 112 | 69 | 84 | 207 | 173 | 144 | 236 | 380 |
| Tuscany | 272 | 509 | 363 | 454 | 1,182 | 416 | 524 | 1,074 | 1,598 |
| Umbria | 48 | 337 | 408 | 359 | 825 | 327 | 430 | 722 | 1,152 |
| Marches | 169 | 421 | 470 | 404 | 1,093 | 371 | 322 | 1,142 | 1,464 |
| Lazio | 1,488 | 3,34 | 3,668 | 1,949 | 8,363 | 2,172 | 4,869 | 5,666 | 10,535 |
| Abruzzo | 312 | 1,027 | 855 | 583 | 2,197 | 580 | 1,252 | 1,525 | 2,777 |
| Molise | 68 | 256 | 223 | 170 | 577 | 140 | 426 | 291 | 717 |
| Campania | 1,06 | 8,457 | 8,913 | 5,435 | 21,636 | 2,229 | 18,277 | 5,588 | 23,865 |
| Puglia | 823 | 3,324 | 4,208 | 2,504 | 9,687 | 1,172 | 7,325 | 3,534 | 10,859 |
| Basilicata | 423 | 1,26 | 1,39 | 1,4 | 3,663 | 810 | 3,13 | 1,343 | 4,473 |
| Calabria | 293 | 1,608 | 2,135 | 1,248 | 4,733 | 551 | 4,402 | 882 | 5,284 |
| Sicily | | | | | | | | | |
| Sardinia | 797 | 2,027 | 1,472 | 1,016 | 4,153 | 1,159 | 2,95 | 2,362 | 5,312 |
| Total | 7,572 | 24,504 | 25,775 | 17,268 | 62,65 | 12,469 | 46,684 | 28,435 | 75,119 |

*Source:* Parliamentary Report on "Socially Useful Jobs," I Semester, 1997

**Table 2.8**
**Workers Engaged in "Socially Useful Jobs" by Region and Type of Social Protection Coverage, 1997**

| | Workers whose social insurance benefits expired | Workers with no previous social insurance coverage | Workers on mobility rolls | Workers on short-term compensation | Other Categories | Total |
|---|---|---|---|---|---|---|
| Val d' Aosta | 51 | 61 | 19 | | | 131 |
| Piedmont | 380 | 2,517 | 427 | | 152 | 3,476 |
| Lombardy | 98 | 164 | 318 | 20 | 31 | 631 |
| Liguria | 97 | 1,050 | 107 | | 113 | 1,367 |
| Trentino A. A. | | | 5 | 1 | | 6 |
| Veneto | 38 | 366 | 317 | 15 | 7 | 743 |
| Friuli | 52 | 44 | 248 | 5 | | 349 |
| E. Romagna | | 312 | 68 | | | 380 |
| Tuscany | 490 | 607 | 397 | 44 | 60 | 1,598 |
| Umbria | 1,033 | | 106 | | 13 | 1,152 |
| Marches | 801 | 393 | 270 | | | 1,464 |
| Latium | 6,958 | 1,566 | 1,335 | 201 | 475 | 10,535 |
| Abruzzo | 496 | 1,011 | 1,116 | | 154 | 2,777 |
| Molise | 271 | 102 | 185 | | 159 | 717 |
| Campania | 20,450 | 1,557 | 1,248 | | 610 | 23,865 |
| Puglia | 7,334 | 1,287 | 1,873 | 242 | 123 | 10,859 |
| Basilicata | 1,829 | 845 | 1,308 | 5 | 486 | 4,473 |
| Calabria | 2,773 | 1,158 | 782 | 93 | 478 | 5,284 |
| Sicily | | | | | | |
| Sardinia | 1,858 | 3,454 | | | | 5,312 |
| Italy | 45,009 | 16,494 | 10,129 | 646 | 2,310 | 75,119 |

*Source:* Parliamentary Report on "Socially Useful Jobs," I Semester, 1997

Table 2.8 provides some relevant information to support the point. In detail, the table offers a breakdown of unemployed workers engaged in "socially useful jobs" based on whether or not they received in the past or are currently receiving social insurance benefits. By focusing on the first two columns, one can notice two different patterns. In the North and in Tuscany, workers with no previous social insurance coverage largely outnumber workers having enjoyed such coverage and whose benefits have expired. On the contrary, the latter are absolutely predominant in southern regions but also in the central regions of Umbria, Marches and Lazio. In essence, the first group of regions conceives "socially useful jobs" as a policy instrument primarily targeted at unemployed workers who have always been excluded from social protection. Hence, this policy offers an opportunity for income support and work experience especially to unemployed youth and first-job seekers. In contrast, "socially useful jobs" in the other regions are first and foremost an expedient for providing an extension of coverage once all other social insurance benefits have been exhausted. If we take a closer look at the figures in column 2, related to the number of positions created for the "outsiders," with the exception of Sardinia all other southern regions appear to limit their action to meeting the 15 percent clause set by law. Finally, the data presented in the last two columns suggest that in a very short span of time the group of recipients envisaged by the original legislation on "socially useful jobs" (i.e., workers on mobility rolls and short-term compensation) ended up playing a rather minor role; this certainly weakened the rhetoric on behavioral requirements originally connected to the 1991 law.

Under these circumstances, it is not surprising to find radically diverging comments on the experience of "socially useful jobs" as expressed by the Employment Agencies of Molise and Emilia Romagna in the Parliamentary Report of 1997. According to the former:

> It is unfortunate that up to now, especially in southern regions, the reservoir of potential recipients of the benefits connected to "socially useful jobs" only continues to fill: those who get in do not get out and we are accumulating increasing numbers of beneficiaries. Quite clearly a vicious circle has developed; on the one hand forcing public agencies to draw up new projects for "socially useful jobs" and on the other hand forcing local social and political actors to press for further resources. This clearly makes it possible to continue providing for the workers already engaged in the projects while allowing for new entries into the reservoir.

The considerations put forward by the Employment Agency of Emilia Romagna could not be more divergent in terms of the issues under consideration:

> Resources are allocated according to the rank order of the project. Project ranking is based on qualitative criteria. Starting from the most to the least important these criteria are intended to tap: (a) the extent to which the proposed activity is innovative and meets specific social needs; (b) the prospects for creating permanent job opportunities; (c) the quality of professional services rendered by the workers; (d) the involvement of workers with special placement difficulties; (e) the quality of skill up-grading connected to the project.

We can certainly draw on a variety of other sources to document the ambivalent outcome of "socially useful jobs." While the implementation of the program resulted in undermining its original workfare frame practically everywhere, it is perhaps inaccurate to cast a negative judgment over the experience altogether. Especially where the numbers have been small—as in most northern regions—"socially useful jobs" provided the opportunity to set up a sort of experimental laboratory for innovative practices and policies, particularly in the area of personal social services, environmental protection and urban renewal. Further, the few micro-analyses that have been carried out point to a highly positive psychological effect on participants—a result that cannot be quickly dismissed considering the emotional and the moral suffering entailed particularly by long-term unemployment.

*Phase III: It Was All a Mistake!*

Notwithstanding the above qualifications, the agenda of recent political debate has focused clearly on the record of the massive projects launched in southern Italy. And one can hardly blame politicians for taking this approach. As mentioned previously, the bulk of workers have been engaged in routine administrative activities and certainly not in innovative sectors—counter to the mandates in the original rulings. Moreover, such workers represent an essentially privileged group within the overall category of the unemployed. Hence, it is not surprising that in the third, most recent phase, the thrust of political discourse and decision making has been on how to downsize and ultimately to eliminate altogether these types of jobs.

This phase began—I would argue—in 1997 with the approval of government decree no. 468, usually referred to as the reform of "socially useful jobs."[14] The decree is heralded especially by trade unions as a turning point in ending the misuse of the program. At first glance, the most striking element is the apparently meaningless distinction between the well-known "socially useful jobs" and the newly introduced category of "public service jobs" (*lavori di pubblica utilità*). But in fact the nominal differentiation reflects a clear-cut distinction between what are considered in essence dead-end jobs and those jobs that can instead be turned into permanent market positions. While the former are depicted as the basic problem that needs to be handled and hopefully solved during the transition period of 1998-1999, the latter are fully legitimated as a piece of the puzzle making up prospective "activation" policies. The decree's financial arrangements provide perhaps the clearest evidence of the government's priorities. Starting with the year 2000, regional employment commissions will be required to allocate 80 percent of the relevant state funding for "public service jobs" and projects especially designed for skill up-grading in innovative sectors. As a result only 20 percent of the resources handed down by the central state is left for the traditional type of "socially useful jobs."

But what exactly is meant by "public service jobs"? In essence, these jobs are supposed to represent an "embryo enterprise" or to put it differently they reflect a temporary opportunity offered to the unemployed, formally and exclusively geared to an occupational outcome in the market. The actual possibility of setting up stable and self-sustaining job positions in the private market must be demonstrated through the submission of a detailed enterprise plan drafted by a certified employment promotion agency. As in the case of "socially useful jobs," participation in any such project does give workers the formal status of an employee.[15] Finally, once the publicly financed program is over, the decree especially envisages mixed companies (with at least 51 percent of private capital) and cooperatives for the management of the relevant activities.[16]

As noted, "public service jobs" are largely projected into the future. Actually, one gets the impression that this represents a stubborn attempt to save at least something from the last decade's cumulative theorizing and experience. Not surprisingly, the phrasing emphasizes work insertion along with punitive rules and sanctions. In the case of projects not resulting in the creation of market positions, the rules stipulate a 50 percent reimbursement of public funding. But what in fact is politically crucial in this piece of legislation is the phasing out of traditional "socially useful jobs." Decree 468 clearly sets the guidelines for such a delicate procedure listing a wide range of exit options for unemployed workers previously or currently engaged in these projects. The details were left to a subsequent ministerial decree but the process is unequivocally set in motion. Indeed, in the following months the press paid special attention to these measures and their impact, largely disregarding all other parts of the decree and at least in the major newspapers frequently referring to "emptying the reservoir of socially useful jobs."

Actually, the list of measures approved just a few months later by ministerial decree in favor of the 120,000 unemployed workers meeting the requirements widens even further the range of opportunities envisaged by the original government provision. The list includes the following: (a) a 50 percent bonus of residual social contributions for workers missing five years to retirement age and an immediately reduced pension; (b) a lump sum of 20 million lira for each worker setting up a new activity (including a cooperative enterprise) by December 1998; (c) 18 million lira (divided in three yearly installments) for each worker employed by a private firm, mixed company or agency placing workers on short or fixed term contracts; (d) deed loans of up to 50 million lira; (e) a premium of 3 million lira for each person successfully reintegrated into the work force by the newly introduced private placement agencies.

In light of the above, the comment offered by the Deputy Minister of Labor Antonio Pizzinato in an interview to the Italian leading financial newspaper *Il Sole—24 Ore* ( 23 April 1998) appears most appropriate: "At this point in time we need to move from the stage of polemics to an extraordinary effort to close a chapter."

## The Second Half of the Decade: Towards a Comprehensive Redefinition of Labor Policies

The third phase of "socially useful jobs" that we have just discussed actually took place within the context of an overall acceleration in the reform and reorganization of unemployment policies. This acceleration is clearly connected to the Prodi government that came into power in June 1996, and in particular to the very active stance taken by the Minister of Labor and Social Security Tiziano Treu, a leading Italian scholar in the field of labor law and industrial relations. The strong commitment by the Minister to rationalize and innovate labor policies and to bring Italy in line with the rest of Europe is reflected in what is usually labeled "the Treu package." This is a comprehensive law (law no. 196 of 1997) originally initiated by Minister Treu and passed by Parliament which set the relevant guidelines and empowered the government to revise legislation on a wide range of issues pertaining to employment policies. The topics subject to government review included: (a) new types of work (fixed-term contracts, temporary work, part-time); (b) working time and over-time work; and (c) the whole system of vocational training. The government was also entrusted with responsibility for drafting a special employment plan for the *Mezzogiorno* and devising a set of incentives promoting the transition of firms from the irregular to the formal sector of the economy.

The other side of the coin is represented by the decentralizing strategy pursued by the government and epitomized in government decree no. 469 of December 1997. This legislation opened a new phase in the development of Italian active labor policies, putting an end to the confusion and overlap of functions between the regional and the central levels of government (Pinelli 1998). The role of the state was in fact restricted to a well-defined set of areas[17] while the region emerged as the pivot point of the newly designed system. In particular, the responsibility for job placement was transferred from the national Ministry of Labor to the regional governments and a new definition of this policy realm was provided. Indeed, it is worth recalling that the performance of public placement offices has always been dramatically poor. According to a study by *Confindustria*, the major employers' association, in recent years only between 5 and 8 percent of those getting jobs found them through public placement offices.

In line with European Union suggestions, the new rules emphasized individual counseling and job orientation in an attempt to eliminate the bureaucratic blueprint attached to the old system. This approach was further complemented by opening job placement to the private sector. The issue had long been debated and the Prodi government actually took action before the ECJ's judgment against Italy's public monopoly in the field.[18]

It goes beyond the scope of this paper to attempt a comprehensive review of this wide-ranging reform process. Yet, we certainly need to call attention to the crucial input by the special commission on the reform of the Italian welfare state, set up by the Prodi government. The Commission, usually referred to as the Onofri Commission in the name of its president, provided a very sharp and lucid analysis of the sins and ills of Italian unemployment policies. In order to overcome the blatant inequities and gaps in existing arrangements, the Commission proposed to establish a three-tier system of social shock-absorbers. The first tier is represented by short-term compensation, duly revised in order to extend coverage and standardize eligibility criteria. The second tier corresponds to the ordinary unemployment benefit. With respect to the current situation the benefit should be upgraded from 30 to 60 percent of previous earnings while functionally equivalent benefits (as mobility allowances) would be eliminated.[19] Finally, the third tier refers to a hitherto nonexistent public assistance safety net which would be gradually introduced in compliance with EU recommendations.

These suggestions did not lead to immediate results. Indeed, the broad range of proposals put forward by the Commission was not promptly taken on board by the government, thus causing heated political debate and controversy. But with respect to our area of concern, the above guidelines have attracted growing consensus, setting the stage for subsequent policy developments and culminating in the 1999 parliamentary law that delegates the government to provide a comprehensive reform of social shock absorbers as recommended in the guidelines. Hence, the scenario stemming from the Commission's proposals provides a good reference point to assess where Italian unemployment policies are heading and what role workfare will play in the global picture.[20]

Elements of workfare can definitely be found in a number of the Commission's proposals and subsequent policy measures, but they were not in the forefront—perhaps because the structural pre-conditions for this kind of discourse were simply not there. If we compare the Italian situation with that of the British the point is unequivocal. Given that in Britain the number of people on unemployment benefits soared during the eighties, irrespective of political leaning one can appreciate why the Conservatives' main purpose was to get people off the register. The case of Italy is radically different. Unemployment steadily increased over the eighties and the situation was not reversed in the nineties. By the second half of the decade almost 3 million workers were unemployed (table 2.5). However, as illustrated in section 2 only a small minority actually received social protection. Under these circumstances, with wide disparities in coverage and treatment the paramount features of the system, behavioral requirements and sanctions could hardly be expected to represent the bottom line of any reform attempt.

Attention appears to be focused instead on three main questions. The first one defines a tight linkage between passive and active labor policies and concentrates in particular on the structural weakness of the Italian training system and the embryonic stage of active labor policies. The underlying assumption is that the inadequacy and inefficiency of the current system—including both initial and continuous training—bears at least partial responsibility for the difficulty encountered by the unemployed in finding new jobs. On the one hand, one might recall that only 1.6 percent of the employed participate in some kind of training program while even in a similar country such as Spain the equivalent figure is 13 percent. On the other hand, it is worth noticing that, especially in southern regions, vocational training represents a policy area heavily penetrated by clientelism and fraudulent practices, as different judiciary inquiries have documented. Hence, the thrust of this focus is on enhancing an appropriate and consistent set of policy measures designed to facilitate re-employment starting with a thorough revision of training programs.

The second crucial issue refers to the introduction of a minimum income program within the public assistance sector, finally ending Italy's anomalous position within the European context. This was actually done by government decree 237 of 18 June 1998. One should immediately add that the program was only launched experimentally for a restricted number of municipalities. However, despite the limited nature of the measure, it would be misleading to consider it a symbolic policy. Lack of resources certainly influenced the choice of a gradual start. I would also argue that along with the stringency of Italian budgetary policies in the 1990s, the markedly increased contribution offered to policy making by experts gradually sharpened government's attention to the issues of performance and monitoring. Moreover, in this case the executive showed particular energy in meeting its commitment. By the following December the Minister of Social Solidarity had already issued the relevant administrative rulings—definitely a good record by Italian standards. As a result, the program has actually taken off and been implemented in 39 municipalities.

Without entering into all the relevant details, it is most interesting for the purpose of this paper to notice the presence of workfare language. However, Italy approaches unemployment, poverty and social exclusion from a cultural perspective that resembles more closely that of France than of Britain (Barbier and Théret 1999). More precisely, Italian rulings refer to a compulsory agreement to be signed between the applicant and the local authority in charge of the training or working project. But the emphasis is clearly on the social insertion component as in the French *revenu minum d'insertion* and not on the sanctions in case of non-compliance. Considering the diversity in political orientation and the widely differing institutional capabilities of local authorities, it would certainly be very interesting to analyze and compare the implementation of the program in the northern and the southern parts of the country.

The analyses we have offered also suggest a comment of a different nature. Policy transfer mechanisms seem to be at work in the Italian case but they appear very distinctive. With respect to the health sector, Freeman (1999) notes that Italy is apparently copying the British example by explicitly referring to the experience of managed competition while engaging in something quite different. In the case of social shock absorbers the issue is not so clear-cut. However, as we noticed in the previous sections, various elements typical of workfare ideology actually inform legislative provisions. The point is that they quickly disappear as soon as the policy is put into action. Is it because the emergency situation of Italian unemployment dampened the initial zeal? Or was the copying simply a relatively superficial operation that overlooked the objective conditions of the Italian context? Perhaps, the answer is more simply, that the current approach is the result of a learning process taking advantage of the innovative but makeshift attempts of the early nineties.

Finally, the third major theme—in part overlapping with the second—refers to the overall redefinition of social shock absorbers and the effective establishment of the three-tier system described above. This is precisely the task that still another special commission set up by the Ministry of Labor is currently trying to fulfill, at least with respect to the first two tiers and following the recent guidelines set by Parliament. But despite all the energy and good will that the commission might display, the impression is that the crucial questions will not be solved until the government takes care of the pension problem. It is hard to imagine far-reaching reforms in employment policy and other increasingly important but dramatically underfunded areas of the Italian Welfare State—especially when contrasting the 10,000 billion lira available for unemployment policies against the 300,000 billion for pensions!

## Notes

1. As is well known, the Netherlands had an extremely low female participation rate until the 1970s, but has since expanded enormously women's working opportunities, although especially in the area of part-time jobs.
2. The situation is slightly better in the case of Spain with a coverage of 60 percent for men in the age group 25-64 and around 40 percent for men under 25.
3. The Prodi government introduced in 1998 an experimental minimum income program which has just started operating. The issue is discussed in the next section.
4. Out of the three measures only work and training contracts were quite extensively implemented, although the trade unions lamented that: (a) the training component was largely disregarded by employers, and (b) the temporary jobs created under the program were never converted into permanent positions. However, in general, work and training contracts allowed employers to hire workers for low-skilled jobs at a lower cost while offering young unemployed an opportunity to acquire at least some working experience. In contrast, work-sharing contracts were considered unsatisfactory by both workers and firms. Such contracts were supposed to represent an alternative to short-term earnings compensation, by spreading the burden of working time reductions over the whole workforce in the firm. But the financial rulings of the latter program continued to make it more attractive: Workers could count on a smaller wage reduction than usually entailed by work-sharing contracts while employers could handle redundancies by shifting the cost on the state. Not surprisingly the situation changed as the reforms of 1988 and 1991 made it more burdensome for employers to resort to CIGS.
5. Regional Employment Commissions are established bringing State and Regional representatives together with representatives of the trade unions and the employers. Whereas these are essentially political bodies entrusted with the negotiation, the selection and the monitoring of the newly financed projects, ad hoc Regional Agencies are created to promote active labor policies. These administrative structures are further complemented by Regional Observatories on the labor market which are supposed to provide the relevant quantitative and qualitative information on regional labor market trends.
6. Actually this time limit is extended for longer periods depending on whether the worker is over 40, over 50 or whether the firm is located in the *Mezzogiorno*.
7. The laws under consideration (which also cover other issues) are the following : (a) law no.236 of July 19, 1993; (b) law no. 451 of July 19, 1994; (c) law no. 608 of November 28, 1996.
8. We are referring to legislative decree no.31 of February 8, 1995 confirmed by subsequent decrees and finally converted into law 608 of 1996, mentioned in note no.10.
9. The information provided in this section is largely based on parliamentary documentation, in particular Camera dei Deputati, Servizio Studi, XIII legislatura, *Dossier Provvedimento* no.395, second part, June 1997.
10. The original provisions are suspended in particular by legislative decrees no. 31 and no. 232 of 1995.
11. The aim of getting projects approved as quickly as possible results in defining imaginative procedures, unheard of in the Italian administrative system and for that matter close to violating the Constitution. For instance, Municipal councils are not

required to approve projects in this area, in contrast with all rulings on their responsibilities. A decision by the Mayor's board is considered sufficient, so long as it receives the approval of the Government Commissioner.

12. These projects are the result of inter-regional cooperation or more often they are directly promoted and organized by State Ministries such as the Ministry of Education, the Ministry of Environmental Protection and the Ministry of Cultural Affairs.
13. Both figures refer to workers actually engaged in "socially useful jobs" on 30 June, 1997. Considering the projects already approved but not yet activated the figures would be even higher. In the case of inter-regional projects the number would in fact be 20,271.
14. The decree is actually the end result of a chain of previous legislative provisions. In 1996 law 608 was passed by Parliament providing temporary regulation on the subject. The next step was represented by Parliamentary approval of what is commonly labeled as "Treu Package"—by the name of the proponent: the Labor and Social Security Minister Tiziano Treu. This law set the guidelines for reforming "socially useful jobs" along with other parts of active manpower policy and delegated the government to approve the relevant decrees. The issue is taken up in the next section.
15. As a result, the worker remains on the unemployment register and the engagement period is not considered for pension purposes. The whole issue—actually regulated by previous legislative provisions—was always strongly contested by trade unions. The government refused to give in on this point in order to avoid the risk of massive public hiring as experienced in the late seventies with youth unemployment programs.
16. Again the rulings on mixed companies are the end result of a series of provisions approved in 1995 and 1996 which turned out to be largely unsuccessful. According to these provisions, public administration was offered the opportunity to contract out the services originally provided through "socially useful jobs" to the aforementioned companies (Marimpietri 1997, 23-24). Despite the favorable conditions set for these companies, their establishment proved extremely difficult and prerequisites were progressively loosened. For instance, the original capital endowment was substantially reduced.
17. In detail, the areas are the following: income maintenance, temporary and structural redundancies plus control and oversight over employment.
18. Following the agreement reached in the tripartite employment pact of 1996, the question was initially addressed by law 196 of 1997. The relevant legislative process was still under way when the European Court of Justice intervened on the subject with the ruling of 11 December 1997.
19. The Commission particularly stresses the need to strengthen training opportunities, counseling and orientation in the first period of unemployment in order to help workers not to fall into long-term unemployment: a strategy that should also contribute to reduce the financial burden otherwise falling on the third tier.
20. A detailed and very informative discussion of the recent scientific and political debate can be found in the special issue of *L'assistenza sociale*, nos. 3-4, 1998, devoted to social shock-absorbers, active labor policies and workfare.

## References

Barbier, J.C., & Gautié, J. (1998). *Les politiques de l'emploi en Europe et aux Etats-Unis*. Paris: Presses Universitaires de France.

Barbier, J.C., & Théret, B. (1999). "Welfare-to-work or work-to-welfare: The French case?" In N. Gilbert (ed.), *From welfare to work: Comparative perspectives on active social policy*, New Brunswick, NJ: Transaction Publishers (forthcoming).

Commissione per l'analisi delle compatibilità macroecomiche della spesa sociale. (1997). *Le politiche del lavoro- documento di base n.2.*

Deacon, A. (1997). "Welfare to work: Options and issues." *Social Policy Review*, 34-49.

Dell'Aringa, C., & Samek Lodovici, M. (1996). "Policies for the unemployed and social shock absorbers: The Italian experience." *South European Society and Politics*, I (3), 172-197.

European Commission. (1996). *Labour Market Studies—Italy, by Fondazione Giacomo Brodolini.* Luxembourg: December.

European Commission. (1997). *Observatoire de l'emploi–Tableau de bord 1997.* Bruxelles.

Fargion, V. (1996). "Social assistance and the north-south cleavage in Italy." *South European Society and Politics*, I (3), 135-155.

Fargion, V. (1997). *Geografia della cittadinanza sociale in Italia.* Bologna: Il Mulino.

Ferrera, M. (1996). "The 'southern model' of welfare in social Europe." *Journal of European Social Policy*, 6 (1), 17-37.

Ferrera, M. & Gualmini, E. (1998, October). "The adjustment of national employment and social policy to economic internationalization: The case of Italy." Paper presented at the Workshop on The Adjustment of National Employment and Social Policy to Economic Internationalization , European University Institute.

Freeman, R. (1999, February). "Policy transfer in the health sector." Paper presented at the Conference Beyond the Health Care State, European University Institute.

Geroldi, G. (1997). "Ammortizzatori sociali e incentivi all'impiego nel quadro dei nuovi strumenti di politica del lavoro." *L'assistenza sociale* (3), 95-114.

Giubboni, S. (1999). "Flessibilità e diritto della previdenza sociale." *Spunti ricostruttivi*', unpublished paper, European University Institute.

Gualmini, E. (1998). *La politica del lavoro,* Bologna: Il Mulino.

Jones, M. (1997). "Full steam ahead to a workfare state?" *Policy and Politics,* XXIV (2), 137-157.

Marimpietri, I. (1997). "La disciplina dei lavori socialmente utili." *Lavoro Informazione,* XVI (9), 13-28

Ministero del Lavoro e della Previdenza Sociale. (1998). *Relazione semestrale sull'andamento dell'utilizzo dei lavoratori impegnati in lavori socialmente utili- I semestre 1997*, Roma.

Perrone, C. (1996). "I lavori socialmente utili: un bilancio." *Lavoro Informazione* XV (12), 5-13.

Pescetto, G. (1996). "Omogeneità e diversità nelle azioni e nelle esperienze." *Lavoro Informazione* (15-16), 25-33.

Pinelli, C. (1998). "Conferimenti di funzioni a Regioni ed Enti Locali e riforme del mercato del lavoro." *Le Regioni,* XXVI (1), 47-57.

Ponzi, S. (1998). "Gli ammortizzatori sociali: un quadro legislativo." *L'assistenza Sociale,* (3-4), 201-223.

Regini, M. & Regalia, I. "Employers, Unions and the State: The Resurgence of Concertation in Italy?" *West European Politics*, 210-230.

Regione Toscana—Agenzia per l'impiego della Toscana. (1998). *I lavori socialmente utili in Toscana—Relazione 1 gennaio 1997/31 Marzo 1998*, Firenze.

Reyneri, E. (1996). *Sociologia del mercato del lavoro*, Bologna: Il Mulino.

Reyneri, E. (1997). *Ocuupati e disoccupati in Italia*, Bologna: Il Mulino.

Rhodes, M. (1995). "A Regulatory Conundrum: Industrial Relations and the Social Dimension." In S. Leibfried & P. Pierson (eds.), *European Social Policy Between Fragmentation and Integration*, Washington D.C.: Brookings.

# 3

# Work-Oriented Reforms: New Directions in New Zealand

*Ross Mackay*

## Introduction

Welfare-to-work is a relatively new idea in the social security world. Although there have been American experiments in this area for the best part of thirty years—some under the flag of the narrower and more pejorative term "workfare"—it is really only over the past decade or so that welfare-to-work approaches have come to be accepted as a core part of mainstream policy in the U.S., while their adoption elsewhere in the world is of even more recent date.

New Zealand is one of the more recent converts to the idea of welfare-to-work. Although a work requirement has always existed for claimants of Unemployment Benefit, more widespread application of welfare-to-work approaches has only recently become established. The climate has evidently favored their growth, however, and they have quickly borne fruit. The recent burgeoning of these ideas owes some of its vigor to the grafting of imported American varieties onto the native root-stock. If the new policies have the characteristics of a distinct New Zealand species, they nevertheless also bear the traces of a genetic link to their American progenitors, and in particular to a prolific cultivar, which we might conveniently refer to as "Wisconsinia."

As a result of such an infusion of new ideas, social security policy in New Zealand has undergone a fundamental transformation and welfare-to-work now occupies a central place in this terrain. The language tends to be used a little differently in New Zealand, however, and "welfare-to-work" is not yet a commonly used term. Rather the discourse has been conducted in other terms—such as "active assistance," "positive income support," and "reciprocal obligations." Yet there is no mistaking the fact that welfare-to-work is now a dominant paradigm for New Zealand social security policy.

The change has involved a number of dimensions: the establishment of a stronger set of expectations of beneficiaries in return for the support they receive (in particular that they will move into work as soon as they are able); the creation of a stronger set of financial incentives to encourage beneficiaries to take up work opportunities; the development of enhanced forms of assistance to lubricate transitions into work; and reformation of the institutional structures to give best effect to these reforms. Each dimension has involved a range of particular changes, which make their own individual contribution to the overall goal of promoting movement off benefit and into employment. The changes have been accompanied by efforts to promote the renewed vision of welfare. In sum, the various changes constitute a coherent package of reforms, which revolve around the central idea of welfare-to-work. They also represent a significant shift away from the traditional view of the role of social security in New Zealand and have transformed interactions with income support claimants.

This paper is intended to document the transformation in the policy environment, by describing the particular changes that have been made in each of these areas. The changes are placed in context, against an account of the historical development of New Zealand's social security system, with particular emphasis on the relationship between welfare and work, and a sketch of the way in which the new ideas assumed prominence. First, though, it is useful to set down more systematically what we mean by the term "welfare-to-work."

### *What Do We Mean by Welfare-to-Work?*

Gardiner (1997) defines welfare-to-work as "any policy intervention that encourages or facilitates a transition from benefits to paid employment." Such interventions may aim to stimulate the supply of labor (through the provision of incentives to beneficiaries aimed at encouraging them to search for work or otherwise increase their supply of labor, and through the provision of facilitative assistance aimed at enabling them to identify and surmount barriers to their employment) or the demand for labor (through the provision of incentives to employers aimed at encouraging them to increase their use of beneficiaries as employees, and through investment in the human capital of beneficiaries aimed at making them more attractive to employers). Many programs involve a combination of these approaches.

A whole battery of policy tools is available for this purpose—in the form of both carrot- and stick-like approaches, as well as facilitative measures aimed at lubricating the transition back into the labor market. Carrot-like measures might include subsidization of job-related costs (such as child care), subsidization of private sector wages, and provision of in-work benefits. Stick-like approaches might include requirements to undertake job search or to accept suitable offers of employment, time-limiting of benefits, and provision for the reduction or extinction of entitlement to benefits in cases of non-compliance with program requirements. Facilitative approaches might include job search assistance, vocational guidance counseling, referral to specialized assistance, and customized case management.

These policy approaches are generally applied in the context of a "work-testing" framework, within which beneficiaries are required to search actively for work and to accept any suitable offer of employment. Such work-test requirements almost always apply to unemployment beneficiaries, but their application beyond this group is variable. As this paper will demonstrate, one of the most innovative aspects of recent policy development in New Zealand is the way in which the focus of welfare-to-work initiatives is being extended beyond the unemployed through expanded applications of the work-test.

Before describing the recent emergence of welfare-to-work approaches as a new development in New Zealand's social security system, it will be useful to give a brief account of the historical development of the system, with emphasis on the relationship between work and welfare.

## Historical Background

### *The Early Years of Social Security in New Zealand*

New Zealand's statutory welfare system had its origins in the late nineteenth century, with the passing of the Old Age Pensions Act 1898 (McClure 1998; Mackay 1998). Other provisions for people who were unable to provide for themselves followed in the first quarter of the twentieth century: widows in 1911, disabled miners in 1915 and blind persons in 1924. Other people, and especially the able-bodied, were expected to support themselves, and their families, through their labor. There was no provision for people who could not find work, apart from private charity. In a colonial economy dependent on exports of primary products, there were periodic fluctuations in the demand for labor, which meant that there were intermittent surges of unemployment (notably in the "long depression" during the 1880s and early 1890s). By the onset of the Great Depression in 1929, however, it was some thirty-five years since New Zealand had to confront the reality of mass unemployment.

There were signs of an incipient unemployment problem before the onset of the depression. Registered unemployment, which had averaged 425 in 1925, had grown to more than 3,000 by mid-1928. This is certainly an underestimate of the true level of unemployment, as the figures excluded both women and Maori. In addition, as there was no statutory provision for unemployment relief, the only benefit of registering was to gain access to help in finding work. Many more people would have been out of work without bothering to register.

By 1928 the situation was serious enough for the Government to appoint a Committee to investigate unemployment in New Zealand, which noted that:

> It is not a new problem in New Zealand; in fact for many years past we have not been entirely free from it except during the war period. It has been dealt with always in the past in the same way—by the undertaking of public works by the State and by local bodies. Sometimes a public-works program has been speeded up to enable more men to be employed than would normally be required at other times, when the demand for work has been greater, special works have been undertaken, not because there was necessity for them, but with the sole object of providing employment temporarily for those for whom no other employment was offered. (New Zealand Government, 1929a, p. 1)

In the same year, the government convened an Industrial Conference which, although it achieved little else, resulted in the Unemployment Act 1930 and thus established a new basis for unemployment relief (Simpson, 1990).

## *The Great Depression*

By now, though, the country was in depression and the numbers of unemployed had climbed vertically. From around 3,000 in mid-

1928, they mounted to 11,000 in December 1930, 51,000 in 1931, and then 72,000 in 1933. By then, there were also 18,000 men on relief work. The problems were exacerbated by Government retrenchment, with cutbacks in public expenditure, a 10 percent reduction in public service salaries and changes to the Arbitration Act, which permitted parallel reductions in private sector wages.

The 1930 Act was ill-equipped to deal with a problem on such a scale. It had established a new Unemployment Fund to provide for sustenance payments to unemployed adult males, but the assistance was limited to those engaged on special work schemes. As the numbers of unemployed grew, it became increasingly difficult to find them suitable work. By 1932, "the Government's unemployment program was in tatters" (Richardson, 1981).

### *The Social Security Act 1938*

The 1935 general election brought in a Labour Government for the first time. The new government boosted the economy through guaranteed prices for primary produce, restoration of salary and wages to their previous levels, and increases in relief pay. Significant additional expenditure was devoted to development works. As a result of these combined measures, the numbers of registered unemployed dropped to around 35,000 by 1937, although recovery to a position of full employment had to wait until the advent of war in 1939.

In 1938, one of the crowning achievements of the first Labour Government—the Social Security Act—was passed. This systematised the prior system of provisions for various groups and provided a more comprehensive basis for social protection. A new statutory Unemployment Benefit was established for anyone who was unemployed, had the capacity and willingness to carry out suitable work, had taken reasonable steps to obtain suitable work, and had lived continuously in New Zealand for not less than twelve months. To satisfy the legislative requirement that claimants were "willing to undertake suitable work," they were required to register for work with the Department of Labour and to report to the Department each week to ascertain whether any suitable work was available.

The new Unemployment Benefit was distinguished from other statutory benefits in having a work-test applied in this way. The Royal Commission on Social Security (1972) drew a distinction in another respect:

> The "disability" from which it is "designed to safeguard the people of New Zealand" is not, like the other disabilities of age, sickness, or widowhood, something which is bound to afflict a number of people at any one time it is a symptom of internal and external factors affecting the national economy as a whole. And it is through the working of the whole economy that the State's primary responsibility in this matter will be carried out it is unlikely that the New Zealand Government will be able to escape from public insistence that it must so manage the economy that there is a market for the services of all who are able and willing to work. The provision of income support through social security or, for that matter, the creation of jobs at times and places where circumstances warrant it, are only secondary protections (p. 291).

The latter part of this statement serves to demonstrate how much assumptions about government's role and powers in managing economic conditions have changed over the past two and a half decades. For the period following the Second World War (which had cured the unemployment problem of the 1930s) right through to the early 1970s, government was considered not only to have a duty, but also the capacity, to avert the rise of unemployment.

### *The "Golden Years" of the Post-War Period*

The reality was that, over these years, New Zealand had (almost literally) no unemployment. During the 1950s, the numbers were, in hindsight, astonishingly low. In the annual statistics reported to Parliament for 1956, only two people were recorded as receiving Unemployment Benefit at fiscal year-end. For the entire decade of the 1950s, the average number of people receiving Unemployment Benefit at fiscal year-end was 63. Although the numbers began to climb inexorably after 1977, as late as 1974 as few as 483 people were reported as receiving Unemployment Benefit in official statistics.

No doubt higher numbers of people were out of work at any one time during these years, but for the most part unemployment was frictional and people who found themselves out of work saw little need to register as unemployed or to claim benefit because another job could always be found quickly.

### *The Turbulent Times from the Mid-1970s*

New Zealand had thus had no recent experience of unemployment (indeed over forty years had passed since the worst year of the Great Depression) by the time the numbers began to go wrong in the late 1970s. In a similar pattern to the experience of other Western countries, the New Zealand economy began to encounter difficulties in the mid-1970s. The numbers of people receiving Unemployment Benefit first began to surge in 1975 when they jumped from 483 to 2,894, and they increased further to 5,127 in the following year.

Similar spikes had been experienced before, but this time the surge was no temporary blip. In 1978, the numbers shot up to 17,484 in a near four-fold increase and from this point they rose relentlessly higher, passing 50,000 in 1983, 100,000 in 1989, and 150,000 in 1991. In the fifteen years between 1977 and 1992, the numbers grew from 3,651 to 170,367—an increase of 4,566 percent. The number who were registered as unemployed was even higher and passed 215,000 in 1992. In this year the official unemployment rate peaked at 11.1 percent.

The reasons for this cataclysmic shift have been well-documented elsewhere (Shirley et al. 1990; Mackay 1998). A malign combination of a long, slow deterioration in terms of trade, the progressive loss of assured markets for the country's primary produce—its main source of export earnings—after Britain joined the European Economic Community, and the steep rise in the cost of imports following the two oil shocks of the 1970s meant that the New Zealand economy was in deepening difficulty. The social and political consequences of the change were to be considerable.

### *Recent Trends in Receipt of Income Support*

Following 1992, when the unemployment rate peaked at 11.1 percent, the economy performed better with an average growth rate of 4.8 percent over the next three years. By 1996, the unemployment rate had come down to 6.2 percent and the numbers receiving Unemployment Benefit had declined by more than 20 percent from their 1992 peak. However, despite declining unemployment, the total numbers on income support continued to remain high, due to continuing growth in numbers on Sickness Benefit, Invalids Benefit and Domestic Purposes Benefit (which is primarily received by single parents). For this reason, policy attention began to shift to these groups. While government's initial attention was directed towards solving the unemployment problem, it became increasingly evident that there was a wider issue of welfare dependency.

Thus, by the mid-1990s, New Zealand was confronting a number of pressures on its income support system for people of working age. First, levels of unemployment remained relatively high and began rising again after 1995 when economic performance again declined.

Secondly, the numbers of people on other benefits had continued to grow even when unemployment was falling, especially those for sickness, invalids and single parents. Thirdly, a significant proportion of people were remaining on benefit for longer periods and found increasing difficulty in re-entering the labor force as their skill levels atrophied, as their work habits dissipated and as their motivation to search for work eroded. Fourthly, dependence on benefit was disproportionately experienced by particular sub-groups, in particular Maori and Pacific Islands people, and young people. And fifthly, while dependence on benefit was a deeply corrosive experience for individuals who had lost jobs and were unable to find others, the growing levels of dependence on benefits was also a divisive experience for New Zealand society, as whole communities now had high proportions of people who were reliant on benefits and as the perceptions of other New Zealanders began to focus on the ever-escalating cost.

## Initial Responses to the Unemployment Problem

Government's initial responses to the growing unemployment problem in the late 1970s and early 1980s were dominated by two concerns: to mop up the numbers of registered unemployed, which were becoming a political embarrassment; and to contain costs as the numbers claiming Unemployment Benefit significantly inflated the spending requirement on income support.

The responses took three general forms. The first, and most instinctive, response was to establish a range of job creation programs aimed at absorbing some of the accumulating numbers of unemployed. A second equally instinctive response was to implement a range of cost-containment measures, aimed at reducing the escalating cost of income support. The third response involved the institution of a range of prototype welfare-to-work programs aimed at assisting people to move off benefit and into work. While the first two responses constituted traditional reactions to unemployment, the third represents a more forward-looking response, which anticipates initiatives more fully expressed in the recent round of welfare reforms aimed at assisting movement off benefit and into work.

### *Job Creation*

Government's initial, instinctual response when faced with upwardly spiralling levels of unemployment was to use the power of the state to create work which would mop up the numbers of people on the unemployment register. In this it was motivated not only by the desire to provide work for those who were unable to find it elsewhere, but also by a desire to keep the numbers of unemployed from becoming a political millstone round its neck. As well as serving this political end, and demonstrating that the government was taking active steps to combat the problem, this response also bore the worthy imprimatur of tradition, since it had been the predominant response of earlier governments in responding to the challenges of the Great Depression. But this also meant that it was backward looking and unlikely to provide a long-run solution to the new and more intractable conditions the New Zealand economy was now facing, which were at the root of the unemployment problem.

The particular approach favored by government involved large-scale fully subsidized job creation schemes within the public sector. The main program was the Project Employment Program, which was established in 1980 and ran through to 1985. It provided 100 percent wage subsidies to public sector employers—such as government departments, hospital boards, local authorities, and education boards—for people engaged on specified projects for periods of up to six months. To protect against substitution and displacement of other workers, the work was required to be additional to the organization's normal workload, which would not have been carried out by other means.

The Project Employment Program was aimed at reducing levels of long-term unemployment and targeted at people who had been registered as unemployed for 26 weeks or more. It was intended to provide eligible job seekers with temporary work which would enable them to maintain and develop their skills, reinforce work habits and avoid loss of motivation. It grew to absorb a significant proportion of the unemployed. As McKenzie (1997) notes, in 1983/84 51,908 people participated in the program, at a time when the number of registered unemployed was around 70,000 and the number of people who were receiving Unemployment Benefit was around 50,000.

One of the initial advantages of the program to government was that it took people off the unemployment register, which indeed was part of the point of instituting it. However, as time passed and numbers on the program grew, this advantage diminished as commentators acquired the habit of adding the numbers participating in the program to the registered unemployed to derive a "true" level of unemployment. Although Bertram (1987) notes that it "probably yielded net benefits for employers and workers," its high administrative costs and the lack of any direct evidence that it improved the long-term employability of participants (McKenzie, 1997) meant that it fell from favor in the mid-1980s and new approaches came to be preferred.

*Cost-containment*

A second and equally instinctual response of government when faced with an expenditure blow-out on its income support programs was to institute a range of cost-containment measures. These took three primary forms: increased waiting time for benefits; curtailment of entitlements to programs among selected sub-groups of claimants, especially the young; and reductions in the rates at which benefits were paid.

*Increased waiting time for benefits*. One means of reducing expenditure on income support is by increasing the waiting period for benefits. Initially this was done in a targeted way, focusing on particular groups. In 1983, the waiting period for unmarried persons without dependants was increased from one to two weeks. An additional waiting period of up to four weeks was also introduced for higher income earners. In 1990 a two-week waiting period was introduced for all benefits.

In the following year the waiting periods for Unemployment Benefit were extended dramatically for particular groups. For high income earners, the waiting period was extended to a maximum of ten weeks. For those who were made redundant, the maximum waiting period was 26 weeks, the actual period being dependent on the size of the redundancy settlement. For people who had become voluntarily unemployed, or who had been dismissed because of misconduct, or who refused an offer of work or training, the waiting period was also extended to 26 weeks. For the latter group, the waiting period was now effectively a sanction for non-performance with the work test requirement.

*Curtailments of entitlement to benefits*. Another way of reducing costs is by restricting entitlements to benefits among particular subgroups. Young people, in particular, were the targets of such policies. In particular, a change was made in 1990 which raised the minimum qualifying age for Unemployment Benefit from 16 to 18 years, although 16 and 17 years olds who were married and had dependent children remained entitled to the benefit. The minimum age for receiving Domestic Purposes Benefit was also increased from 16 to 18 in 1991 (again except for those who were legally married), and that for Sickness Benefit was increased from 15 to 16.

Young people who were disqualified from entitlement to benefits under these changes would now be reliant on their parents for support. To cover cases where there had been an irretrievable breakdown in family relationships, a new provision—the Independent Youth Benefit—was introduced. This provided support for young people aged 16 or 17 who were unable to live with their parents or to be supported by them. Another new provision—the Job Search Allowance—was also added to provide temporary support for young people aged 16 or 17 who had previously been self-supporting.

*Reductions in benefit rates*. The most direct means of cutting costs is by cutting benefit rates. This option was taken in 1991, when the payment level of most main benefits was reduced by varying amounts. The background to this decision was a projected increase in the budget deficit. The fiscal position had been deteriorating during the course of 1990 as the economy slid into recession and the deficit was projected to rise possibly as high as 6.3 percent of GDP.

The reductions in rates were not uniform, but varied across the different categories of benefit. Indeed, not all rates were reduced; some were preserved at the existing rate and a small number were increased. The hardest hit were single unemployment beneficiaries aged 20-24 without children, whose payment rate dropped from $143.57 weekly to $108.17, a decrease of 24.7 percent. The steepness of the reduction for this group derived from the fact that they were, in effect, being subjected to two changes at the one time. In addition to the rate cut, a separate policy change was an upward move of the age band for the youth rate of benefit from 19 to 24. Young persons aged 20-24 were moved to the lower paying youth rate of benefit (payable at a 20 percent lower rate than the adult rate), while the youth rate was itself cut by 5.8 percent.

The rate reductions for other unemployment beneficiaries were smaller. Single adults aged 25 or more without dependants took a cut of 6.9 percent, while, among those with dependent children, a larger cut was imposed on single people than on couples—for example 10.7 percent and 8.5 percent, respectively, for those with one child. Cuts to sickness benefit rates were of a similar order. For this group too, the age band for the youth rate was raised to include single people aged 20-24 without dependants, for whom this meant an effective rate cut of 20 percent.

Recipients of the Domestic Purposes Benefit fared differently depending on their status. The largest group (single parents) faced cuts of the same order as single parents on other benefits. Women alone faced a higher cut of 16.7 percent, while those providing domiciliary care for dependent relatives had their rate preserved at existing levels.

Invalids beneficiaries fared best. Those without dependants had their rates preserved at existing levels, as did single persons with dependants. Couples with dependant children received a rate increase. For example, those with one child had their rate increased by 5.2 percent from $297.08 to $312.44 per week.

The effect of the cuts on the fiscal position was mitigated by the increases in rates of receipt of benefits as the recession intensified. Between 1990 and 1993, when the economy was in considerable difficulty with virtually no growth, the numbers of people receiving the five main benefits (Unemployment, Sickness, Invalids, Domestic Purposes and Widows Benefits) increased by 16 percent. Real expenditure growth over the same period was held to around 11 percent, largely as a result of the cut in benefit rates.

### *Prototype Welfare-to-Work Programs*

A third response to the unemployment problem—more forward-looking, but rather embryonic in the particular forms it took—was the institution of a range of new programs explicitly aimed at assisting beneficiaries to make the transition from benefit to employment. Two particular examples of such programs are discussed here, selected from a range of new initiatives.

*Transition to work allowance.* In 1987, a Transition to Work Allowance was introduced to encourage long-term beneficiaries to move into employment by ensuring that, at least for the first three months of employment, they would be at least $20 per week better off working than they were on the benefit. The rate was calculated on the difference between previous benefit income and employment income. A ceiling, representing the maximum rate payable, was set at $40 per week.

The program was not successful, for reasons, which are not totally clear, but which probably have to do with the fact that it was a rather isolated initiative, and not supported by other policies in a more comprehensive welfare-to-work agenda. It was only ever taken up by minuscule numbers of people, primarily single parents. For example, in the first year only 108 allowances were approved, and rather than growing from this modest beginning, uptake actually declined in subsequent years to 62 in 1989, and 43 in 1992. The program was eventually disestablished in 1996. Its failure means that the types of bridging programs that have been used in other countries to ease transitions into employment have not yet been effectively explored in New Zealand.

*Stepping out.* In 1988, another new program—known as Stepping Out—which was aimed at facilitating the movement of sole parent beneficiaries off benefit and into employment was introduced on a pilot trial basis. It was a rather minimal program, however, which comprised only a mailed information package containing a list of local contacts for training, employment and social service assistance. In one site, a slightly more intensive approach was used, involving the use of two field workers who made personal visits to offer more direct assistance to members of the target group. Unsurprisingly, an evaluation of the program found that it had very little impact on movement of beneficiaries into employment. Following the evaluation, the trial was discontinued.

While these two initiatives now appear rather puny in comparison with the Herculean proportions of the problem they were opposing, they at least represent the first stirrings of a new approach to the problem. They represent qualitatively different responses from the other changes and reflect a recognition that new thinking was needed, since the traditional remedies were evidently not making significant inroads into the problem. Both responses point to the future and were to be considerably elaborated in subsequent policy.

However, at this point they represented only an embryonic form of welfare-to-work policy, and they tended to exist only on the periphery of the income support system. The system largely continued to function as a passive payment system, seeing its role as being restricted to the assessment of eligibility for benefits, and arrangement of payments where eligibility was established. What was still lacking was a welfare-to-work focus which would bring the various elements of policy together in a unifying framework.

Such a focus has gradually emerged over the past decade and has provided a sounder and more coherent foundation for the recent round of benefit reforms. It is useful to take a little time here to examine the origin of the new ideas which have animated these reforms and which have provided the philosophical core of the renewed vision of welfare embodied in the recent reforms.

## Context for the Recent Benefit Reforms

### *Welfare-to-Work as the New Governing Idea*

Early indications of the new direction were set out in the 1991 Budget, in particular in a supplementary paper entitled "Social Assistance: Welfare That Works." The title provides a new indication of the emerging thinking through a slightly complex verbal play, by signifying not only that the system needs to be fixed so that it "works" or functions more effectively, but also, more obliquely, by implying that the way forward is to be found through "work." And indeed, the tenor of the reforms that have followed the 1991 Budget have been increasingly focused on the governing idea of "welfare-to-work."

The thinking was further developed in a document produced by the Department of Social Welfare in 1995 entitled "Income Support: Strategic Directions 1995-2005." The paper argued that a renewed vision for the income support system was needed and proposed that such a vision should be based on the concept of "positive income support," which would not only preserve the traditional role of income support—to provide support for the disadvantaged—but would add a new aspiration—to promote the development of those receiving support. In return, it was argued, recipients of income support had a responsibility to make a reciprocal contribution for the assistance they were afforded.

The paper noted further that efforts in the past to assist people towards self-sufficiency had tended to be focused on the unemployed, but that future policy would need to broaden the focus to the wider group of working-age beneficiaries. In addition to the fact that levels of receipt of benefit among the wider group had been continuing to rise even in times of economic buoyancy when unemployment was dropping, it was noted that many of the wider group—including sole parents, and people with illnesses, disabilities or injuries—wished to increase their work involvement and become self-reliant, but saw little opportunity to do so. Thus the policy was premised not only on the need to reduce the costs of dependency, but also on the view that employment was a fundamental good to which people who were currently disadvantaged needed to be given improved access.

The thinking in this document was still somewhat embryonic, but was about to be strengthened by an awakening awareness of parallel developments elsewhere in the world and especially in America.

*The Influence of American Welfare Reforms*

If modern communication means that ideas can now be exchanged across the world almost simultaneously in the virtual realm, it still remains true that the physical realm, involving exchanges and visits, is important if new ideas are to take secure root in new locations. With this in mind, if one were to construct a plot of all overseas visits made by officials from the New Zealand Department of Social Welfare, it would show a heavy line, denoting significant traffic, between Wellington in New Zealand and California and Wisconsin in the United States. Like much of the rest of the world with developed welfare states, New Zealand administrators have taken considerable interest in American welfare reforms, and in particular those undertaken in California and Wisconsin, which have been the leading proponents of welfare reform. Like the other visitors, the New Zealand observers came to witness the new ideas about welfare-to-work in action. To adapt the words of T. S. Eliot, they came to verify, to instruct and to carry report.

A number of elements of the American reforms engaged the attention of the New Zealand observers. First, the strengthened work requirement fitted with the emerging direction in New Zealand, and it was instructive to see a fully developed system operating which had this idea at its core. The simplicity of the ideas, which easily lent themselves to conversion into messages that could be promoted ("for those who can work, only work should pay"), was also attractive, especially to an organization that was riding the crest of its own wave of institutional reform and was seeking to find ways to focus its new-found energies and to promote its ideas.

The results which were being adduced from the reforms were also impressive. In Wisconsin, for example, in the ten years since 1987 when Governor Tommy Thompson had taken office and began reforming the welfare system, the state's welfare caseload had dropped by 55 percent. More recent figures were even more impressive: in a paper delivered to the Beyond Dependency Conference held in Auckland in March 1997, Jean Rogers of Wisconsin's Department of Workforce Development reported that, in the preceding year, the caseload had dropped by 33 percent and was continuing to fall at a rate of 2.75 percent per month. The strong and charismatic leadership of Governor Thompson was seen to be an important component of the process and the way the energy flowed outwards from the center was duly noted and chimed with the experience of New Zealand officials. Finally, the interest of New Zealand officials was not solely, or perhaps even primarily, focused on the policy content. There was particular interest in operational delivery, and the way in which this cohered around the need to promote the message to all claimants about the new work expectation.

The ground in New Zealand was fertile and ripe for receipt of these new influences. The Department of Social Welfare—a classic example of an old-style government department, with significant problems of inefficiency, lack of accountability, customer dissatisfaction and poor public image (Petrie, 1998)—had just gone through a major restructuring in which the former Benefits and Pensions Division had been transformed into the New Zealand Income Support Service (its title subsequently truncated to, simply, Income Support). The new income support delivery organization was characterised by Petrie as a high-performance service provider, which had largely overcome the above problems. In particular, the new organization had a charismatic leadership, an energised workforce and was above all highly committed to a customer focus.

Perhaps, then, the New Zealand observers were primarily drawn to Wisconsin and California because they saw there a reflection of their own values, and a realization of their own vision. This reinforced the view that the reshaping of the New Zealand system was on the right track and gave additional impetus to the new energy and zeal that flowed through Income Support for operational delivery reforms which were centered around the idea of welfare-to-work.

### *The Beyond Dependency Conference*

Another significant development in the emergence of a more comprehensive vision of welfare-to-work, which also began the process of making a public case for the reforms, was the Beyond Dependency Conference. This brought a number of high profile visitors to New Zealand, not only from America but from a range of countries, most of whom preached the message about the need for new thinking about welfare and especially for a focus on welfare-to-work.

Although it generated some local controversy, with some commentators noting an ironic clash between the content of the conference and its up-market positioning and lobby groups establishing a rival concurrent "Beyond Poverty" Conference, the event was regarded as a considerable success. Even the controversy was regarded as not entirely a bad thing, since it considerably increased the media coverage, thus giving greater exposure to the new ideas. What the conference signalled, above all, was a new confidence on the part of New Zealand officials in the new ideas, which were now beginning to be expressed though reforms in the realms of both policy and operational delivery.

### *A Renewed Vision of Welfare*

Out of these multifarious origins, and drawing on various sources, a new vision of welfare has emerged, which has underpinned the recent round of benefit reforms and which revolves around the central motivating idea of welfare-to-work. While the core purpose of the welfare system—to provide assistance to those who are unable, for one reason or another, to provide for themselves—remains intact, the new vision has involved the elaboration of a set of new ideas about the nature of the obligation that claimants to income support assume in return for the assistance they receive, in particular the obligation to take up work as soon as they are able to do so.

The assumptions which underpin the new vision of welfare can be summarised as follows:

- work is an important norm which has economic and social benefits for individuals and their families;
- most people are capable of working, even if not on a full-time basis;
- some beneficiaries—including those who are medically incapable of working and lone parents with pre-school children—should not be expected to work;
- other beneficiaries, who form the great majority, should be expected to be available for work and required to take active steps to seek work; and
- income support should be seen, for the great majority of beneficiaries, as providing transitional assistance whilst they are without work.

The increased emphasis on work has implications for the overall design of the income support system and each component of the system needs to reflect this emphasis. In particular, there is a requirement for:

- a clearly expressed expectation that most beneficiaries will be available for work and will actively seek work as soon as they are able to do so;
- a set of clear economic incentives for beneficiaries to move into work;
- a range of different forms of assistance to help people make the transition into work and to help them stay in work;
- a regime of sanctions for those who do not meet the work expectation; and
- an emphasis on the work expectation in all contacts with beneficiaries.

## Recent Benefit Reforms

Building on the base of these new ideas—partly imported and partly home-grown—the recent round of benefit reforms represents a coherent body of changes which embody the central motivating idea of welfare-to-work. The changes encompass a range of different initiatives all aimed at encouraging and facilitating movement off benefit and into employment.

The changes fall into four broad categories. To date, most emphasis has been placed on the establishment of a new set of expectations of income support recipients, which revolve around the notion of reciprocal obligations (primarily conceived in terms of movement towards employment). Secondly, efforts have been made to enhance the financial incentives for movement off benefit and into work. Thirdly, attention has been paid to developing a range of different assistance to help beneficiaries to make the transition to work. Fourthly, changes have been made in the operational infrastructure to create a service delivery environment which is likely to give best effect to these changes.

### *Establishing Expectations: The Idea of Reciprocal Obligations*

For much of its history the income support system imposed few expectations on beneficiaries, apart from requiring them to demonstrate their eligibility for entitlements. The role of the system was largely seen as involving the assessment of claimants' eligibility and, where entitlement was established, arranging payments as prescribed by statute and regulation. Once they were on the welfare rolls, little further attention was paid to recipients of benefits. In particular, little effort was made to encourage them to move off benefit into employment—apart from unemployment beneficiaries who were subject to a work test. Even for this group, though, the work test was largely perfunctory.

The system worked well enough in times of economic buoyancy, sustaining people while they were out of work—which wasn't generally for long as jobs were in plentiful supply, at least until the mid-1970s. As economic difficulties began to accumulate after this time, however, the increasing flows onto benefit, and increased competition facing jobs for those who wished to exit, translated into upwardly spiralling levels of benefit receipt and increasing rates of long-term benefit dependency. Policy makers began to realize that attending to the in-flows might not be sufficient and that it was becoming increasingly necessary to pay attention to the process by which people moved off benefit.

The idea of reciprocal obligations crystallized out of these concerns. It was set out in a Post-Election Briefing Paper to the incoming Minister of Social Welfare in 1996 in the following terms: "the notion of reciprocal obligation is the idea that receipt of benefit creates a responsibility to take action towards enhancing capacity to be self-reliant, minimising the duration of dependence, or improving the well-being of family or community." While this notion is a potentially broader idea, in practice reciprocal obligations have tended to be framed in terms of a requirement to be available for and to actively search for work, or (in cases where a beneficiary may not yet be able to compete effectively in the labor market) to take active steps towards work readiness.

The new emphasis on reciprocal obligations (and in particular the strengthened work requirement) has been given effect through various provisions, including tightening of the work test, extension of the work test to a broader range of beneficiaries, restructuring of benefit categories, strengthened sanctions for non-compliance with the new requirements, assessment of the capacity to work of people with a disability, injury or sickness, and provision for people to be required to undertake community work as an alternative to paid employment.

*Tightening the work test.* Recipients of Unemployment Benefit are the only group who have traditionally been subject to a work requirement in New Zealand. This requires them to be "able and willing to undertake suitable work and [take] reasonable steps to find it" (Department of Social Welfare, 1998). An assessment of whether unemployment beneficiaries meet this requirement is known as the "work test."

The nature of the work test has varied over the years. Unemployment beneficiaries are required to register as unemployed. Until the late 1970s, there was considered to be little need to impose any other obligation on them, since only small numbers of people were registered as unemployed and since there was plenty of work available for those who were seeking it. In more recent years, as economic difficulties developed and the numbers of registered unemployed increased, the work test has come under closer policy scrutiny. In 1991, it was given a more precise operational definition: unemployment beneficiaries were considered to be in breach of the work requirement if they turned down a second offer of work (including subsidized work) or if they failed to attend a second job interview to which they had been referred.

*Expansion of the work requirement.* Another significant change has been the broadening of the work test to encompass a wider range of beneficiaries. Rather than focusing solely on recipients of Unemployment Benefit, the new policy applies to the wider group of beneficiaries of working age. This was largely a consequence of the failure of policies which focused narrowly on the unemployed to bring down overall rates of dependency on income support. Recent history had seemed to show that any gains during periods of economic buoyancy from reducing numbers on Unemployment Benefit were counterbalanced by increasing numbers on other benefits; in addition, during flatter periods in the economy, additional numbers were being added to all benefits. The lesson was drawn that, if progress was to be made in reducing total numbers of people on income support, then the focus would have to be widened to the whole of the population of working age.

This has led to the extension of the work-test requirement to include a wider range of beneficiaries. Three new groups were brought within the ambit of the new requirement: spouses of unemployment beneficiaries: sole parents and widows beneficiaries with older children; and people with a disability, injury or sickness, who may formerly have qualified for Sickness or Invalids Benefits.

For single parents and widows, the work test was expanded in two stages. The initial requirement, announced in 1997, was a relatively modest step affecting only those with children aged 14 or over, who were required to seek part-time work or undertake part-time training or education. Those with a youngest child aged 7 or older were required to attend an annual interview to identify the steps needed to prepare for work readiness. A year later, the requirement was substantially strengthened. Single parents with a youngest child aged between 6 and 13 were now required to seek part-time work, while those with a youngest child aged 14 or older were now required to seek full-time work.

These requirements were backed up with some additional assistance: a child care subsidy is available to low-income working parents with children aged between 5 and 13 to cover the costs of out-of-school care. Additional job search and training assistance is also provided to assist those who need help to meet their new obligations.

*Work capacity assessment for sick and disabled people.* The third group of people who will be subject to the new work requirement are people with a disability, sickness or injury who are assessed as having a capacity for full-time work. This has required the development of a new procedure to test the work capacity of people claiming income support who have such a condition. The procedure is currently under development and will be used to determine both the particular benefit that the claimant is eligible for and the nature of the reciprocal obligations he or she is required to fulfil—in particular whether he or she will be subject to a work test.

The procedure will be operated by specialist assessors who will conduct an in-depth interview with claimants and make a determination of the amount of time that a claimant could be expected to work. This determination is to be made from a choice of three categories: able to work fewer than fifteen hours per week; able to work between fifteen and thirty hours per week; or able to work more than thirty hours per week. The assessment will also give consideration to what assistance might be necessary to enable the claimant to work successfully. Those who are assessed as having a work capacity of thirty hours or more per week will be subject to a full-time work requirement.

The new procedure is being introduced on a trial basis and will be evaluated in selected pilot sites, following initial testing of the reliability of the procedure.

*Strengthened sanctions for non-compliance with the work-test requirement.* The work requirement is backed up by a menu of intensified sanctions, which can be applied in cases of non-compliance with the requirement. Sanctions can be applied in a range of circumstances, including failure to accept an offer of suitable work, failure to participate in an organized activity (such as work assessment, training, job interview, work experience or medical or psychological assessment), unsatisfactory performance in an organized activity, and voluntary unemployment (including dismissal for misconduct).

The sanctions regime is a graduated one, with penalties becoming increasingly severe for repeated instances of non-compliance. For a first failure to accept a suitable job offer, the benefit may be suspended for a minimum period of one week and until such time as the person complies with the requirement. For a second failure, the benefit may be suspended for a period of thirteen weeks. Single parents, however, are liable to have only 50 percent of their benefit suspended.

Unsatisfactory performance in organized activities may result in a reduction in the amount of benefit payable. Again a graduated scale of sanctions applies. For late arrival or absence, the penalty depends on how much time is lost, beginning at an 8 percent reduction for absences of 15 minutes to two hours, and rising to a maximum reduction of 40 percent for absences of more than eight hours. A 10 percent reduction can also be applied in cases of failure to complete organized activities. Failure to participate in a mandatory interview may result in a 20 percent reduction in the amount payable for the week in which the failure occurred.

*Restructuring of benefit categories.* A central feature of the recent reforms is the establishment of the new Community Wage program, which replaced the former Unemployment, Sickness and Training Benefits in October 1998. Recipients are expected to be available for and actively seeking work and may be required to participate in community work, training or some other organized activity. The program is intended to help job seekers to maintain their work skills and confidence and to enhance their chances of moving into paid employment. On application, claimants are required to sign a Job

Seeker Agreement, through which they contract to undertake an active search for paid employment and to be available for any appropriate organized activity in which they may be required to participate. Receipt of payments is conditional on the signing of a Job Seekers Agreement.

This restructuring of benefit categories allows people with temporary medical conditions (formerly covered by the Sickness Benefit which was not subject to work test provisions) to come under the provisions of the Community Wage work test. People transferring to the new Community Wage program from the former Sickness Benefit, and new applicants for Community Wage who have a disability, injury or sickness, are required to sign a Job Seeker contract, but may be granted a temporary deferral of the work-test requirement. To obtain a renewal of this deferral they must be assessed as unfit for work by a medical practitioner. As noted above, a new procedure for assessing the work capacity of people who seek a deferral from the work test requirement under the Community Wage program is currently under development.

*Provision for community work.* One of the activities that may be required is community work. Beneficiaries receiving the full rate of Community Wage may be required to undertake up to 20 hours' community work per week, while those receiving a reduced rate of benefit because they are working part-time may be required to undertake up to 10 hours' community work. Community work placements are provided by sponsoring organizations, such as voluntary agencies and work trusts. In order to avoid displacement of other workers, sponsoring organizations are required to sign a declaration stating that the work would not be done by any other means if workers were not available under the Community Work program.

A flat rate "participation allowance" of $21 per week on top of the standard payment rate for the Community Wage is payable for those undertaking community work. Those who face additional costs are also eligible to be reimbursed an additional $20 per week for "actual and reasonable" costs.

In summary, these various changes mean that claimants of income support now face a much clearer set of expectations that they will take up work as soon as they are able to do so. The expectations cover the great bulk of beneficiaries of working age, while the nature of the work test has been more clearly defined and a graduated range of sanctions for non-compliance has been established. In the absence of sufficient opportunities to place in work all who are subject to a work test, beneficiaries may also be required to undertake community work.

*Creating Incentives: Enhanced Returns from Work*

Establishing expectations that beneficiaries will move into work as soon as they are able to do so, however, is only part of the task. It is also necessary to ensure that they face positive financial incentives to take up employment and that they receive an appropriate level of financial gain from their effort. Aside from the dampening effect that a poorly designed incentives regime is likely to have on movement into work, it could also be argued that it is unfair to coerce people into taking up jobs which leave them financially worse off.

Recent policy changes have therefore been aimed at enhancing the returns from work for people who move off benefit. This has been done by a range of methods, including relaxation of the abatement regime for earned income for targeted groups, and introduction of tax credits for low-income working families. The incentive structure was also significantly altered by the benefit cuts implemented in 1991. These cuts had the effect of broadening the gap between wage and benefit levels and thus enhancing replacement rates.

*Dual abatement regime.* In 1996, a change was made to the abatement regime for earned income (that is, the rules which govern the way benefit payments are withdrawn as earned income increases). The income disregard was increased to $80 for all beneficiaries, and the rate of withdrawal of assistance was reduced from 70 percent to 30 percent between $80 and $180 of earnings for specific groups of beneficiaries (in particular single parents and those with disabilities or chronic health conditions). For other beneficiaries, earnings above $80 per week continued to be subject to a 70 percent abatement rate.

This means that there is now a dual abatement regime in effect, which provides better returns from part-time work for people with responsibilities for children and people with disabling health conditions. This recognizes the fact that people in such circumstances are often only able to take up part-time work.

The changes have had a significant impact on the return from part-time work for the targeted group of beneficiaries by reducing the effective marginal tax rate or EMTR (which expresses the amount by which earnings are reduced after taking into account both taxation and withdrawal of benefit as earnings rise). In 1987/88, according to one published study (Compton and Euller, 1992), single parent DPB recipients faced an EMTR of 90 cents on the dollar or higher for each additional dollar of earnings from around $3,000 to around $18,000. While the figures will have changed somewhat over the past decade, it is nevertheless likely that, prior to the change, these beneficiaries were still facing comparably high EMTRs in the income band between around 15 percent and 60 percent of average ordinary time earnings. The effect of the change is likely to have reduced the EMTR to around 50 percent in the income band between 15 percent and 30 percent of average ordinary time earnings. Given that beneficiaries moving into work command lower than average earnings, these groups may experience an income gain for possibly up to around 20 hours' work per week.

There is a cost trade-off for this improvement, however, and it comes in the form of an elevation in EMTRs for higher levels of earnings. In effect, the change has pushed the high EMTR zone further up the income band, so that these beneficiaries will be facing high EMTRs between around 30 percent and 75 percent of average ordinary time earnings. This means that, while there is now a stronger incentive for movement into part-time work, there is also a higher barrier in moving from part-time to full-time work. This might have the effect of trapping these groups in a low-income zone, making it harder for them to improve their income. Other beneficiaries continue to face high EMTRs in the band between around 15 percent and 60 percent of average ordinary time earnings.

The abatement change appears to have had a modest initial impact on the labor supply behavior of Domestic Purposes beneficiaries, primarily in terms of patterns of hours worked by those who were in employment. The proportions who reported other income increased from 19 percent to 22 percent between 1996 and 1997: among the group who did report other income, the amount of income also increased, with 53 percent reporting more than $80 per week in 1997 compared with 36 percent in 1996 (Department of Social Welfare, 1997, 1998).

*In-work benefits*. In 1986, a tax credit was introduced for full-time working families with children. This was the guaranteed minimum family income or GMFI (subsequently repackaged as the Family Tax Credit or FTC). It was intended to guarantee a minimum standard of living to low-income earner families and additionally to provide a margin between benefit levels and the minimum disposable income available to full-time earners. To qualify, a sole parent had to be employed for at least 20 hours per week and a couple had to have a combined total of at least 30 hours' employment per week. Subsequently, in 1996, a new tax credit, the independent family tax credit or IFTC (subsequently also repackaged as the Child Tax Credit or CTC) was added. This was available to lower-income families not receiving a benefit.

No systematic research has been undertaken into the impact of these programs on labor supply behavior and so it is not possible to draw any firm conclusions about their effectiveness as part of the overall welfare-to-work reform program. However—although firm figures are hard to come by—it is known that take-up of both programs has been relatively low. There would appear to be a relatively low level of awareness and understanding of the nature and purpose of both programs among the general community, which is likely to be related to the lack of any significant effort to promote them. This raises a question as to the effectiveness of their contribution to welfare-to-work goals.

*Reductions in level of basic benefit.* The cuts to benefit rates, which were discussed earlier, also served to change the structure of the financial incentives facing beneficiaries as they consider employment opportunities. Although the decision to cut benefit rates was prompted by a deterioration in the fiscal accounts—which was presented as the rationale for the change when it was announced by government—it was also motivated by a desire to increase the differential between benefit levels and low wage rates, so as to provide a greater financial incentive for beneficiaries to move into work. This had become more imperative with the passing of the Employment Contracts Act 1991, which had reformed the industrial relations and wage-fixing structures and infused more flexibility in the labor market. This was likely to create downward pressure on wages for low-skilled jobs, thus reducing the incentives for people on benefits to move into employment.

These various changes have made some difference to the structure of financial incentives faced by beneficiaries when weighing up decisions about work opportunities. However, it is probably fair to say that the changes have not entirely succeeded in overcoming the problems they were aimed at addressing. Several problems remain which may be compromising the extent to which beneficiaries can perceive clear financial advantages in taking up work.

In the first place, the systems in place involve somewhat complex provisions which may not be fully understood by all who are subject to them. There is some evidence that the abatement rules are not fully understood by beneficiaries, while (as noted above) there also seems to be a relatively low level of awareness and understanding of the tax credit programs. This is a serious concern, since perceptions about the nature and purpose of such programs, and the way they alter returns from work, are crucial to the effectiveness of the contribution they can make to welfare-to-work goals.

Secondly, even where the provisions are fully understood, the high effective marginal tax rates that some beneficiaries face may continue to act as a disincentive to taking up work. Although some groups (single parents and invalids) have benefited from relaxed abatement rules and, as a result, will be significantly better off after working part-time, others still stand to gain little from taking up part-time work and need to find full-time jobs before they will see any significant gains from their work effort. For some of these people, a better understanding of the rules may even serve to dampen their work efforts.

Thirdly, the complexity of these provisions are intensified by their interaction with other programs. The widespread use of income testing in the income support system and its expanding use in other areas of social policy (especially in targeting health care and tertiary education study assistance) mean that net returns from work are harder to compute where more than one type of assistance is being received. There is no co-ordination between income testing regimes used in different policy domains, which means that the already high EMTRs erected by the income support system will be exacerbated by income tests in these other domains. In some cases, the actual EMTRs are likely to be well in excess of 100 percent for people who are receiving assistance across a range of social policy domains. This is likely to compromise the value of the improvements made in the changes made to date.

Fourthly, for some beneficiaries the additional costs of taking employment—such as buying clothes or equipment, transport or child care—may still outweigh the financial gains from the enhanced returns from earnings. For single parents, in particular, the costs of child care—even assuming its availability and accessibility—when added on top of the EMTR may mean that many are still likely to be worse off after taking up work. For other people, the start-up costs in taking up a new job—because of the need to buy new clothing or special equipment, or have repairs made to a vehicle—may mean that the net income effect is negligible or even negative, especially if the job is a temporary one. There may also be discontinuities in financial assistance when beneficiaries move into employment, arising from the fact that the tax credit programmes, payable to families in work, are administered by a different department of government from the income support programmes.

Fifthly, for many beneficiaries the only type of work opportunity that arises may be rather insecure in nature—perhaps casual, part-time and temporary—which does not offer much security in terms of a future income stream. The risk of moving into such work and forgoing the certainty of a guaranteed income stream from the benefit may, for many people, outweigh the financial advantage that may accrue from it, if any. Higher incentives may be therefore required to movement into work if aversion to the risk of being stranded without income is a significant barrier to taking up employment.

Taken together, these various considerations mean that it is likely that further reforms will be needed in order to develop a financial incentive structure which offers clear and unequivocal advantages to the bulk of beneficiaries as they confront choices about whether to take up an employment opportunity.

### *Lubricating the Transition to Work*

A third focus of reform effort has been on assisting beneficiaries to make the transition off benefit and into work. Even where people face both clear expectations that they will search for work and positive incentives to take up any opportunities that arise, some will still need assistance in preparing themselves for job readiness and in locating appropriate opportunities. This has led to the development of initiatives which are aimed at lubricating the transition from benefit to work.

A range of programs has been instituted aimed at this goal, including such diverse approaches as facilitative case management, human capital development and job search assistance. The common thread is that they all seek to improve beneficiaries' capacities both to locate and compete effectively for jobs. These changes have been complemented by initiatives aimed at stimulating employer demand for the labor of beneficiaries, primarily through wage subsidies.

*Facilitative case management.* Particular emphasis has been laid on facilitative case management. This involves attention to the particular circumstances and needs of individual beneficiaries with the goal of assisting them to chart a course to self-reliance.

Two programs operated by the former Income Support are discussed here, which had different emphases: customized service was adopted as the standard business model for managing interactions with income support claimants, while the Compass program was specifically targeted at single parent beneficiaries.

*Customized service.* Under the customized service approach, each beneficiary is allocated to an individual case manager who takes responsibility for all contact involving that beneficiary. The one-to-one relationship provides a context in which the case management officer can help the customer to plan a course to employment and eventual self-reliance. This will involve setting goals, identification of barriers to employment and plotting a course to overcome these barriers, with the help of referrals to education, training and employment opportunities. It is also anticipated that the close one-to-one relationship between staff and beneficiaries will reduce the need for emergency payments, as well as the potential for benefit debt and fraud.

*Compass.* Increasing attention began to be paid to single parent beneficiaries in the late 1980s as the numbers of people receiving Domestic Purposes Benefit continued to climb at higher than projected rates of growth. One response was the establishment of the Compass program, which is aimed at assisting single parent beneficiaries into education, training and employment. The program, which was loosely based on the successful Australian Jobs Education and Training (JET) program, provides enhanced individualized assistance to single parent beneficiaries to assist them to prepare for work readiness and overcome barriers to employment. Participation in the program is voluntary.

The program was piloted in four Income Support offices from March 1994 to March 1995 and was extended as a nationwide pilot until June 1997. Results from the trial showed that Compass produced a modest but significant improvement in the rate at which people move off benefit and a more substantial take-up of education and training opportunities. It has now been adopted as a permanent component of New Zealand's income support system.

Income Support has now been merged with the former New Zealand Employment Service, which operated its own individualized employment assistance program based on job action interviews with job seekers. The task for the newly created organization Work and Income New Zealand is to develop a unified case management approach to its whole customer base.

*Human capital development programs.* One of the functions of the case management process is to identify any barriers that might prevent beneficiaries from being able to compete effectively for jobs in the labor market. One of the most significant barriers is a lack of skills. Beneficiaries who lack marketable skills are at especial risk of long-term dependency on welfare. A range of programs is available to provide long-term beneficiaries with basic skills which will better enable them to compete for jobs. Two of the most significant upskilling programs have been the ACCESS training program (which had a parallel Maori ACCESS analogue) and the Training Opportunities Program (TOP).

*ACCESS.* The Access training scheme was established in 1987 and was aimed at improving the job prospects of unemployed people, especially those who were disadvantaged in the labor market and for whom traditional training programs were either unavailable or unsuitable (Dominick, 1992). In 1990, over 70,000 people were enrolled for ACCESS training and over 13,000 were attending courses at any one time. The average amount of time spent in training by ACCESS enrollees during 1990 was fourteen weeks.

An evaluation of the effectiveness of the program found that it had some effect in improving the labor market prospects of participants, but that the impact tended to diminish over time (Dominick, 1992). The evaluation also found that the program was effective in improving the employment prospects of individuals in sub-groups of particular disadvantage (especially those with low levels of education, Maori, those who had been in long-term unemployment and those with little work experience), but that for the most disadvantaged (who had all of these characteristics) fourteen weeks' training was too short to equip them properly to compete for and retain work.

*Training Opportunities Program (TOP).* The ACCESS program was replaced by TOP in 1993, and the Maori ACCESS program was progressively mainstreamed into TOP from this date. The new program was more closely targeted at the longer-term unemployed and at unemployed youth than its predecessors. It is specifically linked with the National Qualifications Framework and is designed to furnish trainees with educational credits recognized under that framework (ETSA, 1998). Over the course of the fiscal year ending June 1998, the average number of trainees was around 15,000.

The available evidence suggests that the program is useful both in furnishing trainees with skills and in improving their employment chances. Of those who completed training in the year ending June 1998, 90 percent attained at least 70 percent of the credits for which they were assessed and 42 percent were subsequently placed in employment, with another 12 percent going on to further education or training outside the program within two months of leaving it (ETSA, 1998).

*Job matching and job search services.* Another potential barrier for job seekers is locating employment opportunities and presenting themselves to employers as a suitable employee. A range of programs are provided to help job seekers to find work opportunities and prepare themselves for applying for vacancies. One of the primary functions of the former New Zealand Employment Service was matching job seekers with job vacancies. This function has now been taken over by the newly created state agency Work and Income New Zealand.

Job matching involves a range of activities. Job seekers are provided with information on vacancies through the Job Bank, while employers are provided with information on job seekers through the Talent Bank. Both databases are available through the agency's website. Job seekers are referred to appropriate employment opportunities, or to related activities aimed at helping them to enhance their employment prospects, such as training programs and work experience placements. The agency also runs an array of seminars to assist people in preparing themselves for job readiness, ranging from general seminars on job search techniques to targeted courses for specific groups, such as single parents, women returning to the workforce, Maori and Pacific Islands people.

*Work experience programs.* Many job seekers who lack skills, and especially those who have been out of employment for long periods, may need additional assistance before they are able to compete effectively for unsubsidized jobs in the open labor market. One way of providing such people with the chance to develop work skills in a work context is through work experience placements.

The new Community Work and Training program, introduced in October 1998 to provide work placement opportunities for job seekers, also has benefits for communities. Placements of up to 20 hours per week are aimed at building work skills, confidence, motivation and self-esteem of job seekers. Placements are intended to resemble a paid work environment as closely as possible.

The program is being developed on the basis of existing programs. In particular, it involves the expansion and further development of the Community Task Force program which has been operating since 1991. By June 30, 1997, around 2,500 medium-to long-term job seekers were participating in the Community Task Force (Department of Labour, 1997). The scale of the program was expanded during the year and by June 30, 1998 8,168 job seekers were participating in community work projects (Department of Labour, 1998). A further 2,840 were involved in training outcomes.

The training element of the new program is also being based on existing programs, such as Job Link (which provides work placements and on-the-job training for up to four weeks for longer-term job seekers who have recently completed a TOP course), Job Intro (which provides work experience placements of up to four weeks for young job seekers) and Task Force Green (which is similar to the Community Task Force program, but with a particular emphasis on projects focused on environmental goals).

*Wage subsidy schemes.* In addition to these programs which are aimed at enhancing the skills that job seekers offer to employers, incentives are also provided to employers to engage people off the welfare rolls, primarily in the form of wage subsidies.

The high tide of New Zealand's use of wage subsidies was in the early 1980s when the Project Employment Project was sustaining more than 50,000 people in fully subsidized work. Since that scheme was phased out in 1985, New Zealand has been somewhat chary in its use of wage subsidy schemes, primarily out of concern about their net impact on total employment, which may be small unless care is taken to reduce the risks of substitution of other job seekers and displacement of other employment. Nevertheless, a range of programs currently provide wage subsidies. The main one is the Job Plus Scheme.

Under the Job Plus Scheme employers are paid a wage subsidy to hire disadvantaged job seekers in full-time permanent positions. The program is targeted at those who have been unemployed for 26 weeks or more. The level of the subsidy is negotiable, with a ceiling linked to the adult rate of Unemployment Benefit. The subsidy is available for up to one year and is typically paid for around six months. The program generally provides wage subsidies for between 20,000 and 25,000 job seekers at any one time.

Although no comprehensive evaluation has been undertaken of the scheme, the various facts that are known about it suggest that it is achieving mixed results. One study showed that six months after the subsidy, 39 percent of workers were in the same job and 65 percent were working at least ten hours per week in some job, although not necessarily with the same employer (New Zealand Employment Service, 1994). However, the same study showed that 41 percent of participants had left the original employer one month after the subsidy had ended and 62 percent had left six months later. More than half those who had left said they were made redundant or had been dismissed. This suggests that the program is not always being used to recruit people to permanent positions, and that a significant proportion of employers may be making more opportunistic use of it and terminating the job once the subsidy has expired.

The Job Plus program is complemented by two other related programs, Job Plus Training—where the subsidy covers a period of short-term training which is linked to a specific vacancy—and Job Plus Maori Assets—where the subsidy covers employment for up to a year by a Maori group or organization involved in the development and management of multiple-ownership Maori assets. Both of these programs operate on a comparatively small scale.

In addition, the very long-term unemployed (those who have been out of work for four years or more) have access to an additional program, entitled Job Connection, which provides fully subsidized six-month work placements which are designed to assist them to re-establish their work skills and develop a work record which will improve their chances of being able to compete for unsubsidized work. This program also operates on a small scale.

These various initiatives represent a reasonably full palette of options for easing the transition from benefit to employment—by enhancing the degree to which beneficiary job seekers are perceived by employers as a useful potential source of labor, and by better equipping such job seekers to search and compete for vacancies. A key instrument in this range of tools is the case management process. Case management, by focusing on the individual circumstances and attributes of a particular job seeker, has the capacity to optimize the use of program resources by drawing on those which are likely to provide the best chances of a successful employment outcome. However, in order to achieve such optimal use of program resources, more complete understanding is needed about what types of assistance are most effective for individuals in different circumstances. There is a need for research and development effort to educate the selection of an appropriate service mix for individual job seekers.

*Reforming the Institutional Environment*

The above changes constitute a significant reform package at the level of both policy and service delivery. The changes have been accompanied by institutional reforms which have been intended to support the welfare-to-work focus and to give best effect to the reforms.

Historically, government's employment policies have been managed separately from its income support policies. The former were delivered through the New Zealand Employment Service (NZES), which was part of the Department of Labour. The latter were delivered through Income Support (IS), which was part of the Department of Social Welfare. This arrangement meant that applicants for work-tested benefits had to deal with two separate agencies: IS would process applications for income support, while NZES would provide job search assistance and manage the practical application of the work test.

With the growing emphasis on welfare-to-work programs, however, the separate delivery structure for these two sets of services made less sense, since more income support programs were paid on the expectation that the recipient would be seeking work. Part of the point of the customized service programs being developed within IS was to ensure that customers were aware of the requirement to seek work and to provide additional support in preparing them to compete for jobs. This means that there was an increasing risk of overlap between the services delivered by the two agencies.

*Coalescence of income support and employment services.* On October 1, 1998, IS and NZES were separated from their parent organizations and brought together into a single new entity—Work and Income New Zealand (WINZ)—which became a new government department in its own right. This change has effectively created a one-stop shop that will not only address people's income support needs but will also focus on their training requirements and help with job search. This will allow the development of a more tightly integrated set of services which, for the beneficiary population of working age, will focus more strongly on welfare-to-work programs.

*Promoting the New Vision of Welfare*

All of these changes are backed up by efforts to promote the new vision of welfare and to change public perceptions about the nature and purpose of income support. This has involved a range of particular initiatives already discussed—including the rebranding of the Unemployment Benefit as the Community Wage and the staging of a high-profile international conference entitled "Beyond Dependency." More generally, there has been a change in the public rhetoric about welfare, which has involved a shift in emphasis from the notion of welfare as a set of unattached entitlements to a more contingent notion based on the principle that the system is to provide temporary support while people are unable to provide for themselves, and that those who have the capacity to work should take every opportunity to do so.

*"From welfare to well-being."* Efforts have also been made to promote the idea that welfare dependency is not solely central government's concern, but that local communities and private business also have a role to play at a local level. An initiative entitled "From Welfare to Well-being" was developed to promote this idea and to mobilize local community and business leaders to develop local employment initiatives. As no additional funds are available to resource the initiative, it mainly relies on a process of relationship-building by local WINZ managers—who undertake a range of speaking engagements and meet regularly with local community and business leaders—together with a mix of suasion and exhortation to employers to take on staff from the unemployment rolls.

Little research has been carried out on public attitudes to welfare, which means it is difficult to form judgments about what impact these initiatives might have had. Nevertheless, it is likely that there will have been shifts in public attitudes to welfare over the course of the past decade—as there have been shifts in public views about many other aspects of public life—and especially about the respective roles of individuals, families and state. In keeping with these more general trends, it is likely that any shift in public sentiment will have been away from provision of open-ended state entitlements and towards forms of support which place greater emphasis on personal responsibility.

## Concluding Comment

Over the course of the past decade, there has been a fundamental change in the premises on which the New Zealand income support system is based. Until the early 1990s, income support benefits were seen as entitlements which people could avail themselves of, if they fell into any one of a number of categories covered by benefit provisions. Anyone who was a widow, a single parent, or an invalid, or anyone who was unemployed, sick, or disabled could lay a claim to being supported by the state, provided that the qualifying criteria were met.

The role of income support administration was largely restricted to assessing the entitlement of claimants and, where an entitlement was verified, arranging payment as set down by statute and regulation. Receipt of income support was considered to entail little obligation, apart from the need to establish that one met the qualification criteria. People who were unemployed were expected to be available for, and actively seeking work, although there was little formal testing of whether they were in fact doing so. No work requirement existed for any other category of beneficiary and little attention at all was paid to the reinsertion of these other groups back into the labor force. In summary, the system operated in what is now characterized as a very "passive" way.

The rules of the game have now been totally transformed. The income support system is no longer viewed in such a passive way and has taken on the character of a much more active system. This has involved several dimensions of change. First, a new set of expectations has been established of people who receive income support, largely that those who are capable of work will seek out and take up work opportunities as soon as they are able to do so. Secondly, efforts have been made to improve the financial incentives that beneficiaries face when considering employment opportunities. Thirdly, new and enhanced forms of assistance have been developed to assist beneficiaries make the transition off benefit and into work. Fourthly, the institutional structures have been reformed to give best effect to these changes. Finally, attention has also been given to changing public attitudes to welfare.

Most emphasis has been placed on establishing new expectations of claimants to income support, expressed in the form of reciprocal obligations for the support they receive. The primary obligation is that people who are capable of work will search for and take up employment as soon as they are able to do so. This expectation has been expressed through a number of particular policy shifts. The work requirement has been expanded to encompass not only the unemployed, but the whole population of beneficiaries of working age who are assessed as being capable of work. The work test itself has been tightened, and a stronger regime of sanctions has been introduced, with graduated penalties for repeated instances of non-compliance with the work requirement. The range of activities that may be required has been broadened to include community work as an alternative to paid work, in recognition both that work is not currently available for all people who are subject to a work requirement, and that some people may not yet be ready for an unsubsidized job.

Hand in hand with these changes have gone efforts to improve the financial incentives for people to move into work. Primary emphasis has been placed on improving returns from work, through the introduction of in-work benefits and improvements to the abatement regime. The relativity between benefits and wages was also adjusted by a round of cuts to benefit rates in 1991. As a result of these changes, more beneficiaries now stand to gain financially from their work efforts. Single parents and invalids, in particular, who are more likely to be able to work only part-time, now retain more of their part-time earnings.

Taken together, the above changes provide a clearer signal to beneficiaries about the importance and financial benefits of work. Many beneficiaries will be able to respond to these signals through their own efforts. Others, however, will need assistance to do so. For this reason, further changes have been implemented on the service delivery side aimed at lubricating the transitions from benefit to employment. These changes have pivoted around the key idea of case management, under which the individual needs of beneficiaries are assessed and a course to employment and self-reliance mapped out which is tailored to their individual circumstances. A range of assistance is available to beneficiaries, including job matching and job search assistance. For people who are assessed as being not yet work-ready, a broader range of human capital development programs and work experience placements are available.

Institutional reforms have also been carried out to give best effect to these changes. In particular, a new state agency—Work and Income New Zealand—was created which brings together both income support and employment service functions. The integration of these two functions will allow a stronger emphasis on welfare-to-work goals through the explicit linking of receipt of benefit to the work requirement via the notion of reciprocal obligations.

The whole set of changes has been backed up by efforts to promote a new vision of welfare, centered around the idea of welfare-to-work. This has been expressed in various ways—through the rebranding of benefits to give higher prominence to the work expectation, through the staging of a high-profile international conference focused on welfare dependency issues, through the mobilization of local communities to tackle problems of welfare dependency at a local level and through changes in public rhetoric about welfare, emphasizing the notion that welfare is intended to provide temporary support for those who are unable to provide for themselves and that those who are able to work should seek every opportunity of doing so as soon as they are able.

These are all relatively recent developments and as yet little research has been carried out on their effectiveness in achieving welfare-to-work goals. Nevertheless, even in the absence of any hard information about the outcomes of the changes, it is possible to make some comments on the comprehensiveness, consistency and coherence of the total reform package.

It is worth noting, to begin with, that the changes outlined in this paper constitute a relatively coherent package comprising a set of related initiatives which are aimed at a similar goal and whose strength is likely to lie in their conjoint action. None of the particular changes is likely to have a significant impact in isolation; taken together, however, the changes are likely to be mutually reinforcing and, when the individual contributions of each component are aggregated together, have a good chance of achieving a significant impact.

However, there remain a number of problems to be resolved. In particular, the improvements to the structure of financial incentives faced by beneficiaries can be considered, as yet, to have made only modest gains and more reform may be needed to ensure that the great bulk of people who take up employment will be significantly better off for having done so. In particular, many beneficiaries continue to face high effective marginal tax rates over a relatively broad band of potential earnings. Single parents and invalids now face lower EMTRs as a result of the introduction of a dual abatement regime, but many other beneficiaries still face a considerable disincentive, in the form of high EMTRs, when facing decisions about employment. For these other groups, part-time work will not deliver much higher income than remaining on benefit and they will need to find full-time jobs to achieve a significant income gain.

Secondly, the problem of high EMTRs is exacerbated by the use of income testing across a range of social policy domains in an uncoordinated way. Within the income support system, the income test gives rise to EMTRs which approach 100 percent across relatively wide earnings bands for many beneficiaries. When the additional impact of income tests operated in connection with health user charge subsidies and tertiary study assistance are taken into account, it is likely that many families will be facing EMTRs which are well over 100 percent, which means that they will be worse off after increasing their work effort.

Thirdly, the costs associated with work mean that a further slice of income is lost over and above the effect of the EMTR. Many single parents who have to fund child care out of their earnings would be likely to find that it does not make financial sense to move into work, despite the improvements that have been brought about by the dual abatement regime. There may therefore be a need to provide additional assistance to help single parents meet the costs of child care before many of them perceive work as being worthwhile.

Fourthly, there is some evidence that low take-up of the tax credit programs may be hampering their effectiveness in contributing to welfare-to-work goals. It is important that these programs are well understood by beneficiaries and that they are actively promoted if they are to function properly in providing an impetus for movement into work. If they are not widely known or well understood, beneficiaries will be taking decisions about employment opportunities without full information on the probable return from work, which may lead them to estimate the potential returns as being lower than they are in fact. This would be likely to have a dampening effect on movement into work.

Fifthly, if the tax credit programs do begin to function effectively in assisting people to move into work, this will mean that instead of reducing the fiscal costs of income support by the full amount of benefit that is no longer being paid, part of the cost will simply be shifted from income support programs to the tax credit programs. Many beneficiaries who move into employment as a result of welfare-to-work programs will be equipped only to carry out low-skilled work, which means both that they will command low wages and that their prospects of income growth are low. Taken together these facts mean there is likely to be a significant demand for in-work benefits from former beneficiaries and that many will need this additional assistance for long periods.

Such costs are likely to be regarded as worth meeting, since they will enable beneficiaries to access the wider benefits of employment. Nevertheless, this raises a number of other issues. In particular, it means that the problem of the poverty trap, with high EMTRs posing a significant disincentive to work effort, will be replicated in the lower reaches of the earnings distribution. Low-income workers receiving in-work benefits will face high EMTRs on the next dollar of earnings as a result of the combined effect of taxation and abatement of in-work benefits as their earnings rise. By erecting a barrier both to increased work hours and to efforts to advance in the labor market, this may have the effect of trapping workers in a perpetual low-income zone.

Sixthly, there is a relatively high rate of return to benefit of former beneficiaries who had moved into work. Wilson (in press) estimates the rate of return of former beneficiaries to benefit within two and a half years of exiting to work at more than 50 percent for most classes of benefit. While a certain amount of churning between benefit and work is to be expected, especially given the nature of recent changes in the labor market—with less security of employment, especially in low-skilled jobs which are more likely to be temporary and casual—this rate seems high and suggests that many beneficiaries find it difficult to re-establish themselves in sustained employment after exiting from benefit.

Current policy settings are primarily configured around the goal of assisting people to move off benefit and into work and have placed less emphasis on maintenance in sustained employment. There is thus scope for the further development of policy which is aimed at this goal. A range of policy options exist for this purpose—including bridging assistance, which is designed to help people over the financial hump during the early period of employment, and post-placement support, which is designed to assist with the various adjustments they need to make to the demands of their new positions. Such approaches have not been tried extensively in New Zealand to date, and perhaps ought to be the subject of consideration. If the rate of return to benefit can be dampened down even slightly by the use of such approaches, this has the potential to deliver significant gains—not only in terms of fiscal savings, but in terms of the improved prospects of former beneficiaries in the labor market.

Scope also exists for further reform in other areas. In the area of case management, in particular, there are opportunities for further advance. One of the challenges facing case management officers is selecting the right mix of services which an individual beneficiary needs to maximize his or her chances of moving off benefit and into work. There are many pitfalls in this process and to get it right requires a deep understanding of what types of assistance are of most benefit to people in different circumstances. At present, it is fair to say that the available knowledge does not allow such decisions to be made with total confidence. There is a role, then, for further research into this question.

In the final analysis, the degree to which New Zealand is successful in reducing its current high levels of receipts on welfare will depend on the way in which the economy performs in creating employment. The reforms are therefore part of a wider picture and their success will be contingent to a high degree on the success of government in managing the macro-economic environment, and that of private business in creating demand for labor. Under adverse conditions, and in the absence of continuing job growth, efforts to change the labor supply behavior of beneficiaries will be largely ineffective and may even be self-defeating if they engender frustration on the part of those who are unable to find work despite their best efforts. At best, under such a scenario, welfare-to-work programs are capable only of stirring the pot and sharing the pool of unemployment among a wider pool of people.

Under more propitious circumstances, and given a prospering economy, the welfare-to-work changes have good prospects of success, especially if they place emphasis on human capital development, by assisting those who lack marketable skills to improve their capacity to compete for jobs. The real challenge for welfare-to-work programs lies here: to ensure that when the economy is performing at times of peak demand job seekers on the welfare rolls are perceived by employers as useful potential recruits to the workforce.

The evidence from the past is that the business cycle has an important impact on levels of unemployment and benefit receipt, not only in the obvious sense that more people are out of work when demand in the economy is low, but also through the more pernicious effect of hysteresis (according to which the troughs in the business cycle increase levels of welfare dependency to a greater extent than the peaks reduce them). The current high levels of welfare dependency are largely the legacy of this effect over the past two decades.

To adapt an idea from Shakespeare, the business cycle is a tide which must be taken at the flood if it is to lead on to fortune. Significant reductions in the welfare rolls are only possible at such a time, and unless they are achieved, there will be no realistic prospect of solving the problem. Government policies must therefore be well configured to ensure that the chance is taken, by ensuring that the highest number of people are work-ready and capable of carrying out the types of work required by employers. Unwinding the legacy of the past will be a stern challenge. Yet it must be done, and welfare-to-work approaches perhaps constitute the best available set of tools to do the job.

## References

Bertram, G. (1987). "Evaluation of employment programs." In *The April Report: Report of the Royal Commission on Social Policy*, Volume III, Part Two Future Directions: Associated Papers. Wellington: Royal Commission on Social Policy.

Brown, R., & Quilter, H. (1997). "New directions at a watershed for welfare." In *Conference Proceedings: Beyond Dependency Conference*. Wellington: Department of Social Welfare.

Compton, J., & Euller, R. (1992). "Effective marginal tax rates." In M. Prebble and P. Rebstock (eds.), *Incentives and labour supply: Modelling taxes and benefits*. Wellington: Institute of Policy Studies.

Department of Labour. (1997). *Annual report*. Wellington: Author.

Department of Labour. (1998). *Annual report*. Wellington: Author.

Department of Social Welfare. (1995). *Income support: Strategic directions 1995-2005*. Wellington: Author.

Department of Social Welfare. (1996). *Social welfare in New Zealand: Strategic directions: Post election briefing paper*. Wellington: Author.

Department of Social Welfare. (1998). *Statistics report*. Wellington: Author.

Dominick, C. (1992). *The effectiveness of ACCESS training*. Wellington: Education and Training Support Agency.

Education and Training Support Agency. (1998). *Annual report*. Wellington: Author.

Gardiner, K. (1997). *Bridges from benefit to work*. York: Joseph Rowntree Foundation.

Gray, A., & Neale, J. (1984). "Study of the project employment programme." In *Studies of employment and training programmes*. Wellington: Government Printer.

Hawke, G. R. (1985). *The making of New Zealand: An economic history*. Cambridge: Cambridge University Press.

Hawke, G. (1991). "Commentary: Belonging and participating in constrained circumstances." In G. R. Hawke (ed.), *A modest safety net? The future of the welfare state*. Wellington: Institute of Policy Studies.

King, M. (1981). "Between two worlds." In W. H. Oliver (ed.), *The Oxford history of New Zealand*. Wellington: Oxford University Press.
Mackay, R. (1998, January). "Targeting in social security: The New Zealand experience." Paper presented at the 2nd International Research Conference on Social Security, Jerusalem.
McClure, M. (1998). *A civilised community: A history of social security in New Zealand 1898-1998*. Auckland: Auckland University Press.
McKenzie, A. (1997). "Workfare: The New Zealand experience and future directions." *Social Policy Journal of New Zealand*, Issue 8.
New Zealand Employment Service. (1994). *An evaluation of job plus*. Wellington: Author.
New Zealand Employment Service. (1998). *Job plus maori assets*. Wellington: Work and Income New Zealand.
New Zealand Government. (1929a). *Unemployment in New Zealand. First Section of Report of Committee Appointed by the Government on 17th October, 1928, and 26th February, 1929*. Wellington: Author.
New Zealand Government. (1929b). *Unemployment in New Zealand. Second Section of Report of Committee Appointed by the Government on 17th October, 1928, and 26th February, 1929*. Wellington: Author.
Olssen, E. (1981). "Towards a new society." In W. H. Oliver (ed.), *The Oxford History of New Zealand*. Wellington: Oxford University Press.
Petrie, M. (1998). *Organisational transformation: The income support experience*. Wellington: Department of Social Welfare.
Prebble, M., & Rebstock, P. (1992). *Incentives and labour supply: modeling taxes and benefits*. Wellington: Institute of Policy Studies.
Prime Ministerial Task Force on Employment. (1994a). *Employment: The issues*. Wellington: Author.
Prime Ministerial Task Force on Employment. (1994b). *Employment: addressing New Zealand's biggest challenge: Proposals for action*. Wellington: Author.
Richardson, L. (1981). "Parties and political change." In W. H. Oliver (ed.), *The Oxford history of New Zealand*. Wellington: Oxford University Press.
Rogers, J. (1997). "The Wisconsin approach—Innovations in welfare reform." In *Conference Proceedings: Beyond Dependency Conference*. Wellington: Department of Social Welfare.
Royal Commission on Social Security. (1972). *Social security in New Zealand: Report of the Royal Commission of Inquiry*. Wellington: Author.
Shipley, J. (1991). *Social assistance welfare that works: A statement of government policy on social assistance*. Wellington: GP Print Ltd.
Shirley, I., Easton, B., Briar, C., & Chatterjee, S. (1990). *Unemployment in New Zealand*. Palmerston North: Dunmore Press.
Simpson, T. (1990). *The slump: The 1930s depression: Its origins and aftermath*. Auckland: Penguin Books.
Wilson, M. (in press). *The duration of benefit receipt: New findings from the benefit dynamics dataset*.
Work and Income New Zealand. (1998). *Job plus training*. Wellington: Author.

# 4

# From Welfare to Work Fare: Dutch Policies in the Nineties

*Piet K. Keizer*

## Introduction

Many socioeconomic auditors consider the Netherlands' social and economic performance to be very positive and use Dutch policies as a guideline for their own policies. The Dutch approach has become known as the Polder model. Not long ago, however, the situation in the Netherlands was characterized as "the Dutch disease." One of the symptoms of this disease was a structural increase in the number of social benefit recipients, including people who were "on welfare." The principal causes were a macro wage level that was too high to be competitive and the rigid institutional structure of the labor market. The negative financial effects were large resulting in governmental budget deficits and a growing governmental debt ratio from the 1970s on. At the end of that period unemployment began to rise, higher than that found in surrounding countries. When looking at the number of social benefit recipients both the number of unemployed and the number of ill and disabled people rose sharply. The ratio of the volume of benefit recipients to the workers, the so-called inactivity ratio, approached the level of one to one.

In 1982 a coalition of Christian-Democrats and Liberals formed a cabinet that made to an important policy shift. The government consulted the central unions and employers' organizations and in November 1982 the social partners signed a Central Agreement, that formulated the principles of the new approach. The main policy resulting from this agreement involved a long-term wage restraint and cuts in governmental expenditures in exchange for employment commitments from the employers' organizations. The work-related efforts by the employers would especially be focused on labor time reduction and the creation of part-time jobs. This appeared to be the beginning of a significant economic recovery in terms of economic growth and a structural increase in the level of employment. Especially in the nineties, the quantity of demands for labor began to rise. If the micro labor markets are perfectly flexible, created vacancies lead to an increase of the level of employment. In reality, however, there is never a perfect match between supply and demand, making it necessary for the government and the social partners to see whether they can improve the match, so as to diminish the number of benefit recipients and to increase the number of people employed.

Analyzing the course of Dutch policy this chapter begins with an overview of the historical development of labor market institutions, the current framework of which has emerged less from a conscious political process to implement an ideal type welfare state blueprint, than from a set of incremental policies that sometimes may conflict with one another. The next section sketches the inactivity problem of growing numbers of benefit recipients, together with declining numbers of employed people. Figures will show that Dutch inactivity as far as it can be influenced by policies is especially to be found in the reservoirs of sick, disabled and unemployed people. These people receive benefits that are rather high under programs designed to prevent those who have to live on "welfare" benefits from becoming outsiders. Although three cabinets headed by Lubbers have developed important policies to combat the problem of inactivity, figures over the period 1982-1994 still show an increase. We then move to examine the policies of the cabinet headed by Kok. Profiting from the positive financial effects of the economic policies of former cabinets and from a significant increase in the volume of international trade, this cabinet has intensified its efforts to get the inactivity ratio down. Latest figures show some success in this respect and future projections made by the Dutch Central Planning Bureau reveal an optimistic picture for the near future. This makes it possible to spend an increasing amount of money to move a significant portion of the people who live on welfare back to work. In the next section we describe the purple cabinet's approach with respect to Public Assistance, which was once meant to be a safety net and social service of last resort, but became a structural service for a relatively large group. In the period 1994-1998 policies to get these people back to work has intensified. In the last section of this chapter attention is paid to the organization of the system of Public Assistance, the purple cabinet's approach in this area, and special considerations with respect to ethnic minorities. The chapter ends with a summary and discussion of prospects for the future.

## History of Dutch Labor Market Institutions

The institutions of the Dutch labor market can best be described as a mature welfare state. A century ago the situation was quite different (Windmuller, 1969). The economy in the nineteenth century was organized along conservative lines of classical liberalism and can be typified as free enterprise capitalism. The polity was organized along conservative lines which favored limited suffrage and the idea that the basic task of the government was to maintain law and order. The family was considered the cornerstone of society. This implied that in case of injury or unemployment of the breadwinner, other family members would assume his role. In the conservative view the role of government was that of a tough father rather than a caring mother for all citizens. There were two major sources of opposition to the conservative view. First, were the Marxists, who considered society a battlefield, more than a naturally ranked hierarchy. They tried to organize the proletariat who were seen as victims of a capitalistic system racked by internal contradictions. According to the Marxists, in the competitive struggle, employers could not afford to give labor a just wage or to provide reasonable aid for those outside the labor force. Lack of central coordination was the reason why the capitalistic system would die out, and necessarily be followed by a system of socialist planning that guaranteed the central coordination and distribution of resources. Second, opposition to conservative thought came from Christians who considered the outcome of capitalism to be unacceptable from a social point of view. The Bible teaches that we are our brother's keeper. So we must care for the poor and the outsiders. Because families are not always able to deliver all the services that they may need, the government has a moral duty to intervene and legally support organizations designed to aid the poor.

In the first half of the twentieth century the institutions of the labor market changed drastically. Under pressure from the groups mentioned above the government started to develop a legal framework to protect people against poverty.[1] Income transfers were arranged in case of illness, disability and unemployment of the breadwinner, while unions and employers' groups became involved in the organization of these services. In the 1930s the Great Depression led to significant changes in industrial relations, with the adoption of a system of collective bargaining with nationwide coverage. Simultaneously the government declared itself responsible for the creation and maintenance of full employment. During WWII Dutch politicians worked out schemes that regulated the labor market in a quite corporatistic way, creating the foundation for a postwar welfare state.

After the Second World War, social policies were no longer merely concessions to left-wing groups for the purpose of avoiding social unrest. Large segments of the population and most of the established political parties embraced the ideology that the government should be responsible for full employment and the care of people who are unable to earn a living. Once the economy had recovered and economic growth reached unprecedented heights, governments were pressured by unions and other left-oriented organizations to set up social security and social assistance arrangements for those unable to earn their own living.[2] Thus, a system of social services was set—to transfer income to the outsiders.

The Dutch social system came into trouble in the 1970s when two oil crises hit the world economy, leading to a worldwide recession. Social insurance schemes were unable to deal with huge macro problems. The massive use of benefit threatened to overwhelm the system. Strong increases in the social premiums were leveled or evaded and put the system under heavy pressure.

## The Necessity of Restructuring the Institutions of the Welfare State

To restore economic growth we have to realize that the basic determinants of prosperity are to be found in the extent to which people are able and willing to innovate and renew production processes. The constant evolution in our knowledge makes it necessary to continuously increase the skills level of our human resources. The flexibility necessary to remain competitive has increased during the last decades. This has led to a growing attention to human resource management on every level of production and management: firm, industry, vocation, region, nation. In economics these policies have become known as "active labor market policies." In The Netherlands, labor offices had the task of supporting unemployed people in their search for a job. Because economic developments have become more complex and dynamic the employment problem has also become more complicated. The labor offices appeared to lack the necessary infrastructure to do the job. In 1990 a law was adopted that formed the legal framework for a new, tripartite organization to develop a modern strategy to shape national human resource management. At the same time, the role of private work agencies has been extended.

The historical overview of the Dutch welfare state suggests that many pieces of the system are developed quite separately from each other, without references to a comprehensive design of the big picture. Societal improvements always appear to be the result of a process of trial and error. But it is efficient to now and then look back and see whether one can improve the coordination between the different policy areas. In the case of the Dutch welfare state we can distinguish among its complementary roles and functions of the following sub-"systems":

1. monetary and budgetary policies stabilize the effective demand on full employment level;

2. income policies, including the system of collective bargaining on labor conditions combine social requirements formulated in terms of fairness with economic requirements formulated in terms of market clearing relative factor prices;

3. social security policies financially release people if they are (temporarily) unable to earn their own living;

4. active labor market policies support job seekers (and employers who search for the workers they need).

These policies have been developed, proposed, adopted and implemented by different organizations. The big question now is whether these policies, which all try to manipulate events that are mutually interdependent, are well coordinated. In other words, when we take the welfare state institutions as a whole, can we judge them as operating within a consistent framework? If the institutional framework works well, the number of people for which there is no employment, is reduced to a minimum. Because the focus of our chapter is

**Figure 4.1**
**Benefit Recipients as % of the Labor Force 1982-1995**

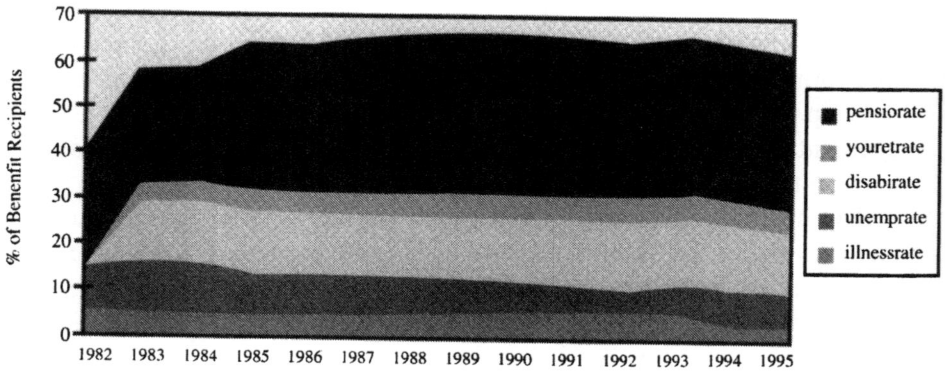


the flow of people from welfare back to work, we will answer this question for subsystems 3 and 4.

## The Dutch Problem of Inactivity

The introduction of the Dutch welfare system is not only generous and extensive, it is also widely used. The Dutch population has, to a growing extent, discovered the opportunities that its government has offered, to receive social transfers in many different ways. The system that was built up during the fifties and the sixties became widely used through the seventies and eighties. In figure 4.1 we see the number of benefit recipients from 1982 through 1995.

During the 1980s, the unemployed and disabled recipients appeared to consume the bulk of benefits. If we compare Dutch figures for sick leave, then one may get the impression that the Dutch people were in bad shape in the 1980s and early 1990s. One of the instruments to reduce unemployment and to create career opportunities for the younger generation was the offering of early retirement. Nevertheless, the problem of Dutch inactivity, as expressed by the inactivity ratio, was aggravated. If we add to this the trend towards longer periods of education for the average teenager, then we have mentioned the main factors that led to an unacceptably high figure for Dutch inactivity. In the next few subsections we will describe the developments with respect to sickness leave, disability and unemployment in more detail and consider how Dutch politics has treated these problems during the 1980s and the early 1990s.

### *Sickness Leave*

In 1981, the Dutch parliament adopted important changes in the Illness Act. The two main elements were a decrease in the benefit rate and a sectoral premium differentiation. The first measure was meant to give sick people a stronger financial incentive to care for their own health as much as possible. The second measure was meant to stimulate employers' organizations and unions to negotiate budgets for the creation of healthier working conditions. Unions, however, were strongly against the first measure and they were able to negotiate with the employers' organizations a financial supplement on top of the official sickness benefit. It took about ten years before the government made a second attempt to reduce sickness leave that was more successful. The new law obliged employers to arrange sickness contracts for their personnel. This made the employers responsible and gave them an incentive to set up sophisticated policies to prevent sickness as much as possible. Figures over the period right after the adoption and implementation of the new legislation show a remarkable effect. The state of illness leave declined by about one-third from 1993 to 1995.[3]

### *Disability*

Because of huge increases in expenditures, measures were considered to decrease the volume and to lower the cost of the social security service for disabled people. In 1992, a law was adopted that introduced a so-called bonus-Malus system. If an employer would hire a disability benefit recipient, he could claim a subsidy; but if he fired a worker who would then become eligible for a disability benefit, the employer had to pay a penalty. In 1993, a law was adopted that intended to lower the number of eligible persons by requiring a clear relation between the disability and the characteristics of the vacancies refused. In other words, the relationship between the job characteristics on the one hand and previous education and skills on the other, was not necessary anymore. So in searching for suitable posts the sphere of work possibilities has largely been extended. The law also arranged for all disabled people younger than 50 years old to be medically re-examined to find out to what degree they were considered to be disabled. The medical reports could also function as a guideline in the search for suitable posts.

*Unemployment*

If fired for reasons other than a person's work performance, one is entitled to receive an unemployment benefit. The level of the benefit is linked to the level of the last earned wage. The duration of the right to receive benefits depends on the amount of time spent in the work force before becoming unemployed. The level as well as duration of benefits have been tightened in an attempt to increase the incentive for the unemployed to search for a job. Nevertheless, many experts consider the small difference between the earned wage and the social wage a severe deterrent to a quick return to the labor market.

The problem of unemployment is not only a matter of size, but also a matter of duration. If many people were unemployed just for a short period of time, unemployment might have been interpreted as an expression of labor market flexibility. So we can imagine an optimal level of frictional unemployment (as workers move among jobs), which must not be reduced artificially. The daily reality of many unemployed people is different, alas. Unemployment is an important social problem, that must be interpreted as an expression of social inequality. Particular groups of people are excluded from the production process for a very long time or are constantly commuting between job and benefit. They are the real outsiders and reintegration of these people is very important, although at the same time, very difficult.

In the next section we will describe recent Dutch social policy.

*People on Welfare*

At the start of the 1980s, the number of people on welfare rose sharply. From 1985 on, the number shows a slight decrease, increasing again in the period from 1994-1996. Due to the positive forecasts for the Dutch economy, the Central Planning Bureau expects a slight but ongoing decline in the number of people on welfare. In table 4.1, we have given the time series over the period 1980-1998. Added

Table 4.1
Number of People on Welfare (in thousands)

| | | | | | | | |
|---|---|---|---|---|---|---|---|
| 1980 | 341 | 1986 | 597 | 1992 | 498 | 1998 | 449 |
| 1981 | 380 | 1987 | 590 | 1993 | 496 | 1999 | 436 |
| 1982 | 448 | 1988 | 585 | 1994 | 505 | 2000 | 428 |
| 1983 | 536 | 1989 | 578 | 1995 | 510 | 2001 | 430 |
| 1984 | 646 | 1990 | 547 | 1996 | 502 | 2002 | 431 |
| 1985 | 590 | 1991 | 516 | 1997 | 483 | 2003 | 433 |

Source: Min. of Soc.Affairs and Empl., *Sociale Nota 1999*, Vuga, The Hague, 1998, p.154.

to it are forecasted figures over the period 1998-2003, made by the Central Planning Bureau.[4]

## The Purple Approach

### *Introduction*

In 1994 a remarkable change took place in Dutch political relations. From the very first beginning of the system of universal suffrage in 1917, the Christian-Democrats had played a central role. But now they had to leave the cabinet, and became the largest opposition group in parliament. The (red) Social Democrats formed a coalition with the (blue) Liberals. Where the Christian Democrats had always valued the role of the so-called "social partners," the purple cabinet made clear that the market mechanism had to play a more important role. Whether this strategy has led to a smaller role for the social partners is not yet clear. It has at least not led to a smaller role for the government. When one wants markets to function according to the economic principles of optimal allocation, then a consistent institutional framework must be designed to let market forces work. The slogan of the purple coalition was "jobs, jobs, jobs...." In 1994, unemployment had begun to grow again and the inactivity ratio was still unacceptably high. This performance was rather disappointing, because the economic recovery of the 1990s had given rise to expectations of a good social performance as well. The cabinet decided to intensify policy effort focused on the reintegration of social benefit recipients. In this respect cabinet Kok (1994-1998) could profit from the efforts of the preceding three cabinets headed by Lubbers (1982-1994), which had restructured government finance and relative factor prices.

Historically, Social Democrats have stressed the importance of institutions other than the market, and classical liberals have stressed the importance of markets as against the effectiveness of governmental rules. In light of their differences it is interesting to examine the purple coalition's efforts, both policy proposals and pieces of legislation, to design new labor market institutions. In order to get a good overview of the policies proposed and implemented over the last four years, we make a distinction between macro and micro policies. We will also distinguish between micro policies that try to adjust people to jobs on the one hand and micro policies that try to adjust jobs to people on the other hand. Finally, we discuss attempts to restructure the whole organization of labor market policy.

### *Macro Policies*

Having a small open economy The Netherlands is highly dependent on international developments; most of its trade is with EU-partners. This makes it necessary to coordinate macroeconomic policies with those partners. Unfortunately, this coordination does not take place, making the countries competitors. The only policy left is to consider the Dutch economy as a firm operating on international markets and applying basic neoclassical microeconomic principles, forgetting the lessons some people have learned from Keynes. In this respect the macro policies of the purple cabinet did not deviate from the lines of macro policies of former cabinets. Unemployment can be reduced by wage decrease, the interest rate lowered by reducing budget deficits and the tax burden lightened by cutting governmental expenditures. These cost decreases make the Dutch firm cheaper to run, ideally cheaper than their EU-competitors on the international market. To achieve wage decreases central consultations are held yearly, to evaluate the outcomes of collective bargaining on labor conditions. In 1994, tripartite consultation led to the observation that the lowest negotiated wages were significantly higher than the legal minimum wage, which makes it unnecessarily difficult for low-skilled workers to find a job. The three parties agreed that in the next rounds of wage negotiations more functions would be created in the lowest wage scales legally allowable. Whether or not these vacancies can be filled with unemployed people is a micro problem, which is the topic of the next section.

*Micro Policies*

An important characteristic of developments in our production processes is the strong increase in necessary skill levels of workers. Technological progress implies a complementary development in terms of increasing human capital. When we look at those who do not participate in the production process and are entitled to a benefit, we see a large skill deficit. Most of the unemployed are low-skilled and cannot find a suitable job, even when jobs are available. This makes it worthwhile to examine the efficiency of developing governmental policies to support the necessary flow of people from outdated industries and from the "social welfare sector" to the profitable and growing industries. When firms have to operate in complex and dynamic markets employers as well as employees have to be flexible. Governmental policies must focus on promoting flexibility in an efficient and justified way. The stimulus must not only be sought in the financial sphere; rules that allocate rights and responsibilities must function as an incentive for suppliers as well as demanders of labor to get matched.

Now we will describe the most important measures taken by the government in the last four years to re-integrate an increasing number of persons.

1. With respect to sick employed persons two laws were adopted to shape the policy focused on a reduction of sickness leave. Taken together these laws make employers responsible for their personnel. They are obliged to insure the employed against the risk of having no income in case of illness. The laws also oblige employers to conclude a contract with a firm that can deliver ARBO services. These services are focused on the improvement of working conditions so that they meet legal requirements. The ultimate goal of ARBO services is the prevention employee illness.

2. Because the number of disabled persons, who receive a disability benefit is astonishingly high in The Netherlands, the government is still working on a more satisfactory arrangement. In 1993, a law was adopted that required the medical re-examination of all disabled persons under 50 years old who receive benefits. This examination aims to establish the degree of disability and deliver the medical information necessary to decide which types of jobs would be suitable for partially disabled persons. The examination of all disabled benefit recipients will, according to the planning, take four years (1994-1998). At the moment legislation is in preparation that specifies the responsibilities of employers, the employed and the organizations who are responsible for the payment of the benefits. Most legislative changes concern the differentiation of premiums among branches of industry, the conditional permission to conclude disability insurance contracts with private

insurance companies, and the rules that make the employers co-responsible for the eventual re-integration of their former workers who became disabled. With the new purple cabinet recently installed, one of the hot topics is the problem of the privatization of disability insurance. Of particular concern here is the question of whether evaluation of disability claims must be done by a governmental body or whether it is possible to delegate even this decision to private agencies.

## Public Assistance

For those who are not entitled to receive any benefits, Public Assistance is organized as a social service of last resort. In 1854, the first steps were taken by the Dutch government to create a bare minimum for every household (Roebroeck, Hertogh,1998). A poor law was adopted that structured charitable action and guaranteed a minimum income to those who fell outside the voluntary, mostly clerical, systems. In the beginning the benefit was quite low. But in the course of time the service became more extensive and generous. It endured until 1965, when parliament adopted a law that guaranteed a benefit to every person unable to earn a living. This law, the Law of Public Assistance, consisted of several parts. For those who were unemployed for already more than two years and for those who became unemployed but were not entitled to receive an unemployment benefit, special rates were arranged. A means test and a partner test were added to the arrangement, to avoid allocating benefits to wealthy people or to allowing people with an income-earning partner to receive the same benefit as those without such a partner. In 1972, the law was reformed to avoid disparities in local policies. And in 1985 adjustments were made to consider a live-in relationship equal to marriage.

Originally meant as a temporary financial support, the service grew into a structural transfer to a rather large group. The main causes for this development were the increasing rate of divorce, growing structural unemployment and social security retrenchment policies. Notwithstanding the serious attempts of subsequent cabinets the number of benefit recipients did not decline. Politically the question of how to get at least part of the group back to work became urgent. In this respect the basic dilemma is the tension between poverty relief on the one hand and the back-to-work responsiveness on the other hand. In the next subsection we will deal with the way the purple cabinet, headed by Kok, approached this dilemma.

### *Purple Public Assistance Policies (1994 - 1998)*[5]

The name purple indicates the coalition of the red Social Democrats with the blue Liberals. The reds traditionally focus on fairness and poverty relief, while the blues traditionally counter by stressing the relevance of (financial) incentives. Dutch purple policy appeared to be a combination of (1) general cuts in the level of the benefit, (2) extra allowances for those with special needs, and (3) a deliberate attempt to activate people on welfare to search for suitable posts. This activation policy meant the creation of various opportunities for low-skilled and handicapped people, with the well-organized support of specialized civil servants to guide these job seekers in their search. This guidance included both carrots—the delivery of relevant information on jobs and training possibilities—and sticks—the threat of sanctions for those who did not make sufficient efforts. One can imagine that such an approach can only be successful, if it is based on careful research with respect to the processes that play a role in the decisions of the (potential) employers, the (potential) employees/benefit recipients and the civil servants of the Public Assistance Agency. This research must especially be focused on the considerable use of discretion by the civil servants who make the allocative decisions in Public Assistance programs. While other programs for allocating benefits can use unambiguous concepts like age, sex and professional status, Public Assistance is a reservoir for those who are not accepted by other social agencies. The difficulty here is not simply to accept anyone, but to judge whether a particular person deserves the benefit or has not been active enough in searching for a job. Research with respect to the functioning of Public Assistance has shown that the exercise of discretion cannot be avoided; it is basically in the nature of the service to be provided.[6] Need is not always self-evident or easy to define. In the first place, there is often a high degree of subjectivity in the determination of need for a particular person. In the second place, important cultural changes have confounded criteria of need; for example with increasing longevity and cohabitation the age criterion and that of marital status are more difficult to interpret in relation to need.

When the opportunities for finding a job are negligible, the problem of bureaucratic discretion in activating the unemployed is not as pressing (as was the case in the 1980s). But when economic recovery takes place (as happened in the 1990s) and the government is initiating many measures to stimulate employment for less productive people, the exercise of discretion increases. Then the content and procedures through which activation policies are implemented really matter. Recently some personnel were offered the opportunity to become trained as "activation officers." Research shows that these experts appear to focus their activities only on those benefit recipients who, in their opinion are promising in terms of policy effectiveness.[7] They make distinctions among three groups. First those who have been receiving a benefit for less than a year and have promising characteristics (they are expected to be able to find a job themselves). Second, those who have been receiving benefits for more than a year and have characteristics that severely limit their prospects of employment. Finally, there is a third group, consisting of people who are expected to have a reasonable chance for employment when extensively supported and monitored—this is the target group for activation. The activation officers develop personal relationships with their clients. Those who appear to be unwilling to make an effort are expelled from the target group and become "members" of the group seen as having severely limited chances for employment. Although the law prescribes sanctions for those unwilling to follow activation plans, research shows that in a majority of the cases these clients are not penalized by a reduction in benefits.[8] It also appears that the experts develop clear-cut ideas about the effectiveness of particular rules they have to apply. If they consider certain rules to be unworkable, they simply do not apply them.

If we consider the behavior of the activation officers and the clients, we can understand their reaction pattern, especially when interpreted as a principal-agent relationship. The experts are focused on maximizing the number of people who exit their client group—an outcome measure that is easily monitored by their principals. They do not invest much time or effort on other relevant objectives like penalizing uncooperative clients. That would create a lot of trouble and would be very costly for the organization. Those who supervise the activiation officers are not very interested in "buying costly units of justice," in part because they are not able to make a distinction between costs imposed by fair and tough policies and trouble caused by incapable civil servants.

To improve the use of civil servants' discretionary power requires clearly formulated objectives and detailed protocols that limit arbitrary differences in decisions made by various agencies and activation officers. To this end, the following measures have been taken:

1. Training of civil servants that is especially focused on problems that may develop when one has to work with people who need help. In some cases the needy are not very friendly or grateful. In that respect this training is not only directed towards the acquisition of knowledge about job opportunities, but also aimed at developing the skill of understanding ("verstehen") the clients and their situation (without identifying with clients so strongly that the worker cannot be objective).

2. The buildings of the Public Assistance agencies have been restyled so as to be more welcoming. They have become more customer oriented, but also incorporate a number of subtle design measures to protect the officers against possible violence.

3. The new job opportunities being created are especially meant for low- skilled people, since at least one-third of the benefit recipients do not have more than basic schooling. Various measures taken in this regard include:

   - To stimulate employers to hire more low-skilled people, the government has increased the Special Reduction in taxes for people who earn a wage that is lower than 115 percent of the minimum wage. For workers who are unemployed for longer than a year and are going to earn a wage that is lower than 130 percent of the minimum wage, there is a Supplementary Reduction. In total the reduction is maximally f 8,160.—which is about 23 percent of the wage.

   - To stimulate benefit recipients to accept a job, two laws have been adopted, the Law on the Use of Job Seekers and the Law on the (Re)integration of Handicapped People. These laws are meant to create jobs both in the private and in the public sectors. Private employers are subsidized if they create special jobs that do not compete with regular jobs. Most special jobs are found in the public sector however. In 1994 the government asked the local municipalities to make employment plans for, in total, 40,000 jobs in the period 1994-1998. Later social benefit budgets were re-allocated to local governments for another 20,000 jobs. In 1998 the government decided on another increase of 10,000 jobs in the level of created employment. Some of the jobs are so-called work-experience jobs. These are temporary for which the employer receives a subsidy from the local government.

   - The Law on the Social Employment Creation was renewed at the beginning of 1998. Until then "social employment" meant that people worked in special firms or agencies. But the renewed law makes it possible to subsidize jobs that are designed for handicapped workers—anywhere (so called adjusted jobs). The handicap is not necessarily based on a physical but may also be the result of a mental deficiency. Besides the possibility of adjusted jobs, there is also the possibility of a guided job, especially for those who lack work experience.

- Employers can also get subsidies if they are willing to create jobs on an experimental basis (so called experimental jobs). These jobs then are designed for long-term unemployed social assistance benefit recipients for two years.

4. The renewed Law on Public Assistance cut benefits from 70 percent to 50 percent of the official minimum wage for singles. For single parents benefits were reduced from 90 percent to 70 percent and for couples the benefit now is 100 percent of the official minimum wage. This reduction may lead to the impoverishment of a relatively large group of people. To compensate for this loss, the task and the financial resources of the local municipalities are extended.

5. Every local government is allowed to increase the benefit of particular persons to a maximum of 20 percent of the official minimum wage. If a person can prove that one's income is too low to pay for a number of necessary goods, the municipality subsidizes the purchase of those goods. Examples of necessary goods and services concern dentist costs, glasses, child care, consumer durables like a washing machine and the like. This special assistance is not only meant for people who are receiving public assistance benefits. Also people who have to live on a state pension, a low unemployment or disability benefit or on the official minimum wage, are allowed to ask for special financial assistance. Although the system is very young, the first results show significant differences between the various municipalities.

## Ethnic Minorities

Policy developments are coming to pay particular attention to the position of a number of ethnic minorities, especially the Turkish people, the Maroccans, the Surinams and the Antillians. Besides the fact that these groups are relatively low skilled and have difficulties with the Dutch language, it is generally accepted by experts that part of the problem they experience involves outright discrimination. This makes it more difficult for these groups to integrate into Dutch society via the normal channel of employment. For the Labour Foundation, which organizes regular central consultations of unions and employers' organizations, the vulnerability of minorities was a reason to pay extra attention to employment measures for these groups. Under the agreement they reenacted for the period 1997-2000 ("With Minorities More Possibilities"), together with a law proposed by the government (but not yet adopted by parliament), measures are in preparation that must improve the situation of job seekers of different ethnic origin. The proposed law tries to create a more coherent legal framework that will facilitate the flow of members of the target group to firms. Obligations of employers in this respect are formulated more clearly and administrative procedures are simplified.

Moreover, new projects will be started to get ethnic minorities out of the social assistance funds and into the firms.

## The Organization of Labor Market Policies

When we look at the organizational structure of the Dutch labor market, including the system of welfare, it appears quite chaotic. The reason is that this structure is not the result of a conscious design. The evolution started with union pressure for financial relief for breadwinners cases of unemployment and on-the-job accidents. Later, the government got involved in the delivery of these social services. Social security was initially organized as a cooperative venture between social partners, in some cases including the government and in other cases without government involvement. Regulated by legislation participation of workers became obligatory, giving the system its social, that is collective, character. Beyond relief for those unemployed or injured on the job, unions were highly committed to setting up a well-functioning system of collective bargaining around labor conditions. For them a reasonable wage was not only a matter of fairness, but also an important building block of an economy that would be able to maintain full employment. This means that the first level of protection was designed for those who could not work, although there were a sufficient number of jobs available. The second level of protection rested on collective bargaining, that was meant to create and maintain a high degree of employment that paid a living wage.

As already described in previous sections, the crises in the 1970s introduced the first big test of the robustness of the welfare state. Then the hybrid structure appeared to be a severe barrier to an efficiently functioning welfare system. Many benefit recipients who had to stay "on welfare" just temporarily, stayed there for the rest of their lives. So the big challenge of the 1980s and 1990s was and still is how to provide social protection while increasing the efficiency of welfare state programs—how to integrate social security and social assistance on the one hand and match job suppliers and job seekers on the other hand. Many pieces of new legislation offer partial solutions to the problem of coordination. For instance the Law on the Re-integration of Job Seekers and the Law on the Re-integration of Handicapped People are dealing explicitly with the problem of coordination.

At the moment the cabinet is preparing a law on the organization of social security that seeks to pull together lots of small programs and develops a comprehensive picture of the distribution of responsibilities and authorities. An important principle of this law will be that every person of an age between 15 and 65 who is willing to work will fall under the responsibility of a particular organization. This responsibility means an obligation to help participants search for a job, while delivering a benefit, if the person involved is entitled to one. If a worker becomes ill, the employer is responsible for the payment of an illness benefit. If a worker becomes unemployed, an employer remains responsible for him for a specified period of time and must help in the search for a job, in the meantime paying the laid-off worker his wage (at the moment this is 13 weeks, but there are proposals to make it up to 26 weeks). After the employers have discharged their responsibility, if the worker is still unemployed the responsibility shifts to a local organization that must pay the benefit to which workers are entitled. As long as the person is unemployed and entitled to the benefit, this organization is also responsible to help search for a new job. If these local organizations do not have the expertise in searching for jobs, then they must buy these services on the market, from, for instance, the governmental "Labor Service." Thus, receiving a benefit is, in most cases at least, considered a temporary arrangement. In this institutional design it is clear who is co-responsible for the job search at every stage in the process. The organizations in charge of particular activities must get budgets that are allocated in such a way that the budget system has a consistent set of incentives for the organizations to strive for the achievement of the official goals as efficiently as possible. To discover what are efficient budgets, markets must be introduced in all cases where performance can easily be measured and the scale of production does not lead to a monopoly. As already noted, this law is still on the drawing board, and subject to hot debates in periodicals, newspapers and TV programs.

## Summary and Prospect

The historical development of the Dutch welfare state, does not openly appear to be based on a national comprehensive plan. Progress could only be made under specific economic, social and political circumstances. But in the 1970s most progressive politicians were of the opinion that the work was almost done. In the same period however, the system proved to be vunerable to structural macroeconomic disequilibria. Moreover, it became too expensive because of its discouraging effects on the labor supply. Economic recovery required policies of social retrenchment.

Many of the new policies seemed to contradict the intentions of the initial social welfare policy makers. In that respect the system had to turn back to reassess its own basics elements. The massive use of sickness and disability benefits had to be limited to a "natural" rate. The use of Public Assistance had to be restricted to a minimum; serving only those who are really unable to earn their own living and are not entitled to receive any other income.

The Dutch economy, as in many countries, turned into a Kondratieff-like recession during the 1970s, and the system of social protection was reformed in the 1980s. Things turned around in the 1990s. Under the influence of a recovery of the global economy and the successful restructuring of government finance and the moderation of wages, the Dutch economy recovered. Production and employment growth created the financial room to work on a qualitative improvement of the social system. While significant benefit cuts were implemented during the first half of the 1990s, the first purple cabinet of Kok (1994-1998) worked on restructuring the organization of the system and spent a rather large amount of money to get benefit recipients back to work. Looking at the numbers, there is a slight decrease in the total number of benefit recipients. In terms of expenditures there is a slight increase, but expressed in percentages of GDP there has been a decrease during the last few years (25.5, 24.4, 23.8 and 23.5 for the years 1994, 1995, 1996 and 1997, respectively).

The prospects of the Dutch welfare state in general, and the Public Assistance program in particular strongly depend on the developments in the global economy. For a small economy like that of the Netherlands, with a marginal import quote of more than 60 percent, political discretion has a limited impact on economic trends. If the threats coming from the Asian recession and from the Russian failure to reform its economy are not strong enough to affect the global economy as a whole, then the Dutch appear able to continue the policies that have led to positive results so far. It goes without saying that a global recession or even depression changes the prospects radically. In the absence of a global recession, the big challenge for the near future will be to "solve" the dilemma between assisting the unemployed and the poverty trap. A huge amount of empirical research has been done over the last years on this dilemma.[8] But the explanation is not the same as solution. If we accept that "free markets" are the principal way of measuring a person's productivity, then we must admit that some, if not many, persons, notwithstanding all the training facilities offered by the community, do not have the productive capacity that is sufficient to earn a decent living. If we want to offer them social benefit that provides a decent living, then we weaken the incentive to make efforts to improve their productivity. If we make the incentve stronger by reducing social benefit, then we leave these people in less than decent circumstances. Although the dilemma cannot be entirely resolved, innovative policies can diminsh the tension between work-incentives and humane social benefit.

## Notes

1. In The Netherlands the law against child labor passed in 1874 is often interpreted as the beginning of Dutch social policy. But many proposals took a very long time before they were adopted as pieces of legislation and legislative production did not become really significant after the First World War.
2. See Keizer (1992) for an analysis of the situation in terms of a bilateral monopoly model.
3. Source: CTSV (1996).
4. See Ministry of Social Affairs and Employment, *Sociale Nota 1999*, Vuga, The Hague, 1998.
5. The sources of information that are used when preparing this part of the paper are: CPB (1997,1998) and the Ministry of Social Affairs (1996, 1997, 1998) and the latest series of brochures that are available at the desk of the Public Assistance in Maestricht.
6. An interesting analysis of the use of the discretionary room in terms of the principal-agency approach is to be found in Teulings, Van der Veen, Trommel, 1998. They also discuss the results of empirical research in this respect.
7. See the Ministry of Social Affairs, *De sociale nota*, 1998.
8. See the Ministry of Social Affairs, *De sociale nota*, 1998.
9. See for instance the readers edited by Rita Asplund et al. and by Stephen Bazen et al.; see the list of references.

## References

Centraal Planbureau. (1997 & 1998). *Centraal economisch plan*, Staatsuitgeverij, 's Gravenhage.

Centraal Planbureau. (1997 & 1998). *Macro economische verkenning*, Staatsuitgeverij, 's Gravenhage.

Centraal Toezicht Sociale Verzekeringen (CTSV). (1996). *Kroniek van de sociale verzekeringen*, Zoetemeer.

Elgar, E. (1998). In R. Asplund, P. J. Sloane, & I. Theodossiou (eds.), *Low pay and earnings mobility in Europe*, Cheltenham, U.K.

Elgar, E. (1998). In S. Bazen, M. Gregory, & W. Salverda (eds.), *Low-wage employment in Europe*, Cheltenham, U.K.

Keizer, P. K., (1992) Union power in a welfare state, *Labour, Review of Labour Economics and Industrial Relations*, (6), 3.
Ministerie van Sociale Zaken en Werkgelegenheid. (1996, 1997, & 1998). *De sociale nota*, Staatsuitgeverij, 's Gravenhage.
Roebroeck, J., & Hertogh, M. (1998). *"De beschavende invloed des tijds,"* Staatsuitgeverij, 's Gravenhage.
Teulings, C., Veen, R. van der., & Trommel, W. (1998). *Dilemma's van sociale zekerheid*, Staatsuitgeverij, 's Gravenhage.
Windmuller, J. (1969). *Labor relations in the Netherlands*, Ithaca, NY: Cornell University Press.

# 5

# Welfare-to-Work or Work-to-Welfare: The French Case

*Jean-Claude Barbier* and *Bruno Théret*

## Introduction

In assessing welfare-to-work social assistance programs in different countries, a preliminary issue must be addressed in the case of France: Is it possible to construct some sort of "functional equivalent" of "welfare-to work" (WTW) in the French context where "welfare" is an alien concept? Social assistance in France is based on the sociological and philosophical idea of solidarity as opposed to the rather negative Anglo-Saxon notion of welfare (Barbier, 1998). With the emergence of neo-liberal ideology and the present economic context of mass unemployment, "welfare" has increasingly become the subject of many normative discussions concerning future social policies among French political elites. Nevertheless, it remains difficult to identify the functional equivalent of typical welfare-to-work programs and to single out the French equivalent of "social assistance" programs. To understand the French system we must explain the substance and scope of what is officially termed "social assistance" (*aide sociale*) in France.

The core logic of French social assistance schemes stands in contrast to the liberal Anglo-Saxon understanding of "welfare." The first section of this chapter will describe the programs that constitute the French solidaristic assistance system and its logic. The second section of the chapter will broaden the field of analysis in order to try and delineate the entire array of programs composing the French

WTW equivalent. This broader framework will encompass programs from within the social assistance system as defined in the first section—RMI (*revenu minimum d'insertion*) programs and the relatively recent "*insertion*" model—as well as additional functionally equivalent programs drawn from outside the traditional "solidaristic assistance" system, which will include specific employment programs traditionally classified as labor market programs or policies (employment and training ones). The third section of the chapter will assess the evaluations of the selected programs, and the fourth section will discuss the relevance of these findings.

## Social Assistance Programs: A Description

The French social protection system was built under the hegemony of social insurance principles and has been mainly funded by social contributions based on payroll collected by a social security system legally and politically distinct from the state. Thus, social assistance has been conceived and institutionally designed essentially as an extension of workers' solidarity to specific categories of vulnerable citizens—those chronically or temporarily unable to enter the labor market and workers unable to earn enough to get them out of poverty. Nevertheless, inasmuch as social assistance is also inherited from previous non-democratic forms of state social protection, there are some elements of this "social assistance" system that do not fit into the new logic of solidarity and citizenship. That is, there is a distinction within the assistance system, between *solidaristic (modern) assistance and residual (traditional) welfare* (the latter mainly consisting of childhood assistance and voluntary social action by local authorities). Since it is not linked to labor market participation, this latter part of the welfare sector of social assistance will be left out of our analysis. At the same time, the traditional field of social assistance shall be enlarged beyond its official boundaries in order to encompass all programs based on a solidaristic assistance philosophy. In our definition of social assistance, we shall thus include the whole gamut of *minima sociaux* (various basic incomes) either state or social insurance funded.

### Social Assistance: A Reconstructed Definition

At first sight, the French system of social protection (SSP), despite its complexity, may be divided as the American SSP into two segments: a "social security" system and a "welfare" system. In the French case, however, such an abrupt dichotomy and comparison with the U.S. is somewhat misleading. The French SSP differs dramatically from the U.S. system because of its extensive social security component that provides a quasi-universal coverage, the benefits of which are predominant compared to social assistance. These social security programs are funded by social insurance resources. Thus, French social protection rests mainly on social insurance institutions administered by "social partners" under central state supervision and organized at the local level.

Four main national financial institutions, legally independent from the state, support the system: CNAV (*Caisse Nationale d'Assurance Vieillesse*) for old age and widowhood insurance, CNAM (*Caisse Nationale d'Assurance Maladie*) for sickness, motherhood, disability insurances and industrial accident and diseases, CNAF (*Caisse Nationale des Allocations Familiales*) for family and housing benefits, and UNEDIC-ASSEDIC for unemployment insurance (UI). Apart from these "general regime" funds, which cater to the mass of employees and workers, a range of smaller social insurance organizations cater to specific professions or groups (fifteen "special" or "autonomous" old-age insurance regimes for the public sector employees and "independent trades"; complementary old-age regimes for employees; nineteen health insurance regimes for specific trades, farmers and professionals; and so on). The contributions collected by the social security system ("*cotisations sociales*") provide for more than three-quarters of the total resources of the SSP. Only roughly 20 percent comes from general taxes, which represents the direct financial engagement of the state in social protection (whose participation is concentrated in assistance programs). On the spending side, social security represents 88.5 percent of the total "compulsory" social expenditure in 1995. In addition, unlike the U.S. system, boundaries between social security and social assistance are blurred in France. Social security includes not only social insurance but also *solidarité,* i.e., specific assistance benefits provided by insurance funds to individuals not entitled to social insurance because they have not (or not fully) paid the required contributions. Moreover, a large part of these assistance benefits, even when delivered through social security organizations, are state funded, mainly through so-called "solidarity funds" (for old age, disability or unemployment), i.e., funds financed from general taxes. Thus, social security funds account for an important part of assistance benefits.

Finally, what could at first sight be termed a French "welfare system" is also split into two different types of social policies: one is *aide sociale* (social assistance) legally binding on the public authorities because it is considered as a public debt of solidarity (recognized in the Constitution); the other is *action sociale* (social action) which is voluntary and extralegal, an optional intervention of local public authorities or of social security institutions. The legally binding social assistance (*aide sociale*) pertains to solidarity as well as the non-contributive benefits provided by social insurance funds. That is why, in 1953, "*assistance publique*" was renamed "*aide sociale*" in order to avoid the negative connotation of welfare and to emphasize its solidaristic dimension (Thévenet, 1992, p. 54). Only "social action" could be possibly equated to public "welfare," in its stigmatized American meaning, but it accounts for a small fraction of the total social protection expenditures.

Thus, from a comprehensive institutional point of view, the French SSP may be described as a system divided into four hierarchically intermingled parts: social insurance; solidaristic assistance linked within the social security system; government social aid (another kind of solidaristic assistance); and social action. The whole system is institutionally linked by state supervision and financial mechanisms of social security which deliver all kinds of benefits (social insurance, solidaristic assistance, and voluntary social action). Social security dominates the system; the solidarity level of assistance is defined as special coverage either by social security or by the state for those who have not contributed enough for regular coverage under social insurance; finally, at the lower level, the residual failures of the solidaristic assistance net are addressed through local authorities' social action. Again, we must note that social action (an equivalent of a "pure welfare" part in French social assistance) is marginal when compared to the solidaristic part of the French system of social protection.

For a deeper understanding of the French SSP, a distinction must be drawn between the sharing of institutional responsibility among social security funds and the different tiers of the state apparatus, on one hand, and the concepts of social insurance and assistance on the other hand. Shared financial administration and accountability of social insurance and assistance must not be interpreted as if the difference between their two procedural rationalities had vanished altogether. Benefits pertaining to both types of programs may be highly interdependent and might look very similar for the "clients" of the Welfare-state. From an analytical point of view, however, it is necessary to differentiate between the logic of social insurance and assistance, if only to understand how they are joined in the SSP. In such an institutionally intricate SSP as the French one, procedural autonomy and institutional interdependence of social insurance and assistance are present at the same time. More generally, in modern democratic Welfare-states, social protection may be seen as an alliance between social insurance and assistance, and the form of the Welfare-state regime as a product of this alliance (Théret, 1996a, 1996b, 1997, 1998). Thus, despite the blurring of institutional boundaries between social insurance and public assistance within the welfare-mix (Rein & Rainwater, 1986), specificities of both should be retained to define their respective fields in order to allow international comparisons of national assistance systems. In other words, social assistance has to be reconstructed from a theoretical perspective that goes beyond its official institutional definition, which is why this chapter starts by specifying what we consider as "social assistance" before coming to the description of the main schemes fitting into our definition.

While social security based on social insurance is divided into different domains of risks in the life course of every individual, social assistance, based on the traditional government logic of life protection, is divided into types of "clientele." Assistance schemes refer to limited categories of the population defined by special status and specific needs deriving from physical or social deficits, which limit their life chances. Social insurance addresses general risks faced by everyone during some periods of their life; social assistance addresses categorical needs and underprivileged status. Moreover, even if both assistance and social insurance are positive rights of citizens in modern democracies, these rights emanate from different sources. Insurance creates rights when a monetary contribution is paid in anticipation of different recognized risks—insured people are thus private creditors of the social security system; on the other hand, assistance deals with human rights forming the traditional life debt of sovereign authorities. Assistance is the modern form of this debt, i.e., the social debt that the state, in the name of the community, constitutionally recognizes to have contracted vis-à-vis any individual belonging to the community at his or her birth—citizens are thus collective creditors of the state. For example, in the French conception of social assistance, "public reliefs are a sacred debt. Society owes subsistence to its unfortunate citizens, either by providing them with work or by providing means of existence to those unable to work" (French 1793's Declaration of the human rights). Assistance is "a very food bond whose debitor is the public community and the creditor the person asking for it" (Thévenet, 1992, p.55). As a consequence of this community duty or social debt, the right to life of persons in need must be honored by the state as soon as civil society fails to meet their needs.

Thus, from a comparative perspective, the concept of social assistance benefits can be distinguished from other program benefits in the SSP according to two criteria: they must be non-contributory benefits but at the same time tied to citizenship rights and public duties. This definition excludes benefits from "*action sociale*" programs because they are not a public duty, and because they are not a citizenship right. Childhood assistance (ASE, *aide sociale à l'enfance*) will also be excluded from our study. It consists of services in-kind provided to orphans, abandoned, abused, and delinquent children. Though these services are non-contributory benefits delivered by public agencies on a compulsory basis, state intervention of this kind amounts to a tutelary substitution of parenthood and implies no recognition of social rights. They are not, in our view, part of social assistance in its modern democratic meaning, but pertain to the traditional parental function of the tributary state.

The structure of the French system of social protection is illustrated in figure 5.1. Here, programs based on legal state duties and citizenship's rights, so-called "general assistance" (Thévenet, 1992), which were legally established at the end of the nineteenth century, are placed in the same category of "solidaristic assistance" as the *minima sociaux* (social minima incomes) delivered by social insurance funds (either from their own resources or state funding). Each of these entitlements has the following features: it is "a *subjective* right, a privilege recognized to anybody who can ask for specific benefits; a *personal* right, untransferable and impossible to renounce; a right *tied to a notion of need*, which can be certified; and a right *subordinated* to specific conditions (maximum of income, specific deficiency—illness, disability, old-age—residence, etc.)" (ibid., p.55). Accordingly, benefits are *specialized*, in the sense of being linked to specific conditions defining the actuality of the rights; they have a "*food*" character; they are *subsidiary*, provided only when all other possibilities opened to society to pay the life debt have been exhausted; and they are *recoverable* from the beneficiary's income when he or she later improves his/her economic situation, or from the recipient's assets (and his/her heirs) in case of death (ibid.).

Does it follow from these characteristics that we must also define social assistance in general, in order to distinguish it from social insurance, as the whole set of "resource-tested benefits" (Gough, et al., 1997, p. 19), under which eligibility is determined by a means-test (income or wealth test) or a need or poverty test (Morel, 1997, p. 212-13)? In our view, even if means-tests are applied in most of the French assistance programs, such a definition is too restrictive and unnecessary. Applying it within our conceptual framework would not be appropriate because on one hand it would exclude parts of social minima incomes, and on the other hand it would include some voluntary "social action" programs. Means-tests appear as criteria used to define specific targeted groups' entitlements to assistance rights but are not necessarily an exclusive criterion. As will be seen, a significant part of social minimum incomes are not means-tested but only linked to a specific lack of social insurance rights. Thus it seems conceptually more consistent to apply a more general definition of social assistance, which meets the French notion of solidarity.

Our description of social assistance will be focused on what we term "solidaristic assistance." The very issue of welfare-to-work, when presently discussed in the French context, must be situated within this subsystem of social protection, precisely questioning the solidaristic philosophy of past social policies (Bec, 1998). To sum up, in the French context, the definition of social assistance exceeds the range of "general assistance" programs and policies (where claimants are asked to prove their actual need, and prove that society has not given them the opportunity of a self-reliant life keeping them out of poverty). Social assistance also encompasses social minimum incomes, social security funded and non means-tested. Turning now to specific programs, we shall describe in order of importance, assistance for handicapped (and disabled) persons, old-age assistance, medical aid, and family and housing assistance; then, we shall come to the unemployment assistance schemes within which we also consider Revenu Minima d'Insertion (RMI), which we examine in greater detail in the second section of this chapter. In fact, RMI was a dramatic innovation in the French traditionally solidaristic assistance framework: it is not a categorical but a universal assistance scheme. The second section of the chapter explains why it is the major French assistance program that may strictly be analyzed in WTW terms. Nevertheless, this doesn't imply that RMI is the only scheme relevant to our comparative perspective in the French context. Notably, due to the fact that young people under 25 years are only entitled to RMI in exceptional cases (Amrouni et Math, 1998a, p. 38), our functional equivalent will also encompass other programs related to the labor market policies. As will be explained in a later section, these policies do not pertain to traditional social policies but to employment programs (or active labor market policies).

## Program Descriptions

Since 1984, strictly denominated "general assistance" programs have been mainly under the political and financial auspices of local

**Figure 5.1**
**Interdependence and Institutional Hierarchy within the French National System of Social Protection**

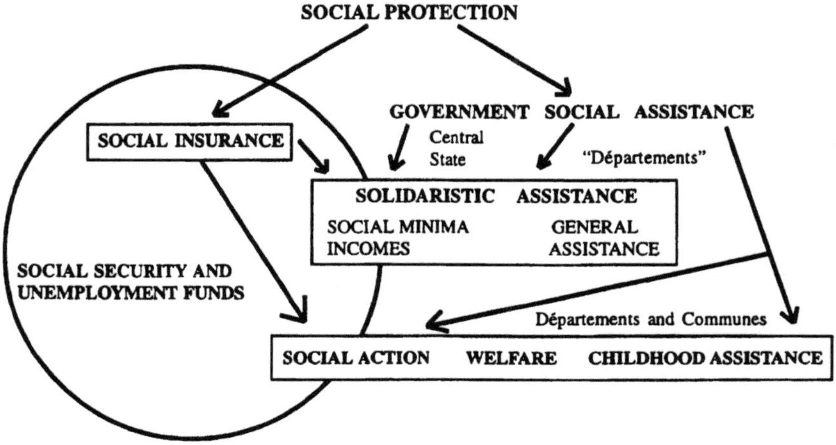

## Table 5.1
## Overview of General Assistance Programs

| Benefits 1996 | Category | year of creation | Administration | Funding source | monthly maximum amount[1] | mean amount | maximum reouces[2] | Maximum duration | Number of benficiaries |
|---|---|---|---|---|---|---|---|---|---|
| AAH | Handicapped | 1975 | CAF<br>MSA | State | 3433 ff<br>(60%) | 2910 | single: 3402 ff<br>couple: 6805 ff<br>+ 1 child: 1701 ff | No limit | 631 145 |
| AES | Handicapped | 1963 | CAF<br>MSA | social security | 665 ff en 1995 | | | till the child is 20 | 104 00 |
| Compensatory allowance | Handicapped<br>Old age | | Department | Department | from 2169 ff to 4337 ff (1995) | | ceiling AAH+ allowance amount | No limit | 300 00 |
| Disability minimum income | disabled under 60 | 1930<br>1956 | CAM-<br>MSA<br>CAVTNS | social security<br>FSI | single 3433<br>(basic: 1428 ff)<br>(supp. 2004 ff) | | 3516 ff | till 65 | 102 541 |
| Old age minimum income | +65 | 1941<br>1956 | CAV<br>CAM<br>CDC | social security<br>FSV | single 3433 ff<br>hh. 6159 ff<br>basic: 1429 ff<br>(30% for basic) | 1260 ff<br>(2nd st.)<br>429 ff<br>en 1995<br>(1st st.) | single: 3402 ff<br>household: 5960 ff | till death | 1000 00 |
| Old age home care 1995 | | | | | 1384 ff | | single: 3402 ff<br>household: 5960 ff | till death | 115 000 en 1994 |
| Old Age simple allowance | Specific catagories | | State | State | single 3433 ff<br>hh. 6159<br>(basic: 1429 ff) | | single 3516 ff<br>household: 5960 | till death | 5600 en 1992 |
| API | single parent | 1976 | CAF<br>MSA | social security | pregnant: 3163 ff<br>one child: 4217 ff<br>each child: +1054 | 2348 ff | pregnant: 3163 ff<br>one child: 4217 ff<br>+1 child: 1054 ff | 1 years or till child is 3 years old | 161 220 |
| ASF | single parent | 1970 | CAF | CAF | one parent absent: 468 ff<br>two parents 624 ff | 722 ff | | | 582 000 |
| Window-hood Insurance | Window with children under 55 | 1980 | CAV<br>MSA | social security | 1st year: 3073 ff<br>(57% en 1995)<br>2nd year: 2019 ff<br>(65% en 1995)<br>other year: 1537 ff<br>(77% en 1995) | 2186 ff<br>(1995) | 3841 ff<br>(1.25 amount of allowance) | 3 years or till 55 in some cases | 17 600 |

**Table 5.1 (cont.)**

| | | | | | | | | | |
|---|---|---|---|---|---|---|---|---|---|
| APJE | families with children under three years | 1985 | CAF | CAF | 955 ff<br>suppl.<br>1st categ. 499 ff<br>2nd categ. 1497 ff<br>3rd categ. 5422 ff<br>(1995) | 1063 ff<br><br><br><br><br>1032 ff | single, 1 child 6370 ff<br>single, 2 children: 10566 ff<br>2 incomes, 2 children: 13397 ff<br>+1 child: 2113 ff<br>(1995) | universal till 3 months<br><br><br>means-tested till 3 years | 419 000<br><br><br><br>1128 000 |
| CF | families with more than 2 children | 1978 | CAF | CAF | 866 ff<br>(1995) | | idem APJE | | 953 000 |
| APE | families with more than 2 children, 1 third child[2] 3 years and I parent ceasing to work | 1985 | CAF | CAF | (1995) full stop of working: 2964 ff<br>part time<br>[2]50%: 1960 ff<br>50-80%: 1482 ff | | | no means-test | 448 000 |
| ALF | | | CAF | State-CAF | | | | | 1103 040 |
| ALS | | | CAF | State-CAF | | | | | 1996 273 |
| APL | | | CAF | State-CAF | | | | | 2743 668 |
| AI | Specific categories | 1979<br>1984 | ASSEDIC | Solidarity fund | 1311 ff | | single: 3933 ff<br>couple: 7866 ff | one year | 16 500 |
| ASS | long term unemployed | 1984 | ASSEDIC | State solidarity fund | usual rate: 2251 ff<br>extra rate[4]: 3233 ff<br>(85%) | 2265 ff | single: 5180 ff<br>couple: 8141 ff | renew. every 6 month. till retirement | 516 300 |
| RMI | 25-65 years poors (under 25 years if family) | 1988 | CAF<br>MSA | State | single[5]: 2402 ff<br>1 child: 3604 ff<br>2 child: 4325 ff<br>+1 child: 961 ff<br>couple: 3604 ff<br>1 child: 4325 ff<br>2 child: 5046 ff<br>+1 child: 961 ff | 1925 ff<br>(metro)<br>1625 ff<br>(DOM) | single[6]: 2402 ff<br>+1 child: 3604 ff<br>+2 child: 4325 ff<br>each child: 961 ff<br>couple: 3604 ff<br>1 child: 4325 ff<br>2 child: 5046 ff<br>+1 child: 961 ff[7] | No limit but periodic controls and renewal | 1010 500 |

Sources: CSERC, 1997; Amrouni et Math, 1998b; CNAF, 1998.

authorities—*départements*. In terms of social assistance recipients, the criteria for attribution of competencies is the domicile, central state financial responsibility being retained for the homeless and the unemployed (Chauchard, 1994, p. 446). Entitled *départements* programs recipients also receive conditional benefits that have a purely national dimension and are provided by social insurance funds. Thus, although reviewing programs according to domains and categories of recipients, as defined by state legislation, we shall also examine the solidaristic benefits social insurance funds allocate for each category. An overview of these programs is presented in table 5.1.

### Assistance for Handicapped Persons

Handicapped persons constitute the most important assistance category. "The idea of a reparation due to every victim of a deficiency or disability is very old" (Marie, 1995, p. 31); it is one of the main aspects of the life debt involving society and of the sovereign's liabilities. But the concept of handicap as a general category including persons suffering from congenital, war, civil and industrial-related disabilities was only legally established in 1957, and the introduction of this general category did not alter the various regimes of protection linked to different causes of disability. It only resulted into the gradual introduction of a new assistance regime of financial compensation and social integration for all the handicapped people not covered by other regimes (war invalids' pensions, industrial accidents compensation rents, disability pensions). In order to claim a benefit, the handicapped person must first be assessed by a technical commission at the *département* level (COTOREP). *Aide sociale* for this category then consists of two main types of benefits: compensation for the handicap and *insertion professionnelle* (integration in employment).

*Départements* are accountable for providing benefits related to housing and special accommodations: housing of persons completely unable to work, covering then the costs of placement in special establishments; compensatory allowances (*allocation compensatrice pour tierce personne*) in cash that covers the recipient's need for daily services delivered by a third party. The special housing aid covered 75,000 recipients in 1992 for a mean monthly cost of about 8500 in 1995 French Francs per person. A monthly individual mean amount of 2730 French Francs (in 1995 FF)[1] for home care (*alloca-*

*tion compensatrice* plus *aide ménagère*) was paid to 262,000 beneficiaries in 1992 and 300,000 in 1996.

A state benefit (*allocation adulte handicapé*, AAH) provides for income compensation; it is mainly (93 percent in 1996) distributed by local agencies (CAF - *Caisses d'allocations familiales*) of the CNAF. This allowance is part of the so-called "minima sociaux" (social minima incomes). The term paradoxically refers to the fact that the benefit is differential and capped. When the minima sociaux are added to the recipients' other incomes, if any, the total amount must not exceed a maximum sum, which is generally close to a legal living minimum income. At the end of 1996, more than 631,000 individuals received AAH compensation, which benefited nearly one million people when household members are included; about 20 percent of beneficiaries got an AAH supplement, and 60 percent received a full benefit. In 1996 the average AAH monthly benefit was FF 2860, 83 percent of the maximum amount. Although the number of beneficiaries has grown by nearly 30 percent in ten years, the mean benefit has remained roughly stable during this period.

Since "the AAH was instituted to compensate for the deficiencies of the disability minimum," it seems appropriate to review this "disability minimum income" initiated in 1930 under the same rubric (notwithstanding the fact it significantly differs from the AAH). In 1945, the health social security branch was unable to provide victims of irreversible diseases (or of accidents that dramatically diminished their work capacity) with sufficient pensions because of the duration of contributions required to be fully vested. Consequently, the previous assistance benefit was retained, creating a two-tiered system. Under the first tier, social security programs (a health insurance fund for employees and old-age insurance funds for independent workers) pay a minimum pension. For example, in 1995, a flat-rate non-means-tested pension of FF 1428 was paid when the recipient lacked entitlement to normal old-age insurance benefits. Moving to the second tier, this minimal benefit is then supplemented by a "first stage" means-tested benefit (special state disability funded) which amounts to a minimum "threshold"—FF 3343 in 1996 (CSERC, 1997, p. 155). In 1995, 105,000 individuals (102,500 in 1996) received this disability minimum income. Between 1986 and 1995, the number of recipients decreased by more than 24 percent and the mean benefit amount, 1250 FF, lost 11 percent of its 1985 value in 1995 constant Francs.

A third benefit, the allowance for special education (AES) is provided to families with handicapped children under 20 years to compensate for additional education costs when their rate of disability exceeds 80 percent (or 50 percent when the child lives in a special institution). This non-means-tested benefit was paid by local social security agencies (CAF) to 104,000 families in 1996, at a monthly allowance of FF 1430.

The legal recognition of the rights of handicapped persons to work provides the major avenue of support for their integration into the labor market. Firms employing more than 20 workers must comply with a minimum quota of full-time or part-time handicapped employees amounting to 6 percent of their workforce or pay a special contribution to a fund for the handicapped. In 1992, only one-third of the French firms complied with the legal rate of 6 percent—employing 26,000 handicapped workers. The remaining 40 percent of firms had to pay a contribution to a special fund dedicated to the "professional insertion" of handicapped people (Marie, 1995, p. 35). Finally, the handicapped unable to work in an ordinary or protected environment, or at home, are catered to by another state program. Paid productive activities similar to ordinary work are organized in special establishments ("Aid by Labor Centers" - CAT), which pay 70 percent of the minimum wage. These wages are possibly supplemented by AAH up to 1.3 times the minimum wage (SMIC) (Marie, 1995, p. 35; CSERC, 1997, p. 157). In 1994, 82,000 handicapped people benefited from this program; that year the monthly mean state expenditure per beneficiary was FF 4960 (Join-Lambert et al., 1997, p.416).

### *Old Age Assistance*

As in the case of the handicapped, old-age assistance administered by the *départements* covers two types of expenditures, special housing and home care. Overall *département* expenditure for old-age assistance has declined slightly, whereas spending for the handicapped has grown rapidly. Expenditure for housing in special establishments is steady because on one side there has been a decline in the number of aged who depend on social assistance and on the other side there has been an increasing risk of dependence for very old people (Audirac et Rattier, 1996, p. 464-65). In 1994, there were 138,000 beneficiaries for whom the monthly mean "*departementat*" expenditure amounted to an average of FF 3300. Concerning home care, compensatory allocations are provided which are not reported as old-age benefits because the aged who get these benefits are considered handicapped. Expenditures only cover home care in-kind (*aide ménagère*), for which there were about 115,000 recipients in 1994 at an average monthly cost of FF 1240 per person.

Moreover, as is the case for the handicapped and disabled persons, old-age assistance consists of a minimum income paid by the Old Age Insurance Funds (CNAV) and a specific Old Age Solidarity Fund (FSV) to people over 65 years. This old-age assistance benefit is very similar to the two-tiered disability minimum income. The first tier, initiated in the forties, consists of a non-contributory flat rate pension (or supplement of pension—AVTS for employees) awarded to old people who did not contribute for enough years to be fully vested. In 1996, this basic allowance funded by old-age insurance was FF 1403. This basic allowance has been supplemented since 1956 by a means-tested differential allowance funded by a special state fund (FSV, *fonds de solidarité vieillesse*) the aim of which is to raise the income of every retired person to a minimum threshold. The old-age minimum income works very similarly to disability minimum for married pensioners. The threshold for both is the same as for AAH. It is important to note that only 30 percent of the claimants get social security basic allowances, and that these recipients are not automatically entitled to the second stage benefit, due to different entitlement rules for both allowances (Amrouni et Math, 1998b, p. 55). Despite the long-term decline in the number of recipients of the old-age minimum income (due to the progressive extension of social insurance covering pensioners with full pensions), one million people nevertheless received help in 1996, at which time the mean monthly FSV allowance was FF 1260.

### *Medical Aid*

Assistance under this heading concerns both medical care for poor people who are sick and health insurance coverage for those in need. Entitlements are means-tested and closely linked to gaps in social insurance coverage. Free medical assistance was legally instituted by the state in 1893 long before the creation of health insurance;

since 1945 this assistance has become a declining residual category due to sickness insurance, which has gradually extended to provide almost universal coverage. Nevertheless, it began to grow again during the eighties, as the share of health expenses covered by social insurance declined and rates of long-term unemployment increased. Four categories of expenditures must be considered here.

Firstly, *départements* cover personal contributions (*cotisations*) to health social insurance for individuals entitled to medical assistance (*aide médicale*). Since 1990, this item has become prominent, because of the growing number of Revenu Minima d'Insertion (RMI) claimants automatically entitled to medical aid. In 1994, nearly three hundred thousand people received medical assistance benefits at an average monthly cost of FF 764 per person.

Secondly, for medical aid claimants, *départements* are accountable for hospital costs (either entirely or for the extra costs not covered by social insurance—*forfait hospitalier, ticket modérateur*). Expenditure for this item has declined, even as the number of beneficiaries (number of admissions in the year) has been growing. In 1992, the mean monthly cost of each admission was only 232 (in 1995 FF) compared to 1984 costs of FF 545. The decline in per person costs reflects the fact that with the extension of insurance coverage, funded by the *départements* or social security, medical aid has increasingly been needed only to cover extra costs.

Thirdly, *départements* pay for home care under conditions similar to hospital costs. The number of persons served has not been well documented since 1984, at which time there were roughly half a million admissions a year (at a mean monthly cost of FF 190 per admission). Finally, *départements* cater to people suffering from mental diseases and tuberculosis. Serving around 23,000 persons, the *départements* average monthly spending per person declined from about FF 1480 to 670 between 1984 and 1991.

There are two areas in which medical aid also involves the central government. One is voluntary abortions, which is financially marginal, representing an expenditure of FF 6 million 1991 for 7,700 beneficiaries. The second is hospitalization for homeless people, which is of more importance. Over the last decade, medical assistance for the homeless has served a fairly stable number of around 80,000 persons, but the individual monthly cost has declined from an average of FF 1760 in 1984 to FF 1270 in 1991.

### *Family and Housing Assistance*

In entering the field of social assistance related to family benefits, we leave the realm of general assistance programs that are mainly under the auspices of *départements*. Most benefits in the areas of family and housing assistance stem from the family allowance funds (CAF). This situation is consistent with a field of social assistance where the evidence of solidarity is very strong. Three types of programs must be distinguished here: first, two *minima sociaux*, minima incomes to single parents (API) and widows; second, two means-tested benefits—young child allowance and "*complément familial*"; third, three other means-tested housing benefits (ALF, APL, and ALS).

The "widowhood insurance allowance" is the only benefit under this heading (although linked to single parent status like API) which is not served by the CAF. Funded by Old Age Pensions Schemes or Agriculture Mutuality, this temporary means-tested allowance is available to widows under 55 years of age who have raised (or raised for at least 9 years) at least one child. The allowance is given for 3 to 5 years if widowhood occurs when the survivor is 50 or more. At the end of 1996, the monthly allowance was FF 3019 for the first year, FF 1984 for the second and FF 1510 for the following years. The monthly income ceiling at which assistance stops equals 1.25 times the amount of the first year allowance. There were 17,600 recipients in 1996, the number of claimants holding steady at around 17,000 for the last 10 years, with a mean monthly individual benefit of FF 2186.

More important is the single parent allowance (API: *allocation de parent isolé*) delivered by the family allowance funds (CAF) to 161,220 persons in 1996 (covering a family population of around 430,000 in 1995) with a mean monthly cost of FF 2348. API is a temporary minimum income aimed at supplementing regular family allowances in case of single parenthood. Benefits are paid either for 12 months or until the youngest child reaches three years of age; the income ceiling equals the amount of the allowance which varies with the number of children in the family and takes into account the beneficiary's housing situation. In 1997, before deduction for housing costs, the allowance was FF 4143 for the first child and FF 1035 for any other children. It is important to note that, in practice, API's amount does not increase with the size of the family, since other family allowances that vary by family size are deducted from the API income ceiling. Between 1985 and 1994, the number of recipients has grown dramatically by a factor of 1.35 (although expenditures increased by a factor of 1.24), but since 1994 it began to decrease.

Two means-tested allowances are provided by CNAF to families with a young child. The first one, "Young child allowance" (APJE), concerns families with children under three. From the fourth month of pregnancy to the third month of the child's life, all families are entitled to this allowance on a universal basis. From the child's third month to three years of age, the benefit is income-tested (Afsa, 1996, p. 68). Meunier (1996, p. 61) notes that, of the 1,423,600 recipients of the benefit in 1995, 1,023,800 claim it on a means-test basis. In 1996, the number of means-tested APJE's recipients was 1,128,000, and the mean amount of the monthly allowance was FF 1032. The income test varies according to the number of incomes in the household and the number of children. The second allowance, which has the same income ceilings as the APJE (Montalembert, 1995, p. 94), is "family supplement" (*complément familial*, CF) and covered 953,000 families with more than two children three years old in 1996, at an average monthly cost per family of FF 864.

Finally, there are three housing-related means-tested benefits: "*Allocation logement familiale*" (ALF), "*Aide personnalisée au logement*" (APL), and "*Allocation logement sociale*" (ALS). Served by CNAF they are essentially funded by central state. In 1996, 5,738,474 people altogether claimed one of the three allowances for a mean monthly benefit of FF 1037. These allowances interact in a very complex way with the social minimum incomes through the means-tests. Due to their wide ranging nature, they play an important role within the whole array of French benefits to help the poor. As has been shown in a comparative study of the relative generosity of social minima incomes in 26 countries, France's rank climbs from 20th to 12th place when housing costs and benefits are taken into account (Jankéliowitch-Laval & Math, 1998).

### *Unemployment Assistance*

Unemployment is the last domain of social assistance to have grown in recent years, covering people who have used up their entitlement to insurance benefits or do not have any insurance in the first place. Coverage is provided through three programs: ASS (*allocation de solidarité spécifique*), AI (*allocation d'insertion*), and RMI (*revenu minimum d'insertion*).

ASS is for the long-term unemployed with no insurance rights left. Created in 1984, it is paid by the unemployment insurance funds (ASSEDIC) but funded by state subsidies drawn from the general budget (2/3) and a special proportional solidarity tax paid by public servants (1/3). Conditions of eligibility are strict and they have been limited in 1992 and 1997. They involve income-tests, age limits, and length of work: recipients must be at least 50 and they must have engaged in a salaried occupation for more than five years within the last ten years preceding the end of their labor contract; if they are under 55, they must also actively seek work. The normal maximum benefit was FF 2212 in 1996 (which is supplemented for the unemployed over 55 with 20 years of paid work or when they reach 57.5 with 10 years work experience). According to a March 1996 survey, 85 percent of claimants get a full benefit, and 13 percent receive the supplement. ASS accounts for 77 percent of the recipient's income in one-person households (34 percent for two persons households) (Amrouni et Math, 1998b, p. 57). There were 516,300 ASS beneficiaries in 1996 with a monthly mean allowance of FF 2268. The average benefit increased from 1984 to 1989; it was steady at FF 2500 until 1992; and then decreased to about FF 2268 in 1996. The number of recipients has multiplied by 5.65 since the beginning of the program.

In contrast to ASS, "insertion allowance" (AI, *allocation d'insertion*), also introduced in 1984, is for job seekers with no entitlement to unemployment insurance (young people, single mothers, refugees, recently freed inmates, etc.) and the number of recipients has sharply declined. Whereas nearly 214,000 claimed AI benefits in the first year of its introduction, only 17,000 claimants were paid a monthly mean benefit of FF 1311 in 1995, the value of which has remained unchanged since 1986. Two main institutional factors account for this decline: first, the creation of RMI in 1988 (see below); second, the exclusion from the benefit in 1992 of the two most important categories of individuals initially covered: young job seekers (*"primo-demandeurs" d'emploi*) under 25 and single mothers. AI's importance has thus faded away.

The "insertion minimum income" (RMI, *revenu minimum d'insertion*), the most recent French *minimum social*, has very quickly become a prominent feature of the system of social protection. The RMI may be seen as a key element of "welfare-to-work" *à la française*. The fact has already been stressed that RMI is no "categorical" minimum income, although its creation is clearly linked to the issue of mass unemployment and, especially, long-term unemployment. Precisely because it is completely disconnected from unemployment insurance (whose coverage has been reduced simultaneously), RMI introduces a new logic in the French solidaristic assistance system, or at least a change in the philosophy of solidarity. This said and notwithstanding the specific procedure of the "*contrat d'insertion*" linked to the new philosophy, RMI may be seen as a quite traditional *minimum social*: a means-tested, differential, state-funded (paid by the CAF) benefit. At the end of 1996, there were 1,010,500 claimants earning a monthly mean benefit of FF 1891 in metropolitan France and FF 1596 in overseas *départements* (DOM). The maximum benefit ranges from FF 2077 for a single person with no child and with a housing deduction to FF 5902 for a couple with three children with no housing deduction (for additional children there is a FF 944 supplement) (CSERC, 1997, p. 164). But, in practice, as with API, "the RMI amount paid is relatively independent of the family size" because RMI and other family benefits are taken into account for the income test (Amrouni et Math, 1998b, p. 58). The average monthly income of a RMI recipient was FF 4200 in 1995, with RMI benefits accounting for 46 percent of the total and housing benefits for 18 percent. The number of beneficiaries has grown dramatically since 1989 when the program served only 407,000 people. And, due to a 45 percent increase in the monthly mean individual cost of the benefit, the total cost for the state has multiplied by 3.6 times between 1989 and 1996.

## The Main Characteristics of the French Social Assistance System: Recent Evolutions

To sum up, considered from a comparative perspective, and especially contrasted with the U.S., the French system is characterized by a " solidaristic assistance" consisting of three main types of benefits: (i) social aid mainly provided at the local level (*département*);

(ii) family and housing CAF paid benefits (largely state funded); (iii) social minima incomes with a mixed funding (social security and central state). In 1992, solidaristic social assistance and public welfare programs represented less (FF 222.5 billion) than 10 percent of the total social expenditure (including all public authorities, social security and unemployment insurance) in France, which amounted to—140 percent growth since 1984 (comprehensive data for expenditures on *aide sociale* in more recent years are currently unavailable). Solidaristic assistance amounts to FF 180.4 billion in 1992 and 193.9 billion if RMI is included. The major increase in solidaristic assistance between 1984 and 1992 comes from housing benefits, with expenditures on family benefits, social aid, and social minima incomes excluding RMI remaining fairly constant. The relative shares of each program, which illustrate the proportional increases in RMI and housing benefits are as follows:

| *Relative Shares of Programs* | *1984* | *1991* | *1992* |
|---|---|---|---|
| Total solidarity | 100 | 100 | 100 |
| Minima incomes except RMI | 34 | 32 | 30 |
| Social aid | 20 | 19 | 19 |
| Housing benefits | 25 | 32 | 34 |
| Specific family benefits | 21 | 18 | 18 |
| Total solidarity & welfare | 100 | 100 | 100 |
| Solidarity | 91 | 84 | 82 |
| Welfare | 9 | 16 | 18 |
| RMI | 0 | 7 | 7 |

Two important developments have emerged since 1984. The first is the relative decline of solidaristic assistance in the total, despite the growth of housing benefits. The second is the increase in the state's share of expenditures and the relative decline in the programs funded by social security funds either alone or with state contribution. For the social minima incomes, which are among the most important of assistance programs, expenditures totaled FF 80 billion in 1995. Altogether, these programs serve a population of 3.3 million households (or 15 percent of French households) and nearly 6 million people (or 10 percent of the whole population); 59 percent of the beneficiaries are women; 58 percent are single individuals and 13 percent single parents; 71 percent are not couples (80 percent for the RMI). Minima incomes claimants are very often also receiving family and housing benefits, or *départements'* social aid benefits. The only feature common to all "*minima sociaux*" is that they ensure beneficiaries get a minimum level of resources through the mechanism of a differential benefit capped by a maximum amount (Amrouni & Math, 1998a, p. 27). These minimum and maximum levels for social minima incomes vary among the programs and there are large differences in resources taken into account for the means-tests. As these variations suggest, there is not a unified vision of the appropriate social minimum income allowing a recipient and his-her family to keep out of absolute or relative poverty (Aubert, 1998). The same applies to the relationship between social minima and minimum wage (SMIC).

Examining these benefits from an historical perspective, four successive generations of social minima incomes emerge. The rules governing benefits being much more coherent within each generation than between the generations.

The first generation is sort of a "golden age," which began with disabled and old-age minima in the 50s and ended with AAH in 1975. All three benefits were designed for categories of people unable to find jobs and/or to earn enough resources to keep out of poverty; moreover, initiated during the gradual extension of social insurance, these benefits are linked to social insurance gaps in addressing the particular "risks" for these categories; they nevertheless remain within a solidaristic framework under which the social insurance system is centrally involved with the state. Moreover, this first generation appears as the most generous—with benefits approaching 70 percent of the SMIC (Auber, 1998, p. 76).

Single parent (API) and widowhood insurance benefits mark the second generation. Beginning in the second half of the 70s, when the "welfare state" was still at its apex, both allowances are in tune with the former generation, but somewhat narrower in scope and benefits: temporary compensations for a weakened domestic situation, they do not address as wide a range of claimants as the first generation benefits; they are totally social security funded through social contributions; although less generous than the first generation minima incomes they nevertheless are more generous than those of the third and fourth generations.

The third generation emerged in a period of mass unemployment along with a financial and ideological crisis which challenged the system of social protection. The AI and ASS benefits created in 1984 are the product of Unemployment Insurance's failure (i) to address the issue of the young unemployed with no entitlement to insurance benefits and (ii) to provide "sufficient" resources for long-term unemployed. Tightening eligibility criteria for entitlements to insurance (in 1992, 1993 and 1997) paved the way to a steady expansion of ASS. At the same time, AI declined because most of the previous claimants were simply excluded from eligibility. This third generation of benefits may nevertheless be seen as "classically" solidaristic, for it still uses the solidarity principle to compensate social insurance failures within the conventional framework.

A different approach was introduced under the RMI, the fourth generation. Although directly related to long-term mass unemployment, RMI is disconnected from unemployment insurance and addresses mass long-term unemployment not only as a risk, but as a possible new status. Moreover, RMI is the least generous benefit of all *minima sociaux*. As will be argued in the next section, RMI has indeed new "welfare" features compared to other social minima incomes: it draws on a new conception of solidarity that contradicts the concept of a solidaristic assistance tightly linked to social security and to an egalitarian philosophy. From a certain point of view, RMI no longer reflects solidaristic social aid, and its creation appears to promote the work-to-welfare stigma. For this reason, it is indeed the main and perhaps exclusive element of the French system of social assistance that embodies the WTW policy orientation, but not entirely.

### *A French Equivalent of Welfare-to-Work (WTW) Programs*

*Social assistance and employment programs in the French context.* As should be inferred from the previous section, there are no Welfare-to-Work (WTW) nor workfare schemes strictly speaking in France, the main reason being the absence of a French equivalent of Welfare—in the sense of programs found in the U.S. and the UK. A second reason pertains to radical differences between French and U.S. labor market (or employment) policies (Barbier, 1998b).

In spite of these essential considerations, the first section has tried, within the French context, to formulate a proxy for "social assistance," for purposes of comparison with programs in other countries. Focusing now on the specifics of measures most related to WTW, a comparison will be drawn with two distinct sets of policies/programs: those related to "social assistance" policies and those that pertain to French "employment policies." Both these "sectors" of public social policies cannot, from our point of view, be compared as exact "functional equivalents" of what exists in other countries as long as we accept a theoretical perspective for comparisons based on "structural" (Théret, 1996b, 1997) or "societal" paradigms (Maurice, Sellier, Sylvestre, 1982; Maurice, 1989; Barbier, 1996; O Reilly, 1996; Schmid et al., 1996). Without delving into this matter thoroughly, we will only stress the fact that in any national frame, "sets of elements" are interrelated and acquire their precise meaning from the context of their interrelations. Three essential features that form a coherent national context may be described as follows:

1. The first one concerns "philosophical justifications" of social policies, which have already been addressed in the previous section. We refer to particular sets of norms and values often seen as belonging to national "cultures." On the specific question of the relationship between "social protection" and the labor market (or the link citizens establish with the labor market as a means of obtaining their livelihood and the social protection associated with it), a central distinction may be drawn between the British and U.S. contexts, which stress a "punitive" approach (King,1995), and the French context, which is somewhat different. As Morel (1996a, 1996b) and Barbier (1996, 1998) have shown, the French state's orientation on this matter stresses society's obligations to provide individuals with means, in order to become (and remain) "integrated" within society. For instance, RMI's (*Revenu minimum d'insertion*) entitlement is explicitly associated with the state's obligation to provide beneficiaries with opportunities to "integrate" (*insérer*) without obliging them either to be "available" or to "actively seek work." The distinction, however, should not be overstated: even in the U.S. context of workfare schemes, in the 1980s there remained a "tension" between a "cooperative" approach aimed at "employability" and a "punitive" one, where the intention was to lower the characteristics of "suitable"

employment (Rodgers, 1981, p. 12). The fact that the actual implementation of workfare schemes differs from the stated normative objectives is also well documented (Anspach, 1996). The central justification of the French programs, involves the concept of "*insertion*." Why exactly should "*insertion*" not be translated as "integration?"

"*Insertion*" in France has been extensively used since the 1980s in social policy, but its use can be traced to the 1960s. There is considerable polysemy to the notion. Central at the same time to specific policies' " theories of action " (Chen, 1980) and to practices initiated by the non-profit sector, this notion points to the present difficulties of public social policies and to the partly challenged previous balance and legitimacy of the French SSP. Social assistance programs may be viewed as redistributive policies whereas "*insertion*" schemes involve much more complex types of "services" that necessitate cooperation of a variety of social actors among which the beneficiaries themselves and their willingness to cooperate are key elements. "*Insertion*" in the French context has come to mean:

- a professional sphere of distinct practices of social workers and their institutions directed towards specific target groups (roughly the "socially excluded" or those who are at risk of exclusion, which includes not only those excluded from the labor market); services are delivered in order to "*insérer*" ("integrate") these groups through various types of services—helping them to use their social rights, socializing them through health and housing counseling, facilitating access to benefits, as well as counseling, training and employment schemes explicitly linked to the labor market, and devising individualized pathways to it);

- "*insertion professionnelle*" (or "*insertion économique*") is one aspect of the broad concept of "insertion," which is specifically linked to the labor market. In the 60s "*insertion professionnelle*" was also used in a more limited sense to convey the process of transition from school to work;

- far from being an example of a universal tendency to restrict entitlement to benefits to those recipients who engage in compulsory work or training, French "*politiques d'insertion*" are based on the principle that "*insertion*" involves a comprehensive process tailored to the individual's needs whether they be needs for socialization, needs for better housing, better access to civil rights, health, etc.—a social process supposedly leading eventually to social integration. It is the state's duty to intervene when necessary in this process, as is stated in the 1988 RMI law. In France, as in most of Europe, the shortage of jobs has worsened over the last ten years and the number of potential "socially excluded" (and not only *de facto* excluded persons from the labor market) has come to encompass a very large proportion of the population. Thus, state intervention appears all the more necessary since for many people in the present economy integration no longer occurs spontaneously. As Castel (1995: 435) notes: "Where a social system ensures that there exists a smooth transition between forms of socialization and social stages (from school to work, from employment to old age pension for example), there is no such thing as '*insertion*' ...it would be redundant with the notion of integration. But when slack appears in the functioning of the wage-earners' society, '*insertion*' emerges as a problem which calls for an appropriate technology to solve it. "*Insertion*" refers simultaneously to the distance from integration and to the specific intervention which is supposed to bridge this distance."

- In sum, the main theme in relation to philosophical justifications and values that inform French policies in the realm of an equivalent to WTW would be "*insertion*" in these various meanings.

2. The second element in the societal context is of the French approach to WTW, the "*national system of social protection*" *(NSSP)*, described in the first section of this paper. As has been argued, this system is complex: its "social assistance" element is closely linked to a very developed social insurance system. Strictly speaking, no element of the NSSP is directly linked to a "workfare" or WTW approach. In the "*aide sociale*" sector *institutionally* defined ("*aide sociale à l'enfance*," "*aide sociale aux personnes handicapées*," "*minimum vieillesse*"), the absence of any linkage is obvious. Similarly, a strict definition of workfare would not fit programs in the "social minima incomes sector": for their part, RMI's recipients are not compelled to seek work nor to register at the employment service. "*Allocation de parent isolé*- API," institutionally linked to the administration of family benefits, is given to single parents who are not obliged to work; but in fact many recipients do work and in these cases their wages are deducted from the benefits; for many recipients API is thus an "in-work" benefit—to use an English equivalent (their present rate of activity is estimated at 40 percent; this is consistent with the high rate of the French female participation in the labor market). Single mothers are entitled to the main benefit (API) only until their last child has reached the age of three. Thus, they are not a particularly compelling target for WTW purposes. Nor are the handicapped persons that receive AAH benefits: their share of the population (1.8 percent) has not increased much over the last ten years (1.4 percent in 1987), contrary to other countries (the UK, The Netherlands, for instance); a significant proportion of them (12 percent) work in special institutions (Centre d'aide

par le travail - CAT, see section A). "*Insertion professionnelle*" for the handicapped is conceived of as a right of citizens suffering from disadvantages, whom employers should recruit for the sake of solidarity.

In the social insurance sector, unemployment insurance benefits ("*allocation unique dégressive*" - AUD) and unemployment "solidarity" benefits (ASS) are available when traditional conditions of eligibility are met: being unemployed, available for and seeking work. The registered unemployed must also comply with participation in various employment and training programs to maintain their entitlement to benefits.

On the whole, RMI is the only "social assistance" program where, on the basis of *insertion*, special public activities are specifically designed to make beneficiaries enter jobs or training programs, (at least officially) on a *voluntary* basis, supported by a citizenship right to *insertion*. In addition to RMI, as we will see, some French public employment policies must be taken into account in our attempt to formulate with a French equivalent of WTW policies.

3. *Macro-economic policies* constitute a third element of the "societal context" for understanding the French approach. As elsewhere in Europe, in the past ten years these policies have resulted in a situation where, compared to the U.S., labor markets have provided fewer jobs and thus fewer opportunities for the individuals to rely on them for their sustenance. The result is one of underemployment, particularly for certain groups. The French case is characterized by high rates of female participation in full-time employment; low rates of participation at both ends of age groups (young men and women's rates are among the lowest in Europe). Responding, in part, to the labor market situation, out of the entire French population, a very significant proportion has been covered either by benefits programs or by various employment programs for the last ten years.

### *Recent Developments of Employment and Social Policies*

Following the comparative frame of reference sketched in the previous section, the WTW proxy in France would encompass a two-pronged policy, "social assistance" and "employment policies":

- The social assistance beneficiaries mainly considered here are RMI's claimants; their case is addressed through "*insertion*" policies and programs; it must be repeated again that recipients of other minimum incomes are not likely candidates for WTW interventions;

- On the other hand, and contrary to the U.S. situation, France, as in many European countries with the notable exception of the UK has implemented a broad range of labor market programs in the last twenty years, which have served about 9 percent of the active population (roughly 2 million). Although these programs are targeted generally to the unemployed—a group constituting more than 10 percent of the active population for most of the last ten years and 12 percent in 1998—they focus most specifically on the long-term unemployed (30 to 40 percent of the unemployed, or 1.2 million people in 1998) and other groups considered as being in particular difficulty on the labor market (such as the young with low qualifications and the handicapped). When entering these programs, participants in employment (and training) schemes may be RMI recipients, insurance benefits recipients, ASS recipients or recipients of other benefits of course.

*RMI and social assistance in a WTW comparative perspective.* RMI is a relatively new benefit in France; it was legally instituted in 1988 on the basis of a very thorough consensual parliamentary decision. It was initially envisaged that about 500,000 people would claim RMI benefits; and that claimants would be mainly middle-aged men, single and without children. These expectations were not realized: the number of claimants soared, particularly after the restrictive conditions imposed on the unemployment insurance system in 1993-94; and the population of claimants encompassed young people along with a significant number of couples or single parents with children (those with children were supposed to be sufficiently cared for by the comprehensive French family benefits system).

The RMI's main innovation was the "*contrat d'insertion*," which was legally created to accompany the benefit; this contract is signed both by the administrative body (*commission locale d'insertion*) and the claimant, within three months of claiming the benefit. It describes a "*projet d'insertion*" on which both have agreed, particularly designating the type and schedule of actions the recipient is supposed to undertake. The benefit's amount is determined by law; and is uniform throughout France. Whereas the benefit is state funded, local authorities (*départements*) are legally obliged to fund "*insertion*" activities at a level of at least 20 percent the benefits paid in their district. For that purpose, they are supposed to establish a "*programme départemental d'insertion*—PDI," in accordance with the local representative of the state (*préfet*). The "insertion" activities encompass actions and schemes in the domains of health, housing, various forms of counselling and "*insertion économique*" (specific activities geared towards all forms of employment and training).

When the law was passed in 1988, one of the main debates in Parliament was directly related to the theme of "welfare to work/workfare": a controversy arose about whether the RMI would be conditional: Did the beneficiaries have to discharge certain civic obligations in exchange for society paying their benefits? As Belorgey (1996) has shown, RMI was eventually instituted as an explicit right, universal rather than local, differential and de-facto non-conditional. On the particular question of "conditionality," although a number of left-wing MPs favored providing benefits as an entitlement without any requirements concerning the recipient's behavior, this was not the case for the majority of MPs. The compromise resulted in what Belorgey termed an "ambiguous situation"—falling somewhere between a totally non-conditional benefit and a benefit conditioned by the recipient's compliance with participation in "*insertion*" activities offered to them. In practice, however, since 1988, roughly 50 percent of beneficiaries have constantly not signed "*contrat d'insertion,*" whereas only a very small proportion (5 to 6 percent) have been sanctioned for non-compliance (Barbier, 1996). Moreover, it should be stressed that only a part of "*contrats d'insertion*" have an "*insertion économique*" or "*professionnelle*" content (i.e., a work or training content). Thus, obligations to participate in "insertion" activities are only partially related to WTW. In addition, according to their choice and strategies, RMI recipients may be engaged in employment of some sort without having signed any "*contrat d'insertion.*"

It must be stressed that the various "economic" activities RMI beneficiaries are engaged in relate either to traditional "social policies" or to "employment policies." One of the effects of the increasing number of people concerned with "*insertion*" has been that the frontier between traditional social policies and employment policies has blurred in France. Whereas the main social task in the seventies was to apply specific techniques to limited marginalized groups to help integrate them, the problem today is one of a lack of resources directly linked to unemployment across a wide scope of population. The content of social work has also evolved accordingly (Castel, 1998; Donzelot and Roman, 1998). The institutions concerned are at the same time inadequate and overloaded, like for instance the public employment service (Barbier, 1995).

*Recent Developments in Labor Market Policies (Employment Policies)*

During the last twenty years, France has experienced a tremendous expansion in what we term "*politique publique de l'emploi*"—public employment policy (Barbier, 1997). Suffice it to say that expenditures in this area have climbed from FF 10 billion in 1973 to FF 295 billion in 1995 (DARES, 1996b), representing an increase from 0.9 to 3.99 percent of the GDP. The number of participants in the various employment programs has increased from 100,000 people in 1973 to 2.4 million in 1995, about 9.5 percent of the active population. These employment programs encompass a wide range of interventions including training, temporary public employment, subsidized employment and early retirement schemes. The priority target groups for these programs include: the long-term unemployed; handicapped persons; RMI recipients; young people (under 25) with low qualifications and experiencing difficulties in finding work; and, at times, unemployed or single mothers.

Public employment policy has often been dismissed derogatively by its critics as "*traitement social*" (social treatment), as against what they term "economic treatment"; the latter refers to the gradually increasing use of public policy to lower the cost of labor by, for example, reduction of indirect labor costs, taxes and social security contributions. In contrast, public employment policy or "*traitement social*" mainly consists of five types of schemes: temporary public jobs in public administrations and voluntary organizations ("*contrat emploi solidarité*"—CES, with a derivative form called "*contrat emploi consolidé*"—CEC); training for the unemployed ("*stage d'insertion et de formation à l'emploi*"—SIFE); targeted subsidized jobs (affirmative action) in the private sector ("*contrat initiative emploi*"—CIE); specific "*insertion économique*" activities ("*entreprises d'insertion,*" "*chantiers d'insertion,*" and "*associations intermédiaires*"); early retirement and other schemes that authorize persons not to seek work when remaining unemployed and entitled to ASS benefits. Finally, it must also be noted that a new orientation to social policy referred to as "*politiques transversales*" or "*politiques globales,*" with a particular emphasis on local implementation, coordination, and partnerships, has been devised and implemented over the last 15 years: these are policies seeking to organize pertinent social policy actors on a local basis (for instance, *plans locaux d'insertion économique*) or on a thematic basis (*politique de la ville*);

they give birth to organizational and political coordination programs using standard central government measures such as CES and SIFE.

*The main employment programs.* We will now turn to a detailed description of the four main types of schemes designed to address the potential "*insertion*" population's needs. These would be the closest proxy for a WTW "equivalent" and should be considered as representative, if not exhaustive of contemporary French public policies in this realm. These schemes are summarized below:

**CES (contrats emplois solidarité) and CEC (Contrats emplois consolidés) Date of creation**: 1990 (formerly [1984-89] TUC—*travaux d'utilité collective,* reserved for youth with a trainee status).
**Participants** - (estimated, thousands): 1991 - 200, 1996 - 400
**Target group –** Long-term unemployed (including youth with specific difficulties); unemployed over 50 years of age; handicapped workers; RMI and ASS beneficiaries.
**Theory of action** - Through participation in the scheme, beneficiaries are supposed to gain basic skills to make them more employable; they at the same time regain social rights including unemployment insurance.
**Status** - Regular employee status (standard social rights included)
**Remuneration** - Half the minimum wage (1/2 SMIC = 2.600f net income before tax) is state funded.
**Content of activity and employers** - Clerical or environmental non-skilled jobs in public organizations, voluntary organizations and local authorities
**Duration** - Minimum 3 months, maximum 2 years
**Prescription, rights and sanctions** - Contracts proposed to the registered unemployed by the public employment service; refusal is possible only for valid reasons; non-registered RMI beneficiaries, handicapped and young people are also in the target group.
**State provision** - Remuneration; social rights; possible training
**CEC** - Reserved for a proportion of CES beneficiaries who, for various reasons are deemed unable to find employment or training after completing the CES; mainly full time; duration up to five years, over which period state funding decreases from 80 percent to 30 percent.

**Contrats initiative emploi (CIE)**
**Date of creation**: 1995 (previously *contrats de réinsertion* - CRA, 1987, and *Contrat de retour à l'emploi*, CRE, 1989-95)
**Participants** - (thousands): 1990 - 65, 1996 - 427
**Target group** - Long-term unemployed (including youth with specific difficulties); unemployed over 50 years of age; handicapped workers; RMI beneficiaries.
**Theory of action** - The subsidy is an affirmative action mechanism encouraging private firms to recruit people who are difficult to employ.
**Status** - Ordinary employee status (standard social rights included)
**Remuneration** - Ordinary conditions (wage equal/superior to the minimum wage)
**Content of activity** - Mainly non-skilled jobs but not exclusively
**Duration** - The subsidy (2000F monthly) and national contribution rebates vary according to wages; they last up to 2 years; contracts must last at least one year
**Prescription, rights and sanctions** - Contracts are made with employers (that select registered unemployed people meeting the legal criteria) by the public employment service.

**State provision** - Subsidy; training can be provided and state financed

**Stages d'insertion et de formation à l'emploi (SIFE)**
**Date of creation**: 1993 (previously *Actions d'insertion et formation*, AIF, 1990)
**Participants** - (thousands): 1990 - 70, 1996 - 74
**Target group** - Long-term unemployed; unemployed over 50 years of age; handicapped workers; RMI beneficiaries; very long-term unemployed.
**Theory of action** - Through participation in the scheme, beneficiaries are supposed to gain basic skills and improve their employability.
**Status** - Trainee status
**Remuneration** - State remuneration
**Content of activity** - Training in basic skills
**Duration** - Minimum 40 hours, maximum 1200 hours
**Prescription, rights and sanctions** - Training is proposed to the unemployed by the public employment service; they may refuse only for valid reasons; non-registered RMI beneficiaries, handicapped and young people are also in the target group.
**State provision** - Remuneration; training; social contributions associated with trainee status

The fourth group of activities is relatively minor in quantitative terms; the schemes funded are not strictly separate from the types above; they may draw on general central state measures as CES or CEC. Activities comprise variously funded schemes which share a common broad characteristic: their participants are those deemed to need a special work environment, not being able to engage directly in ordinary private employment or in an ordinary temporary public job on an individual basis. The three forms here selected are the main ones but various other activities exist, aimed at facilitating "*insertion*"; all are organized on a local basis.

**Insertion économique activities: entreprises d'insertion (1990); associations intermédiaires (1989); chantiers école**
**Target group** - Very long-term unemployed (including young ones with specific difficulties); unemployed over 50 years of age; handicapped workers; RMI beneficiaries
**Theory of action** - **ei**: registered subsidized private firms or voluntary organizations; in two years (maximum), participants are supposed to gain adequate employability for the ordinary labor market. **ai**: registered subsidized voluntary organizations act as intermediaries to lend participants on short-term contracts to firms and private households; contracts supposed to enable participants gradually to find ordinary employment. **cc**: 6 months to 1 year projects where participants regain contact with work before being directed to training or ordinary (possibly subsidized) employment
**Status** - **ei**: employee status (rights associated) possibly linked with CIE. **ai**: short-time employee with specifically regulated contracts. **cc**: if associated with CES contracts, employee; otherwise trainee or assistance claimant
**Remuneration** - **ei**: minimum wage. **ai**: minimum wage (hourly). **cc**: 1/2 minimum wage (part time)
**Content of activity** - **ei**: mainly non-skilled jobs. **ai**: service to persons-households service to small firms (non-skilled). **cc**: services and environment (non-skilled)

**Duration** - **ei**: maximum 2 years. **ai**: 750h a year is the maximum. **cc**: 6 months to 1 year (part time)
**Prescription, rights and sanctions** - **ei**: contracts are proposed to beneficiaries by social services; entitlement allows participants to gain new social rights. **ai**: contracts are proposed to beneficiaries by social services; entitlement allows participants to gain limited new social rights. **cc**: contracts are proposed to beneficiaries by social services; see CES.
**State provision** - **ei**: training is provided and state financed. **ai**: training exceptional. **cc**: possible training associated.

In addition to the main schemes described above, it must be added that new forms of organization and coordination of public interventions in employment and social policies have been devised over the last ten years. Their objectives are twofold: to facilitate "partnerships" between central state and regional/local authorities that reinforce their political cooperation; to coordinate the provision of services of numerous administrative departments and actors that participate in "*insertion*." The main forms of this public intervention are:

- The local plans of "*insertion*" (*Plans locaux d'insertion économique* (PLIE) and *Programmes départementaux d'insertion* (PDI). These plans provide a framework within which local authorities and the state are supposed to organize individualized "pathways" for the potential client population of "*insertion*";

- The central state has also developed general coordinating policies that address specific thematic domains of social policy: the best example of these is probably "*politique de la ville*" (for cities); within these open-ended policies, coordination of various sectoral interventions (housing, revitalization of derelict urban zones, economic development, employment, and so on) is organized by local and regional representatives of the state, involving all other relevant local and regional actors and political authorities.

## *Current Directions of Social and Employment Policies in France*

To complete the rapidly sketched description of the main schemes related to what we have considered here as an equivalent to WTW programs, two points remain to be stressed. The first one concerns public employment policy. For the last ten years, and decidedly from 1986 on, an important element of this policy has been the objective of lowering indirect costs of labor; this is achieved through various tax subsidies and national insurance contributions exemptions. Whereas such a policy is not focused on individual contracts for assistance recipients, it has an indubitable influence on the general functioning of the labor market. The degree to which jobs are created for those excluded from the labor market is a matter of debate among experts (DARES, 1996b) due to deadweight and time scale effects. Such a policy must of course be interpreted within the national context of institutions we referred to previously, and especially the interrelation with the national system of social protection and the way it is financed through insurance contributions. In recent times, three new programs were being designed and considered for implementation:

- Legislation to reduce working hours to 35 hours a week—it is not known how it will affect the local labor markets;

- In December 1997, the government started its new "*emplois jeunes*" program aimed at creating 350,000 five-year public jobs for the young under 25 years of age; a small proportion of these will be reserved for non-skilled youngsters and the ones "excluded" from the labor market (part of our "assistance" population); this will undoubtedly affect the provision and allocation of places in the schemes described earlier;

- In February 1998, a new spate of schemes was announced, aimed at the "excluded" within a new "*loi contre l'exclusion.*" Financial means are reinforced and a special new scheme (TRACE, *trajet d'accès à l'emploi* - pathways to employment) is being discussed for young people deemed to be the least employable.

### Evaluation Results

*Evaluation culture in France and types of policies/programs.* Countries have diverse cultures of social policy evaluation. Some features of the French approach to evaluation deserve mention before examining the specific studies and data available in the field. Evaluation research in France is more recent that in the U.S. (Monnier, 1992) and a specific French conception has emerged (Duran, Monnier et al. 1995), which is wary of strict "program evaluation" (Barbier and Simonin, 1997; Barbier, 1998a) or "managerialist" evaluation. This conception also finds echoes in other European countries (Schmid, 1997, Schmid et al., 1996).

The programs reviewed in the previous sections are embedded in the context of open-ended and much broader social policies. These policies are not definable by the simple aggregation of a number of isolated programs, so that the real challenge of evaluation is not to choose among programs those that work and those that don't but to answer the question why these particular programs, in the broader context of the French social policy pattern appear to have such results, considering a relatively robust testimony of causality may be produced. Suffice it to say that the French approach to evaluation challenges the rational assumptions underlying the bulk of program evaluation, namely that causes and effects are easily connectable, effects clearly measurable, programs clearly defined and objectives stable in time (Barbier, 1998a; Schmid, 1997). This explains, for instance, along with deontonlogical considerations also relevant in the French context, why very few studies have been conducted using control groups. In the past ten years, evaluation expertise has spread extensively in France.

*RMI Evaluation*

The 1988 RMI law is one of a relatively small number of laws where explicit provision was made for a strict evaluation; initially the law was passed for a limited period of time (1988-1992). A special "*Commission d'évaluation du RMI*" was nominated in 1989 and produced a comprehensive report (Commission nationale, 1992) on the first years of implementation.

The commission notes that evaluating RMI is a difficult business, which requires assessing a highly complex set of programs. RMI is a policy that reaches all sectors of the French NSSP; and involves at least two tiers of local administration (mainly *départements* but also *communes*) along with numerous non-profit operators, and many different ministerial departments. Evaluation difficulties, the commission stresses, are also related to the fact that longitudinal measures are required to assess the impacts of RMI efforts on the recipient population. Quantitative longitudinal panel studies were conducted, with representative populations, to measure effects on resources and the effectiveness of "*insertion*" activities (social or economic *insertion*). Numerous qualitative studies were also conducted on implementation.

Based on the initial results of the evaluation (which contributed to the passage of a law in 1992 making RMI permanent) the commission formulated three main conclusions (Commission nationale, 1992):

- RMI was judged as making "undoubtable social progress" in terms of income support distributed to an aggregate 950,000 recipients at the end of 1991 (570,000 in stock at that date), who otherwise would not have had access to this support;

- the RMI benefits resulted in improvement of the recipients' living conditions (housing, health and so on);

- however, the "insertion" part of the law had known only limited achievement.

The first conclusion was linked to the important fact that the structure of the claimant population was different from that initially predicted; 50 percent of the claimants were under 35; 60 percent were isolated people without children; and 16 percent were couples with children. As for their link with the labor market, 50 to 60 percent were registered with the public employment service, a figure that seems to have remained stable up to now. At this early stage of implementation, 75 percent of beneficiaries were non-skilled and only 7 percent had completed secondary education. The commission noted that in 1991, 40 percent of beneficiaries had been on the roll for more than two years (66 percent more than one year) but that new entrants tended to leave it quicker. Based on the criterion of living without benefits for at least 7 months, a "permanent leaving rate" of 44 percent was registered for all recipients.

As for WTW, only 40 percent of claimants had access to a "*contrat d'insertion*," which led to the third main conclusion. On the whole, only 15 percent of beneficiaries had access to "*insertion professionnelle*" activities [mainly the schemes described above: CES, AIF (later to be transformed in SIFE) and CRE (to be renamed as CIE)]. But, in any year, 25 percent of beneficiaries had taken paid work for some time. Of those who left the RMI rolls, 50 percent went to work and most of the rest (34 percent) shifted to other benefits (pensions, 7 percent; AAH, 6 percent; API, 7 percent and unemployment benefits, 14 percent).

This last finding is consistent with one of our hypotheses concerning the overall logic of the recent shifts in the French NSSP: notwithstanding large turnover within the population of beneficiaries of both employment schemes and RMI, a feature of the system is as much a type of "work to welfare" as the reverse, inasmuch as a significant proportion of beneficiaries are shifted into intermediary statuses and not into employment in the "ordinary" labor market. It is also consistent with the fact that the age limit of 25 has been maintained throughout the implementation of RMI: young people continue to depend on families and family benefits and are supposed to enter the job market or stay in education but they are not considered as potential welfare recipients. When they claim RMI, they don't do it massively at their 25th birthday (CREDOC, 1996) and they leave the rolls rapidly (see later).

*Recent monitoring—administrative data on "insertion" activities.* The SESI-CNAF monitoring system has conducted regular surveys representative of the portion of RMI beneficiaries that signed a "*contrat d'insertion*." The latest available data are for 1993 (SESI, 1995). They indicate that the rate of contracts on the whole population (with huge discrepancies among *départements*) has more or less remained steady (roughly 48 percent in 1995). Administrative sources nevertheless tend to caution that this figure should not be taken as a relevant and comprehensive indicator of "*insertion*" in the larger sense. Two-thirds of the signed contracts include job search activities and activities promoting access to employment; 10 percent include training; both these rates have remained stable for the last years. Obviously these contractual items do not mean that there is effective integration into employment for all. Estimates in 1993 indicate that out of a population of 700,000 recipients, about 200,000 had access to a job or training as RMI claimants (263,000 out of 841,000 in 1995, or roughly 30 percent, DARES, 1996a).

One of the main findings from the SESI monitoring system revealed the changing structure of the claimant population—as the proportion completing secondary education rose from 9.3 percent in 1991 to 14.6 percent in 1993.

*1995 CREDOC study.* In 1996, CREDOC issued new interesting results from a survey of 900 RMI recipients, representative of new claimants in 1995. Of these claimants, one-third had left the RMI rolls in 1996; a small minority had already claimed in previous years (14 percent). New claimants are younger than the bulk of the population (40 percent are ages 25-29). The size of the group reflects the increasing difficulty of transitioning from school to work. Ninety percent of all new entrants come from unemployment and 50 percent are looking for a job. Significant educational differences exist between claimants according to age: whereas 25 percent of all new claimants completed secondary education, the rate was 30 percent among those under 30.

One year after their 1995 claim, 10 percent of recipients were inactive (a majority of them women); 50 percent were looking for a job; 6 percent were in training; 5 percent were sick or disabled and

27 percent were in employment, half of whom had benefited from the employment schemes (CES, CEC, CIE, etc.). Those employed often consider their jobs precarious, and most are in part-time employment and would prefer to work longer hours. It must also be noted that when interviewed half of those in employment still claimed RMI (as long as their effective income was below the minimum income): in that case, RMI is an "in work" benefit.

As has already been noted, within a year one-third of the new claimants were no longer receiving RMI; of this group, 53 percent ceased to be eligible because they took a job or paid training, but the other 47 percent give reasons that are somewhat different from those found in the 1992 study cited above (Commission nationale, 1992): 8 percent shifted to unemployment benefits compared to 14 percent in 1992; 5 percent to the API compared to 7 percent in 1992; 4 percent to the AAH compared to 5 percent in 1992. And 12 percent left the RMI because of family reasons: mainly their partners being entitled to other incomes.

## Evaluation of Other Main Schemes

*CES* - Regular evaluations of CES outcomes for beneficiaries are being conducted through panel studies which supplement the Ministry of Labor monitoring data. The latest findings are drawn from a panel study initiated in 1994, where participants were interviewed 3 times (DARES, 1997). There are also numerous qualitative in-depth studies on this scheme, which represents one of the most important measures of French employment policy over the last ten years.

The latest panel study results show that 54 percent of participants interviewed 18 months after entering the scheme in 1994 were unemployed; 42 percent had never been employed and 12 percent worked for some time before becoming unemployed; roughly 40 percent of the CES participants were employed at the time of the interviews and one-third of these in subsidized jobs. Evaluations thus show that those who leave the scheme to enter jobs are a significant minority, but the impact of CES goes far beyond this apparently limited outcome: CES is at the same time a scheme that contributes to a turnover among the unemployed, provides an opportunity to gain a limited income (amounting to half the minimum wage) for a significant portion of the unemployed, and serves as a means to maintain links to the labor market and to social integration for beneficiaries, including the provision of significant access to training. Surveys show a high degree of satisfaction among CES participants; however, participants also register strong dissatisfaction with the prospects for stable jobs. One of the questions not clearly answered by these studies concerns the degree to which unemployed participants return in the schemes after a period of time. There is no precise measure that identifies the number of the unemployed or assisted population that is constantly (or recurrently) of these various schemes and never returns to stable or "ordinary" employment contracts. It is assumed that a significant part of this beneficiary group amounts to a "trapped" population but data to test the hypothesis are not currently available. As for rates of recurrence in RMI, it is estimated that 10-15 percent of all claimants since 1989 have been constant beneficiaries up to now.

*CIE* - From the beneficiaries' point of view, the outcome of CIE (formerly CRE) schemes is mainly positive, inasmuch as the affirmative action objective is generally achieved. Regular evaluations (DARES, 1997c) show that, assessed in terms of immediate results, the scheme is effective. In 1996, 300,000 persons found a job via the scheme, all of which were for at least one year, and two-thirds involved contracts with unlimited duration. One-fourth were part-time jobs. Two-thirds paid from 1 to 1.1 SMIC (minimum wage). Two-thirds of the persons recruited were among the priority target groups: long-term unemployed (more than two years)—16 percent; handicapped employees—7 percent; RMI claimants—10 percent; young with particular difficulties—22 percent.

*SIFE* - If CES is the main measure concerning temporary public employment for the potentially socially excluded, and CIE its counterpart for subsidized private sector jobs, SIFE has been the main training scheme for this target group for the last ten years (under different designations) serving an average of 60-70,000 participants annually since 1988. Those who leave this scheme may enter CES, the relation between SIFE and CES theoretically constituting part of a "pathway" to integration in ordinary employment.

The latest panel study (DARES, 1997b) results show that 51 percent of participants interviewed 18 months after entering the scheme in 1994 were unemployed; 32 percent had never been employed and 19 percent had worked before becoming unemployed; roughly 1 out of 2 participants were employed at the time of the interviews and half of them in subsidized employment (mainly CES). As with CES and other schemes for the socially excluded, it is difficult to know the proportion of the target population which is continuously unemployed.

*Associations intermédiaires and entreprises d'insertion*—Intermediary "*insertion économique*" institutions are quantitatively less significant than other programs, but the way they operate is most appropriate for our quest for WTW equivalents. Overall, a CREDOC survey (CREDOC, 1997) reveals three groups of participants with different employment trajectories: 40 percent of participants were in insecure employment; 20 percent were in stable employment and the remaining were excluded from the labor market. Recent surveys on the *entreprises d'insertion* (DARES, 1997d) examine the type of employees participating and their employment situation in the year after they left (three years after their recruitment in the institutions). The majority of participants are men (70 percent), equally distributed among the age bands of under 26, 26-34, 35 and over. Half of them had no qualifications. When interviewed, 58 percent were either unemployed or inactive, whereas 42 percent were active. Among the active respondents, two-fifths were still employed in the same institution or another *insertion* structure and the others were in ordinary jobs.

Compared to participants in *enterprise d'insertion*, those who participate in *associations intermédiaires* (in fact working for households or firms but employed by the *association*) are more skilled (50 percent have completed secondary education) and more likely to be women (60 percent) (DARES, 1997e). Interviewed one year after the start of their participation, the vast majority are employed: 46 percent employed in the same *association* or another of the same type; 18 percent in ordinary jobs; and 12 percent in subsidized employment. But 21 percent are unemployed, 90 percent of whom are seeking work. The outcomes for both of these programs, notwithstanding the differences in target groups, show that a majority of participants are in the *insertion* sector for a long time and that only a minority (20-25 percent) of participants experienced these schemes as a kickstart for a return to the regular labor market.

## France, What Case for WTW Policies?

To conclude, we will first examine the main implications of the preceding evaluations and then address the question of whether WTW is a relevant concept in the French context.

A prominent feature of the French system is that over the last 15 years a very large proportion of the active population has been served by assistance, employment and training schemes of various sorts. Participation in these schemes is never strictly compulsive and in most programs, participants regain social rights albeit not thoroughly equivalent to those associated with ordinary jobs. The combination of social assistance minimum incomes and of employment programs leads more to the creation of a "secondary market" (although not a closed one, where participants flow to and from the first labor market) than to a WTW logic, which emphasizes a direct flow from assistance to employment.

Evaluations of RMI effectiveness show the limited achievement of its "*insertion*" dimension, though the value of other non-work-related activities in the program should not be ignored. Surveys suggest that RMI operates with a dual and contradictory logic. On one hand, RMI is seen and actually used as a standard minimum income benefit and a way to give the poor access to social rights when they are stigmatized as "unemployable" on the labor market. Roughly half the beneficiary population never sign a "*contrat d'insertion*," and a large part of the contracts signed do not lead to effective integration on the labor market. Conversely, a significant proportion of claimants develop and maintain links with employment through RMI's *insertion* activities. Roughly every other claimant is registered with the public employment service and a quarter of all take paid work (half of them via specific employment and training programs). Thus considered, RMI seems to operate effectively as a WTW program. Nevertheless, its basic characteristics should not be ignored: RMI is not a coercive scheme as the *de facto* "non obligation" to sign a contract demonstrates. The majority of claimants enter the program with the provisional status of welfare recipient before trying to move into the labor market or other more valued statuses (as evidenced by the high turnover of claimants). In strict "*insertion professionnelle*" terms, RMI retains the main features of an "in work" benefit, resulting in a reduction of the cost of unskilled labor; surveys show that it does not usually provide access to the "ordinary" labor market but to a new "secondary" market of unstable and second-rate jobs (short time; limited rights). In that sense, RMI is connected to the whole set of recent employment and training programs described above and targeted at long-term unemployed and non-skilled young newcomers on the labor market. However, both main employment schemes (CES for the public or voluntary sector and CIE for the private) have different outcomes: CES provides a limited number of beneficiaries immediate access to employment, helps to maintain social links and delivers a modest income; CIE successfully promotes affirmative action for employment by private firms, especially for the better skilled in the target group. Both schemes significantly impact the population of the unemployed and especially those on RMI, along with the young. Training schemes for the long-term unemployed are very much linked to the CES. As for the much smaller *insertion économique* sector, results suggest that the majority of participants remain in the schemes or in unstable employment for a rather long period of time.

At the same time, recent surveys have shown that part-time jobs and the whole array of special employment contracts play a significant role in the development of the "working poor," which has become an issue in France. Concialdi (1997) has shown that the proportion of the labor force receiving low wages (less than half the median wage) and very low wages (less than three-quarters of the median wage) has climbed in recent years. The former now account for roughly 5 percent of the wage labor force, and the latter for 10 percent, notwithstanding the minimum wage. The 15 percent total in 1995 is up from a total of 11 percent in the low and very low wage groups in 1983.

Despite references to the necessary *insertion* of claimants, RMI and related employment and training schemes do not (yet?) operate as proper welfare-to-work programs. There is a historic reason for this: before RMI's creation in 1989, there was no "welfare" for citizens in the French SSP. RMI may be viewed as the program that created "welfare *à la française*" in a rupture with the secular tradition of solidaristic assistance. From a labor market perspective, in that sense, RMI amounts at least partly to a transition from "work to welfare"—i.e., from "unity" to "duality" of the labor market; from an SSP perspective, it is a transition from solidarity to welfare—i.e., from a unified national system of social protection under the umbrella of social security to a two-pronged "welfare state" divided into social insurance and social assistance institutions. These new trends might thus be envisaged as the "first stage" of a wider movement towards the implementation of a "welfare-to-work reconfiguration" of the French social assistance system. But considered in the wider framework of the French context, while there clearly are signs of a WTW trend in the articulation of RMI with employment and training policies, there are also obvious signs of strong institutional counter forces. These counter forces at the moment seem to be capable of limiting the reconfiguration of French policies from work (and full-employment policies) towards "welfare" and dual labor market (which would alter the traditional French philosophy of solidarity).

One reason that limits the development of a strong WTW orientation pertains to the structure of the French labor market where, in many sectors, especially for the non-skilled labor force, demand for jobs widely exceeds the supply. France does not experience significant problems of work incentives. Thus, public policies do not need to employ coercive measures to promote obligations to work. This explains why many social policies have aimed (implicitly or explicitly) at reducing rates of participation of certain groups in order to lower the rate of unemployment: for example, the resort to massive early retirement and the relaxing of the "actively seeking rule" for ASS recipients when they reach 55 or 57; in a similar vein, family policies have introduced incentives for parents with young children to at least temporarily quit their job (or work part time) and education policies have extended the duration of schooling for the young. These policies seem partially effective, especially in regard to female participation in the labor force. In the French value structure work appears not as a penance, but rather as a reward, a representation that goes along with the idea that work is the only real way out of poverty and dependency vis à vis the family and public authorities. Herein lies, perhaps, the main problem of social and employment policies in the new international and neo-liberal configuration: in the French national system of values, work looks desirable, but only inasmuch as it functions as a means to get a relief from economic necessity and political dependency. This cultural outlook limits the legitimacy of WTW policies that create an underclass of working poor. Another important feature of French culture, which impedes the implementation of WTW programs along the British or U.S. model, is the traditional representation of citizenship, from a Rousseauist perspective. This perspective supports a commanding role for the central state in the French context, which stands at odds with the U.S. Lockean conception of a fair relationship between state and the individual. The French state's strength is derived from the transfer of its citizens' sovereignty, with the state holding the sovereign power up to the point of acknowledging that this power is being given to it by individual citizens, society's members. The transfer of individual sovereignty to the state (seen as society's deputy) is the initial gift for which the state is indebted to its individual citizens. Having received this gift, the state is obliged to provide a secure life for all citizens. Therefore, in the political exchange between state and citizens, if the state is unable to provide individuals with a secure life by the way of work opportunities, either by ensuring society yields such opportunities, or by delivering these itself, the state is liable for assistance in last resort. Assistance duties are compulsory for the state as is also compulsory the duty to reimburse debts contracted. This conception of the fair relationship between state and citizens in the French system of social values explains the specificities of the "*insertion* requirement" in RMI. The idea that the citizen has a debt or obligation to the state is inconsistent with the traditional solidaristic social assistance which the state is compelled to provide. The question is not even raised, the state being reputed as the borrower in the social debt relationship. Rights are available to categories of individuals in need—those to whom society has failed to adequately settle its debt of solidarity. The state has to compensate these citizens in need in order to maintain the social bond and to legitimate the delegation of sovereignty from which it benefits. On the surface RMI represents a rupture in the French tradition, due to the introduction of a "compulsory" requirement for the beneficiaries. However, the cultural tradition of solidarity has limited the day-to-day administrative and institutional application of compulsory measures under RMI. In practice, as evaluations findings show: administrative implementation of individual obligations under RMI is quite weak. The interpretation of the nature of the individuals' responsibilities as being not so much directly related to a work as to social integration, is perhaps of more importance: the former is only a mediation towards the latter. In fact, individuals are asked to confirm that they recognize themselves as citizens, as members of the society; they must manifest their willingness to participate in the community; this demand may take the form of *insertion professionnelle*, but not automatically. In fact, the outstanding condition required is to demonstrate willingness to participate in society as a whole. In France, it can be argued that the transition from the present stage of work-to-welfare to a second stage of welfare-to-work policies will not come easily, even if economic forces push strongly in this direction. RMI and present employment policies undoubtedly demonstrate a French path to wage relationship flexibility and to reducing low-skilled labor costs by relaxing or getting around institutional protections against poverty for wage-earners. A next step toward increasing flexibility that would involve coercive pressures upon RMI claimants to accept part-time and low-paid jobs, will surely encounter strong opposition, even if its main effects would be a significant reduction of unemployment rather than a reduction of real wages. Further attacks on the traditional form of social aid would have to bear not only on the margins of the active population, but on the core system of values which has governed social relations in French society since the revolutionary nineteenth century. It would have to reverse the notion of social obligations in the relation between state and citizens—the whole framework on which democracy has been built in the French context.

Finally, to sharpen our analysis of the French system we would contrast it with the social system in the U.S., where the idea of workfare seems consistent with prevailing values. The U.S. model of citizenship and the notion of social debt and citizen obligations differ from the ideas of citizenship and social debt in France. These differences are reflected in each country's welfare and solidarity models of social assistance. In the U.S., individuals do not make the gift of their life capital to society, with the state as its deputy. The state is conceived of as an outside power, a foreign body the aim of which is to dominate the society of individuals. This society of individuals emerges naturally from their interdependencies and the invisible hand of the market, which is the main device resulting in the social bond. Consequently, the state is not a sovereign power, there is no sovereignty but that of the consumer's in the marketplace. In that representation of the relation between state and individuals where no sovereign public power has the monopoly to represent society as a whole, the state is neither organically, nor mechanically linked to parts of society; in order to exist, states must take the initiative of making the gift—the distribution of welfare—finding opportunities to enter into such gift exchanges with individuals on the grounds of market failures. Individuals receiving the stated gift of welfare, then have the duty to discharge their social responsibilities in order to close the relationship.

Thus, we may see the origin of workfare in the U.S. as an extension of public assistance in the context of a society which is quite different from France. We think that the specific character of the French equivalent of WTW schemes implemented in the past years has to be ascribed to the differences between both countries' systems of values. The adoption of the U.S. style of workfare in the French setting is then doubtful. French reforms over the last fifteen years reflect more of what can be termed "work-to-welfare" than "welfare-to-work" in the context of our present comparison.

## Note

1. All the figures in this chapter for costs in French Francs will be given in constant 1995 FF.

## References


Afsa, C. (1996). Les prestations familiales: quelle complexité (!) (?). Recherches et prévisions CNAF, 43, 67-77.

Aillet, V. (1998). La force symbolique de l'allocation de parent isolé. Recherches et prévisions CNAF, 50-51, 7-15.

Alfandari, É. (1989). Action et aide sociale. Paris: Dalloz.

Amira, S. (1996). L'indemnisation du chômage en France de 1985 à 1994 (pp. 446-452). In INSEE (eds.), Données sociales 1996. La société française. Paris: Author.

Amrouni, I. & Math, A. (1998). Quelques caractéristiques démographiques des bénéficiaires de minima sociaux. Recherches et prévisions CNAF, 50-51, 27-40.

Amrouni, I. & Math, A. (1998). Une part importante des bénéficiaires des minima sociaux les perçoit à un taux réduit. Recherches et prévisions CNAF, 50-51, 49-59.

Anspach, M. (1996). L'archipel du welfare américain, âge d'abondance, âge de pierre. *Revue du MAUSS semestrielle*, 7, 37-83.

Aubert, B. (1998). Seuils de pauvreté et montants des minima sociaux. Recherches et prévisions CNAF, 50-51, 69-79.

Audirac, P. & Rattier, M. (1996). Aide sociale départementale: Le paradoxe de la croissance (pp. 458-467). In INSEE (eds.), Données sociales 1996. La société française. Paris: Author.

Barbier, J.C. (1995). Politiques publiques de l'emploi: De la production de services à leur évaluation, *Cahiers du Centre d'études de l'emploi*, 34, 79-102.

Barbier, J.C. (1996.). Comparer insertion et workfare, *Revue française des affaires sociales,* 4, 7-26.

Barbier, J.C. (1997a). Le plein emploi au Royaume Uni ? *CEE- 4 Pages,* n° 23, septembre, 4 p.

Barbier, J.C. (1997b). *Les politiques de l'emploi en Europe*. Collection Domino. Paris: Flammarion.

Barbier, J.C. (1998a). A propos des usages de l'évaluation dans le cadre du Fonds social européen objectif 3 en France. communication à la Conférence européenne sur les pratiques d'évaluation en matière de politiques structurelles, Séville, 16-17 mars, 17 p.

Barbier, J.C. (1998b). La logique du " workfare " dans les politiques sociales en Europe et aux Etats Unis: Limites des analyses universalistes, *L'Assistenza Sociale*, n° 1/1998, Roma, 22 p.
Barbier, J.C. & Simonin, B. (March, 1997). European social programmes: Can evaluation of implementation increase the appropriateness of findings? Paper presented at the Conference of the European Evaluation society, Stockholm, (publié dans *Evaluation*, Vol. 3, n°4, October 1997, p. 391-407).
Barthe, M., Gazier, B., Leprince, F., & Noguès, H. (1992). Protection sociale et RMI. Paris: SYROS.
Bec, C. (1998). L'assistance en démocratie. Paris: Bélin.
Belorgey, J.M. (1996). Pour renouer avec l'esprit initial du RMI. In *Revue du MAUSS semestrielle*, 7, 297-299.
Brudney, J.L. & England, R.E. (1983). Towards a definition of the coproduction concept. *Public Administration Review*, 43, 59-65.
Caisse Nationale des Allocations Familiales. (1996). Prestations familiales recettes - dépenses - bénéficiaires année1996. Statistiques CAF et tous régimes. Paris: CNAF.
Castel, R. (1995). *Les métamorphoses de la question sociale, une chronique du salariat.* Paris: Fayard.
Castel, R. (1998). Du travail social à la gestion sociale du non-travail. *Esprit*, 28-47.
Chauchard, J. (1994). *Droit de la sécurité sociale*. Paris: LGDJ.
Chaupain, S. & Guillot, O. (1998). Au sortir de l'allocation de parent isolé. Résultats d'une enquête auprès des allocataires de Meurthe-et-Moselle. Recherches et prévisions CNAF, 50-51, 17-25.
Chen, H.T. (1990). *Theory-driven evaluation.* London: Sage.
Commission nationale d'évaluation du revenu minimum d'insertion. (1992). RMI, le pari de l'insertion, 2 tomes, Documentation française, Paris.
Concialdi, P. (1997). Les bas salaires en France, 1983-95. Document de travail, 97-2, IRES, septembre, 54 p.
Conseil supérieur de l'emploi, des revenus et des coûts. (1997). Minima sociaux. Entre protection et insertion. Paris: La documentaton française.
CREDOC. (1996). Les nouveaux arrivants au revenu minimum d'insertion. *Rapport*, 173, 165.
CREDOC. (1997). L'insertion par l'activité économique, renouer avec le travail, mais rarement avec un emploi stable. *Consommation et modes de vie*, 121, 4.
DARES. (1996a). L'insertion professionnelle des allocataires du RMI de 1989 à 1995, par B (171-174). In Charbonneau & F. Landais (eds.), Bilan de la politique de l'emploi en 1995, *Dossier DARES,* Vol. 8-9.
DARES. (1996b). *40 ans de politique de l'emploi*. Paris: La Documentation française.
DARES. (1997a). *La politique publique de l'emploi*. Paris: La Découverte.
DARES. (1997b). Après un CES ou un SIFE. *Premières informations, 97*.
DARES. (1997c). Les contrats initiative emploi en 1996. *Premières Informations*, 97, 8-33.
DARES. (1997d). Le devenir des salariés passés par une entreprise d'insertion. *Premières informations,* 97.
DARES. (1997e). Le devenir des salariés des associations intermédiaires. *Premières informations*, 97.
Delhoume, B. (1995). L'aide sociale (pp. 67-74). In M. de Montalembert (Ed.), *La protection sociale. Les notices*. Paris: La documentation française.
Delhoume, B. (1995). L'aide sociale à l'enfance (pp. 75-80). In M. de Montalembert (Ed.), *La protection sociale. Les notices*. Paris: La documentation française.
Donzelot, J. & Roman J. (1998). 1972-98, les nouvelles donnes du social, *Esprit*, 7-27.
Duran, P., Monnier, E., & Smith, A. (1995). Evaluation *à la française*: Towards a new relationship between social science and public action, Vol. 1, p. 45-64.

Esping-Andersen, G. (1990). *The three worlds of welfare capitalism*. Cambridge: Polity Press.

Employment Policy Institute. (1998). *Employment Audit*, 6.

Esping Andersen, G. (1996). Welfare States in transition: National adaptations in global economies. London: Sage.

Fay, R.G. (1996). *Enhancing the effectiveness of active labour market policies (ALMP): Evidence from programme evaluations in the OECD countries* (labor market and social policy occasional papers). Paris: OECD.

Friot, B. (1998). *Puissances du salariat. Emploi et protection sociale à la française*. Paris: La Dispute.

Friot, B. & Rose J. (1996). *La construction sociale de l'emploi en France*. Paris: L'Harmattan.

Gazier, B. (1996). Evolution des marchés du travail et des politiques d'emploi: Vers une approche comparative (pp. 225-233). In B. Friot and J. Rose (eds.), La construction sociale de l'emploi en France. Paris: L'Harmattan.

Gomel, B. & Simonin, B. (1995). L'utilité du contrat emploi-solidarité, *Lettre du CEE*, 35, 12.

Gough, I., Bradshaw, J., Ditch, J., Eardley, T., & Whiteford, P. (1997). Social assistance in OECD countries. *Journal of European Social Policies*, 7, 17-43.

Gourio, F. & Volovitch, P. (1996). La protection sociale (pp. 432-445). In INSEE (eds.), *Données sociales 1996. La société française*. Paris: Author.

Guibentif, P. & Bouget, D. (1997). *Les politiques du revenu minimum d'insertion dans l'Union européenne*. Lisbonne: Unico das Mutualidades Portuguesas.

Jankéliowitch-Laval, É. & Math, A. (1998). Revenus minima garantis et incittion au travail: Une comparaison internationale. *Recherches et prévisions CNAF*, 50-51, 81-107.

Join-Lambert, M., Bolot-Gittler, A., Daniel, C., Lenoir, D., Meda, D. (1997). *Politiques sociales*. Paris: Presses de Sciences Po et Dalloz.

King D. (1995). *Actively seeking work: The politics of unemployment and welfare policy in the United States and Great Britain*. Chicago: University of Chicago Press.

Lamiot, D. & Lancry, P. (1989). La protection sociale. Les enjuex de la solidarité. Paris: Nathan.

Lebeaupin, A. (1996). L'aide à domicile: Des prestations matérielles croissantes (pp. 474-479). In INSEE (eds.), *Données sociales 1996. La société française*. Paris: Author.

Lebeaupin, A., Nortler, F. (1996). Les personnes âgées dépendantes: Situation actuelle et perspective d'avenir (pp. 468-473). In INSEE (eds.), *Données sociales. La société française*. Paris: Author.

Leca, J. (February, 1997). L'évaluation comme intervention, sciences sociales et pratiques administratives et politiques. Paper presented at L'évaluation des politiques publiques, GAPP-CNRS-ENS, Cachan.

Madec, A. & Murard, N. (1995). *Citoyenneté et politiques sociales*. Paris: Flammarion.

Maquart, B. (1995). Le chômage (pp. 101-107). In M. de Montalembert (ed.), La protection sociale. Les notices. Paris: La documentation française.

Marie, H. (1995). Les handicapés (pp. 31-35). In M. de Montalembert (ed.), *La protection sociale. Les notices*. Paris: La documentation française.

Mathieu, F., Renouard, S., & Yakubovitch, Y. (1998). Les allocataires de l'AAH, de l'API et du RMI au 31 décembre 1996. *Recherches et prévisions CNAF*, 50-51, 61-67.

Maurice, M., Sellier F., & Silvestre J. (1982). *Politique d'éducation et organisation industrielle en France et en Allemagne, essai d'analyse sociétale*. Paris: PUF.

Maurice, M. (1989). Méthode comparative et analyse sociétale: Les implications théoriques des comparaisons internationales. *Sociologie du travail*, 2, 175-191.

Meunier, P. (1996). Le recensement des allocataires des Caisses d'allocations familiales. Résultats au 31 décembre 1995 et évolutions sur les dernières années. *Recherches et prévisions CNAF*, 45, 57-63.

Meunier, P. (1997). Le recensement des allocataires des CAF au 31 décembre. Analyse des évolutions annuelles par prestation. *Recherches et prévisions CNAF*, 48, 65-69.

Ministère de l'emploi et de la solidarité. (1997). *Les revenus sociaux. Solidarité Santé. Études statistiques*. Paris: La documentation française.

Monnier, E. (1992). Evaluations de l'action des pouvoirs publics (2nd edition). Paris: Economica.

Morel, S. (1996a). France et Etats Unis, les politiques d'insertion et de *workfare* en matière d'assistance sociale, *Interventions Économiques*, 27, 47-75.

Morel, S. (1996b). L'évaluation des politiques sociales aux Etats-Unis: L'exemple des programmes d'intégration à l'emploi pour les allocataires de l'assistance sociale. *Politiques et management public*, 14, 33-58.

Morel, S. (1996c). La contrepartie dans la protection sociale américaine. *Revue française des affaires sociales*, 4, 61-88.

Morel, S. (1997). Le worfare et l'insertion: une application du cadre théorique commonsien (pp. 211-231). In *Les avancées théoriques en économie sociale et leurs applications*, XVIIe Journées de l'Association d'Economie Sociale, 11-12 septembre, Dijon: IREDU-LATEC.

ODAS. (1998). 1983-1998, Quinze ans de décentralisation. In *La Lettre de l'ODAS*, May 1st.

O' Reilly, J. (1996). Theoretical considerations in cross-national employment research (Discussion Paper, WZB, FS I 96 203).

Paugam, S. (1997). *La disqualification sociale. Essai sur la nouvelle pauvreté*. Paris: PUF.

Raymond, M. (1995). Pauvreté, précarité, RMI (pp. 37-44). In M. de Montalembert (ed.), La protection sociale. Les notices. Paris: La documentation française.

Recherches et Prévisions. (1998). Eclairages sur les minima sociaux. CNAF.

La Revue du Mauss semestrielle. (1996). Vers un revenu minimum inconditionnel? 7, Paris: La Découverte/Mauss.

Revue française des affaires sociales. (1996a). La contrepartie: entre droits et créances. 3, Paris: Ministère du travail et des affaires sociales

Revue française des affaires sociales. (1996b). La contrepartie: les expériences nationales. 4, Paris: Ministère du travail et des affaires sociales.

Rein, M., & Rainwater, L. (eds.) (1986). Public/private interplay in social protection. A comparative study. Armonk: Sharpe.

Rodgers, C. S. (1981). Work tests for welfare recipients: The gap between the goal and the reality. *Journal of Policy Analysis and Management*, 1, 5-17.

Schmid, G., O'Reilly, J., & Schöman, K. (1996). *International handbook of labour market policy and evaluation*. Cheltenham: Edward Elgar.

Schmid, G. (1997). The evaluation of labour market policy: Notes on the state of the art. *Evaluation*, 3, 409-434.

SESI. (1995). Profils des signataires et nature des contrats d'insertion du RMI. *Documents statistiques*, 220.

Théret, B. (1996a). Les structures élémentaires de la protection sociale. *Revue francaise des affaires sociales*, 4, 165-188.

Théret, B. (1996b). De la comparabilité des systèmes nationaux de protection sociale: essai d'analyse structurale (pp. 439-503). In MIRE–Rencontres et Recherches, *Comparer les systémes de protection socialeen Europe, Vol. II, Rencontres de Berlin*. Paris: MIRE.

Théret, B. (1997). Méthodologie des comparaisons internationales, approches de l'effet sociétal et de la régulation: fondements pour une lecture structuraliste des systémes de protection sociale. *L'année de la regulation*, 1, 163-228.

Théret, B. (1998). L'État-providence a l'épreuve des comparaisons internationales (pp. 114-130). In P. Auvergnon, P. Martin, P. Rozenblatt, & M. Tallard (eds.), *L'État a l'épreuve du social*. Paris: Syllepses.

Thévenet, A. (1992). L'aide sociale en France. Paris: PUF.
Vernières, M. (1997). L'insertion professionnelle, analyses et débats. Paris: Economica.
Viossat, L. (1995). La sécurité sociale (pp. 57-64). In M. de Montalembert (ed.), La protection sociale. Les notices. Paris: La documentation française.
Viossat, L. (1995). Protection sociale et institutions sociales (pp. 51-56). In M. de Montalembert (ed.), La protection sociale. Les notices. Paris: La documentation française.

# 6

# Moving People from Welfare to Work in the United States

*Neung-Hoo Park and Rebecca A. Van Voorhis*

## Background: Welfare Dimensions

Social policy in the United States has a long-standing tradition of using social assistance based programs for the provision of aid to needy families. The federal program of Aid to Dependent Children (ADC), introduced as part of the original Social Security Act in 1935, was designed to support poor children without fathers. Eligibility for the ADC benefit was means-tested and recipients were primarily widows and their dependent children. Policy makers predicted that the ADC program would be eliminated or at least diminished over time as more people became vested in the social insurance programs of the Social Security Act. However, the ADC caseload did not decline—it remained relatively constant from 1935 to the early 1960s. In 1962, the ADC program was renamed Aid to Families with Dependent Children (AFDC), which reflected a change in policy intended to protect the family unit. (Prior to this time, children were ineligible for aid if an unemployed yet able-bodied parent/father was living in the home. The policy effectively established desertion as a condition for AFDC eligibility, inspiring lawmakers to establish AFDC-UP [AFDC-Unemployed Parent].)

Like ADC, AFDC was a federally mandated program that allowed states to define need, set benefit levels and administer the program. Federal funds covered between 50 and 80 percent of total costs (both benefits and administration), with individual states paying the remainder. The proportion of state financial responsibility was determined by a formula which allowed states with lower per capita income to receive more federal financing than wealthier states. States determined need standards, and families were ineligible for receiving any aid if they earned more than 185 percent of the gross income limit. States were also allowed to set benefit levels, resulting in a high degree of regional variation. For example, in 1996 prior to the enactment of the welfare reform, the monthly maximum AFDC cash benefit for a family of three ranged from $923 in Alaska to $120 in Mississippi (Gallagher et. al., 1998).

The name change to AFDC occurred at the same time that the federal government was launching the "War on Poverty" programs, dedicated to reducing poverty in the U.S. Between 1960 and 1970, the AFDC caseload increased dramatically from 1.7 to 4.1 percent of the population (U.S. Social Security Administration, 1961; U.S. House of Representatives, 1997). There have been two AFDC caseload explosions since 1968. The initial increase occurred from the late 1960s through the early 1970s, when the economy was strong and the general poverty rate was shrinking. This growth is explained by the liberalization of the AFDC program, an increase in the real value of welfare benefits (Moffitt, 1992), expanded eligibility criteria (Bane and Ellwood, 1994), and a reduction in the stigma attached to welfare recipiency due to its association with the civil rights movement (Illig, 1993). The second increase between 1989 and 1993 is attributable to the growth of female-headed households and, to a lesser extent, the weak economy (Peskin, et al., 1993). Besharov (1996) is more specific, linking the growth in out-of-wedlock births and the breakdown of traditional family structures to inflated welfare rolls, citing census survey research that indicates 70 percent of the new caseload between 1989 and 1991 were never-married mothers (Gabe, 1992). While the number of welfare users reached an all time high in 1992, the national caseload has declined by 44 percent since the passage of the Personal Responsibility and Work Opportunity Act in 1996 (U.S. Department of Health and Human Services, 1999).

The interrelationship between cost and caseload is complicated. Between 1970 and 1993, the number of recipients increased 91 percent, from 7.4 to 14.1 million. The number of families receiving aid increased 163 percent during the same time period, indicating a decrease in the size of the average family on AFDC. As the caseload grew, costs also rose although not proportionally to the number of recipients. When controlling for inflation, federal benefit expenditures increased 44 percent from $15.5 billion in 1970 to $22.3 billion in 1993, with the total bill for AFDC peaking at $26.7 billion in 1976. After 1976, AFDC costs fluctuated between $20 billion and $25 billion, as the caseload continued to grow. These figures include expenditures for both benefits and administrative costs. While the percentage of expenditure devoted to administration has decreased from 19 percent in 1970 to 13 percent in 1993, after accounting for inflation the average monthly benefit per family declined by 45 percent during the same period of time (U.S. House of Representatives, 1994).

Despite the sizable debate surrounding the AFDC program, the proportional cost of AFDC compared to other public expenditures is quite small. For example, the $22.3 billion spent for AFDC benefits in 1993 constituted 1.6 percent of total social welfare expenditures and 10.1 percent in public aid expenditures (U.S. Social Security Administration, 1996; U.S. House of Representatives, 1996).

However, public disapproval had less to do with the cost of the program than with the concern that welfare usage was becoming a way of life for many recipients. Bane and Ellwood (1994) found that while 36.1 percent of welfare recipients collected AFDC for less than two consecutive years during a 21-year window, another 29 percent were recipients for more than 8 years, with an overall average length of 6.2 years for all recipients. Furthermore, long-term users were less likely to leave AFDC permanently, and more likely to re-enter the rolls even after exiting for short periods of time. A related concern is that of inter-generational welfare usage. Several studies found a positive correlation between a mother's welfare use and the subsequent use by their daughters (Gottshalk, 1990; Hill and O'Neill, 1991).

## The Shift to Workfare

The precipitous caseload growth that began in the early 1960s fueled a national debate on the program, which critics accused of fostering problems of motivation, out-of-wedlock teenage pregnancies and dependency. Various legislative attempts to curb welfare dependency were promulgated throughout the 1960s, 1970s, and 1980s. One of the first efforts to address this problem was the 1962 Amendment to the Social Security Act which extended rehabilitative services to AFDC clients. Using the "casework approach," social workers visited recipients' homes, inspected the environment, evaluated clients' needs, and intervened in the recipients' problems. These services were expected to reduce welfare and promote the return of clients to the work force. Instead, however, the AFDC caseload climbed by almost 1 million recipients between 1962 and 1966, an outcome which served to heighten concerns about the problem of dependency (Day, 1989; Bane and Ellwood, 1994).

The disappointing results of the casework strategy led to the 1967 Amendments of the Social Security Act, which authorized the Work Incentive (WIN) program. WIN aimed to make work more attractive than welfare by employing a "carrot and stick" strategy. The carrot involved lowering the "benefit reduction rate" from 100 percent to 67 percent, which allowed working AFDC families to retain part of their earnings while continuing to receive assistance. The stick imposed work requirements—AFDC parents whose children were over the age of 6 were required to register with employment programs and to accept jobs when offered. Any adult who refused to participate in required work-related activities could be disqualified from receiving AFDC benefits, unless incapacitated or needed at home. The threat of disqualification, however, was a stick rarely employed to force clients to work.

The Omnibus Budget Reconciliation Act (OBRA) of 1981 reinforced the WIN emphasis on self-sufficiency and increased state autonomy. OBRA introduced the Community Work Experience Program (CWEP), which allowed states to require welfare recipients to participate in public work projects in exchange for the AFDC grant. OBRA also authorized 3-year WIN demonstration programs that encouraged states to design more ambitious workfare devices subject to approval by the federal government. Overall WIN was not much of a success, more often resulting in registering recipients than actually involving them in program activities or employment (Smith, Fortune, and Reid, 1975; Gueron and Pauly, 1991; Cunningham, 1993; Handler, 1995). However, a few of the WIN demonstration projects, Massachusetts Employment and Training Program (ET), California Greater Avenues to Independence (GAIN) Program in Riverside County, boasted significantly better results than the national average.

By the late 1980s, the success of some pilot projects and mounting public sentiment that favored the civic obligation to work, fueled deliberations about the future of entitlement programs in the U.S. At issue was the appropriate balance between the social right to welfare benefits and the social responsibility to be self-sufficient. This ideological discussion evolved into a practical debate as policy analysts and politicians entered the arena, which eventually led to the passage of the Family Support Act of 1988 (FSA).

The FSA sought to reform AFDC along several dimensions, with both theoretical and practical ramifications. The increasing emphasis on individual responsibility focused on welfare-to-work approaches that introduced an element of participant involvement into the welfare equation (Gueron, 1996). The FSA reform heightened efforts to connect welfare benefits and incentives to work (Gilbert, 1995). Mothers with children over the age of three were required to enroll in work-training or education programs, and to seek employment when the programs were completed. The explicit expectation was that the AFDC recipient would become self-sufficient, with the benefit of education or job-training, and thus no longer be a burden to the state. Day-care services, and a year-long continuation of Medicaid insurance were offered as incentives to assist in the transition from welfare recipient to self-sufficient employee. While most attempts to cultivate personal responsibility focused on encouraging AFDC recipients to work, another component of the FSA required that paternity be established upon the birth of a child to an AFDC mother so that fathers could be held responsible for child-support payments (Garfinkle and McLanahan, 1990).

The centerpiece of the Act—the Job Opportunity and Basic Skills (JOBS) program—was envisioned as the vehicle of deliverance from dependency to self-sufficiency for poor families. JOBS replaced the WIN programs, and required that states provide education, training and employment to needy families with children. New federal matching funds for state welfare-to-work initiatives were available. While federal policy identified goals for targeting and participation, the details of program design were left largely to the states (Gueron and Pauly, 1991). Unlike WIN, the initial outcome of JOBS-related programs was somewhat more encouraging; state projects demonstrated employment-directed services and mandates for single mothers on AFDC could be implemented effectively and show moderate rates of success in encouraging work (Gueron, 1996).

Since the advent of FSA, continuous efforts have been made to define the parameters of both rights and responsibilities in relation to welfare benefits. While the contested boundaries are subject to political, social and fiscal influences, there appears to be no retreat from the initial movement toward balancing the equation in favor of personal responsibility. Attempts to formulate a normative consensus concerning rights and obligations dominated the welfare policy discourse in the 1990s. Although the debate tended to reflect conservative rhetoric, it is important to note that there was bipartisan support for exacting obligations from public aid recipients. President Clinton's 1992 campaign promise "to end welfare as we know it" focused shifting the balance toward the obligation to be self-sufficient (Ellwood, 1996). The defection from welfare advocacy by the Democratic party signified a dramatic movement which some suggest has left the poor without a voice (Teles, 1996).

The Personal Responsibility and Work Opportunity Act of 1996 (PRWO) was the culmination of several decades of welfare policy adaptation and retrenchment. This Act targets the least popular and most maligned sectors of public assistance for substantial change. It affects four different federal programs—AFDC, Supplemental Security Income (SSI, means-tested public assistance for blind, aged, and disabled people), Food Stamps, and Medicaid (means-tested health insurance)—resulting in the most comprehensive welfare reform movement of the twentieth century. The most significant impact of this law was to dismantle a cornerstone of federal protection for the poor, with the elimination of AFDC—the 61-year-old federal guarantee of cash assistance for the nations' poorest families. In its place a new program was created, Temporary Assistance for Needy Families (TANF), which provides time-limited cash assistance delivered by states and funded through federal block grants. TANF places a five-year limit on public assistance to any family during their lifetime, and requires most adults to work within two years of receiving aid. However, states can both set stricter limits or exempt up to 20 percent of families from the time limit for reasons of hardship. TANF also mandates that all able-bodied adults work after two years on assistance.

In addition to the work requirement for individuals, TANF obligates states to have a specific portion of their caseload involved in work-related activities. The level of participation in work-related activities for single parents was set at 25 percent in 1997, increasing to 50 percent in 2002. For two-parent families, the required level was 75 percent in 1997 rising to 90 percent in 1999. Parents with children under age 6 may satisfy the 20-hour-per-week work condition by engaging in subsidized or unsubsidized employment, on-the-job-training, community service, vocational training, or child-care provision services to other individuals participating in community service. The minimum requirement increases to 30 hours per week for single parents without a child under age 6, and 35 hours per week for two-parent families.

While AFDC was an open-ended federal entitlement program, TANF will be funded by block grants that place a cap on the amount of federal funds available. The formula for establishing state grants is a function of prior state expenditure, allowing states to receive the greater of three alternative calculations tied to fiscal spending (APWA, 1996). While the TANF block grants restrict the amount of federal funds available, the Act affords states unprecedented authority in the design of their welfare programs. In creating block grants, policymakers sought to encourage welfare experimentation and to allow for more exact tailoring of programs to local needs and conditions (Ellwood, 1996; Kaus, 1996).

Although TANF affords states increased and expansive opportunity to run their own welfare and work programs, the federal government has not abdicated total responsibility. In order to maintain a modicum of control and continuity, provisions link federal funding to elements of state programs. To receive their full block grant allocation, states must maintain their current spending efforts at 75 percent of their 1994 spending, or 80 percent if they fail to meet work participation requirements established by the Act (Borkowski, 1996). (The parallel between state penalties for failure to meet federal goals, and harsh consequences for welfare recipients' noncompliance with work obligations, demonstrates the emerging tendency toward the use of financial sanctions to motivate organizational and individual behavior.)

Financial sanctions are also reflected in contractual obligations with welfare clients, through which the Act demands heightened responsibility and dispenses severe penalties for failure to comply. States may refuse payments to unwed teenage mothers if they do not stay in school or live with an adult; may require heads of households to secure work within two years, or lose welfare benefits; and may deny benefits to people convicted of drug felonies. The stringent work requirements linked to welfare are consistent with early attempts to move families off public aid, but move beyond prior endeavors.

Finally, TANF promotes retrenchment of public delivery through privatization. Proposals to privatize delivery of welfare benefits via a fixed-price contract with corporate sponsors offer an attractive option to states faced with decreasing budgets and financial penalties for failure to meet new employment requirements (Bernstein, 1996). In addition, many states are exploring ways to develop "partnerships" with private employers as an alternative form of privatization. For example, some states are experimenting with the use of employer wage subsidies and tax credits, which may encourage businesses to hire recipients (Kilborn, 1996). The transactions appear to benefit all parties: the employer receives a financial incentive, the recipient a job and the opportunity to develop skills, and the state the possibility of decreasing welfare enrollment. These developments reflect the states' growing acceptance of important private market principles—infusion of competition, maximization of benefit for all parties, and the need for customized services—as a means to effectuating lasting change.

## Research on Dimensions of Welfare-to-Work Leading to TANF

A vast number of studies on various aspects of welfare dependency and work-oriented public assistance reforms have been performed during the past twenty years. The studies include independent reviews of workfare programs funded by foundation and other private sources and federally mandated evaluation studies conducted by researchers under contract with the state. The studies vary in their methods, design, and evaluative criteria, often addressing and measuring different questions concerning welfare usage. Our discussion of the research leading up to TANF in this chapter will focus on five primary issues concerning: labor force participation; the effects of grant size and mandatory work requirements on employment rates; duration of aid; factors affecting the duration of aid; and programmatic variations in the attempt to move people from welfare to work.

### *Labor Force Participation*

A large number of studies have investigated the employment status of welfare recipients. Although earned income would reduce the size of their welfare benefits, AFDC recipients have been permitted to work without terminating eligibility for aid. Despite this policy, designed to permit work among recipients, official government data would suggest that while the labor force participation of the female population climbed sharply in recent decades, AFDC mothers' work force participation decreased dramatically between 1975 and 1992. As shown in table 6.1, female heads-of-household on AFDC had the lowest overall rates of employment among all women. For example in 1992, official government data show 63.9 percent of married and spouse-present women, 43.4 percent of never-married women, and 65.3 percent of divorced, separated, or widowed women were employed in 1992, while only 6 percent of AFDC mothers were employed that year. Another noticeable feature of AFDC mothers employment rate is the abrupt drop from 14 percent to 6 percent between 1981 and 1982 and the continuing stability around 6 percent, during a period when other subgroups have experienced an increasing rate of employment. The sharp decline in 1982 resulted from the implementation of OBRA in 1981, which reduced the amount of earned income a recipient could make and still qualify for the AFDC program (Moffitt, 1992). Prior to OBRA of 1981, an initial $30 in monthly earnings plus one-third of the remaining earnings, work expenses (including child care costs) were "disregarded"—that is, these earnings were not counted toward the total household income which determined the amount of the overall grant. The rationale was that disregarding income encouraged employment behavior that would lead to self-sufficiency. However, the OBRA amendments severely limited the amount of disregarded earnings and prohibited states from paying an AFDC grant to any family whose household income exceeded 150 percent of the state's standard of need. The perverse effect of the policy was to generate higher levels of welfare dependency by lowering the percentage of welfare recipients who worked for wages.

However the official data in table 6.1 do not capture non-reported work. In contrast to government accounts, some researchers have found significantly higher levels of employment among female heads of households on AFDC. As shown in table 6.2, Marcenko and Fagan (1996) report that 29 percent of welfare mothers who participated in the Head Start program held a paid job for a one-year time window. An analysis from the National Longitudinal Survey of Youth (NLSY) dataset indicates that 49.4 percent of the female recipients of AFDC, aged 27-34, participated in paid jobs during the one-year period of 1991 (O'Neill, O'Neill and Ellenoff, 1997). Harris (1993) also reports that 51 percent of the AFDC mothers had some work activity during a three-year period.

**Table 6.1**
**Percentage of Employed Mothers in Various Women's Subgroup with Children under 18**

| Year | Married, spouse present | Never married | Divorced, separated, widowed | AFDC mothers |
|---|---|---|---|---|
| 1975 | 40.5 | 32.1 | 56.8 | 16.1 |
| 1980 | 50.9 | 39.9 | 63.0 | n.a. |
| 1981 | 52.1 | 38.3 | 62.9 | 14.0 |
| 1982 | 51.6 | 36.2 | 61.9 | 6.0 |
| 1983 | 52.4 | 34.5 | 58.4 | 4.9 |
| 1984 | 54.9 | 36.3 | 62.8 | 5.0 |
| 1985 | 56.8 | 39.2 | 63.0 | n.a. |
| 1986 | 57.6 | 37.8 | 65.6 | 5.8 |
| 1987 | 60.4 | 40.2 | 66.2 | 6.0 |
| 1988 | 61.9 | 40.2 | 65.9 | 6.4 |
| 1989 | 63.1 | 43.1 | 65.9 | 6.0 |
| 1990 | 63.5 | 45.1 | 67.9 | 6.7 |
| 1991 | 63.2 | 44.0 | 66.1 | 6.4 |
| 1992 | 63.9 | 43.4 | 65.3 | 6.6 |

*Source*: O'Neill , O'Neill and Ellenoff, 1997. p. 19; The employment of AFDC mothers is from U.S. House of Representatives, each year and Moffitt, 1992.

**Table 6.2**
**Employment Rate of Various Subgroup of AFDC Mothers**

| Study | Source of data | Population | Length of time window | Employment rate |
|---|---|---|---|---|
| Marcenko & Fagan (1996) | Interview | Participants in Head Start Program | 1 year | 29% |
| O'Neill, O'Neill & Ellenoff (1997) | NSYL: 1991 | Aged 27-34 | 1 year | 49.4% |
| Harris (1993) | PSID: 1984-1986 | All AFDC mothers | 3 year | 51% |

Note: NSYL: National Longitudinal Survey of Youth; PSID: Panel Study of Income Dynamics.

Welfare mothers receive payment for employment in cash and in-kind, and undertake work in the formal and informal labor market (Kemp, et al., 1996). Payments in-kind for which valuation can be difficult, are unlikely to be reported as income. Similarly, cash payments in cash from the informal labor market (which includes both legitimate work and illegal underground work) are often not reported to the welfare office in order to avoid grant reduction. Strong evidence corroborates these findings that a large proportion of AFDC mothers did not report work activities. Data from in-depth interviews revealed that whereas only 2 percent of welfare mothers in Boston and 9 percent in Charleston reported employment, an additional 44 percent of welfare mothers in Boston and 36 percent in Charleston were involved in paid jobs which were not reported to the welfare office (Edin and Lein, 1997). The authors observed similar situations in two other cities, as shown in table 6.3.

Edin and Lein's 1997 study suggests that estimates of AFDC employments based on administrative data are significantly lower than the actual employment rates. The high rates of unreported work suggest that despite work-oriented reforms up through the early 1990s AFDC programs placed few demands on welfare recipients and rarely monitored their compliance with the requirement to report income.

### *Effect of Grant Size on Employment*

A second area of research concerns the extent to which the grant size affects welfare rolls. Several empirical studies have analyzed the effects of changing the maximum benefit level on labor force participation. The Seattle/Denver Income Maintenance Experiments (SIME/DIME) conducted between 1971 and 1978 provided inter-

**Table 6.3**
**Percentage of Welfare Mothers Involved in Various Work Activities in Four U.S. Cities**

| | Boston | Chicago | Charleston | San Antonio |
|---|---|---|---|---|
| Total | 44 | 60 | 36 | 41 |
| Reported work | 2 | 2 | 9 | 6 |
| Unreported work | 36 | 52 | 32 | 35 |
| Underground work | 7 | 19 | 2 | 3 |

Note: Percentage for subcategories will not sum to total percentages because of mothers engaged in multiple work activities. *Source*: Edin and Lein, 1997. Table 3.

esting data on the behavior of the poor with respect to labor supply (SRI International, 1983). The SIME/DIME projects were the largest, most complicated and most scientifically controlled income-maintenance experiments ever conducted. Using an experimental design, nearly 5,000 families were enrolled as subjects, 44 percent of whom were assigned to a control group with the remainder distributed among eleven experimental groups. Participants in each experimental group received three different levels of guaranteed income, and were taxed at varying rates. After three years of treatment, the results showed that labor force participation of single female heads of household in the experimental group was 50 percent lower than that of the control groups, which received no guaranteed incomes (SRI International 1983, p.122). Although the median AFDC grant ($187 per month or $2,244 in 1971 dollars) was less than the minimum guaranteed level of the SIME/DIME ($3,800 in 1971 dollars) the findings suggest that any guaranteed income provides a negative work incentive (U.S. Social Security Association, 1997).

Wiseman (1984) examined the effects of changes in the benefit level on AFDC recipients' work efforts, utilizing historical variations in welfare parameters in Alameda County, California, from 1968 to 1981. Participants were observed at the end of each of two consecutive three-month periods, and a person was counted as employed if she was employed at either of those two sampling times. Wiseman's results showed that a 10 percent increase in the benefit level reduced the probability of employment by 25 percent when all other variables were held constant.

Within a somewhat longer time frame, Moffitt (1992) also investigated the effects of AFDC grant amounts on the labor force participation rate. Because AFDC guaranteed benefits have fluctuated annually, the rate of employment in each year itself may represent an effect of the AFDC grant level. Moffitt's study concluded that there is no apparent relationship between the employment rate of welfare recipients and the level of AFDC benefits. However, it should be noted that there are many factors which affect the employment rate of welfare recipients that were not controlled in Moffitt's study.

An alternative way of manipulating grant size involves the mechanism of the benefit reduction rate (BRR), which was altered twice in the history of the AFDC program. The BRR is the amount the AFDC benefit is reduced for each dollar earned. The first change lowered the BRR from 100 percent to 67 percent in 1967, and in 1981 the

BRR was restored to 100 percent (as previously noted in table 6.1, employment of AFDC mothers declined dramatically after 1981). These changes provided good opportunities to investigate the precise effect of the benefit reduction rate on the employment of welfare recipients by simulating a quasi-experimental design. The traditional economic assumption is that a lower benefit reduction rate will encourage employment among AFDC recipients by not penalizing work.

Garfinkle and Orr's (1974) study using national cross-sectional data from the 1967 AFDC Survey, found that a 35 percent decrease in the benefit reduction rate increased the employment rate by 5 percent. However, given the fact that Garfinkle and Orr treated variations across states as if they were variations among individuals under the same AFDC benefit rules, the results of their analysis should be viewed with caution.

Using 1968 data from the Panel Study of Income Dynamics, Levy (1979) examined the labor force participation rate of all female household heads with children instead of confining the analysis only to AFDC recipients. Levy found that a reduction in the tax rate rarely induced nonworking AFDC recipients to join the labor force. Instead, the increased break-even level caused by the lower BRR made a number of initially ineligible families newly eligible for AFDC, and confronted them with new work disincentives. Thus, a lowering of the benefit reduction rate can decrease labor force participation on net if a decline in the labor force participation by those newly eligible to receive AFDC outweighs the increased work effort of those initially on the AFDC rolls. However, it should be underlined that Levy is not arguing that the benefit rate reduction decreases the work incentive of existing welfare recipients. His claim is that overall labor force participation of female household heads with children may decrease by reducing the 100 percent tax-rate, i.e., the dollar-for-dollar tax on welfare benefits for each dollar earned.

Hutchens (1986) examined the effects of the increase in the benefit reduction rate that occurred in 1981. After analyzing six data sets derived from different sources, including the General Accounting Office Study, the Institute for Research on Poverty Study, and the Minnesota Study, he found different effects according to the initial working status of the welfare recipients. For initially working recipients, the increased BRR did not lower their propensity to work. For people who were initially nonworking welfare recipients, the increased BRR reduced the possibility that they would participate in the labor force. The studies of Levy (1979) and Hutchens (1986) provide complimentary perspectives on the impact of changing BRRs. Their findings suggest that although raising the benefit reduction rate does not affect the work activities of welfare recipients, who were already participating in the labor force, it will dampen the propensity to work for welfare recipients who were not initially employed in the labor market. Conversely, if the BRR is lowered, the possibility increases that initially nonworking welfare recipients will seek employment, but those welfare recipients who are working are unlikely to increase efforts to find a job.

Hutchens' study also provides interesting implications for the average earnings of welfare recipients. When the BRR is reduced, if an increase of employment occurs mainly in the initially nonworking group while the initially working group does not increase its hours of employment, there is a possibility that the *average amount* of earnings of *all working* welfare recipients will not increase even though more welfare recipients participate in labor market. This is because a larger number of newcomers into the job market usually earn less than those already working, which reduces the overall average earnings of workers.

### *Duration of Aid and Welfare Dynamics*

Since the mid-1970s, a number of studies have increased our understanding of the dynamics of welfare use. Bane and Ellwood's (1983) work on welfare dynamics refuted the widely held assumption that most recipients experienced welfare dependency in a similar way. Instead, Bane and Ellwood found the welfare population to be heterogeneous in terms of its length of use. In their initial research using the Panel Study of Income Dynamics (PSID) over a 12-year period, Bane and Ellwood (1983) provided a longitudinal dynamic analysis of patterns of welfare use. They examined 554 AFDC spells that began between 1968 and 1979, and found that about half of all welfare spells last 2 years or less and that two-thirds of all spells end within 4 years. Only a relatively small fraction of recipients—17 percent—have spells lasting 8 or more years. It should be noted that they analyzed only the first spell instead of total time of welfare use in this study. By looking only at the duration of a single spell of welfare, one ignores the fact that the recipient may have previously been on welfare or that she may use it again after the current spell ends. Considering the problem of single spell analysis, Ellwood (1986) updated the first study with 15-year PSID data, and once again Bane and Ellwood (1994) updated with 21-year PSID data, focusing on welfare recidivism and multiple spells.

As previously noted, the latest results show that 36.1 percent of welfare recipients stayed less than 2 years on welfare during the 21-year time window, while 29 percent stayed more than 8 years on the welfare rolls; the overall average length of receipt was 6.2 years, a noticeably longer duration than the first study. Bane and Ellwood (1994) explain this discrepancy by recidivism. Many women who leave welfare return to the rolls. Recidivism is more common in the first few years, which means the longer recipients stay off welfare the less likely they are to return. During the six years following exit, 32 percent of those who leave welfare will have returned.

O'Neill, Wolf, Bassi, and Hannan (1984) provided a comparable analysis to Bane and Ellwood's first study, both repeating their analysis on the PSID and using the National Longitudinal Survey (NSL) and AFDC case records. Their findings from the three data sets were very similar to each other but somewhat different from those of Bane and Ellwood. About half of all spells end within a year, 16-18 percent last five years, and 5-7 percent go for ten years. These results indicate considerably higher exit rates in the first few years of welfare receipt than those observed by Bane and Ellwood. They suggest that the difference comes from the fact that Bane and Ellwood, from their analysis, observed welfare cases that reported receipt of less than $250 in benefits in one year.

Although these studies conveyed a good picture of welfare dynamics, they had one drawback. They all used annual data, which provides information only on whether a household received any welfare benefits over an entire year. This approach tends to produce an image of longer and more continuous spells on AFDC than occur in reality.

Boskin and Nold (1975) conducted one of the early studies using monthly data from the State of California AFDC five-year survey of 440 California households that began receiving benefits in 1965. They found that the median length of total time for a household to receive welfare was 14 months and only 17 percent of the cohort received welfare for the entire 60 months.

Another study conducted by Plotnick (1983) used monthly information from the Denver Income Maintenance Experiment (DIME) covering the period from January 1971 to December 1974. His analysis of 384 spells including multiple spells showed an average welfare duration of 20 months, much less than the result from the annual data. However, Plotnick's findings should be interpreted with caution; because the DIME data set covers a relatively short time period—48 months—it could not avoid the problems of censoring time periods from both sides. Left censoring occurred because many cases were already on welfare in January 1971 and their starting dates were unknown. Right censoring occurred when many cases did not leave welfare before December 1974 and their ending dates were unknown.

Blank (1989) also used monthly data from the Seattle/Denver Income Maintenance Experiments (SIME/DIME) to analyze welfare spells, but she expanded the time frame to 72 months and took only the first spell, which means she excluded second and thereafter spells. Among the total 508 spells observed as a first spell, 323 (64 percent) were completed during the 72 months, and the residual 185 (36 percent) were right censored. Her analysis shows that the average length of first completed spells was 13.3 months, significantly shorter than Plotnick's result. It also shows that 62 percent of completed spells occurred within the first 12 months. Even if we consider the right censoring of the data, the high exit rate is somewhat striking.

Beginning in 1984, the Panel Study of Income Dynamics (PSID) survey, which had been an important source of yearly data, began to collect retrospective reports of monthly welfare receipt and employment status for the previous year. Using this monthly information from PSID, Harris (1993) analyzed 238 spells with observed beginnings over a 36-month period from January 1984 to December 1986, which means she excluded the left censored spells. Of the 238 spells with observed beginnings, 116 spells (48.7 percent) were true first spells and 122 spells were returned cases. Her findings show that almost half (51.2 percent) of all spells ended by 18 months. Beyond 2 years of receipt, however, the rates of welfare exit declined dramatically so that 31 percent did not end the spell within a 36-month time window.

Barton and Pillai (1994) analyzed data from the Wisconsin Department of Health and Social Services' Computer Reporting Network (CRN), which contains a monthly record of AFDC cases. They chose cases that experienced the start of a spell between April 1987 and September 1989, a time window of 30 months. They did not consider whether the case is a true first spell case or a returned spell case. They included only the first observed spell and assumed that the spell ended at the last month of the observed period if it was still on welfare. Under these restrictions and assumption, they found that median spell length of the AFDC-FG case was 10.4 months, and for the AFDC-U case it was 6.4 months.

In general, by illuminating the dynamics of welfare use, these various studies have helped policy makers to distinguish at least three categories of welfare users: those who come on for a relatively short term and then go on to achieve self-sufficiency; those who stay on the rolls continuously for many years, and those who exit the rolls for a period of time and then return—cycling in and out of welfare.

*Determinants of Length of Spell*

Boskin and Nold (1975) found that persons facing the prospect of very low wages and/or high rates of unemployment in the labor market are less likely to leave welfare and more likely to return to welfare. They also found that nonwage income and race affect spell durations: for persons with more nonwage income the duration on welfare was shorter than for those with less nonwage income; whites were more likely to leave the welfare rolls in the short term than nonwhites.

A somewhat broader model, developed by Bane and Ellwood (1994), reveals five characteristics of welfare recipients that have strong relationships with the length of welfare spells: Race, education, marital status, work experience, and disability status. They found that women who have never been married at the time they begin their first spell of AFDC will spend 6.1 continuous years on the welfare rolls during this spell, while married women will spend only 1.7 years in their first spell. Those five variables also have a substantial influence on recidivism. For instance, for the never-married women, average duration of repeated spells is 3.0 years, but it is 1.4 years for the married women. On the other hand, Bane and Ellwood's study indicates that the age of the female head, the age of the youngest child, and the number of children in a household did not affect the length of spell.

Along this same line, O'Neill, et. al., (1984) found that an individual's market productivity, an individual's attitude, amount of

AFDC guarantee, and economic cycle as well as number of children, education, marital status, and race are important factors affecting the length of spell. The results are quite similar to Bane and Ellwood's except for the effect of children. Although Bane and Ellwood's analysis shows no significant effect of number of children or age of children, O'Neill et. al. found that the number of children is negatively related to the exit rate and the effect is strong. Regarding the effect of program parameters, they found that a higher AFDC guarantee lowers exit rates.

Plotnick (1983) included 11 variables in his estimation model including age, race, education, guarantee level, wage, and other income. Of those variables, age of female head-of-household, guarantee level, and nonwage income significantly affect the exit rate. For the entry rate, those three variables and the expected wage are important. He found the same result as O'Neill et. al. for the effect of the guarantee level: Given the wage rate, a higher guaranteed level of welfare benefit increases the duration of spells on welfare significantly, while it decreases the duration of spells off welfare.

Blank (1989) also found that age of female head-of-household, race, and other income are important variables in determining the duration of welfare spells, confirming the results of previous studies. However, her findings that education, guarantee level, and unemployment rate did not significantly affect the duration of welfare spells were somewhat contradictory to other studies.

Harris (1993) focused on exits occurring through work. She found that women who have smaller families, have finished high school, have more advantaged family backgrounds, are younger, and are never-married are more likely to leave the welfare rolls when they work, while women who have more children, fewer family resources, and less human capital are more likely to remain on welfare even when they get jobs. The finding that never-married women are more likely to leave welfare when they work than married women appears to contradict the fact that never-married women have longer welfare spells. However, the probability of never-married women working is much lower than that of married women, so on average they stay on welfare longer.

In summary, a number of studies have investigated the demographic and psychosocial characteristics of welfare recipients as well as AFDC policy parameters and socioeconomic variables that might help explain why women remain on welfare for varying lengths of time. A common finding was that higher guaranteed levels of support prolong the spell of welfare use, while reducing the length of time off welfare. These studies also showed that other variables including education, race, work experience, marital status, other income, economic cycle, age of female head-of-household, and number of children significantly affect length of welfare spell.

**Evaluation of Programs to Move People from Welfare to Work**

Finally, many studies have compared the results of different welfare reform projects. One of the most comprehensive efforts is an analysis conducted by the General Accounting Office (GAO) which summarizes the findings of ten different experimental programs in eight states seeking to move clients from welfare to work (GAO, 1994). A unique feature of the GAO report is the impressive experimental designs of the programs evaluated. Comparison groups and random assignment were standard features of each program, allowing for a more rigorous comparison of outcomes within and between projects. The state projects were undertaken as part of the JOBS program created by the Family Support Act of 1988, and featured varied efforts to decrease welfare usage by creating stricter work requirements, increasing work incentives, time-limiting receipt of benefits, and offering employment services and support.

The GAO found that the most successful of the programs, as measured by higher rates of employment, offered numerous employment-related activities combined with mandatory work requirements, and had sufficient funding to implement program initiatives. Table 6.4 summarizes the welfare-to-work strategies employed by the four most successful of the ten projects studied, and ranks the programs from negative to positive on four outcome criteria—earnings, employment, AFDC receipts, and AFDC payments. For each outcome of each study, treatment group participants (those receiving the program services) were compared to the control group, and where statistically significant differences were found (significance = .05 level), a program effect or outcome was designated.

All but three of the ten experiments (ASSETS, TSMF and FIP) had at least one statistically significant outcome variable. Four of the programs received a positive ranking on all four outcome variables (as shown in table 6.4), the remainder showed a positive effect on only one or two outcomes. However, since many programs provided more than one treatment to an experimental group at a time (e.g., both a mandate and income disregard), it is impossible to accurately evaluate the effectiveness of a single program feature. In order to compensate for this methodological problem, the GAO based its conclusions concerning program effectiveness on comparisons of projects with similar and dissimilar features, and by evaluating the cluster of features of the more successful program experiments. However, this introduces subjective judgments concerning the selection of features and how they are clustered.

The four most successful projects—San Diego's SWIM (Saturation Work Initiative Model), Massachusetts' ET (Employment and Training) program, California's GAIN and Riverside County's GAIN project—show statistically significant effects on all four GAO outcome variables, and provided a similar mix of employment services (including child care), education and training, and some form of mandatory participation requirement. Although the programs in Florida and Ohio offered a similar menu of treatment services, the less positive results are in part attributable to funding problems which delayed or altered the full experiment.

**Table 6.4**
**Four of the Most Successful Treatments That Were Tested in Welfare-to-Work Evaluations and Their Outcomes**

| | | Treatment | | | | Outcome | | | |
|---|---|---|---|---|---|---|---|---|---|
| Program | Mandate | Income disregard | Support service | Employment and training | Merge programs | Earnings | Employment | AFDC Receipt | Payment |
| Calif. SWIM | Monthly participation; fixed activity sequence | No | Child care | Emphasis: job search. Also CWEP, education, and training | No | Positive | Positive | Positive | Positive |
| Mass. ET | Work registration only | No | Child care; transitional care | Emphasis: voluntary education and training Also CWEP job search | No | Positive | Positive | Positive | Positive |
| Calif. GAIN | Work registration; activity sequences | No | Child care; transitional care | Emphasis: basic education and training. Also job search and vocational education. | No | Positive | Positive | Positive | Positive |
| Riverside GAIN | Work registration; activity sequences | No | Child care; transitional care | Emphasis: job search. Also basic and vocational education and job training. | No | Positive | Positive | Positive | Positive |

Source: United States General Accounting Office. (1995, ably). Welfare to work: State programs have tested some of the proposed reforms. Report to the Honorable Daniel Patrick Moynihan, US. Senate. Washington, D.C.: Author.

However, the effects of even the most successful of the projects were disappointing and only modestly reduce welfare dependency. While a variety of explanations are offered for limited success in moving welfare recipients into self-supporting employment—too few support services, low levels of education and skills of project participants, and low wages—after 3 years, only 25 percent of program participants were both employed and off welfare. The results in less successful programs (Florida's FPI and Ohio's TI) were even more modest. Based on these data, the GAO reached several conclusions. First, successful programs offer a large package of employment and education related-services, dictate a specific participation requirement, and have adequate funding. Second, even utilizing the prescribed formula and increasing investment in employment and support services is unlikely to significantly reduce caseloads or dependency. Finally, the GAO concluded that additional research is necessary to develop better and more successful approaches toward ending welfare dependency, and understanding the barriers to the labor market.

*Workfare under TANF: Implications for Welfare*

Since the GAO's 1994 evaluation, the Personal Responsibility and Work Opportunity Act has been implemented which replaced AFDC with the more stringent Temporary Aid to Needy Families (TANF) program and the caseload size has dropped significantly. In 2000, although the full implications of TANF are not yet evident, the removal of AFDC from the federal framework is a radical change in federal tolerance, protection, and entitlement which may provide precedent for reexamination of federal obligation and responsibility across a broader spectrum of programs.

The data consistently confirm that the welfare caseload diminished significantly by 44 percent from 1994 to 1999 (U.S. Department of Health and Human Services, 1999). Regarding what became of the former welfare recipients after leaving welfare, a 1998 GAO study, which examined seven states (California, Connecticut, Louisiana, Maryland, Oregon, Texas, and Wisconsin) considered to be representative of national experience, reveals a sharp increase in the proportion of former recipients who entered the labor market (Pear, 1998). Of the seven states in the study, all but one showed a significant increase in job placement rates from 1995 to 1997, with California, Louisiana, and Maryland's job placement rate more than doubling and Oregon and Washington's rising an impressive 70 percent. A second finding reveals an acceleration in the number of welfare users leaving public assistance rolls—three- quarters of the overall caseload reduction from January 1993 until March 1998 occurred after January of 1996.

Proponents of welfare reform interpret these data as positive indication of the PRWO Act's ability to end the cycle of welfare dependency. However, several larger questions remain unanswered. First, while fewer families are receiving public aid, the effects of this change on the welfare of children is unknown. Second, those users who were able to leave welfare most easily were those with higher levels of skills, education and determination than the users still receiving aid. Therefore the impressive job placement rates may not be sustainable. Third, there are no longitudinal data reflecting the ability of welfare recipients to maintain their employment and therefore stay off of aid. And finally, the increased employment rates have occurred during a period of economic expansion, with unemployment rates at a 30-year low, which may not be sustainable.

These questions are partially addressed in a recent study by Loprest (1999) who analyzes NASF data (National Survey of America's Families). Her findings depict a less optimistic view of life after welfare reform than painted by its proponents. For example, more than 25 percent of former welfare recipients work at night, and more than half experience work and child-care scheduling conflicts. A third or less of welfare-leavers have employer-sponsored health insurance, and about 20 percent of former recipients have no known form of support—from employment, government benefits, or a working spouse. More discouraging is Loprest's finding that nearly 30 percent of those who left the public assistance rolls between 1995 and 1997 had returned to welfare by the end of 1997.

Despite the lack of conclusive data concerning the long-term effects of the PRWO Act, the Act itself demonstrates three persistent trends away from uniformity, entitlement, and universal allocation. First, as the role of the federal government in the provision and delivery of social welfare benefits decreases, and state discretion and funding burdens expand, regional variations in benefits and programs are likely to increase. Additional differences may arise as states privatize welfare efforts by contracting with major corporations (Lockheed, EDS, and Andersen Consulting) for welfare delivery and programs. The "corporate welfare" alternative may explode in popularity if it proves to be both cost-effective and humane. However, the market-driven world of corporate providers may create incentives to deny aid if the providers' profits are linked to reducing the welfare roll. A conflict between efficiency and efficacy of welfare dispensation may re-ignite the debate concerning the appropriateness of privatized social services.

A second trend advanced with the passage of PRWO is the movement away from entitlement and toward obligation. A federal grant to poor mothers with dependent children is no longer guaranteed; in its place are heightened expectations of self-sufficiency, and the requirement of increased personal responsibility. Food stamps to able-bodied poor without dependents are limited, unless the recipient complies with new "work requirements" (APWA, 1996). Viewed collectively, these shifts reveal a tightening definition of eligibility, predicted on recipients' participatory efforts. The development toward increased individual obligation reflects what some policy makers see as the need for a more balanced relationship between social rights and civic responsibilities. This view is emphasized by the communitarian movement, which asserts that a civil society demands both accountability and participation from its members. Contribution and active enrollment in the community are prerequisites to deservedness (Etzioni, 1993). The communitarian model challenges the assumption that citizenship alone affords civil, political, and social rights—a belief which has shaped the contours of federal policy since the 1960s (Marshall, 1963). At the same time citizenship has become a necessary, but not sufficient, criterion for welfare eligibility. Under the PRWO, legal immigrants are less able to rely upon the safety net of federal assistance, as SSI and food-stamp eligibility requirements are tightened.

The decline of entitlement is closely linked to the third trend: The revival of the sharp distinction between the "deserving" and "undeserving" poor created by the English Poor laws. The PRWO Act targets what the public view as the "undeserving poor": Long-term welfare recipients. However, despite the rising tide of public intolerance towards entitlement programs and their recipients, the PRWO permits a 20 percent waiver to the five-year lifetime limit to public aid. This provision of TANF recognizes that a proportion of welfare recipients may be unable to achieve self-sufficiency—the *hardcore* poor who lack the skills or ability to find gainful employment. What the future holds for this group is uncertain.

## Notes

1. For a more detailed analysis of this topic, see R. A. Van Voorhis (forthcoming), "The development of American welfare: The trend toward a workfare state," in M. Borrel (ed.), *Postwar Trends in the Evolution of French and American Industrial Societies,* Berkeley: International Area Studies, University of California, or N. H. Park, *An Evaluation of Work Incentive Provisions in Welfare Reform: California Work Pays Demonstration Project,* University of California, Berkeley.
2. In 1940 about one-third of all children entered the ADC program because of a deceased parent, about a third due to an incapacitated parent, and the remaining third for alternative reasons including divorce, separation, and no marriage tie. The 1961 caseload reflected dramatic change—the children of widows accounted for only 7 percent, 39 percent were children of divorced or separated parents, and only 20 percent were children of never-married parents. However, by 1993 children of never-married mothers represented the largest proportion of the AFDC caseload at 55 percent, with a decline in number of children of widows (1 percent) and divorced or separated parents (29 percent). (Besharov and Gardiner, 1996).
3. It is interesting to note that only 11 states have modified their benefit levels as a result of the change from AFDC to TANF, with 5 increasing benefits and 4 lowering benefits. In two states, TANF and food stamps benefits have been combined into a single benefit since July 1996. The remainder have retained the same benefit levels that were in effect in July 1996. (Gallagher, et.al., 1998).
4. Although the notion of welfare could be construed to include a variety of governmental programs including various types of corporate welfare, mortgage interest deductions, and other tax credits, the term welfare here is used to refer to AFDC usage.
5. The three levels of guaranteed income for a family of four persons were $3,800, $4,800, and $5,600 in 1971 dollar value. Four negative tax rates were implemented—two constant (50 percent and 70 percent) and two variable rates (70 and 80 percent respectively, that declined as income increased). Using the $4,800 grant and the constant 70 percent tax rate as an example, a family earning no income would receive $4,800 per year. However, the $4,800 subsidy would be reduced by 70 cents for each dollar earned. Gilbert and Terrell (1998).
6. A spell of welfare use is defined as a period of continuous welfare receipt, where continuous receipt refers to sequential months or years in which AFDC was received. However, the vast majority of people who leave welfare return to welfare and many of them repeat going off and coming back, a pattern referred to as *welfare recidivism.* Because of recidivism, recipients may have multiple spells of relatively short episodes in a certain time window. Thus, the length of a spell is distinguished from total time of welfare use. The total time on welfare can be calculated by aggregating multiple spells of a recipient observed during the whole time period.
7. Exit type tells us what kind of event leads people to end welfare receipt. Of the exit types, ending welfare through work has been of primary interest in most studies because work is viewed as a means to end welfare dependency. Bane and Ellwood (1994) categorized exit types. From their analysis of 21-year panel data, they found that welfare receipt of a female head ends through one of following events: marriage (29.4 percent), earnings increase of female head (25.0 percent), transfer income increase (12.1 percent), no longer eligible child (10.8 percent), earnings increase of other family member (6.7 percent), reduction of family size (5.4. percent) family moving (1.6 percent), unidentified (9.2 percent). The finding shows that only 31.7 percent of people leave welfare due to increased earnings of her own or of another

family member. This number is much lower than that observed in other studies: 49.2 percent from Blank's (1989) study; 70.2 percent of first spell endings and 67.2 percent of returned spell endings from Harris' (1992) study.

Considering the low rate of exit through work, Bane and Ellwood tried to reinterpret their findings and admitted the possibility of a higher rate of exit through work. Because they assigned only one type per exit, and the scheme was hierarchical, if a woman who marries and has substantial earnings in the year she leaves welfare, she will be classified as having left due to marriage, and the increased earnings will be ignored as a reason of exit for the woman. As a result, the rate of exit through work is under-estimated in their analysis.

Harris (1996) provides interesting findings on the relationship between exit type and the proportion returning to welfare. She compared the proportion of women returning to welfare by three types of prior welfare exit: work exit, marriage/cohabitation exit, and other exit. By the end of the 72-month observation period, 57 percent of all former welfare mothers had returned to welfare. However, the proportion returning varied according to prior welfare exit type. Fifty-four percent of the work exits, 58 percent of marriage/cohabitation exits, and 63 percent of other exits returned to welfare by the end of observation period. She also found that other exits result in more rapid returns in the first six months following welfare exit, whereas work exits and marriage exits cumulate more returns over time.

8. Three of the programs evaluated were conducted in the state of California; one, the state program of the GAIN (Greater Avenues for Independence) implemented in numerous California counties, a pilot project called SWIM, and a GAIN program in Riverside, which was sufficiently different from the larger GAIN study to treat it separately.

## References


American Public Welfare Association (APWA). (1996). *The Personal Responsibility and Work Opportunity Reconciliation Act of 1996, Summary*. Washington, D.C.

Bane, M. J., and Ellwood, D. T. (1983). *The Dynamics of Dependence: The Route to Self-Sufficiency.* Cambridge, MA: Urban Systems Research and Engineering, Inc.

Bane, M. J. and Ellwood, D. T. (1994). *Welfare Realities: From Rhetoric to Reform.* Cambridge, MA: Harvard University Press.

Barton, T. R., and Pillai, V. K. (1994). "Differences in Spell Lengths Between the AFDC-Basic and AFDC-Unemployed Parents Programs." *Journal of Social Service Research.* Vol. 19, No. 1/2.

Bernstein, N. (1996, September 15). "Giant companies entering race to run state welfare programs." *New York Times,* pp. 1, col. 1.

Besharov, D. (1996). "Poverty, welfare dependency and the under class: Trends and explanations," in M.R. Darby (ed.), *Reducing Poverty in America* (pp. 13-56). Thousand Oaks, CA: Sage.

Besharov, D., and Gardiner, K. N. (1996). "Paternalism and Welfare Reform." *Public Interest,* 122: 70-84.

Blank, R. M. (1989). "Analyzing the Length of Welfare Spells." *Journal of Public Economics.* Vol. 39.

Borkowski, M. (1996, August 1). "Points of agreement, and disagreement, on the welfare bill." *New York Times,* pp. A8, col. 1.

Boskin, M. J., and Nold, F. C. (1975). "A Markov Model of Turnover in Aid to Families With Dependent Children." *The Journal of Human Resources.* Vol. 10, No. 4.

Cunningham, Patrick M. (1993). *Welfare Reform: A Response to Unemployed Two-Parent Families.* New York and London: Garland Publishing, Inc.

Day, Phyllis J. (1989). *A New History of Social Welfare*. Englewood Cliffs, NJ: Prentice Hall.

Edin, Kathryn, and Lein, Laura (1997). "Work, Welfare, and Single Mothers' Economic Survival Strategies," *American Sociological Review*. Vol. 62, No. 2.

Ellwood, D. T. (1986). *Working off of Welfare: Prospects and Policies for Self-Sufficiency of Women Heading Families*. Madison: University of Wisconsin.

Ellwood, D. T. (1986). *Targeting 'Would Be' Long-Term Recipients of AFDC*. Princeton, NJ: Mathematics Policy Research.

Ellwood, D. T. (1996). "Welfare reform as I knew it." *The American Prospect*, May/June 1996.

Etzioni, A. (1993). *The spirit of the community*. New York: Crown.

Finder, A. (1996, August 25). "Welfare clients outnumber jobs they might find." *New York Times*, pp. 1, col. 2.

Gabe, T. (1992). *Demographic Trends Affecting Aid to Families with Dependent Children (AFDC) Caseload Growth* (CRS Report to Congress). Washington, DC: Library of Congress: Brookings Institute.

Gallagher, L. J., Gallagher, M., Perese, K., Schreiber, S, Watson, K. (1998). *One Year after Federal Welfare Reform: A Description of State Temporary Assistance for Needy Families (TANF) Decisions as of October 1997*. Washington, D.C.: The Urban Institute.

Garfinkle, I., and McLanahan, S. (1990). "The effects of the child support provisions of the family support act of 1988 on child well-being." *Population Research and Policy Review*, 9, pp. 205-234.

Garfinkle, Irwin, and Orr, Larry L. (1974). "Welfare Policy and the Employment Rate of AFDC Mothers," *National Tax Journal*. Vol. 27, No. 2.

Gilbert, N., and Terrell, P. (1998). *Dimensions of social welfare policy* (4th ed.). Englewood Cliffs, NJ: Prentice Hall.

Gilbert, N. (1995). *Welfare justice*. New Haven: Yale University Press.

Gottshalk, P. (1990). "AFDC Participation Across Generations." *American Economic Review*, 80:21.

Gueron, J.M., and Pauly, E. (1991). *From welfare to work*. New York: Russell Sage Foundation.

Gueron, J. M. (1996). "Welfare and poverty: Strategies to increase work." In M. R. Darby (ed.), *Reducing poverty in America* (pp. 235-250).

Handler, Joel F. (1995). *The Poverty of Welfare Reform*. New Haven, CT: Yale University Press.

Harris, Kathleen Mullan. (1993). "Work and Welfare among Single Mothers in Poverty." *American Journal of Sociology*. Vol. 99, No. 2.

Harris, Kathleen Mullan. (1992). "Work and Welfare among Single Mothers in Poverty," presented at the APPAM Annual Research Conference, October 29, 1992 in Denver, CO.

Hill, M. A., and O'Neill, J. E. (1991). *A Study of Intercohort Change in Women's Work Patterns and Earnings*. U.S. Department of Labor, Bureau of Labor Statistics.

Hutchens, Robert M. (1986). "The Effects of the Omnibus Budget Reconciliation Act of 1981 on AFDC Recipients: A Review of Studies." *Research in Labor Economics*. Vol. 9, Part B.

Illig, David C. (1993). *Welfare Reform: History, Legislation, Strategies, and Options for Reforming the State's Aid to Families with Dependent Children Program*. Sacramento: California Research Bureau.

Kaus, M. (1996). "Clinton's welfare endgame." *Newsweek*, August 5, 1996.

Kemp, Alice Abel, Jenkins, Pam, and Biehl, Molly. (1996). "Reconceptualizing Women's Work: A Focus on the Domestic and Eligibility Work of Women on Welfare." *Journal of Sociology and Social Welfare*. Vol. 23, No. 3.

Kilborn, P. T. (1996). "Previously reluctant states moving on welfare changes." *New York Times*, December 16, 1996, pp. 1, col. 1.
Levy, Frank. (1979). "The Labor Supply of Female Household Heads, or AFDC work Incentives Don't Work Too Well." *The Journal of Human Resources*. Vol. 14, No. 1.
Loprest, P. (1999). *How Families that Left Welfare are Doing: A National Picture*. Washington, DC: The Urban Institute.
Marcenko, Maureen O., and Fagan, Jay. (1996). "Welfare to Work: What are the Obstacles?" *Journal of Sociology and Social Welfare*. Vol. 70, No. 3.
Marshall, T. H. (1963). *Sociology at the crossroads and other essays*. London: Heinemann.
Moffitt, Robert. (1992). "Incentive Effects of the U.S. Welfare System: A Review." *Journal of Economic Literature*. Vol. 30, No. 1.
O'Neill, Dave M., O'Neill, June Ellenoff. (1997). *Lessons for Welfare Reform: An Analysis of the AFDC Caseload and Past Welfare-to-Work Programs*. Kalamazoo, MI: W.E. Upjohn Institute for Employment Research.
O'Neill, J. E., Wolf, D., Bassi, L. J., and M. T. Hannan. (1984). *An Analysis of Time on Welfare*. U.S. Department of Health and Human Services.
Park, N. H. (1998). *An Evaluation of Work Incentive Provisions in Welfare Reform California Work Pays Demonstration Project*. Dissertation, University of California, Berkeley.
Pear, R. (1998, June 19). "Millions Leaving Welfare are Getting Jobs—GAO Study Answers Big Question." *San Francisco Chronicle*, pp. A3, col. 1.
Peskin, J., Tapogna, J., and Marcotte, D. (1993). *Forecasting AFDC Caseloads with an Emphasis on Economic Factors*. Washington, DC: Congressional Budget Office.
Plotnick, Robert. (1983). "Turnover in the AFDC Population: An Event History Analysis." *The Journal of Human Resources*. Vol. 18, No. 1.
Smith, Audrey D., Fortune, Anne E., Reid, William J. (1975). "Notes on Policy and Practice: WIN, Work, and Welfare." *Social Service Journal*. Vol. 49, No. 3. Social Security Administration (1996). *Annual Statistical Supplement, 1996*. Washington D.C.: Government Printing Office. SRI International. (1983). *Final Report of the Seattle-Denver Income Maintenance Experiment. Volume 1: Design and Results*. Washington, D.C.: U.S. Government Printing Office.
Teles, S. M. (1996). *Whose welfare?* Lawrence: University Press of Kansas.
U.S. Congress, Committee on Ways and Means, House of Representatives. (1996). *Overview of Entitlement Programs, 1996 Green Book: Background Material and* Data on Programs within the Jurisdiction of the Committee on Ways and Means. Washington, D.C.: U.S. Government Printing Office.
U.S. Congress, House of Representatives. (1994). *Overview of Entitlement Programs, 1994 Green Book: Background Material and Data on Programs within the Jurisdiction of the Committee on Ways and Means*. Washington, D.C.: U.S. Government Printing Office.
U.S. Congress, House of Representatives. (1997). *Overview of Entitlement Programs, 1994 Green Book: Background Material and Data on Programs within the Jurisdiction of the Committee on Ways and Means*. Washington, D.C.: U.S. Government Printing Office.
U.S. Department of Health and Human Services. (1999).
U.S. General Accounting Office. (1995). *Welfare to Work: Current AFDC Program Not Sufficiently Focused on Employment* (GAO/HEHS-95-28). Washington, DC: U.S. Government Printing Office.
U.S. Social Security Administration. (1997). *Social Security Bulletin: Annual Statistical Supplement, 1996*. Washington, D.C.: U.S. Government Printing Office.
U.S. Social Security Administration. (1961). *Social Security Bulletin: Annual Statistical Supplement, 1960*. Washington, D.C.: U.S. Government Printing Office.

Van Voorhis, R. A. (forthcoming). "The development of American welfare: The trend toward a workfare state." In M. Borrel (ed.), *Postwar Trends in the Evolution of French and American Industrial Societies*. Berkeley: International Area Studies, University of California.

Wiseman, Michael. (1984). *Work Incentives and Welfare Turnover*. Welfare and Employment Studies Project, Working Paper 84-01. Berkeley: University of California, Department of Economics.

# 7

# The Emergence of Active Policy in Switzerland

*François Xavier Merrien*

## The Emergence of Active Policy in Switzerland[1]

During the mid-twentieth century, all the continental European countries introduced social insurance against unemployment, even the countries where the idea of voluntary unemployment was very strongly embedded in national culture, such as Switzerland (Lalive d'Epinay, 1988). The idea that the main cause of unemployment was economic cycles was partially recognized. Unemployment insurance for the worker was implemented in order to guarantee him near maintenance of his standard of living during periods of unemployment.

With the growth of unemployment and poverty rates during the 1980s and the 1990s, governments have changed their views. Arguments that generous social benefits affected the recipients' economic and social behavior, which had previously belonged to the conservative critique of the welfare state, are now gaining partisans in all countries, whatever the dominant party is (Gilbert, 1992). The neoliberal paradigm is gaining ground in many countries.

Welfare schemes, particularly unemployment benefits, are considered to create a situation of unemployment. High replacement rates are perceived as leading to an unemployment trap, where there are few incentives to take up paid employment. One argument is that no one will accept a job unless they earn more than they would have received from unemployment benefits or welfare benefits (the poverty trap). Another and more sophisticated argument is to be found in the theory of moral hazard. Many social reforms in Europe are now based on incentives such as requirements to work, job training, and sometimes enactment of punitive forms of workfare supposed to move people out of unemployment and poverty. In most European countries, conditions for social benefits have been tightened during the last years, unemployment schemes have been time-limited, and cuts in benefits have been made.

In all countries, these ideas have been supported by experts and international organizations. This new paradigm may be interpreted in the context of larger economic and societal changes as an effect of a shift from Fordism to post-Fordism (Boyer, Durand, 1998) and from a Welfare state to a Schumpeterian workfare state. The main characteristic of this evolution is to subordinate social benefits to economic behavior.[2] In tackling this problem, most countries have tried to reorient their global labor market programs. Welfare benefits have been reduced in order to suppress the incentive to stay unemployed. Moreover, from the 1990s, labor market policies have been characterized by a gradual shift to more active measures aimed at tightening the incentives and constraints faced by the unemployed. A large part of these active measures are targeted to the hardest to employ: the youth, the long-term unemployed and the disabled. Nevertheless, some analysts have shown that the possibility of introducing radical changes into social and unemployment policies is somewhat difficult and depends on institutional structures (Pierson, 1994; Ferrera, 1995; King, 1995).

From a comparative point of view, Switzerland is a very interesting case. First, in that country, and in comparison with other European countries the development of unemployment is new. Secondly, even if growing, it stays at a relatively low level. Third, it produces a shock in public opinion and the feeling of the end of a golden age. Fourth, Switzerland has been successful in implementing new measures proposed by the international experts, but to a certain extent only.

This chapter tries to cope with the Swiss paradoxes: the paradox of slow growth without the development of unemployment during the 1970s and the 1980s; the paradox of policy failures in the early 1990s. Finally, it aims to emphasize some factors which can explain the specific features of labor market reforms in Switzerland during the mid-1990s.

This chapter is structured in three sections. In section 1, I will explain briefly the main characteristics of the Swiss political system—as a "consensus democracy"—and its influence on the development of social policies in Switzerland, and follow with a short account of the Swiss "production regime" as a coordinated market economy. Finally, I will develop the necessity to emphasize the duality of the Swiss economy between an export sector employing mainly highly qualified and Swiss people, and a sheltered sector employing many unskilled foreign workers. Section 2 traces the economic and employment situation before the 1990s. I will then describe the growth of unemployment in the last few years and the new policies measures introduced to cope with the new emergent problem: the development of unemployment schemes and the development of active policies. Section 3 attempts to highlight theoretical perspectives along the line of a new institutionalist theory. First, we should try to underline that, to a large extent, the shift in labor market policy is the result of past lock-in policies and a paradigm crisis. Then, that formal political institutions explain the shape of new policies recently introduced in Switzerland.

## The Swiss Political, Economic, and Social Model: Inheritance of the Past

From a political point of view, factors that distinguish Switzerland are federalism and "consociational" politics. In political economic terms, it has been an example of a liberal corporatist system (Katzenstein, 1985) or of a "coordinated market economy" (Soskice, 1999). In institutional terms, it presents very specific characteristics of a weak state. Swiss federalism was designed to restrict power at the federal level. The legislative arena is divided into two chambers and legislation is subjected to direct popular veto (referendum). Federal council power is limited to specific areas (Kriesi, 1995).

This atypical design is the result of history: the slowness of state-building, and political conflicts between conservative Catholics, opposed to a strong national state as to free trade, and liberals. After the "Sonderbund civil war" (1847-48), the 1848 constitution was specifically modeled on the American Constitution with the expectation of limiting the power of the federal government. The 1874 revision of the Constitution expanded these powers, but it also added further constraints in the form of the referendum.

The country is a federation of cantons united by a two-chamber government. The cantons are highly autonomous, each having its own constitution. Regulation of financial and organizational processes between the confederation and the cantons operates at three levels: delegation of traditional tasks (civil law and penal code, public health, police, traffic, etc.), new obligations for cantons accompanied by financial support from the confederation, and thirdly, cooperation (federal legislation implemented by cantons).

In international comparisons, the Swiss political system is generally classified as a typical case of "concordance democracy" (Lijphart 1984, Kriesi 1995). The most remarkable and important feature of consensual politics is arguably the composition of the federal government. The four main parties, Catholic Conservative Party (e.g., the Christian Democratic Party), the Swiss People Party (formerly the Farmers' Party), the Radical Democratic Party, and the Socialist Party together ruled the country, sharing ministerial posts and administrative departments between them. Government policies thus tend to be compromised in order to be acceptable to all coalition partners. This approach, however, is not always accepted by Parliament, where right-wing parties have a majority (Papadopoulos, 1997).

In practice, consensual politics in Switzerland implies that legislative change is negotiated by social partners and other interest groups even before reaching Parliament. Until very recently, Parliament had relatively little impact on legislation. A key factor of consensual policy making is the opportunity for unsatisfied minorities to call a referendum (Kriesi, 1995). As a result, the legislative process in Switzerland is characterized by an unusually large series of stages opening access points to interesting parties.

Switzerland can be considered a "liberal neo-corporatist" country, or a "coordinated market economy." According to this model, the state sets only very general rules rather than intervening actively in the economic process, which is dominated by employers' associations and the unions. Katzenstein (1985) proposes Switzerland as the paradigmatic case of "liberal democratic corporatism." As a small country, it has an open economy. The corporatist arrangements are the functional effects of its position in the international economy. Having accepted the imperative of successful competition in open world markets, the actors are pushed to find a national consensus that facilitates the handling of international change. While social democratic corporatists countries counter the effects of external dependence by expanding social policies to counter the effects of external dependance, Switzerland, as a liberal corporatist country, has rather relied upon private spendings (high wages), regional development and educational (technical) policies and spending. From a general point of view the Katzenstein thesis still seems to be salient.

From a theoretical point of view, however, the "production regime" hypothesis[3] developed by Soskice (1999)—partially compatible with Katzenstein's theory—offers a better fit to the data. Switzerland, according to Soskice, is a case of what he calls a "coordinated market economy regime"—in contrast with an "uncoordinated market economies model" dominant in Anglo-American countries. The levels of cooperation between bank and industry, on the one hand, and employers and unions on the other are high. The coordination between the four main "economic" systems: the financial system, the industrial relation system, the intercompany system and the education and training system, is strong. The degree of coordination between business is high, as well as the degree of coordination in wage determination The institutional framework tends to encourage cooperation at all levels and across different actors. The coordination between sectors is the main explanation for Switzerland's high level of productivity and international competitiveness. It is a typical example of an industry-coordinated economy. It produces diversified quality export products, which depend on skilled and experienced employees on whom responsibility can be devolved (Kappel and Landmann, 1997).

Switzerland is not simply an industrial country. Indeed for a long time, it has been a service economy. In 1965, the service sector (especially banking and insurance companies) represented 40 percent of the whole economic sector, today it represents 67 percent. In the industrial sector, importations and exportations are nearly equal, but, the balance of services is always positive.[4] Other unusual characteristics are a low rate of public employment and a low rate of fiscal and social expenditures.

But we must underline further aspects underestimated by many analysts. The Swiss economy is a dual economy with a segmented labor market. For decades Switzerland, like Germany (Manow, Seils, 1998), resorted to attracting migrant workers from southern European countries (Portugal, Spain, Italy, and Yugoslavia) and frontier workers from France and Italy rather than increasing female employment.

**Table 7.1**
**Taxes and social Security Contributions as a Percentage of GDP**

| | 1970 | 1980 | 1990 | 1997 |
|---|---|---|---|---|
| USA | 27.4 | 26.9 | 26.7 | 28.5 |
| Australia | 24.2 | 28.4 | 30.6 | 30.4 |
| Switzerland | 22.5 | 29.1 | 30.9 | 34.6 |
| UK | 37.0 | 35.2 | 36.6 | 35.3 |
| New-Zealand | 27.4 | 33.0 | 38.0 | 36.4 |
| Germany | 32.9 | 38.2 | 36.7 | 37.5 |
| Netherlands | 37.1 | 45.2 | 44.6 | 43.4 |
| Austria | 34.9 | 40.3 | 41.0 | 44.4 |
| Italy | 26.1 | 30.4 | 39.2 | 45.0 |
| France | 35.1 | 41.7 | 43.7 | 46.1 |
| Belgium | 35.7 | 43.7 | 44.0 | 46.5 |
| Denmark | 40.4 | 45.5 | 48.7 | 52.2 |
| Sweden | 39.8 | 48.8 | 55.6 | 53.3 |

Sources, OECD, Revenue Statistics, 1999.

The second, distinct industrial sector employs mainly foreign workers with low qualifications and low wages.[5]

"Liberal neo-corporatism" allows little space for a full welfare state. Generally speaking, welfare is the result of arrangements between employers' associations and the unions, or, for non-working people, it is the responsibility of the communes or eventually the cantons (Bütschi, Cattacin, 1994). In this respect, Switzerland is one of the richest countries in the world, the level of revenue per capita is high, but it is a welfare laggard.

The first attempts to create a Swiss welfare state were designed, as in Germany, to cope with the "Arbeiter Frage" ("the labor question"). The introduction of social insurance by Bismarck in the 1880s was widely seen as an example to be followed (Gilland, 1990). But the overall impact of referendums and consensual politics on the development of social insurance was to limit the scope of programs that had already been agreed upon by Parliament (Immergut, 1992).

On one hand, confessional, liberal and conservative parties are the main political forces that push toward the creation the Swiss "Sozial Staat." For this reason, its features have a Christian Democratic flavor (van Kersbergen, 1995). On the other hand, for institutional reasons, it is a welfare laggard in comparison with other continental welfare-states (Gilliand,1990, 1997; Bonoli, 1997). For example:

- A basic pension scheme was only accepted by Swiss voters in 1948. The scheme (AHV/AVS), which has been amended a number of times since then, is universal in its coverage. It is financed through contributions and receives a state subsidy .

- In the field of health insurance, Switzerland still constitutes an exception in Europe because it does not have a public health insurance scheme. In 1899, a coalition of the medical profession, farmers, and existing mutual societies subjected the new health insurance law to a referendum and the law was rejected (Gilliand, 1990; Immergut, 1992). Later, in 1910, a law which established the foundation of the current health care system was adopted. Affiliation was not compulsory and financing was based on premiums, unrelated to earnings. In 1994, affiliation became compulsory. The new law also aimed to create a competitive market between mutual funds and introduced targeted subsidies towards people with low incomes.

- Unemployment insurance was introduced into the Swiss constitution in 1947, but the first federal law on the unemployment insurance was adopted only in 1951. Under the law, the affiliation was not compulsory, the cantons were free to create public funds or to delegate the responsibility of the unemployment insurance to the mutual funds already existing (Bois, Greber, 1982).

## From the Golden Age to the Crisis: Economy, Employment, and Social Policies in Switzerland

### *The Golden Age*

In Switzerland, from 1950 up to the 1990s, contrary to other European countries, unemployment was not an important issue. Indeed, economy continues to grow. Table 7.2 illustrates that unemployment remained under 1 percent. It was clearly a seasonal or conjunctural unemployment, not a structural one.

**Table 7.2**
**GDP Growth and Unemployment in Switzerland**

| | 1950 | 1955 | 1960 | 1965 | 1970 | 1975 | 1980 | 1985 | 1990 | 1995 |
|---|---|---|---|---|---|---|---|---|---|---|
| PIB* | +7.4 | +6.2 | +6.8 | +3.2 | 6.6 | -7 | +4.0 | +3.5 | +2.5 | +0.1 |
| Unemplt* | 0.01 | 0.01 | 0.01 | 0.1 | 0.1 | 0.1 | 0.2 | 0.7 | 0.5 | 4.2 |

*Sources: OCDE
*Sources: OFIAMT

How can we explain Swiss exceptionalism? First, we must emphasize economic factors. Switzerland has followed a "niche strategy." It is a producer and an exporter specializing in both some products and services: the machines industry, the chemistry industry, the watch-making industry, finance, insurance and tourism.[6] The level of productivity in most of these sectors is very high and specialization has produced comparative economic advantages. The level of inflation is very low, and Switzerland is able to export manufacturing products and services to European and world markets.

But the productivity of Swiss industry relies also on social and policy factors. It is a result of its comparative institutional advantages (Soskice, 1999) resulting from its productive institutional framework.

If we go into details, we must emphasize two main factors which can explain the economic growth as well as the low level of unemployment up to the 1990s. The first one relates to corporatist arrangements between trade-unions and employers associations[7] (Katzenstein, 1984, 1985) which guarantee a continuing process of adaptation to economic changes, few strikes and what is called "Work peace."[8] The state does not intervene in industrial relations. The social partners themselves, establish collective conventions. They can be negotiated at different levels: national, regional or local by the competent professional organizations. Every enterprise is invited to conform its practice to their prescriptions. Such a system privileges the negotiation between the social partners if every partner respects the terms of the agreement (according to the Convention of Work Peace concluded by 1937). Negotiations determine working conditions, periods of notice, modalities of notice, working hours, salary and holidays. When economic conditions change, new negotiations have to take place. In case of disputes, a referee's court with parity composition has to be consulted; 54 percent of 3.5 million salaries are affected by this global work agreement, for 18 percent of them the agreement is of obligatory nature. The clause of price increase is included in almost all collective wage agreements; salaries should therefore regularly be adjusted to take into account any increase in the national index of consumption prices. Some companies propose their own agreement and this accounted for 11 percent of the wage earners in the private economy sector in 1992.

The second reason relates to the dual system of education[9] and the existence of the apprenticeship system—based on practical knowledge combined with a theoretical education in a specific technical teaching establishment. The dual system works on a corporatist basis of consensus-building between the concerned professional groups and teaching institutions. Federalism leaves a large margin to cantons and to the professional organizations. Federal agencies set quality standards and pay subsidies to technical schooling institutions. The legal frame is set by the federal level, but implementation is largely left to the cantons. Enterprises are forced to respect guidelines in technical teaching. Thus, the regulation of professions leads to a sound education adaptable to regional economic disparities and cantonal differences. The strong apprenticeship system is considered to ensure a steady supply of young, skilled and highly productive labor.[10]

These two facts are of special importance in the production regime explanation. But—even if important—these factors are not sufficient to explain the very low rate of unemployment during 40 years. We must add two different and specific factors very often neglected by international commentators. The first one is economic. When we speak of the competitive and successful Swiss economy, we must not forget that it represents only a partial view of that economy. Alongside an externally oriented and competitive sector, exists a large internally oriented and protected sector. For decades, agriculture was subsidized and sheltered from international competition by private and public arrangements: cartels, price maintenance, and monopolies (Sciarini, 1994, Mach, 1997). This explains why the price of goods produced for the internal market is very high, but also why over a long period of time workers in these sectors were protected from external competition.[11]

The other hidden factor is the use of a strict migration policy. The use of strict migration policy is a long established feature of Swiss policies to control the labor market and it is in contrast with the European tradition. Swiss government is able to limit the number of annual permits relative to the employment situation. When the economy needs workers, the quota of work-permits is increased.[12] On the contrary when a recession occurs, seasonal workers and frontier workers are forbidden to work in Switzerland. For example if the recession of the seventies did not produce mass unemployment, it is mainly due to the fact that 360,000 foreign workers were compelled to leave.[13] For decades, this policy allowed Switzerland to escape a rise in the unemployment rate (Bonvin, 1996). Thus, the amount of foreign workers varied across economic cycles.

The continuing growth of Swiss economy explains why unemployment insurance, implemented after the Second World War, was non-compulsory. Few workers were affiliated to unemployment insurance funds. Owing to the very low unemployment rate most workers chose at that time not to join the mutual funds. The affiliation rate remained extremely low (19.8 percent in 1974). The economic crisis in the mid-seventies pushed the Swiss government to modernize the legislation. The principle of obligatory affiliation was introduced in the constitution in 1977 and the Federal Law on Compulsory Unemployment Insurance (LACI) was enacted in 1982, coming into effect in 1984. These laws prescribes that:

- The funds were financed by contributions from employers and employees (0.8 percent of the payroll equally distributed between both);
- The funds were administered by the cantons;
- The benefits granted up to 70 percent of the last salary for childless unemployed people and 80 percent for those with dependent children;[14]
- The maximum duration was 85 working days for childless unemployed people and 250 for the others which, at that time, was not very generous by international standards;
- The funds staff whether the unemployed people fulfill the legal conditions (relating mainly to the length of the contribution period) to qualify for benefits;
- The OFIAMT (Federal Office of Industry, Arts and Crafts and Labour) is responsible for implementation control and attempts to combat abuses.

The 1982 legislation also introduced active measures for the labor market (subsidies for professional training, benefits aimed at job insertion...), but these opportunities were rarely exercised. The placement activities were generally left to the local labor offices but most of the work in this field was done by private agencies.

In fact, until the end of the 1980s, the level of unemployment stayed very low. For example, even during the recession of the 1970s, the unemployment rate remained under 0.5 percent even though employment rates reduced over 7 percent. In this respect, immigration policy remained an efficient mechanism.

Up to 1990, a situation of full employment prevailed in Switzerland. The unemployment insurance fund made large financial profits. These economic and social performances fostered the belief that Switzerland was an exceptional country (*Sonderfal*): different and better. This constitutes one of the main reasons for the popular rejection (Referendum) to join the European Economic Area (EEA) on December 1992. The "no-camp" dramatized the debate, pointing to a series of negative effects: massive immigration, the rise of unemployment, the decline of wages, and the loss of sovereignty. The EEA Treaty was rejected by 50.3 percent of the voters and 16 cantons out of 23. The arguments given by the "no-camp" voters were criticism of the EU, fear of foreigners, fear of unemployment, fear for the culture of traditional Switzerland (Kriesi et al., 1993; Sciarini and Listhaug, 1997).

*The End of the Golden Age: The Turning Point of the 1990s*

The situation, however, changed dramatically in the early 1990s when recession arrived and unemployment rose to unprecedented levels in Swiss post-war history. Since the beginning of the 1990s, Switzerland had been undergoing a round of economic difficulties. Between 1990 and 1995, the average growth of PNB was 0.3 percent, the weakest in Europe. Today, experts agree on the four main factors that explain the recession which occurred in Switzerland in the early 1990s. The first one is a monetarist policy to fight inflation which, in turn, produces high interest rates that discouraged productive investments and the growing strength of the Swiss franc relative to the DM and other European currencies (+15 percent between 1993 and 1995) which, in turn, penalized exports and tourism. The second explanation points low growth in countries which are the principal customers of Swiss products (Germany, France, EU). A context of low economic growth is a dramatic change for a country bent on growth strategies.[15] The third factor is the crisis in the building sector following a wave of speculation in the real estate industry. The fourth emphasizes the effect of the restriction of public deficits by the federal and cantoral governments which, in turn, limited public consumption.

Moreover, new immigration policies had "negative effects." During the 1970s crisis the Swiss government was able to push a large part of the working population outside its borders, in others words it was able to distribute its "surplus" outside. But, during this period xenophobia increased, and the government decided to change its immigration policy.[16] The possibility of obtaining an annual or permanent permit was limited (by canton and differed from the country of origin of the worker). By contrast, there were less limitations to recruit seasonal workers and no more to recruit frontier workers. The idea behind this policy was: when recession occurs, the return to a market equilibrium is fast and the cost to public finance is zero. But, in fact, this brilliant idea produced unexpected effects in the 1990s.

In the 1970s, more than 70 percent of workers had annual or seasonal permits. In the 1990s, the figure is 25 percent. Most of the migrant workers have permanent permits and can no longer be legally pushed out.[17] Moreover, the level of wages in some sectors employing seasonal or frontier workers is very low and unattractive to Swiss workers. Restrictive migration policies could no longer be used to solve the problem of unemployment.

From 1990 to 1997, the number of unemployed people rose from 18,000 to 190,000 and the rate of unemployment grew from 0.5 percent to 5.2 percent. While a 5 percent unemployment rate might be low by European standards,[18] it is slightly higher in the Italian- and French-speaking parts (7.6 percent in the Ticino canton, 6.8 percent in the Geneva canton, and 7.3 percent in the Vaud canton). We must add that the frontier workers are not taken into account in the statistics. This group is of special importance in the border cantons of Switzerland.[19] An average of 5.8 percent of the whole coun-

**Table 7.3**
**Unemployment by Category: 1980, 1985, and from 1990 to 1997 (in percent figures)**

| | Total | | Men | | Women | | Swiss Foreign Workers[43] | | | |
|---|---|---|---|---|---|---|---|---|---|---|
| Source | OFIAMT | ESPA | OFIAMT | ESPA | OFIAMT | ESPA | OFIAMT | ESPA | OFIAMT | ESPA |
| 1980 | 0.2 | - | 0.2 | - | 0.2 | - | - | - | - | - |
| 1985 | 1.0 | - | 0.8 | - | 1.2 | - | 0.7 | - | 1.6 | - |
| 1990 | 0.5 | - | 0.4 | - | 0.6 | - | 0.4 | - | 0.9 | - |
| 1991 | 1.1 | 1.8 | 1.0 | 1.2 | 1.2 | 2.5 | 0.8 | - | 2.1 | - |
| 1992 | 2.5 | 2.8 | 2.5 | 2.3 | 2.7 | 3.5 | 2.0 | - | 4.5 | - |
| 1993 | 4.5 | 3.7 | 4.4 | 3.1 | 4.7 | 4.6 | 3.5 | - | 7.8 | - |
| 1994 | 4.7 | 3.9 | 4.4 | 3.5 | 5.2 | 4.4 | 3.7 | 2.9 | 8.4 | 5.7 |
| 1995 | 4.2 | 3.3 | 3.9 | 2.9 | 4.8 | 3.9 | 3.2 | 2.6 | 8.0 | 5.1 |
| 1996 | 4.7 | 3.7 | 4.4 | 3.4 | 5.1 | 4.1 | 3.3 | 2.6 | 9.3 | 7.7 |
| 1997 | 5.2 | 4.1 | 4.9 | 4.3 | 5.7 | 3.9 | 3.6 | 2.8 | 10.7 | 8.8 |

Sources: OFIAMT/OFS[44], in Bonvin, Bertozzi, 1998, see note 1.

try, it nevertheless represented 24.9 percent of the working population in Ticino canton and 16.8 percent in Geneva canton in 1993 (Fluckiger, 1996).

Unemployment rates among those aged 15 to 24 is low by international standards, lower than the rate for those aged between 24-49, and even lower than the rate for the total labor force. As in Germany, this result is the effect of the system of vocational training (largely imported from Germany!). Unskilled workers and women—who are more often unskilled—are more prone to unemployment. We must underline that, amongst the 168,630 unemployed persons, 55 percent are Swiss (88,000), 45 percent (75,000) are foreign workers. The level of unemployment amongst foreign workers[20] is explained by the fact that they are less skilled workers and employed in economic sectors subjected to conjunctural economic variations: tourism, building, leather, shoes and textile, plastic and rubber.[21] This explains partially why the level of unemployment is higher in the border cantons.

The unexpected growth in unemployment created a much greater financial burden both on federal unemployment insurance and on cantons and Communes which had to meet the social assistance costs. Confronted with this problem, the Federal Council adopted several Federal Urgent Decrees (AFU)[22] aimed at a quick adaptation of the legislative provisions. Thus the maximum duration of the entitlement to benefits was progressively reduced to 400 working days. The notion of suitable work was introduced in the law and the unemployed had to accept any job with a salary amounting to at least 70 percent of the last wage. The contributions were also modified and passed to 3 percent of the payroll, equally distributed between the employer and the worker. In spite of these measures, the number of registered long-term unemployed increased regularly. The phenomenon was assuming unexpected proportions which meant a much greater financial burden both for the federal unemployment insurance and for the cantons and Communes which had to take charge of social assistance expenses. In these circumstances a remodeling of the whole system proved inevitable. After 18 months of negotiations a new project was proposed and adopted after a long debate by the Parliament in 1995.

The new legislation constitutes a turning point from a rather passive policy to an active one (Tabin, 1998).[23] The new law introduces innovations in the organization of job placements. In order to improve the efficiency of public service employment a new structure was set up in 1995: the Public Regional Placement Office (ORP).[24] The ORP uses specialized placement officers. Another service performs the administrative tasks: registration, stamping, control. The entitlement to passive benefit payments is reduced from 400 days in the previous arrangements to 150 days.[25] Afterwards, benefit payments are contingent upon entry to an active labor-market program. Failure to do so will result in sanctions including a 60-day benefits' suspension period. Participation to active measures would not generate further new periods of entitlement to federal benefits as was the case in the past.

Cantons are obliged to supply temporary job programs according to the number of inhabitants and the unemployment rate. If no active program is available the unemployed are entitled to receive benefit payments for 80 more days, but unemployed persons must agree to take an adequate job, which is now defined in terms of salary (at least equal to the amount of the benefits), of compatibility with the skills of the recipient and with distance (a 2-hour journey is regarded as adequate). The maximum duration of the benefit payment is 520 days.[26] In order to insure the implementation of the activation principle, the cantons are called on to supply 25,000 active labor market program slots, avoiding competition with private sector activities (which would create further unemployment). This number is distributed among the cantons according to the number of inhabitants and the unemployment rate. Financial incentives are also introduced to encourage the cantonal cooperation: 3,000 Swiss francs are paid by the cantonal fund for each yearly active program. However, the canton has to assume 40 percent of the benefit payments in case the allowed quota is not respected. In this way active measures are presented as a duty both of the public authorities and of the job-seekers.

All these active measures can be divided into two categories: training programs on one side and temporary jobs on the other. The administration insists on the presence of at least one training aspect in every program. Temporary jobs allow the unemployed to have an activity and earn wages. The salary is fixed by the employer and paid by the unemployment fund. It corresponds to the usual minimum wage in the branch and place of employment; if inferior to the benefit levels, unemployment insurance makes up the difference. The temporary work must not be used by employers as a substitute for ordinarily productive work. This principle concerns both the private sector and the public institutions. As a general rule the social partners and the economic spheres must give their agreement before the beginning of a program and a tripartite commission has to examine the controversial cases.

The period from 1991 to 1997 shows a considerable increase in the active expenses and in the number of persons in the active programs as shown in tables 7.4 and 7.5. The unemployed have still a right to unemployment, but they have the duty not only to be available to work, but also to undertake active measures. Officials of the ORP have the new role of checking unemployed individuals and helping them to find adequate training or a temporary job. However, some analysts (Sheldon, 1998) view the new policy measures with skepticism. It seems to them that active measures are not sufficiently targeted towards the long-term unemployed, and that some measures, such as offering courses to old/low-skilled workers are inefficient.

**Table 7.4**
**Labor Market Programs Expenses, 1990-1998 (in Swiss Francs millions)**

| | 1990 | 1991 | 1992 | 1993 | 1994 | 1995 | 1996 | 1997 |
|---|---|---|---|---|---|---|---|---|
| Courses | 7.6 | 12.6 | 42.8 | 93.8 | 139.7 | 165.2 | 205.6 | 296.8 |
| Temporary Jobs | 5.7 | 5.4 | 8.1 | 26.2 | 145.9 | 328.3 | 577.7 | 813.1 |
| Job insertion allowances | 2.8 | 3.4 | 7.8 | 14.1 | 29.3 | 32.1 | 24.8 | 31.7 |
| Training Allowances | 0 | 0 | 0 | 0 | 0 | 0 | 0.8 | 3.9 |
| Subsidy to the setting up of independent activities | 0 | 0 | 0 | 0 | 0 | 0 | 7.2 | 8.5 |
| Participation to transport expenses | NA | NA | NA | 2.2 | 2.8 | 3 | 3.4 | 4 |
| TOTAL | 16.1 | 21.4 | 58.7 | 136.3 | 317.7 | 528.6 | 809.5 | 1158 |

**Table 7.5**
**Number of Persons in the Labor Market Programs, 1990-1998**

| | 1990 | 1991 | 1992 | 1993 | 1994 | 1995 | 1996 | 1997 | 1998 |
|---|---|---|---|---|---|---|---|---|---|
| Number of persons | 6480 | 11,670 | 39,800 | 51,070 | 75,752 | 90,700 | 157,000 | 210,000 | 235,000 |

Sources: Bonvin in Merrien, dir 1998.

*Redefining assistance.* In the 1990s, an increase in the number of unemployed people and in the number of recipients of social assistance occurred at the same time (Cunha, 1998). It provoked very different legislative adjustments at the level of the cantons. For forty years, assistance was considered as the last local safety net for people having exhausted their entitlement to social insurance. The amount of this means-tested social benefit was fixed according to the needs of the individuals and was repayable.[27]

However, the level of the financial help and the type of help there differed according to cantonal legislations. Implementation was generally left to the communes. With the recession, new problems appeared on the public agenda. A common issue was the distribution of financing. The cantons feared that the long-term unemployed, having used up their right for insurance benefits, now would have to be financed by cantonal and municipal social assistance. So, new measures were adopted by the local authorities. It is possible to roughly distinguish two categories in the new measures adopted by the cantons. There was a clear distinction between the linguistic regions. The policies established by the Swiss Latin cantons considerably differ from those implemented in the German part of Switzerland.[28]

Most Swiss German cantons have not yet developed a new social assistance scheme and their employment policy relies exclusively on the active measures introduced by the revised Unemployment Act. Even when new mechanisms have been set up, they follow the approach of the federal legislation and try to provide the long-term unemployed with temporary jobs that are as close as possible to the primary labor market. These jobs allow the unemployed to earn a social wage instead of receiving a social benefit, and they are considered the best way to escape the poverty trap.

The principle governing the action of the Swiss German cantons and main cities is: "Rather work than welfare." By contrast, in every

Swiss French speaking canton as well as in the Italian speaking canton (Ticino), policies have been adopted that include minimum income maintenance schemes. In all cases the benefits payment is subordinate to the acceptance of carrying out community work. Despite these divergences, all of these new schemes have a common feature, namely "reciprocity." The payment of social benefits to the unemployed always relies more on the acceptance of carrying out an active program.

The Esping-Andersen classic typology of Welfare States, cannot provide a useful framework for understanding the evolution of social assistance in Switzerland. Esping-Andersen includes Switzerland in the liberal model of Welfare regimes. However, attacks against welfare program as well as the shift from "the war against poverty to the war against the poor" (Gans, 1995) has never occurred in that country. In addition, the level of cantonal safety net is considerably higher in Swiss cantons than in U.S. states. New social assistance measures are based on incentives such as requirement to work and job-training. The main characteristic of this evolution is to subordinate social benefits to economic and civic behavior. But the reform of social protection also includes new measures aimed at giving more adequate assistance to designated segments of the population (the poor, the long unemployed, women etc). In that sense, they cannot be called pure "conservative policies."

## Institutions and Welfare State Reforms in Switzerland

One can argue (Hall, 1989, 1993; Jenson, 1989; Merrien, 1990, 1993; Rein, Schon, 1993) that during periods of crisis anomalies and unanticipated developments tend to discredit past policies and open windows to new ideas and policies (King, 1985). In the 1990s, low economic growth, and the rise of unemployment, produced a shock in public opinion. Continuing economic crisis undermines the current interpretative framework.

In the case of Switzerland, until the beginning of the 1990s, the idea of Swiss "Sonderfall" was a cognitive obstacle to new ideas and new policy measures. When problems occurred, Swiss policy makers tried first the old kind of policy measures: pushing foreign workers outside, subsidizing infrastructure investment program, etc. But in the 1990s, these policies have failed. Restrictive migration policies can no longer be used to solve the problem of unemployment. Public investments do not lead to an economic growth, but to growing deficits. This has led to growing dissatisfaction and criticism of these traditional policy measures. Policy failure and a new belief system are pushing the state to change its strategy.

On the one hand, the 1990s represent a "recognition" that the traditional way of thinking and doing is over and that the neo-liberal paradigm and its policy proposals are the solution to the problems of the new economic era. On the other hand, we must not underestimate institutional constraints the state confronts in trying to implement new policies particularly in a federalist country with a very weak state and a large number of veto points (Immergut, 1992 ).[29] In the case of Switzerland—as history has shown—welfare reform policies are rather difficult. Nevertheless, from a new-institutional point of view, if able to achieve neo-corporatist compromises with interest groups and civil society, a weak state can even have a stronger capacity to act than a strong state (Merrien, Bonoli, forthcoming). Even if, of course, the need for consensus limits the extent to which this new policy diverges radically with past policies.

The last part of this chapter concentrates on these two points: (1) how new liberal ideas influenced policy makers; and (2) how the political system favored the implementation of some ideas and blocked others.

*A Paradigm Shift?*

It is clear that, despite Christian-Democrat traditions, the neo-liberal agenda has taken on a special importance since the early 1990s. From the early 1990s, neo-liberal ideas, which were hardly embraced by Swiss elites, spread very rapidly in the economists' networks, the high ranking officials' circles, the employers' networks,[30] and political parties of the right. The OCDE reports, notably the 1992 report,[31] as well as other experts,[32] exerted a strong influence on elites. Most of the economists, experts, officials,[33] and many politicians agree on the idea of implementing a more deregulated market.

The new policy imperatives were to suppress cartels and other obstacles to economic competition, to follow strict monetarist policies, and to limit public deficit and the growth of the welfare state. At the national level federal deputies strive to increase Swiss companies' competitiveness. They regularly propose cutting taxes which they perceive as an excessive burden on their economic activity.[34] Social security contributions (for which employers must contribute a little more than 25 percent of the payroll) are often considered a handicap for the competitiveness of Swiss business and any proposal to increase the non-wage labor costs gives rise to considerable discussion. In this context the appearance of new social security schemes or the development of those already existing would add burdens, expenses perceived to be intolerable. Discussions about reorganizing social security along neo-liberal lines are no longer a taboo. The role and importance of economic promotion in regard to structural unemployment is on the agenda. Entrepreneurs criticize the rigidity of work contracts. In addition, some enterprises have chosen to stop following the collective conventions and try to find their own way out of the crisis. The growing budget deficit has become a dominant issue. For many of these groups, New Zealand's new orientation is an example to follow. In 1995, the neo-liberal thesis of the book *Accepting challenges,*[35] received large play in the mass media and particularly in publications of employers' associations (Mach, 1997).

Nevertheless, all members of the Swiss elite were not convinced by the new trend in ideas. On one hand, employers' associations and right-wing parties call for a policy of welfare reorientation and retrenchment, and greater labor market flexibility. On the other hand, other elites, influenced by Christian-Democrat ideas and members of the conservative radical party, defend the idea of a Swiss "social model": high wages, high regulation of the labor market and the development of social pacts between unions and associations of employers. In addition, as in other EU countries, trade unions, the socialists and the green parties, churches advocate a stronger welfare state, a better social protection of the workers, better unemployment benefits and a more generous poverty policy.

Controversies over policies in Switzerland are not very specific. The problem the country has to face is that social organizations, religious charities, communal authorities play a major role in social welfare, which is adequate in normal times, but not in times of recession. With the development of mass unemployment, the first question on the agenda was how to deal with a problem that traditional actors could not cope with, not how to reduce a big welfare state or welfare dependency because neither conditions were existent.

Secondly, the social and political inheritance is composed of what is called a liberal-democratic-corporatism based on a dual economy.

In the export sector workers are highly qualified and receive high wages, the labor market is highly regulated. The competition between companies in the same sector is limited. Workers share loyalty towards their company. The evolution towards an "uncoordinated market economy" would mean an economic revolution: wage bargaining, competition among firms and workers, dispersion of wages. It would be a complete transformation not only of the welfare state, or of the sheltered economic sector, but of the economic system as a whole. Even if they agree with neo-liberal ideas on a ideological level, and if they wish more autonomy to fix working conditions, employers have few incentives to change an economic and social system which proves to be very productive and efficient even in times of economic troubles.[36] This limits the evolution towards a deregulated market system. In addition, for historical reasons, "social ideals" are strongly embedded in Switzerland. Even right-wing parties such as the Christian Democrats and the Parti Radical are opposed to an evolution towards an U.S.-style society. Deregulation has not influenced the core of the coordinated economic model: in most economic sectors the coordination, not competition, among industries is still prevalent, industrial relations have remained well established, and the vocational system has not been profoundly change.

Furthermore, the experts (OECD, OFAEE) do not recommend such a revolution. Most analysts agree on the idea that neither the system of wage fixing, nor the level of taxation, nor the welfare system, nor labor-market policies affect the level of unemployment. The questions in Switzerland are how to change working conditions to meet the intensification of competition in the world markets without ruining the system of industrial relations, how to implement new measures to combat unemployment and finally, how to limit social exclusion without creating welfare dependency.

The unemployment policies of the mid-1990s are first characterized by an attempt to cope seriously with the problem of unemployment by improving social policies. On one hand, we can define these measures as "progressive" measures. They include more money for training and job creation schemes. On the other hand, the architecture of the reforms shows the strong influence of new ideas and practices diffused by the experts. Some issues such as savings, to avoid moral hazard and to introduce active measures, are main themes of them. We must note:

- the reduction of entitlement to passive benefit payments;
- the subordination of benefit payments to the entry in an active labor-market program;
- the fact that the participation to an active labor program does not generate a new period of entitlement to federal benefits.

All the new measures are close to the recommendations of the OECD experts.[37] They are aimed at limiting the "unemployment gap." Benefits are less readily available. They imply concomitant obligations by the recipient to take active steps to re-enter employment. Unemployed people who are not able to find a job within two years can rely on social assistance programs for support, which in Switzerland are weak and decentralized. However, due to political reasons, the Swiss government has not been able to implement the new labor market program in its entirety:

- the government has not been able to reduce the level of benefit payments, which is still relatively high in comparative perspective;
- the job has to be compatible with the skills of the recipient;
- the job must not be too far (2-hour journey);[38]
- many free active measures are proposed to the unemployed (training courses, etc.);
- the proposed temporary work must take into consideration the training and the qualifications of the unemployed.

*Implementing Social Reforms in Switzerland*

Consensual politics and federalism are factors that might facilitate innovations. But, in this country as in many others, institutions constrain changes (Weaver, Rockman, 1993). At the ideological levels, a trend towards a more free-market ideology occurred. Unemployed persons are more often being treated not as victims of economic mutations, but either as being unproductive or unwilling to work. There is a clear tendency to stigmatize unemployed people as lazy, profiting from unemployment benefits.[39] However, there are conflicting ideological interests as to the objectives of social policies. But at the level of implementation, ideology is not sufficient.

The institutional rules of a federal system like Switzerland have major implications for social policymaking, and create a major difficulty for the definition and the implementation of completely new policies. First, direct-democracy offers the unions and other interests-groups the possibility to oppose controversial measures. If the powerful employers' associations base their conception of reform on heightened competitiveness and productivity, the trade unions generally stand for social protection and the status quo concerning working conditions.[40] Secondly, the federal system, unlike centralized systems, implies the existence of three major administrative levels, each of them having specific powers and budgets. Conflicts between cantons and the Confederation concerning their respective powers and the distribution of financial charges have important effects. Reducing the generosity of benefits would imply a massive burden on communal or cantonal schemes.

These two features of the Swiss political system explain why some legislative initiatives were rejected. Two cases provide very interesting examples: the first one concerns deregulation of the working hours, the second one cuts in unemployment benefits. With regard to the first point, a large majority of the deputies and the social partners (chambers of commerce and trade unions) agreed on the necessity to adapt this legislation to the new conditions defined by the globalization of the economy.[41] After long negotiations the social partners reached an agreement acceptable to both parties, but the representatives of the righties parties strove to give a more radical turn to the suggestions of the social partners. The project they finally voted on contained many controversial points concerning deregulation in key matters: night shifts, supplementary working hours, etc. The trade unions decided to launch a referendum against the new proposals. During the campaign a deep split divided the supporters of the revised provisions and those who interpreted it as worsening the working conditions. In December 1996 the referendum resulted in a clear defeat of the representatives' project and everything had to be negotiated again.

The second point directly concerns this chapter: In 1997 the Federal Council adopted a new AFU in order to reduce the level of unemployment benefit payments (1 percent or 3 percent less according to the categories of unemployed). But a referendum was launched and in September 1997 the Swiss people rejected the proposals adopted by the Federal Council. Thus the precedent level of benefits was restored. For the second time in one year the federal authorities were defeated in a popular vote.

Generally, the partners are able to find a compromise between opposite positions. At the level of parliament, the three dominant parties of right or center-right with a similar orientation have a political majority. They are able to vote controversial acts. But, as acts can be subjected to a referendum, they are generally very cautious, and when they try to go too far, they lose (Kriesi, 1995. Papadopoulos, 1997). A new political process seems to be emerging, to propose reforms but, at the same time, to offer compensations to the opposing camp (Bonoli, 1997). The new policy measures which were adopted in the mid-1990s largely are in the mainstream of neo-liberal ideas diffused by the dominant international epistemic community.[42] But, as Switzerland is a federalist and "consensus democracy," the implementation of the new policies results in a political process of trial and error.

## Conclusion

Finally, the Swiss case confirms that the path dependency phenomena exists but that it does not impede new reforms. It means rather that the possibility of implementing new measures depends largely on their congruence with general values and interests of major political actors. And, in the case of Switzerland, it seems that there are no incentives to change the production regime but that labor market policies have to be adapted to new national and international conditions.

From a comparative point of view, the historical legacy is largely different. By contrast with the United States, the number of really underprivileged people (the "underclass") is very low. Contrary to other European countries, the Swiss political authorities have not used either early retirement policies—as in France and Germany (Kohli, Guillemard, 1995) or public employment, as in Nordic countries (Cameron, 1978)—in order to limit the growth of unemployment. The constraints of past public policies are relatively weak.

Contrary to the policies introduced in the Anglo-American family of nations (Castles, 1993), Swiss policies are less targeted than in Scandinavian countries. Active labor market measures reach all of the unemployed. Their aim is to intervene to prevent the need for local or cantonal assistance, not to extract people from it like in "liberal welfare states." The new policy measures mean on one hand a shift from a tradition of welfare passivity to a new philosophy of welfare. On the other hand, the reforms are compatible with Swiss culture and economic philosophy. Consensual politics is one way to avoid "blame avoidance." Its consequence is to limit the scope of reforms.

## Notes

1. This paper was prepared for the weekly seminar of the European Forum of the European University Institute. It derives from a work conducted by a research team of the university of Lausanne under the direction of F-X Merrien. It is part of an European research project: Policies of Social Integration in Europe in collaboration with CERAT:France, Poleis:Italy, IFS: Germany, conducted under the auspices of the European Commission (DG XII), contract number SOE-CTR97-3036 . The author thanks Jean-Michel Bonvin, Olivia Strobel, and Fabio Bertozzi who worked on this part of the research that contributed to this paper. I also benefited from comments of my distinguished colleagues at the European Institute Forum. I am particularly grateful to Fiona Ross for helpful comments.
2. We can distinguish between Keynesian active labor market measures associated with institutional, or social democratic welfare regimes and workfare measures of neo-liberal inspiration.
3. "By a production regime is meant the organization of production through markets and market-related institutions. It analyses the ways in which the micro-agents of capitalists systems—companies, customers, employees, owners of capital—organize and structure their interrelationships within a framework of incentives and constraints or "rules of the game" (NB:FXM: the institutional framework)..." The most important of the institutions contributing to the institutional framework are the financial system, the industrial relations system, the education and training system, the inter-company system" (Soskice, 1999, p 101).
4.

| | 1990 | 1991 | 1992 | 1993 | 1994 | 1995 |
|---|---|---|---|---|---|---|
| Balance of trade | -10 | -8.5 | -1.4 | +2.5 | +2.2 | +1.0 |
| Balance of services | +13 | +14.7 | +15.1 | +16.8 | +16.1 | +14.9 |

Mds CH Francs. Sources: OCDE, Suisse: 1997.

5. We lack missing data but we may extrapolate from this figure (Ticino canton 1980):

| Qualification/men | Suisse people (percent) | Foreign Workers B+C | Frontiers Workers (percent) |
|---|---|---|---|
| | | | |
| High/very | 14.5 | 7.6 | 1.3 |
| | | | |
| Middle | 38.1 | 18.6 | 8.7 |
| | | | |
| Low/unskilled | 47.4 | 73.8 | 90 |

Source, Fabio Bertozzi, Les nouvelles politiques de l'emploi au Tessin, Masters dissertation, University of Lausanne, 1999.

6. In the 1960s, the share of exports and imports in GPD is yet around 60 percent.
7. Switzerland generally is considered as being a partial neo-corporatist country, as trade unions are fragmented and employers' associations are more centralized and organized, informal network arrangements are highly asymmetrical. Using a scale of indicators to measure the power of employers' associations and workers' movements, Katzenstein concludes that in comparison to 6 other small European countries, in the range of employers' associations, the Swiss are first; in the scale of the workers' movement the Swiss are last in the seventh position.
8. "Lost working days" due to strikes or lock out:
1733 (1975), 5178 (1980), 662 (1985), 4090 (1990), 51 (1992), 14380 (1994), 351 (1995); sources, OECD, 1997.
9. The proportion of young people choosing this kind of education reaches 60 percent in Switzerland, in comparison to 24 percent in France.
10. Comparison based on a review of cross-country evidence suggests that the apprenticeship system does yield a better outcome in terms of employment and pay; see P. Ryan, 1998, 'Is apprenticeship better? A review of the economic evidence' in *Journal of Vocational Education and Training*, London, vol. 50, n. 1.
11. Switzerland is first in the transfer of resources to agriculture, Norway is second (sources: OECD). Changes occurred only recently. Following negotiations in the Uruguay Round of the GATT and with the EC, Switzerland has begun to reform its agricultural policy and its concurrence policy (Sciarini, 1994, Mach, 1997).
12. There are 4 kinds of work permits: the A, B and C and the frontier worker permit. The C is "permanent." Workers must have worked in Switzerland a minimum of 5 years without interruption. Even in this case it is very hard to obtain the Swiss naturalization. The B is limited to one year but eventually reconducted. The family of the worker has the right to come to Switzerland only one year after he receives the permit. The A permit is the seasonal permit. The worker can work only 9 month a year. He has no guarantee to obtain a new permit and no right to unemployment benefits. His/her family cannot join him/her. The frontier worker must go home every night.
13. This accounts for more than three-quarters of the employment decline in Switzerland.
14. Up to a maximum of 5,800 Swiss francs.
15. cf Solde de la balance commerciale: (Mds CH Francs): -7.1 (1991), -0.2 (1992), +3.5 (1993), +3.2 (1994), +1.8 (1995), +1.9 (1996) , sources: OECD, 1997)
16. In 1970-71 the xenophobe Schwarzenbach initiative calling for a strict limitation of the foreign population was refused by the Swiss people but the result was very tight. From that time, political authorities deliberately chose to integrate some of the xenophobe claimings in the legislation in order to avoid the referendal process.
17.

| | Permanent | Annual | Seasonal | Frontier-workers |
|---|---|---|---|---|
| 1975 | 21 percent | 52.1 | 18.6 | 9 |
| 1993 | 57.6 percent | 18.1 | 7.6 | 16.7 |

Sources: Office fédéral de la statistique.

18. By comparison, since 1977 the rate of unemployment in France is over 5.1.
19. Source: Rossi M., 1994.
20. It means here foreign workers with an annual or permanent working permit.
21. We are missing data, but in Ticino canton, 85 percent of the working population in these sectors is composed of foreign workers (Bertozzi, 1999).
22. Some of these measures had to undergo a referendal process in 1993 but more than 70 percent of the voters approved the Federal Urgent Decrees.
23. In 1994 active measures accounted for little more than a quarter of the public expenditure on labor market programs and the three-quarters remaining served to pay the income support programs.

24. Until 1994, private agencies were responsible for three-quarters of the placements.
25. 250 for people above age 50 and 400 above age 60.
26. In the case of accepting the proposed active measures or of non-availability of such programs.
27. In the mid-1990s, Ian Gough underlined that in Switzerland: "Assistance consists of localized, discretionary relief, linked to social work and with wider kin obligations. Benefit levels are above average yet relatively few people claim assistance. This is partly due to the record of full male employment, and partly to low take-up, which is attributable to stigma and the substantial powers of intervention accorded to social welfare workers" (1997, p 37).
28. To a certain extent the regional distribution of the unemployment rate accounts for these divergences.
29. In terms of implementation capacity, most studies highlight the superiority of strictly parliamentary regimes. They generally can rely on stable and disciplined minorities (Weaver and Rockman 1993).
30. Notably the industries of the export sector (machine industry, chemistry industry...). By contrast, the associations of the sheltered sector (USAM, USP) agree with some measures but were opposed to the liberalization of the internal market.
31. OCDE, 1992, Etudes économiques, Suisse, 1991/1992.
32. Some academics: Professor Borner (Bâle University) and Professor Borner (University of Saint Gall), have been very influential experts.
33. Notably high official members of the OFAEE (Office fédéral des affaires économiques extérieures); the administrative department which conducted discussions with the EC and for the GATT Treaty. Management consultants (in Switzerland the Arthur Andersen group has been very often consulted) also played an important role in selling new ideas and policies.
34. For instance, such supplementary fiscal gifts accounted for about half a million Swiss francs in 1997.
35. In the book, coedited by David de Pury—former diplomatic head of the Swiss delegation to the Uruguay round, former manager of the firm ABB (Asea brown Boveri), now manager of the Swiss newspaper *Le Temps*—nineteen entrepreneurs, managers and professors (Hauser) propose radical reforms.
36. Solde la balance des opérations courantes (Mds CH Francs): +15.2 (1991), +21.3 (1992), +28.8 (1993), +24.4 (1994), + 25.0 (1995), +25.1 (1996), source: OECD, 1997.
37. OECD, Employment Outlook, 1994; OECD, Implementing the Strategy, 1995. We must add that from 1993, Switzerland followed the recommendations of the ILO to count the number of unemployed people.
38. Largely less than what most of the Parisian workers do every day.
39. The scandal around Volker Kind, former vice-director of the OFDE (federal office for economic development and employment), illustrates this stereo-type. Mr. kind publicly stated in July 1997 that two-thirds of the disoccupied were lazybones. alcoholics, and social cases.
40. The most important of them are the Vorort (association of employers), the Union Suisse des Arts et Métiers and the Central Union of employers' associations. The major trade union is the Union Syndicale Suisse, as well as unions of specific branches.
41. Since the beginning of the twentieth century the legislation about labor had been revised only two times.
42. "Pour revitaliser l'économie suisse en général, le gouvernement fédéral a adopté en 1995, *conformément aux recommandations de l'Etude de l'OCDE sur l'emploi*, d'importantes réformes de la législation du travail....La réforme assez radicale de

l'assurance-chômage a durci...," Cité in Etudes économiques de l'OCDE: Suisse, 1997, p 8.

43. Without seasonal and frontier-workers.
44. The statistics published monthly by the OFIAMT concern only the registered unemployed and this notion brings about considerable distortions with international standards. It covers the « persons registering with labor offices who do not have a job and are immediately available for employment. Following the ILO recommendations, the Federal Office of Statistics (OFS) set up in 1991 the « Swiss Labor Force survey » (Enquête Suisse sur la population active or ESPA). The results are then extrapolated according to intricate statistical procedures.

## References


Bertozzi, F. (1999). "Les nouvelles politiques de l'emploi au Tessin." Masters dissertation, University of Lausanne.

Bois, S., & Greber, P. Y. (eds.). (1982). *Emploi et politiques sociales*. Lausanne: Réalités Sociales.

Bonoli, G. (1997). "Social insurance in Switzerland." In J. Clasen (ed.), *Social insurance in Europe*. Bristol: The Policy Press.

Bonvin, J. M. (1996). Les réponses Suisse aux phénomènes migratoires. *L'Année Sociologique*, 46, 442-473.

Bütschi, D. & Cattacin, S. (1994). *Le modèle Suisse de bien-être*. Lausanne: Réalités Sociales.

Cameron, D. (1978). "The expansion of the public economy: A comparative analysis." *American Political Science Review, 72*, 1243-1261.

Castles, F. (ed.). (1993). *Families of nations. Pattern of public policy in western democracies*. Aldershot: Dartmouth.

Cunha, A., Leresch, J. P., & Vez I. (1998). *Pauvreté urbaine*. Lausanne: éditions Réalités Sociales.

Esping-Andersen, G. (ed.). (1996). *Welfare states in transition*. London: Sage.

Esping-Andersen, G. (1990). *The three worlds of welfare capitalism*. Cambridge: Polity.

Evans, P., Rueschemeyer, D., & Skocpol, T. (eds.). (1985). *Bringing the state back in*. New York: Cambridge University Press.

Ferrera, M. (1996)." Modèles de solidarité, divergences, convergences: perspectives pour l'Europe." *Revue Suisse de Science Politique*, 2, (1), 55-72.

Fischer, F., & Forrester, J. (1993). *The argumentative turn in public analysis and planning*. London: UCL and Duke University Press.

Flückiger, Y. (1996). "Analyse socio-économique des différences cantonales de chômage." In F. Helveticum (ed.), *Le chômage en Suisse: bilan et perspectives*, Lenzbourg.

Fragnière J. P., & Greber, Y. (eds.). (1997). *La sécurité sociale en Europe et en Suisse*. Lausanne: Ed Réalités Sociales.

Gilbert, N. (1992). "From entitlements to incentives: the changing philosophy of social protection." *International Social Security Review*, 45.

Gilliand, P. (ed.). (1990). *Pauvreté et sécurité sociale*. Lausanne: Réalités Sociales.

Gilliand, P., & Rossini, S. (1997). *La protection sociale en Suisse*: Lausanne: Réalités Sociales.

Gough, I., & Bradshaw, J. (1997). "Social assistance in OECD countries." *Journal of European Social Policy*, 17-43.

Hall, P. (ed.). (1989). *The political power of economic ideas. Keynesianism across nation*. Princeton, NJ: Princeton University Press, 361-391.

Hall, P. (1993). "Policy paradigms, social learning and the state." *Comparative Politics*, 23, 275-96.

Immergut, E. (1992). *Health politics. Interests and institutions in Western Europe.* New York: Cambridge University Press.
Jenson, J. (1989). "Paradigms and political discourse: Protective legislation in France and the United States before 1914." *Canadian Journal of Political Science*, XXII.2, June.
Jobert, B. (1995). *Le tournant néo-libéral en Europe.* Paris: L'Harmattan.
Kappel, R., & Landmann, O. (1997). *La Suisse dans un monde en développement.* Fribourg: Presses Universitaires.
Katzenstein, P. (1985). *Small states in world markets. Industrial policy in Europe.* Ithaca, NY-London: Cornell University Press.
Katzenstein, P. (1984). *Corporatism and change. Austria, Switzerland, and the politics of industry.* Ithaca, NY: Cornell University Press.
King, D. (1995). *Actively seeking work. The politics of unemployment and welfare policy in the United States and Great Britain.* Chicago: The University of Chicago Press.
Kingdom, J. (1984). *Agendas, alternative and public policies.* Boston: Little, Brown.
Kohli, M., Guillemard, A. M., & Rein, M. (1995). *Time for retirement.* New York: Sharpe.
Kriesi, H., Longchamp, C., Passy, G., & Sciarini, P. (1993). "Analyse de la votation fédérle du 6 décembre 1992," Genève/Bern, *Département de science politique,/Gfs Forschungsinstitut*, n° 47.
Kriesi, H. (1995). *Le système politique suisse.* Paris: Economica.
Lalive d' Epinay, C. (1988). *Le mythe du travail en Suisse.* Genève: Georg.
Lijphart, A. (1984). *Democracies. Pattern of majoritarian and consensus government in twenty-one countries.* New Haven, CT and London: Yale University Press.
Mach, A, (1997). "Quelles réponses politiques face à la globalisation et à la construction européenne? Illustration à partir de la loi Suisse sur les cartels." *Communication,* International Congress of Political Science: Seoul.
Manow, P., & Seils, E. (1998). *The Adjustment of national employment and social policy to internationalisation.* Workshop, Florence: European University Institute.
March, J., & Olsen, J. (1989). *Rediscovering institutions.* New York: The Free Press.
Merrien, F. X. (1990). "Etat et politiques sociales: contribution à une théorie néo-institutionnaliste." *Sociologie du travail,* no. 3, 267-294.
CRESAL. (Ed.). (1993). "Les politiques publiques, entre paradigmes et controverses." *Les raisons de l'action publique. Entre expertise et débat.* Paris: L'Harmattan.
Merrien, F. X. (1997). *L'Etat-providence.* Paris: Presses Universitaires de France.
Merrien, F. X., & Bonoli, G. (forthcoming). "Implementing big reforms of the welfare-states. A new-institutionalist approach." In S. Kuhnle (ed.), *Survival of the European Welfare-State.* London: Routledge.
Morosoli, C. (1994). *Il mercato regionale del lavoro. Concetti teorici e applicazione al caso del Cantone Ticino.* Bellinzona: Istituto Ricerche Economiche/Meta Edition.
OCDE. (1997). *Suisse. OCDE: Etudes economiques.* Paris.
OCDE. (1994). *New orientations for social policy.* Paris.
OECD. (1994, 1995). *OECD Employment outlook.* Paris.
OECD. (1995). *Implementing the strategy.* Paris.
Papadopoulos, Y. (1997). *Les processus de décision fédéraux en Suisse.* Paris: L'Harmattan.
Pierson, P. (1994). *Dismantling the welfare state? Reagan, Thatcher and the politics of retrenchment.* Cambridge: Cambridge University Press.
Pierson, P. (1995). "Fragmented welfare-states: Federal institutions and the development of social policies." *Governance,* 8 (4), 449-478.
Rein, M., & Schon, D. (1993). *Reframing policy discourse.* In F. Fischer, & J. Forrester, (eds.), 145-166.
Rossi, M. (1994). "Emploi, chômage et travailleurs frontaliers: évolution récente dans les régions frontalières de l'Europe occidentale." *Periodico dell'IRE,* 3.

Schmitter P. (1981). "Interest intermediation and regime governability." In S. Berger, (ed.), *Organizing interests in Western Europe*. Cambridge: University Press.

Sciarini, P. (1994). *Le système politique Suisse face à la Communauté européenne et au GATT: Le cas test de la politique agricole*. Genève: Georg.

Sciarini, P., & Listhaug, O. (1997). *Single cases or a unique pair? The Swiss and Norwegian not to Europe*. Robert Schuman Centre, European University Institute, Working papers, RSC, 97/25.

Sheldon, G. (1998). "Le chômage de longue durée en Suisse: diagnostic et thérapie." *La Vie économique* (8), 45-51.

Soskice, D. (forthcoming). "Divergent production regimes. Coordinated and uncordinated market economies in the 1980s and 1990s." In H. Kitschelt, P. Lange, G. Marks, & J. Stephens, (eds.), *Continuity and change in contemporary capitalism*. Cambridge: University Press.

Tabin, J. P. (1998). "Chômeur ancien, chômeur moderne: persistance des représentations?" *Revue Suisse de Sociologie, 24* (2), 209-236.

Van Kersbergen, K. (1995). *Social capitalism. A study of Christian Democracy and the welfare state*. London and New York: Routledge.

Weaver, K., & Rockman, B. (eds.). (1993). *Do institutions matter? Government capacities in the US and abroad*. Washington, DC: The Brookings Institution.

# 8

# Sweden—Still a Civilized Version of Workfare?

*Sven E. O. Hort*

"Some might argue that the centrist Swedish model is simply defunct. But Swedish voters have made a conscious choice to trade off higher taxes for better services and to aim for high-skill jobs. There is no conclusive evidence that this condemns them to permanent low growth."

—*Financial Times*, 15 April 1998

## Introduction: The Swedish Work-Welfare Dilemma in a Period of Increasing European Unemployment

Unemployment, work avoidance, and welfare dependency are recurrent phenomena—both as practices and rhetoric—in advanced capitalist "work and welfare" societies. Such societies are perceived as organizations or systems of social institutions and social relations where the working-age individual tries hard to be able to participate in the consumption of societal goods, not only to care for basic needs, and deliberately avoid the ghost of unemployment. In contrast, those who avoid a societal-defined normal amount of workload and, furthermore, manage to receive community support through improperly withdrawing from the chains of wage slavery, are in public opinion most often comprehended as unworthy deviants or welfare scroungers.

These were the macro characteristics of the modern postwar industrial society, not least in Europe; on the micro level related objectives were achieved through a combination of bureaucratic social control and primarily economic incentives both at the family, enterprise, and the societal level. To put it bluntly, in most cases a blend of sticks and carrots make people work in advanced society. However, in some cases this combination does not function and thus becomes a headache for parts of or society as a whole. As a remedy, a new mixture of the three components—unemployment, work avoidance, and welfare dependency—is needed to overcome what was once thought of as solving the problems at the margins of society.

In some countries, perhaps more so in the Anglo-Saxon world, these phenomena have tended to be blurred more often than in others. Less so in the case of Western Europe where, for instance, the conservative continental welfare regime through work-related unemployment insurance in the core countries of the European Union has created a rather stable social safety net for the great majority of the working population, males in particular (Carroll 1999; Korpi 1991). Nevertheless, due to a slowdown in the creation of new jobs a substantial proportion of the age group 20-60—for instance sole mothers—has been trapped in the "new poverty" and thus has had to rely on different, often means-tested, cash benefit programs (Berghman & Cantillon 1993). There, too, in the most recent decades the idea of welfare-to-work and work-to-welfare programs have seen the light of day.

Thus, also in Europe the notion of workfare—most often defined as activation of individuals through "flexible" participation on the labor market instead of "real jobs"—has become more widespread as the practice of the welfare state has come under intense scrutiny. However, where fundamental social rights—either through the labor market or as part of national citizenship—had been established prior to the breakthrough of the Reagan-Thatcherite anti-welfare rhetoric, various social policy institutions became strongholds of resistance to neo-liberal attempts at dismantling the welfare state. Yet two decades of fierce retrenchment policies did contribute to a steady retreat from the traditional priorities of the European welfare state. Demands for the expansion of social rights and for full employment became less frequent, and most political parties and other institutional actors began to elaborate a new agenda which included the idea of workfare.

Workfare is a concept that has entered the welfare debate in the last quarter of the twentieth century. It is generally defined as a a method to force people to work for less than the minimum wage, and sometimes there is even a requirement that employable public or social assistance recipients receive benefits only if they work off their grants in unpaid jobs. Few countries operate a pure workfare program, but many have more or less voluntary workfare schemes for the unemployed, with or without the sanction of loss of benefits if someone chooses not to participate.

To understand the contextual differences of workfare in various countries, from the start it is necessary to emphasize the stark contrast in the interpretation of the notion of welfare in most of Western Europe, on the one hand, and on the other hand in the Anglo-Saxon world and in particular in the United States. In Europe, following the establishment of Bismarckian social insurance schemes and later on the universalist Beveridge model, welfare and state were combined in a complex network of institutions—from social security to comprehensive education—to protect families and individuals against the insecurities of the market and to enhance individual life chances through active labor market participation (Marshall 1950; Titmuss 1958; Wilensky 1975; Flora 1986; Rokkan 1999). In contrast, in the United States the welfare concept has become the equivalent of tax payer support to the most vulnerable groups and individuals in society (Gilbert 1994). Welfare is synonymous with hand-outs to those living in squalid poverty, the (un-)deserving poor, and, for instance, separated from the working population's earned entitlements (eligibility) to social security.

## The Early Swedish Workfare, or Work-to-Welfare Model

Perhaps the blurring of unemployment, work avoidance, and welfare is even less true for the far north of Europe, Scandinavia. During the second half of the twentieth century in particular in Sweden unemployment has become recognized as a central societal dilemma and not an individual pathology. Previously, unemployment was generally regarded as self-inflicted and equated with poor relief problems. Gradually the mutual obligations between the individual citizen and society have become the norm of the day. Only to the extent that the individual met her or his responsibilities did society-at-large assume responsibility for income protection towards the individual worker and his or her family. The responsibility of the individual consisted of actively seeking work and accepting the challenge of skill development. This was the essence of the right to work enshrined in the 1974 Swedish Constitution (Olsson 1993a). The right to laziness, on the other hand—a right made famous by Paul Lafargue, the son-in-law of Karl Marx—has never been accepted as a social right in this still extremely Lutheran country of the far north. Welfare benefits as social rights or entitlements were aimed at the deserving working population—or those vulnerable and involuntarily unable to support themselves (various groups labeled handicapped and disabled)—and not at the undeserving poor and able-bodied, drunkards and vagrants. However, also in this society of workaholics the current wave of secularization has tested the tender balance between rights and obligations.

To understand the peculiar features of Swedish state and society as well as its manpower policy—the active labor market policy—it is necessary to make a few analytical distinctions and point out some trenchant institutional characteristics (Olsson 1993b). As is shown in figure 8.1, on the one hand there is the spatial or synchronic division between state and civil society, or community as the everyday notion is in the U.S. On the other hand there is the temporal or diacronic axis ranging from pre-modern forms of social institutions to the modern ones. Social insurance or social security is the modern form of institutional social protection closely linked to the current institutions of the labor market while poor relief was its archaic relative. However, for many years, up to the early 1980s, the two forms of social support were operating side-by-side in Swedish society although there was a notional shift in the mid-1950s from poor relief to social assistance.

**Figure 8.1**
**The Welfare Society of Sweden**

State

Local governments
(Church parishes)

Social assistance
(Municipal)

Poor relief
security

Social

Social organizations
(Popular movements)

Labor market
(Active manpower policy)

Civil Society/Community

The simultaneous century-long existence of two institutional forms of social protection is of course of diacronic nature but related to the syncronic axis. Poor relief was the traditional obligation for local communities whether in the old form of the parishes of the Lutheran State Church, or later through the latter's secular sequel, the municipalities (and the county councils responsible for medical services and hospitals). However, the local authorities were for long closer to civil society than to the central monarchic state as the former was run by elected laymen, in this primarily rural country dominated by small landowners or free farmers, or in the few towns by merchants and artisans (Stenius 1999). Lay activists in the revivalist free church movement as well as in the temperance (prohibitionist) movement played a crucial role in the transformation of pre-modern Sweden into a distinct modern though for long only semi-urban, industrial society. With the extension of suffrage—universal suffrage for both men and women was achieved after World War I—and the simultaneous establishment of parliamentary democracy both at the central and local levels, another segment of community or civil society, members of the popular social movements came to dominate local politics, in particular the Agrarian (later Center) and Social Democratic parties, and became responsible also for the proper distribution of resources to the—working as well as non-working—poor and also the education of the latter to respected, responsible and sober citizens.

In the aftermath of the breakthrough of political citizenship, in particular after World War II, came the gradual development of the welfare state—a state based on the idea of social rights on par with civil and political rights, or the principle that the welfare of every individual is the collective responsibility of the community. The distinction between state and civil society became blurred as both the central state and local governments as well as a set of representative bottom-up organizations, most often based on the popular social mass movements, became involved in the daily running of various welfare state agencies both at the central and the local level. In particular the labor movement—the Social Democratic party, the trade unions and the housing and retail coops in particular—but also rural social movements and organizations such as the Agrarian producer coops and its adjacent political party, the Agrarian Association, became significant societal players apart from the employers in a corporatist but fairly decentralized welfare state. Moreover, at the community level of society, the municipalities gathered forces and created their own corporatist lobby at the central level through the self-governed National Association of Local Authorities (Ramel 1998).

The establishment of the modern institutions of social rights such as universal social insurance was, thus, a blend of civil society and central state initiatives, sometimes consensual, at other times conflictual. The popular social mass movements, in particular the trade unions but also for instance the temperance movement, were heavily involved in the set-up of the various branches of social security, in particular sickness insurance. Even more important was the establishment of the tripartite active labor market policy during World War I with the central state, national labor unions as well as employer associations at the peak level as the main players. Thereby, a hierarchy between employment and social security policy was established at the central state level, which put job creation ahead of cash support for those on the dole. The work-first principle became the governing principle of Swedish labor market policy although it was not undisputed by the just-mentioned partners involved. For a while, this policy initiative was challenged from civil society by some major labor dominated municipalities, with the tacit support of the many trade unions, as the first era of twentieth century active labor market or workfare policy was characterized by harsh wage conditions and, even more important, anti-strike work obligations as the liberal conception of wage formation at the start dominated this policy (Unga 1976). Job creation as first principle remained intact when, from the early 1930s, the labor movement or Social Democracy became the long-term ruler of the central state and made the anti-strike rules more favorable for trade union members and cash support more generous for workers. As important, the employers remained active players in this policy arena and supported the new workfare policy. Furthermore, as a complement to full employment policy, state subsidies became available to voluntary but trade union organized unemployment insurance funds, a cash benefit support system for people with a long work experience and with the possibility to expel members-beneficiaries who refused to take suitable jobs recommended by the local employment exchanges (Rothstein 1996; 1992).

Throughout the postwar period the active labor market or full employment policy was the jewel in the crown of the Swedish welfare state. In the 1960s an important shift occurred as the concept of manpower and gainful employment not only came to include males but also adult females. Before the 1990s, unemployment never exceeded 4 percent and during economic slowdowns active measures to create new jobs reached at most 3 percent of the labor force. Work-to-welfare—the right to become a wage-earner and thus a taxpayer—or work activation was the hallmark of the National Labour Market Board (AMS), a corporatist, tripartite central state agency with close ties to the labor movement, and operating throughout the country by a network of local employment exchange offices. In the early decades such offices were most often run by non-bureaucratic former trade unionists, not traditional civil servants with a formal education (Rothstein 1980). AMS also supervised, and still supervises, the complementary trade union controlled unemployment insurance benefit societies/funds, and from 1974—through the local employment guidance and exchange offices—had its own complementary cash allowance system, at an extremely low reimbursement level, for those who for various reasons were/are not members of the voluntary benefit societies, or not qualified for insurance payments despite membership in such societies because of too short labor market experience.

Job creation through a variety of either, in the jargon of economists, demand- or supply-side measures, has been and still is the main duty of this agency. Following the Rehn-Meidner model, a labor market theory developed in the late 1940s by two trade union economists and pupils of Nobel laureate Gunnar Myrdal, the AMS Board encouraged structural change and did not support declining branches of industry. Apart from the employment exchange monopoly, AMS distributed subsidies to new industries in backward regions, organized training and retraining of unemployed and those threatened by unemployment as well as handed out mobility grants to those prepared to move to regions with labor shortage. Temporary public work projects were only considered a last resort in the arsenal of active labor market policy measures. For several decades, this was considered an exceptionally successful form of manpower policy but the shadows of the Anglo-Saxon anti-welfare rhetoric also fell over this market interventionist model as Keynesianism in general came into disrepute in the late 1970s (cf. Therborn 1985). However, as late as after the 1991 general election the British neo-liberal and pro-market journal *Economist* concluded that while other parts of the Swedish model might well be abandoned, its "active labour market policies are well worth saving" (cf. Olsson Hort 1993).

In the meantime, the Labour Market Board developed and enlarged its manpower policy arsenal as well as developed its organizational structure, a kind of state within the state. In 1980, the local sheltered workshops for handicapped and disabled persons run by AMS local employment offices or regional boards were fused into a national state company, *Samhall*, still mainly operating in the shadow of AMS and its rehabilitation units. In 1986, the educational wing of the Board—responsible for organizing labor market training and retraining courses throughout the country—was split off and became a Board on its own—*AMU*—although operating as a specialized subcontractor to AMS. In the early 1990s this latter agency was transformed into a state company—still named AMU—competing on the educational market for contracts with AMS with other non-state-owned sub-contractors, although AMU in most cases has remained the preferred choice. Furthermore, in the 1980s, the AMS Board became involved in a series of cooperative endeavors with other government agencies, in particular the National Social Insurance Board and the regional and local affiliates under its supervision—the Social Insurance Offices—to rehabilitate those who more or less permanently had left the labor market with cash support from various social insurance programs, in particular disability pension without being considered severely handicapped, and hence a case for Samhall. In toto, the visible hand, still had a say in Swedish society.

As mentioned, during this period of full employment simultaneously the old form of poor relief remained the last resort of support for those without any means of survival. In contrast to labor market policy and social security administration, the municipalities continued to be responsible for the welfare of citizens and community residents unable to support themselves. The policy ambition continued to be to turn such claimants into self-sustaining persons with a secure foothold on the labor market. There was still a fair number of social welfare clients that received temporary cash payments—for instance when housing costs increased without an immediate increase in wages—but had a steady foot on the labor market. Long-term recipients, however, tended to be people without strong labor market ties, and they were often looked upon as the major target group of municipal support. Poor relief, thus, tended to develop into a safety net for people with special problems such as heavy alcohol addiction, severe family breakdowns and mental illness.

In the mid-1950s poor relief changed its name to social assistance. At the same time the administration of social assistance not formally but in reality changed hands from lay politicians in the municipal social committees to professional social workers. As a profession, social workers and in particular the Association of Social Service Managers managed to hook up with other social organizations, and hence became influential lobbyists in Sweden in the field of social welfare (Hort & McMurphy 1997). The actual recipient rate of social assistance, however, continued to be closely linked to an increasingly lowered unemployment curve. Under pressure through the 1970s from a broad lobby of local politicians, professional social workers and representatives from various client organizations, a new Social Service Act was adopted by Parliament in 1980 (in effect as of 1982). Thereby the residualist character of cash assistance was transformed into the language of universal social policy, the discourse of citizen rights and entitlements. Social assistance clients were empowered while means-testing continued as an obligation for municipal professional social workers, a not very popular duty within this profession. Despite the new law, the work-welfare dilemma continued to haunt the social services.

Hence, during the postwar decades the administration of poor relief continued to be a high profile or controversial policy area while it simultaneously became less significant both as a national and municipal budget item. The welfare state grew in terms of programs, money, personnel and resources in particular at the local level. In the 1980s, this was further stressed as decentralization became a domestic Social Democratic answer to the international wave of neoliberal privatization (Olsson 1989). Swedish municipalities entered new welfare fields as responsible for part of universalist social programs—in particular personal social services to families and children, the handicapped and the aged—subsidized by generous (central) welfare state grants. However, most of these programs contained an element of needs-test carried out by professional social workers under the auspices of elected politicians in the municipal social committees. This kind of testing, though controversial in individual cases, never became a detested activity within the new profession of social workers. Overall, these were welfare program activities that were separated from the daily workings of the active manpower or work-to-welfare administration.

## The Workfare Crisis of the First Half of the 1990s

While most countries in Europe since the early 1970s have faced persistent unemployment problems Sweden entered into such a state of disease only in the early 1990s. Sweden was long known as a country of full employment where an active labor market policy based on the activation or work-first principle at an early stage intervened in the spontaneous workings of the market. Full employment was the main goal of government policy. Labor market measures were combined and complemented with other welfare state arrangements—such as risk-decreasing social insurance programs, state-subsidized child care facilities and, of course, competence development through general education—that encouraged a high labor market participation also among females (Hort 1997). High labor force participation, and often also labor shortage with inflationary pressure, became the typical characteristic of this model. In the 1990s, however, more people than ever have been dependent on cash benefits including not only non-means-tested social insurance benefits but also means-tested municipal social assistance (Salonen 1996). Social assistance as a municipal budget item tended to out-crowd other important municipal welfare objectives such as personal social services to children (including general education), the handicapped and the elderly.

The rapid and sudden increase in the unemployment rate coincided with a dramatic policy change as the Social democratic government in early 1990 declared that, instead of full employment and a fair distribution of income and other resources, low inflation had reached the top of the government agenda. This was in stark contrast to the postwar agenda of Swedish Social Democracy. Actually, it was a preparation for Swedish membership in the European Union, during the Cold War, an extremely controversial issue in neutral Sweden. In the aftermath of the Fall of the Berlin Wall, in the fall of 1990 the Swedish Social Democratic government declared that a membership application would be handed over to Brussels in due course (this was formally done in the Hague on June 30, 1991, and in January 1995 Sweden became a member-state of the union). At this time, a financial and budgetary crisis was underway, and soon followed a rapid increase in the open unemployment rate, from less than 2 percent in 1989 to well over 8 percent three years later. Labor force participation rapidly fell as well. Sweden was hit by the worst economic downturn since the Great Depression. In 1990, 83 percent of the age group 20-64 belonged to the active labor force, six years later this percentage figure had decreased to 72.

In 1990, the Social Democratic government for the first time ever proposed and later made cutbacks in welfare benefits (Stephens 1996). In the general election of 1991, voters expressed their dissatisfaction with this new course and the traditional rulers of Sweden received its worst election result in more than 60 years (37 percent of the votes) (Korpi 1993). In the midst of this social and economic turbulence, a non-experienced conservative-led coalition cabinet took over. The new government encouraged deregulation, entrepreneurship and increased competition within or marketization (commercialization) of the public sector but overall whatever neo-liberal element the new government had on its agenda, it quickly disappeared. The most ambitious labor market policy initiative from the new non-socialist government was to extend social rights and make unemployment insurance compulsory—i.e., less trade union controlled—and, thus, universal for the entire labor force as of mid-1994 (only to be overruled by the new Social Democratic government as of January 1995). Second, it tried to put an end to payouts from the insurance system, i.e., a final limit for the duration of benefits, but pro-union controlled lobbyists were strong enough to prevent such a parliamentary decision (Olsson Hort 1995). Third, with labor support the new cabinet managed to decrease the benefit level, but this consensus was only achieved in the midst of a strong attack against the Swedish krona, and by the Social Democratic opposition seen as a necessary attempt to restore confidence in the global financial markets (Olsson 1993).

Otherwise, the new government continued along the lines of the traditional active labor market policy, and at the Labour Market Board the pro-labor bureaucracy remained in charge. However, already in 1994, social expenditure on passive measures (unemployment insurance cash support) overshadowed expenditure on active measures (training and retraining, employment guidance, mobility and rehabilitation grants etc); a break in a four-decade-long trend. Hence, all of a sudden a government program—the active labor market or manpower program—prepared to cope with an unemployment rate of less than 4 percent, and able to mobilize resources to take care of 3 percent of the labor force had to face double digit unemployment figures and with less resources had to double its capacity to activate and retrain those unexpectedly out of work. Volume replaced excellence as the main objective of labor market measures. In the first half of the 1990s, a number of cheap programs were invented to take care of the growing numbers of unemployed—often in cooperation with the municipalities—while more costly measures such as labor skill upgrading and increased competence building had to give way as demand was exceptionally low even for such labor power. But those belonging to an unemployment fund and eligible for benefits, often older workers with a fair amount of work experience, so called insiders, had the right to receive an offer of a six-month relief job or retraining from the AMS local employment office when their benefit period expired in order not to be expelled from their voluntary insurance benefit society. Thus, active manpower measures became in practice only another waiting period for unemployment cash support. Moreover, the gap between labor market insiders and outsiders increased (Lindbeck 1997). For those in the age group 55+, early retirement was offered but this alternative was rather restrictively used as rules were tightened (Olofsson & Pettersson 1994).

In particular fairly unskilled young persons, in many cases even with a high school degree, were not any longer considered interesting by employers, and thus, not able to enter the regular labor market. The number of young labor market outsiders increased as thousands and again thousands of high school pupils had nothing but the dole to look forward to after graduation. This was in policy circles considered a nightmare, in particular for those graduating in 1992-94. The harsh reality of an intentional loophole in the universal welfare state—voluntary unemployment insurance as a secondary complement to active labor market policy—created a social and economic duality between labor market insiders and outsiders. Moreover, the traditional work-to-welfare active manpower programs operated for all those who had got a job during earlier decades, but were not to the same extent open to young or newly arrived foreign migrants, for instance the considerable number of refugees from Bosnia that arrived in Sweden in 1992 and 1993.

Municipal social assistance again became the last resort for many of those outside the main welfare system, in particular those without previous work experience, the young high school graduates (of course, even worse off were young high school drop-outs) and newly arrived Swedes (immigrants) from abroad. After a while the municipalities received extra money for the refugees' first years in Sweden, and together with the national labor market authority, AMS, they also created some jointly run labor market activation programs for the young and unskilled unemployed. However, these people were ineligible for unemployment insurance cash support when the activation period elapsed. In some cases, though, they became eligible for the above-mentioned supplementary unemployment cash allowance. In most cases, however, again they had to rely on municipal social assistance. After their first years in Sweden on central state cash support also many refugees have had to rely on municipal cash assistance. These victims of national system rule and global development, in Sweden have been blamed as typical welfare scroungers. Furthermore, many working poor applied for temporary supplementary cash support in times of hardship. Social assistance recipients as well as social expenditure on social assistance more than doubled in the first half of the 1990s. Social assistance was no longer a residual safety net for drunkards, vagrants and other social deviants on the margins of society. Still, this benefit system remained apart from the labor market support system. No obligation to work was in general part and parcel of this local welfare system.

## The New Workfare, or Municipal Welfare-to-Work Project: The Uppsala Model

In the early 1980s, the historical legacy of poor relief was supposed to have disappeared from municipal social assistance and, as mentioned, this means-tested cash support had become a social right as an element of the new Social Service Act. However, this legislation was not rule-driven but a frame law and hence gave considerable leeway for local government interpretation. Furthermore, the level of cash support was firmly decided on the local level although the National Board of Social Welfare—a national agency with much less power and authority than the above-mentioned National Labour Market Board (AMS)—wrote annual recommendations in tandem with the self-governed National Association of Local Authorities. During the 1990s, the principles and practices governing the Social Service Act—and in particular the local right to self-determination over cash support—was challenged by a growing number of politicians and other voices in public opinion (Sunesson et al 1998).

Already in the second half of the 1980s the number of social assistance recipients and expenditure on social assistance had continued to grow despite that the employment situation became better

(Salonen 1993). This was in contrast to earlier developments when the social assistance rate with a slight time-lag had closely followed the unemployment rate. Some municipalities interpreted this in a controversial manner: the hand-out of social assistance had become less stringent as it had become an enacted social right to cash assistance. It was in this context that the Uppsala workfare or welfare-to-work model was developed, named after the fifth largest municipality in Sweden, although it was not confined to this urban municipality.

Today, the Uppsala model includes careful means testing, requires frequent visits to the municipal social welfare office, demands that full-time efforts to find paid employment are carried out as a condition what is usually the case in Sweden (Milton & Bergström 1999). The responsibility—obligation—of the individual for earning a living consists in a requirement to participate in tripartite discussions with social welfare officers as well as employment guidance officers working at the local level for the National Labour Market Board. If the client is unwilling to follow these rules, the Uppsala model recommends sanctions in the form of cut-off from benefit payments. Furthermore, social welfare officers have frequent in-house meetings with special group leaders to evaluate and elaborate the individual career plan whereby the claimant—the case—is scrutinized by a greater number of social work professionals. By following these principles, the inventor of this model thought that the benefit period would be shortened. Another idea was that also more or less permanent solutions to the maintenance of the client, either through work or education, to a greater extent than earlier would be found (Rönnlund 1992). In rare cases the municipal workfare approach has been extended to include a rule saying that the recipient has to accept a job in the municipality as a reciprocity for receiving social assistance. The recipient has been obliged to take any job offer from the municipality, but this has been practiced only in a few, rather small local authorities and, thus, not particularly widespread.

From the start, the Uppsala model was considered extremely provocative but as the unemployment crisis deepened in the early 1990s, and demands for municipal participation in job creation increased, the National Association of Local Authorities began to support this workfare or welfare-to-work model as it was considered cost-saving (Svenska Kommunförbundet 1992). However, the Association has no executive power and can only recommend various solutions. At most roughly 30 municipalities or some 10 percent of Swedish local governments paid tribute to the Uppsala model, most of them fairly small ones (Karlsson 1995). No major municipality other than Uppsala followed suit but a few individual social service agencies also in other big municipalities have applied this approach. Advocates believed that this model would encourage people to reach positive changes in their lives and enable them to make the most of their skills, while critical commentators have viewed it as a regression to the old poor relief or social control practice in which a social problem is considered as an individual problem of welfare dependency and work avoidance. Furthermore, it has been looked upon as an instrumentalization of the client-professional relationship, thus a deprofessionalization of social work, and as an example of the utilitarian ethics of "the end justifies the means" (Karlsson 1995). Nationwide, critics from within the professions of social work as well as social researchers pointed out that people were insulted, degraded and confronted with impossible demands (Sunesson et al. 1998). Many local politicians—Agrarians and Conservatives as well as Social Democrats—have hesitated to follow the recommendations from their own Association, and in at least two of the upcoming political parties, the ecological Green Party and the feminist Left party there has not been much support for harsher measures towards social service claimants. Another new political party, the Christian Democratic party, although decidedly neo-conservative, has not been outspoken on this issue.

Instead, further collaboration at the local level between municipal and county council agencies and national players such as the labor market employment offices as well as social insurance offices have become the typical pattern of Swedish workfare policy. This has not been an uncomplicated love affair as the rules governing the various welfare fields have been difficult to combine. Though experiments through exceptions from existing laws were allowed, national legislation has been slow to adapt to new circumstances (see for instance Egon Jönsson and Hammarsköld 1997)). At the local level several authorities have been involved and have had to adapt to new circumstances. Agency cooperation and coordination have been recommended and various economic incentives tried, but later national authorities hesitated to go ahead further.

At the national level, one state commission has replaced the other without reaching definite conclusions and legislative change in Parliament. At the local level, though, in some cases such undertakings have been exceptionally successful in particular when public resources—money and personnel in particular—have been distributed in new ways or through new channels. Also the above-mentioned National Social Insurance Board and the regional Social Insurance Offices under its supervision as well as the National Board of Social Welfare and the new Public Health Institute have participated in these endeavors (for a successful local example, cf. Axelsson 1998).

## Halving Open Unemployment by Year 2000

During most of the first half of the 1990s Sweden was ruled by a rather inexperienced non-socialist coalition cabinet which had to deal with rising unemployment and a burgeoning public deficit. Before the regular election of 1994, the Social Democrats promised to restore public finance by decreasing welfare benefits as well as increasing already high taxes, and finally to combat unemployment. With this program the party made an impressive victory (46 percent of the votes) and pretty soon had restored confidence in the financial market. Interest rates soured/decreased as welfare benefits including unemployment insurance benefits were decreased (to 75 percent of an average worker wage). Without protest from the invisible hands of the financial market, in 1998 the government restored the benefit level in most of the social insurance system to 80 percent in advance of the upcoming election. The fight to combat unemployment has been more of an uphill battle but in 1996 the party and the government under a new Prime Minister—the former, and for two years successful, Minister of Finance—presented a major program to cut unemployment in half before the year 2000. At that time, the unemployment rate was well above 8 percent and another 5-6 percent in labor market activities. Apart from traditional Swedish active measures the government decisively increased educational opportunities on every level including adult education. A special program for upgrading skills—economically supported by a new benefit program at the level of unemployment insurance cash support—among adults without a high school degree has been set up all over the country. The work-first principle was transformed into a work-and-competence-first principle. Likewise, the number of students in tertiary education has doubled in the 1990s as new universities and colleges have opened throughout the country.

The arsenal of active labor market measures has come to include for instance an individual career plan for every unemployed job seeker, old as well as young. In the latter case, newly unemployed young persons are usually transferred to municipal workfare programs. The municipalities have become involved to a much greater extent than during earlier decades in particular regarding young unemployed. As the age of secondary education increased, the municipalities already in the 1980s became responsible for those few who were outside the school system, first before reaching age 18, later age 20. Those without paid jobs more or less automatically become part of an activation program and receive a daily benefit similar to the supplementary unemployment assistance benefit (non-insurance). During the 1990s the age of participation in such programs has risen considerably, and in early 1998 a youth development guarantee was implemented for those age 20-24 (Statskontoret 1999). As a condition to receive a place in an activation program and thereby an activation benefit, they had to be unemployed for 100 days as well as active labor seekers. As a consequence of the increase of municipal involvement the volume of workfare program has grown. As a complement to activation benefit the municipalities may pay additional housing cost through social assistance (Svenska Kommunförbundet 1999). Those youngsters who refuse to participate in such program are also denied the latter benefit (as well as the central state financed activation benefit). Thus, they are denied existing social welfare benefits and have to support themselves through other means (for instance, non-state intra-family benefits, "black or gray sector" jobs, etc).

Young people have also been encouraged to continue their education either through "adult" secondary education or academic studies. As mentioned, during the 1990s various governments have increased the slots at the present centers of tertiary education as well as opened new university colleges. Thereby an increasing number of persons in the age group 20-30 have been eligible to apply for study loans (with a 10 percent study allowance as part of the loan). This way, most young people have been kept outside the core social insurance programs. No pension points, no rights to sick pay, work injury payments, paternal insurance benefits, etc., and, of course, no rights to occupational welfare benefits. Young parents without work experience and no pay-related parental benefits (except at the minimum level), have been hit by the crisis.

The emphasis on active measures for long-term unemployed, i.e., activation rather than benefit and wage reduction, carrots rather than sticks, has meant that the municipalities have also been forced to take care of older workers whose unemployment (insurance) benefit is in danger of expiring. With central state grants municipalities employ these people for a six-month period at the rate of the unemployment benefit or with a small increase if the job is part of a special program. These unemployed have in general only one purpose for participation in an activity—to regain his or her right to an unemployment benefit. In particular in the first half of the 1990s, activation measures were adapted to the unemployment situation: cheap programs were invented to take care of a large increase in the level of unemployment.

Carrots have dominated for those already within the unemployment insurance system. Furthermore, there have been an emphasis on improving the skills and work experience of the unemployed instead of increasing their mobility and job seeking efficiency at a time when there were few jobs to move to and few to seek. Activation still undoubtedly involves a great deal of discipline and punishment, but it also tends to break the social isolation of the unemployed and helps to improve their social capacities, technical skills and, not least, their self-confidence or cultural resources. The goal of the Rehn-Meidner workfare model has always been to improve the political resources of those threatened by unemployment, i.e., empowerment through a right to work. This is the inner core of the civilized version of workfare.

The 1996 government program also included an ambition to increase the sticks in the systems, in particular through a limit in the duration of cash benefits. However, the power base of Social Democracy, the trade union movement, opposed such a measure and manage to defer a decision despite that the other part of the informal government coalition, the Agrarian Center party, insisted on such a step. The government also set up several state commissions to investigate new ways of supporting poor and unemployed people both within the present social insurance system and as a separate alternative to municipal social assistance. But apart from the above-mentioned adult education support no new benefit programs have yet seen the light of day. The commissions continue to work and much smoke has entered the legislative battlefield. In particular a limitation in the duration of unemployment benefit has created a lot of unrest within the labor movement, and no decision is in sight. A citizens income has been proposed by the Green party but other players in the field seem reluctant to adopt such a change. A citizen or basic income has been interpreted as a move away from the traditional work-first principle toward a cash-first principle. Instead, municipal social assistance has been streamlined as a rather low national baseline has been introduced. Thereby the traditional emphasize on local power was overruled but with tacit support from the municipalities as they hoped to get economic support from the central state in exchange. So far no grant have been paid but municipalities in population-decreasing areas have been promised additional money as of the year 2000.

When the Social Democrats after four years in power had to face the voters in the regular election of September 1998 the electorate was not impressed. The party received only 37 percent of the votes, close to the all time low of 1991. Its partner, the Agrarian Center party, was also seriously wounded and their joint vote was not enough to support a majority government. Due to a split among the center-right parties and other victorious center-left (green) and leftist parties the Social Democrats managed to avoid a resignation and continued at the helm. When the new government program was presented a few weeks later the government upheld the earlier promise to cut unemployment in half before the year 2000 as well as increase labor force participation to the late 1980s level (above 80 percent of the population in the age group 20-60) before the year 2004.

In particular the latter addition should be taken as a significant step in restoring the traditional active manpower policy. If achieved it could be a major victory for Social Democracy. If it fails, the long march downward of Social Democracy most likely would continue more rapidly. At present, at the EU level the Swedish government has continued to emphasis the employment goal inscribed in the 1997 Amsterdam declaration, and has fought battles against more neo-liberal social democratic governments within the union, for instance the U.K. Blair government. In particular the idea of a more "flexible" workforce—i.e., less job security—has been criticized by the Swedish government. Thus, the workfare or welfare-to-work policy has remained at the top of the policy agenda although competing with an overarching economic growth through low inflation goal. Approaching the crucial year 2000 the government remained silent on the issue of a limit of unemployment cash support as well as other issues controversial to their new political partners. Still, no work obligation—work-in-exchange-for-benefit—has been seriously proposed or enacted apart from the development guarantee for the young unemployed on municipal social assistance. But two state commissions presented their proposals in late 1999, one from the Ministry of Social Affairs and the other from the Ministry of Industry (cf. Socialdepartementet 1999).

## Summary and Conclusions: Still a Centrist Model or Civilized Version of Workfare?

Restoring and empowering unemployed and otherwise marginalized people—regardless of class, gender or ethnicity—so that they can participate in mainstream society and escape poverty demands both social and political commitment as well as economic investment. In Sweden, carrots have been preferred at the expense of sticks. For decades, however, a carrot meant a job, not money. This was considered the social basis of individual self-respect (cf. Kildal 1998). At the level of social collectivity, the national priority of Swedish governments of different colors was for decades to put people in work, i.e., what in the late 1980s in the U.S.—as it was debating AFDC or welfare reform—was called a civilized version of workfare.

In the 1990s the Swedish welfare system has faced some strains such as a growing budget deficit and for some years also a combined unemployment rate of 13 percent. Apart from financial difficulties also the national consensus behind the policy has weakened, at least at the elite level, if not among voters (Svallfors 1996). In particular the state financial problems forced the labor market authorities to reinterpret the work-first-principle into a bridge-over-principle to make people eligible for continued unemployment benefits after a six-month period in paid employment. Likewise, many local authorities had to reduce spending on social welfare and to look for new ways of dealing with increasing hand-outs of social assistance. These problems contributed to a growing critique of the overall high-tax-and-benefit system, and a rethinking of some sacred cows in Sweden.

The idea of a stronger element of obligations—more emphasis on sticks instead of carrots or, for instance, an obligation to work or more actively seek jobs in reciprocity for social assistance benefits—in an otherwise social-right-dominated welfare system (i.e., carrots) created some controversial measures at the level of local authority. The most typical example was the so-called Uppsala-model which included more stringent evaluation of benefit claimants as well as a greater emphasis on job seeking. This model can be viewed as a welfare-to-work model, although far from the extreme Anglo-Saxon type of workfare. It has, despite strong support from the National Association of Local Authorities, never been able to take root among the great majority of municipalities but remained a provocative alternative at the margin. Most municipalities have continued to hand out means-tested cash benefits as a right although at lower benefit levels, in particular after the national norm was put in place in 1997. The obligations of social welfare clients have not been standardized at the national level but remained open for municipal interpretations. Only youngsters have been an object of increased stress on the obligation to work or continue education.

Thus, it is the old Swedish active manpower policy—or centrist model—administered by the National Labour Market Board and its local employment offices combined with a new emphasis on general and academic education among young people as well as adult—the work-and-competence-first-principle—that have come to dominate efforts to cut unemployment and increase labor force participation. This is where the Swedish work-first principle has always been institutionally placed, and where it still remains. Despite a number of difficulties in the first half of the 1990s, the national active manpower policy has survived. Maybe it has even been rejuvenated when an extreme unemployment rate challenged previous ways of dealing with its mission. It is too early to give a definite judgment as things are still at the crossroads. However, empowerment rather than local control and individual punishment has continued to be the priority of the policies adopted also in the late 1990s. To summarize, it is in essence a neo-statist strategy as the element of central state regulation is still stronger than the self-regulation of local governance networks (cf. Benner 1997).

As the economy has been restored during the second half of the 1990s, there has been an increasing emphasis on labor force participation and thus workfare policy. But this should not be interpreted as a give-in to pressure from outside in the direction of a neoliberal welfare regime. This is a continuation of an earlier policy with new and other means. At the approach of the year 2000, the economic is growing at a steady rate and the unemployment rate has been lowered considerably. In June 1999 the figure was 5.6 percent, the forecast for the year 2000 is roughly 4.4 percent (Ministry of Finance August 1999). Thus, more than one and a half percent remains before the government goal of 1996 is fulfilled, maybe less than half a percent if the forecast comes through. As these lines are written another four and a half years remain until the most distant but no less demanding complementary goal of a labor force consisting of more than 80 percent of the age group 20-60 is in harbor. Whether this goal will be achieved is, of course, to early to make any speculation about. But the presence of such a goal is an indication that the civilized version of workfare is still alive although challenged as a practice and ideologically called into question.

## References


Axelsson, C. (1998). *Hela kedjan GAIA*. Esklilstuna: Centrum för välfärdsforskning

Benner, M. (1997). *The Politics of Growth: Economic Regulation in Sweden 1930-1994*. Lund: Arkiv (diss.).

Berghman, J. & Cantillion, B. (eds.). (1993). *The European Face of Social Security*. Aldershot: Avebury.

Berglind, H., Gullberg, A., & Elofsson, S. (1996). "Work or welfare—a dilemma in the declining Swedish welfare state." *Scandinavian Journal of Social Welfare*, Vol. 5, pp. 148-153.

Clapton, R., & Pontusson, J. (1998). "Welfare State Retrenchment Revisited." *World Politics*, Vol. 51 (Oct) pp. 67-98.

Carroll, E. (1999). Emergence and Structuring of Social Insurance Institutions— Comparative Studies on Social Policy and Unemployment Insurance. Stockholm: Swedish Institute for Social Research (diss. No. 38).

Edebalk, P. G. (1975). Arbetslöshetsförsäkringsdebatten—en studie i svensk socialpolitik. Lund: Department of Ekonomic History (diss.).

Gilbert, N. (1994). *Welfare Justice—Restoring Social Equity*. New Haven: Yale University Press.

Hammarsköld, C-G. (1997). *Finsam—Förändring av en välfärdsorganisation genom försöksverksamhet*. Lund: Bokbox.

Hort, S.E.O. (1997). "Advancing for Children in the Advanced Welfare State: Current Problems and Prospects in Sweden." In G.A. Cornia & S. Danziger (eds.), *Child Poverty and Deprivation in the Industrialized Countries*. Oxford: Clarendon Press.

Hort, S.E.O., & McMurphy, S.C. (1997). "Sweden." In N. Mayades, T. Watts & D. Elliott (eds.), *International Handbook on Social Work Theory and Practice*. Westport, CT: Greenwood Press.

Flora, P. (eds.). (1986). *Growth to Limits—the West European Welfare State Since World War II*. Volumes I & II. Berlin & New York: Walther de Gruyter.

Karlsson, U. (1995). "Uppsalamodellen—ett nygammalt arbetssätt inom socialt arbete." *Nordisk socialt arbete*. Vol. 10, No. 5, pp. 243-257.

Kildal, N. (1998). "The Social Basis of Self-respect: A Normative Discussion of Politics against Unemployment." *Thesis Eleven*, No. 54, pp. 63-77.

Korpi, W. (1993). "Politik och väljare bakom valutgången 1991" (Politics and voters behind election result in 1991) in *Sociologisk Forskning*, Vol. 30, No 1, pp. 3-28,

Korpi, W. (1991). "Political and Economic Explanations for Unemployment: A Cross-National and Long-Term Analysis." In *British Journal of Political Science*, Vol. 21, No. 2, pp. 315-48.

Lindbeck, A. (1997). *The Swedish Experiment*. Stockholm: SNS.

Marshall, T. H. (1950). *Citizenship and Social Class*. Oxford: Oxford University Press.

Milton, P., & Bergström, R. (1999). *Uppsalamodellen och socialbidragstagarna—en effektutvärdering*. Stockholm: Centrum för utvärdering av socialt arbete.

Olofsson, G., & Pettersson, A. (1994). "Sweden: Policy Dilemmas of the Changing Age Structure in a 'Work Society'." In F. Naschold & B. Van der Vroom (eds.), *Regulatring Employment and Welfare: Company and National Policies at the End of Worklife in Industrial Countries*. New York: Walther de Gruyter.

Olsson, S. E. (1989). "Decentralization and privatization: strategies against a welfare backlash in Sweden." In R. Morris (ed.), *Testing the Limits of Social Welfare*. Hanover: Brandeis University Press.

Olsson, S. E. (1990; 1993b). *Social Policy and Welfare State in Sweden*. Lund: Arkiv (first ed. 1990; second ed. 1993).

Olsson, S. E. (1993a). "Freiwillige Arbeitlosenversicherung und umfassende soziale Sicherheit—der Widerspruch der Swedischen Vollbeschäftigungspolitik." In G. Lottes (ed.), *Soziale Sicherheit in Europa*. Heidelberg: Physica-Verlag.

Olsson Hort, S. E. (1993). "Welfare Policy in Sweden." In T.P. Boje & S. E. Olsson Hort (eds.), *Scandinavia in a new Europe*. Oslo: Scandinavian University Press.

Olsson Hort, S. E. (1995). "Sickness and Unemployment Insurance in Sweden." In E. Brunsden & M. May (eds.), *Social Policy Review 1995*. London: Social Policy Association.

Ramel, C. (1998). "The National Association of Local Authorities." Stockholm: Department of Sociology (mimeo).

Rokkan, S. (1999). *State Formation, Nation-Building and Mass Politics in Europe—the Theory of Stein Rokkan*. Oxford: Oxford University Press (edited by Peter Flora, Stein Kuhnle, and Derek Urwin).

Rönnlund, E. (1992). *Socialt arbete—att se möjligheter*. Stockholm: Almqvist & Wiksell.

Rothstein, B. (1996). *The Social Democratic State—the Swedish Model and the Bureaucratic Problem of Social Reform*. Pittsburgh: Pittsburgh University Press.

Rothstein, B. (1992). *Den korporativa staten*. Stockholm: Norstedts.

Rothstein, B. (1980). "AMS som socialdemokratisk reformbyråkrati." In *Arkiv för arbetarrörelsens historia* no. 18.

Salonen, T. (1996). *Övervältringar inom socialsektorn. Effekter av statliga nedskärningar på socialbidragshushåll*. Stockholm: Kommentus.

Salonen, T. (1993). *Margins of welfare—A study of modern functions of social assistance*. Lund: Hällestad Press (diss.).

Socialdepartementet. (1999). *Samverkan för färre bidrag och fler i jobb*. Stockholm: Ministry of Health and Social Affairs.

Statskontoret. (1999). *Utvecklingsgarantin för ungdomar*. Stockholm: The Swedish Agency for Administrative Development.

Stenius, K. (1999). *Privat och offentligt i svensk alkoholistvård—arbetsfördelning, samverkan och styrning under 1900-talet*. Lund: Arkiv (diss.).

Stephens, J. (1996). "The Scandinavian Welfare States: Achievements, crisis and prospects." In G. Esping-Andersen (ed.), *Welfare States in Transition*. London: Sage.

Sunesson, S., Blomberg, S., Edebalk, P-G., Harrysson, L., Magnusson, J., Meeuwisse, A., Petersson, J., & Salonen, T. (1998). "The flight from universalism." *European Journal of Social Work*, Vol. 1, No. 1, pp. 19-29.

Svallfors, S. (1996). *Välfärdsstatens moraliska ekonomi*. Umeå: Borea.

Svenska Kommunförbundet. (1999). *Utvecklingsgarantin—som kommunerna ser det*. Stockholm: National Association of Local Authorities.

Therborn, G. (1986). *Why Some Peoples Are More Unemployed Than Others*. London: Verso.
Titmuss, R. (1974). *Social Policy*. London: Unwin.
Wilensky, H (1975). *The Welfare State and Equality*. Berkeley: University of California Press.

# 9

# The Norwegian Work Approach in the 1990s: Rhetoric and Reform

*Espen Dahl and Jon Anders Drøpping*

## Introduction

In this chapter we describe and analyze the activation policies which have been the official guideline for virtually all social policy initiatives in Norway in the 1990s. Focusing on both the rhetoric and program level, a primary ambition is to assess the degree to which the government's wishes, intentions, and objectives are detectable in actual policies, i.e., whether the good intentions come true in reality. The chapter consists of four parts. First, we sketch out some salient features of recent changes and trends in socioeconomic conditions in Norwegian society. We also give a brief exposition of the welfare system in Norway, a system known as the "Nordic Model," and address some of its tensions and dilemmas. Second, we describe and discuss the Norwegian version of activation policies, the "Work Approach" (*arbeidslinjen*), on a rhetoric level. We track down the origin of the term and define its substance. Part three describes the ways in which a number of specific programs and benefits have become more activation-oriented during the 1990s. We assess this question by looking at four program characteristics: changes in institutional settings, organization, expenditures, and number of "activated" participants. Finally, we discuss some of the implications of our investigation. Among the themes we address are the following: what is new, if anything, with the activation approach; do the reforms succeed in making "work the first choice" of the citizens; and what are the implications and the unintended consequences of this social policy?

*Socioeconomic Trends*

The Norwegian economy has shown a favorable development in recent years. The upturn in the Norwegian economy has now lasted about five years. Employment increased by 121,000 persons from 1993 to 1996 and unemployment declined. Total labor force participation has risen sharply the last 25 years, exceeding in 1995 the level recorded in the previous peak year, 1988. The growth in the labor force is primarily caused by an increase in female participation rates. Higher levels of educational attainment among women, better day-care coverage and more flexible maternity leaves may contribute to a further increase in labor force participation among women in the years ahead.

Unemployment, measured as a share of the labor force, was reduced by 1.5 percentage points from 1993 to 1996, and in 1999 the unemployment rate is close to a modest 2.5 percent. Long-term unemployment and youth unemployment have shown a particularly sharp decline. Some groups, however, seem to experience problems in gaining a labor market foothold. This applies, in particular, to people with disabilities and immigrants from eastern Europe and the Third World.

The rise in prices is low, and so are interest rates. The current balance of payments is in large surplus and the government budget also shows a surplus. A tight fiscal policy and responsible and solidaristic behavior on the part of the social partners have been decisive factors behind a simultaneous recovery of activity and low price and wage increases. Norwegian industry has regained market shares in traditional export markets and has penetrated new markets. Side by side with the favorable development of the sectors exposed to external competition, the purchasing power of the individual wage earner has increased.

The Norwegian economy is dependent on off-shore oil production and therefore vulnerable to fluctuations in oil prices. For the future, there is a deep concern regarding the situation after the oil reserves run dry around 2050. Currently, there are some signs of a labor shortage in some labor market segments. A further reduction in unemployment without triggering higher wage growth will require employment and manpower policies carefully adapted to the demand for labor. Labor force participation among older persons, especially men, has declined steadily over the past few decades; a trend which is at odds with official retirement policies. In the long run, this means that the economic burden of (early) retirement placed on the work force will be heavier than predicted solely by demographic developments.

*The Nordic Welfare Model and Some Current Challenges*

In an international context, Norway's welfare system may be described by referring to the features of the Nordic model, as laid out by Esping-Andersen (1990). The coverage of welfare is universal, the benefits are relatively generous, and benefits and services are provided by public agencies (on the state or municipal level). The level of equality is relatively high and citizens' opportunities for "decommodification" are abundant and liberal. In this model there is a particular structural configuration of economy, state, and civil society. A publicly financed and organized welfare state depends on a high level of taxation, which, in turn, depends on high employment among the able-bodied population. Thus, the Nordic welfare model has "always" been based on the premise of "full employment" (Esping-Andersen, ibid.: 28). Between the two world wars, Swedish social democrat economists denoted this principle "productive justice." Shortly after World War II similar views were expressed in Norway. In this sense, "activation" has for long been a basic premise of the Nordic model. One expression of this is the traditionally high employment rates in groups which elsewhere are far less attached to the labor market, e.g., women and the elderly (Kolberg and Esping-Andersen, 1992). For women, the welfare state serves as a gigantic employment machine in itself. This is the model in a simplified, pure, and harmonious form. However, due to internal and external developments, it has been put under pressure (Esping-Andersen, 1999; Kautto et al., 1999).

Several symptoms of severe tensions and contradictions call for adjustments. Let us just mention a few related to the macro-economic performance and viability of the system. The "second demographic transition" is obviously not unique to Norwegian society. All industrial nations face a rising surge of elderly, as the generation of the postwar baby boomers grows old. What is peculiar for Norway, however, is that the culmination of this surge is predicted to coincide with the lowest oil revenues for more than fifty years. The trend describing the transfers to age and disability pensions points steeply and steadily upwards to the year 2030, while the trend depicting the oil revenues drops equally steadily in the same period; thus leaving a huge gap to be filled (Welfare White Paper 1995 [WWP]). Right or wrong, this image has been a premise for the public debate on how Norwegian society shall fulfil its pension commitments for the elderly in the future. It adds to the problem that each new cohort of elderly persons–males in particular–retires earlier and lives longer than the previous. It is a paradox that this occurs in a situation where the elderly are healthier than ever before in history. Thus, in the long run full employment among the able-bodied seems more vital than ever for the economic viability of the present system.

## The Norwegian "Work Approach": Origins and Substance

First, it might be useful to define what we mean by "activation policies." Our notion is fairly broad: the term covers public policies, programs, and measures that enable, encourage, or even compel the citizens to be active, in some way—in contrast to being passive recipients of benefits. By "being active" we have a wide range of different work and work-related activities in mind: working in an ordinary job, working in a sheltered or created job, actively seeking work, moving to a place where jobs are more abundant, attending qualifying courses or taking formal education.

This section offers an account of the activation rhetoric in Norwegian welfare policy in the 1990s, the main information source of which is a selection of relatively recent public documents which may be perceived as representative with respect to the essence of the current catchword in social policy discourse. It is important to bear in mind, however, that neither the term "Work Approach" nor the principles upon which the strategy is based are novelties in Norwegian social policy.[1] The Work Approach of the 1990s amounts to a resurrection of ideas which served as ideological underpinnings of the legislation in the 1950s and 1960s.

### *The Work Approach in Public Rhetoric*

The introduction of the term Work Approach (*arbeidslinjen*) in Norway is commonly attributed to the 1992 White Paper on Rehabilitation, WPR (*Attføringsmeldingen*). The WPR signals the advent of a Government offensive to deal with the tendency of increasing exclusion and expulsion from the labor market observed throughout the 1980s.[2] The magnitude and complexity of the problem inspired a strategy comprising a number of initiatives along several paths, the lowest common denominator of which was the supremacy of *work* as a bedrock of individual welfare. Hence, the Work Approach is presented as a concerted set of measures ultimately aimed at increasing participation and activity:

> The basic premise...is that the social insurance system should provide security for those unable to participate in gainful employment due to contingencies of health, or for some other reason temporarily find themselves outside the labour market. At the same time, the basic premise is that individual rights are not exclusively tied to cash benefits; each individual has, as far as possible, a right and a duty to work, to participate in rehabilitation programs or enter education....Social insurance schemes should be designed so as to make the "Work Approach" the first choice for all affected parties, and prevent unnecessary exclusion and expulsion of vulnerable groups from the labour market. (St.meld. nr. 39 (1991-92): 8, our translation)

In addition to a number of administrative changes, one of the most significant imprints of the Work Approach thus outlined was a suggestion to make eligibility for sickness benefits more explicitly conditional upon proved willingness to participate in rehabilitation programs.

A Green Paper on "A National Strategy for Increased Employment in the 1990s" (NOU 1992:26) was issued later in 1992. The commission—an exceptionally broad group of representatives from all political parties, union representatives, high-ranking civil servants and experts—conducted its discussions on labor market strategies with explicit references to the Work Approach, but it felt no need to elaborate on the underlying rationale of the term. Considering the prominence of active labor market policies (ALMP) in the "Nordic Model" of social policy, a signaling of continued reliance on ALMP is hardly striking. A central concept in the commission's recommendations was reservation wage, which was presented as an argument for introducing cuts in the replacement rate of unemployment benefit.[3] This is an interesting observation inasmuch as the underlying assumption informing the reservation wage theory was *explicitly* rejected in 1977.[4]

In 1995, the Welfare White Paper (WWP) reviewed the social insurance system within the overall context of the Work Approach. The WWP maintains that the Work Approach serves as a means of achieving a number of objectives,[5] and a number of reasons for protracting the Work Approach were explicated in the document.

Some of these highlighted individual concerns and others were based on considerations of the national economy. The result is a *conjunction* of the two rationales:

> There is a close relationship between work and welfare, both for the individual and the national economy... [Work] offers an opportunity to fulfil personal abilities and possibilities. A high level of employment bestows economic growth for society and a broader and safer economic basis for our collective welfare.¼ The government therefore seeks to protract the Work Approach in welfare policy. (WWP, St.meld. nr. 35 (1994-95): 89, our translation).

The practical consequences of these and other initiatives are discussed later. The main observation at present is that the WWP furthered and consolidated the Work Approach as outlined in the WPR three years earlier.

*Critical Assessments of the Work Approach*

This review of public documents is far from exhaustive, but it goes a long way in terms of identifying the origins and essence of the Work Approach. More specifically, the Norwegian (and Nordic) activation discourse conveys reassurance and public acquiescence in highlighting the Work Approach as a means of conjoining individual advantages with benefits for society as a whole (Drøpping et al., 1999: 138): at least on the level of rhetoric, the Work Approach means social integration and independence for the individual and economic sustainability and social cohesion for society.

This point is further illustrated by Kildal (1998), who—based on a detailed analysis of the arguments with which the Work Approach was forwarded in the WPR and the WWP–identifies a number of key arguments related to both the "societal" and "individual" level.[6] Kildal assesses each argument with reference to the controversial discussion on whether they amount to "adequate reasons to turn down benefits claims" (ibid.: 19), and the analysis suggests that—although some of the arguments in the public rhetoric may support this claim—neither of them, jointly or independently, constitute a valid basis for denying basic economic support: the arguments are almost exclusively based on *normative assumptions*. Kildal concludes that a *moral* message permeates and propels the arguments (ibid.: 28).

With respect to the most fundamental rationale of the Work Approach, Hvinden (1994) asserts that–despite rhetorical efforts to balance the view–a concern with growth in expenditures was the most fundamental and dominant premise informing the discussion over the Work Approach in the early 1990s. Consequently, Hvinden maintains, the character of reform initiatives has been more or less predictable. In contrast to the period of welfare state construction in the 1950s and 1960s–a period in which control mechanisms were promoted as a means of propelling welfare state expansion–the rationale of the Work Approach in the 1990s appears to be an ambition to enforce *contraction* (ibid.: 14).

Altogether, the rhetoric of the Work Approach constitutes a bridge between potentially conflicting social policy issues. Indeed, Midré (1995) suggests that the very concept "Work Approach" obtains much of its ideological potency precisely from this ambiguity: it may entail right *and* duty; coercion *and* care; exclusion *and* inclusion.[7] Most significantly, however, the Work Approach balances and makes use of two conflicting conceptions of the notion of work itself: while the *positive* version highlights pro-active policies as a means of achieving the right to work, the *negative* conception vindicates cutbacks in benefits and welfare privileges more generally (ibid.: 203).

Alarming trends regarding the future of the de-commodifying welfare state may indeed constitute a case for change, and it appears that the main challenge confronting policy makers is how to administer a *de facto* reorientation of social policy while conveying reassurance to the supporters of a welfare system which generally enjoys wide public support (see e.g., Goul Andersen et al., 1999). The rhetoric accompanying the introduction and continuance of the Norwegian Work Approach in the 1990s suggests that stated attempts to balance change with continuity produces an ambiguous social policy discourse. In the next section we examine whether the strategy has been equally ambiguous on the *practical* level.

## Recent Reforms in Social Policy

In this part we present brief accounts of the main features and relevant changes in the most important schemes in the Norwegian system of social protection. The following policy areas are singled out: (1) the disability benefit/pension; (2) medical/vocational rehabilitation allowance/services; (3) sickness benefit/sick pay scheme; (4) social assistance; (5) active labor market programs; (6) unemployment benefit; and (7) transitional benefit for single parents. Developments in most of these policy areas are illustrated by means of national statistics in absolute numbers. As an aid in drawing mean-

**Table 9.1**
**Labor Force (1000) and Expenditures of the National Insurance Scheme (million NOK), 1990-1998**

| | 1990 | 1991 | 1992 | 1993 | 1994 | 1995 | 1996 | 1997 | 1998 |
|---|---|---|---|---|---|---|---|---|---|
| Labor force | 2142 | 2126 | 2130 | 2131 | 2151 | 2186 | 2239 | 2285 | 2317 |
| Social security expenditures | 121,054 | 107,062 | 114,579 | 119,340 | 121,811 | 126,198 | 132,535 | 139,359 | 150,848 |

Source: Statistics Norway; The National Insurance Administration

ingful inferences from these figures, table 9.1 describes developments in the total labor force and expenditures in the National Insurance Scheme throughout the 1990s.[8]

With respect to activation orientation, we focus on four aspects or levels of these programs: the institutional level: are there important changes in the legislation; the organizational aspect: are there alterations in the ways the services and benefits are delivered; the budget level: is more money used for activation purposes; and finally the participation level: are more people subjected to activation regimes?

### *The Disability Benefit/Pension: Tighter Eligibility Rules and Intensified Follow-Up Activity*

In one sense, initiatives in this area of social policy did spearhead the social policy reorientation of the 1990s. Regarding health-related benefits (and services) in general, the strategy can be summarized as a two-pronged approach: stricter qualifying criteria/tighter eligibility rules and intensified follow-up activity.

In practical terms, one of the most significant modifications in the National Insurance Scheme (NIS) has been the introduction (in 1991) of more stringent claims to occupational and geographical mobility for claimants of disability pension (as well as unemployment benefit, see Section 3.5). The main thrust of this particular initiative was to strike down on incidences of "geographical disability," which was perceived as a major source of premature exit. In the same vein and also in effect from 1991, eligibility to disability pension was made conditional on more strict claims to the direct causal relationship between the medical condition and the vocational disability (reduced earnings capacity). Third, as a means of stimulating labor market reentry, the NIS was modified in 1993 to increase the frequency of disability pension reassessment. This modification is part of a general trend in the 1990s to encourage the utilization of residual/remaining work capacity, a trend in which easier access to combining work and benefits constitutes another important ingredient.

While the overall message and general tendency of these institutional modifications amount to an intense battle against labor market exclusion, the statistics presented in Table 9.2 indicate a turning operation of only limited success.

The growth rates for both indicators did slow down around 1993; a fact attributed in particular to the 1991 tightening of causality between medical condition and vocational status (Bragstad et al., 1996: 212). However, the positive effects proved to be of a temporary nature as both numbers continued to grow from around 1995, and the numbers are anything but declining at present. On the contrary, the number of disability pensioners during the first half of 1999 increased by 4.7 percent compared to the previous year, which amounted to a 3.6 billion NOK increase in expenditures (Aftenposten, 30.8.99). Indeed, the recent (April 1999) government appointment of a committee to investigate issues related to the growth in sick leave and the disability pension scheme testifies to the persistency of the problem. Considering that the 1990s set off with two green papers on roughly the same issues (see Section 2.1), the next decade appears to commence in the same way as the previous one.

### *Vocational and Medical Rehabilitation: Transfer of Responsibilities*

Rehabilitation (and other "active" measures) runs to the core of the Work Approach. In line with the objectives of the work-oriented welfare regime, *vocational* rehabilitation has been particularly prominent. Consequently–in an attempt to tie efforts of vocational rehabilitation more directly to the labor market–the budgetary and administrative responsibility for vocational rehabilitation was trans-

**Table 9.2**
**Number of Disability Pensioners (1000 cases) and Levels of Expenditure on the Disability Pension Scheme (million NOK), 1990-1998**

| | 1990 | 1991 | 1992 | 1993 | 1994 | 1995 | 1996 | 1997 | 1998 |
|---|---|---|---|---|---|---|---|---|---|
| Pensioners | 234.4 | 238.5 | 236.2 | 232.4 | 233.7 | 236.3 | 239.4 | 246.5 | 258.1 |
| Expenditure | 16 117 | 17 595 | 18 256 | 18 707 | 18 940 | 19 934 | 23 474 | 25 183 | 28 125 |

Source: Statistics Norway; The National Insurance Administration

ferred from the National Insurance Administration to the Labour Market Authorities in 1994. This administrative modification implied a more distinct separation between *vocational* and *medical* rehabilitation.[9]

On the institutional level, two modifications of significance to the medical rehabilitation scheme were introduced in 1993: a reduction in maximum duration of income replacement benefits to one year; and a tightening of the concept of "sickness" in relation to benefit eligibility. The main reason for cutting the maximum duration was the assumption that treatment of *de facto* medical (as opposed to social) problems would produce positive results after a relatively short period. With respect to the concept and definition of "sickness," the modification is a close parallel to the tightening of claims to causality between medical condition and earnings capacity in the disability pension scheme. The definitional emphasis is, moreover, closely associated with the general modification in the sickness benefit scheme (see below).

While declining figures in disability pension and sickness absence would be important indications of a successful Work Approach, the opposite development would be true for "preventive" measures such as vocational and medical rehabilitation. Both schemes displayed a generally increasing tendency throughout the 1990s (the pre-1994 numbers in medical rehabilitation are not comparable to the numbers from 1994 and onwards), a development in line with stated intentions.

### *Sickness Benefit: Earlier and Intensified Intervention*

The list of modifications in the sickness benefit/sick pay scheme is more comprehensive than in the other health-related schemes de-

**Table 9.3**
**Total Number in Receipt of Vocational Rehabilitation Allowance and Medical Benefits (1000 cases), Annual Averages, 1990-1998.**

| | 1990 | 1991 | 1992 | 1993 | 1994[1] | 1995 | 1996 | 1997 | 1998 |
|---|---|---|---|---|---|---|---|---|---|
| Vocational | 24.2 | 27.8 | 27.3 | 25.9 | 30.8 | 30.4 | 31.0 | 30.6 | 30.6 |
| Medical | 28.6 | 32.8 | 35.0 | 31.7 | 19.8 | 18.8 | 20.7 | 23.4 | 26.5 |

[1] The method of calculating medical rehabilitation claimants changed in 1994
Source: National Insurance Administration

scribed above. We attribute the intensity of reform activities in this area partly to the reoccurring debates on absence rates, and partly to the overall importance ascribed by the Work Approach to prevention and early intervention. Either way, the general impression is one of more systematic attempts to facilitate early intervention and return to work for people in receipt of sickness benefits. Another observation is the tightening of the conception of "sickness" as a condition of benefits eligibility. The objective and effect of this tightening has been to single out the cases most likely to benefit from *de facto* medical treatment–and thus most likely to re-enter the labor market.

The fight against sickness absence and premature exit was boosted in 1988 with the introduction of "medical certificate II" (*sykmelding II*), which made eligibility for sick pay exceeding eight weeks contingent on reassessment. The formal authority to make this reassessment was eventually transferred to the National Insurance Administration. In a similar vein, a second "checkpoint" was introduced in 1993, when sick pay exceeding twelve weeks became contingent on confirmation from the national insurance authorities in addition to the medical doctor's assessment. 1993 also marked the introduction of "active sick leave" (*aktiv sykmelding*), under which a person in vocational rehabilitation at the workplace (*bedriftsintern attføring*) can receive sick pay up to 12 weeks (longer if the training is necessary for the person to retain the position in the firm).

Three other modifications were introduced in 1991. First, the replacement level of sickness benefit for the unemployed was reduced to match the compensation level of the "mainstream" unemployment benefit. The main purpose of the revision was to avoid a situation in which a *de facto* ("able-bodied") unemployed managed to shun the typical requirements otherwise placed on the unemployed—while at the same time enjoying a relatively more generous benefit. Second, 1991 marked the launching of the "Sick-Leave Project" (*sykefraværsprosjektet*), a tripartite project between the government, the Norwegian Federation of Trade Unions (*Landsorganisasjonen* - LO), and the Central Employers Organisation (*Næringslivets hovedorganisasjon* - NHO). The parties to the project ambitiously committed themselves to reduce sick leave by 20 percent during the period 1991-1993 in order to prevent changes in the existing sick pay scheme (Andersen, 1994).[10] Third, the advisory role of medical doctors was strengthened in order to reach more accurate medical diagnoses and contribute to drawing up rehabilitation plans at an early stage.

1992 witnessed a proposal to double the sick pay period financed by the employer from two to four weeks. The main purpose of the proposal was to underline employers' shared responsibility in prevention through improvements in the occupational environment and to induce employers to implement preventive measures. The proposal was initially rejected, but the employer period was extended to three weeks in 1998.

As indicated by table 9.4, it has proved difficult to check the incidences of sickness absence and expenditures on sickness benefits, despite the number of initiatives to curb them. In terms of expenditures in the long run, however, the real increase in sick pay has been relatively stable compared to other major National Insurance schemes; the expenditure level in 1995 was a modest 5 percent above the 1980 level in fixed prices (Pedersen, 1997: 37). It is, nevertheless, difficult to explain the relatively steep rise over the last few years. On the one hand, we may be witnessing a case of the seemingly inverse relationship between the unemployment level and sickness absence rate (Olsen and Mastekaasa, 1997: 33-40); on the other hand, the trend may actually indicate that there exists a lower limit to sickness absence rates (Pedersen, ibid.: 15-17; Bragstad et al., 1996: 218). The latter interpretation suggests that even a successful Work Approach will be imperfect inasmuch as integration of the genuinely "residual" labor reservoir is bound to reach a point of negative returns. Either way, the most recent statistics testify to further problems: the sickness absence rate increased by 6 percent during the first half of 1999, which represents an 11 percent increase in expenditures (Aftenposten, 30.8.99).

**Table 9.4**
**Incidences of Sickness Absence (1000 cases) and Expenditures (million NOK) on Sickness Benefits, 1990-1998**

| | 1990 | 1991 | 1992 | 1993 | 1994 | 1995 | 1996 | 1997 | 1998 |
|---|---|---|---|---|---|---|---|---|---|
| Incidences | 381 | 366 | 335 | 321 | 325 | 348 | 376 | 463 | 490 |
| Expenditures | 11,508 | 12,173 | 11,581 | 11,025 | 10,442 | 11,377 | 13,221 | 14,788 | 16,600 |

Source: Statistics Norway; The National Insurance Administration

## Norwegian Social Assistance: "Workfare" Initiatives and Municipal ALMPs[11]

With the enactment of the Social Services Act in 1991, a new principle was introduced into modern Norwegian social assistance. For the first time in sixty years local authorities were allowed to require that recipients of minimum protection carried out work in exchange for benefits. The subheading of the paragraph regulating conditions for aid states, "It can be made a condition that the recipient performs suitable work in the town of residence for as long as the person receives benefits."[12]

Even if this reform was a breach of practices established in the postwar period, the re-introduction of work requirements is best understood as a culmination of curtailments in the access to social assistance, which started towards the end of the 1980s. As such, the reform is part of the general change towards a renewed emphasis on work and activity—as opposed to the passive provision of aid.

The work requirement is targeted at young people, offering an individually tailored program with the aim to further labor market integration. The work is supposed to be of limited duration, and the social services are obligated to cooperate with the labor market authorities in implementation. The regulation of workfare in Norway is limited to a condition to the receipt of benefits that may or may not be used by the local authorities. There are, however, very few binding specifications designed to ensure that these principles are followed in implementation. The consequence is a great variety in the local implementation of the work requirement (Lødemel, 1997). In Norway, there is no tradition for central government to supervise the welfare targeted at the small minority falling outside state programs. In a tradition dating back to the poor law, assistance has remained the financial and administrative responsibility of local government. As a part of this scheme, a detailed regulation would have introduced a breach with a strong tradition of local autonomy.

In 1995, 34 percent of the approximately 510 local social assistance administrations ran workfare programs (Lødemel, 1997). A more recent survey indicates that this figure has dropped to 25 percent (Vik-Mo, 1999: 88). Lødemel (1997) estimated that less than 1,500 persons participated in workfare programs within social assistance in 1995. While few, this is a tremendous increase, since virtually none were offered such programs prior to 1993. The total costs of these policies are unknown, and so are the development in number of participants during the subsequent years.

Recipients of social assistance subjected to work requirements may participate in ordinary governmental ALMPs shoulder to shoulder with recipients of unemployment benefit.[13] In addition, many municipalities have developed their own "home-tinkered" activation programs, and the work requirement is often used as a means within this local context. A survey from 1998 demonstrates that about 44 percent of the municipalities have built up municipal employment programs and apparatuses alongside the governmental ALMPs. In contrast to governmental ALMPs, which in principle are targeted at ordinary job seekers, the local programs are targeted at recipients of social assistance with multiple problems (Vik-Mo, 1999). Nearly 60 percent of all the social assistance clients who where activated in 1997 participated in municipality programs (Statistics Norway, 1997). The number of people subjected to work requirement is unknown. If the present government's plans are put into practice (St.meld. nr. 50 (1998-99)), municipal ALMPs are likely to grow also in the years to come.

*Active Labour Market Programs (ALMPs): Huge Fluctuations*

A comprehensive and varied bulk of ALMPs is considered one of the major characteristics of a social democratic welfare state regime (Kolberg and Esping-Andersen, 1992). Norway has a history of such programs dating back to the early 1980s. Up to 1993, these programs grew in size, scope, and diversity. The programs are funded by the government and are administered by the regional Labour Market Administrations. The primary target groups of ALMP are the young, immigrants, and long-term unemployed.

Altogether, there are nine different programs and measures (Directorate of Labour, 1998). The most important of these in terms of the number of participants (in 1996) are Labour Market Training (*arbeidsmarkedsopplæring*); Stand-in place for unemployed (*vikarplass for arbeidsledige*); Wage compensation for employers (*lønnstilskudd*); Competence, training for work and job creation for unemployed people (*KAJA*); and Mentor assisted practice place (*praksisplass med fadderordning*) (St.meld. nr. 4 [1996-97]).[14]

The expenditures and number of participants in ALMPS are presented in table 9.5.

**Table 9.5**
**Costs of Ordinary ALMPs (million NOK) and Number of Participants (1000) in ALMP, 1990-1998**

| | 1990 | 1991 | 1992 | 1993 | 1994 | 1995 | 1996 | 1997 | 1998 |
|---|---|---|---|---|---|---|---|---|---|
| Expenditures | 4422 | 4623 | 5362 | 6363 | 6072 | 4921 | 4049 | 2656 | 1778 |
| Participants | 40 | 42 | 44 | 57 | 56 | 45 | 34 | 23 | 15 |

Source: Directorate of Labour; Statistics Norway: Statistics Weekly 26.8.99.

The number of participants peaked at 57,000 in 1993 (3 percent of the labor force). Beyond this, the development pattern shown in table 9.5 closely corresponds to changes in the unemployment level. Part and parcel of current employment policy, these fluctuations are indeed intended. According to the government's "Long-Term Program" (1998-2001), labor market measures are intended to play an important role in "stabilization policy" which means that they are scaled back during economic upturns and increased during downturns. The argument is that in a situation with high demand for labor it is important to ensure that as many job-seekers as possible are available for ordinary employment (see also OECD, 1996). A limited duration for labor market training courses is also important in order to limit the recruitment of persons who primarily seek an education, and who should thus make use of the mainstream education system. These policies are reflected in the planned reduction to 8,000 places in 1999 (Revised National Budget, 1999).

Even in a booming economy, however, targeted efforts for groups that experience particularly difficult situations in the labor market are still considered necessary. These will primarily encompass the long-term unemployed, including those who are no longer eligible for unemployment benefits as well as persons who have little or incomplete education, and limited work experience. A high-priority task for the government is to prevent inactivity among young people as a result of prolonged unemployment.

Put briefly, the magnitude and design of the ALMPs are adapted to and coincide with the fluctuations in the labor market. As an integrated part of activation policies, the question whether ALMPs are on the rise or on the decline depends to a substantial degree on the situation in the labor market.

*Unemployment Benefit: Stricter Time Limit and Less Eligibility*

The Unemployment Benefit (UB) is an integral part of the Social Security Scheme and is administered by the Labour Market Authorities. Entitlement to UB is determined by earnings in the year(s) previous to the spell of unemployment.[15] The compensation rate is normally 62.4 percent of the calculation base. The maximum duration of benefits is now 3 years, after which re-qualification is contingent upon a new period of ordinary work or participation in a temporary employment program. The present legislation (enacted in 1996) differs from its predecessor in three important respects: first, the new rules impose a strict time limit; second, the earnings threshold is raised (thus excluding groups of part-time workers and low-income earners from entitlement); and third, the former 10 percent reduction in benefit level for long-term unemployed is removed.

The UB is (still) a relatively comprehensive and generous system for income maintenance. As such, and according to common orthodoxy, it may undermine work motivation. Thus, recipients of UB are required to accept job offers or a place in a labor market program, and the rules emphasize that benefit recipients shall be available to the labor market. This implies that the claimant is expected to move to areas where jobs are available. This requirement was strengthened in 1995, particularly for young people (Directorate of Labour, 1996: 5). Benefits may temporarily be suspended if the person concerned is considered to be unemployed by his or her own choice, refuses to take a suitable job or participate in labor market measures, or fails to attend to the employment office when summoned. The local labor market officers may also employ "softer" measures like personal talks where motivation and encouragement are the core elements. The claimants' own responsibility is stressed in these meetings.

*Transitional Benefit for Single Parents: "Work-Related Activity" Requirements and Stricter Time-Limits*

Unlike most, perhaps all, Western countries' transitional benefit for single parents is an integral part of the social security system. Up to 1998, a single parent had the right to receive transitional benefit until the youngest child was ten years old, but this was drastically reduced to three years in September 1998. When the youngest child is three years old,[16] the parent is required to be in "work-related activity" in order to preserve benefit eligibility. Work-related activity comprises formal job-seeking or working/studying at least half-time.[17] Provided that the lone parent is studying, the eligibility period may be extended to 5.5 years. Parallel to the introduction of a stricter time limit, the annual benefit has been increased by about NOK 10,000.

Social security also provides childcare benefit and education benefit for single parents. Childcare benefit is granted until the child is ten years old. In order to assist and enable single parents in activation, the Social Security Administration has set up a system of so-called user-contacts in all municipalities. This arrangement is intended to provide a social network for the target group of single parents, and to offer help, assistance, and counseling on their trajectory to self-sufficiency.

At present, there are about 60,000 recipients of transitional benefit in Norway. In September 1998, the Social Security Administration estimated that between 12,000 and 18,000 single families would face the new activation requirements (Aftenposten 2.9.1998). According to The Ministry of Social Affairs and Health the overall cost reductions of the reform will amount to about NOK 300-400 million annually (Innst. O. nr. 46 [1996-97]). The bulk of this reduction is attributed to stricter time limits. The costs associated with the enforced activation regime are estimated to NOK 95 million annually (Ot.prp. nr. 8 [1996-97]): 29). Various aspects of this reform are currently considered for evaluation.

## Summary and Discussion

### *Summary*

In this chapter we have reviewed the major income maintenance programs in the Norwegian welfare system with respect to (changes in) the degree of activation orientation. We have focused on developments in the institutional and organizational frameworks, expenditures, and number of participants. The general impression of the 1990s is a shift towards more activation-oriented policies. Most of the adjustments are fairly small, but they all point in the same direction. We may describe them as iterative adaptations to the overarching ideology of the Work Approach. They reflect a committed political will to change the profile of the programs and emphasize the obligations of the citizens.

Focusing on five central domains, table 9.6 summarizes the main trends in the Norwegian Work Approach in the 1990s. "Eligibility" pertains to whether eligibility criteria have been tightened or not; "duration of benefits" summarizes changes in length of maximum eligibility; "level of benefits" relates to whether benefit levels have been changed or not; "behavioral requirements" charts whether messages of conduct are conveyed to claimants; and "activation" refers to the institutional linking between eligibility and activation.

First, we have not observed any *de facto* reductions in benefit levels. On the contrary, the levels of unemployment and transitional benefits have increased somewhat —partly to "compensate" for cuts in maximum duration of these benefits. Second, we witnessed tightened eligibility and a general trend towards cuts in duration. Indeed, both the carrot and the stick have been used, but while other countries have opted–more or less successfully–for cutbacks in benefits replacement levels (Pierson, 1994), the incentive effects of financial benefits in Norway have mainly been discussed with reference to *eligibility criteria* ("accessibility") and intensified follow-up activities rather than the relative "generosity" of benefits *per se*. It is plausible to interpret these tendencies in light of Norwegians' "passion for equality" (see Section 1.2). Finally, all schemes are tightly linked with some sort of "activation" requirement (i.e., work, training, education). This is in line with the objective of designing social insur-

**Table 9.6**
**Main Trends in the Norwegian Work Approach**

| | Eligibility | Duration of benefits | Level of benefits | Behavioral requirements | "Activation" |
|---|---|---|---|---|---|
| Disability benefit | Tightened | No change | No change | Yes | No |
| Vocational rehabilitation | No change | No change | No change | Yes | Yes |
| Medical rehabilitation | Tightened | Reduced | No change | Yes | No |
| Sickness benefit | Tightened | No change | No change | Yes | No |
| Social assistance | No change | No change | No change | Yes | Yes |
| ALMP | Tightened | Reduced | No change | Yes | Yes |
| Unemployment benefit | Tightened | Reduced | Increased | Yes | Yes |
| Transitional benefit | No change | Reduced | Increased | Yes | Yes |

ance schemes in a manner which corresponds with the Work Approach (see Section 2). This observation does not, of course, apply to disability, sickness, and medical rehabilitation, whose beneficiaries by definition are (temporarily) exempted from "activation."[18]

*Countertrends?*

In concentrating on reforms in already existing programs, we have omitted any new programs launched in this period. Although not directly relevant to the rest of our discussion of the Work Approach, we nevertheless want to mention an important newcomer, Cash Benefit for Families with Small Children (*kontantstøtten*). Launched in 1998, it is paid to all families (lone parents as well as couples) with small children (up to three years old) provided that they do not use a day care center that receives as state grant.[19] The cash benefit has three major objectives: first, to allow the families to spend more time with their children; second, to enhance the freedom to choose the child-care of preference; and third, to increase equity in the subsidies to families with small children (Ot.prp. nr. 56 [1997-98]: 1). One may note that neither the intentions nor the (probable) consequences of the cash benefit are in line with the notions of the Work Approach. On the contrary, inasmuch as it presents parents with an incentive to stay away from (or even leave) the labor market, the cash benefit marks a fairly clear breach with the reigning idea in welfare policy. The cash benefit thus represents an anomaly, and it is far too hasty to declare the end of the Work Approach.

The present Centre Coalition Government recently launched the idea of a "softer Work Approach" in a white paper on Income and Living Conditions (St.meld. nr. 50 [1998-99]). This version of the Work Approach appears to rest on the idea that the occupational life should allow room for people who are chronically incapacitated by poor health and enable more people to combine a social security benefit with remunerated work.[20] It is difficult to see how these objectives differ from the ones of former governments, and the concrete measures proposed are unlikely to cause much opposition in the political establishment.

*Recent Developments Seen in a Historical Perspective*

An activation discourse is certainly discernible in Norwegian social policy of the 1990s. We have noted that the Work Approach is not a qualitatively new approach, and the most accurate assessment of the recent development is probably that it represents a resurrection of the term and an accentuation of its principles. These principles can, in brief, be summarized under such slogans as "care before cash" and "help to self-help." We may thus conclude that the activation discourse represents a renewed focus on the blessings of work and activation; a focus summarized as dichotomies: from social rights to obligations, from passivity to activity, from benefits to services, etc.

This reorientation gives rise to some crucial questions with regard to the near social policy history: Did a focus on the (individual) right to passive income replacement permeate the general conception of "welfare"? Did this conception hold sway over the (social) obligation to participate to the best of personal abilities? In which way and to what extent does the Work Approach signify an actual change from previous practices? It is not easy to answer the first two questions with any degree of certainty, but we believe that it is possible in the past to discern a move away from the principles upon which the idea of social security was originally based. One expression of the "care before cash" philosophy, for instance, is the formal requirement to exhaust all possibilities of medical and vocational rehabilitation prior to granting disability pension, a requirement only moderately enforced in practice (Hvinden, 1991; 1994; Kjønstad, 1992). Related examples which all add to the financial burden of the de-commodifying welfare state are the growth in the sickness absence rate throughout the 1970s and 1980s; the trend towards a lower *de facto* age of old-age retirement; increase in the number of single parents; and the rate of unemployment.

Consequently, we do not attribute the underlying rationale of the Work Approach to widespread irresponsible attitudes and a general erosion of the population's moral fibre, but focus, rather, on the very institutions of the de-commodifying welfare state. More precisely, we maintain that a significant part of the problem can be attributed to reluctance to bear the political costs and inability to design effective means of *balancing* the rights-based welfare state with the institutional thresholds necessary to prevent it from overload. Inasmuch as the explanation can be found in an erosion of these "balancing principles" at the institutional level, it is probably appropriate that the reaction is a spirit of firm resolve to balance the rights of citizenship with the obligations. Thus, we conclude that the Norwegian

Work Approach is an attempt to reshape welfare in accordance with its original principles rather than dismantle it.

*Success or Failure?*

"The proof of the pudding lies in the eating," and whether the Work Approach signifies a genuine change in social policy depends, ultimately, on the extent to which "activity" is promoted. It will be recalled that official statistics from the 1990s paint a rather discouraging picture of the achievements so far. While a more detailed analysis of this important question is beyond the scope of the present article, we can nevertheless present some evidence from evaluations of most of the schemes discussed here (the reform in the Transitional Benefit Scheme is not yet evaluated).

First, in their summary of research on *sickness absence* in the period 1980-1996, Olsen and Mastekaasa (1997: 10) points to a high correlation between research focus and the currents of the public debate on the issue. However, while Norwegian and international studies on both sickness benefits, labor market trends, and working conditions are surveyed, none of them appear to be directly inspired by the Work Approach. While instantly puzzling, this observation may be attributed to the fact that issues related to the Work Approach (both in sickness absence and other schemes) has not informed Norwegian studies until quite recently. Focusing on income sources for three cohorts of long-term recipients of sickness benefit (1991, 1992 and 1993), Blekesaune (1998) investigates the impact of the 1993 modifications in sickness benefit on long-term sick leave. The duration of sick leave declined and the proportion of previous recipients in receipt of labor wage increased after 1993. However, the proportion in receipt of health-related benefits were tangent to the pre-1993 level after three years. This particular observation is parallel with the findings in a similar study of the impact of restricted eligibility to vocational rehabilitation allowance on the transition from rehabilitation to paid work for those with marginal labor market relations the two years preceding receipt of rehabilitation allowance (Blekesaune, 1999). Both studies thus report positive effects in the short run but uncertain long-term effects. Second, various aspects of the transfer of responsibility for *vocational rehabilitation* to the Labour Market Authorities in 1994 have been investigated by Ford and Hvinden (1997) and Jessen (1997). While Ford and Hvinden's studies focus on *administrative* processes and adaptations within and between the

Labour Market and National Insurance Authorities, Jessen investigates the users' experiences with the new administrative design. As a means of spelling out the purpose of the individual rehabilitation process more explicitly, one intention of the 1994 reform is to encourage the users to take part in and design the rehabilitation process (i.e., an upgrade of status from "client" to "customer"). The degree of positive feedback seems to be positively correlated with the users' background and resources, a finding which leads Jessen to conclude that there is a tension between the Labour Market Authorities' goal of personal motivation and the interest of the less resourceful group of users. Third, evaluations of governmental ALMPs and municipal activation programs do indicate that they work as intended. Although generally positive, their effects are often quite modest (Pedersen, 1998; Aakvik, 1999). The new "workfare" regimes in social assistance are not yet evaluated, but will be within a year (Dahl, forthcoming).

A final remark is that although some activation measures have proved efficient (especially in mainstream ALMP), it would be an exaggeration to attribute the excellent labor market performance in recent years solely to these programs. We strongly believe that the primary moving force behind this fortunate development is the booming international economy—which is alpha and omega for the soundness of a small, open economy such as the Norwegian.

### *Some Dilemmas of a Successful "Work Approach"*

We argue that a successful Work Approach warrants a second look at the idea of "welfare." One downside of a reformed regime may, paradoxically, be to contribute to exclusion rather than integration. The mainstream labor market may indeed be the nuclear arena of social interaction, but a one-sided focus on (paid) work may exclude a number of people from enjoying the fruits of *other* activities, e.g., various sorts of voluntary/charity work, local community-based projects, etc. A second negative aspect may arise from tightened eligibility criteria to cash benefits. Less predictability in "passive" income security may be an implicitly intended consequence of the Work Approach, but offering financial incentives to work is only successful to the extent that the labor market is able (and willing) to absorb those so induced. Restricted eligibility may also serve only to postpone–rather than prevent–exit from the labor market. Clear tendencies of this kind of trend are shown for claimants of disability benefit (Westin, 1994). Unless thoroughly examined in advance and carefully monitored, work-oriented rehabilitation and activation schemes may be a lost cause from the start, in which case efforts of "activation" may add to the insecurity experienced by the individual. From a principal point of view, finally, there is little doubt that the Work Approach implies less autonomy and freedom of choice on the part of the individual, particularly in the new "workfare" initiatives in social assistance. The paternalistic message conveyed may, ultimately, compromise the notion of rights to an extent not reconcilable with the notion of de-commodification (Drøpping et al., 1999). "The new paternalism" (Mead, 1997) makes a strange bedfellow with the demands that modernity puts on the individual. In modernity individuals are expected to be autonomous, reflexive, to make informed choices, to plan their life courses, and to realize their life chances (Giddens, 1994; Beck, 1986). These entries seem at odds with the renewed paternalistic elements in Norwegian social policy.

We believe that de-commodification will remain a key objective and salient feature in the future Norwegian (and Nordic) model, but argue that the Work Approach is part of a *re-commodifying* process: when welfare amounts to work and *vice versa*–and policies become increasingly designed in line with this rationale–we expect rights-based de-commodification to become a more conditional notion. With its ability to merge rights and obligations in a seemingly non-conflictual manner, the Work Approach is an appealing notion. While appealing, however, the Work Approach offers no welfare state cure-all in itself. The political commitment to change may be present, but the ability to transform a system so resilient to change is the real test on policy makers.

## Notes

1. The term was coined by the Torp-Committee as early as 1952 (Kommunal- og arbeidsdepartemente, 1952). In the committee's report, which accompanied the White Paper on "Qualification and Employment of the Partially disabled" (St.meld. nor. 48 [1953]), the Committee suggested a move away from the previously dominant "Benefits Approach" (*stønadslinja*) in favor of the "Work Approach" (*arbeidslinjen*).
2. The process was initiated in the late 1980s with the appointment of the Committee on Disability Pension and the committee on the Sick Pay Scheme. The Green Papers submitted by the two committees (NOU 1990/17; NOU 1990/23, respectively) provided a baseline for the recommendations in the WPR.
3. The reservation wage is the lowest level of payment an unemployed individual is willing to accept in considering (return to) work; a level influenced both by condi-

tions on the labor market and the design and generosity of the Unemployment Benefit Scheme. The theory is based on the assumption that individuals enjoy a freedom a choice which allows them to base their decision on rational calculations with respect to potential economic rewards (cf. also Midré, 1994: 23-4).

4. During the preparations to the 1978 Sick Pay Scheme, the Ministry of Social Affairs expressed doubts with respect to the individual freedom of choice assumed in the theory (Ot.prp. nr. 68 (1976-77): Section 2).
5. For example, enhanced and more equitable redistribution of welfare; reduced need for redistribution from the occupationally active population to social security beneficiaries; and increased numbers of persons in position to contribute in financing the system.
6. The main arguments of relevance to the "societal" level are concerns with "the National economy" (a sound economic foundation for welfare conditional on a high employment rate) and "integration" (work as a means of social integration). On the "individual" level, Kildal identifies three principal arguments: the "qualification" argument (participation in active measures is a means of improving human capital); "work as an asset" (work is a means to economic independence/social inclusion); and, finally, the "reciprocity" argument (individual rights are conditional on compliance with obligations and performance of anticipated social roles).
7. More generally, Midré (1994: 21-2) refers to this phenomenon as the "social function of imprecise concepts."
8. The National Insurance Scheme (NIS) comprises the following arrangements: Old Age Pension; Disability Benefit, Rehabilitation Assistance; Benefit for Surviving Spouse and Single Mothers; Occupational Injury; Sickness, Unemployment; and (from 1998) Cash Benefit for Families with Small Children. Social assistance and expenditures related to active labor market programs are not covered by the NIS.
9. The 1992 White Paper on Rehabilitation introduced a distinction between the terms vocational and medical rehabilitation. While the former term is reserved for initiatives aimed directly at assisting people with disabilities back to the labor market (*yrkesrettet attføring*), the latter refers to restoring, maintaining, and developing basic functional abilities (*medisinsk rehabilitering*).
10. While the LO wanted to prevent curtailments in the Sick Pay Scheme, the NHO was induced by the fear of increase in the sick pay period financed by employers.
11. This section is heavily influenced by Lødemel, forthcoming.
12. Social Services Act, 1991 §5-3.2.2.
13. There are at least three important differences between the "workfare" clients and the recipients of unemployment benefit. The normal participants in ALMP-schemes are not subjected to the Social Services Act and have therefore entered into them on a voluntary basis. Second, the ALMP-schemes are organized, and benefits are provided, by the local Labour Market Administration. Third, unemployment benefits are generally higher than social assistance benefits, and an incentive for participation is therefore in place.
14. Recipients of social assistance previously qualified for KAJA, but they are now excluded.
15. The income threshold for benefits is at present NOK 56, 713—the preceding calendar year, or NOK 45,370—as an average during the three preceding years (Ministry of Health and Social Affairs. The Norwegian Social Insurance Scheme. An introduction 1999).
16. To be accurate, the single parent is eligible for transitional benefit for up to three years until the child is eight years old. "Everyone," including the government, acknowledges that this in practice means that the entitlement will be used during the child's three first years of living.

17. Single parents without adequate childcare, or those having a child with an incapacitating illness, are exempted from the work requirement.
18. On the other hand, recipients of disability benefit are obligated to report "significant improvements in health status," and medical rehabilitation represents, in itself, an effort to overcome the basic physical obstacles to work.
19. A monthly full cash benefit is equivalent to one month's state subsidy of care for one child in a public preschool (for the time being NOK 2363). If the child is in a state-sponsored day care center for less than 30 hours weekly, the family will be entitled to a reduced cash benefit. Combined with maternal allowance for one year, it thus enables (one of the) parents to stay at home to take care of a child for three years.
20. The main components of this work approach will be experiments with: a five-year wage subsidy to people with reduced earnings capacity (extended from a maximum of three years); eligibility for disability pension from 30 percent disability (reduced from 50 percent); increased efforts of re-activating of disability pensioners through "networks of motivation;" and activation of long-term social assistance claimants.

## References


Aftenposten: 2.9.1998: 30.8.99.

Andersen, L. (1994). *Sykefraværsprosjektet 1991-1993*. Trondheim: SINTEF.

Aakvik, A. (1999). Five essays on the micro-economic evaluation of job training programs. *Dissertation in Economics No. 15*. University of Bergen: Department of Economics.

Beck, U. (1986, 1992). *Risk society*. London: Sage.

Blekesaune, M. (1998). Virker arbeidslinja på de langtidssykmeldte? *NOVA-rapport 1998:10*. Oslo: Norsk institutt for forskning om oppvekst, velferd og aldring.

Blekesaune. M. (1999). Innstramming I rehabiliteringspenger. Hvke følger fikk den? *NOVA-rapport 1999:2*. Oslo: NOVA.

Bragstad, T., Kristoffersen, P., & Østvold, J. (1996). Konsekvenser av innstramminger i folketrygdens regelverk. In *Det XIV nordiske sosialforsikringsmøte*. Oslo: Rikstrygdeverket.

Directorate of Labour. *Månedsstatistikk for arbeidsmarkedet (various issues)*. Oslo: Arbeidsdirektoratet.

Directorate of Labour. *Annual reports* 1990-1998. Oslo: Arbeidsdirektoratet. Directorate of Labour. (1998). *The book of measures ("Tiltaksboka")*. Oslo: Arbeidsdirektoratet.

Drøpping, J. A., Hvinden, B., & Vik, K. (1999). "Activation policies in the nordic countries." In M. Kautto et al.

Esping-Andersen, G. (1990). *The three worlds of welfare capitalism*. Oxford: Polity Press.

Esping-Andersen, G. (1999). *Social foundations of postindustrial economies*. Oxford: Oxford University Press.

Ford, M., & Hvinden, B. (1997). Samling av ansvaret for yrkesrettet attføring I arbeidsmarkedsetaten. *NOVA-rapport 1997:9a*. Oslo: NOVA.

Giddens, A. (1994). *Beyond left and right. The future of radical politics*. Cambridge: Polity Press.

Goul Andersen, J., Pettersen, P. A., Svallfors, S., & Uusitalo, H. (1999). "The legitimacy of the nordic welfare states: trends, variations and cleavages." In M. Kautto et al.

Hvinden, B. (1991). "Attføring i uføresaker. Praktisk virkemiddel eller uforpliktende symbol?" In A. Hatland, (ed.), *Trygd som fortjent?* Oslo: Ad Notam.

Hvinden, B. (1994). "Arbeidslinjen i ny og gammel drakt." In *Marginalisering og integrasjon på arbeidsmarkedet, Arbeidsforskningsinstituttets konferanse, mai 1994*. Oslo: Arbeidsforskningsinstituttet.

Innst. O. nr. 46. (1996-97). Oslo: Ministry of Social Affairs and Health.
Jessen, J. T. (1997). Brukere i attføringsapparatet. Tilfredshet og medvirkning. *NOVA-rapport 1997:9b*. Oslo: NOVA.
Kautto, M., Heikkilä, M., Hvinden, B., Marklund, S. & Ploug, N. (eds.). *Nordic social policy. Changing welfare states*. London/New York: Routledge.
Kildal, N. (1998). "Velferd og arbeidsplikt. Om arbeidslinjens begrunnelse." *Tidsskrift for velferdsforskning, 1*, 18-34.
Kjønstad, A. (1992). *Folketrygdens uførepensjon*. Oslo: Universitetsforlaget.
Kolberg J. E., & Esping-Andersen, G. (1992). "Welfare states and employment regimes." In J. E. Kolberg, (ed.), *Between work and social citizenship*. London: Sharpe Inc.
Kommunal- og arbeidsdepartementet. (1952). *Kvalifisering og sysselsetting av yrkesvalgshemmet arbeidskraft (Torp-komitèen)*.
Lødemel, I. (1997). "Pisken i arbeidslinja. Om iverksetjinga av arbeid for sosialhjelp." *Fafo-rapport 226*. Oslo: Fafo.
Mead, L. (ed.). (1998). *The new paternalism*. Washington, DC: Brookings Institution Press.
Midré, G. (1994). "Arbeid eller trygd? Om ideologiske spenninger i velferdsstaten." In *Marginalisering og integrasjon på arbeidsmarkedet, Arbeidsforskningsinstituttets konferanse, mai 1994*. Oslo: Arbeidsforskningsinstituttet.
Midré, G. (1995). *Bot, bedring eller brød*? Oslo: Universitetsforlaget.
Ministry of Finance. (1999). *Revised national budget 1999*. Oslo: Ministry of Finance.
National Insurance Administration. *Trygdestatistisk årbok (various issues)*. Oslo: Rikstrygdeverket.
NOU 1990:17: *Uførepensjon*.
NOU 1990:23: *Sykelønnsordningen*.
NOU 1992:26: *En nasjonal strategi for økt sysselsetting i 1990-årene*.
OECD. (1996). *The OECD jobs study. Enhancing the effectiveness of active labour market policies*. Paris: OECD.
Olsen, K. M., & Mastekaasa, A. (1997). Forskning om sykefravær–en oppsummering og vurdering av perioden 1980-96. *ISF-rapport 1997:3*. Oslo: Institute for Social Research.
Ot.prp. nr. 68 (1976-77). *Om lov om endring i Folketrygdloven av 1966 (sykelønnsordningen)*.
Ot.prp. nr. 56. (1997-98). *Om lov om kontantstøtte til småbarnsforeldre (kontantstøtteloven)*.
Ot.prp. nr. 8. (1996-97). *Om lov om endringer i folketrygdloven og i enkelte andre lover(Oppfølging av Velferdsmeldingen)*.
Pedersen J. T. (1998). "Er arbeidslinjen egnet til å hjelpe klientene ut av stønadsrollen?" *Rapport 1998:4*. Universitetet i Oslo: Seksjon for trygdemedisin.
Pierson, P. (1994). *Dismantling the welfare state*. Cambridge: University Press.
Statistics Norway. *Statistisk årbok (various issues)*. Oslo: Statistisk sentralbyrå.
Statistics Norway. (1997). *Sosialstatistikk 1997*. Oslo: Statistisk sentralbyrå.
St.meld. nr. 48. (1953). *Om kvalifisering og sysselsetting av delvis arbeidsføre*.
St.meld. nr. 39. (1991-92). *Attføring og arbeid for yrkeshemmede. Sykepenger og uførepensjon(Attføringsmeldingen)*.
St.meld. nr. 4. (1996-97). *Langtidsprogrammet 1998-2001*.
St.meld. nr. 35. (1994-95). *Velferdsmeldingen*.
St.meld. nr. 50. (1998-99). *Utjamningsmeldinga. Om fordeling av inntekt og levekår i Noreg*.
Vik-Mo, B. (1999). "Arbeidsplikten i sosialhjelpen. Kommunenes iverksetting av vilkåret om arbeid for sosialhjelp." *Hovedoppgave i statsvitenskap*. Trondheim: NTNU.
Westin, S. (1994). "Pasienter i klemme på arbeidsmarkedet." *Tidsskrift for den norske Lægeforening*, 114, 1804-5.

# 10

# Activating the Unemployed: The Challenge Ahead

*Neil Gilbert and Rebecca A. Van Voorhis*

The case studies in this book have analyzed various methods crafted to activate the unemployed in a range of modern welfare states. In summing up the lessons drawn and issues raised by these studies we move from analyses of specific countries to more general observations about the trends and concerns associated with the development of work-oriented policies. We recognize that when formulating broad observations from analyses of specific cases one usually skates onto thin ice. However, the case studies of these countries reveal several trends that would seem to support the weight of generalization.

Since the mid-1980s, policy reforms have been initiated to limit and reshape the major programs serving unemployed people—public assistance, unemployment, and disability—along several dimensions, beginning with access to benefits, which usually has been made more restrictive. Thus, for example, in Switzerland the period of entitlement to passive unemployment benefits was reduced from 400 days to 150 days, after which recipients must enter an active labor market program including temporary work in the public sector; New Zealand raised the minimum age to qualify for unemployment benefits, reduced benefit rates, and tightened the work test, while expanding the requirement to work to encompass people receiving disability and public assistance benefits; The Netherlands established procedures to re-examine recipients of disability benefits in order to determine more precisely the degree of disability and the jobs that would be suitable for partially disabled persons, and reduced the general level of public assistance benefits, while pressing recipients to seek work, backed by the threat of sanctions; in Norway claimants for unemployment benefits are expected to move to regions of the country where jobs are available; welfare reforms in the U.S. now require public assistance recipients to work after two years and limit their lifetime eligibility for benefits to five years. The trend toward more restrictive access to welfare benefits is partly a response to the proliferation of welfare entitlements between 1960-1980 after which it became clear that at some point the accumulation of easy access to generous benefits with long periods of duration tends to discourage work effort.

Policies to restrain access to social assistance, unemployment, and disability benefits have been accompanied by the expanded use of incentives and sanctions designed to facilitate entry into the labor force. This is not to suggest that the use of incentives in social welfare policy is a new idea, but to recognize that it is an idea which has gained considerable support and momentum in recent times. Incentives and sanctions are designed generally: (a) to facilitate movement to work by providing child care, education, subsidized jobs in which to gain work experience, and treatment services for people with psycho-social problems; (b) to enhance the financial gain of those who work through adjusting the marginal tax rates on public benefits and offering refundable tax credits; (c) to impose financial penalties by reducing (sometimes even eliminating) cash benefits for those who refuse to accept work or participate in work-related activities.

These various measures to narrow the entrance to social benefits and to broaden the exit off welfare rolls and into the regular labor force or other work-related activities underscore an increasing emphasis on the obligation to work, which is reshaping the daily practices of administrative agencies. Indeed, the introduction of "contractual agreements" is a crucial development in professional practice that has flowed out of the major work-oriented policy reforms. Public assistance, disability, and unemployment schemes have introduced quasi-contractual arrangements (sometimes referred to as "activation plans"), which are formulated by mutual agreement between clients and administrative officials. These plans specify the clients' obligations and rights to participate in education, training, job search, subsidized work, and other activities to improve their chances for paid employment along with the agency's duty to provide a range of supports and opportunities aimed at facilitating the movement of clients from welfare to work (Van der Veen and Trommel, 1997; Hatland, 1998). This development has altered the way unemployment, disability, and social assistance schemes operate. Administrative procedures for the allocation of benefits have moved away from the impartiality and anonymity of social rights framed by bureaucratic formulas toward the more individualized and discretionary dispensation of benefits based on case-by-case management. A corollary of this trend is the heightened differentiation among clients of social security schemes. In social assistance programs efforts are made to distinguish those ready-to-work, in need of training, and in need of special intervention; unemployment programs seek to differentiate the needs of youth, mobile unemployed, and long-term unemployed; and disability schemes seek to discern finer degrees of disability and the range of work that might be undertaken by disabled individuals in the different categories.

## The Emerging Challenge

All the countries reported on in this volume have initiated reforms changing the rules of access, increasing the use of incentives, and broadening the sphere of administrative discretion. Although the degree of change has varied among countries, the general intent and direction has been to shift the systemic objectives governing unemployment, disability, and social assistance schemes away from the provision of a safety-net of financial support in times of need, toward a system designed to integrate beneficiaries into the primary labor market. This increasing emphasis on work-oriented policy reforms has given rise to a number of issues with which social security officials are coming to grips. The challenges ahead concern :

1. How to do it— the appropriate role of government in promoting work-related activities.
2. What the "it" is—the practical definition of "activation," "insertion," and work-related activities.
3. How to insure fair treatment—under policies that expand the sphere of administrative discretion.
4. How to make work pay—enough to provide a decent standard of living.
5. How to deal with the problem of success—when only the hardcore are left.

6. How to measure the effects of efforts to activate the unemployed—on economic as well as social dimensions.

First, on the matter of how to do it—there are at least five broad strategies that have been employed to promote work-related activities. These involve:

- Measures designed to increase the availability of work, which operate either directly through the creation of public employment opportunities or indirectly by providing financial incentives, such as tax credits and wage subsidies, for employers to hire welfare, disability, and unemployment clients or by offering lump-sum grants for unemployed persons seeking to create new enterprises. In the U.S., for example, a business that employs a welfare client at the minimum wage in the state of Florida can be subsidized by the amount of the client's welfare check and for companies that provide on-the-job training the state offers to reimburse up to 50 percent of a client's wages during the training period. In addition to trying to increase the number of jobs through subsidized employment, recently efforts have been made in France to spread the current work by regulating overtime work.

- Efforts to upgrade worker skills involve a range of educational, training, and work experience opportunities designed to increase their chances of employment.

- Motivational programs address long-term unemployment partly as a psychological problem. Various therapeutic services are being offered to raise the client's self-esteem, confidence, and general level of motivation. In Australia, for example, the Special Intervention Program provides therapeutic intervention for the long-term unemployed who do not respond to the standard case management services (Eardley, 1997). And a British study suggests that cognitive-behavioral therapy may have beneficial effects in helping the long-term unemployed find work (Proudfoot et al., 1997).

- To overcome barriers to work, diverse measures have been employed to provide supportive services such as day care, transportation, and extended medical coverage.

- Finally, financial sanctions have been introduced in many programs to discipline those who might reject fair offers of activation (such as work, training, and community service).

Although it conveys only a partial and highly condensed version of the policy options, this list suggests that there are important choices to be made about the degree to which the mix of work-oriented interventions features what might be termed "public investment" versus "social incentive" strategies in relation to both individuals and the market. In regard to individuals, public investment strategies aim to improve chances for employment by enhancing human capital through publicly subsidized education and training programs; in contrast, social incentives focus on creating financial benefits and sanctions—the proverbial carrots and sticks—designed to encourage movement into the labor force at the individual's current level of skill, which exerts no upward pressure on wages. In regard to the market, public investment strategies seek to create new jobs for the unemployed through public works while social incentives rely on tax credits and other benefits and sanctions aimed at encouraging private enterprises to hire welfare recipients.

Second, on the issue of the meaning of work—the increasing emphasis on "activating" (sometimes referred to as reintegration or insertion) beneficiaries of public assistance, disability, and unemployment programs raises questions about what ultimately qualifies as work and work-related activities. When eligibility for social benefits requires participation in work or work-related activities: Is voluntary community service a work-related activity? While one might assign vocational education as work-related activity, what about the more general liberal arts education? How should self-employment be viewed, particularly for those such as artists, writers, and street-corner musicians whose work often may generate little or no income? Should caring for children, the elderly and infirm relatives qualify as a form of work or active participation, as Scherer (1997) proposes? How long does one count looking for work as a work-related activity?

One of the debates that has emerged regarding the definition of work in the United States concerns the relation between the level of compensation for participating in a program which requires community service in exchange for a grant and the level of compensation received by city employees for performing the same type of service. For example, more than 1,400 workfare participants in San Francisco, California, performed work such as janitorial duties in public buildings, sweeping city streets, and cleaning public transit vehicles for grants that amounted to less than one-half the hourly wage paid to union employees engaged sometimes side-by-side in similar jobs. Welfare advocates claim that the city is taking advantage of needy applicants forcing them to work at below union scale. City officials claim that the workfare recipients are doing community service in a program designed to teach basic work habits: showing up on time; working in a team, and accepting supervision. The issue, in part, revolves on the length of time a recipient spends in the program. That is, after a year or so on the job one would not expect there is much more to be gained in the way of developing basic work habits.

The debate in California took place within the context of a robust economy with the lowest unemployment rates in more than a decade. Questions about the meaning of "work" and the place of public employment schemes take on even greater weight in societies with high unemployment and future prospects of jobless growth, where the public sector may find itself the employer of last resort. In Italy "socially useful jobs" created by public agencies were supposed to avoid routine activities and place the unemployed in special innovative projects dealing with, for instance, environmental protection and urban renewal. However, in practice, most of those enrolled in the publicly subsidized "socially useful jobs" ended up engaged in routine paper-pushing administrative activities.

Third, concentrated efforts to develop case-be-case contractual agreements or "activation plans" between agencies and social welfare recipients have expanded the sphere of administrative discretion—raising the issue of how to insure that all clients receive equitable treatment. Depending on where in their country citizens reside, they may or may not be required to participate in "activation plans." In Sweden, for example, the Uppsala model of activation involves not only an individual career plan developed in consultation with social welfare and employment guidance officers, but frequent meetings to evaluate and elaborate the plan and to scrutinize the claimants efforts—a more intense and intrusive process than that experienced by social welfare claimants in most other municipalities. In Norway, although the Social Services Act of 1991 allowed local authorities to require that social assistance work in some capacity in exchange for their benefits, surveys suggest that the work requirement has been implemented by between only 25-34 percent of local agencies. In France, the *contrat d'insertaion*, an agreement between claimants and their local authorities (specifying the work-and-training-related activities that would be undertaken by claimants) was a major innovation of the Revenu Minimum d'Insertion (RMI) program introduced under national legislation in 1988. Since the program's inception, however, almost 50 percent of RMI beneficiaries have not signed a *contrat d'insertion* and only 5-6 percent have been sanctioned for non-compliance.

In the Netherlands research indicates that activation officers tend to distinguish among claimants on the bases of those who are most likely to obtain employment on their own, those whose characteristics severely limit their prospects for employment, and those who have a reasonable chance of obtaining a job if their efforts are well-supported and monitored; it is the latter on whom activation efforts are concentrated. Although financial penalties are prescribed by law for claimants who do not follow activation plans, such sanctions are rarely implemented by the local civil servants. To limit inequitable treatment of claimants because of arbitrary decision making by activation officers, the Dutch have instituted several measures, including efforts to create new jobs for low-skilled people and the provision of special training for civil servants, aimed at helping them to better understand their clients life-situations and how to work with people who may express hostility under the pressures of activation.

The fourth issue concerns how to make work pay—since the process of activation is likely to enlarge the ranks of the working poor (or very low-paid workers). There are several methods that can be advanced to make work pay. The first and most obvious approach is to require a high minimum wage, which insures a decent standard of living to the lowest paid workers. The problems with this approach, however, are that: (a) it may encourage capital to move to other countries where labor costs are low, particularly if the work involved would be otherwise low-paying in the absence of regulated minimum wages because the jobs only require a low level of skill, which is available among workers in other countries, and (b) it may discourage the development of certain business that could not afford to pay a high minimum wage. The second approach involves ameliorative measures, such as the Working Families Tax Credit recently introduced in the United Kingdom, the Family Tax Credit in New Zealand, and the Earned Income Tax Credit in the U.S. (at a maximum of $3,756 to low-income working families with two or more children), which subsidize workers through the system of tax expenditures. The way the U.S. scheme operates is that the value of the EITC rises by 40 cents for every dollar of income until earnings reach $9,390, and only begins to decline after earnings go above $12,250. The EITC is a refundable credit, so workers with two or more children who are earning $9,390 to $12,250 (and do not benefit from the normal tax deductions available to middle-income citizens) are eligible for the maximum $3,756 refund from the government. The EITC is a case of federal and state governments mediating between the individual and market, providing an adequate income to those who work by topping up salary earnings with a social transfer. Although the EITC can be seen as a response to the market's failure to provide an adequate standard of living for workers with families, it can also create a form of market failure by "over-subsidizing" low wage jobs--dampening political pressures to raise the minimum wage when an increase would not reduce the level of profit in low-wage occupations to the point that many jobs would be lost.

Coming at taxes from another angle, a third approach involves reducing the effective tax rate on earned income for low-paid workers. This can be achieved by lowering or eliminating social security taxes on low-incomes. In addition, the financial rewards for the unemployed who receive assistance from social programs and then move into the paid labor force (facing withdrawal of these social benefits) can be raised by adjustments that lower the rate at which benefits are withdrawn as earned income increases. This approach, however, can create perverse incentives for some, tempting people currently at work in low-paid positions to leave their jobs long enough to establish eligibility for social benefits (Weaver, 1992; Kaus, 1986). It can also encourage people to move into part-time jobs, which yield the best combination of earned income and social benefits, while creating a disincentive for full-time employment. Another way, of course, to reward work by increasing the gap between wages and social benefits is to cut the level of social benefits.

While transfers such as the EITC and measures that lower tax rates on earned income and withdrawal rates on welfare payments can provide social supplements to make employment pay for workers able to enter the labor force, those left behind pose a greater challenge. As the people most willing and able to work are drawn out of the unemployment, disability, and social assistance beneficiary pools, those remaining will embody beneficiaries of public aid who are the most difficult to employ for reasons of physical and mental health, behavioral troubles and intellectual limitations. This will lead to a sharpening of stratification along cognitive and behavioral lines ultimately requiring other policy choices, which brings us to the next issue.

How to deal with the problem of success? As work-oriented policy reforms create pressures and opportunities for employment, we may expect that an increasing number of clients receiving public assistance, disability, and unemployment benefits will move into the paid labor force. Already, in the U.S., welfare policy reforms and a robust economy have contributed to a decline of almost 48 percent in public assistance rolls between 1993 and 1999. As those most willing and able to leave welfare are drawn out of the recipient pool, those remaining will represent a tremendous challenge to work-oriented policies. For example, an analysis of the National Adult Literacy Survey, which tests an individual's ability to apply math and reading skills to every-day situations, indicates that 35 percent of public assistance recipients in the U.S. score in the lowest of five levels of literacy; people in this category are unable to perform tasks such as locate an intersection on a street map, fill out a government benefits application, and total the costs on an order form (Levenson, Reardon, and Schmidt, 1997).

Although the issue of what to do about the most disadvantaged and least employable recipients of public aid is not yet as salient as the issue of how to activate the unemployed in general, one can sketch out several approaches to dealing with those hardest to employ. Some policy analysts have argued that the employment prospects for people with extremely low levels of literacy and basic skills are so limited that public efforts should begin by trying to improve the life chances of their children through monitoring the recipient's child rearing practices, offering special educational and social services to the children, providing training to enhance parental functioning of welfare recipient, and placing teenage mothers and their children under adult supervision in group homes (Gilbert, 1995; Wilson 1996). Another option, favored by those who emphasize the value of paid work involves the expansion of public employment in protected settings for social welfare recipients who cannot function competitively in the normal labor market; this approach would include community service activities. Finally there is always the option of trying to compensate for deficiencies in basic skills and behavioral problems through intense efforts at education and rehabilitation, which would prepare even the most difficult to employ welfare recipients for regular work. Although presented as alternatives, practically speaking these choices are not mutually exclusive in the sense that a mix of polices can be tailored to various segments of the long-term welfare recipient population, recognizing that this is a diverse group, which contains many types of problems and faces various obstacles to employment. In the end, however, there may remain a group for whom work-oriented policies are not the answer—a group composed of the most vulnerable and least competent, for whom honorable dependency may be the best arrangement the community has to offer.

Sixth, the issue of how to evaluate the effects of programs to activate the unemployed is gaining greater attention among administrators and public officials—as these efforts multiply through the use of diverse work-oriented strategies. Many studies have been conducted and more are underway assessing individual contracts, varying packages of service, fiscal incentives, and sanctions. Using a matched comparison group design, a major evaluation of the Work Trials program in the U.K. (reviewed in chapter 1), for example, found that after six months 59 percent of subjects in the intervention group were employed compared to only 25 percent of the control group. These results indicate a high degree of success within the initial period. The firmness of these results were somewhat qualified, however, by a differential response rate between the groups and differences in the characteristics of the two samples (despite efforts to match them on relevant attributes).

In regard to the methodology of evaluative studies, the classical experimental research design—random assignment of subjects to intervention and control groups—is the most robust method for controlling group differences and assessing the effects of various policy measures. Over the last decade, this approach has been increasingly employed, particularly in the U.S. where millions of dollars are currently invested in evaluations using experimental designs. A meta-analysis by the U.S. General Accounting Office (described in chapter 6), for example, of findings from ten random-assignment-experimental studies of welfare-to-work programs in eight states showed that the most successful projects in terms of the participants' earnings and rates of employment provided a mix of employment-related activities, such as education, training, and child care, along with mandatory work requirements.

Although the experimental design works neatly in laboratory settings, several problems arise when applying this method in field settings. To begin with, random assignment is often difficult to achieve due to ethical reasons that argue against denying a control group services or benefits that would be beneficial. Even when random assignment is employed, it can be distorted by allowing control groups other forms of compensatory treatment and by the inability to restrict members of the control group from going elsewhere to receive the intervention services. Field studies, whether using matched group comparisons or random assignment, designs cannot prevent differential attrition between control and experimental groups, which may also contaminate the results. And no matter how carefully they are implemented, randomized experiments cannot control for the systemic impact of the experiment itself. When subjects are aware that an experiment is underway and what the desired effects are—having fewer children, finding a job, going to school—they may adjust their behavior in response to the changing normative environment, which would confound the experimental-control group comparison (Besharov, Germanis, Rossi, 1997).

Beyond broad methodological issues about the type of research designs to employ and their limits in evaluating the effects of activation policies, there are more specific questions concerning the time frame for analyses and what exactly to measure. Longitudinal analyses of active employment policies would allow policy makers to assess how these measures function in periods of economic growth, stagnation, and recession. But over the long term the activation measures implemented would be likely to vary with economic conditions, making it difficult to find equivalent comparisons. Still, even in the short term of say one month to several years, there is a strategic question of over how long a period activation schemes should be operating before efforts are made to measure their effects. And then comes the question of what effects to measure. Most studies to date have examined the immediate economic consequences of activation policies, focusing on variables such as rates of employment, earnings, and public costs or savings.

Relatively little attention has been devoted to the social consequences of activation measures, particularly the impact on children, family life, and informal caring and other voluntary activities. The issue here is largely a matter of values and the type of society that is seen as desirable. Work and financial independence are highly valued as are family care for its dependent members and personal freedom to direct one's course in life.

Thus, after policy makers have dealt with all of these emerging challenges—a larger, more profound philosophical question remains. That is, at what point are we to interpret the shift toward work-oriented policies as simply a necessary adjustment—"fine-tuning"—

of social policy designed to nurture individual responsibility, to empower citizens, and to promote social inclusion by activating people and joining them with others in gainful work on the labor market? And at what point should we begin to view these uplifting claims of empowerment, responsibility, and social inclusion as, perhaps, a billowing smoke screen for the triumph of free market economics under which the state is becoming merely a handmaiden to the market rather than an effective counter force that once offered, not activation, but social protection to labor against the vicissitudes of modern capitalism? The words we use are important. If the choice is posed between "active" and "passive" social benefits—there is little doubt that most people would prefer to be "active." The word "active" speaks of life's energy, whereas "passive" suggests a state of mild depression. But if the choice is between "activation," which presses people into the labor force, and "social protection" against the risks of modern capitalism, the tendency to embrace 'activation" might be less compelling. As governments pursue more active policies, it is important to question the real choices at stake and to temper the current trend toward activation with concerns for protection. To put it bluntly, is the emphasis on work-oriented policies going to give people more freedom to live fuller lives or is it going to make human labor more like other commodities that must be sold at whatever price clears the market? As governments move to embrace active work-oriented policies it is vital to clarify where they will land on the continuum between "fine tuning" policy and a fundamental decline in social protection.

## References

Besharov, Douglas, Peter Germanis, and Peter Rossi. (1997). *Evaluating Welfare Reform: A Guide for Scholars and Practitioners*. College Park: University of Maryland.

Eardley, Tony. (1997). "New Relations of Welfare in the Contracting State: The Marketisation of Services for the Unemployed in Australia," Social Policy Research Center Discussion Paper 79. SPRC, University of New South Wales.

Gilbert, Neil. (1995). *Welfare Justice: Restoring Social Equity*. New Haven: Yale University Press.

Hatland, Askel. (1998). "The Changing Balance Between Incentives and Economic Security in Scandinavian Unemployment Benefit Schemes," paper presented at the 2nd International Research Conference on Social Security, Jerusalem, Israel, January 25-28.

Kaus, Mickey. (1986). "The Work Ethic State." *New Republic*, October 6, pp. 22-23.

Levenson, Alec, Elaine Reardon, and Stefanie Schmidt. (1997). "Welfare Reform and the Employment Prospects of Welfare Recipients." *Jobs and Capital* VI:3 (Summer), pp. 36-41.

Proudfoot, J., D.Guest, J. Carson, G. Dunn, and J. Gray. (1997). "Effect of cognitive-behavioral therapy training on job-finding among long-term unemployed people." *The Lancet*, 305, 12 July, pp. 96-100.

Scherer, Peter. (1997). "Socio-economic Change and Social Policy." In *Family, Market, and Community*. Paris: OECD.

van der Veen, Romke and Willem Trommel (1997). " Managed Liberalization of the Dutch Welfare State." Presented at the SASE Conference on Rethinking the Welfare State, Montreal, July 5-7.

Weaver, Carolyn. (1992). "Reassessing Federal Disability Insurance." *Public Interest* 105 (Winter), pp. 108-21.

Wilson, James Q. (1996). "Beginning with our Children." *Policy Review* 76 (March-April).

# Contributors

Jean-Claude Barbier is Director of research (sociology) at the Centre d'études de l'emploi and associate Professor at University Paris VII Denis Diderot.

Espen Dahl is a sociologist and works as a Research Director at the Institute for Applied Social Science (Fafo) in Oslo, Norway.

Jon Anders Drøpping is a political scientist from the Norwegian University of Science and Technology, and a researcher at the Institute for Applied Social Science (Fafo) in Oslo, Norway.

Valeria Fargion is Senior Lecturer in the Political Science and Sociology Department, University of Florence. In 1998-99 she was European Forum Fellow at the EUI in Florence.

Neil Gilbert is Chernin Professor of Social Services and Social Welfare at the University of California, Berkeley, and Director of the Center for Comparative Study of Family Welfare and Poverty.

Sven E. O. Hort is Senior Lecturer in Sociology at Sødertørn University College, Stockholm, Sweden, and a visiting professor at the Department of Comparative Politics at the University of Bergen, Norway, past president of the Scandinavian Sociological Association.

Ken Judge is Professor of Social Policy at the University of Kent at Canterbury and Director of the Personal Social Services Research Unit.

Piet K. Keizer is Associate Professor Institutional Economics, at the Faculty of Economics and Business Administration, University of Maastricht.

Ross Mackay is Special Advisor in the Social Policy Agency of the New Zealand Department of Social Welfare.

François Xavier Merrien is Professor of Comparative Political Sociology at the University of Lausanne, Switzerland.

Neung Hoo Park is Director of the Social Security Research Division of the Korean Institute for Health and Social Affairs.

Bruno Théret is Directeur de recherche au Centre National de la recherche Scientifique, France, and was Directeur de l'Institut de

Recherche Interdisciplinaire en Socio-économie (IRIS) at the Paris Dauphine University when writing his contribution to this book.

Rebecca A. Van Voorhis is Assistant Professor in the Department of Sociology and Social Services at the California State University, Hayward.

# Index

For Product Safety Concerns and Information please contact our EU representative GPSR@taylorandfrancis.com
Taylor & Francis Verlag GmbH, Kaufingerstraße 24, 80331 München, Germany

www.ingramcontent.com/pod-product-compliance
Ingram Content Group UK Ltd.
Pitfield, Milton Keynes, MK11 3LW, UK
UKHW022004180926
475701UK00003B/181

* 9 7 8 0 7 6 5 8 0 7 6 7 0 *